Lecture Notes in Computer Science 6192

Commenced Publication in 1973
Founding and Former Series Editors:
Gerhard Goos, Juris Hartmanis, and Jan

T0092404

Astrid M.L. Kappers
Jan B.F. van Erp
Wouter M. Bergmann Tiest
Frans C.T. van der Helm (Eds.)

Haptics: Generating and Perceiving Tangible Sensations

International Conference, EuroHaptics 2010
Amsterdam, July 8-10, 2010
Proceedings, Part II

 Springer

Volume Editors

Astrid M.L. Kappers
Helmholtz Institute, Utrecht University
Padualaan 8, 3584 CH Utrecht, The Netherlands
E-mail: a.m.l.kappers@uu.nl

Jan B. F. van Erp
TNO Human Factors
PO Box 23, 3769 ZG, Soesterberg, The Netherlands
E-mail: Jan.vanerp@tno.nl

Wouter M. Bergmann Tiest
Helmholtz Institute, Utrecht University
Padualaan 8, 3584 CH Utrecht, The Netherlands
E-mail: w.m.bergmanntiest@uu.nl

Frans C.T. van der Helm
Delft University of Technology
Mekelweg 2, 2628 CD Delft, The Netherlands
E-mail: F.C.T.vanderHelm@tudelft.nl

Library of Congress Control Number: 2010929195

CR Subject Classification (1998): H.1.2, I.6, C.3, H.5, I.2.6, I.2

LNCS Sublibrary: SL 3 – Information Systems and Application, incl. Internet/Web
and HCI

ISSN   0302-9743
ISBN-10   3-642-14074-2 Springer Berlin Heidelberg New York
ISBN-13   978-3-642-14074-7 Springer Berlin Heidelberg New York

springer.com

© Springer-Verlag Berlin Heidelberg 2010
Printed in Germany

Typesetting: Camera-ready by author, data conversion by Scientific Publishing Services, Chennai, India
Printed on acid-free paper   06/3180

Preface

Welcome to the proceedings of EuroHaptics 2010. EuroHaptics is the major international conference and the primary European meeting for researchers in the field of human haptic sensing and touch-enabled computer applications. We were proud to have received more submissions for presentations, demonstrations and special sessions than ever before. This shows that the topic and the conference's quality and approach appeal to an increasing number of researchers and companies.

We received more than 200 submissions for oral and poster presentations, demos and pre-conference special workshops. A team of 25 associate editors and 241 reviewers read the submissions and advised the four volume editors. We owe the associate editors and reviewers many thanks. We accepted 43 submissions as oral and 80 as poster presentations, 7 pre-conference workshops were approved and more than 20 demos could be experienced 'hands-on' during the conference. The proceedings contain all oral and poster presentation papers. No distinction between the two presentation types was made because selection was not on the basis of submission quality but on relevance for a broad audience. We were proud to add three distinguished keynote speakers to the conference program: Mark Ernst, Rosalyn Driscoll and Patrick van der Smagt.

Besides the authors, presenters and reviewers, we would like to express our gratitude to our supporting organizations, The Netherlands Organisation for Applied Scientific Research TNO, VU University Amsterdam, Utrecht University and Delft University of Technology, and to our sponsors, especially our four gold-level sponsors: Force Dimension, Engineering Systems Technologies, TNO and Moog.

Traditionally, EuroHaptics aims at a multidisciplinary audience from (scientific) fields such as neuroscience, perception and psychophysics, rendering and software algorithms, hardware development and applications. To further increase the multidisciplinary approach, we adapted a new setup for the conference program by organizing the sessions across and not along scientific disciplines. We hope that this will further increase the crosstalk between the disciplines involved in haptics, which we consider a prerequisite for the further development of the field. Reading through the proceedings will show you that the field is already maturing rapidly and has a bright future ahead.

Finally, it is my honor and pleasure to acknowledge the Organizing Committee and acknowledge their roles in making EuroHaptics 2010 a memorable event: Astrid Kappers (Program Committee Chair, editor), Wouter Bergmann Tiest (editor, proceedings coordinator), Jeroen Smeets (local host, treasurer), Peter Werkhoven (sponsors), Frans van der Helm (editor), Tom Philippi (webmaster, treasurer) and Anne-Marie Brouwer (demos and social program).

Jan van Erp

Organization

Organizing Committee

Jan van Erp (Chair)	TNO Human Factors, Soesterberg, The Netherlands
Jeroen Smeets	VU University, Amsterdam, The Netherlands
Astrid Kappers	Utrecht University, Utrecht, The Netherlands
Frans van der Helm	Delft University of Technology, Delft, The Netherlands
Peter Werkhoven	Utrecht University, Utrecht, The Netherlands
Wouter Bergmann Tiest	Utrecht University, Utrecht, The Netherlands
Anne-Marie Brouwer	TNO Human Factors, Soesterberg, The Netherlands
Tom Philippi	Utrecht University, Utrecht, The Netherlands

Editors

Astrid Kappers (Editor-in-chief)	Utrecht University, Utrecht, The Netherlands
Jan van Erp	TNO Human Factors, Soesterberg, The Netherlands
Wouter Bergmann Tiest	Utrecht University, Utrecht, The Netherlands
Frans van der Helm	Delft University of Technology, Delft, The Netherlands

Associate Editors

David Abbink	Delft University of Technology, The Netherlands
Cagatay Basdogan	Koç University, Turkey
Seungmoon Choi	Pohang University of Science and Technology, South Korea
Göran Christiansson	SKF Engineering & Research Center, The Netherlands
Herman Damveld	Delft University of Technology, The Netherlands
Knut Drewing	Justus-Liebig-Universität Gießen, Germany
Abdulmotaleb El Saddik	University of Ottawa, Canada
Berthold Färber	University of the Bundeswehr, Munich, Germany
Manuel Ferre	Universidad Politécnica de Madrid, Spain
Antonio Frisoli	PERCRO, Scuola Superiore S. Anna, Pisa, Italy
Martin Grunwald	Universität Leipzig, Germany
Matthias Harders	ETH Zürich, Switzerland
Vincent Hayward	Université Pierre et Marie Curie, Paris, France
Thorsten Kern	Continental Corporation, Germany
Abderrahmane Kheddar	CNRSUM2 LIRMM, Montpellier, France

Dong-Soo Kwon   KAIST, Daejeon, South Korea
Ki-Uk Kyung   ETRI, Daejeon, South Korea
Karon MacLean   University of British Columbia, Vancouver,
                                     Canada
Mark Mulder   Delft University of Technology, The Netherlands
Haruo Noma   ATR Media Information Science Labs, Kyoto,
                                     Japan
Miguel Otaduy   URJC Madrid, Spain
William Provancher   University of Utah, Salt Lake City, USA
Chris Raymaekers   Hasselt University, Belgium
Jeha Ryu   Gwangju Institute of Science and Technology,
                                     South Korea
Jeroen Smeets   VU University, Amsterdam, The Netherlands

Reviewers

Jake Abbott	Oliver Braddick	Marc Ernst
Marco Agus	Jean-Pierre Bresciani	Thomas Ertl
Hyo-sung Ahn	Stephen Brewster	Paul Evrard
Fawaz Alsulaiman	Andrea Brogni	Ildar Farkhatdinov
Mehdi Ammi	Etienne Burdet	Irene Fasiello
Hideyuki Ando	Gianni Campion	Mark Fehlberg
Michele Antolini	Ozkan Celik	Peter Feys
Hichem Arioui	Pablo Cerrada	Alessandro Formaglio
Angelo Arleo	Jongeun Cha	Antonio Frisoli
Carlo Avizzano	Elaine Chapman	Ilja Frissen
Mehmet Ayyildiz	Hee-Byoung Choi	Yukio Fukui
José Azorín	Seungmoon Choi	Ignacio Galiana
Sarah Baillie	Göran Christiansson	Fabio Ganovelli
Soledad Ballesteros	Q. Chu	Marcos García
Karlin Bark	Salvador Cobos	Pablo García-Robledo
Kenneth Barner	Edward Colgate	Carlos Garre
Jorge Barrio	Chris Constantinou	Roger Gassert
Cagatay Basdogan	Koen Crommentuijn	Christos Giachritsis
Gabriel Baud-Bovy	Andrew Crossan	Frederic Giraud
Massimo Bergamasco	Herman Damveld	Brian Gleeson
Wouter Bergmann Tiest	Joan De Boeck	Pauwel Goethals
Antonio Bicchi	Nienke Debats	Daniel Gooch
Marta Bielza	Barbara Deml	Florian Gosselin
Hannes Bleuler	Massimiliano Di Luca	Burak Guclu
Juan Bogado	Andrew Doxon	Hakan Gurocak
Raoul Bongers	Knut Drewing	Gabjong Han
Monica Bordegoni	Christian Duriez	Sung H. Han
Gianni Borghesan	Mohamad Eid	Gunter Hannig
Diego Borro	Abdulmotaleb El Saddik	Riender Happee
Martyn Bracewell	Satoshi Endo	Matthias Harders

Mitra Hartmann
William Harwin
Wataru Hashimoto
Christian Hatzfeld
Vincent Hayward
Thomas Hazelton
Andreas Hein
Morton Heller
Denise Henriques
Constanze Hesse
Jim Hewit
Sandra Hirche
IIsin-Ni IIo
Robert Howe
Barry Hughes
Inwook Hwang
Jung-Hoon Hwang
Rosa Iglesias
Ali Israr
Miriam Ittyerah
Hiroo Iwata
Caroline Jay
Seokhee Jeon
Li Jiang
Lynette Jones
Christophe Jouffrais
Georgiana Juravle
Kanav Kahol
Lukas Kaim
Marjolein Kammers
Idin Karuei
Sebastian Kassner
Thorsten Kern
Dirk Kerzel
Shahzad Khan
Abderrahmane Kheddar
Sang-Youn Kim
Yeongmi Kim
Roberta Klatzky
Alois Knoll
Umut Kocak
Ilhan Konukseven
Gabor Kosa
Katherine Kuchenbecker
Tomohiro Kuroda
Yoshihiro Kuroda

Hoi Kwok
Dong-Soo Kwon
Ki-Uk Kyung
Mung Lam
Patrice Lambert
Piet Lammertse
Anatole Lécuyer
Susan Lederman
Vincent Levesque
Ming Lin
Robert Lindeman
Claudio Lo Console
Javier López
Karon MacLean
Charlotte Magnusson
Florence Marchi
Davide Mazza
Thorsten Meiß
Christopher Moore
Konstantinos Moustakas
Winfred Mugge
Masashi Nakatani
Marko Nardini
Fiona Newell
Günter Niemeyer
Verena Nitsch
Farley Norman
Ian Oakley
Shogo Okamoto
Marcia O'Malley
Sile O'Modhrain
Keita Ono
Jun Oohara
Miguel Otaduy
Martin Otis
Krista Overvliet
Miguel Padilla-Castaneda
Karljohan Palmerius
Jaeheung Park
Jinah Park
Jerome Pasquero
Volkan Patoğlu
Ricardo Pedrosa
Angelika Peer
Myrthe Plaisier
Daan Pool

Dane Powell
Carsten Preusche
Roope Raisamo
Markus Rank
Jyri Rantala
Jacqueline Rausch
Chris Raymaekers
Stéphane Régnier
Miriam Reiner
Gerhard Rinkenauer
Gabriel Robles De La
    Torre
Andreas Röse
Emanuele Ruffaldi
Jee-Hwan Ryu
Jeha Ryu
José Sabater
Eva-Lotta Sallnäs
Roopkanwal Samra
Krish Sathian
Joan Savall
Thomas Schauß
Stefania Serafin
Sascha Serwe
Shahin Sirouspour
Lynne Slivovsky
Massimiliano Solazzi
Edoardo Sotgiu
Jonas Spillmann
Mark Spingler
Christoph Staub
Arno Stienen
Hong Tan
Jean Thonnard
Nikolaos Tsagarakis
Brian Tse
Dzmitry Tsetserukou
Costas Tzafestas
Sehat Ullah
Ana Rita Valente Pais
George Van Doorn
René van Paassen
Dennis van Raaij
Lode Vanacken
Emmanuel Vander Poorten
Iason Vittorias
Frank Wallhoff

David Wang
Carolina Weber
Joel Carlos West
Eleonora Westebring-Van
    der Putten

Maarten Wijntjes
Alan Wing
Raul Wirz
Mark Wright
Juli Yamashita

Gi-Hun Yang
Hiroaki Yano
Yasuyoshi Yokokohji
Mounia Ziat

Table of Contents – Part II

Texture and Surfaces

Virtual Reality

Grasping and Moving

Performance and Training

Table of Contents – Part I

Mass, Force, and Elasticity

Teleoperation

Novel Approaches

Part I
Texture and Surfaces

Fingernail-Mounted Display of Attraction Force and Texture

Masataka Niwa, Tomoko Nozaki, Taro Maeda, and Hideyuki Ando

Graduate School of Information Science and Technology, Osaka University
2-1 Yamada-oka, Suita, Osaka, Japan
{niwa,nozaki.tomoko,t_maeda,hide}@ist.osaka-u.ac.jp

Abstract. The paper studies two methods of haptic. One is an attraction force display that can induce attraction force by a cyclic movement of a weight with asymmetric acceleration. Another is a texture display that induces a sensation of texture by giving off vibration while a subject traces a finger over a flat surface. In this paper, we propose a novel design that can induce both attraction force and texture feeling. The prototype consists of four vibration motors, which are controlled to generate asymmetric acceleration and vibration. The device is evaluated by experiments.

Keywords: haptic interface, tactile display, pseudo-attraction force, pseudo-texture.

1 Introduction

We have developed devices adopting a pseudo-texture display [1] and a pseudo-attraction force display [2] in the past. These techniques focused on the ability to use vibration, and later a prototype fingernail-mounted display [3] was constructed to achieve the above two functions using four vibration motors. This device recreates the target vibration wave shape. However, the device could not provide pseudo-attraction force or pseudo-texture because it failed to achieve the required performance at a practical output torque and frequency.

In this research, we propose a new mechanism that solves these problems and discuss the development of a device that can provide pseudo-attraction force and pseudo-texture.

2 Fingernail-Mounted Attraction Force and Tactile Display

2.1 Tactile and Attraction Presentation Technique

When a small mass in a handheld device oscillates along a single axis with asymmetric acceleration (strongly peaked in one direction and diffuse in the other, Fig. 1), the person holding it typically experiences a kinesthetic illusion characterized by the sensation of being continuously pushed or pulled by the device. Furthermore, when the rotation speed of weights is 5–9 Hz, people tend to perceive pseudo-attraction force easily.

A.M.L. Kappers et al. (Eds.): EuroHaptics 2010, Part II, LNCS 6192, pp. 3–8, 2010.

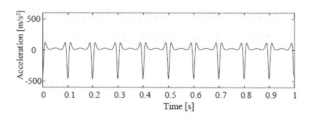

Fig. 1. Ideal acceleration for presenting pseudo-attraction force

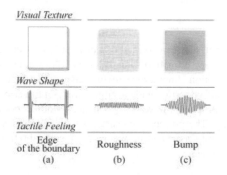

Fig. 2. Vibration waveform for texture presentation

On the other hand, if the vibratory stimulation is given when the object is traced by the finger, it has been shown to cause a pseudo-texture (Fig. 2) in the finger pad. This stimulus needs to have a vibration frequency of 100–200 Hz.

In this research, we aim to present these two types of vibration stimuli in a single device. The vibrational pattern is generated by controlling the phase of an eccentric weight's rotation.

2.2 Generating a Vibration Pattern by Phase Control

Four eccentric weights are attached to one fingernail, where two weights rotate clockwise and the other two rotate counterclockwise, with all weights rotating at the same frequency. If there were no phase control, the rotation of the eccentric weights would make a random vibration. However, when the weight of each phase in the same rotational direction shifts 180 degrees, the weights' centrifugal forces cancel each other out, thus producing a non-vibration state (Fig. 3 (a)). Moreover, centrifugal forces other than the element of the symmetrical axis can be negated by turning to the line symmetry the weight that rotates in the opposite direction. Under such a condition, when the weight rotates, a pseudo-attraction force can be presented in an arbitrary direction (Fig. 3 (b)). Furthermore, when the weights stop and are then driven by the high frequency of the non-vibration state, a vibration is generated for the current pseudo-texture (Fig. 3 (c)).

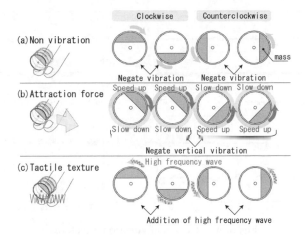

Fig. 3. How to generate a vibration pattern

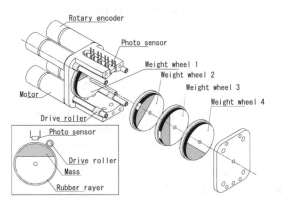

Fig. 4. Proposed fingernail-mounted display mechanism

2.3 Prototype Display

The previous fingernail-mounted device [3] was built with vibration motors (Namiki Precision Jewel, 4CR-1002W-07). This device can operate in a narrow band of vibration frequency. Moreover, the weak torque of the motor and the motor's vibration resonate with each other, causing a problem that could not be controlled by phase.

Therefore, in this paper we propose a friction drive mechanism to drive the eccentric weights (Fig. 4). This mechanism is designed to achieve large drive torque and wide-band vibration frequency. The motor used is the Maxon RE8, where the reduction gear ratio is 6:1, the radius of the eccentric weight is 18 mm, and each weight is 2 g. The size of this device is 20 × 25 × 42 mm, and its mass is 30 g. The positions of the weights were found by a photo sensor, and the rotary encoder's microcomputer (Microchip Technology, dsPIC33FJ128) conducted feedback control.

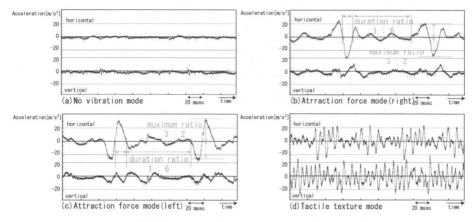

Fig. 5. Acceleration of vibration waveform

3 Performance Evaluation of Prototype Device

3.1 Acceleration of Vibration Waveform

Figure 5 shows the display placed on the fingernail, where an accelerometer (Frees-cale Semiconductor, MMA7361L) measures the vibration of the display. In this case, the motor is driven at 10 Hz and the vibrational frequency used to present the texture is 100 Hz. The non-vibration mode in Fig. 5 (a) nearly cancels out the horizontal and vertical acceleration. Figure 5 (b), (c) shows the attraction force mode, where the duration ratio is 1:6 and the maximum ratio is 3:2. As shown in Fig. 5 (d), a vibration of 100 Hz is generated.

3.2 Perceptual Characteristics

In order to confirm the existence of a pseudo-attraction force created by the display, the subjects wore the display on a fingernail, and a vibration stimulus was applied by the display for the subjects. The subjects were four adult men, all of whom were right-handed.

3.2.1 Experiment of Pseudo-attraction Force Perception
The nail-mounted display was worn on the right hand's index and middle fingers. First, the display worked in the non-vibration mode. Next, the display worked in the attraction force mode (to right or to left), and the stimulus was presented for three seconds. After the presentation, the display again worked in the non-vibration mode. The stimulus was presented 10 times each in the right and left directions. The stimuli were presented in random order. Subjects responded to the perceived direction of the attraction force by selecting from three choices: "Right," "Left," or "I do not know."

Table 1. Correct answers for perceived direction of pseudo-attraction force (percent)

Subject	A	B	C	D	(Average)
Percentage of correct answers	90%	95%	80%	100%	(91%)

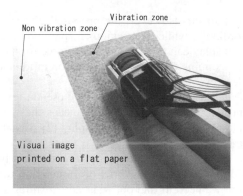

Fig. 6. Conditions for presenting pseudo-texture

Table 1 shows the results of correct answers for the perceived direction of pseudo-attraction force. The introspective reporting by subjects of "felt my fingers pulled" is listed.

3.2.2 Experiment on Pseudo-texture Perception

The subjects traced over flat paper with the printed visual texture by their fingers (Fig. 6). If the subject's fingers traced in the non-vibration zone, the display worked in the non-vibration mode; similarly, if the subject's fingers traced in the vibration zone, the display worked in the texture mode. Trace speed and direction of subject's finger are unrestricted, and tracing was done for 30 seconds. After the tracing, subjects were given a choice as to whether they felt the texture, the vibration, or nothing.

As a result, all of the subjects felt the texture. The introspective reports of subjects included "felt like the friction grew on the visual texture" and "felt like the finger dropped down when it moved from vibration zone to non-vibration zone."

4 Discussion

From the experimental results on the perception of pseudo-attraction force, all subjects achieved a rate of correct answers higher than 80%. This indicates that traction was presented. Moreover, the subjects only gave incorrect answer in the case where the left attraction force was presented at the right side. We can conclude that the display's center of gravity moved to the right, caused by the distributing cable. To solve this problem, a soft and light cable should be adopted to prevent it from influencing the posture of the device.

The previous pseudo-attraction force display [1] could provide attraction force in only one direction. To provide the attraction force in any direction, the display needs to physically rotate. However, the proposed display can provide attraction force in any direction by itself, which is the major advantage of this display.

Consequently, the maximum ratio of the proposed display's acceleration waveform is only 3:2, significantly smaller than the ratio of 3.5:1 achieved by the previous display. The relationship between maximum ratio and perception of acceleration force has not been discussed so far. However, the proposed display can provide pseudo-attraction force. Accordingly, while the previous display provides attraction force for the arm, the proposed display can provide attraction force for the finger. In the future, it will be necessary to examine the frequency, duration ratio, and maximum ratio for fingernail-mounted devices.

From the experimental results of the perception of pseudo-texture, all subjects were able to feel the texture on their finger pad. This means that the proposed display is able to provide pseudo-texture. The previous display [2] was able to vibrate enough gain only near the resonant frequency by using a voice-coil-type tactor, but the proposed display is able to vibrate at any frequency. This means that the proposed display is able to provide more texture patterns of stimulation than the previous one. Therefore, in the future we need to find out what new textures the proposed device is able to provide.

5 Conclusion

In this paper, we proposed and developed a fingernail-mounted display to utilize pseudo-attraction force and pseudo-texture. Furthermore, perceptual experiments were conducted using the proposed device. As a result, the proposed display was able to provide pseudo-attraction force and pseudo-texture.

In the future, we would like to investigate the parameters of the proposed display that are effective in providing the pseudo-attraction force and the pseudo-texture. In addition, the display will be made more lightweight and compact.

Acknowledgments. This research was supported by JST, CREST. Research Collaboration and "Global COE (Centers of Excellence) Program" of the Ministry of Education, Culture, Sports, Science and Technology, Japan.

References

1. Amemiya, T., Ando, H., Maeda, T.: Lead-me interface for a pulling sensation from hand-held devices. ACM Transactions on Applied Perception, Vol. 5, No. 3, Article 15 (2008)
2. Ando, H., Watanabe, J., Inami, M., Sugimoto, M., Maeda, T.: A fingernail-mounted tactile display for augmented feality systems. Electronics and Communications in Japan, Part II Vol. 90, No. 4, pp. 56-65 (2007)
3. Nozaki, T., Ando, H., Maeda, T.: The nail-mounted attraction force/bump display. Proceedings of the 13th Annual VRSJ Meeting (in Japanese), pp. 469-470 (2008)

Contact Force and Duration Effects on Static and Dynamic Tactile Texture Discrimination

Hoi Fei Kwok[1], Kerry Darkins[1], Calogero M. Oddo[2], Lucia Beccai[3],
and Alan M. Wing[1]

[1] Sensory and Motor Neuroscience, School of Psychology, University of Birmingham,
Edgbaston, Birmingham B15 2TT, United Kingdom
[2] Advanced Robotics Technology and Systems Laboratory, Polo Sant'Anna Valdera,
Viale Rinaldo Piaggio, 34, 56025 Pontedera, Pisa, Italy
[3] Center for Micro-BioRobotics, Italian Institute of Technology, Viale Rinaldo Piaggio, 34,
56025 Pontedera, Pisa, Italy
h.f.kwok@bham.ac.uk

Abstract. Tactile roughness magnitude estimates increase with contact force. However, it is not known whether discrimination thresholds are affected by contact force and other parameters, such as duration and tangential movement. The effects of these factors on roughness discrimination thresholds were determined using an adaptive staircase procedure for coarse and fine texture discrimination during active touch. The presence of tangential movement (dynamic touch) significantly reduced thresholds in coarse and fine texture discrimination compared to static touch, with effects more marked with fine textures. Contact force did not affect discrimination except in static touch of coarse texture when the threshold was significantly higher with low force. Within the perspective that texture discrimination involves distinct vibratory and spatial mechanisms, the results suggest that spatial-dependent texture discrimination deteriorates when contact force is reduced whereas vibration-dependent texture discrimination is unaffected by contact force. Texture discrimination was independent of contact duration in the range 1.36s to 3.46s, suggesting that tactile integration processes are completed relatively quickly.

Keywords: Tactile discrimination, roughness, contact force.

1 Background

Tactile roughness has been extensively studied using dot patterns, gratings, sandpaper and emery cloth. Early studies of roughness perception were based on the use of subjective magnitude scaling [1]. However, the discrimination threshold is an alternative measure of tactile sensibility which is less susceptible to individual bias. Lamb (1984) found that the 75% threshold for discrimination of periodic dot patterns could be as low as 2% in normal subjects [2]. Using gratings, the mean discrimination threshold of normal subjects was found to range from 4% [3] to 10% [4, 5] in terms of change in spatial period and the minimum threshold could be as low as 1.4% in some subjects [6].

A.M.L. Kappers et al. (Eds.): EuroHaptics 2010, Part II, LNCS 6192, pp. 9–16, 2010.
© Springer-Verlag Berlin Heidelberg 2010

It is not known if factors such as contact force, contact duration and scanning velocity affect the discrimination threshold. Perceived tactile roughness is related to the mean and variation of the neuronal activity of slowly adapting type 1 (SA1) mechanoreceptors [7, 8]. SA1 mechanoreceptors respond to skin indentation [9] which in turn is affected by the contact force. The variation of their activity is affected by how fast the finger moves across the tactile surface. Therefore, both contact force and scanning velocity could affect roughness perception. Longer contact duration giving more time for the brain to process incoming sensory information may also affect roughness perception. Subjective roughness estimates have been shown to be affected by contact force [1] but not by scanning velocity [10]. However, there have been no published reports of the effects of contact duration nor whether the discrimination threshold is affected by force, velocity or contact duration.

It has been found that discrimination ability differs in static and moving touch. Hollins and Risner (2000) compared the ability to discriminate two pairs of textured surfaces under stationary and moving conditions [11]. The two pairs of textured surfaces were two fine sandpapers (particle size 9 and 15μm) and two coarse sandpapers (particle size 141 and 192μm). They found that the discriminability (assessed by percentage correct response) was significantly reduced in the stationary condition for the finer pair of sandpapers. This finding is in agreement with Katz's (1925) theory that the tactile perception of surface textures is a complex process, depending on a "spatial sense" for discernment of coarse textures and a "vibration sense" for an appreciation of finer textures [12]. However, the contact force and contact duration were not controlled during these experiments. Therefore, it is not clear if the difference in effect was due to different force conditions. The objective of the present study is to study the effect of contact force and contact duration on roughness discrimination of fine and coarse textured materials under moving and static touch conditions.

2   Effects of Contact Force and Movement on Texture Discrimination

2.1   Methods

Participants. Twelve paid volunteers (8 females and 4 males), all but one were right-handed, took part in the experiment. They were all naive to the purpose of the experiment. None had any history of hand or wrist injury or disease. All provided informed consent.

Apparatus and materials. The apparatus, depicted in Figure 1, consisted of a custom designed active touch platform with 6df load cell (Nano43, ATI Industrial Automation) which recorded three axis force (Fx, Fy, Fz) and three axis torque signals (Tx, Ty, Tz). Sandpapers of grit number 80, 100, 120, 180, 220, 240, 320, 360, 400, 500, 600, 800 and 1000 were used as tactile stimuli. During the trial, the platform was hidden from the view of the participants. The contact force (vertical force Fz) exerted by the participant during the experiment was displayed in real-time as a variable height bar on computer screen controlled by custom software written in LabView 7 (National Instruments), in order to allow the subject to track the target force level. White noise was played to the participant through a headphone during the exploration process to mask any auditory cues to texture.

Fig. 1. The active touch experiment platform with two textured stimuli

Task and procedure. The roughness discrimination threshold was determined using a two-interval forced-choice paradigm with a Zwislocki 3-1 staircase [13]. Two standard surfaces were used: 100 grit sandpaper (coarse texture) and 1000 grit sandpaper (fine texture). Participants were told to touch the sandpaper using the pad of their right index finger. During the touching procedure, the participant had to look at the screen, lower the fingertip and adjust the contact force to within 0.1N of the target contact force (0.3 or 0.8 N). In some blocks, the participant was asked to scan their finger across each surface once (moving touch) and in some blocks, the participant was asked to simply touch and not to displace the finger sideways (static touch).

Participants washed and dried their hands before the experiment in order to standardise skin friction conditions. The experiment procedure was explained and then participants were seated in front of the apparatus and the computer screen with headphones on. At the beginning of each block, participants were familiarised with the force needed for the block trials in a brief series of 12 trials. They were then given two surfaces to touch with white noise played through the headphone at the same time and asked to report which surface was rougher. The test stimulus for the first trial of each block was 180 grit for the 100 grit standard and 600 grit for the 1000 grit standard. The test stimulus was changed according to the response given. The difference between the stimuli was reduced after three non-consecutive correct responses and it was increased (reversal) if an incorrect response was given. No feedback was provided but there was an unrecorded easy trial after every 10 trials in an attempt to reduce performance shifts sometimes observed in the absence of feedback. The trial was stopped after six reversals at the same level. Alternatively, if participants answered correctly for the surface that differed from the standard by one grade in more than 8 out of 10 consecutives trials, the trial was stopped.

Experimental Design. There were eight blocks for each participant with a 2 x 2 x 2 design (texture x force x movement). The sequence of the blocks was randomized across all participants.

Data analysis. In the Zwislocki 3-1 staircase [13] the 75% threshold is between the two steady state reversal levels. However, grit numbers are not on a linear scale and it is not appropriate to average the two levels. Therefore, we report the threshold as the number of grades away from the standard. In the off-line analysis, the F/T data from the load cell were low-pass filtered (10Hz, 3rd order Butterworth filter). In addition, the centre of pressure was calculated from the F/T measurements and the distance of the fingertip/stimulus interface from the load cell surface. Fingertip trajectory, contact duration and scanning velocity were estimated from the centre of pressure data.

2.2 Results

The mean normal contact force was .276 (±.008) N and .665 (±.012) N in the .3 and .8 N force conditions respectively. There were no reliable differences in contact force between moving and static condition for either coarse or fine sandpaper trials. The mean scanning velocity was 27.3 (±3.2) cm/s, with no significant difference between static and moving conditions. However, the average contact duration during static touch was significantly shorter than moving touch (1.855 ± 0.667 s vs 3.017 ± 1.510 s, p<.001).

The discrimination thresholds in the eight conditions are shown in Figure 2. Friedman tests showed that the discrimination thresholds were significantly higher in static touch compared to moving touch for both fine ($X^2(23,1)=19.6$; p<0.001) and coarse textures ($X^2 (23,1)=13.2$; p<.001). Friedman tests also revealed a significant effect of force on the discrimination threshold for coarse texture ($X^2 (23,1)=5.2$, p=0.02). Comparing moving touch and static touch using sign-rank tests, the discrimination threshold was significantly increased during static touch compared to moving touch in the 0.3N force condition (p<0.01) for the coarse sandpaper series and in the 0.8N force conditions (p<0.001) for the fine sandpaper series. The discrimination threshold for coarse sandpaper under the high force condition appears similar for moving and static touch (Figure 2). However, the majority of the participants

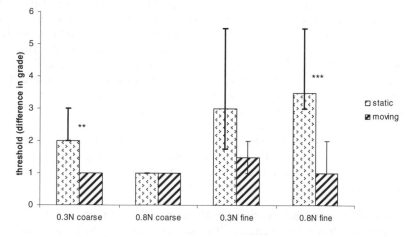

Fig. 2. The median and interquartile range of the discrimination threshold as a function of normal contact force and sandpaper type. **: p<0.01, ***: p<0.001 by sign-rank tests.

(9 out of 12) could differentiate between the sandpaper closest to the standard even in static touch. It could be the case that any improvement in performance due to the presence of movement could not be detected by the experiment as we were unable to obtain sandpaper between 100 and 120 grit. We examined the percentage correct for differentiating 100 grit and 120 grit sandpapers in these nine participants where the threshold lay between these two sandpapers. The mean percentage correct for the static and moving touch were 81.9 ± 1.5 and 96.3 ± 1.9 respectively. The performance in moving touch was significantly better (p<0.001, t(8)=-7.55) than in static touch.

3   Effects of Contact Duration on Texture Discrimination

The previous experiment showed that the discrimination threshold was higher during static touch than during moving touch. However, the contact duration was also longer during moving touch which may have contributed to improved performance. The following experiment investigated whether contact duration affects roughness discrimination.

3.1   Methods

The experiment was conducted using the same materials and apparatus as described in Section 2.1. The task and procedures were also the same, except that the participant was asked to lower the finger to start touching when the white noise started and to lift the finger off the surface when the white noise stopped. The duration of white noise was 1 s for the short contact duration trials and 3 s for the long contact duration trials.

Participants. Nine paid volunteers (3 females and 6 males, mean age 24 ± 4) were recruited from the undergraduate and postgraduate population. They were all naive to the purpose of the experiment. None had any history of hand or wrist injury or disease. They were all right-handed.

Experiment design. There were eight blocks for each participant with a 2 x 2 x 2 design (texture x contact duration x movement). The sequence of the blocks was randomized across all participants.

3.2   Results

Mean contact durations were 1.372 (±.062) s and 3.422 (±.052) s for the short and long duration conditions respectively. Two-way ANOVA showed no significant effects of texture and movement on contact duration in either case. Three-way ANOVA indicated no significant effects of texture, movement or contact duration on the mean contact force.

The discrimination thresholds are shown in Figure 3. The roughness discrimination threshold was significantly greater in static touch compared to moving touch with (p=0.01; X^2 (1,9) = 6.74) and (p=0.01, X^2 (1,9)=18.96) respectively using Friedman tests on data from coarse and fine texture trials. Contact duration did not have any significant effect on roughness discrimination with (p=0.66; chi X^2 (1,9) =0.66) and (p=0.97; X^2 (1,9) = 0.01) respectively for coarse and fine texture trials.

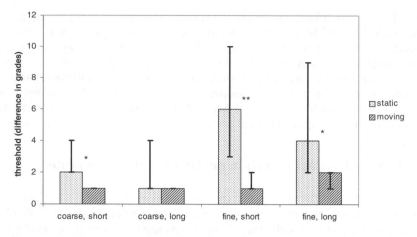

Fig. 3. The median discrimination threshold under static and moving conditions as a function of contact duration and sandpaper type. *: p<0.05 with sign-rank test; **: p<0.01 with sign-rank test.

4 Discussion and Conclusions

The results show that roughness discrimination is not affected by contact force except in static touch of coarse textures. It was also not affected by contact duration. The first result appears to contrast with previous findings that subjective roughness magnitude estimation increases with greater contact force [1]. However, in the discrimination paradigm used in the present study, roughness magnitude could have been been affected by similar amounts during the exploration of the standard and the test stimuli, i.e., the slope of the magnitude estimation curve would have remained the same throughout the roughness range used. This implies that in moving touch, as long as the force used during the exploration of the standard and test stimuli remains the same, the roughness discrimination threshold should not be affected. However, it remains to be seen if the discrimination threshold is affected when different forces are used for the standard and test. In static touch of coarse textures, lower contact force tended to reduce discriminability. Lower contact force might reduce skin indentation by the microstructure of the material and so increase the discrimination threshold. The overall results suggest that spatial-dependent texture discrimination deteriorates when the contact force is reduced whereas vibration-dependent texture discrimination is not affected by contact force.

The study also showed that roughness discrimination thresholds were greater in static than dynamic touch for both fine and coarse texture, although the effects were more pronounced in fine texture discrimination. This departs somewhat from previous findings [11] where fine texture discrimination was found to be significantly worse in static touch but there was no effect of movement in coarse texture discrimination. The mean particle size of the sandpaper used as the coarse texture standard in the current study was 162 µm, which is comparable to those used in [11] (192 µm and 141 µm). However, the difference could be due to different methodology being used in the two studies. Here we measured the 75% discrimination threshold, whereas in [10] the percentage correct response to differentiate two stimulus surfaces was recorded. If movement affects the psychometric function, the curve will be shifted to one side. However, if performance is assessed at the upper or lower end of the curve, the shift may not be apparent. If it is measured at the point of the steepest slope (the 75% discrimination threshold), then the difference can be detected more easily.

The results suggest that vibration sense plays a role in coarse as well as fine texture perception although its importance may be greater in the latter case. A lack of vibration information reduces the discriminability in both fine and coarse texture perception. However, one aspect that is not clear is whether there is a sharp demarcation point at which performance becomes spatial-dependent from vibration-dependent, or if there is a gradual transition between the two modes.

Although the contact duration in the static condition was reliably shorter than that of the moving condition, the second experiment showed that the discrimination threshold is not affected by contact duration. The mean contact durations used in the second experiment were comparable to those of the first experiment. Indeed, in the second experiment, the actual contact durations in the 'short duration' conditions were slightly shorter and in the 'long duration' conditions were slightly longer. Therefore, if the results of first experiment were affected by the contact duration in any way, they should have been revealed by the second experiment. The lack of an effect of contact duration on discrimination threshold indicates that the information needed to determine the roughness magnitude is gathered in the first 1.4 s of the touch process. In future research the effects of short contact duration (down to less than 1 s) on roughness discrimination should be investigated to determine the minimum time needed for making roughness judgments.

Acknowledgments. This study was funded as part of the EU FP6 project NanoBio-Tact (Contract no. 033287).

References

1. Lederman, S.J., Taylor, M.M.: Fingertip force, surface geometry and the perception of roughness by active touch. Perception and Psychophysics 12, 401–408 (1972)
2. Lamb, G.D.: Tactile discrimination of textured surfaces: peripheral neural coding in the monkey. J. Physiol. 338, 567–587 (1983)
3. Sathian, K., Zangaladze, A., Green, J., Vitek, J.L., DeLong, M.R.: Tactile spatial acuity and roughness discrimination: impairments due to aging and Parkinson's disease. Neurology 49, 168–177 (1997)
4. Tremblay, F., Mireault, A., LeTourneau, J., Pierrat, A., Bourrassa, S.: Tactile perception and manual dexterity in computer users. Somatosensory and Motor Research 19, 101–108 (2002)
5. Morley, J.W., Goodwin, A.W., Darian-Smith, I.: Tactile discrimination of gratings. Experimental Brain Research 49, 291–299 (1983)
6. Nefs, H.T., Kappers, A.M.L., Koenderink, J.J.: Frequency discrimination between and within line gratings by dynamic touch. Perception and Psychophysics 64, 969–980 (2002)
7. Blake, D.T., Hsiao, S.S., Johnson, K.O.: Neural coding mechanisms in tactile pattern recognition: the relative contributions of slowly and rapidly adapting mechanoreceptors to perceived roughness. J. Neuroscience 17, 7480–7489 (1997)

8. Yoshioka, T., Gibb, B., Dorsch, A.K., Hsiao, S.S., Johnson, K.O.: Neural coding mechanisms underlying perceive roughness of finely textured surfaces. J. Neuroscience 21(17), 6905–6916 (2001)
9. Johnson, K.O.: The roles and functions of cutaneous mechanoreceptors. Current Opinion in Neurobiology 11, 455–461 (2001)
10. Meftah, E.M., Belingard, L., Chapman, C.E.: Relative effects of the spatial and temporal characteristics of scanned surfaces on human perception of tactile roughness using passive touch. Experimental Brain Research 132, 351–361 (2000)
11. Hollins, M., Risner, S.R.: Evidence for the duplex theory of tactile texture perception. Perception and Psychophysics 62, 695–705 (2000)
12. Katz, D.: The world of touch (L.E. Krueger, trans.). Erlbaum, Hillsdale (original work published 1925) (1989)
13. Zwislocki, J.J., Relkin, E.M.: On a psychophysical transformed-rule up and down method converging on a 75% level of correct responses. Proc. Nat. Acad. Sci. 98, 4811–4814 (2001)

Causality Inversion in the Reproduction of Roughness

Michaël Wiertlewski[1,2], José Lozada[1],
Edwige Pissaloux[2], and Vincent Hayward[2]

[1] CEA, LIST, Sensory and Ambient Interfaces Laboratory, 18 route du Panorama, BP6, 92295
Fontenay-Aux-Roses, France
{michael.wiertlewski,jose.lozada}@cea.fr
[2] UPMC Univ Paris 6, Institut des Systèmes Intelligents et de Robotique, 75005, Paris, France
{pissaloux,hayward}@isir.upmc.fr

Abstract. When a finger scans a non-smooth surface, a sensation of roughness is experienced. A similar sensation is felt when a finger is in contact with a mobile surface vibrating in the tangential direction. Since an actual finger-surface interaction results in a varying friction force, how can a measured friction force can be converted into skin relative displacement. With a bidirectional apparatus that can measure this force and transform it into displacement with unambiguous causality, such mapping could be experimentally established. A pilot study showed that a subjectively equivalent sensation of roughness can be achieved betweem a fixed real surface and a vibrated mobile surface.

Keywords: Roughness simulation; Haptic devices; Virtual reality.

1 Introduction

Roughness is an important attribute of things we touch [1]. Concomitantly, there is a need for ever increasingly realistic virtual environments that can reproduce the various attributes of objects, including their roughness. To date, the approaches used to simulate roughness include the use of force feedback devices to replicate the microgeometry of surfaces, directly, or by reproducing its effects; see [2] for an extensive survey. Other approaches modulate the friction force that arises when a finger slips on an active surface. To this end, electrostatic fields [3], surface acoustic waves [4], or the squeeze film effect [5,6], can be employed.

Finger-Surface interaction. The steady slip of a finger on a surface induces a frictional force. If the surface in question deviates from smoothness, then the interaction force varies over time as a result of a complex interaction taking place between the finger and the surface. Microscopically, the variation is the consequence of the space-and-time-varying traction distribution (i.e. tangential force per unit of contact surface) at the interface between the finger and the surface. The traction distribution depends on the relative geometries of these two bodies, on the materials they are made of, and on the possible presence of fluids and foreign bodies.

In spite of this complexity, integration of traction over the (unknown) contact surface results in a net force that can be measured. It is known that the variations of this

A.M.L. Kappers et al. (Eds.): EuroHaptics 2010, Part II, LNCS 6192, pp. 17–24, 2010.
© Springer-Verlag Berlin Heidelberg 2010

force correlate strongly with a sensation of roughness [7,8]. While there is much debate regarding the manner in which the nervous system mediates the sensation of roughness peripherally and centrally, there is evidence that a variety of mechanisms are at play. Because of the multiplicity of these mechanisms, diverse stimulation methods can contribute to elicit roughness, see [9] among others.

Present Study. The present paper explores the possibility of stimulating the cutaneous system in order to create roughness sensations through the simplest method possible: that of vibrating tangentially a smooth surface in non-slipping contact with the finger, as the finger undergoes net motion. Yet, when it comes to design a display based on this idea, this simple approach poses a basic question which must be clearly answered: During tactile exploration, does the finger-surface interaction force "cause" the finger to deform or does the deformation "cause" the interaction force? Visual or auditory displays, by-and-large, radiate the same energy regardless of how they are looked at or listened to, so the causality is clear, but for haptic displays the causality question cannot be answered so easily, see [10] for elementary notions. The same question can be rephrased as follows: Should the measurement and the simulation be based on the skin displacement or on the force applied to it?

Bidirectional apparatus. To study this question, we build an apparatus that unambiguously establishes a causal relationship between the measurement and the stimulation by operating both as a sensor and as an actuator. In these two cases, the device was engineered to be very stiff, that is, five orders of magnitude stiffer than a fingertip. This way, when used as a sensor, the interaction force is known regardless of the finger movements and deformations; when used as an actuator, displacement is specified independently from the interaction force. To complete the symmetry, during recording operations, the sensor is fixed with respect to the ground and the finger slips on a rough surface. During restitution, the actuator is mounted on a slider and remains fixed relatively to the scanning finger touching a flat surface. In both modes, the device operates with a bandwidth spanning from 20 to 600 Hz, and has a maximum displacement of 0.2 mm in actuator mode, thereby covering the range useful for conveying roughness.

Main result. We performed a preliminary psychophysical experiment aimed at finding the subjective equivalence of roughness elicited by a rapidly varying measured force or by an imposed displacement, hence realizing a causality inversion between the measurement and the display. This approach is in contrast with the one employed with conventional haptic devices where a force is measured, or computed, and then specified with impedance devices; or where a displacement is computed and then specified with admittance devices. It was found that, indeed, such subjective equivalence of roughness could be established.

2 Apparatus

Referring to Figs. 1a and 3a, the apparatus comprises a rigid plate, A supported at one end by a low stiffness blade, B, and connected to a multilayer piezoelectric circular bender (CMBR07, Noliac Group A/S, Kvistgaard, Denmark), C, at the other. As a sensor, a textured surface is glued to the plate and during scanning the interaction force is measured within a very large dynamic range. As an actuator, the assembly is mounted on a linear guide and the smooth plate is vibrated tangentially.

2.1 Sensor Operation

The piezoelectric bender converts tangential forces due to the interaction with the finger into electric charges. These charges are transformed into voltage by an instrumentation amplifier (LT1789, Linear Technology Corp., Milpitas, CA, USA) as shown in Fig. 1b. The signal is then digitized by a 16-bit data acquisition board (PCI-6229, National Instruments Corp., Austin, TX, USA). The piezoelectric transducer acts like a generator V_p in series with a capacitor C_p and a charge resistance R_s. The RC circuit corresponds to a 20 Hz high-pass filter. Such charge-based force sensor is capable of a very high dynamic range response unachievable with conventional strain-gauge-based force sensors.

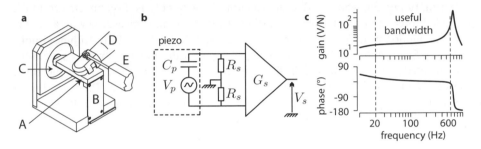

Fig. 1. Sensor operation. **a**: Setup. The finger position, measured by E, and the interaction force, measured by C are recorded when the finger, D, slips on the surface, A. **b**: Signal conditioning. **c**: Frequency response of the sensor.

The position of the finger, D, is measured with a linear variable transformer transducer (LVDT), E, (SX 12N060, Sensorex SA, Saint-Julien-en-Genevois, France) fastened to the fingernail. The response, Fig.1c, shows a sensitivity of 26 V/N in the range from 20 Hz to 600 Hz. The range is limited upward by the mechanical natural resonance. Output noise is lower than 20 μN/$\sqrt{\text{Hz}}$ and 16-bit digital conversion provides 50 μN of resolution at a 2 kHz sampling rate. The high stiffness of the bender ($70 \cdot 10^3$ N/m) ensures that the small deformation hypothesis is valid. Low frequency force components are measured by a conventional force sensor (Nano 17, ATI Industrial Automation, Inc., Apex, NC, USA) mounted on the load path between the assembly and a firm mechanical ground.

The interaction force components F_t and F_n and finger position $x(t)$ are acquired by the sensor during scanning, see Fig 2a. A typical measurement is seen in Fig. 2b. Notice how the tangential force F_t rises at the beginning of the motion and then oscillate around a value. The high-pass filter preserves the variation of the tangential force occurring within a wide dynamic range that a conventional force sensor would be unable to resolve, as shown in Fig. 2c. The initial stick to slip transition and ensuing transients have been edited out for clarity. This diagram is representative of the rich variations of the friction force due to a finger slipping on a periodic grooved surface.

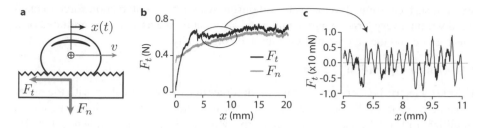

Fig. 2. Measurement **a**: The components F_n and F_t of the interaction force during scanning. $x(t)$ is measured by a LVDT. **b**: Typical force measurement from the conventional force sensor. **c**: Wide range dynamic measurement of sliding interaction measured by the piezoelectric sensor.

2.2 Actuator Operation

Referring to Fig. 3a, when used as an actuator, the assembly is disconnected from the grounded force sensor and placed on a slider, E. Its position is measured with a 7.5 μm linear resolution using an incremental encoder, F, (Model 2400, Fritz Kübler GmbH, Villingen-Schwenningen, Germany). The participant's third phalanx rests on a cradle, G, connected to the slider so that the fingertip rests on the active surface, A. As the finger scans to and fro, the transducer is driven by a voltage amplifier (Apex Precision Power PA86U, Cirrus Logic Inc., Austin, TX, USA) such that the skin in contact with the active surface is entrained by its oscillations without slip.

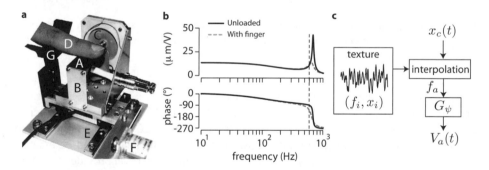

Fig. 3. Actuator operation. **a**: The stimulator, C, mounted on a linear stage, E, is fixed relatively to the finger, D. **b**: Frequency response of the none loaded actuator (black line) and with a finger pushing at 1 N (dash line). **c**: Control.

In order to ascertain performance, the output displacement was measured with a laser telemeter (LT2100, Keyence Corp., Osaka, Japan). The response, Fig. 3b, shows that the system is able to produce a displacement of $\pm 20\,\mu$m/V from DC to 600 Hz, limited by the system's natural resonance. For a 5V input, the actuator is able to achieve a maximum displacement of 100 μm.

The actuator is driven by a 2 kHz periodic realtime thread that reads the encoder position $x_c(t)$, interpolates a force value f_a from a given texture profile, multiplies it by a gain G_ψ and refreshes the amplifier output $V_a(t)$, see Fig. 3c. This control thread runs under the LabVIEW™ environment on an ordinary computer equipped with the digital input-output board already mentioned.

3   Experimental Procedure for Perceptual Calibration

Having unambiguously converted a varying interaction force into a skin displacement during the scanning of a surface by means of an apparatus designed to establish robust causal relationships not achievable with conventional haptic devices, the question now arises of the value of the conversion factor that could elicit an equivalent sensation of roughness. Furthermore, if such a factor exists, does it vary from person to person? To address these questions, a calibration procedure was carried out with six participants in order to establish the point of subjective equivalent roughness between the natural texture and its simulated version. A 2-alternative forced choice, constant stimuli procedure was employed to find the gains $\hat{G}_\psi$ that would elicit an equivalent sensation of roughness.

Stimuli. The standard stimulus was a triangular grooved grating of 1 mm spatial period with 0.1 mm of depth. Without relative motion, the roughness of this texture was not perceptible. The scanning force with this grating was measured using the sensor described earlier with the help of a "standard" participant. During recording, the speed v and the normal force F_n were held constant with a 10% tolerance. The signal was processed as described in Section 2.1, then normalized to ± 0.5 V. The filtered signal, expressed in Newton, and its Fourier transform are shown in Fig. 4b. The comparison stimulus was provided by the stimulator described in Section 2.2. Fig. 4a illustrates the precautions that were taken so that both stimuli were presented in exactly the same conditions: (a) The participants had their proximal phalanx resting in cradles connected to sliding guides so that the fingertip rested on the grooved texture or stimulator in same manner; (b) Both surfaces were made in polycarbonate; (c) The two sliders were mechanically connected so the same inertia and the same friction was felt for the standard and the comparison stimuli. The experimental setup was hidden by a curtain to avoid visual bias. Subjects wore sound isolation headphones (model K518, AKG Acoustics, Harman International Industries) playing white noise.

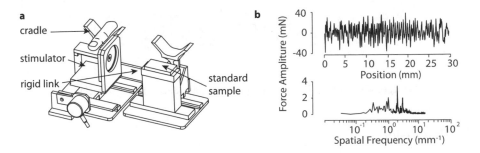

Fig. 4. a: Experimental setup. **b**: Stimulus and its spectrum. The scanning process transforms a simple surface waveform into a complex, broadband force signal.

Subjects and Procedure. Six volunteers participated in the experiment, two female and four male, all right-handed, aged from 24 to 31 years. They were from CEA LIST and two of them were familiar with haptic technology. Their hand was guided to explore the setup and after short instructions they were asked to judge whether the standard or the comparison stimulus was rougher and to give an answer via a keystroke. Like in [11], no definition of roughness was given except that "roughness is the opposite of smoothness". Neither training nor feedback was provided during the tests. Gain G_ψ was randomly chosen in a range of 1 to 10. Each value was tested at least 10 times.

4 Results

Subjects responded to gain changes following a typical psychometric curve, as shown in Fig. 5. The data were fitted with a cumulative Gaussian distribution $f(x) = 0.5 \left[1 + \mathrm{erf}\left((x - \mu)/\sqrt{2}\sigma \right) \right]$ where x is the gain, μ the mean gain and σ^2 the variance. The data fitting was achieved using a nonlinear least-square fitting procedure.

The point of subjective equivalence (PSE) was extracted from the gain that corresponds to a 50% probability of judging the comparison rougher than the standard. Figure 6 shows the distribution of PSE's. The average across subjects is $\bar{G}_\psi = 3.99$ with a standard deviation of 0.93.

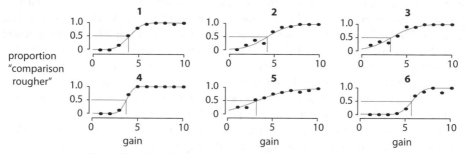

Fig. 5. Results of each participants and their sigmoid fitting

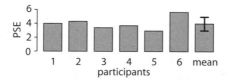

Fig. 6. Value of the Point of Subjective Equivalence of each subject

5 Discussion

The results indicate that the interaction force variation can be converted to skin displacement variations to elicit an equivalent sensation of roughness for a virtual surface compared to a real one. As a result, this particularly simple stimulation method is shown to be effective at simulating the roughness of a surface. Moreover, participants frequently commented on the perceptual similarity of the sensations themselves between real and simulated surfaces.

These results support the idea that as far as fine textures are concerned, spatial information can be completely eliminated from the simulation, yet, the conscious experience can be that of a non-smooth surface. While similar observations have frequently be reported in the past, our experiments, given to the care that we put in controlling the causality as well as the quality of the transmitted signals, make it now possible to quantify the conditions under which such phenomenon occur. Another aspect of our results worthy of some comments is the relative constancy of the conversion factor among individuals. Of the six individuals who lent themselves to the experiment, five obtained very similar numbers. Only one required a significantly higher displacement stimulus to achieve an equivalent level of roughness. Our efforts will be directed in the future at understanding these individual differences.

6   Conclusion

With the help of a carefully engineered sensor, sliding frictional forces could be acquired within a very high dynamic range. The same device was turned in a stimulator having, by construction, a compatible dynamic range that could convert this frictional force into a displacement able to provide a simulated sensation.

This study has so-far considered only one texture for perceptual calibration. We plan to investigate other aspects of texture signals, such as spectral content, in addition to amplitude, and to study the conditions under which perceptual equivalence can be achieved. The distribution of roughness perception across gain values was found to be a monotonic function. As a result, one could employ fast calibration procedures such as accelerated staircase methods as in [11].

A final implication of the present experiment is the possibility to replace force feedback stimulation by cutaneous displacement stimulators which may lend themselves to more favorable engineerings tradeoffs, particularly with subminiature devices. Such miniature devices could for instance be embedded in the gripping surfaces of conventional force feedback devices.

Acknowledgment. The authors would like to thanks Margarita Anastanova for her helpful comments on the experimental setup. This work was supported by the French research agency through the REACTIVE project (ANR-07-TECSAN-020).

References

1. Lederman, S.J., Taylor, M.M.: Fingertip force, surface geometry, and the perception of roughness by active touch. Perception & Psychophysics 12(5), 401–408 (1972)
2. Campion, G., Hayward, V.: On the synthesis of haptic textures. IEEE Transactions on Robotics 24(3), 527–536 (2008)
3. Yamamoto, A., Nagasawa, S., Yamamoto, H., Higuchi, T.: Electrostatic tactile display with thin film slider and its application to tactile telepresentation systems. IEEE Transactions on Visualization and Computer Graphics 12(2), 168–177 (2006)

4. Takasaki, M., Kotani, H., Mizuno, T., Nara, T.: Transparent surface acoustic wave tactile display. In: IEEE/RSJ International Conference on Intelligent Robots and Systems, IROS 2005, pp. 3354–3359 (2005)
5. Biet, M., Giraud, F., Lemaire-Semail, B.: Squeeze film effect for the design of an ultrasonic tactile plate. IEEE Transactions on Ultrasonics, Ferroelectrics and Frequency Control 54(12), 2678–2688 (2007)
6. Winfield, L., Glassmire, J., Colgate, J.E., Peshkin, M.: T-PaD: tactile pattern display through variable friction reduction. In: Second Joint EuroHaptics Conference and Symposium on Haptic Interfaces for Virtual Environment and Teleoperator Systems. World Haptics, pp. 421–426 (2007)
7. Smith, A.M., Chapman, E.C., Deslandes, M., Langlais, J.S., Thibodeau, M.P.: Role of friction and tangential force variation in the subjective scaling of tactile roughness. Experimental Brain Research 144(2), 211–223 (2002)
8. Smith, A.M., Basile, G., Theriault-Groom, J., Fortier-Poisson, P., Campion, G., Hayward, V.: Roughness of simulated surfaces examined with a haptic tool; effects of spatial period, friction, and resistance amplitude. Experimental Brain Research 202(1), 33–43 (2010)
9. Maeno, T., Otokawa, K., Konyo, M.: Tactile display of surface texture by use of amplitude modulation of ultrasonic vibration. In: IEEE Ultrasonics Symposium, pp. 62–65 (2006)
10. Hogan, N.: Impedance control: An approach to manipulation. Journal of Dynamic Systems, Measurements, and Control 107, 1–7 (1985)
11. Campion, G., Hayward, V.: Fast calibration of haptic texture synthesis algorithms. IEEE Transactions on Haptics 2(2), 85–93 (2009)

Laterotactile Rendering of Vector Graphics with the Stroke Pattern

Vincent Lévesque[1] and Vincent Hayward[2]

[1] Department of Computer Science, University of British Columbia
201-2366 Main Mall, Vancouver, BC, V6T 1Z4, Canada
vlev@cs.ubc.ca
[2] UPMC Univ Paris 06, UMR 7222
Institut des Systèmes Intelligents et de Robotique, F-75005, Paris, France
vincent.hayward@isir.fr

Abstract. Raised line patterns are used extensively in the design of tactile graphics for persons with visual impairments. A tactile stroke pattern was therefore developed to enable the rendering of vector graphics by lateral skin deformation. The stroke pattern defines a transversal profile and a longitudinal texture which provide tactile feedback while respectively crossing over the stroke and tracing its length. The stroke pattern is demonstrated with the rendering of lines, circles and polygons, and is extensible to other vector graphics primitives such as curves. The parametric nature of the stroke allows the representation of distinctive line types and the online adjustment of line thickness and other parameters according to user preferences and capabilities. The stroke pattern was informally evaluated with four visually impaired volunteers.

Keywords: assistive technology, tactile graphics, tactile display, haptic rendering, laterotactile rendering.

1 Introduction

The accessibility of graphical content is gaining in importance for persons with visual impairments as visual representations of information become increasingly ubiquitous in applications ranging from home appliances to computer interfaces. The accessibility of graphics is particularly critical in education where visually impaired students require equal access to visual teaching aids such as technical diagrams [1,2]. Tactile graphics, however, are generally produced on physical media such as embossed paper or thermoformed plastic [1] which are cumbersome to produce and distribute, often deteriorate with use, and do not afford access to dynamic content such as interactive geographic maps.

These issues could potentially be addressed through the development of virtual or refreshable tactile graphics interfaces. Force-feedback interfaces have for example been used to allow single-point interaction with virtual environments or surfaces (e.g. [3]). An alternative consists of using a transducer known as a tactile display that produces distributed tactile sensations by deforming or otherwise stimulating the skin [4]. A first class of tactile displays presents a large, programmable surface to be explored by the

A.M.L. Kappers et al. (Eds.): EuroHaptics 2010, Part II, LNCS 6192, pp. 25–30, 2010.

fingers or hands, often in the form of an array of actuated pins (e.g. [5]). A second class produces a large virtual surface out of a smaller tactile display by dynamically altering the sensation produced in response to displacements of the device (e.g. [6]).

The work presented in this paper leverages a novel approach to skin stimulation that produces virtual tactile graphics by laterally deforming the fingerpad skin with the Tactograph, a haptic interface that combines a STReSS[2] laterotactile display and an instrumented planar carrier (Fig. 1a-b). The latest STReSS[2] consists of an array of 8×8 independent piezoelectric actuators forming a dense array of 64 laterally-moving skin contactors within an area of 1 cm^2 [7]. The tip of each actuator can be deflected towards the left or right by a maximum of approximately 0.1 mm. Virtual tactile graphics are produced by stimulating the skin with the tactile display as it slides within the carrier's 21×15 cm workspace.

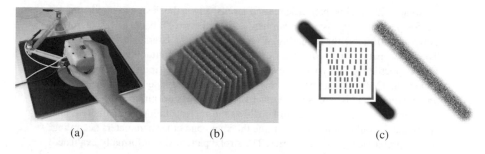

(a)   (b)   (c)

Fig. 1. Pictures of (a) the Tactograph and (b) its array of skin contactors, and (c) simulation of actuator activation over 5-mm wide stroked lines

Laterotactile rendering algorithms can be described as sets of deflection functions $\delta_{i,j}(P,\theta,t)$ that define the behaviour of each actuator i,j as a function of time t as well as the position P and orientation θ of the tactile display. Rendering algorithms can often be simplified such that the deflection $\delta(p)$ of an actuator depends solely on its position p within the virtual canvas. Vibration can also be rendered by introducing a time-varying sinusoidal oscillation with variable amplitude and a maximum frequency of 50 Hz. Virtual tactile graphics are illustrated as shown in Fig. 1c by mapping local deflection and vibration to pixel intensity and white noise respectively.

Previous work has demonstrated that complex illustrations, simple shapes and textures can be produced with rendering algorithms that generate localized vibrations, grating patterns and raised dots based on bitmapped modulation masks [8,9]. The work presented in this paper introduces vector graphics capabilities to this framework through the development of a tactile stroke pattern that emulates the properties of a raised line. The stroke pattern is defined by a transversal profile which triggers the sensation of crossing over the stroke, and a longitudinal texture which provides feedback as the stroke is traced. The stroke pattern can be applied to a variety of vector graphics primitives and is demonstrated with the rendering of lines, circles and polygons. Strokes and stroked shapes were informally evaluated with four visually impaired volunteers.

2   Stroke

The stroke is similar in concept to a brush stroke or raised line and defines the tactile appearance of a shape's outline. A stroke's rendering is composed of a transversal deflection profile that depends on the distance r across the shape's path as well as a longitudinal texture varying with the distance l along its length.

The transversal profile triggers the sensation of brushing over a raised line when moving across the stroke by causing a sinusoidal swing in actuator deflection. A smooth profile (Fig. 2a) results in a natural sensation which becomes increasingly subtle as the stroke thickness is increased. The sharpness of the stroke is restored by shortening the sinusoidal transition at its edges (Fig. 2b). Sharp edges, however, can create the sensation of touching two distinct lines when separated by a certain distance. This effect can optionally be embraced and reinforced by rendering the stroke as an outline with maximal actuator swing at its edges (Fig. 2c). A transversal texture in the form of a sinusoidal oscillation can finally be superposed over a scaled-down deflection profile (Fig. 2d).

The transversal profile provides only minimal feedback when following the length of a stroke. A longitudinal texture is therefore introduced to provide additional tactile feedback while tracing a shape's contour. The resulting stroke deflection is produced by modulating the stroke profile with a grating waveform varying along the length of the shape's path. The grating texture imitates the sensation of brushing against a corrugated surface by producing smooth swings in actuator deflections that are perceived as raised bumps or ridges [8]. A grating cycle is composed of a sinusoidal swing that creates the sensation of a ridge followed by an optional gap that reinforces the salience of the tactile feature. Although otherwise effective, a dense texture can interfere with the perception of the profile by introducing breaks in the edges (Fig. 2e). The frequency of edge breaks can be reduced through the use of a sparse grating texture (Fig. 2f). As an alternative, an outlined stroke (Fig. 2g-h) can be produced to reinforce the stroke's edges. The salience of the grating texture is dependent on its physical extent and hence affected by the width and sharpness of the stroke profile.

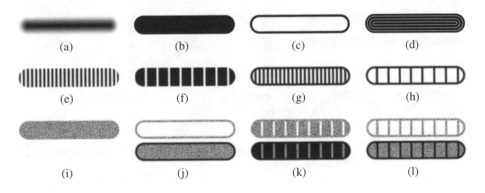

Fig. 2. Examples of the use of (a-d) transversal profiles, (e-h) longitudinal textures and (i-l) vibrations in the rendering of a stroked line

Vibration can also be used to reinforce the intensity of a stroke and to allow it to be felt even in the absence of exploratory movement. Vibration can be applied either to the active or inactive pattern of a stroke (Fig. 2i-l).

3   Shapes

Shapes are rendered by applying the stroke pattern according to the definition of a coordinate system that specifies both a transversal distance r from the shape contour and a longitudinal distance l along its length. The concept is described below for lines, circles and polygons but could easily be generalized and adapted to other common vector graphics primitives such as curves, arcs and open paths.

A line is rendered by defining the transversal distance r and the longitudinal distance l respectively as the minimal distance to the line segment and the distance to the actuator's projection along its length. This results in rounded lines caps through which the longitudinal texture extends gracefully (Fig. 3a). A circle is similarly rendered by defining r and l as the minimal distance to its contour and arc length along it respectively (Fig. 3b). Continuity is ensured by fitting a whole number of texture cycles within the circle's circumference.

A polygon is rendered by defining the transversal distance r as the minimal distance to the its contour, which corresponds to the minimum transversal distance to its line segments. The definition of the longitudinal distance l is more ambiguous due to complications at the vertices. The simplest approach consists of extending the longitudinal path to the midline of the joints. This definition, however, causes discontinuities in the rendering at the junction of the line segments which can be eliminated by rounding the longitudinal path. A further complication is encountered close to the arc's pivot point where the spatial frequency of the texture increases without bounds. This singularity can be moved out of the stroke by defining the longitudinal path as if for a wider stroke, resulting in the early onset of the rounding near joints. All three approaches are illustrated in Fig. 3c. Texture continuity is enforced such that a whole number of cycles fits within the length of the selected longitudinal path.

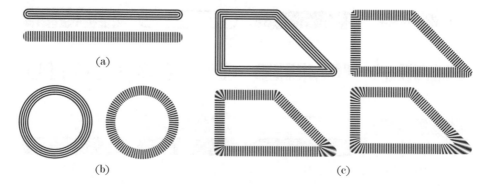

(a)

(b)   (c)

Fig. 3. Illustration of the transversal and longitudinal coordinate system for stroked (a) lines, (b) circles, and (c) polygons

Fig. 4. Examples of polygons with (a) vertex markers and (b) a fill texture

Markers can also be superposed on a polygon's vertices to improve their salience, facilitate their localization and hide discontinuities in their rendering (Fig. 4a). Vertex markers have a conic shape that extends from the point of intersection of the joint's edges and are rendered either as plain or vibrating patterns. Their angular coverage can either be fixed or set according to the properties of the joint. A filling texture such as a grating [8] can similarly be applied to the interior of a polygon or circle (Fig. 4b). The texture begins at the inner edge of the stroke and fades in linearly over a small distance to avoid discontinuities, with an optional gap for increased contrast.

4   Discussion

The effectiveness of strokes and stroked shapes was informally evaluated by soliciting feedback from four visually-impaired volunteers. The following discussion forms a synthesis of the preliminary insights gained from their comments.

Although individual preferences vary, alteration of the sharpness, thickness and texture of a stroke results in distinctive tactile patterns that can be used to produce contrasting line types. Smooth strokes are noisy when thin and weak when thick, but otherwise usable for a range of approximately 2 to 10 mm. The edges of sharp or outlined strokes, on the other hand, remain strong but are felt as disjoint lines when the thickness exceeds approximately 5 mm. Transversal and longitudinal textures both add substance to the stroke with the latter providing better tracing feedback. A dense grating with a spatial wavelength of 2 mm is generally preferred and the breaks introduced in the edges do not appear to warrant correction with a sparse grating or a stroke outline. Vibrations result in less pleasant but much more intense sensations than smooth deflections and are therefore ideal to introduce contrast. Vibration, however, may cause tactile adaptation with prolonged exposure and tends to overpower nearby non-vibrating patterns. The geometry of stroked shapes can be traced and understood with relative ease. The rounding of the longitudinal path at polygon vertices appears to slightly weaken sharp corners while the discontinuities otherwise introduced have minimal effect. Vibrating markers are effective at highlighting vertices but their exact shape is not perceptible and should be selected to maximize area. Fill textures are effective but sometimes interfere with the shape contour, particularly in the absence of a gap or clear contrast between the stroke and texture.

This informal evaluation suggests that the stroke pattern has great potential for the laterotactile rendering of vector graphics. The results indicate that stroke parameters could be selected not only for improved perceptibility, but also to present contrasting line types. Stroke parameters could moreover be adjusted online so as to adapt to the user's preferences and capabilities. Much work nevertheless remains to formally evaluate the effectiveness of the stroke pattern and the effect of its rendering parameters on the discriminability and identifiability of strokes and stroked shapes. Preliminary results suggest that stroked shapes should match or outperform the dotted and vibrating patterns evaluated in [8]. The rendering of stroke intersections and the achievable density of stroked patterns may also require further investigation for practical applications. This work is a first step towards a complete vector graphics drawing library which could enable the automated adaptation of vector graphics content such as those produced using the increasingly popular Scalable Vector Graphics (SVG) format.

References

1. Edman, P.K.: Tactile Graphics. AFB Press, New York (1992)
2. Aldrich, F.K., Sheppard, L.: Tactile graphics in school education: perspectives from pupils. British Journal of Visual Impairment 19(2), 69–73 (2001)
3. Rassmus-Gröhn, K., Magnusson, C., Eftring, H.: User evaluations of a virtual haptic-audio line drawing prototype. In: Proc. Workshop on Haptic and Audio Interaction Design (2006)
4. Vidal-Verdú, F., Hafez, M.: Graphical tactile displays for visually-impaired people. IEEE Trans. Neural Syst. Rehabil. Eng. 15(1), 119–130 (2007)
5. Watanabe, T., Kobayashi, M., Ono, S., Yokoyama, K.: Practical use of interactive tactile graphic display system at a school for the blind. In: Proc. Fourth International Conference on Multimedia and Information and Communication Technologies in Education (m-ICTE), pp. 1111–1115 (2006)
6. Jansson, G., Juhasz, I., Cammilton, A.: Reading virtual maps with a haptic mouse: Effects of some modifications of the tactile and audio-tactile information. British Journal of Visual Impairment 24(2), 60–66 (2006)
7. Wang, Q., Hayward, V.: Compact, portable, modular, high-performance, distributed tactile display device based on lateral skin deformation. In: Proc. Haptics Symposium, pp. 67–72 (2006)
8. Lévesque, V., Hayward, V.: Tactile graphics rendering using three laterotactile drawing primitives. In: Proc. Haptics Symposium, pp. 429–436 (2008)
9. Petit, G., Dufresne, A., Lévesque, V., Hayward, V., Trudeau, N.: Refreshable tactile graphics applied to schoolbook illustrations for students with visual impairment. In: Proc. ACM Conference on Computers and Accessibility (ASSETS), pp. 89–96 (2008)

Discrimination Capabilities of Professionals in Manual Skills in a Haptic Task Not Related to Their Expertise

Marcos Hilsenrat and Miriam Reiner

Laboratory of Virtual Reality and Neurocognition, Department of Education
in Technology and Science Technion – Israel Institute of Technology Haifa, Israel
{marcos,miriamr}@technion.ac.il

Abstract. In this study we present a comparative research between the discrimination capabilities of two populations: Professionals in manual skills and non-professionals, in a task that was not related to their field of expertise. The task was, in a psychophysical test, to discriminate between surfaces of different roughness by indirect touch, using a 3D hapto-visual virtual reality (VR) device. In a texture-difference recognition test subjects glided a pen-like stylus on a virtual surface. The surface was divided into five areas: one central, and four surrounding areas. The roughness of the central area was kept constant throughout the experiment. In each run, three of the four surrounding areas were kept at the same roughness as the central surface, and one, randomly, was different. From run to run, surface roughness was changed following a binary search paradigm. If a subject recognized the portion of the surface with a different roughness, then the roughness was reduced by half; if not, the roughness increased, and so on, until the desired degree of accuracy was achieved. Five professionals from different haptic expertise fields and five non professionals participated in the experiment. The results of the study showed that laymen were significantly more sensitive than experts on roughness discrimination ($p < 0.01$). These results may suggest that intensive manual activity that demands particular haptic expertise may have a negative impact on manual tasks that are irrelevant to their daily professional activity.

Keywords: experts performance; roughness sensitivity; virtual reality.

1 Introduction

Superior tactile performance in professional pianists was found using a passive psychophysical test [1]. The test was to measure tactile spatial acuity using a simultaneous two-point discrimination paradigm. On the other hand, in a comparative study between professional typists and casual users it was found that in a prototype keyboard with different haptic feedback than in a regular keyboard, non-professionals performed better [2]. It was shown that visual perception of regular golf balls painted as practice balls (heavier than regular balls) affected the weight evaluation of professional golfers. In contrast, non-golfers had no problem judging the balls (painted and white) as having the same weight [3]. This suggests top-down processing in a motor task (weight perception), that is, expertise can have a negative impact on sensory perception.

A.M.L. Kappers et al. (Eds.): EuroHaptics 2010, Part II, LNCS 6192, pp. 31–36, 2010.
© Springer-Verlag Berlin Heidelberg 2010

Contact with a surface by means of a probe or tool generates considerable amount of information about its texture. One of the main qualities of the objects' texture is its surface roughness. Many studies have been conducted on the perception of roughness by the bare finger [4]-[6], and through indirect touch [7]-[9]. Those studies included psychophysical research on subjects' abilities to perceive changes in surface roughness during active and passive touch [7] [10].

The potential role of VR in experimental psychology was already pointed out [11]. Several studies concerning haptic perception using VR interfaces have been made [12] [13].

In this paper we present results from a comparative study between the discrimination capabilities of professionals in manual skills and non-professionals, in a task that was not related to their field of expertise. We took advantage of the programmable capabilities of a hapto-visual interface to assign arbitrary physical properties to virtual objects and to evaluate participants' sensitivity to changes in surface roughness.

2 Method

2.1 Apparatus

We used a 3D virtual reality touch-enabled computer interface (The DESKTOP PHANToM from SenseAble Technologies Inc.) capable of providing users with visual and haptic stimuli, and with the capability of recording applied forces (Fig. 1). The assembly included a computer screen that was tilted 45° and was reflected on a half-silvered horizontal mirror. The participants viewed this reflection from above. A pen-like robotic arm (stylus) gripped and moved as in handwriting or drawing, was placed below the mirror surface and was represented as a stick figure in the visual workspace.

To program surface roughness, we used the Reachin function that simulates something akin to sand paper [14]. To simulate the granularity of sand paper, the haptic device's motion is constantly stopped, and a new starting friction value is randomly calculated using a Gaussian probability distribution with a mean and standard deviation. The two values that can be altered are the mean and the standard deviation. The input in the mean value is the dimensionless friction coefficient μ. The input in the standard deviation allows the randomness to be contained, and it was kept constant through the experiment. A low value of μ means a smoother surface, and as the value of μ increases, the surface becomes rougher.

2.2 Participants

Ten right handed participants, participated in the experiment; five non-professionals (two females, three males) who declared not having a hobby that demands manual expertise, and five professionals (two females, three males) from different fields of expertise: one pianist, one violinist, two dentists, and one reflexologist. All professionals had more than five years of experience, and worked and (or) trained for more than twelve hours per week. The participants reported that they not suffer from any motor impediment. The mean age and standard deviation of the professionals and laymen were 35.2 years, 6.1 years, 37.8 years, 7.3 years, respectively. All procedures were performed in accordance with the ethical standards established in the 1964 Declaration of Helsinki.

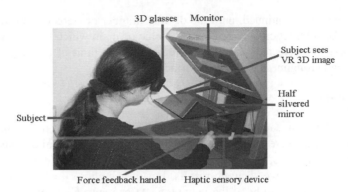

Fig. 1. Experimental array. The participant interacts with a virtual 3D object using a haptic interface. The visual and physical properties of the virtual objects are programmable, and the participant's responses are saved.

2.3 Experimental Setup

A schematic representation of the experimental setup is shown in Fig. 2. The virtual surface was divided into five areas: one central, and four surrounding areas. The roughness of the central area was kept constant throughout the experiment. In each run, three of the four surrounding areas were kept at the same roughness as the central surface, and one area, randomly, was different. This geometrical shape was designed so that the subject was able to move the hand smoothly across the entire surface.

In the central area, and in three of the four surrounding areas, roughness was kept constant with $\mu=\mu_B$, throughout the experiment, and one was randomly with different roughness, $\mu=\mu_n$. The participant was instructed to glide the stylus across the surface, and find the area with μ_n, then, to press the correspondent number on the small cells (see Fig. 2). The choice has visual feedback; if the subject chose correctly, the pressed cell turns to green, and if incorrectly, it turns to red.

The possibility of choosing between four areas reduces the probability of guessing a correct answer to 0.25 for each run, in contrast with conventional methods where the probability is 0.5.

2.4 Experimental Algorithm

The algorithm for evaluation of the limit of aware recognition of differences in surface roughness is based on a binary search paradigm [15]. A similar method was designed for visual contrast detection [16]. The input values are: The background friction coefficient μ_B, the initial friction coefficient that is different μ_1, and the desired number of steps n. The algorithm is built so that always $\mu_1 > \mu_B$. μ_1 is chosen so that a healthy participant will easily recognize the area with this value; if not, the experiment is stopped due to the subject' incapability.

In the next step, the new value of μ_n is set as the average between μ_1 and μ_B. When the subject chooses correctly, the procedure is repeated. If the participant chooses incorrectly, then the next μ_n is obtained by calculating the average between the values of μ when the last correct answer was given, and its present value.

The procedure is continued, until the desired number of steps is achieved. We define μ_{lim} as the subtraction between the last value of μ_n in which the area with different roughness was detected, and μ_B. μ_{lim} represents the limit of aware perception of the difference in roughness for a given surface with μ_B.

2.5 Procedure

The number of runs in each measurement, and the initial value of μ_1 for the area with different roughness were carefully chosen by performing many pilot tests. We concluded that eight steps, allowing 128 equally spaced possible results were the optimal choice to achieve accurate results. For μ_1 we chose $\mu_1 = 2\mu_B$. In the present experiment, μ_B was set to be at the value 0.5. After many pilot runs, we found that this value for the reference stimulus was the most appropriate, since participants felt more comfortable. To allow a suitable statistical analysis, every participant ran each test, ten times.

To avoid hand adaptation, after each test subjects took a short break, and were instructed to perform a manual task that was not related to the experiment.

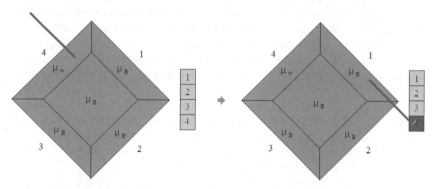

Fig. 2. Schematic representation of the experimental setup, before, and after the area with different roughness was correctly detected

3 Results

The mean and standard deviation of μ_{lim} for each participant was calculated, then, for each group those results were combined, and the general mean and standard deviation were obtained. The results were as follows:

Table 1. Mean value and standard deviation of μ_{lim} for each group

	Professionals	Non-professionals
Mean μ_{lim}	0.152	0.069
SD	0.038	0.017

We performed a one tailed paired t-test between the two groups and we found a significant difference between the means ($p < 0.01$). The post hoc power analysis [17], was: $1 - \beta = 0.97$. Remarkably, we found that the "less sensitive" layman (mean $\mu_{lim} = 0.085$) performed better than the "more sensitive" expert (mean $\mu_{lim} = 0.105$).

All participants reported that the visual feedback and the active exploration of the surfaces increased their motivation in the experiment, avoiding boredom and lack of concentration that are common in long psychophysical experiments.

4 Conclusions

In the present study, we investigated the haptic performance of professionals in several fields of manual expertise, in a task that was not related to their occupation. We evaluated the limit of aware perception for changes in surface roughness. We compared their performance to a corresponding group of non-professionals, and found that the last group was significantly more sensitive than the experts' group.

These results may suggest that the action loop of the perception of a haptic stimulus (down-top) and a motor response to it (top-down) by professionals is "tuned" by their everyday activity. In contrast, laymen are not affected from everyday experience. The use of a binary search paradigm for haptic sensitivity evaluation [15], was possible due the programmable capabilities of the VR. Preliminary results from similar experiments with different haptic stimuli (hardness, vibration), are consistent with the conclusions described above.

In our point of view, the active nature of our experiment, and the high degree of participants' immersion, helps subjects to act naturally, and therefore emphasizes the use of virtual reality as a very useful and often indispensable tool in behavioral research.

Further research will include a similar comparative experiment where professionals will come from one field that includes indirect touch (e.g. surgery). We will build a virtual environment that will resemble their natural working environment. We expect that in such a test professionals will perform better. Then, we will repeat the same paradigm presented in the present paper. Opposite results in both tests will validate our conclusions.

Acknowledgments

This study is supported by the following project: IMMERSENCE 027141.

References

[1] Ragert, P., Schmidt, A., Altenmüler, E:, Dinse, H.R.: Superior Tactile performance and learning in professional pianists: evidence for meta-plasticity in musicians. Euro Journal of Neuroscience 19(2), 473–478 (2004)

[2] Barret, J., Krueger, H.: Performance effects of reduced proprioceptive feedback on touch typist and casual users in a typing task. Behavior and Information Technology 13(6), 673–681 (1994)

[3] Ellis, R., Lederman, S.: The golf-ball illusion: evidence for top-down processing in weight perception. Perception 27, 193–201 (1998)

[4] Lederman, S.J.: Tactile roughness of grooved surfaces: The touching process and effects of macro and microsurface structure. Perception & Psychophysics 16, 385–395 (1974)

[5] Lederman, S.J., Taylor, M.M.: Fingertip force, surface geometry and the perception of roughness by active touch. Perception & Psychophysics 12, 401–408 (1972)

[6] Connor, C.E., Hsiao, S.S., Phillips, J.R., Johnson, K.O.: Tactile roughness: Neural codes that account for psychophysical magnitude estimates. J. Neuroscience 10, 3823–3836 (1990)

[7] Klatzky, R.L., Lederman, S.J., Hamilton, C., Grindley, M., Swendsen, R.H.: Feeling textures through a probe: Effects of probe and surface geometry and exploratory factors. Perception & Psychophysics 65(4), 613–631 (2003)

[8] Klatzky, R.L., Lederman, S.J.: Tactile roughness perception with a rigid link interposed between skin and surface. Perception & Psychophysics 61, 591–607 (1999)

[9] Hollins, M., Lorenz, F., Harper, D.: Somatosensory coding of roughness: The effect of texture adaptation in indirect and indirect touch. J. Neuroscience 26(20), 5582–5588 (2006)

[10] Lederman, S.J., Klatzky, R.L., Hamilton, C.L., Ramsay, G.L.: Perceiving roughness via a rigid probe: Psychophysical effects of exploration speed and mode of touch. Elec. J. Haptics Res. 1(1), 1–20 (1999)

[11] Gaggioli, A.: Using virtual reality in experimental psychology. In: Riva, G., Galimberti, C. (eds.) Toward Cyber Psychology: Mind, Cognitions and Society in the Internet Age, pp. 157–174. IOS, Amsterdam (2002)

[12] Hecht, D., Reiner, M.: Field dependency and the sense of object-presence in haptic virtual environments. Cyberpsychol. Behavior 10(2), 243–251 (2007)

[13] Hilsenrat, M., Reiner, M.: The impact of unaware perception on bodily interaction in virtual reality environments. Presence 18(6), 413–420 (2009)

[14] Reachin API 3.2 Programmers Guide, pp. 10–11 (2003)

[15] Hilsenrat, M., Reiner, M.: Hapto-visual virtual reality as a tool in psychophysical research on roughness sensitivity. In: Proceedings of the 3rd International Conference on Advances in Computer-Human Interactions (ACHI 2010), pp. 139–142. IEEE Computer Society Press, Los Alamitos (2010)

[16] Tyrrell, R.A., Owens, D.A.: A rapid technique to assess the resting states of the eyes and other thrshold phenomena: the modified binary search (MOBS). Behavior Research Methods, Instruments, and Computers 20(2), 137–141 (1988)

[17] Faul, F., Erdfelder, E., Lang, A.G., Buchner, A.: G*Power 3: A flexible statistical power analysis program for the social, behavioral, and biomedical sciences. Behavior Research Methods 39, 175–191 (2007)

Modulations in Low-Frequency EEG Oscillations in the Processing of Tactile Surfaces

Francisco Muñoz, Manuel Sebastián, José Manuel Reales, and Soledad Ballesteros

UNED, Department of Basic Psychology II, Juan del Rosal 10, 28040 Madrid, Spain
`mballesteros@psi.uned.es`

Abstract. The present study investigated low-oscillatory (theta band, 3-7 Hz) modulations induced by tactile roughness stimulations under two attention-demanding conditions. Four levels of roughness were presented under low-demanding and high-demanding conditions. In both conditions, an oddball paradigm was used to present three target surfaces varying in roughness (low, mid, and high levels of roughness), and a nontarget flat surface. The results showed that centro-parietal theta oscillations are involved in allocating atten-tional resources when participants have to update new information induced by incoming haptic stimuli. Theta power was higher in the high-demanding task compared to the low-demanding. Furthermore, theta power varied depending on tactile roughness but not in a linear manner. This was interpreted as that theta oscillations were sensitive not only to task difficulty but also to physical properties.

Keywords: tactile roughness perception, brain oscillations, attentional demands, theta band.

1 Introduction

A growing body of evidence indicates that oscillatory electrical activity plays a key role in the recruitment of cognitive systems during the processing of information [1]. In recent years, event-related spectral perturbation (ERSP) and inter-trial coherence (ITC) have been revealed as crucial for understanding the nature of brain electrical activity. ERSP measures and ITC would reflect the state of the neuronal assemblies involved in the task [2]. It has been proposed that event-related low-frequency oscilla-tory activity in the theta frequency band (3-7 Hz) increases during the processing of information in working memory tasks [3]. For example, in an auditory oddball para-digm it has been shown that tasks requiring high attentional demands are associated with an increase in theta frequency [4].

While many studies have investigated event-related oscillations in the auditory and visual modalities [5-7], studies in the tactile modality have been very scarce. In elec-troencephalographic (EEG) studies, mechanical tactile stimulation to the skin may entail some jittering between stimulus onset and the triggering to the system. Hence, event-related brain potentials (ERPs) averaged trial-by-trial are not phase-locked with the stimulus onset. Event-related brain oscillations offer an alternative to the ERPs as

A.M.L. Kappers et al. (Eds.): EuroHaptics 2010, Part II, LNCS 6192, pp. 37–43, 2010.

they allow the averaging of responses that are not phase-locked to the stimulus [8]. This might overcome the jittering issue.

The aim of the present study was to investigate theta oscillations while the participant perceived tactile stimuli using mechanical stimulation. We tested two hypotheses. The first was that different levels of tactile roughness would induce variations in theta power. To test this hypothesis, we presented four types of tactile stimuli varying in roughness to the perceiver's fingertip using a specific-purpose machine [9]. One stimulus was completely smooth and always unattended, whereas the other three stimuli with different levels of roughness were always attended.

A second hypothesis was that event-related theta oscillations would be modulated by attentional task demands. We used two different tasks involving higher and lower attentional demands. In the low-demanding task, one target was discriminated to the non-target stimuli in each block, while in the high-demanding task, three targets had to be discriminated to the non-target in a single sequence. This may lead to increase the participant expectancy to the unexpected ongoing stimulation to be discriminated.

In the high-demanding task, three targets had to be discriminated from the non-target in a single sequence, which should imply participants' expectancy to the unexpected ongoing stimulation to be discriminated.

2   Method

2.1   Participants

Twelve participants (mean age 33.1, SD. 5.7 years) performed the low-demanding task and 14 participants (mean age 29.4, SD. 5.9 years) performed the high-demanding task. The mean age did not differ between the groups ($t_{1,24}=1.7$; $p>0.1$). All participants were right-handed undergraduate students. The study was approved by the UNED Ethics Committee and the study was performed in accordance with the ethical standards laid down in the 1964 Declaration of Helsinki.

2.2   Materials

Stimulus set. We used four different hard-plastic blocks in which there were embossed three triangular gratings with different wavelengths (0.4 mm, 1.6 mm 2.8 mm, referred as rough-2, rough-3, and rough-4, respectively) and one flat surface (rough-1). The embossed surface was 50 mm X 40 mm. The amplitudes of the triangular gratings were: 0 (rough-1), 0.5 (rough-2), 1.1 (rough-3), and 1.8 mm (rough-4).

Apparatus. The stimuli were presented in the *Tactile Spinning Wheel* [9], an electro-mechanical device specifically designed to deliver textured surfaces to the static index fingertip. It is composed by two main components: (1) a circular platform that spins at a certain velocity controlled by the experimenter; and (2) an interface that connects the apparatus to the EEG recording system. The device was made of black methacrylate that did not allow visual contact with the stimulus. The spinning platform was a horizontal-revolving disc provided with sixteen rectangular sockets located in the upper surface of the platform to which the textured blocks were fastened. The device was specially designed to allow ERPs recording for a series of stimuli by the synchronization between the stimulus-onset and the trigger delivered to the EEG recording system. The rotation speed of the platform can be controlled by a potentiometer placed in the interface.

2.3 Procedure

During the experimental session, the participant sat in a chair in front of the apparatus. The right arm and hand was supported in a horizontal platform with a special hole allowing the right index fingertip to contact the stimulus. The finger was immobilized horizontally in the holder. Participants were instructed to maintain a light and constant pressure on the stimulus. The stimulus presentation platform rotated counterclockwise at a speed of 140 mm/s. At this speed, the finger was in contact with the stimuli during 560 ms, and the inter-stimulus interval (ISI) was 1280 ms. To make sure that participants paid attention to the stimuli, they were instructed to detect and keep a running mental count of all the targets.

Low-demanding task condition. Participants were presented with three random sequences of textured surfaces. Each sequence consisted of just one target stimulus (rough-2 or rough-3 or rough-4) intermixed with several instances of non-target stimuli (rough-1). Each sequence comprised 104 stimuli presented in sets of 8 stimuli (one run of the spinning-wheel platform). The relative probability of target/non-target stimuli was $P=0.2$ and $P=0.8$, respectively. The subject had to discriminate a single target from the nontarget in each block. At the end of the block, the experimenter recorded the subject's tally.

High-demanding task condition. Participants were presented with a single randomized sequence of the three target stimuli and the non-target ($P=0.2$ and $P=0.8$, respectively). To make both conditions as much comparable as possible rest periods were introduced every 104 stimuli and the participant's response was reported at the end of each presentation. In this task, participants have to count all the targets, irrespective the kind of roughness.

Although engaging attention is obviously required in both tasks, the main difference between low and high demanding conditions was the amount of attentional resources used to continuously update the incoming information.

2.4 EEG Recording and ERSP Data Analysis

The electrodes were attached prior to seating the participant at the presentation apparatus, which was located inside a soundproof, electrically shielded room. Continuous EEG activity was recorded with tin electrodes from 32 scalp sites of the extended 10-20 system through 32 channels using an EEG amplifier (NuAmps, Neuroscan, Inc.). The EEG was digitized with a sampling rate of 250 Hz and on-line band-pass filtered from 0.1 to 70 Hz. Linked-earlobes were used as reference and AFz electrode as ground. The overall electrode impedance was maintained below 10 kΩ. Four additional electrodes were placed above and below the left orbit and on the outer canthus of each eye to monitor the electro-oculographic (EOG) activity. Segments were made for each trial from 200 ms pre-stimulus to 1024 ms post-stimulus. Trials containing extra-cranial artifacts were removed from the analysis. Eye movement and muscle artifacts were corrected by spatial filtering methods. Only artifact-free segments were selected for averaging after baseline correction (200 ms pre-stimulus).

To study time-frequency modulations of the electrical activity elicited by the target, single trials (from 200 ms before to 1s after targets) were convoluted time locked to each stimulus using a sinusoidal wavelet (short-time DFT) transform. Each wavelet consists of a single cycle at 3 Hz, increasing progressively until 10 cycles at 40 Hz, in each data window (window-size 260 ms). ERSP modulations (increase or decrease of power respect to baseline) were analyzed in relation to averaged spectral power in the baseline period of 200 ms. This calculation was carried out by EEGLAB using custom spectral decomposition techniques [8].

ERSP data were computed using two consecutive time-frequency windows: early-theta band (250-400 ms) and late-theta band (400-550 ms). Both windows were selected from the averaged spectral maps (see Figure 1) in nine electrodes (F3/4, Fz, C3/4, Cz, P3/4, Pz). In order to compare ERSP between conditions of roughness and experimental conditions, we analyzed the mean theta power for each time-window using mixed ANOVAs. The following factors were included in the analyses: Presentation conditions (high-demanding, low-demanding) as between-subject factor, and Roughness (rough-1, rough-2, rough-3 and rough-4) x Anterior-Posterior Axis (frontal, middle and posterior) X Laterality (left, central and right) as within-subject factors. For repeated measures analyses, multivariate statistics are reported. Statistical significances for intra-subject factors were computed using Greenhouse-Geiser correction. In all post-hoc contrasts, the level of significance was Bonferroni adjusted ($\alpha = 0.05$).

3   Results

3.1 Behavioral Results

The mean counting for low- and high-demanding tasks were 62.3 (SD 8.3) and 73.6 (SD 22.9), respectively. One-sample t-test compares the actual with the right performance (value of 60 targets) in both tasks. The counting in the low-demanding task was not different of the expected value ($t_{11}=0.1$, $P=0.3$). By contrast, the counting in the high-demanding task was significantly different ($t_{13}=2.23$, $P=0.04$). The high deviation in counting indicates that target discrimination was more difficult in the high-demanding task.

3.2 Time-Frequency Results

Time-frequency analysis for EEG channels in individual subjects revealed a similar enhancement of oscillatory activity in theta (3-7 Hz) band beginning after 200 ms from the stimulus onset mainly over centro-parietal electrodes. Figure 1 (left) displays the spectral plots of event-related oscillations for the low-demanding condition. They were obtained from the mean ERSP power corresponding to frontal, central and parietal electrodes. A stronger ERSP power is observed in the theta band corresponding to rough-3 at centro-parietal sites comparing to the other textures. Figure 1 (right) shows

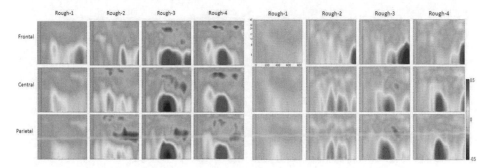

Fig. 1. ERSP for the low-demanding (left) and high-demanding (right) tasks

the spectral plots of event-related oscillations corresponding to the high-demanding condition. It shows a stronger ERSP power in the theta band corresponding to the rough-3 at frontal sites, whereas it was quite similar at centro-parietal sites.

The analysis revealed a main effect of Roughness ($F_{3,72} = 4.2$; $P<0.01$) in the 250--400 ms time-interval. Post-hoc analyses revealed that theta power to rough-1 (0.62 dB) differs significantly from both, rough-3 and rough-4 (1.7 and 1.6 dB, respectively), regardless of the presentation condition. Theta power to rough-1 and rough-2 (1.3 dB) did not differ significantly. In general, theta power increased significantly at centro-parietal sites compared to frontal sites. In the 400-550 ms time-interval, similar results were obtained. Theta power for rough-1 (0.61 dB) differed significantly from both rough-3 and rough-4 (2.1 and 1.9 dB, respectively), regardless of presentation condition. The topographical distribution increased at centro-parietal sites. In this 400-550 ms time-window, theta power was higher on the mid-right hemisphere compared to the left hemisphere. The four-way interaction (Roughness X Anterior-posterior axis X Laterality X Presentation) was significant. The three way interaction Roughness X Anterior-posterior axis X Laterality was modified by task demands (see Figure 2). Specifically, theta power increased in rough-2 compared with rough-1 at left-frontal ($P=0.09$) and left-central ($P=0.06$) sites, and at right-frontal ($P=0.08$), right-central ($P=0.02$) and right-parietal ($P=0.03$) sites. These differences were not significant in the low-demanding condition. However, theta power increased in rough-3 compared with rough-2 at left-central ($P=0.05$) and left-parietal (0.02) sites, at mid-central ($P=0.005$), mid-parietal ($p<0.005$) and right-central ($P=0.05$), right-parietal ($p<0.01$) sites in the low-demanding condition.

Table 1. Main ANOVA results in each time window

Time Window (ms)	Roughness			Anterior-Posterior Axis			Laterality			Roughness x Anterior-posterior Axis x Presentation Condition		
	F	P	η^2	F	P	η^2	F	P	η^2	F	P	η^2
250-400	4.2	<0.01	0.15	14.3	<0.0001	0.37						
400-550	7.2	<0.0001	0.23	10.9	<0.0001	0.31	9.0	<0.0001	0.27	2.3	<0.001	0.01

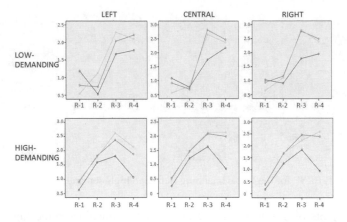

Fig. 2. Interaction Roughness X Anterior-posterior Axis X Laterality X Presentation

4 Discussion

In the present study, we investigated event-related theta oscillations while participants perceived tactile stimuli varying in roughness under two different demanding conditions. The main ERSP results were found at the 400-550 ms time-window, showing a differential modulation in event-related theta power depending on both stimulus characteristics and attentional demands. Under the low-demanding condition, discrimination between the rough-2 and the non-target stimulus did not correlate with changes in theta power. This effect could reflect a lack of responsiveness in the theta frequency when processing very similar stimuli. Thus, textures with similar roughness might be evaluated as non-informative at the first stages of information processing, so it is probably that, differences between rough-0 and rough-1 stimuli were hardly detected in the low-demanding task. In contrast, when the task required more attentional resources, a different pattern of results was observed in the high-demanding task. It appears that when the task required more attentional resources, the representation of the non-target is updated with the detection of the next incoming rough-1 stimulus.

Regarding theta power for rough-3 and rough-4 stimuli, a stronger synchronization was found when processing these targets as compared to rough-2. While in the low-demanding task a significant change was obtained from rough-2 to rough-3, this change was observed for the whole set of stimuli in the high-demanding condition. In both tasks, targets that were discriminated easily (rough-3 and rough-4) from the non-target did not yield any significant change in theta frequency. This might reflect that detecting and categorizing information from these targets seem to recruit similar amount of attentional resources.

These findings are in agreement with previous ERP results in the auditory modality (for a description of the relationship between theta band and P300 component, see [11]). For instance, Fitzgerald and Picton found that a high-demanding odd-ball task confers a higher level of expectancy, as revealing by the P300 amplitude [10]. High-demanding tasks yield a higher capability to evaluate and update mental representation of targets from non-targets, even more as discrimination is hardly to perform. In such situation, low-demanding task did not yield any change in theta power. To summarize, centro-parietal theta oscillations may be functionally involved in allocating attentional resources when the task performed involves the updating induced by incoming stimuli [6]. This updating is difficult to achieve under low-demanding task conditions in which targets and non-targets have similar levels of roughness. However, high-demanding tasks require the allocation of higher attentional resources, increasing the capability to evaluate the incoming stimuli and update the mental representations of the textured stimuli. These findings shed light to the knowledge of the cognitive processes in haptic perception.

Acknowledgments. The research reported in this paper was supported by the European Community: NEST-2005-Path_IMP, grant 043432 (SOMAPS project) to SB. FM and MS were funded by the European project SOMAPS. SB also acknowledges the support of the Comunidad de Madrid (Multiparametric imaging of vascular competence – MULTIMAG: 2006/BIO-170).

References

1. Lakatos, P., Karmos, G., Mehta, A.D., Ulbert, I., Schroeder, C.E.: Entrainment of neuronal oscillations as a mechanism of attentional selection. Science 320, 110–113 (2008)
2. David, O., Harrison, L., Friston, K.J.: Modelling event-related responses in the brain. Neuroimage 25, 756–770 (2005)
3. Yordanova, J., Devrim, M., Kolev, V., Ademoglu, A., Demiralp, T.: Multiple time-frequency components account for the complex functional reactivity of P300. Neuroreport 11, 1097–1103 (2000)
4. Spencer, K.M., Polich, J.: Poststimulus EEG spectral analysis and P300: attention, task, and probability. Psychophysiology 36, 220–232 (1999)
5. Digiacomo, M.R., Marco-Pallarés, J., Flores, A.B., Gómez, C.M.: Wavelet analysis of the EEG during the neurocognitive evaluation of invalidly cued targets. Brain Research 1234, 94–103 (2008)
6. Ishii, R., Canuet, L., Herdman, A., Gunji, A., Iwase, M., Takahashi, H., Nakahachi, T., Hirata, M., Robinson, S.E., Pantev, C., Takeda, M.: Cortical oscillatory power changes during auditory oddball task revealed by spatially filtered magnetoencephalography. Clinical Neurophysiology 120, 497–504 (2009)
7. Oniz, A., Başar, E.: Prolongation of alpha oscillations in auditory oddball paradigm. International Journal of Psychophysiology 71, 235–241 (2009)
8. Delorme, A., Makeig, S.: EEGLAB: an open source toolbox for analysis of single-trial EEG dynamics including independent component analysis. Journal of Neuroscience Methods 134, 9–21 (2004)
9. Reales, J.M., Muñoz, F., Kleinboehl, D., Sebastián, M., Ballesteros, S.: A new device to present textured stimuli to touch with simultaneous EEG recording. Behavioral Research Methods 42, 547-555 (2010)
10. Fitzgerald, P.G., Picton, T.W.: Event-related potentials recorded during the discrimination of improbable stimuli. Biological Psychology 17, 241–276 (1983)
11. Spencer, K., Polich, J.: Post-stimulus EEG spectral analysis and P300: attention, task, and probability. Psychophysiology 36, 220–232 (1999)

Power Consumption Reduction of a Controlled Friction Tactile Plate

Frédéric Giraud[1], Michel Amberg[1], Romuald Vanbelleghem[2],
and Betty Lemaire-Semail[1]

[1] Univ Lille Nord de France, F59000 Lille, France
frederic.giraud@polytech-lille.fr
[2] INRIA Lille Nord Europe, F59000 Lille, France

Abstract. This paper describes design improvements of a friction reduction based tactile device, which yields to reduction of the supply power. We first evaluated the power consumption of four different plates. We found that a convenient design could cut the power losses down by 90%. To explain these changes we propose a modelling of the dielectric losses in the piezoelectric actuators and of the vibration amplitude.

Keywords: haptic interface, tactile interface, surface friction, power reduction.

1 Introduction

One way to enhance interaction between man and the machine is to provide tactile stimulation to the user. By this way, information can be provided through the sense of touch. To achieve that, many tactile displays have been designed and can be divided into three groups, according to their working principle. Devices made up with a large number of pins arranged in an array [1][2] reconstruct the geometry of a virtual surface. Other tactile stimulators don't create the exact geometry of a virtual surface, but the *effect* of this geometry on the finger pulp. For example, [3] uses an array of small pins that vibrate to excite each R.A. mechanoreceptor independently. In [4][5], the skin is stretched to give the sensation of touching a real bump or a hole. Those two types of tactile stimulator create a *local* stimulation. But tactile stimulators using a *global* stimulation can be found as well. Devices based on friction reduction belong to this category. They use a vibrating plate at very high frequency (typically above $25kHz$) on which the finger is free to move. The vibration creates an airgap which decreases friction between fingertip and the plate. By turning on and off the power supply of the device, the stimuli generated by this temporal friction variation create the illusion of a more or less finely textured surface. Previous designs of such a tactile plate have been made[6]. This plate, called *the original plate* suffered from the heat generated by the plate, which could hurt users. To solve this problem, we study the design of the tactile plate in the light of power consumption.

The paper is organized as follows. First we describe the original tactile plate and the squeeze film effect. Then we analyze the power consumption of three new designs of the tactile plate. A modelling of the power losses is then proposed, which explains

A.M.L. Kappers et al. (Eds.): EuroHaptics 2010, Part II, LNCS 6192, pp. 44–49, 2010.

the differences in power consumption between the new designs. Finally a discussion highlights the influence of the plate's dimension on power consumption.

2   Presentation of the Original Tactile Plate

The friction reduction occurring between fingertip and a vibrating plate is often explained using ≪squeeze film air bearing≫ theory which is detailed in [7] and applied on a tactile device in [8,9,10]. On a practical approach, an overpressure between the fingertip and the plate is created by the vibrations, resulting in a friction reduction. The plates described in this article use a standing flexural wave which propagates at the plate's surface. This design allows high vibration amplitude with small bulk size. To create the vibration, 28 piezo cells are bonded onto a copper substrate; when supplied by a sinusoidal voltage, they bend the substrate as shown in figure 1.

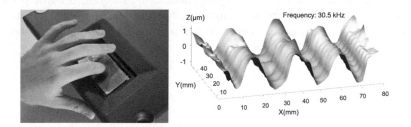

Fig. 1. An ultrasonic tactile plate and the measured deformed shape

One important thing to explain, is that when moving the fingertip on the plate, users don't feel the vibration by itself, but the effect of the vibration on the tribological behaviour of the contact between the finger and the plate. Moreover, the vibration is not homogenous, due to the vibration nodes and antinodes; however, the squeeze film effect is more or less filtered because touching area is in the same order of size as the vibration wavelength.

To be efficient, the plate should be designed so as to allow vibrations at 25kHz and above, otherwise the squeeze effect is not created. Moreover, a typical vibration amplitude of $1\mu m$ is necessary in order to attain a sufficiently low friction level. The original plate has been designed to offer those performances[6]. Its size was chosen in order to optimize the vibration amplitude for a given voltage amplitude V. However, in this design, plate thickness has been fixed to $2mm$ and the piezo cells'thickness to $1mm$. Moreover, the optimization process paid no attention to the power requirements of the tactile plate, which actually needs a large amount of power to be supplied. Consequently, the device's temperature increases because of the power losses, leading to burning sensations. Reducing the losses is a key issue in these devices to allow a use over a long duration. The following section of this article presents several new designs which help to reduce the required power supplied to the device.

3 Loss Reduction

3.1 Experimental Approach

The tactile plate is built up with piezoceramics bonded on a copper-beryllium substrate. In order to find which design produces less power losses at a given vibration amplitude, we built up several tactile plates with different sizes:

- plate **0**: the original plate, the wavelength of which is $\lambda = 20.6mm$,
- plate **1**: same as the plate **0** but the substrate's thickness is set to $0.7mm$,
- plate **2**: same as plate **1**, but the ceramics' thickness is changed to $0.5mm$,
- plate **3**: a new plate with $\lambda = 15.6mm$, a substrate's thickness of $0.75mm$ and piezo ceramics' thickness of $0.5mm$.

We then measured the required power as a function of W. Results are presented in figure 2. As it can be seen, the supply power required for the original tactile plate dramatically increases with the vibration amplitude. Moreover, it appears that plates with thicker piezoelectric cells exhibit larger vibration amplitude for the same amount of power consumption.

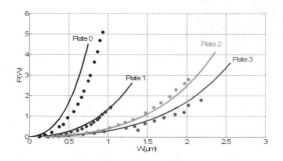

Fig. 2. Required power as a function of the vibration amplitude, for several plate designs. line: modelling, dots: experimental measurements.

We also measured the vibration of the plate as a function of the supply voltage. The results are presented in figure 3. It appears that for plate **0** and plate **1**, the deflexion saturates to almost $1\mu m$. When trying to vibrate more than $1\mu m$, and thus providing more voltage to the plates, we supply with much more power but we don't obtain more deflection: the additional amount of power is lost into heat, without increasing the vibration amplitude. The other two designs plates **2** and **3**, also saturate but at a higher level. These designs are more convenient to the use in a tactile stimulator.

Comparing plate **0** and plate **1**, we find that we can reduce power consumption using a thin substrate. In fact, both plates output the same deformation amplitude, but the thinnest plate consumes less. However, those plates saturate at a low level of deflection, and $1\mu m$ is a maximum value one may expect with them. A better design seems to be plates **2** and **3**. For those plates, we used thin piezo cells: those plates don't saturate at

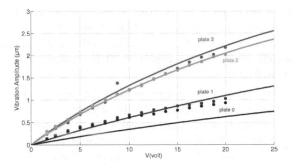

Fig. 3. Vibration amplitude as a function of the voltage supplied to the device, for several plate designs. line: modelling, dots: experimental measurements.

1μm, and the required power is very low compared to the other designs. As a conclusion to this experimental study, we can describe the effect of the plate's parameters as follows:

- reducing substrate's thickness reduces power consumption and has no effect on the maximum vibration amplitude,
- reducing piezoelectric actuator's thickness reduces power consumption and also increases the maximum vibration amplitude.

The next section of this paper explains which role plays the thickness of the piezo layer, and also gives a modelling of the power losses and the vibration amplitude. This step is important to design an optimized plate.

3.2 Discussion

The reason why original plate requires so much power compared to the others is that the design was optimized to produce large vibration amplitude at a given voltage. This design was not optimized to reduce power losses. One mechanism leading to power losses is the presence of dielectric losses inside the piezoelectric cells. The piezo product manufacturer [11] gives the relationship between the voltage supplied to the piezo element V, its capacitance C_0, the working frequency f and the power losses P by introducing the parameter δ:

$$P = (2\pi f)C_0 V^2 \tan(\delta) \qquad (1)$$

The capacitance C_0 is given by the cell's dimension:

$$C_0 = \varepsilon \frac{a \times b}{e} \qquad (2)$$

Where $a \times b$ is cells' surface, ε is the material's dielectric constant and e is the piezo-thickness. Introducing 2 into 1 leads to:

$$P = (2\pi f)\frac{V^2}{e}\varepsilon(a \times b)\tan(\delta) \qquad (3)$$

As it can be seen, the power losses depend on the resonance frequency of the plate. This is verified by experimental data, because the frequency of the three new plates is lower than the original one. In this study, the plates didn't fully fulfill requirements of section 2 because the resonance frequency was around $20kHz$ instead of the required $25kHz$. However, conclusion to the work doesn't change.

Moreover, the power losses are proportional to the ratio $\frac{V^2}{e}$: for a given substrate and piezoelectric material, cells thickness should be as big as possible to reduce power losses. However, this fact is not consistent with conclusion of section 3.1. In fact, in this application, the device doesn't work at constant voltage, but at constant vibration amplitude. This is why, this modelling must be completed with the relationship between the vibration amplitude and the voltage.

This vibration modelling is extracted from [6] to deduce the vibration amplitude as a function of V, allowing the drawing of the curves in figure 3. In this paper, we do not fully describe this modelling, but we focus on the fact that the vibration amplitude is proportional to $Q_m d_{31} \frac{V}{e^2}$ where d_{31} is an elongation factor of the piezoelectric material, and Q_m is a quality factor of the mechanical resonator.

Normally, Q_m and d_{31} are constant; however, to take into account non linearity of the piezo material, and reach to the behaviour shown in figure 3, these parameters should be varying. We decided to make d_{31} vary with the electrical field inside a piezo cell, and we laid down:

$$d_{31} = d_{31n} \times \frac{E_{max}}{E_{max} + \frac{V}{e}} \tag{4}$$

where d_{31n} is a value given by the material manufacturer and E_{max} is a constant parameter depending on the material, not on the plate's size. This modelling is consistent with the experimental data as shown in figure 3, except for the plate **0** for which deflection is under estimated.

Finally, taking into account 4 into 3 yields to writing that P is proportional to $\frac{e^3 W^2 (E_{max} + \frac{V}{e})^2}{E_{max}^2}$: the thinner the piezo layer is, the smaller the power losses. This conclusion is consistent with what is found by experimental measurements.

Consequently, increasing the vibration amplitude can be achieved by choosing thin piezoceramics cells: to reach $1\mu m$, the device needs lower voltage leading to a smaller amount of power. Then there exists a tradeoff between the level of voltage to reach $1\mu m$ and the power consumption leading to an optimized geometry of the tactile plate. By this way, we have shown that it is possible to reduce the power consumption to less than $0.5W$ at the rated vibration amplitude of the plate, while the original tactile plate needed $5W$.

4   Conclusion

This paper presents a study of power losses in a controlled friction tactile stimulator. We found that optimal design should include power consumption in its cost function. Previous modelling used for the plate's design has been extended in order to take into account the power losses.

Finally, we found that a more convenient design could cut the power losses down by 90%. Consequently, the tactile plate doesn't get warm, allowing the user to play a long time with the device. Moreover, the rated power (0.5W) is sufficiently small to allow a power supply from a lightweight power source, or directly from an USB port for example.

Acknowledgement

This work has been carried within the framework of the INRIA Mint project and is supported by the IRCICA (Institut de Recherche sur les Composants logiciels et matériels pour l'Information et la Communication Avancée)

References

1. Wagner, C.H., Lederman, S.J., Howe, R.D.: A tactile shape display using servomotors. In: Proceedings of the 10th Symposium on Haptic Interfaces, pp. 354–355 (2002)
2. Valazquez, R., Pissaloux, H.M., Szewick, J.: Tactile Rendering With Shape-Memory-Alloy Pin-Matrix. IEEE Transactions on Instrumentation and Measurement 57(5), 1051–1057 (2008)
3. Summers, I.R., Chanter, C., Southall, A., Brady, A.: Results from a Tactile Array on the Fingertip. In: Proceedings of the EUROHAPTICS 2001, Birmingham, pp. 26–28 (2001)
4. Levesque, V., Hayward, V.: Experimental Evidence of Lateral Skin Strain During Tactile Exploration. In: Proceedings of EUROHAPTICS 2003, Dublin, pp. 261–275 (2003)
5. Pasquero, J., Hayward, V.: STReSS: A Practical Tactile Display System with One Millimeter Spatial Resolution and 700 Hz Refresh Rate. In: Proceedings of EUROHAPTICS 2003, Dublin, pp. 94–110 (2003)
6. Biet, M., Giraud, F., Lemaire-Semail, B.: Implementation of tactile feedback by modifying the perceived friction. IEEE TUFFC 43(1), 123–136 (2008)
7. Wiesendanger, M.: Squeeze Film air Bearings Using Piezo-electric Bending Elements. PhD dissertation, EPFL Lausanne – Switzerland (2000)
8. Watanabe, T., Fukui, S.: A method for controlling tactile sensation of surface roughness using ultrasonic vibration. Proceedings of IEEE ICRA 1, 1134–1139 (1995)
9. Winfield, L., Glassmire, J., Colgate, J.E., Peshkin, M.: T-PaD: Tactile Pattern Display through Variable Friction Reduction. In: Proceeding of Worldhaptic 2007, pp. 421–426 (2007)
10. Biet, M., Casiez, G., Giraud, F.: Betty Semail: Discrimination of Virtual Square Gratings by Dynamic Touch on Friction Based Tactile Displays. In: Proceeding of the Haptics Symposium 2008, pp. 41–48 (2008)
11. Noliac website, http://www.noliac.com/Material_characteristics_-143.aspx

Psychophysical Evaluation of a Low Density and Portable Tactile Device Displaying Small-Scale Surface Features

Nadia Vanessa Garcia-Hernandez, Nikos Tsagarakis, Ioannis Sarakoglou,
and Darwin Caldwell

Italian Institute of Technology, Advanced Robotics Lab, Via Morego 30, 16163, Genova, Italy
{nadia.garcia,ioannis.sarakoglou,nikos.tsagarakis,darwin.caldwell}@iit.it

Abstract. This work evaluates the haptic rendering capabilities of a low density and portable tactile device displaying small-scale surface features, such as ridge patterns and sinusoidal gratings. Psychophysical experiments were conducted to investigate and compare JND's for distance, angle and wavelength perception of virtual and real surface features. Velocity was monitored during the active exploration of ridges and controlled during the passive-guided exploration of gratings. JND's found for the virtual surfaces are 22%, 12.6% and 13.3% of the standard stimuli (4.2mm, 45° and 5.09mm). JND's for real surfaces indicate that subjects' discrimination ability using the tactile device decreases roughly 65%. Results provide insight of the sensory resolution associated with the tactile device which can guide the development of an improved device, suitable applications and effective tactile rendering methods.

Keywords: evaluation; psychophysics; tactile device.

1 Introduction

Tactile displays are devices that provide spatially distributed cutaneous signals in order to deliver vital tactile information during haptic exploration and manipulation of virtual/remote objects.In particular, tactile shape displays contain an array of active pins that are used to convey the tactile information to the user's hand. They have often been used as a sensory substitution system [1] especially for the visually or hearing impaired (to display Braille, maps or graphs), or as additional interface feedback components in keyboards, mouse and handheld games controllers or in teleoperated systems [2]. An ideal tactile shape display should recreate the skin deformation that humans experience when touching real geometric shapes. To achieve this, studies such as [3] suggest that the display should have high actuator density ($1/mm^2$), high bandwidth (at least 50Hz), large forces ($50N/cm^2$), displacement up to 3mm, while being as small and lightweight as possible. Unfortunately, to design a tactile display that matches all the above requisites is difficult and costly; in fact even the best existing tactile display only partially satisfy the characteristics required.

This work evaluates a tactile display [4] that is light-weight and portable and its low actuator density could limit its capability to replicate cutaneous information in all its

A.M.L. Kappers et al. (Eds.): EuroHaptics 2010, Part II, LNCS 6192, pp. 50–57, 2010.

details. To evaluate the haptic rendering capabilities of the display, a variety of psychophysical experiments were performed to obtain JND's for distance, angle and wavelength perception of virtual small-scale surface features, which have equal or smaller size than the fingertip. For comparison, experiments were also conducted for real small-scale surface features.

2 Background

Much of the psychophysical information found in the literature is focused on vibrating pin arrays used to produce sensations, such as texture [5]. However, very few psychophysical studies are found on tactile pin-based display [6]. Moreover, few studies have compared the perception of virtual surface features rendered by a tactile display with the perception of real surfaces with the bare finger.

Some works that have studied the use of tactile displays to render shape information include the work of Provancher et al [7] which tried to recreate curvature and object motion by moving a tactile element along the user's fingertip, or the work of Gi-Hun et al [8] which used a 6x5 pin array to study different static tactile patterns, such as polygons, by controlling the normal deflection of the pin array (maximum deflection at $700\mu m$). Other example is the work of Kammermeier et al [9] that evaluated the identification of small geometric objects (using passive touch) rendered by a 6x6 pin tactile shape display, that uses a simple on/off control for the pins. One interesting and important aspect of the testing in the majority of the works mentioned before is the use of the proportion of correct answers as a quantitative method to indicate if the display has a satisfactory performance in replicating the tactile stimulus. Few have used psychophysical methods to measure the sensation produce by the tactile display. In this study, a psychophysical method is used to obtain subjects' tactile acuity in discriminating small surface features.

3 Experiments

Three types of small surface features Fig. 1, whose spatial parameters can be specified precisely and varied independently, were used in the following experiments to obtain the JND's for distance, angle and wavelength perception:

Exp. 1 Distance discrimination (d) between two parallel ridges (Fig. 1a).
Exp. 2 Inclination angle discrimination (α) of a ridge (Fig. 1b).
Exp. 3 Wavelength discrimination (λ) of sinusoidal gratings (Fig. 1c).

In Exp. 1 and 2, subjects had full control over their movements (active exploration) and the exploratory velocity was monitored. In Exp. 3, subjects' movements were guided (passive and guided exploration) at a constant velocity of 20 mm/sec, in a way that the perception of the spatial parameter could only depend on the temporal frequency (f $=v/\lambda$).

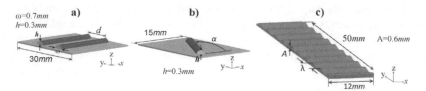

Fig. 1. Small-scale a) two-parallel ridges, b) inclined ridge and c) sinusoidal gratings

4 Materials

4.1 Tactile Display System

The tactile system evaluate in this work (see Fig.2) consists of a 4x4 pin array actuated by 16 miniature dc motors (1.5mm pin diameter and 2mm pin center-to-center spacing). The pins have an effective continuous displacement between 0-2mm and can exert a maximum force of 1.2N, it has a bandwidth of 8Hz at the maximum displacement of 2mm, although displacements at 23Hz can reach the amplitude of 0.5mm and create texture sensations. The actuator module measures 14cmx6cmx4cm and weighs approximately 275g. of which less than 15g. are loading the finger. The use of the cable permits mounting the module on the forearm reducing users loading and enables the finger to freely explore the virtual environment in a more natural way. The actuator module contains all the motors, controller system and batteries for over 2hrs continuous use.

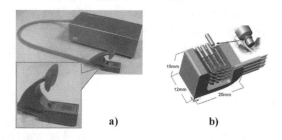

a)   b)

Fig. 2. a) Portable-wearable tactile display [4] and b) section view of the display

4.2 Experimental Setups for Tactile Exploration

Setups of Fig. 3a,b were used in Exp.1 and 2 and allow subjects' fingertip move freely back and forth (along the longitudinal axis of the fingertip) within a range of 3cm and choose the velocity they consider most appropriate (active exploration). In the setup of Fig. 3a the tactile display was placed in a slotted plastic guide to constrain the subjects' fingertip motion. The setup of Fig. 3b has a rotational base structure holding the surface features in individual slotted compartments. The rotational motion of the structure is done manually and offers an easy and fast way to change pattern. Setups of Fig. 3c,d were used in Exp. 3 and guide subjects' tactile exploration by controlling their arm-hand-finger motion in one direction at a constant velocity (passive- guided exploration).

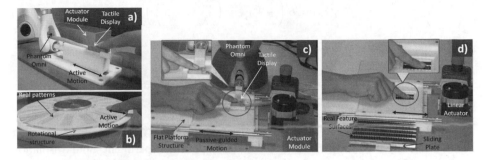

Fig. 3. Experimental setups for a-b) Exp.1 and 2 and c-d) for Exp.3

During the test, subjects' arm was resting horizontally on a flat platform structure and their index finger placed on top of the tactile display (Fig. 3c) or on top of the real feature surface (Fig. 3d). The flat platform motion was controlled by a SMC linear rodless actuator. Setup of Fig. 3d has a sliding plate with the real feature surfaces which is placed under the flat platform structure and inside a rack guide to allow moving the plate. Subjects explore the surface feature through the square hole located in the flat platform structure. The Phantom Omni read the display position and control the motion of the pins.

The real surface features used in this work were produced with a 3D printing system for rapid prototyping and manufacturing which can elaborate complex plastic objects with fine feature details.

5   Methods

5.1   Tactile Rendering

The tactile display reproduces the tactile features by individually controlling the normal displacement (perpendicular to the object surface) of each pin. When subjects explore a surface by moving their index finger within a planar limited area, the pin's displacement corresponds to the height of the exploring surface.

The ridge patterns were created using the sinusoidal profile of Eq.(1), where Z_n represents the normal displacement of each pin, ω the width of the ridge and $C = h * K$ the amplitude of the ridge h multiplied by the scalar factor between the ridge amplitude and pin normal displacement K. For the two parallel ridges pattern $Y_n = y_n$, where y_n corresponds to the y-position of the pin n, whereas for the inclined ridge pattern Y_n is equal to $\frac{y_n}{\sqrt{1+(tan\alpha)^2}}$, where α is the inclination angle of the ridge. The virtual sinusoidal gratings were created using Eq.(2), where G_n represents the normal displacement of each pin, λ the wavelength of the gratings and $B = A * K$ the amplitude of the gratings A multiplied by the scalar factor between the grating amplitude and pin normal displacement K.

$$Z_n(Y_n) = C \left(sin \frac{Y_n}{\omega} \pi \right) \tag{1}$$

$$G_n(Y_n) = B \left(\frac{1}{2} + \frac{1}{2} \cos \left(\frac{2\pi}{\lambda} y_n - \pi \right) \right) \tag{2}$$

5.2 Subjects

For the experiments, subjects between 22 and 35 years old and without any previous experience in tactile psychophysical experiments, participated in the study. Five subjects (3 males and 2 females) participated in Exp. 1, five (3 males and 2 females) in Exp. 2 and seven performed Exp. 3 (5 males and 2 females). All subjects were right handed and chose their right index finger to execute the experiment. Sound isolation headphones were used to avoid using auditory cues coming mainly from the display tendon transmission system.

5.3 Psychophysical Procedures

In all experiments, individual psychometric functions for each subject were obtained by implementing a method of constant stimuli (2-interval forced choice procedure [10]) which consist of the following:

a) In one trial, two tactile pattern stimuli T_S and T_C were displayed in two intervals separately by a time space (1-2sec) and presented randomly with equal probability.
b) T_S corresponds to the standard stimulus and T_C is selected from a set of comparison stimuli (standard stimulus plus increment).
c) There are two possible responses after each trial, R_1 or R_2. Subjects indicate R_1 if the bigger stimulus was perceived in the first interval and R_2 if it was perceived in the second interval.
d) P_{R1} represents the proportion of correct R_1 and P_{R2} of correct R_2.
e) P_{Tc} is the proportion of the "greater" responses for each T_C. $P_{Tc} = 1 - (P_{R1} + P_{R2})$ when $T_C < T_S$, and $P_{Tc} = P_{R1} + P_{R2}$ when $T_C > T_S$.

Each psychometric function was constructed by analyzing the proportion of the trials (P_{Tc}) in which each T_C was perceived "greater" than T_S. Subsequently, it was found the function that fit best to the proportion values by using cumulative Gaussians. The JND (Just Noticeable Difference) was defined as the half of the difference between the comparison stimuli corresponding to the 0.25 and 0.75 value of the Proportion of "greater" responses (P_{Tc}).

In Exp. 1, $T_S = 4.2mm$ and $T_C = 2.7, 3.4, 3.7, 4.1, 4.3, 4.7, 5.8$ or $6.7mm$. In Exp. 2, $T_S = 45°$ and $T_C = 30, 40, 43, 44, 46, 47, 50$ or $60°$. In Exp. 3, $T_S = 5.09mm$ and $T_C = 3.5, 4.08, 4.47, 4.85, 5.3, 5.95, 6.64$ or $7.5mm$. The exploration time of each stimulus was of equal duration, 4sec in Exp.1 and Exp. 2 and 5sec in Exp. 3. The velocity of exploration in Exp. 3 was fixed at 20mm/sec. All experiments were performed in two sessions each in different day (Session I for virtual patterns and Session II for real patterns) to isolate the effects of learning and fatigue. In each session, the comparison stimuli were presented 16 times, resulting in a total of 128 trials which were randomized and divided in three parts with 5min breaks. For Exp. 1 and 2, Session I took ≈60min and Session II ≈45min. For Exp. 3, Session I took ≈50min and Session II ≈60min.

6   Results and Discussion

Subjects' JND from Exp. 1 for the standard distance of 4.2mm are plotted in Fig. 4a. For virtual parallel ridges, the average JND is 22% (Mean=0.922mm, SD=0.11mm) of the standard distance. For real parallel ridges, the average JND is 4.7% (Mean=0.197mm, SD=0.02mm) of the standard distance. Analysis of variance (ANOVA) revealed a highly significant difference between the average JND for real and virtual parallel ridges ($F_{1,8} = 54.19, p < 0.001$). Comparing the results, the discrimination ability of virtual surface features decreases (JND increase) roughly 79% with respect to the discrimination ability of real surface features.

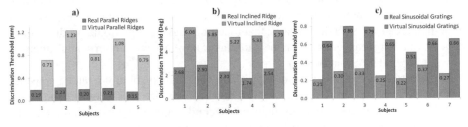

Fig. 4. JND's obtained from a) Exp. 1, b) Exp. 2 and c) Exp. 3

Fig. 4b displays the JND's of each subject from Exp. 2 for the standard inclination of 45°. For virtual inclined ridges, the average JND is 12.6% (Mean=5.66°, SD=0.18°) of the standard inclination. For real inclined ridges, the average JND is 5.4% (Mean=2.43°, SD=0.22°) of the standard inclination. ANOVA indicates a significant difference between the average JND for real and for virtual inclined ridges ($F_{1,8} = 158.2, p < 0.001$). Comparing the results, the discrimination ability of virtual surface features decreases (JND increase) roughly 55% with respect to the discrimination ability of real surface features. The result reported in this study for virtual inclined ridges is quite similar to that reported by Wall et al [1] which conducted a similar experiment on virtual horizontal lines rendered by the VTPlayer mouse (4x4 pins) and found that subjects could discriminate lines within roughly 5 of a horizontal line. The exploration average velocity of Exp. 1 and Exp. 2 are shown in Table 1. ANOVA failed to reveal a significant difference between the resulting velocities for real ridge patterns ($F_{1,6} = 0.06, p = 0.817$) and between the velocities for virtual ridge patterns ($F_{1,6} = 0.193, p = 0.676$). However, there is a significant difference between the resulting velocities for real and for virtual ridge patterns of Exp. 1 ($F_{1,6} = 43.7, p < 0.001$) and Exp. 2. ($F_{1,6} = 39.93, p < 0.001$). A possible explanation for this significant difference could be that the poor transmission of information through the tactile device makes to subjects move slowly in order to perceive better the surface features.

   The subjects' JND from Exp. 3 for the standard wavelength of 5.09mm are plotted in Fig. 4c. For virtual sinusoidal gratings, the average JND is 13.3% (Mean=0.678mm, SD=0.06mm) of the standard wavelength. For real sinusoidal gratings, the average JND is 5.5% (Mean=0.278mm, SD=0.03mm) of the standard wavelength. ANOVA indicates a significant difference between the average JND for real sinusoidal gratings and that

Table 1. Average Velocity of Exploration and Standard Deviation

	Real Surfaces	Virtual Surfaces
Exp. 1	96.8± 8.7 (mm/s)	41.0±3.0(mm/s)
Exp. 2	95.1± 8.1 (mm/s)	40.8±2.5(mm/s)

for virtual sinusoidal gratings ($F_{1,12} = 83, p < 0.001$). Comparing the results, the discrimination ability of virtual surface features decreases (JND increase) roughly 58% with respect to the discrimination ability of real surface features.

The degradation on performance with the tactile display could be explained by the following reason; first, the tactile display resolution is poor with respect to the resolution of the mechanoreceptors in the fingertip; second, the density of the tactile display is not enough to create the skin deformation that touching real gratings would produce; third, subjects touching real surface with the bare finger have access to both spatial-intensive as well temporal information [12].

In order to improve the tactile display effectiveness, two solutions can be consider; first, increase the actuators resolution [11]; however the size and weight of the device would increase and the portability reduced. Second, explore the use of an additional sensory modality such as sight and sound as it has done by [9].

7 Conclusion

The results emerged from this study reveal that using the tactile display subjects' discrimination ability decreases (JND increase) roughly 65% (79% in Exp. 1, 55% in Exp. 2 and 58% in Exp. 3) with respect to that achieved touching real surface features. More specifically, subjects presented more difficulties to discriminate distance in ridge patterns than inclination in ridges or wavelength in sinusoidal gratings. Considering that the tactile display resolution in comparison with the human finger resolution is very low, then we can say that its performance is quite acceptable. Moreover, the tactile display presents several great advantages; its light weight and portability make it suitable for virtual environments and teleoperation applications, its reduce size allow to easily incorporate it into mechanisms with force feedback and its sufficient displacement (0-2mm) and control of pins allow rendering features of different amplitudes. Finally, the quantification of the subjects performance using the tactile device and using physical surfaces can guide the development of new and improved tactile display, help designers to choose appropriate applications for the tactile display and improve the actual tactile rendering methods.

References

1. Wall, S.A., Brewster, S.A.: Sensory Substitution Using Tactile Pin Arrays:Human Factors, Technology and Applications. In: Signal Processing, vol. 86 (2006)
2. Kontarinis, D.A., Son, J.S., Peine, W., Howe, R.D.: A tactile shape sensing and display system for teleoperated manipulation. In: IEEE International Conference on Robotics and Automation, vol. 1, pp. 641–646 (1995)

3. Moy, G., Singh, U., Tan, E., Fearing, R.S.: Human psychophysics for teletaction system design. Haptics-e, The Electronic Journal of Haptics Research 1 (2000)
4. Sarakoglou, I., Bezdicek, M., Tsagarakis, N., Caldwell, D.G.: Free to touch: A portable Tactile Display For 3D surface exploration. In: Intl. Conf. Intelligent Robots and Systems, pp. 3587–3592 (2006)
5. Kops, C.E., Gardner, E.P.: Discrimination of simulated texture patterns on the human hand. J. Neurophysiol. 76, 1145–1165 (1996)
6. Summers, I.R., Brady, A.C.: Psychophysics experiments on a tactile renderer. In: Proceedings of Materials and Sensations, pp. 39–42 (2008)
7. Provancher, W.R., Cutkosky, M.R., Kuchenbecker, K.J., Niemeyer, G.: Contact Location Display for Haptic Perception of Curvature and Object Motion. International Journal of Robotics Research 24(9), 691–702 (2005)
8. Yang, G., Kyung, K., Srinivasan, M.A., Kwon, D.: Quantitative tactile display device with pin-array type tactile feedback and thermal feedback. In: Proc. IEEE International on Conference Robotics and Automation (2006)
9. Kammermeier, P., Buss, M., Schmidt, G.: Dynamic Display of Distributed Tactile Shape Information by Prototypical Actuator Array. In: Proc. of the IEEE/RSI Int'l. Conf. on Intelligent Robots and Systems (2000)
10. Gescheider, G.A.: Psychophysics: The Fundamental, 3rd edn. Lawrence Erlbaum Associates, Mahwah (1997)
11. Garcia-Hernandez, N., Tsagarakis, N.G., Caldwell, D.G.: Effect of the tactile array density on the discrimination of edge patterns: Implications for tactile systems design. In: International Conference on Advanced Robotics, pp. 1–6, 22–26 (2009)
12. Klatzky, R.L., Lederman, S.J.: Tactile roughness perception with a rigid link interposed between skin and surface. Perception and Psychophysics 61, 591–607

Tactile Perception of a Water Surface: Contributions of Surface Tension and Skin Hair

Michi Sato[1], Junya Miyake[1], Yuki Hashimoto[1], and Hiroyuki Kajimoto[1,2]

[1] The University of Electro Communications
1-5-1 Chofugaoka, Chofu, Tokyo 182-8585, Japan
[2] Japan Science and Technology Agency
{michi,junya,hashimoto,kajimoto}@kaji-lab.jp

Abstract. We investigated the tactile perception of a liquid surface that can be clearly felt as a thin line by a hand moving in the liquid. Although this phenomenon was first reported by Meissner in 1859 and is quite well known, the underlying mechanism is poorly understood. This study aimed to clarify how we perceive the boundary between the atmosphere and water as a cutaneous sensation. We found that skin hair plays a major role in the perception on hairy skin, while surface tension does not significantly contribute to perception of a liquid surface. Furthermore, we found that glabrous skin has a smaller role than hairy skin in this sensation.

Keywords: Cutaneous Sensation, Hair Follicle Receptor, Liquid Surface, Tactile.

1 Introduction

This study investigated the tactile perception of a liquid surface. The history of liquid surface perception is long. In 1859, Meissner reported that we can clearly feel a liquid surface as a thin ring when a finger is immersed in a vessel filled with mercury [1]. This finding was reinvestigated by Bekesy [2], and has been cited in many reports as proof that human skin can perceive spatial and temporal differences in pressure, rather than pressure itself [3][4][5].

However, it has remained unclear which receptors contribute to the perception of a liquid surface.

In contrast, on a daily basis, we perceive a water surface as a thin line when we take a bath, for example. Water has a much smaller surface tension than mercury, and this perception occurs for any part of body, especially the forearm. Therefore, we must reconsider what mechanism underlies this perception.

In our preliminary experiments, we confirmed that we can clearly feel a water surface when we move our arm up and down through the water (Fig. 1). This perception disappears if we stop moving our arm. We also confirmed that mechanoreceptors, rather than thermoreceptors, contribute to this perception because, as the water temperature and body temperature became closer, the sensation became clearer. Although hydraulic pressure is the first candidate, the hydraulic pressure at a

A.M.L. Kappers et al. (Eds.): EuroHaptics 2010, Part II, LNCS 6192, pp. 58–64, 2010.

water surface is 0. Therefore, it is hard to consider that we perceive a water surface by hydraulic pressure alone.

Starting from these facts, this study aimed to clarify how we perceive the boundary between air and water as a cutaneous sensation, particularly at the forearm.

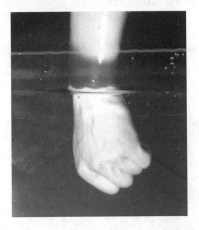

Fig. 1. Feeling a liquid surface in a tactile manner

2 Experiment 1: Evaluation of the Contribution of Surface Tension

Based on the fact that a water surface is perceived, the contribution of the surface tension was considered as the first candidate for the perception of a water surface. Therefore, we performed an experiment to evaluate the contribution of surface tension to perception.

The experiment was conducted with 17 participants who were separated into two groups of different sequences to avoid bias in the results.

We prepared two vessels filled with different liquids. One contained water (surface tension, 63 mN/m) and the other contained a neutral 2% detergent solution (surface tension, 26 mN/m). The liquid temperatures were set to 34°C, which is the temperature of the skin surface. The participants compared the vividness of liquid surface perception by immersing their forearm into the vessels (Fig. 2). The experimental procedure was as follows (Fig. 2).

Group A: 8 participants

i.   Each participant immersed their right arm in water and their left arm in the detergent solution. They were asked to move their arms up and down.

ii. The participants evaluated the vividness of the water perception from 1 to 5, after setting the vividness of the detergent solution perception as 3 (standard liquid).

iii. After swapping the liquids, the arms were moved up and down again.

iv. The participants evaluated the new solutions as described in (ii).

v.   Procedures (i) to (iv) were repeated, but this time the participants evaluated the vividness of the detergent solution perception, after setting the vividness of the water perception as 3 (standard liquid).

Group B: 9 participants
All of the procedures were the same as those for group A, except that each participant started the experiment by immersing their right arm in the detergent solution and their left arm in water.

The results of Experiment 1 are shown in Fig. 3. From these results, we concluded that the contribution of the surface tension to sensation is actually quite small ($p > 0.01$).

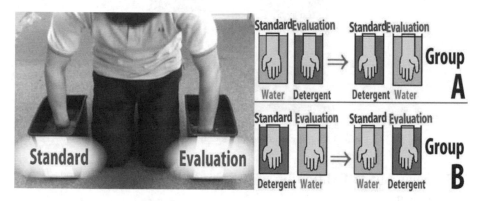

Fig. 2. Setup and procedure of Experiment 1

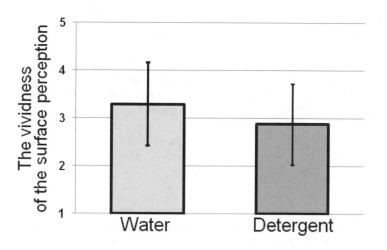

Fig. 3. Comparison of the vividness of the surface perception in Experiment 1

3   Experiment 2: Evaluation of the Contribution of Skin Hair

We considered that skin hair may be another factor behind the perception of a water surface because the hair may be directly moved at the water surface. Therefore, we evaluated the contribution of skin hair to sensation in a second experiment.

The experiment was conducted by 16 participants who were separated into two groups of different sequences, similar to Experiment 1. We prepared vessels filled with water at 34°C. The left arm and the back of the left hand were shaved to lessen the effect of skin hair. Next, the participants compared the vividness of the liquid surface perception by immersing their forearms in the vessels. The experimental procedure was the same as that in Experiment 1 (Fig. 4).

The results for Experiment 2 are shown in Fig. 5. Hairy skin generated a much more vivid sensation than shaved skin ($p<0.01$). Therefore, we concluded that the contribution of skin hair to liquid surface perception is actually quite large.

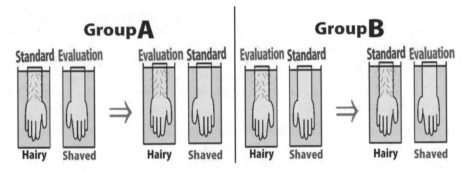

Fig. 4. Procedure for Experiment 2

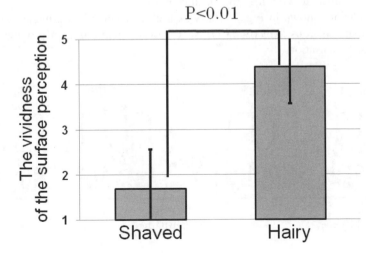

Fig. 5. The results for Experiment 2 show that skin hair plays a significant role in liquid surface perception

4 Experiment 3: Validation of the Perception in Glabrous Skin

From the results of Experiment 2, it seems that skin hair plays an important role in the perception of a liquid surface. However, Meissner [1] described that we can clearly feel a liquid surface as a thin ring when a *finger* is immersed in the liquid, not the arm. Half of the skin of a finger is glabrous skin and, therefore, we need to verify whether the perception of water surface occurs on glabrous skin. If this is the case, how clear is it compared with hairy skin? To answer these questions, we performed an experiment that compared the perceptions on hairy skin and glabrous skin of the hand.

This experiment was conducted by five participants. The experimental procedure was as follows and as shown in Fig. 6.

 i.   The backs of the participants' left hands were covered by liquid bandages (Coloskin®, Tokyo-Koshisha Inc.). Their right hands were left uncovered. Both hands were immersed in water.
 ii. The participants evaluated the vividness of the water perception by their left hand from 1.0 to 5.0, after setting the vividness of water perception for the right hand as 3.0 (standard perception).
 iii. The palms of participants' left hands were covered by liquid bandages. Their right hands were left uncovered. Both hands were immersed in water.
 iv. The participants evaluated the vividness of the water perception by their left hand as described in (ii).

The back of the hand comprises hairy skin while the palm comprises glabrous skin. Therefore, when the palm is covered by a liquid bandage, the perception of a water surface is induced by the hairy skin. Conversely, when the back of the hand is covered, the perception is induced by glabrous skin.

Because the number of participants in this experiment was small, we asked the participants to evaluate vividness to a decimal point.

The results are shown in Fig. 7. Hairy skin clearly generated a much more vivid sensation than glabrous skin ($p<0.01$). Nevertheless, glabrous skin provide a small contribution to sensation.

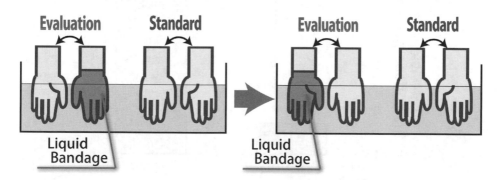

Fig. 6. Procedure of Experiment 3

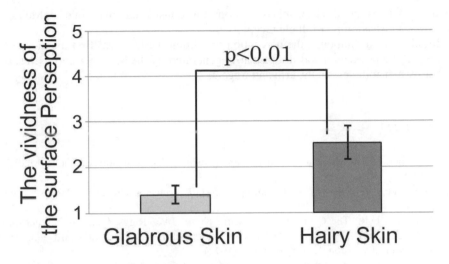

Fig. 7. The results for Experiment 3 show that skin hair plays a significant role in liquid surface perception

5 Discussion and Conclusions

In Experiment 1, we compared two liquids with different surface tensions. The results showed that there was almost no difference between the perceptions of these two liquids, despite the two-fold difference in their surface tensions. From these results, we concluded that the contribution of the surface tension to liquid surface perception is quite small.

In Experiment 2, we compared hairy skin with shaved skin. The results showed that the perception of a water surface became indistinct and almost disappeared when the skin was shaved. Therefore, we concluded that the contribution of skin hair to liquid surface perception is quite large.

Based on these observations, we sought to identify which types of receptors contribute to the sensation of liquid surfaces.

As the contribution of skin hair is dominant, we considered that hair follicle receptors may be involved. This consideration is supported by the following facts. First, the perception of a water surface became vivid when the arm was moved and indistinct when the arm was rested. These observations suggest that RA-type receptors are involved. Second, there are only two types of RA receptors (Pacinian corpuscles and hair follicle receptors) in hairy skin (Meissner corpuscles do not exist in hairy skin [6][7][8]). Third, the spatial resolution of Pacinian corpuscles is quite large, and a "thin line" perception by Pacinian corpuscles seems unreasonable.

This raised another question. Meissner first observed the water surface perception by a finger, which contains both hairy and glabrous skin. Thus, which skin type contributes most in the finger?

In Experiment 3, we compared glabrous skin and hairy skin of the hand. The results showed that the hairy skin generated a much more vivid sensation than the glabrous skin. Although glabrous skin provided some sensation, it was quite small relative to hairy skin. Thus, this sensation was considered to be due to Meissner corpuscles instead of hair follicle receptors.

In other words, although the perception of a liquid surface was first mentioned by Meissner, the perception was not primarily generated by the Meissner corpuscles, but rather by hair follicles, on the arm and fingers.

References

[1] Meissner. G.: Untersuchungen über den Tastsinn. Zeitschrift fur rationelle Medicine (1859)
[2] von Bekesy, G.: Sensory Inhibition, pp. 115–117. Princeton University Press, Princeton (1967)
[3] Kenshalo, D.R.: The Cutaneous Senses. In: Kling, J.W., Riggs, L.A. (eds.) Woodworth and Schlosberg's Experimental Psychology, Sensation and Perception, 3rd edn., Holt, Rinehart and Winston, New York, vol. 3 (1972)
[4] Katz, D., trans. by Krueger L.E.: The World of Touch, p. 213. Lawrence Erlbaum, Mahwah (1989)
[5] Srinivasan, M.A., Dandekar, K.: An Investigation of the Mechanics of Tactile Sense Using Two-Dimensional Models of the Primate Fingertip. Trans. ASME J. Biomech. Eng. 118, 48–55 (1996)
[6] Bolanowski, S.J., Gescheider, G.A., Verrillo, R.T., Checkosky, C.M.: Four Channels Mediate the Mechanical Aspects of Touch. J. Acoustic. Soc. Am. 84, 1680–1694 (1988)
[7] Gescheider, G.A., Bolanowski, S.J., Pope, V., Verrillo, R.T.: A Four-channel Analysis of the Tactile Sensitivity of the Fingertip: Frequency Selectivity, Spatial Summation, and Temporal Summation. Somatosensory Motor Res. 19, 114–124 (2002)
[8] Miyaoka, T.: Mechanoreceptive Mechanisms to Determine the Shape of the Detection-Threshold Curve Presenting Tangential Vibrations on Human Glabrous Skin. In: Proceedings of the 21st Annual Meeting of the International Society for Psychophysics, pp. 211–216 (2005)

A Force and Touch Sensitive Self-deformable Haptic Strip for Exploration and Deformation of Digital Surfaces

Monica Bordegoni, Umberto Cugini, Mario Covarrubias, and Michele Antolini

Politecnico di Milano, Dipartimento di Meccanica
Via G. La Masa, 1, 20146 Milano, Italy
{monica.bordegoni,umberto.cugini}@polimi.it,
{mario.covarrubias,michele.antolini}@mail.polimi.it
www.kaemart.it

Abstract. The paper describes a haptic device whose aim is to permit the assessment of digital prototypes of industrial products with aesthetic value. The device haptically renders curves belonging to digital surfaces. The device is a haptic strip consisting of a modular servo-controlled mechanism able to deform itself, allowing the user to feel the resulting shape with his free hands. The haptic strip is also equipped with two force sensitive handles placed at the extremities, and a capacitive touch sensor along its length, which are used for applying deformations to the digital shape.

Keywords: Haptic linear strip, Virtual Prototyping, Multimodal application.

1 Introduction

The haptic tool presented in this paper, consisting in a continuous servo-controlled physical strip, aims to represent a step forward in the field of digital surfaces manipulation. Such device allows a continuous, free hand contact on a developable strip bended and twisted by a modular servo-controlled mechanism, and is integrated with a multimodal, virtual reality system. The objective of the system is to experiment a new tool that allows designers and stylists to perform the assessment and modification of the aesthetic quality of new products applied directly on the digital prototype, in an intuitive, natural and easy manner.

The motivation inspiring this research is the following. Current digital tools for shape creation and evaluation (CAD tools), nowadays largely used for the design of products with aesthetic value, are too technical for this kind of users. Therefore, we have developed an interface and an interaction modality that allows the designers, more keen on expressing their ideas using their own hands, to craft physical prototypes, to manipulate a digital prototype mimicking operations made during a real evaluation session. The system is based on a haptic device based on the concept of a bendable strip; it permits 6-DOF translation and orientation of a digital prototype, and haptic evaluation of its shape along user-defined geodesic trajectories.

The haptic interface has been described in [1,2]. This paper focuses on the description of the system allowing users to apply deformations to the shape of the digital prototype. This is performed by interpreting the user's intent during his interaction with

A.M.L. Kappers et al. (Eds.): EuroHaptics 2010, Part II, LNCS 6192, pp. 65–72, 2010.

the strip. The deformation to apply is computed through the integration of information coming from the force-sensitive handles positioned at the extremities of the strip, and the capacitive touch sensor placed along its length. The full system functionalities are controlled through four buttons integrated at the strip extremities and used for the selection of menu items.

The paper presents the system specification, the kinematic mechanism of the haptic device, the sensors integrated and an example of use of the device operated by a designer for the exploration and modification of a digital model of a product.

2   Related Works

Most of the research and development activities on haptics have concentrated on point based force-feedback devices. The evolution trend of both research and industrial applications seems to be based on multi-point contacts that is a way to improve and enlarge the field of application not changing the basic approach. Some of the most relevant force feedback technologies are the following [3]: point-based devices like the PHANToM [4], the FCS-HapticMaster [5], and the Haption-Virtuose [6], and multi-point based devices like the Haptex [7] system, and the T'nD system [8].

Another type of haptic device consists of tactile devices. They consist of small patches of sensors/actuators that can render very small surfaces and support limited input forces, usually with small and few pin arrays or vibrators arranged in order to stimulate the skin. Some interesting researches are mainly based on vertical pins displacement for mid-scale virtual surfaces [9], or more recently on a miniature pin array tactile module [10] based on elastic and electromagnetic force for mobile devices, which provides enough working frequency, output force and amplitude to stimulate the human's mechanoreceptors. A small and lightweight tactile display described in [11] is integrated into a haptic glove system. In [12] it is presented a tactile display using airborne ultrasound: the prototype presented provides weak force for users to feel constant pressure, just sufficient for vibratory sensation. In [13] the authors present a haptic interface capable of simulating forces experienced during abdominal palpation using pneumatic actuators. In [14] is described a continuous tangible user interface for modelling free-form 3-D objects, such as landscape models by scanning and illuminating a Clay or a SandScape; nevertheless the actual system is not providing a force feedback. There are several studies using the Immersion CyberGlove [15] the only draw back is that it is quite invasive; the user needs to wear a glove covered by an armature. The only attempt to render a continuous contact along a line is described in [1,2]. It consists of a haptic device able to self-deform as a continuous planar curve and as a geodesic curve. In [16], the authors describe an approach for the perception of shape curvatures using a three DOF robotic-type mechanism in which is used a single finger rather than the complete palm of the hand, which is instead possible in our approach described in this paper.

3   System Description

The deformable haptic strip that we have developed is a part of a multimodal system conceived for the evaluation and the deformation of digital prototypes (http://www.youtube.com/user/SATINproject). The aim of the research is to mimic assessment operations performed on real prototypes using physical splines laid over the surface of the stereoscopic visualization of the virtual object. The interaction modalities provided by the system permit the 6-DOF positioning of the virtual object within the workspace, the haptic rendering of user-defined curves belonging to the surface of the virtual object, inspection of the curve by touching the haptic strip and hearing associated sound for geometrical characteristics like curvature function, inflection points and discontinuities and finally the local and global deformation of the virtual shape using the force-sensitive handles at the extremities of the strip. A structure mounting a DLP projector and equipped with a semi-reflective mirror is able to provide 3D stereo visualization, head tracking, stereo sound system and co-location of virtual model and haptic strip, allowing the user to perceive the strip exactly where it is projected within the virtual workspace [1].

4 Kinematic Mechanism

The haptic strip is connected with two 3-DOF force sensitive FCS-HapticMaster robots (HM) in a configuration as shown in Figure 1-**a**. The geodesic mechanism (**5**) is attached on the two HM devices (**6**) through the sheet metal component (**3**) mounted on the tilt mechanism (**7**).

The haptic strip is able to render geodesic curves, which are defined as the shortest path between two points in a curved space. That means that the mechanism in which the plastic strip lies on needs to apply some bending and twisting deformations in order to render these particular curves. For this reason a spatial and modular mechanism has been designed for providing both bend and torsion effects [2]. We decided to include bending moments through side forces on each module using single push rods. It

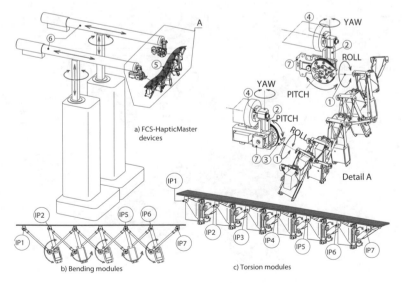

Fig. 1. The haptic strip as 6-DOF platform

is well-known that the curvature in a homogeneous physical spline is proportional to the bending moment induced into the extremities. In a slender beam, both the overall change in length due to stretch and the additional shape change due to shear deformation are negligible compared to the bending deformation. Figure 1-**b** shows the schema for the bending modules and Figure 1-**c** shows the schema for the torsion modules.

5 Force Sensing

The strip can be used in three different modalities: to manipulate (move and rotate) the virtual object, to haptically render a curve on the virtual object and to apply global and local deformations to the virtual object. That means that the user has to handle the strip in some ways for both manipulating and applying deformations to the strip. We have decided to allow the handling through the strip extremities. We have analysed the strain gauge sensor technology to use for retrieving the degrees of freedom required for both manipulation and modification modalities. The first row in Figure 2 shows the six degrees of freedom required for manipulating the haptic strip as a 6-DOF platform. The second row shows the user's intent action for modification (compression, bending and torsion).

A strain gauge is a sensor whose resistance varies with applied force; it converts force, pressure, tension, weight, etc., into a change in electrical resistance which can then be measured and are a typical use for mechanical measurements. They are used for the measurement of strain, (tensile and compressive strain, distinguished by a positive or negative sign). We use these data for both the positioning and modification modalities. We have installed the 1-LY13-6/350 and 1-XY43-3/350 strain gauges models provided by HBM [17] following certified procedures. The shape of the handle and the locations

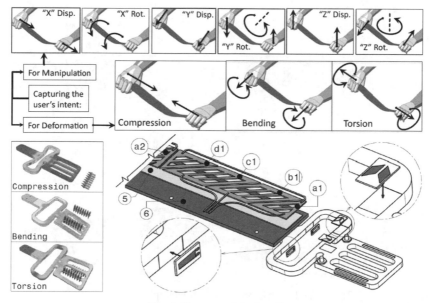

Fig. 2. Force sensitive handle

and characteristics of strain gauges to be used have been designed and verified through structural analysis of the user's conditions.

6   Touch Sensor and Lighting

As mentioned in Section 3, the sound interface of the system gives the possibility to play metaphoric sounds during the user's exploration of the haptic strip. These metaphoric sounds can be played according to the type of local geometric characteristics of the curve (e.g. curvature discontinuities). So, it is necessary to track the user's fingers position on the strip surface. In addition, the modifications via local force application requires the detection of the position of the user's finger on the strip. Taking this into account, we have analysed some technical solutions for tracking the position of the user's fingers and/or of the palm of the hand. We have devised a solution using tactile sensors rather than using gloves or any kind of invasive system. Figure 3-**a** shows the flexible capacitive sensor positioned on top of the strip.

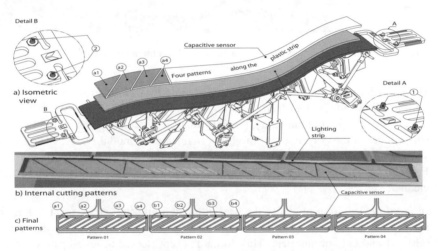

Fig. 3. Capacitive touch sensor

Using a flexible capacitive sensor is an effective solution because the user does not need to apply any pressure to activate it. In fact, the sensor is easily activated through a soft contact. As shown in Figure 3-**b**, we have analysed different patterns. An electric field is formed between the receiver and the transmitter trace. We used four QProx E1101 development boards, which provide excitation to the capacitance sensor, sense the changes in capacitance caused by the user's proximity, and provide a digital output. The final pattern configuration is displayed in Figure 3-**c**. The first board uses the metal traces a1, a2, a3 and a4 to track the user's finger, the second board uses the metal traces from b1 to b4 and so on. In this way we have designed a flexible multi-touch strip.

The sensor includes a lighting system [18] in order to better visualise the physical strip in the 3D stereo visualization system.

7   Use of the Haptic Strip

The integrated system provides three main functionalities:

1. **Positioning:** The user, through the two sensorised extremities, can move and rotate the virtual object using the haptic strip as a 6-DOF platform.
2. **Exploration:** When this option is active, the haptic strip remains still allowing a stable evaluation of the curve represented by the deformed strip. This operation can be performed in the same way than in the real world using both hands. During this operation, the haptic strip conforms according to the geodesic trajectory metaphor in real-time. Figures 4-**a** and 4-**b** show the user's hand while exploring the virtual object.

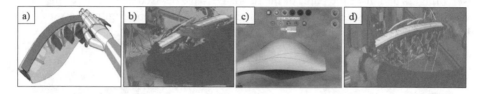

Fig. 4. Haptic strip used in exploration (a and b) and modification (c and d) modalities

3. **Deformation:** Two options have been implemented in deformation modality. These options allows *global* and *local* deformation on the virtual object. When the user selects the deformation modality, the deformation is controlled using the two sensorised extremities of the strip. In *global deformation* modality, the visual representation of the model is deformed as well and the strip description is updated. Figures 4-**c** and 4-**d** show the global deformation applied on a virtual vacuum cleaner.

In *local deformation* modality the user, after defining the curve, must define the surface domain affected by the deformation, as well as the boundary constraints (G0, G1 and G2 continuities). This domain is represented as an ellipsoid surface. By applying forces, the user is able to push or pull the surface using as deformation devices the sensorised extremities.

8   Conclusion

The paper has presented a novel haptic interface for rendering and for applying deformations to digital surfaces. The haptic interface consists of a haptic strip that is bended and twisted by a modular servo-controlled mechanism. The strip conforms to a selected curve belonging to a surface and allows users to evaluate the quality of shapes along a line. The strip is also equipped with force sensors placed at its extremities. By acting on the extremities, the user can apply deformations to the digital object shape.

The tests performed with target users, who are industrial designers, have demonstrated that the use of the haptic strip for the evaluation of aesthetic shapes is effective and supports them in the appreciation of the aesthetic qualities of the shape [19]. The use of the strip for the deformation of the digital surface has also been considered an easy and rapid way for prototyping various forms of the digital object.

Despite the limitation of the haptic strip [2], mainly related to the fact that the exploration and modification of a 3D digital shape occurs through a line, it is indeed a step forward in the development of haptic devices for the manipulation of 3D surfaces.

Acknowledgement

The research work presented in this paper has been partially supported by the European Commission under the FP6-IST- 5-0054525 SATIN Sound And Tangible Interfaces for Novel product design (http://www.satin-project.eu). The authors would like to thank all the project partners for their contributions to the research.

References

1. Bordegoni, M., Ferrise, F., Covarrubias, M., Antolini, M.: A linear interface for the evaluation of shapes. In: Proc. of the ASME 2009 International Design Engineering Technical Conferences & Computers and Information in Engineering Conference IDETC/CIE 2009, San Diego, CA, USA (2009)
2. Bordegoni, M., Cugini, U., Covarrubias, M., Antolini, M.: Geodesic haptic device for surface rendering. In: Proc. of the Joint Virtual Reality Conference of EGVE-ICAT-EuroVR 2009, Lyon, France (2009)
3. Hayward, V., Ashley, O.R., Cruz Hernandez, M., Grant, D., Robles De La Torre, G.: Haptic interfaces and devices. Sensor Review 24(1), 16–29 (2004)
4. PHANToM device, SenSable Technologies Inc., http://www.sensable.com (accessed October 30, 2009)
5. FCS-HapticMaster, MOOG, http://www.moog.com/ (accessed December 30, 2009)
6. Virtuose, Haption, http://www.haption.com/ (accessed December 30, 2009)
7. Haptex system, http://haptex.miralab.unige.ch/ (accessed December 30, 2009)
8. Bordegoni, M., Cugini, U.: Haptic modeling in the conceptual phases of product design. Virtual Reality Journal 9(1), 192–202 (2006)
9. Iwata, H., Yano, H., Nakaizumi, F., Kawamura, R.: Project feelex: adding haptic surface to graphics. In: SIGGRAPH 2001: Proceedings of the 28th Annual Conference on Computer Graphics and Interactive Techniques, pp. 469–476. ACM, New York (2001)
10. Tae-Heon, Y., Sang-Youn, K., Chong-Hui, K., Dong-Soo, K., Wayne, J.B.: Development of a miniature pin-array tactile module using elastic and electromagnetic force for mobile devices. In: Proc. of the World Haptics Conference, pp. 13–17. IEEE Computer Society, Los Alamitos (2009)
11. Seung-Chan, K., Chong-Hui, K., Gi-Hun, Y., Tae-Heon, Y., Byung-Kil, H., Sung-Chul, K., Dong-Soo, K.: Small and lightweight tactile display (salt) and its application. In: Proc. of the Third Joint Eurohaptics Conference and Symposium on Haptic Interfaces for Virtual Environment and Teleoperator Systems, Salt Lake City, UT, USA, pp. 69–74 (2009)
12. Takayuki, H., Takayuki, I., Hiroyuki, S.: Non-contact tactile sensation synthesized by ultrasound transducers. In: Proc. of the Third Joint Eurohaptics Conference and Symposium on Haptic Interfaces for Virtual Environment and Teleoperator Systems, Salt Lake City, UT, USA, pp. 256–260 (2009)

13. Cheng, M., Passenger, J., Salvado, O., Riek, S., Ourselin, S., Watson, M.: Pneumatic haptic interface fuzzy controller for simulation of abdominal palpations during colonoscopy. In: Proc. of Third Joint Eurohaptics Conference and Symposium on Haptic Interfaces for Virtual Environment and Teleoperator Systems, Salt Lake City, UT, USA, pp. 250–255 (2009)
14. Ishii, H., Ratti, C., Piper, B., Wang, Y., Biderman, A., Ben-Joseph, E.: Bringing clay and sand into digital design — continuous tangible user interfaces. BT Technology Journal 22(4), 287–299 (2004)
15. CyberForce device, http://www.vrealities.com/cyberforce.html (accessed April 16, 2010)
16. Wijntjes, M.W.A., Sato, A., Kappers, A.M.L., Hayward, V.: Haptic perception of real and virtual curvature. In: Ferre, M. (ed.) EuroHaptics 2008. LNCS, vol. 5024, pp. 361–366. Springer, Heidelberg (2008)
17. Strain Gages, HBM, http://www.hbm.com/ (accessed July 15, 2009)
18. Lighting Stripes device, Elshine Inc., http://www.elshine.it/inglese/inverter.htm (accessed December 30, 2009)
19. Covarrubias, M., Antolini, M., Bordegoni, M., Cugini, U.: A spline-like haptic tool for exploration and modification of digital models with aesthetic value. In: Proc. of the ASME 2010 World Conference on Innovative Virtual Reality, WINVR 2010, Ames, Iowa, USA, May 12-14 (2010)

Influence of Visual Feedback on Passive Tactile Perception of Speed and Spacing of Rotating Gratings

Anatole Lécuyer[1], Marco Congedo[1, 2], Edouard Gentaz[3],
Olivier Joly[4], and Sabine Coquillart[5]

[1] INRIA Rennes, Campus de Beaulieu,
35042 Rennes Cedex, France
anatole.lecuyer@irisa.fr
[2] ViBS Team, GIPSA-lab CNRS, Domaine Universitaire,
38402 Saint Martin d'Hères Cedex, France
marco.congedo@gmail.com
[3] LPNC, CNRS and Université Pierre Mendès-France,
38040 Grenoble Cedex 9, France
edouard.gentaz@upmf-grenoble.fr
[4] CEA LIST, 92265 Fontenay-Aux-Roses Cedex, France
olivier.joly@cea.fr
[5] INRIA Rhône-Alpes-LIG, 655 avenue de l'Europe, Montbonnot,
38334 Saint Ismier Cedex, France
sabine.coquillart@inria.fr

Abstract. We studied the influence of visual feedback on the tactual perception of both speed and spatial period of a rotating texture. Participants were placed in a situation of perceptual conflict concerning the rotation speed of a cylindrical texture. Participants touched a cylindrical texture of gratings rotating around its axis at a constant speed, while they watched a cylinder without gratings rotating at a different speed on a computer screen. Participants were asked to estimate the speed of the gratings texture under the finger and the spacing (or spatial period) of the gratings. We observed that the tactual estimations of both speed and spacing co-varied with the speed of the visual stimulus, although the cylinder perceived tactually rotated at a constant speed. The first effect (speed effect) could correspond to the resolution of the perceptual conflict in favor of vision. The second effect (spacing effect) is apparently surprising, since no varying information about spacing was provided by vision. However, the physical relation between spacing and speed is well established according to every day experience. Thus, the parameter extraneous to the conflict could be influenced according to previous experience. Such cross-modal effects could be used by designers of virtual reality systems and haptic devices to improve the haptic sensations they can generate using simple (constant) tactile stimulations combined with visual feedback.

Keywords: Touch, Texture, Perception, Illusion, Speed effect, Spacing effect.

1 Introduction

Our everyday activities rely on the simultaneous and interactive involvement of different senses. The exchanges between individuals and environment are mostly

A.M.L. Kappers et al. (Eds.): EuroHaptics 2010, Part II, LNCS 6192, pp. 73–78, 2010.
© Springer-Verlag Berlin Heidelberg 2010

multimodal. There has been increasing interest on multimodal integration and cross-modal interaction, particularly on integration of vision and touch (Hatwell, Streri and Gentaz, 2003; Ernst and Banks, 2002; Lécuyer, 2009). Early studies on integration of vision and touch used situations of sensory conflict and revealed a strong dominance of vision for spatial properties (Rock & Victor, 1964). However, the notion of visual dominance has been further modulated since, because other studies have shown a "compromise" between the two conflicting values (Heller, 1983). It seems that in spatial conflicts vision is usually dominant, but tactual information comes into play abruptly when inter-modal coherence is broken. Moreover, results are different for material properties, which are the domain favored by touch. For instance, tactual perception of textures is as efficient as visual perception and sometimes, for fine textures of abrasive papers, touch surpasses vision (Heller, 1989). Contrary to what was found for spatial properties, Heller (1989) and Lederman (1974) observed no difference between active exploration (participants rub the object with their fingers) and passive one (the object is moved under the immobile fingers). Thus, perception of textures might be less the result of kinesthetic than of cutaneous information. In a conflicting situation on textures properties, with abrasive paper seen and touched, the participants gave compromise responses (Lederman & Abbott, 1981). Their evaluation of the conflicting texture was a mean of the visual and tactual values. Lederman, Thorne and Jones (1986) dissociated two elements of textures: the notion of "roughness" (a material property) and the spatial density of the grains (a geometric property). A tactual-dominant compromise appeared when participants were instructed to estimate roughness, whereas a visual capture appeared when participants were instructed to evaluate the spatial density of the grains. Tactual dominance in the estimation of roughness was also observed in passive exploration (Guest & Spence, 2003).

In few studies, the issue of how the perceptual influence on one parameter influences other parameters physically related to it has been addressed (Lécuyer, 2009). To further investigate this issue, we set up an unusual situation of perceptual conflict regarding the rotation speed of a cylindrical texture (a texture glued on a rotating cylinder). Participants touched (without active movements) a cylindrical texture made of gratings rotating around its axis at constant speed, while watching on a computer screen a representation of a cylinder without gratings rotating at a different speed. The rotation of the visual stimulus was sometimes largely accelerated or decelerated when compared to the actual rotation of the gratings under the finger. Participants were asked to estimate both the speed of the gratings texture under the finger, and the spacing, i.e., spatial period, of the gratings. The reviewed literature suggests that the visual perception of speed could dominate the tactual one. We then expected the tactual perception of speed to be influenced by the visual speed. We also studied the possible influence of the perceptual conflict on the tactual estimation of the spatial period of the texture.

2 Method

Population: Ten adults (6 men and 4 women) took part in this experiment. All participants were right-handed.

Experimental apparatus: The texture used as tactual stimulus was a cylindrical texture of gratings (Figure 1-left). The gratings had a 1.5mm height (or amplitude) and a 5mm spacing (or spatial period). The cylinder on which the texture was glued had a 50mm diameter. The spacing of the gratings texture remained constant since the same texture was used along the whole experiment. The texture was set in rotation by an electrical motor. The texture was touched with the left index, perpendicularly to the axis of the cylinder and thus to the texture. The texture rotated from the interior to the exterior of the finger. The tactual stimulus was hidden to the participants' view by means of a box which enclosed both texture and participants' left hand. The left index rested on the gratings without any motion. As a consequence, the tactual perception of gratings was passive and based exclusively on cutaneous information. A small screen could be positioned between the index and the stimulus in order to enable or disable the contact between the finger and the texture. It was removed when testing the texture and immediately replaced after it.

Fig. 1. Experimental apparatus: (Left) Tactual texture of gratings; (right) Visual scene

The visual scene was made of a rotating cylinder (Figure 1-right). This cylinder had the same radius as the real cylindrical texture (i.e. 50mm) and was 10cm long. The visual texture used and mapped on the cylinder on the screen was a standard image (terra cotta) provided with the O2 graphic workstation of the SGI Company. This texture was considered as "neutral", as it did not provide meaningful information in terms of spacing of the gratings. The visual stimulus was displayed on a computer screen in monoscopic conditions. The participants were seated 30cm in front of the screen. The eyes of the participant were at the same height as the display of the cylinder on screen. The frame rate of the visual stimulus was of 15Hz.

Experimental procedure: During a test, participants were asked to touch the tactual stimulus with their left index while looking at the computer screen. Participants were told that the cylinder displayed on the computer screen was a representation of the rotating shaft on which their finger rested. We used the magnitude estimation method (Lederman, Thorne & Jones, 1986). During each trial, participant began to perceive the speed and spacing of a first texture (reference condition). After a 2-second break, they were asked to perceive the speed and spacing of a second texture (comparison condition). Participants were allowed unlimited time needed to evaluate each texture, but they were asked to perform the trials as quickly as possible. After each trial, the participants were asked to grade both the speed and the spacing of the comparison texture located under the finger, as compared to the reference texture, using a 10-based scale. For example, a speed –or spacing– of the comparison texture estimated as two times faster –or wider– was graded with a 20 value. For the purpose of the analysis, the estimations can be converted into rpm values for the speed and mm values for the spacing.

The spacing of the gratings remained constant throughout the experiment and equal to 5mm. The rotation speed of the texture remained also constant under the finger and equal to 15rpm for both the reference and the comparison conditions. The linear speed of the texture at the surface of the finger was thus equal to 39.27mm/s. In the reference condition, the visual speed of the cylinder on the computer screen was also equal to 15rpm. In the comparison condition, 7 different visual speeds were used (smaller, equal or greater than the tactual one): 7.5, 10.5, 13.5, 15, 16.5, 19.5, and 22.5 rpm. Each comparison pair was tested 4 times, for a total of 4x7=28 trials per participant. The 7 comparison pairs were presented randomly. The experiment lasted around 40 minutes. The participants wore earphones to eliminate noise cues.

3 Results

Estimation of Speed: Figure 2-left shows individual estimations of the tactual speed averaged across the four blocks of trials. The fitted line with all individual estimations (N=70) has equation y=6.87x+0.61. The R-squared value is 0.53. The t-test for the slope being different from zero is significant (t(68)=8.75; p<0.0001). The estimated tactual speed seems thus positively correlated to the visual speed.

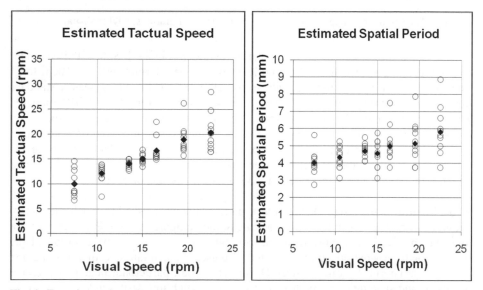

Fig. 2. Experimental results (black circle = one participant, black rhombus = average): (Left) Estimated tactual speed of the texture; (Right) Estimated spatial period of the texture

Estimation of Spatial Period: Figure 2-right shows individual estimations of the spatial period averaged across the four blocks (N=70). With spatial period data converted to rpm values, so to allow comparison with results obtained with Speed estimation, the obtained fitted line has equation y=4.68x+0.71. The R-squared value is 0.67. The t-test for the slope being different from zero is significant (t(68)=11.74; p<0.0001). The estimated spacing is positively correlated to the visual speed. Thus, the tactual estimates of the spatial period of the texture seem also influenced by the speed of the visual stimulus.

4 Perspectives

Summary of results: Our studies explored two cross-modal effects of vision on tactual perception. The first effect, named the "speed effect", concerned the visuo-haptic perceptual estimation of the rotation speed of a cylinder. All participants reported a change in the tactual speed although this speed remained constant during all trials. If the visual and tactual percepts do not agree, the visual feedback was found to influence the tactual perception of the constant stimulus. The second effect, named the "spacing effect", concerned the estimation of the spatial period (spacing) of the gratings texture located on the cylinder. When the visual speed was greater than the real one, the participants reported that the spacing of gratings increased, and when the visual speed was smaller than the real one they reported that the spacing decreased. In this case, no relevant information about spacing was provided by the visual stimulus, but the tactual estimation of spacing was still influenced as for speed. Therefore this experiment shows that when touching gratings which rotate at a constant speed, the tactual perception of both the speed and spatial period of the gratings is influenced by the visual perception of the rotation speed of a "neutral" texture rotating at different speeds. The speed and spatial period of the texture perceived tactually tend to increase (or decrease) when the rotation of the visual stimulus is accelerated (or decelerated). Indeed, the varying visual stimuli influence the perception of the two constant tactual parameters. A relation between stimuli coming from separate modalities is built by the participants, and question of how this phenomenon operates remains open.

Discussion: The speed effect is in line with previous research showing that for spatial properties vision dominates touch in the bimodal integration process. The spacing effect is more surprising. No explicit relation existed in the experimental materials between the parameter estimated tactually and the visual stimulus. There was indeed no relevant information available on the visual scene to provide a notion of spatial period of the gratings. However, a cross-modal association is arbitrarily established between the two stimuli, as shown by Figure 2. An interpretation of the spacing effect consists in considering a texture of rectangular gratings moving at the surface of a finger. A relation does exist between three parameters: the speed of the texture, its spatial period (spacing) and the resulting temporal frequency which corresponds to the temporal activation of the surface of the finger at a single point (Cascio & Sathian, 2001). This relation ensures the physical homogeneity and is given by Equation 1, where P (in mm) is the density or spatial Period of the texture (in our case: the spacing of the gratings), S (mm/s) is the Speed of the texture at the level of the finger, and F (Hz, or s-1) is the temporal Frequency sensed at the level of the finger and induced by the uniform motion of the texture under the finger. Thus, F is the number of consecutive activations at a single point or at a single cutaneous mechanoreceptor. The cross-modal association made by the participants could stem from the physical relation implied by Equation 1.

$$P = S / F \qquad (1)$$

Applications: The two cross-modal effects demonstrated here could be of great interest for the designers of haptic devices and virtual reality systems. Our results suggest indeed that the use of a constant haptic (tactile) stimulus can be combined with varying visual stimuli to generate a wide range of haptic sensations. This implies new uses and requirements for the design of cheap and simple tactile peripherals, augmented by visual feedback.

References

1. Cascio, C.J., Sathian, K.: Temporal cues contribute to tactile perception of roughness. Journal of Neuroscience 21, 5289–5296 (2001)
2. Ernst, M.O., Banks, M.S.: Humans integrate visual and haptic information in a statistically optimal fashion. Nature 415, 429–433 (2002)
3. Guest, S., Spence, C.: Tactile dominance in speeded discrimination of textures. Experimental Brain Research 150, 201–207 (2003)
4. Hatwell, Y., Streri, A., Gentaz, E.: Touching for knowing. John Benjamins Publishing Compagny, Amsterdam (2003)
5. Heller, M.A.: Haptic dominance in form perception with blurred vision. Perception 12, 607–613 (1983)
6. Heller, M.A.: Texture perception in sighted and blind observers. Perception and Psychophysics 45, 49–54 (1989)
7. Lécuyer, A.: Simulating Haptic Feedback using Vision: a Survey of Research and Applications of Pseudo-Haptic Feedback. Presence: Teleoperators and Virtual Environments 18(1), 39–53 (2009)
8. Lederman, S.J.: Tactile roughness of grooved surfaces: The touching processes and effects of macro and microsurface structure. Perception and Psychophysics 16, 385–396 (1974)
9. Lederman, S.J., Abbott, S.G.: Texture perception: Studies of intersensory organization using a discrepancy paradigm, and visual versus tactual psychophysics. Journal of Experimental Psychology: Human Perception and Performance 7, 902–915 (1981)
10. Lederman, S.J., Thorne, G., Jones, B.: Perception of texture by vision and touch: Multidimensionality and intersensory integration. Journal of Experimental Psychology: Human Perception and Performance 12, 169–180 (1986)
11. Rock, I., Victor, J.: Vision and touch: An experimentally created conflict between the two senses. Science 143, 594–596 (1964)

Dimensional Reduction of High-Frequency Accelerations for Haptic Rendering

Nils Landin[1], Joseph M. Romano[2],
William McMahan[2], and Katherine J. Kuchenbecker[2]

[1] KTH Royal Institute of Technology, Stockholm, Sweden
[2] University of Pennsylvania, Philadelphia, USA
nlandin@kth.se,
{jrom,wmcmahan,kuchenbe}@seas.upenn.edu
http://haptics.seas.upenn.edu

Abstract. Haptics research has seen several recent efforts at understanding and recreating real vibrations to improve the quality of haptic feedback in both virtual environments and teleoperation. To simplify the modeling process and enable the use of single-axis actuators, these previous efforts have used just one axis of a three-dimensional vibration signal, even though the main vibration mechanoreceptors in the hand are know to detect vibrations in all directions. Furthermore, the fact that these mechanoreceptors are largely insensitive to the direction of high-frequency vibrations points to the existence of a transformation that can reduce three-dimensional high-frequency vibration signals to a one-dimensional signal without appreciable perceptual degradation. After formalizing the requirements for this transformation, this paper describes and compares several candidate methods of varying degrees of sophistication, culminating in a novel frequency-domain solution that performs very well on our chosen metrics.

Keywords: haptic feedback, vibrations, measurement-based modeling.

1 Introduction

Haptic interfaces are designed to let a user touch virtual and distant objects as though they were real and within reach. For many applications, users would like the haptic feedback provided during these virtual and distant contacts to match the feel of real objects as closely as possible. When you touch a real surface with a tool, you feel low-frequency forces that convey shape, compliance, and friction, and you also feel high-frequency vibrations that reflect the texture of the object and its current contact state with your tool [5,6]. The mechanoreceptors that detect these important high-frequency vibrations are the Pacinian corpuscles (PCs); they are sensitive to vibratory stimuli from 20 to 1000 Hz, with a peak sensitivity between 250 and 550 Hz [1,2]. PCs are also known to respond to vibrations that occur in all directions, with motion parallel to the skin surface being slightly more easy to detect than motion normal to the skin [3].

As described in Section 2, high-frequency acceleration measurements have been shown to enable realistic haptic rendering of surface contact. Although tool vibrations

A.M.L. Kappers et al. (Eds.): EuroHaptics 2010, Part II, LNCS 6192, pp. 79–86, 2010.

occur in all three directions, these previous works have simplified the problem by measuring and recreating only a single axis of the vibration, discarding potentially significant haptic information in the other two axes. One could imagine replicating these single-axis techniques in three orthogonal directions, but such an approach would require significantly more complex vibration models and haptic hardware. Instead, we believe we can take advantage of the human hand's insensitivity to vibration direction by recreating the feel of a full three-dimensional acceleration with a one-dimensional signal. Section 3 lays out our quantitative objectives for this dimensional reduction problem. Section 4 then describes the candidate transformations we have considered, culminating in the presentation of our new approach, DFT321. Finally, Section 5 summarizes the contributions of this paper and lays out future work.

2 Background

Several research teams have succeeded at creating realistic haptic renderings through the use of high-frequency acceleration signals, though all of these efforts have neglected the 3D nature of real vibrations. For teleoperation, Kontarinis and Howe measured uniaxial accelerations at the fingertips of a custom robotic hand and continually played these vibrations for the operator to feel via two inverted audio speakers on the fingers of the master interface [7]. This sensory augmentation improved user performance in bearing inspection and needle puncture tasks. Several other researchers have used uniaxial recordings of real contact accelerations to improve the realism of virtual surface contact, either through parametric models [12,4] or direct playback [8]. In the domain of direct manipulation, Yao, Hayward, and Ellis created a handheld tool that measures accelerations perpendicular to the tool tip and outputs them in the orthogonal direction to improve the user's sensitivity to small surface features [15].

Inspired by this previous research, work in our own lab has focused on capturing and recreating the feel of real surfaces during tool-mediated contact, a process we call haptography [9]. As part of this project, we added a voice-coil actuator to the handle of a Phantom Omni to allow feedback of a single axis of contact acceleration during teleoperation [10]. Though this system was initially configured to replicate accelerations normal to the contacted surface, it was altered to transmit tangential accelerations for a human subject study focused on texture perception [11]. Subjects rated surface renderings as significantly more real when they included vibrations from the dedicated actuator, but no sample achieved a realism rating as high as the real surface. In fact, the highest rated rendering provided vibrations that were 50% stronger than the measured tangential values, indicating that restricting vibration measurement to a single axis may compromise the fidelity of the resulting interaction. Finally, we have also developed a method for distilling a set of recorded accelerations into a texture model for virtual surface rendering [13]; that work used principal component analysis to reduce 3D sensor signals down to 1D, but it did not closely consider the important role this transformation plays in system performance.

3 Transformation Objectives

The human hand detects high-frequency vibrations in all directions but cannot readily distinguish these directions from one another. Thus, we believe haptic rendering systems should be able to model and output 3D contact accelerations as 1D vibrations. Figure 1 shows our experimental setup for capturing and recreating such vibrations. The three-axis accelerometer (ADXL345) is configured for a range of ± 78.5 m/s^2 (± 8 g) and is sampled at 1000 Hz. The stylus is also equipped with a pair of voice coil actuators for vibration output. Figure 2 shows eight seconds of data collected with this device during real contact interactions. Notice that the shape of the time- and frequency-domain signals differs significantly between the three axes. The smoothed version of each spectrum was computed with a variable frequency resolution that matches the 22% Weber fraction for vibration discrimination [2]. Logarithmic scaling causes the smoothed version to appear to be too high in the plot,

Fig. 1. Texture vibrations were captured with a Wacom stylus equipped with a digital accelerometer

though it is correctly positioned. Because the mapping from $\mathbb{R}^3$ to $\mathbb{R}$ is not obvious, we have identified two objectives for measuring transformation performance.

I. Spectral Match. Human perception of high-frequency vibrations relies on the spectral content of the signal [2]. Thus, a dimensionally reduced vibration should feel like it has the same spectrum as the original recorded signal. We formalize this by saying that the synthesized 1D vibration should have the same energy at each frequency as the sum of the energies present at that frequency in the original vibration's three component directions. Consequently, the transformation should preserve the total Energy Spectral

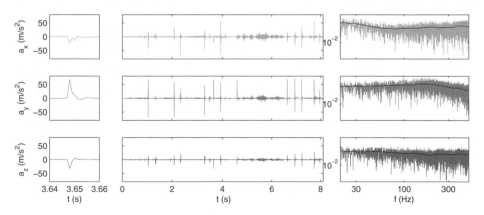

Fig. 2. Sample three-dimensional acceleration data. The user ran the tool tip over several small surface features, dragged across a textured vinyl surface, and then tapped on a hard piece of plastic.

Density (ESD) of the original 3D signal, where the ESD of each component $a(t)$ is $E_s(f) = |A(f)|^2$, where $A(f)$ is the Fourier transform of $a(t)$.

Because raw spectral estimates are noisy, we do not judge spectral similarity directly from the energy spectral density at each frequency. Instead, we have designed a spectral metric that takes into account the limited frequency resolution of human vibration perception, as mentioned in the previous section. Hence, our spectral perceptual comparisons use a frequency smoothing resolution that varies according to this rule, implemented via the spafdr command in Matlab; an example of this smoothing is shown in Figure 2, and we denote the smoothed version of $A(f)$ as $\tilde{A}(f)$. Using $a_s(t)$ to represent the 1D synthesized signal that results from the transformation, we write our spectral match metric as

$$M_{sm} = 1 - \frac{1}{n_f} \sum_{f=20Hz}^{1000Hz} \left(\frac{\left| |\tilde{A}_x(f)|^2 + |\tilde{A}_y(f)|^2 + |\tilde{A}_z(f)|^2 - |\tilde{A}_s(f)|^2 \right|}{|\tilde{A}_x(f)|^2 + |\tilde{A}_y(f)|^2 + |\tilde{A}_z(f)|^2} \right) \tag{1}$$

where n_f signifies the number of discrete frequencies in the sum. Here, we are quantifying the extent to which the synthesized signal preserves the energy in the original 3D signal for frequencies from 20 Hz to 1000 Hz, chosen to match the sensitivity range of Pacinian corpuscles. This calculation provides a strict measure of the average normalized deviation between the 1D signal's smoothed ESD and the 3D signal's smoothed ESD. If the two are identical, the spectral match metric will be one.

II. Temporal Match. While the spectral criterion captures the requirements for the stationary characteristics of the signal, we need to impose another criterion to capture transients. Ideally, peaks and sudden changes of the 1D signal should coincide with similar features in the 3D components. As a simple measure of temporal match, we thus look at the absolute value of the cross-correlation between each of the three original components and the synthesized signal at a time shift of zero; we use the absolute value because the human hand is not sensitive to vibration direction. We write our full temporal match metric as

$$M_{tm} = \frac{1}{3} \left(\frac{|a_x \star a_s|}{\sqrt{a_x \star a_x}\sqrt{a_s \star a_s}} + \frac{|a_y \star a_s|}{\sqrt{a_y \star a_y}\sqrt{a_s \star a_s}} + \frac{|a_z \star a_s|}{\sqrt{a_z \star a_z}\sqrt{a_s \star a_s}} \right) \tag{2}$$

where $\star$ denotes the cross-correlation evaluated at zero time delay. In words, this equation provides the average of the absolute values of the normalized cross-correlations. The resulting value is a measure of simultaneous temporal similarity between the 1D signal and the original components. A signal that correlates (or anticorrelates) perfectly with all three components (though rarely realizable) would have a temporal match metric of one.

4 Candidate Transformations

There are many potential methods for transforming three acceleration values into one value over time. This section describes the approaches we have considered thus far, progressing from the simplest options up to a more sophisticated method that we have newly developed. Each algorithm name includes the suffix 321 to indicate that it reduces the dimensions of a time-domain signal from three to one. This suffix also distinguishes our synthesis algorithms (e.g., DFT321) from the analysis algorithms from which they are derived (e.g., DFT). Figure 3 shows the effects of four of the candidates on the sample data from Figure 2, and Figure 4 shows their performance on a shorter texture-only sample. The corresponding spectral and temporal metric results are presented in Table 1.

Single-Axis (SA321). The simplest solution is to use an axis fixed to the sensor, as done in prior work [10,11]. Since there is no guarantee that the main vibrational energy will occur along that axis, considerable signal loss is expected. This is verified by inspection of the sample data in Figure 2: peaks do not always co-occur between the axes. This approach does not capture the total energy of the vibrations, and its spectral and temporal match metrics are not excellent.

Sum of Components (SoC321). Another computationally simple approach is to merely add the three components together. While correlation between components is

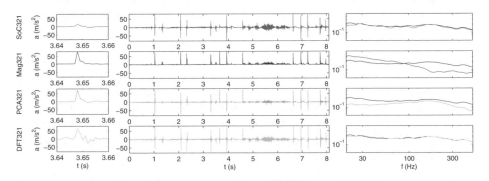

Fig. 3. Four of the candidate transformations applied to the data from Figure 2. The left column shows a detailed time view, and the right column presents the smoothed energy spectral density along with the original signal's smoothed ESD (black line).

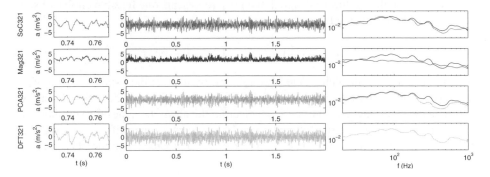

Fig. 4. Four of the candidate transformations applied to a 3D texture vibration

Table 1. Spectral match and temporal match metrics for the candidate transformations on the data shown in Figures 3 and 4

		SA$_x$321	SA$_y$321	SA$_z$321	SoC321	Mag321	PCA321	DFT321
Figure 3	M_{sm}	0.34	0.56	0.10	0.90	0.34	0.56	0.97
	M_{tm}	0.37	0.38	0.39	0.51	0.11	0.40	0.46
Figure 4	M_{sm}	0.27	0.51	0.23	0.48	0.37	0.52	1.00
	M_{tm}	0.69	0.68	0.60	0.62	0.02	0.80	0.64

likely, it may be positive or negative; this approach is thus susceptible to destructive interference between components that have negative cross-correlation. As exhibited in the top panels of Figures 3 and 4, this method does not preserve spectral energy and has inconsistent temporal performance.

Vector Magnitude (Mag321).   One can also take the square root of the sum of the squares of the components, as shown in the second panels of Figures 3 and 4. This transformation is not suitable for the outlined objectives; the magnitude of a 3D vector will always be positive, which introduces a DC-component that does not reflect the feel of the original high-frequency vibration. Also, the spectral contents of the three components are redistributed in a non-linear way that is highly dependent on the magnitudes of the different frequency components.

Principal Component Analysis (PCA321).   As done in [13], we can project the 3D signal onto a single fixed axis that PCA has identified as containing the most energy. This approach may be adequate if the haptic interaction that generated the data was highly constrained, as with the texture exploration data of Figure 4, though it always discards the information in the two perpendicular directions. For a slight improvement, one could divide the signal into segments over time and continually adapt the estimate of the first principal component.

Discrete Fourier Transform (DFT321).   Because none of the above transformations fully satisfies our objectives, we developed a new approach based on the DFT. By expressing each component of the 3D signal as an orthogonal basis function expansion, we can sum the components without destructive interference. In view of the spectral requirements on the synthesized signal, the DFT represents one feasible choice of such basis functions. Following (1), we set

$$\left| \tilde{A}_s \left(f \right) \right| = \sqrt{\left| \tilde{A}_x \left(f \right) \right|^2 + \left| \tilde{A}_y \left(f \right) \right|^2 + \left| \tilde{A}_z \left(f \right) \right|^2} \tag{3}$$

Having obtained the absolute value of $\tilde{A}_s \left(f \right)$ and by that set the local spectrum of a_s, we must assign a phase θ_f that ensures desirable temporal properties. To this end we optimize the phase towards metric (2), neglecting the absolute values for simplicity. In the frequency domain, the sum of cross-correlations at zero time shift can be expressed as $\sum_{i=1}^{3} a_i \star a_s$. It can be shown that this quantity is maximized when the phase of $\tilde{A}_s$ is chosen as follows:

$$\theta_f^{\max} = \angle \sum_{i=1}^{3} \tilde{A}_i \tag{4}$$

The synthesized time-domain signal a_s is then obtained by a square-root, multiplication by $e^{j\theta_f^{max}}$ where $j = \sqrt{-1}$, and inverse DFT. By Parseval's theorem the result will always have the same signal energy as the sum of energies of the components. We call this new dimensional reduction approach DFT321.

For the transient data shown in Figure 3 and online applications, the DFT321 method must be divided in short windows. Here, a window length of 35 ms has been used, which is 10 ms less than the minimum detectable time delay between visual and haptic stimuli [14]. We found that window lengths ranging from 25 ms to 50 ms yield consistently good results, with $0.94 \leq M_{sm} \leq 0.97$ and $0.45 \leq M_{tm} \leq 0.46$. For offline processing of stationary vibrations, such as those shown in Figure 4, no windowing is required, and the spectral content of the vibrations is captured exactly.

5   Conclusion

This paper focuses on possible methods for reducing a three-dimensional high-frequency acceleration signal into a perceptually matched one-dimensional signal. After reviewing previous work in this area, we presented two objectives by which to judge candidate transformations, and we described several possible options, including our new DFT321 method. While DFT321 is a top candidate for both transient and stationary data, one should adapt the choice according to the application and available real-time computational resources. Using dimensional reduction in this way will strongly benefit haptic rendering approaches that rely on high-frequency acceleration measurements: for example, our methods reduce data storage needs and parametric complexity for surface texture models, they diminish the required transmission bandwidth for teleoperation systems, and they facilitate the effective use of one-dimensional haptic vibration actuators. Continuing research will include human subject testing to verify and refine our spectral and temporal match metrics.

Acknowledgments. This research was supported by the National Science Foundation (grant #IIS-0845670) and the University of Pennsylvania's GAANN and Ashton fellowships.

References

1. Bell, J., Bolanowski, S., Holmes, M.H.: The structure and function of Pacinian corpuscles: A review. Progress in Neurobiology 42(1), 79–128 (1994)
2. Bensmaïa, S., Hollins, M., Yau, J.: Vibrotactile intensity and frequency information in the Pacinian system: A psychophysical model. Perception and Psychophysics 67(5), 828–841 (2005)
3. Brisben, A.J., Hsiao, S.S., Johnson, K.O.: Detection of vibration transmitted through an object grasped in the hand. Journal of Neurophysiology 81(4), 1548–1558 (1999)
4. Guruswamy, V.L., Lang, J., Lee, W.S.: Modelling of haptic vibration textures with infinite-impulse-response filters. In: Proc. IEEE International Workshop on Haptic Audio Visual Environments and their Applications, pp. 105–110 (2009)
5. Johnson, K.O.: The roles and functions of cutaneous mechanoreceptors. Current Opinion in Neurobiology 11, 455–461 (2001)

6. Klatzky, R.L., Lederman, S.J.: Perceiving object properties through a rigid link. In: Lin, M., Otaduy, M. (eds.) Haptic Rendering: Algorithms and Applications, ch. 1, pp. 7–19. A. K. Peters (2008)
7. Kontarinis, D.A., Howe, R.D.: Tactile display of vibratory information in teleoperation and virtual environments. Presence: Teleoperators and Virtual Environments 4(4), 387–402 (1995)
8. Kuchenbecker, K.J., Fiene, J.P., Niemeyer, G.: Improving contact realism through event-based haptic feedback. IEEE Transactions on Visualization and Computer Graphics 12(2), 219–230 (2006)
9. Kuchenbecker, K.J., Romano, J.M., McMahan, W.: Haptography: Capturing and recreating the rich feel of real surfaces. In: Proc. International Symposium on Robotics Research (August 2009)
10. McMahan, W., Kuchenbecker, K.J.: Haptic display of realistic tool contact via dynamically compensated control of a dedicated actuator. In: Proc. IEEE/RSJ International Conference on Intelligent RObots and Systems, pp. 3171–3177 (October 2009)
11. McMahan, W., Romano, J.M., Rahuman, A.M.A., Kuchenbecker, K.J.: High frequency acceleration feedback significantly increases the realism of haptically rendered textured surfaces. In: Proc. IEEE Haptics Symposium, pp. 141–148 (March 2010)
12. Okamura, A.M., Cutkosky, M.R., Dennerlein, J.T.: Reality-based models for vibration feedback in virtual environments. IEEE/ASME Transactions on Mechatronics 6(3), 245–252 (2001)
13. Romano, J.M., Yoshioka, T., Kuchenbecker, K.J.: Automatic filter design for synthesis of haptic textures from recorded acceleration data. In: IEEE International Conference on Robotics and Automation, May 2010, pp. 1815–1821 (2010)
14. Vogels, I.M.L.C.: Detection of temporal delays in visual-haptic interfaces. Human Factors 46(1), 118–134 (2004)
15. Yao, H.Y., Hayward, V., Ellis, R.E.: A tactile enhancement instrument for minimally invasive surgery. Computer-Aided Surgery 10(4), 233–239 (2005)

Analysis of a New Haptic Display Coupling Tactile and Kinesthetic Feedback to Render Texture and Shape

Tao Zeng, Frédéric Giraud, Betty Lemaire-Semail, and Michel Amberg

Univ. Lille Nord de France, F-59000 Lille, France
USTL, L2EP IRCICA, F 59650 Villeneuve d'Ascq, France
tao.zeng@ed.univ-lille1.fr,
{Frederic.giraud,betty.semail}@polytech-lille.fr,
michel.amberg@univ-lille1.fr

Abstract. In the domain of haptics, the sensation of touch is normally classed into two types: tactile and kinesthetic. Correspondingly, the haptic display can also be divided into two categories: tactile display and kinesthetic display. The two aspects are commonly addressed separately, but life experience has shown that this is not intuitive and not effective. Therefore, it is a significant work to couple the tactile display and the kinesthetic display. In this paper, we propose a new design of haptic display coupling tactile and kinesthetic feedback for rendering spatial texture (tactile) and haptic shape (kinesthetic).

Keywords: tactile display, kinesthetic display, haptic display, coupling tactile and kinesthetic, spatial texture rendering, haptic shape rendering.

1 Introduction

The sensation of touch (haptic) plays a crucial role in many applications such as teleoperation, interactive simulator, medical training, virtual reality and so on. This haptic sensation can be classed into two types: tactile and kinesthetic. The former helps us perceive object's properties; the latter improves the stability of hand movements. Correspondingly, the haptic display is divided into two categories: tactile display and kinesthetic display. Over the years, both kinds of display have enjoyed great development. However, the two modalities are commonly addressed separately. The experience of daily life has proved that this is not intuitive and not effective. Therefore, simultaneous stimulation of tactile modality and kinesthetic modality is essential. Over the recent years, some haptic displays combining tactile and kinesthetic feedback have emerged [1], [2], [3].

The tactile displays for rendering the sensation of spatial texture are mainly derived from the Braille technologies and consist of an array of arranged pins which depend strongly on the used actuation technology. In recent years, the friction control tactile displays have been developed [4], [5]. This kind of tactile display can create texture sensations through variation of the surface friction. In [6], M.Biet et al have designed a tactile display named *tactile plate* (see Fig. 1) for rendering spatial texture. This tactile plate uses the principle of squeeze film effect: ultrasonic frequency, low

A.M.L. Kappers et al. (Eds.): EuroHaptics 2010, Part II, LNCS 6192, pp. 87–93, 2010.

amplitude vibrations of a flat plate have been shown to create a film of air between the plate and the finger which can change the friction. Using finger's position and velocity feedback, this tactile display allows us to create the spatial texture sensations.

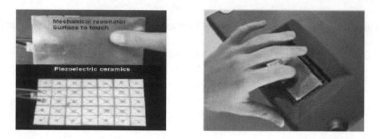

Fig. 1. The friction controlled tactile plate for rendering spatial texture

As for the displays rendering haptic shape, they are sometimes realized by orientating a real plane plate under the fingerpad. In [7],[8], it was observed that, in the process of exploring a large object, the perception of haptic shape depends on the fingertip's deformation, and this deformation is determined by the angle between the fingertip and the object's surface. A flat plate in rolling contact with the fingertip provides the desired moving patterns of finger deformation.

For rendering spatial texture (tactile) and haptic shape (kinesthetic), we propose a new design of haptic display coupling tactile and kinesthetic devices. This concept is realized by mounting a tactile device on a kinesthetic platform (see Fig. 2). Rendering the sensation of spatial texture is achieved by moving our finger forward and backward on the tactile plate designed in [6]. Rendering the haptic shape is through accurate control of this tactile plate's movement thanks to the simultaneous control of the platform. By controlling both the tactile plate's friction coefficient and its movement according to the finger's position, we will obtain a strong coupling between tactile and kinesthetic feedback. Moreover, the tactile device developed in [6] is particularly well adapted to be integrated in such a coupling device.

In this paper, we firstly propose *a shape model*; then, according to the tactile plate's characteristics, we focus on analysis of its motion control rules to reproduce this shape. This analysis leads us to propose finally a three DOF (degrees of freedom) platform to support the tactile plate.

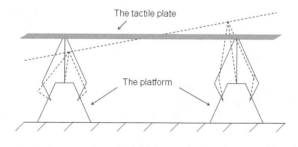

Fig. 2. The sketch map of the device's structure

2   Analysis of the One DOF Platform Movement

2.1   Description

Fig. 3 shows the haptic shape model, in which the arc closed to a section of sphere is the shape we are going to render. This is a typical shape example, whose dimensions, in particular its length, are in agreement with the tactile plate characteristics. M is the contact point; θ is the angle between the finger and the tactile plate at the contact point; U is the length of an arc between the midpoint O and M.

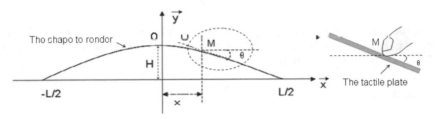

Fig. 3. The haptic shape model (L=0.084m, H=0.01m)

The angle θ determines the deformation of the fingertip during the contact, so it is the most important parameter to render the shape [7],[8]. The relationship between θ and the location of the fingertip on the surface U is deduced by the following steps:

The expression of the shape to render is:

$$y(x) = -\frac{4H}{L^2} \cdot (x - \frac{L}{2}) \cdot (x + \frac{L}{2})$$ (1)

The relationship between the angle θ and the shape is:

$$\tan \theta = \frac{dy(x)}{dx} = -\frac{8H}{L^2} \cdot x$$ (2)

The relationship between x and U is:

$$x = R \cdot \sin(\frac{U}{R}), \quad R = \frac{L^2}{8H} + \frac{H}{2}$$ (3)

Finally, the angle θ functioned on U is determined by:

$$\theta = arc \tan[-\frac{8H}{L^2} \cdot R \cdot \sin(\frac{U}{R})]$$ (4)

For each contact point (the distance between the midpoint and the fingertip is U), there is a corresponding angle θ. The finger's position has to be measured so as to deduce the corresponding value of angle θ by equation (4). Then we control the tactile plate's angular position, in order to make the angle between the finger and the tactile plate respect the angle between the finger and the real surface. Fig. 4 depicts the different angular positions of the tactile plate – given by equation (4) – for several values of U.

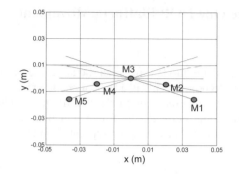

Fig. 4. The evolution of the tactile plate's movement with one DOF. The points M1-M5 are the successive finger's positions on the tactile plate. The corresponding values of U are: 0.040m, 0.021m, 0.000m, -0.021m, -0.040m.

2.2 Analysis

Fig. 5 shows the tactile plate's movement. At the time t_1, the finger's position is at the contact point M_1. As the plate rotates rounding its midpoint, at the time t_2, the point M_1 displaces at the position M'_1 (at this instant, the contact point is M_2). As Fig. 5 shows, the contact point has its own velocity. This velocity will influence the manipulator's feeling when rendering the shape, because in the real environment, the object is static commonly. Therefore, it is significant to analyze this velocity.

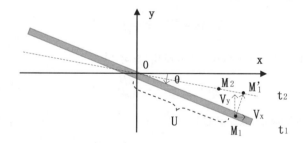

Fig. 5. Illustration of the contact point's velocity during finger exposition

As H is small enough, the whole length of the arc and the whole length of the tactile plate have the same order, we assume that the two lengths are equal. So, we can use the same symbol U to present both the length of arc and the distance between the midpoint and the contact point. If H is large, it needs to convert the arc's length into the tactile plate's length.

Now, let's compute the contact point's velocity.

$$\overrightarrow{OM} = \begin{bmatrix} U \cdot \cos\theta \\ U \cdot \sin\theta \end{bmatrix} \qquad (5)$$

The velocity is the derivative of equation (5).

$$v_M \in plate = \frac{d\overrightarrow{OM}}{dt} = \begin{bmatrix} \dfrac{-\left(\dfrac{8H}{L^2}\right)^2 \cdot \cos(\dfrac{U}{R}) \cdot \sin(\dfrac{U}{R}) \cdot R \cdot \dot{U}U}{\left[1+\left(\dfrac{8H}{L^2} \cdot R \cdot \sin(\dfrac{U}{R})\right)^2\right]^{\frac{3}{2}}} \\[4ex] \dfrac{-\dfrac{8H}{L^2} \cdot \cos(\dfrac{U}{R}) \cdot \dot{U}U}{\left[1+\left(\dfrac{8H}{L^2} \cdot R \cdot \sin(\dfrac{U}{R})\right)^2\right]^{\frac{3}{2}}} \end{bmatrix} \tag{6}$$

Where, $\dot{U}$ is the velocity of the finger. Usually, during exploration tasks, this speed is low and has an average value close to 0.1 m/s [9].

The evolutions of the contact point's velocity on components x and y are shown in Fig. 6. Note that, at U=0.04, the contact point's velocity on component x is 0.014m/s. The finger's velocity on component x is 0.09154m/s ($0.1 \cdot \cos\theta$). So, the ratio between contact point's velocity and finger's velocity is 15.29%. On component y, the ratio is 86.96%. These two ratios are quite large and may induce disturbance in texture and shape rendering. So, we are going on with the analysis to cope with this problem.

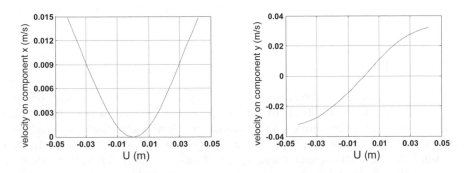

Fig. 6. The evolutions of the contact point's velocity on component x and on component y.

3   Specification for the Moving Platform

To avoid this velocity reduce the quality of shape perception, we propose to solve this problem by adding two DOFs to the system. The idea is to add additional terms $\dot{x}_0$ and $\dot{y}_0$ to the components x and y in equation (6) and let the velocities on components x and y be equal to zero, we get:

$$\dot{x} = \dot{x}_0 + \frac{d\overrightarrow{OM}}{dt}\Big|_x = 0, \quad \dot{y} = \dot{y}_0 + \frac{d\overrightarrow{OM}}{dt}\Big|_y = 0 \tag{7}$$

The integral of $\dot{x}_0$ and $\dot{y}_0$ are the displacements x_0 and y_0. One solution is given by:

$$x_0 = \int \dot{x}_0 dt = -U \cdot \cos \theta, \qquad y_0 = \int \dot{y}_0 dt = -U \cdot \sin \theta \qquad (8)$$

The evolution of the tactile plate's movement is shown in Fig. 7a.

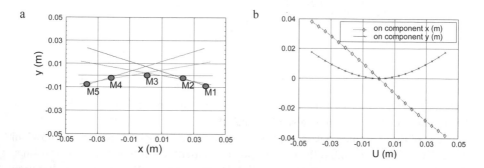

Fig. 7. a) The evolution of the tactile plate's movement with 3 DOF (the same values of U as in Fig.4.). **b)** The displacements x_0 and y_0 for tactile plate's velocity equal to 0 at contact point.

This motion model has three DOF: the DOF of rotation; the DOFs on component x and on component y, their values are calculated by equation (8) and their evolutions are shown in Fig. 7b.

4 Conclusion

In this paper, we have analyzed and proposed a new design of haptic display coupling tactile and kinesthetic feedback to render spatial texture and haptic shape. This concept is realized by mounting a tactile device on a kinesthetic platform. Rendering the sensation of spatial texture is achieved by moving our finger forward and backward on the tactile plate; rendering the haptic shape is through an accurate control of this tactile plate's movement. We focused on analyzing the motion models of the tactile plate. Based on a given typical shape, we get an initial motion model with one DOF which respects the angle between the finger and the tactile plate, but induces a parasitic velocity of the contact point. The motion model with three DOF has solved this problem. Therefore, this motion model is expected to faithfully render both the texture and the haptic shape. Future works will be focused on psychophysical evaluations of the different solutions.

References

1   Sato, K., Kajimoto, H., Kawakami, N., Tachil, S.: Electrotactile Display for Integration with Kinesthetic Display. In: 16th IEEE International Conference on Robot & Human Interactive Communication, pp. 3–8. IEEE Press, Korea (2007)
2   Kim, Y., Oakley, I., Ryu, J.: Combining Point Force Haptic and Pneumatic Tactile Displays. In: Proceedings of the EuroHaptics 2006 (EH 2006), Paris, France (2006)

3   Fritschi, M., Ernst, M.O., Buss, M.: Integration of Kinesthetic and Tactile Display: A Modular Design Concept. In: Proceedings of the EuroHaptics 2006 (EH 2006), Paris, France (2006)

4   Winfield, L., Glassmire, J., Colgate, J.E., Peshkin, M.: T-PaD: Tactile Pattern Display through Variable Friction Reduction. In: Second Joint EuroHaptics Conference and Symposium on Haptic Interfaces for Virtual Environment and Teleoperator Systems (WHC 2007), pp. 421–426. IEEE Press, Japan (2007)

5   Kotani, H., Takasaki, M., Mizuno, T.: Surface Acoustic Wave Tactile Display using a Large Size Glass Transducer. In: Proceedings of IEEE International Conference on Mechatronics and Automation, pp. 198–203. IEEE Press, Harbin (2007)

6   Biet, M., Giraud, F., Lemaire-Semail, B.: Squeeze Film Effect for the Design of an Ultrasonic Tactile Plate. IEEE Transactions on Ultrasonics, Ferroelectrics and Frequency Control 54(12), 2678–2688 (2007)

7   Hayward, V.: Display of Haptic Shape at Different Scales. In: Proceedings of Eurohaptics 2004. Keynote paper, Munich, Germany, pp. 20–27 (2004)

8   Wijntjes, M.W.A., Sato, A., Hayward, V., Kappers, A.M.L.: Local Surface Orientation Dominates Haptic Curvature Discrimination. IEEE Transactions on Haptics 2(2) (April-June 2009)

9   Martinot, F.: The Influence of Surface Commensurability on Roughness Perception with a Bare Finger. In: Proceedings of the EuroHaptics 2006 (EH 2006), Paris, France (2006)

Constraints on Haptic Short-Term Memory

Catherine Monnier[1] and Delphine Picard[2]

[1] Université Montpellier 3, Laboratoire de Psychologie, Route de Mende,
34199 Montpellier Cedex 5, France
catherine.monnier@univ-montp3.fr
[2] Université Toulouse II, EA4156 Octogone-ECCD & Institut Universitaire de France
delphine.picard@univ-tlse2.fr

Abstract. This study examines to what extent limitations in short-term memory capacity in the haptic modality depends on (1) the narrowness of the effective field of view combined with a sequential processing of information, and/or (2) the format in which spatial configurations are represented internally. A total of 64 participants carried out memory span tasks in four different conditions: haptic, visual, visual with a limited field of view, and haptic with visual cues. Results provide support for both hypotheses. Differences in haptic and visual short-term memory disappeared when the visual processing of information occurred within a limited field and when the haptic processing of information was aided by visual cues.

Keywords: Haptic short-term memory; Visual short-term memory; Spatial configurations.

1 Introduction

Although a large body of research has examined the nature of visual short-term memory, few studies have focused on the structure and function of haptic short-term memory [1], [2]. A recent study comparing haptic short-term memory and visual short-term memory [3] showed that the capacity of haptic short-term memory is more limited than visual memory. In the present study we evaluate possible hypotheses for this limitation. Hypothesis 1 attributes the cause to differences in working modes (the narrowness of the effective field of view combined with a sequential processing of information for haptic modality). Hypothesis 2 states that capacity limitations are due to the format in which information is represented in short-term memory (as a sensory trace only or in a visuo-spatial format).

Hypothesis 1

More so than vision, haptics relies on sequential processing of information within a limited perceptual field. This acts to constrain the rate at which information is processed and integrated over time [4], [5]. This likely reduces the amount of information that can be stored in short-term memory in the haptic modality relative to vision. In order to test this hypothesis, we adapted a procedure developed by Loomis and

A.M.L. Kappers et al. (Eds.): EuroHaptics 2010, Part II, LNCS 6192, pp. 94–98, 2010.

Klatzky [4]. In this design, the visual field is reduced artificially to be equal to that of haptics. This ensures that the same level of sequential processing is being carried out in visual and haptic modalities. If the capacity of the haptic modality is constrained by (a) the narrowness of the effective field of view and (b) sequential processing of information, then short-term retention of spatial configurations in the visual modality should be similarly constrained in the visual 'limited field' condition.

Hypothesis 2

Capacity limitations might also be due to the format in which information is stored in short-term memory. Previous research has suggested that spatial information received from the haptic channel was often stored as a sensory trace before being recoded into visuo-spatial format [6]. This means that information may be made available to refreshing or rehearsal mechanisms, which prevent against a rapid decay of information over time. In order to test this hypothesis we included a condition designed to elicit the recoding of haptic information into visuo-spatial format. It was expected that this use of a visuo-spatial recoding strategy would enhance memory performance.

2 Method

2.1 Participants

64 adults (32 females, 32 males) participated in the experiment. Their mean age was 23 years (sd = 4 years). A between-subject design was used in which participants were randomly assigned to one of four experimental conditions (visual, haptic, visual 'limited field', haptic 'with visual cue'). There were 16 participants per condition.

2.2 Materials

Six different patterns composed of three 1.5x1.5 cm squares arranged as an inverted L shape were created. Each square was covered with a piece of smooth or rough abrasive paper (Wolcraft no. 400 and no. 40 respectively). The patterns contained either one smooth and two rough squares or two smooth and one rough squares in different spatial locations. They were painted with black gouache to control for brightness differences between the two abrasive papers (see Fig. 1).

For the memory span task, three sequences of 2, 3, 4, 5 and 6 patterns (i.e., 15 sequences in total) were constructed with the condition that 1) no pattern appeared more than once in any given sequence; 2) each pattern was presented 10 times at varied serial position among the sequences; 3) two successive sequences included different patterns at the first and at the final serial positions. Two additional training two-pattern sequences were drawn up.

Fig. 1. Picture of the six experimental patterns used in the study

2.3 Experimental Conditions

A participant was assigned to one of the following four experimental conditions.

In order to prevent visual feedback in the haptic condition, a vertical screen with a large opening covered by a curtain was used. Participants were asked to keep their forearm motionless and to use the distal pad of their right index finger to explore each square of a spatial pattern one at a time, by means of a lateral motion procedure [7]. Participants first explored the top left square, and then they moved their index finger from left to right and from top to bottom to explore successively the remaining two squares of a given spatial pattern. Haptic exploration of a pattern was completed in 3 seconds. Participants followed instructions from the experimenter (go/stop) to move on to the next pattern.

The haptic 'with visual cue' condition was similar to the haptic condition except that participants were provided with a line-drawing of blank spatial patterns during haptic exploration. Participants were instructed to visualize what they were touching on the line-drawing.

In the visual condition, participants were holding an L-shaped visual screen in their right hand above a sequence of spatial patterns. For each individual pattern, participants were instructed to move the L-shaped screen laterally to the right so that they could see the spatial pattern in full through the aperture. Participants scanned the spatial pattern for 3 seconds. Participants followed instructions from the experimenter (go/stop) to move on to the next pattern.

The visual 'limited field' condition was similar to the visual condition except that participants had their right hand holding a screen with a small square opening permitting to see only one square of a spatial pattern at a time. For each individual pattern, participants were instructed to move the screen laterally to the right so that they could see the top left square of a spatial pattern through the small aperture. They then moved the screen from left to right, and then from top to bottom to scan the spatial pattern starting with the top left square and ending with the bottom right one.

2.4 Memory Span Task

The session started with a short training session, immediately followed by a span task. In the memory span task, sequences of spatial patterns of increasing length (from 2 to 6 patterns) were presented to the participants, either haptically or visually depending on the experimental condition. Participants were instructed to explore all the patterns and to recall the location of the rough squares for each successive configuration in order, by pointing their left index finger on a paper sheet where the blank spatial patterns were drawn. There was no time limit on participants' response. In order to systematically increase task difficulty one spatial pattern was added to a sequence when a participant correctly recalled two sequences of a same difficulty level, given that a maximum of three sequences of the same difficulty level could be proposed. Memory span was scored as the largest number of patterns recalled in the correct order on at least two of the three sequences of a given difficulty level.

3 Results

Fig. 2 shows the mean memory span for each experimental condition. A one-way analysis of variance with experimental condition as a between-subjects factor demonstrated a significant effect of condition, $F(3, 60) = 3.55, p = .02$. Planned comparisons indicated that a) haptic memory span was significantly lower than visual memory span, $F(1, 60) = 6.15, p < .05$; b) memory span for the visual 'limited field' condition was not significantly different from the haptic condition, $F(1, 60) = 0.29, p = .59$; and c) memory span for the haptic 'with visual cue' condition was not significantly different from the visual condition, $F(1, 60) = 1.97, p = .17$.

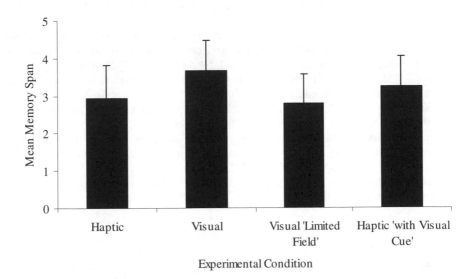

Fig. 2. Mean memory span for each experimental condition

4 Discussion

The present study examined two possible hypotheses for why haptic short-term memory span is smaller than visual span. In support of hypothesis 1, we found that reducing the size of the visual field lowered memory span for visual-spatial configurations to a level similar to that of haptic memory. Consistent with this finding, the effect of a sequential processing of information within a limited perceptual field has been shown to weaken adults' performance at various spatial memory tasks [8], [4]. The sensory constraints inherent to the haptic modality (namely that of sequential processing of information within a limited perceptual field) limit its short-term retention of spatial information. According to our view, this constrains the rate at which information is processed and integrated over time into a coherent representational unit, thereby resulting in a limited haptic memory span.

Our results also show that the availability of a visual cue during haptic exploration enhances haptic memory span to a level similar to that of visual memory. This supports hypothesis 2. We estimate that a visual cue improves haptic information processing for two reasons. First, the availability of visual cues may have reduced the cognitive demands due to the recoding of haptic information into visual format. It is likely that participants used the visual cue as an external mirror for their mental imagery. Second, the availability of visual cues may have facilitated the rehearsal of mental images during haptic processing. This proposed active rehearsal process may have limited the rapid decline of information in haptic short-term memory.

References

1. Gilson, E.Q., Baddeley, A.D.: Tactile short-term memory. Q. J. Exp. Psychol. 21, 180–184 (1969)
2. Miles, C., Borthwick, H.: Tactile short-term memory revisited. Memory 4, 655–668 (1996)
3. Bliss, I., Hämäläinen, H.: Different working memory capacity in normal young adults for visual and tactile letter recognition task. Scand. J. Psychol. 46, 247–251 (2005)
4. Loomis, J.M., Klatzky, R.L.: Similarity of tactual and visual picture recognition with limited field of view. Perception 20, 167–177 (1991)
5. Newell, F., Woods, A.T., Mernagh, M., Bülthoff, H.H.: Visual, haptic and crossmodal recognition of scenes. Exp. Brain Res. 161, 233–242 (2005)
6. Mahrer, P., Miles, C.: Recognition memory for tactile sequences. Memory 10, 7–20 (2002)
7. Lederman, S.J., Klatzky, R.L.: Hand movements: A window into haptic object recognition. Cogn. Psychol. 19, 342–368 (1987)
8. Millar, S., Al-Attar, Z.: What aspects of vision facilitate haptic processing? Brain Cogn. 59, 258–268 (2005)

Part II
Virtual Reality

Design and Development of a
Haptic Dental Training System - hapTEL

Brian Tse[1], William Harwin[1], Alastair Barrow[1], Barry Quinn[2], Jonathan San Diego[3],
and Margaret Cox[3]

[1] School of Systems Engineering, University of Reading, Berkshire, RG6 6AY, U.K.
[2] King's College London, Dental Polyclinic, St Thomas' Hospital, London SE1 7EH
[3] Room 18.1, Guy's Hospital, Tower Wing, King's College London,
Dental Institute, London, SE1 9RT, U.K.
{tsehoyeungbrian,w.s.harwin,a.l.barrow}@reading.ac.uk,
{J.P.San_Diego,barry.quinn,mj.cox}@kcl.ac.uk

Abstract. This paper presents a novel design of a virtual dental training system (hapTEL) using haptic technology. The system allows dental students to learn and practice procedures such as dental drilling, caries removal and cavity preparation for tooth restoration. This paper focuses on the hardware design, development and evaluation aspects in relation to the dental training and educational requirements. Detailed discussions on how the system offers dental students a natural operational position are documented. An innovative design of measuring and connecting the dental tools to the haptic device is also shown. Evaluation of the impact on teaching and learning is discussed.

Keywords: Haptic, Haptic Dental Training, Evaluation of haptic system, Technology-enhanced learning, Virtual Reality.

1 Introduction

In Kings College London (KCL) dental school, at the early stage of dental training, students are required to gain practical experience as well as theoretical. Practical training involves using a physical simulation device called a Phantom Head, which simulates a patient's head. However, there are limitations with the traditional training model:

(1) It has become difficult to use real human teeth because of ethical constraints.
(2) With natural teeth it is not possible to provide identical standard carious lesions (tooth decay) for teaching.
(3) Plastic teeth do not have the range of variability as real teeth.
(4) Procedures cannot be repeated on the same tooth or carious lesion.
(5) Head model does not simulate patient movements, emotions and bleeding.
(6) Post lesson evaluation of student practices is difficult; recording requires high magnification video which may be blocked by the students' head or hand.

A haptic interface based dental simulator could provide a solution to these issues.

A.M.L. Kappers et al. (Eds.): EuroHaptics 2010, Part II, LNCS 6192, pp. 101–108, 2010.

1.1 Project Background

The aims of the hapTEL project include the development of a dental training simulator using haptic technology, and evaluating the educational impact of haptics on dental students' learning. 12 identical systems were integrated into the undergraduate teaching programme at the Dental Institute of King's College London. The research, which is part of the work of the hapTEL project, involved 144 students and about 20 members of the faculty in the Dental School.

1.2 User Requirements

Previous work [1] has identified important user requirements for practical training in dentistry using haptic devices:

(1) System Physical Setup - dental advisors require the correct operational posture to be adopted. This includes a range of factors such as viewing angles, workspace sizes, finger resting positions and physical dental tool positions.
(2) Sensory feedback – All relevant sensory feedback should be present including stereo vision, visual parallax, sound and touch.
(3) 3D Models - The virtual models should accurately represent dental tools, oral anatomy and material attributes.

1.3 Existing Haptic Dental Training Simulator

Previous dental trainers from the research community include VRDTS[1] [2], IDSS[2] and PerioSim [3]. Dental Trainer[3] and Forsslund [4] on the other hand, are commercial dental training units. Unlike previous systems [2,3], Forsslund and Dental Trainer have visual and haptic feedback collocated and positioned in approximately the correct operating position, which should be when the patient is supine.

Wu et al. [5] uses a half silvered mirror to achieve augmented reality (AR), where as the AR described in Rhienmora et al. [6] uses a head mounted display (HMD) with a tracking unit. When using AR, small differences in the hand and visual positions can make usage confusing. Other than Dental Trainer, no other system provides user with a dental tool for operation. The Systems reported in [2,3,5] do not provide users with 3D stereo vision, which is an important feature identified by the dental experts in Diego et al. [1]. The HMD used in [6] has a low resolution (640x480), reducing model quality. Although the Dental Trainer has achieved the visual and haptic requirements related to collocation, tracking of user head movement is not available. Table 1 shows the properties of these systems.

Furthermore, no qualitative evaluation by expert users is reported in the work in table 1. This paper evaluates the hapTEL hardware and software and presents the pedagogical analysis. The design and evaluation of Prototype I are shown in sections 2 and 3 respectively. Section 4 documents the development of Prototype II (hapTEL Prototype Curriculum Version), which is based on the evaluation from Prototype I.

---

[1] VRDTS is produced by Virtual Reality Dental Training system produced by NOVINT: http://home.novint.com/products/medical_dental.php
[2] Iowa Dental Surgical Simulator (IDSS): http://grok.ecn.uiowa.edu/Projects/medsim.html
[3] Dental Trainer by MOOG: http://www.moog.com/

Table 1. Comparison of Existing Dental Training Systems using Haptic Technology

System	Display Type	Haptic Device	Head Tracking	Collocation
VRDTS	LCD/No Stereo	Desktop[4]	No	No
IDSS	LCD/No Stereo	IE 2000	No	No
PerioSim	LCD/No Stereo	Desktop	No	No
Dental Trainer	Multi Projector/Stereo	Customized	No	Yes
Wu	LCD/AR/ No Stereo	Desktop	No	Yes
Forsslund	LCD	Omni[5]	No	Yes
Rhienmora	HMD/AR/Stereo	Omni	Yes	Yes

Section 5 focuses on results of Prototype II and identifies new technical factors based on the feedback from educationalists, dentists and users. Finally, section 6 includes the discussion and conclusion of the research in this paper and future work.

2 Development of Prototype I

Integral to the project was the requirement of a large-scale educational evaluation [7]. This meant that a compromise between quality and number of systems was necessary. After initial quality testing with a number of commercial haptic devices[5], it was decided to produce 12 basic systems using the Novint Falcon and 2 high fidelity systems using the Omega 3[6]. This compromise allowed the large scale evaluation to proceed but also to use the high fidelity systems to explore the potential of the haptic rendering algorithms developed.

Prototype I consisted of a desktop PC, Planar 3D[7] stereo display, camera head tracking unit, Falcon haptic device and a modified dental hand piece. A 3 DoF gimble connector was designed for attaching the dental hand piece to the Falcon. As the Falcon has only 3 positional DoF, an additional 6 DoF passive measurement device, referred to as the POD (Pose Device), was developed and attached to the back of the hand piece. It consisted of a serial chain of 6 linked encoders and the orientation of the hand piece was computed using forward kinematics. During the development of Prototype I, other 3D displays and haptic devices were investigated. Planar 3D was selected as the system display due to the high resolution (1280x1024) properties.

3 Evaluation of Prototype I

The evaluation of Prototype I was based on user feedback, observation and responses from dentists and educationalists. Factors considered included: quality of haptic rendering, teaching impact and student educational value. The results are presented in Table 2, which shows the evaluation results from pilot trials with dental clinicians

---

[4] PHANTOM Desktop™ and Omni™ are haptic devices by SensAble Technology: http://www.sensable.com/
[5] Haptic Device include: PHANTOM Omni™, PHANTOM Desktop™, PHANTOM Premium 1.5™, NOVINT Falcon™, Force Dimension Omega 3™
[6] Omega by Force Dimension: http://www.forcedimension.com/
[7] Planar 3D stereo display: http://www.planar3d.com/

Table 2. Evaluation of 3D Display for Prototype I

Areas (*Priority*)	Functional Evaluation Result	Educational Implication
Head Tracking (*Medium*)	Dentist head movements are tracked and the update rate was satisfactory.	Student can view the model from different positions.
Hand, Eye and Tool Collocation (*High*)	Although hand position is correct, visual display is not collocated due to Planar monitor. This was a particular concern for the dental tutor.	This would limit the realism of the system, making it different from the Phantom Head student experience.
Stereo Vision (*Medium*)	The quality of the 3D display was satisfactory.	The image was regarded as similar to real teeth.
Dental Tools (*High*)	The gimble connecting dental hand piece to haptic device limited orientation; a singularity could occur at certain orientations.	This problem was expected to give unhelpful feedback to students.
Finger Rest (*High*)	Finger rest mechanism collided with the gimble reducing workspace.	Finger rest should enable the learner to move freely around the tooth being drilled.
Oral Tissues (*Low*)	No cheek and gum tissues are presented.	This meant student could position the tool through virtual mouth model with no resistance contrary to the Phamtom Head.
Foot Pedal (*Medium*)	No dental foot pedal was presented. Dental drill speed should be controllable by the user.	A foot pedal was considered as essential to match those used by the control group of students in real teaching lab.
Haptic Device (*Medium*)	The inertia and the weight of the haptic device were considered too high. Vibration of the dental tool cannot be replicated.	The effect of this on learning the task is currently unknown, but as student need to become accustomed to working with a range of overweight instruments, further analysis may show that problem has negative effect.
Software (*High*)	The oral cavity and tooth models were artistic representations. Realism was considered insufficient. 3D model data must be realistic, based on real human tissues sample and accurately represent the enamel, dentine, pulp and cavity of the tooth.	Improvements need to be made to virtual mouth images so students would experience they were treating a realistic mouth.

(Column 2) and implications for teaching dental undergraduates (Column 3). The areas were assigned priorities based on pedagogical necessity and technical limitation.

4   Development of Prototype II (Current System)

Based on the evaluation of Prototype I (see Table 2 above), the second version included both redesigned and additional features. 12 systems, figure 2, were developed for the first phase, large scale evaluation.

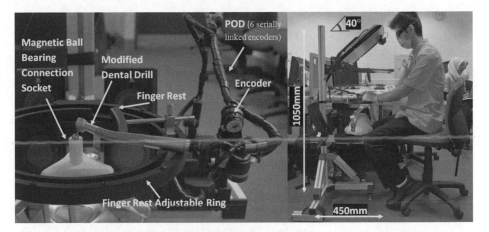

Fig. 2. Kings College London Dental Student using Prototype II

4.1 Achieving Hand, Eye and Tool Collocation

After the development of Prototype I (March 2008), a new type of 3D LCD[8] using shutter glasses became available. This display was used in Prototype II with a front surface mirror (FSM) to reflect the image. Using an FSM removes double reflections. This configuration allowed full hand, eye and tool collocation.

Due to the nature of the LCD monitor and LCD shutter glasses (linear light polarization), when the image is reflected it cannot be seen when wearing the shutter glasses. A quarter wave plate (circular polariser) was placed over each eye of the shutter glasses to change the light polarization and allow it to pass through.

4.2 Novel Magnetic Connectors, Enhancing Dental Tool Orientation

The haptic device was modified to be mounted facing upward, allowing rooms for finger rest and rubber cheek to be installed. In order to solve the dental tool orientation problem mentioned in Table 2, a novel magnetic ball bearing socket system was developed (Fig 2), providing the drill 180 degrees of rotation without singularity issues. The socket embedded a magnet rod (D9, L25, 5900 Gauss), which magnetically locked the modified ball bearing (D8) drill head. The trade off was justified by experienced dentist as an acceptable solution.

4.3 Finger Rest, Pose Device (POD), Foot Pedal and Data Source

The new haptic mounting system allowed an adjustable finger rest to be developed and employed in Prototype II (Figure 2). The space between the magnetic connector and the finger rest were calculated and mechanical collisions were avoided during simulation. The design of the POD in Prototype II is based on Prototype I; additional features were added to take account of the educational pilot evaluation summarised in Table 2. These included self-indexing encoders, which allow quick calibration when

---

[8] 3D LCD Display by Nvidia: http://www.nvidia.com/

the system is initialised, reducing the setup time by the dental tutor. Another additional feature of the POD was removing the singularity issues which happened in some positions in Prototype I. A dental foot pedal has been installed into Prototype II. The pedal has been modified to allow variable drill speed control and sound.

Prototype II had also improved the realism of the virtual mouth model. The model data source such as oral cavity model and jaw model were obtained from CT scan. The models were transformed into a volumetric tetrahedron model using Tetgen[9]. The haptic drilling algorithm used this volume model and added four different types of materials and physical properties. They were enamel, dentine, pulp and cavity. The tooth cavity models were design based on real life scenarios and advice from dentists.

5   Evaluation of Prototype II

As mentioned above, 12 systems based on Prototype II were installed in KCL. The approximated development cost for each system was in the order of £4000. The first phase of the large scale evaluation was conducted and involved 144 year one dental students, 48 of which used the hapTEL system over the autumn term (2009). Observation, video, questionnaires and data capture were used to record students' experiences. The analysis of over 50 data sets are in progress and a future publication will report on the results in detail, particularly the pedagogical aspects. However, from the results to date there are already many important observations which can be made regarding the hardware design and ergonomics.

5.1   Evaluation on Student Operational Body Position

The visual position, dental tool and the hand position are sufficiently collocated to allow the students to adopt an operating position which closely matched the required dental posture. No adjustment of heights, other than chairs, was required for the students to use the workstations demonstrating that the design was accessible for a range of user heights. The handedness of the system was customisable for left or right hand dominant users and neither group expressed any differing accessibility views.

5.2   Hand Position and Interaction with POD, Haptic Device and Dental Tool

The magnetic ball bearing connection socket delivered a range of orientation and workspace which the dentists and students considered satisfactory for operation on the occlusal surfaces of a tooth. The internal friction (approximated static friction 0.34N), inertia and the mass (approximately 155g) of the haptic device linkages were considered too high. Some students therefore rest their wrists on the finger rest ring and used two hands to control the drill head, which they would not need to in the traditional environment. This could potentially affect the quality of student learning. The mass effect on weight was reduced by a gravity compensation algorithm. The inertia and the internal friction were not solved to the dental tutor's satisfaction.

The haptic device did not suffice in quality and could only provide one point of force feedback to the dental tool head. Therefore, no rotational force feedback was

---

[9] Tetrahedral Mesh Generator called Tetgen: http://tetgen.berlios.de/

possible. Students could operate the drill in a position which would not be possible in a real life situation resulting in a possible reduction in educational value. The large scale educational pre and post-tests will show the extent of this effect.

5.3 Effect of Head Tracking and Stereo Vision towards Training

The update rate of the head tracking was reduced by the lighting conditions of the room where research was conducted. This caused students to move their head more slowly than desired. We are currently analysing the feedback form from students, which will reveal whether this was considered a problem by majority of students. It seems from student responses that this was not a serious effect as they take time to plan their work which compensates this slight delay. The tracking area which the system could provide was acceptable. According to the dental clinician and comments from the students, both groups considered the quality of stereo vision was highly satisfactory. However, the monitor resolution meant student preferred to scale up the tooth by visual magnification for accurate caries removal. Brightness, which was already low due to the shuttering effect, was reduced further by the additional circular polarisers. The importance of circular polariser was highlighted as students perform significant head rotation whilst operating.

6 Discussion and Conclusion

Haptic devices have great potential to enhance the learning of skilled manual tasks such as in dentistry. This paper has documented the design, development and the evaluation of the hapTEL prototypes, which have helped to identify many important design considerations including ergonomic factors and dental training needs. There still remain many problems and challenges which will be addressed in future. Rubber 'cheeks' will be introduced around the finger rest so the range of movement of the hand piece more closely approximates reality. The dental mirror system which was trialled in Prototype I will be added to the Prototype II curriculum systems using an equivalent POD as the drill but on the opposite side. The POD provides a general way of measuring hand piece orientation similar to hand digitizer. More sophisticated haptic rendering algorithms for drilling and probing than those used on Prototype I & II are currently under development and it is expected these will further enhance the user experience and value of the system. Software development has undergone a similar prototype-evaluation process and the techniques used and lessons learnt will form the basis of a future paper.

Other areas relating to dental education under investigation include: the importance of colour and texture for identifying dental materials and the benefit of adjustable visual effect such as transparency and movable clipping planes, when understanding the structure of teeth. Such techniques have the potential to enhance learning in ways unavailable in traditional settings. The pedagogical aspects of using haptics and other virtual reality technology in dental training form a core part of the hapTEL. The results of the evaluation of Prototype II will also be the focus of future publications. Prototype II aims to be operated alongside with the Phantom Head in the curriculum, allowing students to benefit from both platforms.

Acknowledgments. We gratefully acknowledge the support and help of the dental tutors and students and from the researchers in the hapTEL project. The hapTEL project is supported under the Technology Enhanced Learning (TEL) jointly funded by the Economic and Social Research Council (ESRC) and Engineering and Physical Science Research Council (EPSRC).

References

1. San Diego, J., Barrow, A., Cox, M., Harwin, W.: PHANTOM Prototype: Exploring the Potential for Learning with Multimodal Features in Dentistry. In: 10th International Conference on Multimodal Interfaces, pp. 201–202. ACM Press, Crete (2008)
2. Buchanan, J.A.: Use of Simulation Technology in Dental Education. J. Dent. Educ. 65, 1225–1231 (2001)
3. Kolesnikov, M., Zefran, M., Steinberg, A.D., Bashook, P.G.: PerioSim: Haptic virtual reality simulator for sensorimotor skill acquisition in dentistry. In: IEEE International Conference on Robotics and Automation, pp. 689–694. IEEE Press, Kobe (2009)
4. Forsslund, J., Sallnas, E.-L., Palmerius, K.-J.: A user-centered designed FOSS implementation of bone surgery simulations. In: EuroHaptics conference, Symposium on Haptic Interfaces for Virtual Environment and Teleoperator Systems, World Haptics 2009. Third Joint, pp. 391–392. IEEE Press, Salt Lake City (2009)
5. Wu, J., Yu, G., Wang, D., Zhang, Y., Wang, C.: Voxel-Based Interactive Haptic Simulation of Dental Drilling. In: International Design Engineering Technical Conferences & Computer and Information in Engineering Conference. ASME Press, California (2009)
6. Rhienmora, P., Gajananan, K., Haddawy, P., Suebnukarn, S., Dailey, M., Supataratarn, E., Shrestha, P.: Haptic Augmented Reality Dental Trainer with Automatic Performance Assessment. In: International Conference on Intelligent User Interfaces. ACM Press, Hong Kong (2010)
7. Cox, M.J., San Diego, J.P., Quinn, B., Harwin, W., Newton, T.W., Barrow, A., Tse, B., Elson, B., Woolford, M., Hindmarsh, J., Reynolds, P., Banerjee, A., Millar, B., Wilson, N., Dunne, S., Robinsons, B., Hyland, L.: Developing and Researching Personalised Learning with Haptics when Teaching with Online Media (PHANTOM): methodological strategies and solutions for technological, curriculum and teaching challenges. In: World Conference on Computers in Education, Bento Gonçalves, RS, Brazil (2009)

Design of a Multimodal VR Platform for the Training of Surgery Skills

Florian Gosselin[1], Fabien Ferlay[2], Sylvain Bouchigny[2], Christine Mégard[2], and Farid Taha[3]

[1] CEA, LIST, Interactive Robotics Laboratory,
18, route du Panorama, BP6, 92265 Fontenay aux Roses, France
[2] CEA, LIST, Sensory and Ambient Interfaces Laboratory,
18, route du Panorama, BP6, 92265 Fontenay aux Roses, France
[3] Amiens University Hospital, Department of Oral and Maxillofacial Surgery
Place Victor Pauchet, 80054 Amiens, France
{florian.gosselin,fabien.ferlay,sylvain.bouchigny,
christine.megard}@cea.fr, taha.farid@chu-amiens.fr

Abstract. There are many ways by which we can learn new skills. For sensory motor skills, repeated practice (often under supervision and guidance of an expert mentor) is required in order to progressively understand the consequences of our actions, adapt our behavior and develop optimal perception-action loops needed to intuitively and efficiently perform the task. VR multimodal platforms, if adequately designed, can offer an alternative to real environments therefore. Indeed they present interesting features: controlled environment, measure of the user's performance, display of quantitative feedback. This paper presents such a platform that was developed for surgery skills training.

Keywords: multimodal platform, training, skills, haptics, surgery.

1 Introduction

There are many applications, as diverse as hand writing, sport, or surgery, which require the mastery of highly specific and precise force position patterns. Training in such domains usually requires long and repetitive practice. It often occurs under the supervision and guidance of an expert trainer or mentor who can help, give feedback and advices or even guide the trainee during the task execution. Consequently, the training efficiency is dependant on the capability to perform regularly (which is not always possible in surgery) and on the teaching qualities of the mentor. On the contrary, VR technologies offer a unique opportunity to overcome these limitations. Current multimodal platforms can realistically reproduce the main components of the task, considering vision, audition and haptics. Moreover, as the task is performed in a controlled environment, training can be focused on its critical steps, allowing more repetitions in the same time period [1] (and for surgery independently of the availability of patients). Training can also be adapted to the trainee's level. Another advantage is the continuous monitoring of the user, allowing quantitative analysis of the performance, and both immediate and a-posteriori feedback [2].

A.M.L. Kappers et al. (Eds.): EuroHaptics 2010, Part II, LNCS 6192, pp. 109–116, 2010.

Due to these advantages, numerous VR training platforms were developed, for example for hand writing [3], sport [2] or surgery [4], [5], [6], [7]. Preliminary results tend to prove the efficiency of using such platforms as a complement to traditional teaching for sensory-motor skills training. An interesting example is found in [3]. This study shows that the fluency of handwriting cursive letters in kindergarten childrens can be increased using a visuo-haptic VR training system. After training, the movements are faster, exhibit less velocity peaks and children lift the pen less often than after training with a pen and a paper. It is stated that the device may help children to change from retroactive control of movement (based on sensorial, visual and kinaesthetic feedback) to proactive control (based on an internal representation of motor acts). Different reviews also discuss the efficiency of VR platforms for surgical training [8] [9]. A study cited in [8] shows that residents who received virtual reality training performed the dissection more quickly, made fewer errors, and had higher economy-of-movement scores during a laparoscopic cholecystectomy than did residents without such training. On the other hand, the transfer of skills from the simulation environment to the operating room is assessed in [10] for laparoscopic gynaecological surgery. After training for a total of 8 hours in a simulator, inexperienced trainees progressed from the performance level of a novice to that of an intermediately experienced gynaecologist. This result was assessed in their first complex laparoscopic procedure (the simulator trained group reached a score equivalent to the experience gained after 20-50 laparoscopic procedures which usually requires a year or more in clinical practice, whereas the control group reached a score equivalent to the experience gained from fewer than five procedures).

The same teaching difficulties and VR training promises are encountered in Maxillo Facial Surgery. The general objective is here to reshape the face in order to correct either malformation, results of trauma or tumors. Such procedures are difficult to perform and to teach with traditional methods which mainly rely on observation as the trainee has only a limited vision of the narrow operating site. Moreover, critical subtasks are mainly based on haptic feedback which is not accessible through observation and is also difficult to explain verbally. In order to improve training in this field, we developed a dedicated multimodal VR training platform.

Section 2 introduces the selected use case. Section 3 presents the general design drivers of the platform. Section 4 gives more details on the actually implemented system. Finally, section 5 shortly introduces the training application.

2   Specifications of the VR Training Platform

Maxillo Facial Surgery includes a large set of procedures among which we chose to focus on the Epker Osteotomy. It is selected because it is considered by surgeons as representative of delicate interventions requiring highly sensitive skills, mainly in haptics and audition [11] which are difficult to teach with traditional methods. In this surgery, the front part of the lower mandible is first separated (corticotomy) then reassembled in a better position (osteosynthesis).

The main difficulty is to drill the bone during the corticotomy without damaging the alveolar nerve which is hidden in the mandible (this nerve is responsible for the sensitivity of the face). Therefore only the cortical part of the bone must be drilled, with as less as possible overshoot in the underlying spongy bone. This operation is very stressful, even for expert surgeons with years of practice, as any injury would be very handicapping for the patient. The most critical subtasks obtained from interviews of three French expert surgeons and real surgery task analysis are:

- localization of the Spine of Spix: this small bone protrusion marks the entry of the alveolar nerve in the lower maxilla. It must be located precisely to protect the nerve before drilling. Novices tend to localize the Spine of Spix using visual indices while experts rely more on haptic information as vision is limited;
- drilling the fraction lines: this task requires drilling the cortical bone along the Epker lines with as less as possible overshoot in the underlying spongy bone. Novices tend to grasp the instruments insufficiently firmly, producing more unstable movements compared to experts. Moreover, in order to avoid entering the spongy bone, they tend to proceed to a superficial and incomplete drilling which can cause a undesirable multiple fracture of the maxilla during distraction;
- distraction: this task requires frank gestures to orient the fracture on the theoretical line. Some young surgeons are not sufficiently self-confident and tend to make too 'shy' movements which lead to a bad fracture.

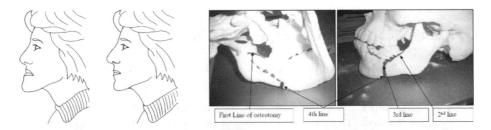

| First Line of osteotomy | 4th line | | 3rd line | 2nd line |

Fig. 1. The Epker Osteotomy consists in moving forward or backward the front part of the lower mandible to correct its positioning. Therefore the most resistive cortical parts of the maxilla are drilled along 4 lines and the natural weakness of the bone is used to proceed to the distraction of the mandible while protecting the integrity of the alveolar nerve (the doted line represents its theorical position).

The tasks analysis shows that these tasks are essentially multimodal, e.g. during drilling the transition from cortical to spongy bone is perceived by a change in bone compliance and colour and by a modification of the drilling sound. A training platform should thus integrate visual, audio and haptic feedback. Moreover, the second hand is used for self-positioning and stabilization of the drilling hand. Hence a bimanual platform is required.

In order to get the quantitative data needed to specify the platform more precisely, we performed a data acquisition campaign on dead bodies in the Anatomy Laboratory of the Rouen University Hospital in France. Three expert surgeons performed the complete corticotomy procedure (exposition, drilling, distraction) on the right side of the mandible of one patient and on the left side of the mandible of a second patient.

Positions of the surgeons forearm, arm and head were captured using a 4 cameras ART Fast Track 2 motion capture system (range ~1 m / 360°, 64 bits, 60 Hz). Forces and torques exerted by the surgeon on the tool were acquired using an ATI Mini 40 SI80-4 force sensor (range ±80 N / 4 Nm, 16 bits, 3 kHz). Accelerations of the tool were obtained in 3D with two Analog Device ADXL330 accelerometers (±30 m/s^2, 16 bits, 3 kHz). We also recorded surgery sounds with 2 Superlux microphones (24 bits, 192 kHz), the first one close to the scene and the second one more distant to capture ambient sounds. Finally, 2 mini DV cameras and a Nikon D60 were used to capture videos (one focused on the mouth and the other one in large field) and pictures from the surgery.

After post-processing and analysis, the data show that the drill moves within a volume included in a 200 mm cube while the maximum continuous / peak force (torque) applied by the surgeons is 12 N / 25 N (0.6 Nm / 1.5 N.m). The maximum bone equivalent stiffness obtained from position and force information is around 13 kN/m. Finally, maximum tool speed is around 0.9 m/s in free space (when the surgeons are repositioning the tool between two drills) and 2 mm/s during the drilling phases. These values were used as a basis to obtain design drivers for the platform's haptic interfaces. On the other side, the movements of the surgeon's head are limited and remain above the patient's head. It is thus possible to implement the visual feedback with a fixed screen placed between the user's hand and head.

3   Multimodal Training Platform Set-Up

The previous data were used to design a multimodal VR training platform for Maxillo Facial Surgery, as shown on Fig. 2. The main components are the following:

- Platform cabinet: the whole platform is integrated in an autonomous mobile cabinet that can easily be conveyed to hospitals or universities for training. The upper part integrates input / output devices while the lower part incorporates PCs, controllers, power supplies and amplifiers. In order to allow taking a natural and realistic posture, the height of the upper part table can be adjusted to cope with the user's size, in the same range of motion as hospitals real operating tables.
- Tangible support: a tangible element figuring the chin is integrated on the platform to allow stabilizing surgeons gestures with finger support (see insert in Fig. 2). It is used as a global reference for the other elements of the platform.
- Haptic interfaces with MFS props: two 6 DOFs hybrid haptic devices (each composed of two 3 DOFs robots connected to a platform supporting a 6th axis in series) are used as input devices as well as for force rendering. Such architecture combines the advantages of serial (large workspace, especially in orientation) and parallel robots (high transparency, especially in orientation) [12]. They are driven by two 9 axes Haption haptic controllers running at 1600 Hz (they run RTAI Linux) and linked to the main application PC via Ethernet. The right hand device is used to control the drill. It is a new interface specifically designed to fit previously mentioned design drivers. It is equipped with a new tactile handle using a piezo actuator to render vibrations of the drill up to 1000 Hz. To overcome the

limited range of motion of such actuators, the gripper is designed to amplify the displacements and give the best possible feedback at the level of the surgeons' fingers (100 μm up to 600 Hz). It is driven by a Piezomechanik LE 150/100/EBW amplifier which is controlled with vibration signals generated by the surgery simulation. The left hand device is used to control the vacuum cleaner. As it mainly interacts with mouth soft tissues, we make use of a pre-existing hybrid haptic interface originally developed for abdominal telesurgery (i.e. soft tissues interaction) [13]. It is equipped with a passive prop figuring the vacuum cleaner and ensuring a natural grasp sensation for the surgeon (to date the integration of the new right hand haptic interface is still in progress and the active prop is mounted on the left hand one in order to allow separate tests, see Fig. 2). The position of both devices is adjusted in order to get optimal performances in the operating regions around the tangible support.

- 3D monitor: a Samsung 2233RZ 22 inches LCD monitor running at 120 Hz is used as 3D screen. It is associated with Nvidia Geforce 3D Vision active LCD shutter glasses. The 3D parameters are adjusted so that the visual feedback is coherent with the position of the tangible support and tool props.

- Head mocap system: a simple motion capture system is integrated to capture the position of the surgeon's head and adjust the visual feedback accordingly. To date we make use of a Track IR solution but we also investigate OMG Vicon's new cost-effective solutions.

- Speakers: we make use of two Genelec 6010A active loudspeakers to implement the audio feedback. They are driven by an Edirol FA-66 (24 bits, 192 kHz) external sound card. Details on sound analysis and synthesis can be found in [14].

- Main application PC: the whole platform is driven by a HP XW8600 workstation (bi-quad core Intel Xeon 5450 running at 3 GHz, Quadro FX5600 graphic card) used to implement the training program and exercises.

- Extra monitor: during the task execution, the tools positions and forces are recorded. The information is then used to display performance feedback curves, indexes and messages on an additional LCD monitor. This information is used both by the trainee to check his performances and by the trainer to monitor the progression towards expertise and compare the trainees' performances.

While most of the existing commercial systems like for example the Lap Mentor from Symbionix (www.simbionix.com), Hystsim from Virtamed (virtamed.com) or LapVR from CAE Healthcare (www.cae.com) concentrate on MIS procedures, allowing a simplified platform design with 3 or 4 DOFs robots and remote visual feedback, and while some research platforms make use of commercially available 3 DOFs force feedback devices [6], our training platform integrates advanced 6 DOFs robots for improved force feedback (larger workspace, higher amount of force in both translation and rotation, larger stiffness), allowing to cover more diverse surgeries. Moreover, the combination of force and tactile feedback up to several hundreds of Hz is new and unique in the field. Another difference compared to the afore-mentioned systems is that the user can look where he manipulates which is required for the training of such open surgery procedures.

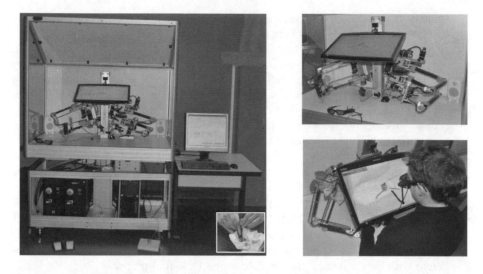

Fig. 2. The multimodal VR training platform is an autonomous mobile cabinet including two 6 DOFs haptic devices equipped with an active tactile drill prop and a passive vacuum cleaner prop, a tangible support figuring the chin of the patient, a 3D screen with stereoscopic glasses, a head mocap system, and 2 loudspeakers. The lower rack integrates the haptic devices controllers, the main PC running the application, the active prop amplifier and the audio sound card. An additional screen is used to display performances feedback.

4   Multimodal Training Program Implementation

Among the afore-mentioned critical subtasks, we decided to first focus on the drilling of the fraction lines. Therefore it is required to be able to hold and move the tools correctly while applying correct forces. The associated skills that we aim at training are perception by touch, fine position and force control, as well as bi-manual coordination and postural control.

Training is organized in simple exercises allowing training those skills before moving to the surgery context. A linear progression is proposed. This progression is based on the logic followed during apprenticeship in which the learner is progressively involved in the surgery with increasing difficulty. A tutorial is first proposed to the trainee. Then he has to train to drill holes (like in [15]), then to drill lines on different complex shapes and finally to perform constrained drilling which are representative of specific Epker gestures (e.g. access is limited during drilling at the basilar edge). Only the first simple exercise is available at the beginning and the other exercises are progressively unlocked as the trainee successfully executes the previous ones three times in a row. For each exercise, it will be studied how haptics, vision and audition can be used to help training (e.g. unimodal feedback, emphasis change, temporary augmented information, number and order of repetitions). Further details on the training program and on the way we aim at accelerating training will be detailed in a forthcoming paper.

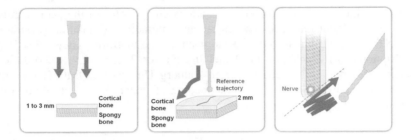

Fig. 3. Example training exercises. First exercises focus on punctual drilling and perception of a change in compliance when moving from cortical to spongy bone. Second exercises focus on fine position and force control during line drilling on different complex shapes. Last exercises correspond to specific situations encountered in the surgery.

All those elements are driven by a mixed Flash/Adobe AIR architecture for the management of the Demonstrator and XDE framework developed at CEA-LIST for the real time simulation. We use a continuous surface representation based on distance fields. The continuity of the surface allows a more consistent force rendering compared to Voxel based representations. The surface is locally displaced upon tool tissue penetration as a function of the drilling parameters (force applied on the tool at the preceding time step, drilling rotation speed, tool-surface angle, local bone density). Contrary to Voxel based methods, this displacement can be smaller than the grid size, thus a smoother force rendering. After the surface displacement, we solve for the geometric contact with a constraint based method yielding at the same time the forces to apply to the tool. This method guaranties that no penetration between the tool and the surrounding tissues remain at the end of the time step. Consequently, no oscillations occur in narrow places like deep cuts produced by the drill. This method is thus much more robust than point-voxel or voxel-voxel volumetric intersections and does not require a multigain approach with non linear stiffness as proposed in [6] in the case of large penetration.

5 Conclusion and Perspectives

In this paper, we introduced a new multimodal VR training platform for maxillo facial surgery. The platform features visual, audio and haptic feedback. Moreover, a specific training program is proposed. The next step will be the identification of the real performances of the system in order to compare them with the task related specifications. Then the platform will be finely tuned to obtain an as realistic as possible feedback compared to real surgery. Finally, we will perform a training campaign to validate the added value of the proposed approach.

Acknowledgments. The authors gratefully acknowledge the support of the SKILLS Integrated Project (IST-FP6 #035005, http://www.skills-ip.eu) funded by the European Commission. The authors also warmly thank the surgeons implied in the project for their cooperation: Dr. P. Delcampe from Rouen University Hospital, Dr. C. D'Hauthuille from Nantes University Hospital. They also thank Mr. B. Beloncle from the Anatomy Laboratory of Rouen. The authors are grateful to the people from the Sensory and Ambient Interfaces Laboratory and Interactive Simulation Laboratory at CEA-LIST who contributed to the development of the platform. They thank Haption (www.haption.com), Technion, the Israel Institute of Technology, EDM Lab from University Montpellier 1, Acoustics from Aalborg University, OMG (www.omg3d.com) for their contribution to this work (lending of material and contribution to the specification of the platform).

References

1. Kneebone, R.: Simulation in surgical training: educational issues and practical implications. Med. Educ. 37, 267–277 (2003)
2. Baca, A., Kornfeind, P.: Rapid Feedback Systems for Elite Sports Training. Pervasive Computing 5(4), 70–76 (2006)
3. Palluel-Germain, R., Bara, F., de Boisferon, A.H., Hennion, B., Gouagout, P., Gentaz, E.: A Visuo-Haptic Device – Telemaque – Increases Kindergarten Children's Handwriting Acquisition. In: Proc. Worldhaptics Conf., Tsukuba, Japan, pp. 72–77 (2007)
4. Sourin, A., Sourina, O., Howe, T.S.: Virtual Orthopedic Surgery Training. Computer Graphics and Applications 20(3), 6–9 (2000)
5. Agus, M., Giachetti, A., Gobbetti, E., Zanetti, G., Zorcolo, A.: Real-time Haptic and Visual Simulation of Bone Dissection. In: Proc. IEEE Virtual Reality, Orlando, Florida, pp. 209–216 (2002)
6. Morris, D., Sewell, C., Barbagli, F., Salisbury, K., Belvins, N.H., Girod, S.: Visuohaptic Simulation of Bone Surgery for Training and Evaluation. Computer Graphics and Applications 26(6), 48–57 (2006)
7. Terada, T., Ogata, M., Kukikawa, T., Hongo, S., Nagasaka, M., Takanami, K., Kajihara, K., Fujino, M.: Virtual Human Body using Haptic Devices for Endoscopic Surgery Training Simulator. In: Proc. 4th IEEE Int. Conf. on Mechatronics, Kumamoto, Japan, pp. 1–5 (2007)
8. Reznick, R.K., MacRae, H.: Teaching surgical skills, changes in the wind. The New England Journal of Medicine 355(25), 2664–2669 (2006)
9. Haque, S., Srinivasan, S.: A Meta-Analysis of the Training Effectiveness of Virtual Reality Surgical Simulators. IEEE Transactions on Information Technology in Biomedicine 10(1), 51–58 (2006)
10. Larsen, C.R., Soerensen, J.L., Grantcharov, T.P., Dalsgaard, T., Schouenborg, L., Ottosen, C., Schroeder, T.V., Ottesen, B.S.: Effect of virtual reality training on laparoscopic surgery: randomized controlled trial. BMJ 338, b1802 (2009)
11. Müller-Tomfelde, C.: Interaction sound feedback in a haptic virtual environment to improve motor skill acquisition. In: Proc. Int. Conf. on Auditory Display, Sydney, Australia (2004)
12. Gosselin, F.: Développement d'outils d'aide à la conception d'organes de commande pour la téléopération à retour d'effort. PhD dissertation, University of Poitiers, 358 p. (2000)
13. Gosselin, F., Bidard, C., Brisset, J.: Design of a high fidelity haptic device for telesurgery. In: Proc. IEEE Int. Conf. on Robotics and Automation, Barcelona, Spain, pp. 206–211 (2005)
14. Hoffmann, P., Gosselin, F., Taha, F., Bouchigny, S., Hammershøi, D.: Analysis of the drilling sound in maxillo facial surgery. In: Proc. Int. Conf. on Multimodal Interfaces for Skills Transfer, Bilbao, Spain, pp. 121–127 (2009)
15. Sewell, C., Blevins, N.H., Peddamatham, S., Tan, H.Z., Morris, D., Salisbury, K.: The Effect of Virtual Haptic Training on Real Surgical Drilling Proficiency. In: Proc. Worldhaptics Conf., Tsukuba, Japan, pp. 601–603 (2007)

Haptic Assistance in Virtual Environments for Motor Rehabilitation

Jaka Ziherl, Domen Novak, Andrej Olenšek, and Marko Munih

Laboratory of Robotics and Biomedical Engineering, Faculty of Electrical Engineering,
University of Ljubljana,
Trzaska c. 25, 1001 Ljubljana, Slovenia
{jaka.ziherl,domen.novak,andrej.olensek,marko.munih}@robo.fe.uni-lj.si
http://robo.fe.uni-lj.si/

Abstract. This paper presents the MIMICS MMS rehabilitation system with a virtual rehabilitation task that includes several modes of haptic assistance. We observed the influence of these different modes of assistance on task performance and work performed toward the target during the pick-and-place movement. Twenty-three hemiparetic subjects and a control group of twenty-three subjects participated in the study. The haptic assistance resulted in improved task performance and lower work performed during pick-and-place movement.

Keywords: haptic interface, haptic assistance, rehabilitation robotics.

1 Introduction

Robotics is advancing into different areas of human lives [1]. One of these is the area of rehabilitation where robot-enhanced physical therapy improves recovery after stroke [2]. In rehabilitation robotics, haptic interfaces combined with virtual reality largely improve the patient's motivation [3]. Several robotic training systems for upper extremities have been developed. For instance, MIT-MANUS [4] with SCARA configuration interactively treats stroke survivors. The MIME [5] system uses a Puma 560 robot manipulator and is capable of four modes of haptic assistance. The robot system for upper limb rehabilitation developed by Deneve et al. [6] uses impedance control to avoid a large movement deviation from the desired trajectory. The Gentle/G [7] system based on the HapticMaster robot includes reach and grasp tasks, correcting movements that stray too far from the correct pathway. These systems use virtual reality and apply different modes of haptic assistance to the patients. The HapticMaster has also been used in other areas, such as haptic modeling of digital shapes [8]. This paper presents the MIMICS MMS (Multi Modal System) rehabilitation system with the HapticMaster haptic robot and a virtual rehabilitation task as well as the results of exercising in hemiparetic subjects and control group. Our goal was to determine how different modes of haptic assistance influence the task performance of the training in stroke subjects. Catching efficiency, pick-and-place movement efficiency and work performed during pick-and-place movement were observed.

A.M.L. Kappers et al. (Eds.): EuroHaptics 2010, Part II, LNCS 6192, pp. 117–122, 2010.

2 Methods

2.1 Haptic System Specification

The HapticMaster (Moog FCS Inc.) is an admittance-controlled haptic interface with one rotational and two translational degrees of freedom. It presents a suitable device for upper extremities in rehabilitation tasks. A grasping mechanism is attached to a gimbal, which allows reorientation of a wrist connection mechanism and therefore the subject's hand. The mechanism is upgraded with a one degree of freedom finger opening and closing subsystem in order to provide grasping and object carrying capabilities. Support of the lower and upper arm is provided by an active gravity compensation mechanism. The graphic environment is presented to the subject on a back-projection screen via two LCD projectors and uses OGRE 3D library for graphic rendering. The projectors have polarizing filters that enable a subject with polarizing glasses to perceive a virtual environment in 3D.

2.2 HapticMaster Blocks in Simulink

The HapticMaster runs on the xPC Target^{TM}(The MathWorks, Inc.) host-target environment that enables the connection of models to physical systems and their execution in real time. The task executes at 2500 Hz. A new library was developed to link together the robot and the Simulink environment. The library includes input and output drivers, control blocks, robot kinematics and dynamics, haptic objects and collision detection blocks. The inputs to the haptic model are the measured forces on the top of the robot and the positions of the three robot joints. The outputs to the robot are the velocities of the joints. The control blocks subsystem includes an admittance model, a PD controller, a direct and an inverse kinematic of the robot and a Jacobian matrix. These blocks provide the bases for development of a haptic virtual environment.

2.3 Haptic Objects and Collision Detection

The haptic environment in Simulink consists of haptic objects and collision detection among them. The basic haptic objects are the sphere, the box, the cone and the wall. For each of the objects we can set parameters: dimensions, mass, initial position and velocity, initial orientation and rotation, stiffness, damping, gravitation, environment translation damping and environment rotation damping. All the combinations of the collisions among objects are available in collision detection blocks. Collision detection blocks involve algorithms from Open Dynamics Engine (ODE) library [9]. The top of the haptic interface is modeled as a point and presents a haptic interaction point (HIP) in the virtual environment. When a collision is detected, a virtual force that effects on the user and the virtual object is computed. With these basic objects, we can develop different haptic scenes in combination with visual environment scenes.

2.4 Virtual Rehabilitation Task

The rehabilitation task is a catch-and-place exercise. A table is positioned in a room with several objects around the scene (Fig. 1). A small sphere and two small cones

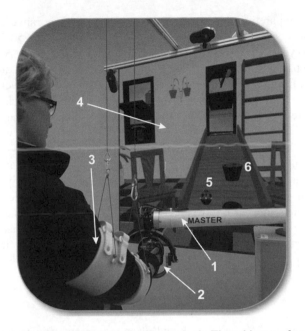

Fig. 1. A subject performing the virtual rehabilitation task. The subject performs the task using the robot (1) and grasping device (2) while his/her arm is supported by cuffs (3). The screen (4) shows a sloped table, a ball (5) and a basket (6).

on the left and right sides of the sphere represent the current position of the robot in the virtual environment. The distance between the cones is proportional to the grasping force. A ball rolls from the opposite side of the sloped table. The subject needs to catch the ball and place it in a basket which appears when the ball is grasped. After the ball is successfully placed in the basket, a new ball rolls down. The task is a combination of catching, grasping, pick-and-place movement and releasing.

The task includes different options for haptic assistance. These include:

1. **Catching assistance.** The catching assistance helps the subject catch the ball. It is an impedance controller that moves the subject's arm in a frontal plane.
2. **Grasping assistance.** The grasping assistance causes the ball to stick to the virtual end-effector. When the subject reaches the place point, the ball is dropped.
3. **Tunnel assistance.** The haptic trajectory tunnel enables movement from the catch point to the place point along a desired trajectory in a virtual haptic environment. An impedance controller prevents the subject from deviating from the desired trajectory. The bisector of the tunnel is generated using B-splines and control points [10]. The control points are approximated by using B-splines from trajectories measured in healthy subjects' movements. The guidance assistance provides a trajectory guidance force in the advancement of the haptic trajectory tunnel.

In the experiment, catching efficiency and pick-and-place efficiency were observed to find how different modes of haptic assistance influence on the outcome of the exercise.

Twenty-three hemiparetic subjects (age 51.0 ± 13.3 years, age range 23-69 years, 16 males, 7 females) and a control group (twenty-three subjects, age 50.5 ± 12.6 years, age range 24-68 years, 16 males, 7 females) participated in the study. As a result of the stroke, 13 hemiparetic subjects suffered from hemiparesis of the left side of the body and 10 suffered from hemiparesis of the right side of the body. All were right-handed before the stroke. The subjects in control group had no major physical or cognitive defects. All were right-handed. The participants had 6 minutes training in virtual rehabilitation task with different haptic assistances. These assistances were activated if subject was unable to perform a particular component of the task. Therefore, 7 patients had catching and tunnel assistance and 16 patients had no assistance. The control group also performed the task without any assistance. Several haptic parameters were measured during training including positions, forces on the top of the robot, catching efficiency and pick-and-place movement efficiency. The listed parameters were analyzed using the t-test to determine significant differences between patients using the assistance and the patients without the assistance as well as between the patients and the control group.

3   Results

We observed catching efficiency, pick-and-place movement efficiency and performed work toward target of stroke group with and without assistance as well as in control subjects (Table 1). The control group caught more balls than the stroke group without the catching assistance during the virtual rehabilitation task ($p < 0.001$). Catching efficiency in stroke group was greater when the catching assistance was applied ($p < 0.001$). Fig. 2a shows the pick-and-place efficiency for stroke and control group, both without the tunnel assistance. The control group performed more successful pick-and-place movements than the stroke nTA group during the virtual rehabilitation task ($p = 0.006$). The stroke TA group pick-and-place efficiency was greater than the efficiency of the stroke nTA group ($p < 0.001$) and the control group ($p < 0.001$). Fig. 2b shows the work performed to move toward the place point. The stroke nTA group performed more work toward target than the stroke TA group ($p < 0.001$). There is not a statistically significant difference of performed work in stroke nTA group and control group ($p = 0.362$).

Table 1. The results of observed catching efficiency (CE), pick-and-place efficiency (PE) and work performed toward the target (WTT). The stroke patients are divided into the groups with catching assistance (CA), without catching assistance (nCA), with tunnel assistance (TA) and without tunnel assistance (nTA).

	Stroke nCA	Stroke CA	Control nCA
CE [%]	63 ± 17	86 ± 14	86 ± 13

	Stroke nTA	Stroke TA	Control nTA
PE [%]	79 ± 14	98 ± 6	91 ± 9
WTT [J]	1.39 ± 0.65	0.12 ± 0.38	1.23 ± 0.91

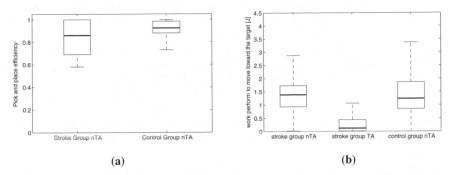

(a) **(b)**

Fig. 2. (a) Pick-and-place efficiency of the stroke group and control group without the tunnel assistance (nTA). (b) Work performed to move toward the target during pick-and-place movement of the stroke group without the tunnel assistance (nTA), stroke group with the tunnel assistance (TA) and control group without the tunnel assistance (nTA).

4 Discussion

The results in patients showed that the catching efficiency of stroke group was greater when the catching assistance was applied. The results are even higher than in control group. The similar holds for the tunnel assistance (Fig. 2a). Therefore as expected the assistances can raise the performance of the exercise. On the other hand, the work toward the target performed during pick-and-place movement in patients was smaller when the assistance was present. There is not a statistical significant difference between the stroke group without the tunnel assistance and the control group. We believe that the subjects benefits the most from the exercising when besides the task efficiency also the performed work is high. In the future, the adaptive haptic support system might substitute the tunnel assistance in the rehabilitation task. We assume that the subjects will be allowed to select the most comfortable movement trajectory and will therefore increase the performed work and maximize the outcome of the exercise.

Acknowledgments. The work was funded by the EU Information and Communication Technologies Collaborative Project MIMICS grant 215756. Moog FCS kindly loaned one of two HapticMaster devices for the MIMICS project. The authors acknowledge the financial support from the state budget by the Slovenian Research Agency (ARRS).

References

1. Kanehiro, F., Hirukawa, H., Kajita, S.: OpenHRP: Open Architecture Humanoid Robotics Platform. Int. J. Robot. Res. 23, 155–165 (2004)
2. Sunderland, A., Tinson, D.J., Bradley, E.L., Fletcher, D., Hewer, R.L., Wade, D.T.: Enhanced physical therapy improves recovery of arm function after stroke. A randomised controlled trial. J. Neurol. Neurosurg. Psychiatr. 55, 530–535 (1992)
3. Mihelj, M., Nef, T., Reiner, R.: A novel paradigm for patient-cooperative control of upper-limb rehabilitation robots. Adv. Robotics 21, 843–867 (2007)

4. Hogan, N., Krebs, H.I., Charnnarong, J., Srikrishna, P., Sharon, A.: MIT - MANUS: A workstation for manual therapy and training I. In: IEEE International Workshop on Robot and Human Communication, pp. 161–165. IEEE Press, New York (1992)
5. Lum, P.S., Burgar, C.G., Shor, P.C.: Evidence for improved muscle activation patterns after retraining of reaching movements with the MIME robotic system in subjects with post-stroke hemiparesis. IEEE Trans. Neural Syst. Rehabil. Eng. 12, 184–194 (2004)
6. Deneve, A., Moughamir, S., Afilal, L., Zaytoon, J.: Control system design of a 3-DOF upper limbs rehabilitation robot. Comput. Meth. Prog. Bio. 89, 202–214 (2008)
7. Loureiro, R.C.V., Harwin, W.S.: Reach & Grasp Therapy: Design and Control of a 9-DOF Robotic Neuro-rehabilitation System. In: IEEE 10th International Conference on Rehabilitation Robotics, pp. 757–763. IEEE Press, New York (2007)
8. Borgedoni, M., Cugini, U.: Haptic modeling in the conceptual phases of product design. Virtual Real 9, 192–202 (2006)
9. Smith, R.: Open Dynamics Engine - ODE (2007), http://www.ode.org
10. Farin, G.: Curves and Surfaces for CAGD. Morgan Kaufmann, San Francisco (2001)

Preliminary Experiment Combining Virtual Reality Haptic Shoes and Audio Synthesis

Rolf Nordahl[1], Amir Berrezag[2], Smilen Dimitrov[1],
Luca Turchet[1], Vincent Hayward[2], and Stefania Serafin[1]

[1] Aalborg University Copenhagen, Medialogy, Lautrupvang 15, 2750
Ballerup, Denmark
{rn,sd,tur,sts}@media.aau.dk
[2] UPMC Univ Paris 06, Institut des Systèmes Intelligents et de Robotique, 4 place Jussieu,
75005 Paris, France
{amir.berrezag,vincent.hayward}@isir.upmc.fr

Abstract. We describe a system that provides combined auditory and haptic sensations to simulate walking on different grounds. It uses a physical model that drives haptic transducers embedded in sandals and headphones. The model represents walking interactions with solid surfaces that can creak, or be covered with crumpling material. In a preliminary discrimination experiment, 15 participants were asked to recognize four different surfaces in a list of sixteen possibilities and under three different conditions, haptics only, audition only and combined haptic-audition. The results indicate that subjects are able to recognize most of the stimuli in the audition only condition, and some of the material properties such as hardness in the haptics only condition. The combination of auditory and haptic cues did not improve recognition significantly.

Keywords: physical models, walking sounds, audio-haptic interaction.

1 Introduction

Multimodality is an increasingly common feature of interactive systems. Whilst most studies focus on the interaction between vision and audition or between vision and touch, interaction between touch and audition is also strong because of two sources of sensory information have high temporal resolution. The perception literature contains many reports of audio-tactile interaction effects, see [1,2,3,4] for examples and surveys, and there has been studies directed at leveraging audiotactile to enhance interaction with virtual worlds [5,6,7,8,9,10].

We typically spend a great amount of our waking hours interacting with the world through our feet, performing simultaneous auditory and haptic probing. However, most studies, so far, both from the perception and from the virtual reality literature, have focused on the hands. A notable exception is the work of Giordano et al., who showed that the feet were also effective at probing the world with discriminative touch, with and without access to auditory information. Their results suggested that integration of foot-haptic and auditory information does follow simple integration rules [11].

Almost all haptic device development research is directed at stimulating the hand but what about the foot? Similarly to research on haptic devices for the hand, the approaches

A.M.L. Kappers et al. (Eds.): EuroHaptics 2010, Part II, LNCS 6192, pp. 123–129, 2010.

to stimulate the foot broadly follow two directions [12]. The force-feedback option has been explored considering either rolling or ground-referenced devices, e.g., [13,14]. This approach typically involves considerable engineering challenges and cost. The vibrotactile option has also been explored. There are two possible ways to provide the signal. Actuators can be embedded in the floor, see [15] for a survey, or they can be embedded in worn shoes. In the later case, however, to our knowledge, there has been no attempt up until now to aim for any kind of reproduction fidelity needed for a virtual reality simulation. Only signaling functions were considered [16,17].

We describe a preliminary study carried out with haptic feedback sandals that employed a newly introduced broadband vibrotactile transducer. The transducers as well as the headphone worn by the participants were driven by the same physical model. The model, presented in greater detail elsewhere [18], is able to represent, for virtual reality purposes, the kind of interaction that one might expect from stepping on solid surfaces that may or may not present the characteristics of a creaking material or be covered by crumpling objects such as dry leaves. Within the auditory modality, this model was already shown to enable good discrimination among these materials.

Here, we used the same model to drive the haptic simulations in order to investigate whether the experience of a virtual world may be enhanced by providing haptic feedback through the feet. In the present study, the participants passively received sensory information through touch and audition which is not the condition in which the system is intended to be used ultimately. Even though sensorimotor coupling was inexistent, as if another person did the walking for the participants, interesting results were obtained.

2   Simulation Hardware and Software

2.1   Haptic Hardware

A pair of light-weight sandals size 43 was procured (Model Arpenaz-50, Decathlon, Villeneuve d'Ascq, France). This particular model has light, stiff foam soles that are easy to gouge and fashion. Two cavities were made in the thickness of the sole to accommodate two vibrotactile actuators (Haptuator, Tactile Labs Inc., Deux-Montagnes, Qc, Canada). These electromagnetic recoil-type actuators have an operational, linear bandwidth of 50–500 Hz and can provide up to 3 G of acceleration when connected to light loads. As indicated in Fig. 1, one actuator was placed under the heel of the wearer and the other under the ball of the foot. They were bonded in place to ensure good transmission of the vibrations inside the soles. When activated, vibrations propagated far in the light, stiff foam. In the present configuration, these two actuators were driven by the same signal but could be activated separately to emphasize, for instance, the front or back activation, to strike a balance, or to realize other effects such as modulating different, back-front signals during heel-toe movements.

The sole has force sensors intended to pick the foot-floor interaction force in order to drive the audio and haptic synthesis. They were not used in the present study. As far as auditory feedback is concerned, it was delivered through closed headphones (DT 770, beyerdynamic, Heilbronn, Germany).

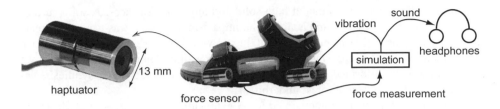

Fig. 1. System (one shoe shown). Left: recoil-type actuation from Tactile Labs Inc. The moving parts are protected by an alumimum enclosure able to bear the weight of a person. Middle: approximate location of the actuators in the sandal. Right: system diagram showing the interconnections. Here the force signal was not used.

2.2 Audio-Haptic Simulation

This model and its discretization is described elsewhere in detail [19]. The model has been recently adapted to the audio simulation of footsteps [18]. Here, we used the same model to drive the haptic and the audio synthesis. It is briefly recalled below.

A footstep sound may be considered to cause multiple micro-impacts between a sole, i.e., an *exciter*, and a floor, i.e., a *resonator*. Such interaction can be either discrete, as in the case of walking on a solid surface, or continuous, as in the case of a foot sliding across the floor.

In the simulation of discrete impacts, the excitation is brief and has an unbiased frequency response. The interaction is modelled by a Hunt-Crossley-type interaction where the force, f, between two bodies, combines hardening elasticity and a dissipation term [20]. Let x represent contact interpenetration and $\alpha > 1$ be a coefficient used to shape the nonlinear hardening, the special model form we used is

$$f(x,\dot{x}) = -kx^{\alpha} - \lambda x^{\alpha}\dot{x} \quad \text{if } x > 0, \quad 0 \text{ otherwise.}$$

The model described was discretized as proposed in [21].

If the interaction called for slip, we adopted a model where the relationship between relative velocity v of the bodies in contact and friction force f is governed by a differential equation rather than a static map [22]. Considering that friction results from a large number of microscopic damped elastic bonds with an average deflection z, a viscous term, $\sigma_2 v$, and a noise term, $\sigma_3 w$, to represent roughness, we have

$$f(z,\dot{z},v,w) = \sigma_0 z + \sigma_1 \dot{z} + \sigma_2 v + \sigma_3 w.$$

The force specified by these models is applied to a virtual mass which produces a displacement signal that is then processed by a linear shaping filter intended to represent the resonator.

Stochastic parameterization is employed to simulate particle interactions thereby avoiding to model each of many particles explicitly. Instead, the particles are assigned a probability to create an acoustic waveform. In the case of many particles, the interaction can be represented using a simple Poisson distribution, where the sound probability is constant at each time step, giving rise to an exponential probability weighting time between events.

We used this approach to model both solid and aggregate surfaces. A solid surface is represented by an impact and a slide. The impact model alone was used to recreate the sound and the feel produced when walking on wood. The friction model was tuned to simulate walking on creaking wood. To simulate walking on aggregate grounds, we used a physically informed sonic models (PhiSM) algorithm [23]. The synthesis was tuned to simulate snow and forest underbrush.

These algorithms were implemented as an extension to the Max/MSP platform[1] to drive both the auditory and haptic feedback.

3   Preliminary Evaluation

We conducted a within-subjects experiment whose goal was to assess the ability of subjects to recognize the surfaces they were exposed to using auditory and haptic stimuli, and a combination of both. The experiment entailed asking three groups of fifteen participants to passively experience the stimuli described in the previous section. The first group received the haptic stimuli only, the second the audio only, and the third the combined stimuli. The synthesis was tuned to evoke four different surfaces: wood, creaking wood, snow, and underbrush. Participants had to select in a list of sixteen different materials one that matched best their experience. They also rated the realism and quality of their experience on a seven-point Likert scale.

Procedure: The participants were asked to wear the sandals, and the headphones described in the previous section, and to sit in a chair. In the condition with haptics only they wore earplugs and sound protection headsets. Participants were asked to recognize the stimuli they were exposed to. They were given a list of sixteen options, made of fifteen materials: wood, creaking wood, underbrush, snow, frozen snow, beach sand, gravel, metal, high grass, dry leaves, concrete, dirt, puddles, water, and carpet plus an additional "I don't know" option. The materials were chosen in order to cover a large set of solid and aggregate materials, which could represent realistic walking surfaces with characteristics similar to the ones simulated. The reason to add the "I don't know" option was in order to allow subjects to express their complete uncertainty in the recognition of materials, which would not have been possible using forced choices. Each of the four simulated surfaces were presented twice in a randomized order. When presented one of the four stimuli, participants had to match it to one in the list and rated the realism and quality of the simulations. At the conclusion of the experiment, participants were asked to leave comments.

Participants: The forty five volunteers (students and faculty at the Engineering college of Copenhagen; 31 men and 14 women; average age =24.5, sd=4.6) were randomly assigned to one of the three groups (audio only, haptic only or audio-haptic) for a total of 15 participants per condition. None reported hearing problems or other sensory impairments. In order for the size of sandals not to affect performance, subjects wore shoes sizes from 41 and 45 (as mentioned before, the sandals were size 43).

---

[1] www.cycling74.com

Results and discussion: Table 1 shows the confusion matrices produced by the three groups.

Table 1. Confusion matrices with: haptics, audio, and combined haptics and audio

		WD	CW	SW	UB	—	FS	BS	GL	MT	HG	DL	CC	DR	PD	WT	CP
haptics	WD	6	2				4	1	2	5		2	6	2			
	CW		11	2	4	5	5	2	1								
	SW		1	13		3	3	2	4		1	2				1	
	UB	1		2	4		10	2	8			1	2				
audio	WD	11	1	1	1	11	1		1	1			1			1	
	CW	1	27				2										
	SW			23			3	2					2				
	UB			2	20	1	2		1			1	3				
haptics and audio	WD	13	1	1		9	1			1			3	1			
	CW		29				1										
	SW			23			2		3						2		
	UB			2	16		6		4				2				

Legend:

WD	wood	CW	creaking wood
SW	snow	UB	underbrush
—	don't know	FS	Frozen snow
BS	beach sand	GL	Gravel
MT	metal	HG	High grass
DL	dry leaves	CC	concrete
DR	dirt	PD	puddles
WT	Water	CP	carpet

From the results, it can be noticed that haptic cues alone gave the subjects the possiblity to recognize surfaces categories but with poor fine discrimination. This is the case for the wood simulation that was easily confused with metal, concrete or dirt. A solid surface was not confused with aggregates such as snow, underbrush, grass or with soft surfaces such as puddles or carpet. Recognition rates with audio stimuli were much higher as seen in the corresponding dominant diagonal. The audio simulation of wood still caused some confusion as seen in the numerous 'don't know' answers that were not present with the haptic experience. The small number of confusions was mostly among the aggregates. When the two stimuli (identical at the signal level) were delivered simultaneously, performance was not necessarily better as if conflict was created; such phenomenon is noticeable during the presentation of simulated underbrush. What is quite interesting is that a similar phenomenon occurs during the multimodal identification of *real* materials [11] (full report forthcoming). In both haptic and auditory modality, the friction simulation was an important cue which facilitated the recognition of creaking wood.

Table 2 shows the degree to which participants judged the realism and quality of the experience. The degree of realism was calculated by looking only at that data from correct

Table 2. Average realism and quality scores from a seven-point Likert scale

	realism				quality			
	wood	creaking	snow	underbrush	wood	creaking	snow	underbrush
haptics	3.3	4.3	4.8	3.2	2.8	4.0	4.2	4.3
audio	1.8	3.5	5.2	5.5	3.2	3.8	5.1	4.9
combined	3.3	3.6	5.3	4.6	4.0	4.7	5.2	4.6

answers, i.e., when the surfaces were correctly recognized. As far as the quality judgement is concerned, the data was based on all the answers different from 'don't know'.

Overall, the aggregate surfaces were considered as more realistic and with a higher quality than the solid surfaces. In all conditions, the addition of the creaking sound to the simulation of wood increased both the rated quality and the realism.

4   Conclusions and Future Work

We described a system able to simulate the auditory and haptic sensation of walking on different materials and presented the results of a preliminary surface recognition experiment. This experiment was conducted under three different conditions: auditory feedback, haptic feedback, and both.

By presenting the stimuli to the participants passively sitting in a chair, we introduced a high degree of control on the stimulation. However, this method of delivery is highly contrived since it eliminates the tight sensorimotor coupling that is natural during walking and foot interaction. It is true for the auditory channel, but even more so for the haptic channel. In spite of these drastically constrained conditions, performance was surprisingly good.

We are currently running follow up experiments allowing subjects to walk in a controlled laboratory, where their steps are tracked and used to drive the simulation. We believe introducing a higher level of interactivity will significantly enhance the recognition rates as well as the perceived quality and realism of the simulation.

Acknowledgments

The research leading to these results has received funding from the European Community 's Seventh Framework Programme under FET-Open grant agreement n. 222107 NIW - Natural Interactive Walking.

References

1. Lederman, S.: Auditory texture perception. Perception (1979)
2. Jousmaki, V., Hari, R.: Parchment-skin illusion: sound-biased touch. Current Biology 8(6), R190–R191 (1998)
3. Shimojo, S., Shams, L.: Sensory modalities are not separate modalities: plasticity and interactions. Current Opinion in Neurobiology 11(4), 505–509 (2001)

4. Bresciani, J.P., Ernst, M.O., Drewing, K., Bouyer, G., Maury, V., Kheddar, A.: Feeling what you hear: Auditory signals can modulate tactile tap perception. Experimental Brain Research 162, 172–180 (2005)
5. Ramstein, C., Hayward, V.: The pantograph: A large workspace haptic device for a multimodal human-computer interaction. In: Proceedings of the SIGCHI Conference on Human Factors in Computing Systems, CHI 2004, ACM/SIGCHI Companion-4/94, pp. 57–58 (1994)
6. DiFranco, D., Beauregard, G.L., Srinivasan, M.: The effect of auditory cues on the haptic perception of stiffness in virtual environments. In: Proceedings of the ASME Dynamic Systems and Control Division (1997)
7. DiFilippo, D., Pai, D.K.: Contact interaction with integrated audio and haptics. In: Proceedings of the International Conference on Auditory Display, ICAD (2000)
8. Pai, D., Doel, K., James, D., Lang, J., Lloyd, J., Richmond, J., Yau, S.: Scanning physical interaction behavior of 3d objects. In: Proceedings of the 28th Annual Conference on Computer Graphics and Interactive Techniques, pp. 87–96 (2001)
9. Sreng, J., Bergez, F., Legarrec, J., Lécuyer, A., Andriot, C.: Using an event-based approach to improve the multimodal rendering of 6dof virtual contact. In: Proceedings of ACM Symposium on Virtual Reality Software and Technology (ACM VRST), pp. 173–179 (2007)
10. Avanzini, F., Crosato, P.: Integrating physically based sound models in a multimodal rendering architecture. The Journal of Visualization and Computer Animation 17(3-4), 411–419 (2006)
11. Giordano, B.L., Mcadams, S., Visell, Y., Cooperstock, J., Yao, H.Y., Hayward, V.: Non-visual identification of walking grounds. Journal of the Acoustical Society of America 123(5), 3412 (2008)
12. Hayward, V., MacLean, K.E.: Do it yourself haptics, part-i. IEEE Robotics and Automation Magazine 14(4), 88–104 (2007)
13. Iwata, H., Yano, H., Tomioka, H.: Powered shoes. In: ACM SIGGRAPH 2006 Emerging technologies, p. 28 (2006)
14. Schmidt, H., Hesse, S., Bernhardt, R., Krüger, J.: Hapticwalker—a novel haptic foot device. ACM Transactions on Applied Perception 2(2), 166–180 (2005)
15. Visell, Y., Law, A., Cooperstock, J.R.: Touch is everywhere: Floor surfaces as ambient haptic interfaces. IEEE Transactions on Haptics 2, 148–159 (2009)
16. Fu, X., Li, D.: Haptic shoes: representing information by vibration. In: Proceedings of the 2005 Asia-Pacific Symposium on Information Visualisation, pp. 47–50 (2005)
17. Magana, M., Velazquez, R.: On-shoe tactile display. In: IEEE International Workshop on Haptic Audio Visual Environments and Games (HAVE 2008), pp. 114–119 (2008)
18. Nordahl, R., Serafin, S., Turchet, L.: Sound synthesis and evaluation of interactive footsteps for virtual reality applications. In: Proc. IEEE VR 2010 (2010)
19. Avanzini, F., Serafin, S., Rocchesso, D.: Interactive simulation of rigid body interaction with friction-induced sound generation. IEEE Transactions on Speech and Audio Processing 13(5 Part 2), 1073–1081 (2005)
20. Hunt, K.H., Crossley, F.R.E.: Coefficient of restitution interpreted as damping in vibroimpact. ASME Journal of Applied Mechanics 42(2), 440–445 (1975)
21. Avanzini, F., Rocchesso, D.: Modeling collision sounds: Non-linear contact force. In: Proc. COST-G6 Conf. Digital Audio Effects (DAFx 2001), pp. 61–66 (2001)
22. Dupont, P., Hayward, V., Armstrong, B., Altpeter, F.: Single state elastoplastic friction models. IEEE Transactions on Automatic Control 47(5), 787–792 (2002)
23. Cook, P.: Physically Informed Sonic Modeling (PhISM): Synthesis of Percussive Sounds. Computer Music Journal 21(3), 38–49 (1997)

Two-Hand Virtual Object Manipulation Based on Networked Architecture

Manuel Ferre[1], Ignacio Galiana[1], Jorge Barrio[1], Pablo García-Robledo[1],
Antonio Giménez[2], and Javier López[2]

[1] Universidad Politécnica de Madrid, Centro de Automática y Robótica (UPM-CSIC)
Jose Gutierrez Abascal 2, 28006 Madrid, Spain
[2] Universidad de Almería, Departamento de Ingeniería Rural, Área de Ingeniería Mecánica
Carretera de Sacramento s/n, 04120, La Cañada de San Urbano (Almería), Spain
{m.ferre,ignacio.galiana,jordi.barrio,p.grobledo}@upm.es,
{agimfer,javier.lopez}@ual.es

Abstract. A setup for bimanual virtual object manipulation is described in this paper. Index and thumb fingers are inserted in the corresponding thimbles in order to perform virtual object manipulations. A gimble, with 3-rotational degrees of freedom, connects each thimble to the corresponding serial-parallel mechanical structure with 3 actuated DoF. As a result, each finger has 6 DoF, movements and forces can be reflected in any direction without any torque component. Scenarios for virtual manipulation are based on distributed architecture where each finger device has its own real-time controller. A computer receives the status of each finger and runs a simulation with the virtual object manipulation. The information of the Scenario is updated at a rate of 200 Hz. The information from the haptic controller is processed at 1 kHz; it provides a good realism for object manipulation.

Keywords: Haptic devices, bimanual manipulation, multifinger devices, collaborative manipulation.

1 Introduction

The use of multi-finger haptic devices provides a higher realism in object manipulation; it also recreates virtual object interaction in a more natural and easy manner. A great step forward in virtual object manipulation has been achieved with only one contact point that simulates palpation or exploration of the virtual object surface. However, at least two contact points per hand are required in advanced manipulation tasks to grasp and properly handle objects. Relevant examples of this advanced manipulation can be found in applications such as telerobotics [1-2] and medical applications [3-4].

In this paper, a haptic interface called MasterFinger-2 (MF-2) [5] has been used for developing a bimanual setup. This setup consists of two MF-2 haptic devices. Workspace and main component of this setup are explained in section 2. Section 3 shows how scenarios are developed for virtual object manipulation considering multiple contact points. An example of a box manipulation is described in section 4 and conclusions are summarized in section 5.

A.M.L. Kappers et al. (Eds.): EuroHaptics 2010, Part II, LNCS 6192, pp. 130–135, 2010.

2 Setup Description

The mechanical structure was designed for the MasterFinger-2 haptic interface in order to enable object manipulation within a virtual environment. The setup design is based on a modular design, in which each finger represents a module managed as a haptic device. Fingers have 6 degrees of freedom (DoF) for movement; therefore any position and orientation can be achieved in the workspace. The first 3-DoFs are actuated by three DC motors. These actuators reflect forces in all directions. The last 3-DoFs are passive, these DoF have a gimble configuration. This gimble allows the end-effectors to be oriented towards any direction so as to increase capability of grasping and ease development of automatic tasks. Mechanical structure of both fingers is connected to the MF-2 base by using an additional actuator. This redundant actuator is located on the horizontal plane and provides an extra DoF to the interface, which significantly increases workspace. Fig. 1 shows the designed modular haptic interface and its workspace, redundant axis is in red. Main difference between MF-2 and the use of 2 common haptic devices can be seen in Fig.1.b and Fig.1.c. Fig.1.b represents the connection of 2 haptic devices (one per finger). Fig.1.c represents, however, the workspace of MF-2 where the redundant axis allows to significantly increase the available space for manipulation.

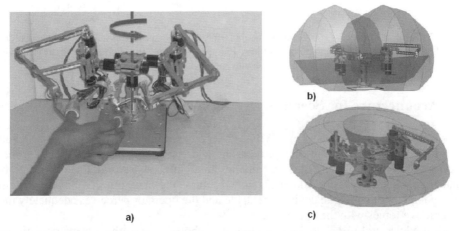

Fig. 1. MasterFinger-2 (a), it is used by inserting thumb and index in the corresponding thimbles. Workspace of each finger (b); workspace of the MF-2 including the additional DoF that allows rotation in a vertical axis (around the device base).

The bimanual setup is made up of two MasterFinger-2, as shown in Fig 2. According to the task configuration, the haptic interface can be used in its original position as shown in Fig.1, or in an inverted position as shown in Fig.2. The second configuration increases the dexterity to perform manual tasks since the central area is free of collisions among the device parts. In addition, the ability of touching, grasping, or moving an object using both hands increases. It provides users with a more realistic manipulation. The distance between both MF-2 bases varies depending on virtual object size. MF-2 base distance should be above 50 cm., so as to avoid collision between different hand's fingers. the distance between bases in Fig.2.b. is 55 cm., so there aren't collisions between both MF-2.

The volume where fingers are able to move considering this setup is shown in Fig.2.b. This workspace represents the area for free movements. In bimanual manipulation, each finger has to be inside its workspace. It implies several constraints in the area where the virtual object can be manipulated, since distance among fingers has to remain constant. As result, the workspace manipulating a box (as shown in Fig2.a) is significantly reduced regarding the workspace of free movements.

a)   b)

Fig. 2. Setup developed for bimanual manipulation (a), user is lifting a box. Workspace depends on the size of the manipulated object. Picture (b) shows the workspace for free movements; when an object is grasped by both hands, new constraints are to be evaluated.

3 Architecture for Scenario Development

The entire system is made up of 2 MF-2, several electronic boards (signal control and power), and software for data processing and scenario simulation. The proper performance of all of these elements implies an architectural design that can properly integrate them. Processing all signals in real time is the main objective of the system and guarantees that haptic devices are stable and the operator perceives adequately the interactive forces with the environment.

A modular and distributed architecture was chosen due to the advantages offered by a system with such characteristics. This design allow simplifying device controllers; it distributes large quantities of processed data, making the simulation faster. Furthermore, it gives the system great flexibility since this open architecture makes the simulation of a large number of applications within multimodal scenarios easier [6]. Each finger is treated as an independent haptic device. This device has its own controller, consisting of a Xilinx Virtex-5 FPGA [7], which closes the control loop of the mechanical device at 1kHz. At each loop step, a reading of the motor encoders and three gimble rotations take place so that finger positions and orientations can be obtained. Additionally, the values of other sensors (thimble contact sensors) are read and the motor electric flows are controlled in order to reflect the manipulation forces. Fig.3 shows the main modules of the architecture.

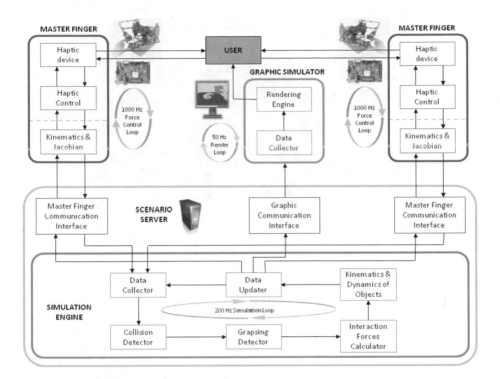

Fig. 3. Diagram of the software architecture required to perform bimanual object manipulation in real time. Each finger has its own controller that acts as a driver. All finger controllers send and received commands and data to the central computer, called scenario server. These data are transmitted via Ethernet.

4 Example of Two Hand Manipulation

The distributed architecture described in Section 3 allows the user to have as many MF-2 as needed thus Simple and complex manipulation tasks can be simulated by using this setup.

The Simulation Engine, integrates a collision detector as shown in Fig.3., this evaluates if two objects are colliding. There are two possible situations when a collision is detected: if both objects are virtual, they will react according to the collision, but if the collision is between the user's finger and a virtual object, the object will react and the MF-2 will exert the user the interaction force based on Hooke's law with dumping.

This collision detector also decides if the user is grabbing the virtual object or if the user is colliding with it.

Most simulations carried out so far focus on analyzing weight discrimination perception difference between grabbing virtual objects using one hand or two hands[8], cooperative tasks done by two users manipulating a common object [9] as shown in Fig.4., and study of trajectories and forces of usual grasping tasks [10].

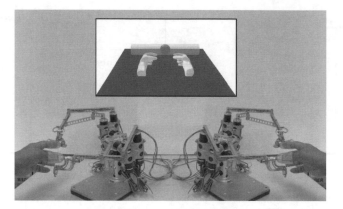

Fig. 4. Two users performing a cooperative task manipulating a cylindrical object, the goal is to cooperate to lift the cylinder and position the sphere in the middle of the cylinder

5 Conclusions

Common haptic interfaces have been used for touching and interacting with virtual environments by applying forces at a single point. More contact points have to be included in order to manipulate virtual objects in a more complex manner. For such purpose, a setup for multifinger haptic interaction has been designed. It allows grasping and manipulating virtual objects by using index and thumb fingers in a wide workspace. This setup proves to be an accurate instrument for manipulating virtual objects. A modular architecture has been implemented in order to run all required processes in real time. This architecture allows developing bimanual manipulation tasks in a more flexible and adaptable manner.

Acknowledgments

This work has been partially funded by the European Commission (IMMERSENCE FP6-IST-027141), and the Spanish *Ministerio de Ciencia e Innovación* (TEMAR, DPI2009-12283) and UPM's Formación de Personal Investigador (RR01/2009).

References

1. Endo, T., et al.: Five-Fingered Haptic Interface Robot: HIRO III. In: Proc. of World Haptics, Third Joint Eurohaptics Conference and Symposium on Haptic Interfaces for Virtual Environment and Teleoperator Systems, Salt Lake City, UT, USA, March 18-20, pp. 629–634 (2009)
2. Peer, A., Buss, M.: A New Admittance-Type Haptic Interface for Bimanual Manipulations. IEEE/ASME Transactions on Mechatronics 13(4), 416–428 (2008)
3. Waldron, K.J., Tollon, K.: Mechanical Characterization of the Immersion Corp. Haptic, Bimanual, Surgical Simulation Interface. In: Proc. of the 8th International Symposium on Experimental Robotics (ISER 2002), vol. 5, pp. 106–112 (2003)

4. Sun, L., van Meer, F., Bailly, Y., Yeung, C.K.: Design and Development of a da Vinci Surgical System Simulator. In: Proc. of the 2007 IEEE International Conference on Mechatronics and Automation, pp. 1050–1055 (2007)
5. Monroy, M., Oyarzabal, M., Ferre, M., Campos, A., Barrio, J.: MasterFinger: Multi-finger Haptic Interface for Collaborative Environments. In: Ferre, M. (ed.) EuroHaptics 2008. LNCS, vol. 5024, pp. 411–419. Springer, Heidelberg (2008)
6. García-Robledo, P., Ferre, M., Barrio, J., Ortego, J.: Advanced Virtual Manipulation based on Modular Haptic Devices. In: International Symposium on Robot Control (SYROCO 2009), pp. 111–116 (2009)
7. Virtex-V from Xilinx (2009), http://www.xilinx.com/products/devkits/HW-V5-L505-UNI-G.htm
8. Giachritsis, C., Barrio, J., Ferre, M., Wing, A., Ortego, J.: Evaluation of Weight Perception During Unimanual and Bimanual Manipulation of Virtual Objects. In: Proc. of World Haptics, Third Joint Eurohaptics Conference and Symposium on Haptic Interfaces for Virtual Environment and Teleoperator Systems, Salt Lake City, UT, USA, March 18-20, pp. 629–634 (2009)
9. Ferre, M., Oyarzábal, M., Campos, A., Monroy, M.: Multifinger Haptic Interfacesfor Collaborative Enviroments. In: Pavlidis, I. (ed.) Human Computer Interaction, pp. 101–112. InTech Education and Publishing (2008)
10. García-Robledo, P., Ortego, J., Ferre, M., Barrio, J., Sánchez-Urán, M.A.: Segmentation of Bimanual Virtual Object Manipulation Tasks using Multifinger Haptic Interfaces. IEEE Transaction on Instrumentation and Measurement (accepted for publication)

Validation of a Virtual Reality Environment to Study Anticipatory Modulation of Digit Forces and Position

Matteo Bianchi[1], Giorgio Grioli[1], Enzo Pasquale Scilingo[1],
Marco Santello[3], and Antonio Bicchi[1,2]

[1] Centro Interdipartimentale di Ricerca "E. Piaggio"
Facoltà di Ingegneria
Via Diotisalvi 2, 56126, Pisa, Italy
{matteo.bianchi,bicchi,giorgio.grioli,e.scilingo}@centropiaggio.unipi.it
http://www.piaggio.ccii.unipi.it
[2] Istituto Italiano di Tecnologia (IIT)
Via Morego 30, 16163, Genova, Italy
http://www.iit.it
[3] Department of Kinesiology, School of Biological and Health Systems Engineering
Arizona State University
Tempe, AZ (USA) 85287-0404
marco.santello@asu.edu
http://kinesiology.clas.asu.edu

Abstract. The aim of this paper is to validate a virtual reality (VR) environment for the analysis of the sensorimotor processes underlying learning of object grasping and manipulation. This study was inspired by recent grasping studies indicating that subjects learn skilled manipulation by concurrently modulating digit placement and forces as a function of the position of object center of mass (CM) in an anticipatory fashion, i.e. by modulating a compensatory moment before the onset of object manipulation (object lift onset). Data from real and virtual grasping showed a similar learning trend of digit placement and forces, resulting in successful object roll minimization. Therefore, the overall behavioral features associated with learning real object manipulation were successfully replicated by the present VR environment. The validation of our VR experimental approach is an important preliminary step towards studying more complex hand-object interactions.

Keywords: VR environment, object grasping, object manipulation, anticipatory grasp control.

1 Introduction

The control of grasping and manipulation in humans has been extensively studied [1]. Two main modes of control are generally recognized: one based on sensorimotor memories, allowing for anticipatory grasp control, and another that relies on online sensing, leading to reactive control (for review see [1]). Anticipatory grasp control has traditionally been quantified by measuring digit forces between contact and the onset of object manipulation (e.g [5]). Examples of reactive grasp control are the force upgrades

A.M.L. Kappers et al. (Eds.): EuroHaptics 2010, Part II, LNCS 6192, pp. 136–143, 2010.

occurring shortly after the onset of object slip [7] or the detection of an unexpected texture shortly after contact [6]. It has been recently shown that anticipatory control of grasping is not limited to digit forces, but extends to digit placement [2,8]. Specifically, when subjects are aware that object properties (object center of mass) do not change across consecutive trials, they modulate digit position before object lift-off in parallel with digit forces, both of these variables being instrumental for preventing object roll during the lift [2,3,4]. The functional role of the anticipatory modulation of digit placement appears to be the optimization of digit force distributions [3]. Furthermore, learning of digit placement and force modulation to object center of mass occurs within one or two trials [3,4]. Such quick learning is likely to depend on the integration of several sensory modalities such as vision (digit placement and object roll), tactile input (forces at and during manipulation), and proprioception (hand shape, relative distance between the digits). However, due to the fact that object manipulation is learned very quickly, it is challenging to dissociate experimentally the role of each sensory modality when manipulating real objects. Virtual reality environments are particularly suited to pursue this question as they allow varying the weight of specific sensory modalities by introducing noise to the perceptual and/or motor processes [9,10]. The present study focused on creating a VRE that could be used to quantify the effect(s) of individual sensory modalities on learning object manipulation. Here we describe human subjects' performance using our VRE in relation to previously published data on manipulation of real objects. We found that subjects in the VRE exhibited anticipatory control of digit forces and position. Furthermore, subjects learned object manipulation in a quantitatively similar fashion as reported by previous studies of manipulation of real objects [3,4]. In these papers, we found that (a) subjects exert a compensatory moment in the direction opposite to that of the external moment generated by a mass added to the object; (b) this compensatory moment is learned within the first 2-3 object lifts; (c) subjects generate the external moment by modulating both digit placement and forces; (d) the digit on the side of the added mass is placed higher than the other digit. Therefore the VRE proposed in the present study offers promising avenues for research into the neural processes underlying the integration of multiple sensory modalities responsible for learning and control of object manipulation.

2   Materials and Methods

2.1   Subjects

Twelve healthy right-handed volunteers (6 females and 6 males, their age ranged from 23 to 33) with normal or corrected-to-normal vision participated in the study. Each subject gave informed consent to participate in the study according to the Declaration of Helsinki, and the experimental procedures were approved by the Institutional Review Board at University of Pisa. All subjects were naive to the experimental purpose of the study.

2.2   Experimental Task

We asked subjects to reach, grasp, lift, and replace a virtual object with their right hand. The object consisted of a vertical block attached to a rectangular base (see Fig.1(b))

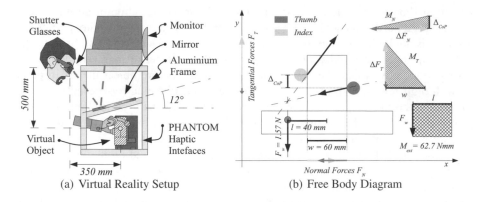

(a) Virtual Reality Setup   (b) Free Body Diagram

Fig. 1. Panel (a) shows the experimental setup. Two PHANTOM desktop devices were attached to the tip of the thumb and the index finger to generate haptic perception of a solid object. The tip of the two digits and the 3D image of the virtual object were visually rendered on a computer monitor and projected through a mirror. Panel (b) shows the free-body diagram of the virtual object and the variables of interest measured by the haptic interface. M_{ext} was produced by applying a suitable force F_w at a distance l from the midpoint of the object base. In condition of equilibrium: $M_{ext} = M_N + M_T$, where M_N and M_T were produced, respectively, by normal and tangential forces exerted by subjects.

similar to the real object we used in previous studies [3,4]. In the manipulation task of real objects, that was simulated in the present work, the behavioral consequences of anticipatory modulation of digit positions and forces are confined primarily to the frontal plane. This is because the added mass introduces an external torque in the frontal plane, whereas it negligibly affects the orientation of the object in the sagittal or horizontal plane during object lift. Therefore, manipulation in our VR was simulated to occur in the frontal plane only by preventing motion in the sagittal plane. Subjects were asked to perform the task using the fingertips of the thumb and the index finger. Note that no instructions were given about where to grasp the object along its vertical sides. Although the visual appearance of the object remained invariant throughout the experiment, an external moment (M_{ext}) of 62.72 Nmm was imposed in order to replicate the change in the center of mass (CM) in the experiment conducted in [2]. In [2], the CM of an inverted T-shaped object, consisting of a cylinder attached to a horizontal base, was changed by adding a mass in one of three slots at the base of the object. According to the position of the slot situated from the midpoint of the object base, the CM locations were indicated as left (thumb side) LCM, center CCM, and right (finger side) RCM, respectively. The same naming was used in this work, considering now the sign of the external moment; LCM for a negative M_{ext}, RCM for a positive M_{ext} and CCM for a M_{ext} equal to 0 (see Fig.1(b)). The only task requirement was to minimize object roll caused by M_{ext} while lifting the object vertically (5–10 cm above the virtual horizontal plane). During the task, subjects were comfortably seated and with the forearm resting on a table. Subjects were instructed to initiate the reach after a verbal signal from the experimenter and perform the task at a self-selected, natural speed. The experiment consisted of three blocks of six trials per CM. On each trial, subjects were provided with the visual-haptic object with a given pre-imposed CM. Each block corresponded to a position of CM. Before starting data collection, subjects were provided with three practice trials for the CCM condition, to allow them to familiarize with the virtual environment. These practice trials were not included in the data set used for analysis. At the beginning of each block, subjects were informed that the object CM was going to be changed, but they were not told the actual CM location. Subjects were also informed that the object CM location would be the same for the entire block of trials. Therefore, on the first object lift subjects were unable to anticipate the direction of M_{ext} before object lift-off. On following trials, however, we expected subjects to anticipate the CM location by generating a compensatory moment (M_{com}; see below) before lift-off. The order of CM presentation was randomized and counterbalanced across subjects. To prevent fatigue, we gave subjects rest periods of 10 seconds and 1 minute between trials and CM blocks, respectively.

2.3   Virtual Object

We presented the virtual object through stereoscopic visualization and haptic rendering. The image of the virtual object was visually rendered such that its visually and haptically perceived locations coincided, thus enabling the integration of these two sensory modalities. The visual feedback of the rendered scene was displayed on a monitor and reflected by a tilted mirror to allow co-allocation of visual and haptic stimuli, in front of the subjects, at a suitable reaching distance (see Fig.1(a)). Haptic rendering of the virtual object was obtained using two PHANTOM Desktop devices [11]. The algorithm for visuo-haptic rendering (and for both positioning of the object in the virtual scene and determination of the fingertips positions) is based on the standard ones contained in the PHANTOM Device software library. The two fingertips are modelled as two spheres with 9 mm radius, whose centers are located in correspondence of the endpoints of the two devices (where the centers of the two real fingertips are). The position resolution of the PHANTOM device is ~ 0.023 mm. The contact model is based on the standard linear visco-elastic contact point model used by the PHANTOM Device software library. The chosen friction coefficient is $\mu = 1.5$, the elastic constant of the surface is $K_e = 0.5$ N/mm. The mass of the simulated mass is equal to $M = 0.16$ Kg and the acceleration of gravity is the same as in the real world $g = 9.8$ m/s^2. Considering that the virtual object is constrained to move in the frontal plane (distance from the subject $\simeq 50\%$ length of the subject's arm, as in the studies with real objects), both the angular momentum and the inertial tensor reduce to scalar quantities. The magnitude of the rotational inertial forces is much smaller than the magnitude of the other forces involved in the experiment. Rotational inertia of the simulated body is equal to 0.64 Kg$\cdot cm^2$.

2.4   Data Recording and Experimental Variables

The virtual environment was rendered at a frequency of about 75 Hz (non-noticeable jitter with a variance inferior to 1 μs). The haptic stimuli were rendered by an autonomous software thread running at a fixed frequency of 1 kHz. The time constant of the main rendering dominates both synchronization issues and sampling rate of position and force. The Phantom interface has a nominal position resolution of about 0.023 mm inside its workspace. This datum, and the stiffness of the virtual object ($K = 0.4$ N/mm), allows for a force resolution of about 9.2 mN. Recorded data consist of an array of five tuples of elements of the type

$$t_i = (Thb_i, Ind_i, Trj_i, Rll_i, t_i);$$

where, for each temporal instant i: Thb and Ind contain the three-dimensional coordinates of thumb and index finger, respectively (from these variables, the vertical distance between contact points, i.e. Δ_{CoP}, was computed); Trj_i and Rll_i contain the spatial coordinates of the cylinder and its roll angle and t_i records the temporal i-instant, from the beginning of the trial.

After recording, data were re-sampled at a fixed frequency of 50 Hz and smoothed using a 4th order filter. Tangential forces exerted by each digit were used to compute the difference between tangential forces (ΔF_T). Anticipatory grasp control was quantified by measuring peak object roll during object lift. For details on the rationale and interpretation of these variables see [2,4].

3   Results

Fig(2) shows representative data from the first, second and sixth trial performed by one subject (right object CM, RCM). Although on the first trial this subject exerted nearly zero compensatory moment (M_{TOT}, bottom trace) at object lift onset (first vertical dashed line), he was able to exert a compensatory moment that gradually approached the external moment (horizontal dash-dotted line) on subsequent trials at object lift-off. The compensatory moment was generated by exerting a larger digit tangential force (F_T) with the index finger than the thumb, while raising the index finger center of pressure (CoP) relative to the thumb CoP. As a result, this subject learned to reduce object roll during the lift.

3.1   Object Roll Minimization

The trial-to-trial changes in compensatory moment and peak object roll described in Fig.2 were common to all subjects Fig.3(b). Specifically, subjects learned to generate compensatory moments as a function of object CM and trial (main effect of both factors: $P < 0.01$). As expected, subjects generated little or no compensatory moment in the CCM condition (interaction CM x Trial, $P < 0.01$). The generation of a compensatory moment at object lift onset resulted in successful minimization of peak object roll during the lift (main effect of Trial, $P < 0.01$; Fig.3(a)), more so for the asymmetrical CMs than the CCM (interaction CM x Trial, $P < 0.05$). Note that these results are nearly identical to those reported by studies of the same task with real objects [3,4].

3.2   Digit Placement and Digit Forces

The compensatory moment is a function of CoP, F_N and F_T. To further examine how subjects learned anticipatory control of the compensatory moment, we performed separate analyses of its three components. Through consecutive lifts, subjects learned to

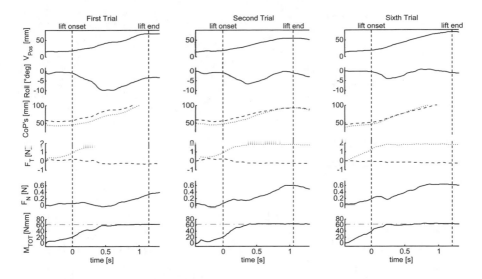

Fig. 2. Grasp performance (object roll) is shown for the first, second, and sixth trial together with object lift (V_{Pos}), digit centers of pressure ($CoPs$, blue dashed line for the thumb and red dotted line for the index finger, respectively), forces (tangential forces of each finger F_T and Average grip force F_N) net moment exerted by the digits (M_{TOT}) relative to the external moment (green dash-dot line).

separate the vertical distance between the thumb and index finger as a function of object CM ($P < 0.01$ and 0.05, respectively). Subjects adapt the CoP in trials of the LCM and RCM type (significant interaction CM x Trial, $P < 0.01$; Fig.3(c)) but not for CCM trials. Similarly, subjects use asymmetrical digit load forces that varied as a function of trial and object CM ($P < 0.01$ and 0.05, respectively), the tangential force difference (ΔF_T) being smallest for the left than right and center CM (Fig.3(d)). Note that an opposite effect of CM was found for the difference of the CoP position for thumb and index (Δ_{CoP}). The Δ_{CoP} is larger for LCM than for RCM (Fig.3(c)). In contrast, the sum of digit normal forces did not change systematically with trials ($P > 0.05$). The trial-to-trial changes in digit CoP and forces as a function of object CM, as well as the inverse relation between Δ_{CoP} and ΔF_T, resemble the results reported by previous work with real objects [3,4].

4   Discussion

The present study was designed to validate a VR environment for the study of object grasping and manipulation. The design of the task was inspired by recent grasping studies indicating that subjects learn to modulate digit placement and forces as a function of object CM [1,3]. The focus of these studies was on anticipatory grasp control, i.e., on the modulation of the compensatory moment before object lift onset. Note that the above cited studies of two-digit [3,4] and five-digit grasping [2] used objects that

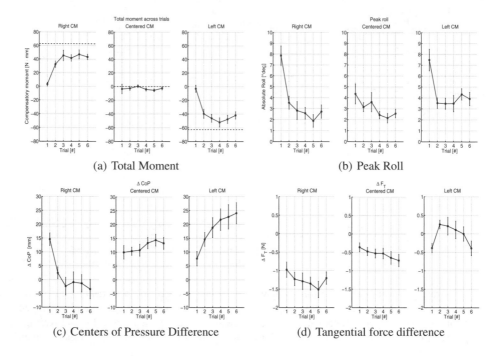

(a) Total Moment

(b) Peak Roll

(c) Centers of Pressure Difference

(d) Tangential force difference

Fig. 3. Panel (a) and (b) show the compensatory moment exerted at object lift onset and peak object roll, respectively, as a function of object center of mass and trial. Panel (c) and (d) show, respectively, The difference between thumb and index finger center of pressure (Δ_{CoP}) and tangential force difference (ΔF_T) as a function of object center of mass and trial. All data are averages of all subjects ($\pm S.E.$).

were significantly heavier (over 10-fold) than the object rendered by our haptic interface. Consequently, previous studies examined the effect of significantly larger external moments on anticipatory grasp control. This difference might account for some differences between present and previous results. Specifically, in previous work subjects used a larger digit CoP for right than left CM, whereas opposite results were found for the VR data. Nevertheless, data from real and virtual grasping showed a similar learning trend of digit placement and forces, resulting in successful object roll minimization. Hence, the overall behavioral features associated with learning real object manipulation were replicated by the present VR environment. The validation of our experimental approach is an important preliminary step towards studying more complex hand-object interactions.

Acknowledgments. This work has been partially supported by the European Commission with the Collaborative Project no. 248587, "THE Hand Embodied", within the FP7-ICT-2009-4-2-1 program "Cognitive Systems and Robotics". The authors wish to thank Qiushi Fu, MS (Department of Kinesiology, Arizona State University) for his comments on analyses and an earlier version of the manuscript.

References

1. Johansson, R.S., Flanagan, J.R.: Coding and use of tactile signals from the fingertips in object manipulation tasks. Nat. Rev. Neurosci. 10, 345–359 (2009)
2. Lukos, J., Ansuini, C., Santello, M.: Choice of contact points during multi-digit grasping. Effect of predictability of center of mass location. Journal of Neuroscience 96, 3894–3903 (2007)
3. Fu, Q., Zhang, W., Santello, M.: Anticipatory Planning and Control of Grasp Positions and Forces for Dexterous Two-Digit Manipulation. Journal of Neuroscience (accepted pending minor revisions)
4. Zhang, W., Gordon, A.M., Qiushi Fu, Q., Santello, M.: Manipulation after object rotation reveals independent sensorimotor memory representations of digit positions and forces. Journal of Neurophysiology (in Press)
5. Johansson, R.S., Westling, G.: Coordinated isometric muscle commands adequately and erroneously programmed for the weight during lifting task with precision grip. Experimental Brain Research 71, 59–71 (1988)
6. Johansson, R.S., Westling, G.: Roles of glabrous skin receptors and sensorimotor memory in automatic control of precision grip when lifting rougher or more slippery objects. Experimental Brain Research 56, 550–564 (1984)
7. Johansson, R.S., Westling, G.: Signals in tactile afferents from the fingers eliciting adaptive motor responses during precision grip. Experimental Brain Research 66, 141–154 (1987)
8. Lukos, J.R., Ansuini, C., Santello, M.: Anticipatory control of grasping: independence of sensorimotor memories for kinematics and kinetics. Journal of Neuroscience 28, 12765–12774 (2008)
9. Ernst, M.O., Banks, M.S.: Humans integrate visual and haptic information in a statistically optimal fashion. Nature 415, 429–433 (2002)
10. Kording, K.P., Wolpert, D.M.: Bayesian integration in sensorimotor learning. Nature 427, 244–247 (2004)
11. Sensable Technologies, Woburn, MA, USA, http://www.sensable.com

On Multi-resolution Point-Based Haptic Rendering of Suture

Wen Shi and Shahram Payandeh

Experimental Robotics and Graphics Laboratory, School of Engineering Science,
Simon Fraser University, 8888 University drive, Burnaby, Canada
{wsa18,shahram}@cs.sfu.ca

Abstract. In this paper we present a point based potential field mechanics model for suture interaction. We study extended models to represent suture behaviors such as bending, stretching, twisting, which can be used in haptic rendering of knotting and unknotting tasks. In this paper, one-dimensional single point-samples and adaptive point-samples are studied and compared. In the adaptive model description, we develop a novel LOD(Level of detail) and re-sampling method using fluid particle flow model. A multi-resolution suture model is constructed based on the proposed LOD. Experimental studies demonstrate the feasibility of our proposed model for knotting and unknotting of the suture and can offer an adaptive and stable modeling environment for both graphic and haptic rendering. In addition, through the tuning of several key parameters, different material behavior such as elasticity can be obtained.

Keywords: point based potential field, SPH(Smoothed Particle Hydrodynamic), fluid flow LOD(Level of Details), adaptive knotting unknotting.

1 Introduction

There exist a number of works which address the haptic rendering of suture/rope. [1] modeled the string to be a rigid chain of links and joints, where during the dynamic simulation, constraining forces such as gravity forces and user input forces are added. In general, variations on single dimension mass-spring model or linear finite element model have been used for modeling ropes, sutures or strings [2] [3]. An approach based on exact dynamics splines which can also offer a real time performance is presented in [4]. However the method fails to provide a framework for accomplishing computational efficiency needed for adaptive resolution framework. [5] presented a spline-based model and [6] presents the adaptive resolution 1D B-spline approach. Through moving a Frenet frame along a thin solid, a specific energy term measuring stretching and twisting deformation is obtained based on Cosserat theory [7] [9]. However, this approach may have drawback when being extended to the case of interactive haptic rendering. [8] presents a model based on Super-Helices, which can capture the behavior of the hair string naturally and smoothly. However, the implementation is computationally complex and do not offer an interactive haptic framework. [10] proposed a modified Finite Element Method suitable for multi-resolution simulation of deformable objects, but which didn't incorporate haptic interaction. [11] also created an adaptive model for dynamically deforming hyper-elastic rods, which doesn't incorporate haptic interaction.

A.M.L. Kappers et al. (Eds.): EuroHaptics 2010, Part II, LNCS 6192, pp. 144–151, 2010.
© Springer-Verlag Berlin Heidelberg 2010

2   Modeling Overview

2.1   Governing Mechanics Model

Potential field mechanical model is first introduced for deformable object simulation in [12], where deformable object is considered to be a collection of points and the deformation is represented by the change of the potential energy of the points due to the influence of external forces. In comparison with mass spring model, there are no pre-defined fixed artificial springs defined between the vertices and the interaction forces between points are defined implicitly. In addition, the potential field can be constructed in such a way that it can be related to the mechanics model and to the elastic potential energy. Different from [12] where 3D object is modeled as potential forces propagating around the 3D volume, we model the 1D suture thread to be a spatially coupled point system and compute the field potential forces between the pairs of points.

The motion of the suture thread is the summation of the motion of each point inside the suture thread. The behaviour of each point can be governed by the linear ordinary differential equation of motion:

$$m_i \ddot{x}_i + \gamma \dot{x}_i + f_i^{int} = f_i^{ext}, \tag{1}$$

where m_i is the mass of each point; $\ddot{x}_i$ and $\dot{x}_i$ are the acceleration and velocity of each point respectively; γ is the damping coefficient; f_i^{int} and f_i^{ext} are the internal and external forces respectively. External forces can be gravity force and user interaction force. Here, the internal force is calculated through the governing definition of potential field model. In order to localize the calculation of the potential energy, a weighting function is implemented [12]. However unlike [12] that dealt with 3D deformable object, of which the points are distributed symmetrically in the controlled volumes, in our 1D suture thread simulation, the mechanical relationships between points are restricted to the order of the points along the length of suture. For example, we can modify the potential calculation of the ith point to only incorporate the two closed neighbors of it as in equation (2) figure (1(a)).

$$\phi_i = \phi(r_{i(i-1)}) + \phi(r_{i(i+1)}) \tag{2}$$

The choice of the potential function is critical to the model. There are several candidates such as elastic potential energy function, electrical potential energy function and Lennard-Jones potential energy function. Among the candidates we choose Lennard-Jones potential model for representation of suture. For example, when a sutre is being fully stretched, it is hard to increase its length. However when the suture is being compressed from two ends along its length, it will buckle along its pushed direction and it can form a knot. On the other hand Lennard-Jones potential function can create long range attraction force and short range repulsion force, which is more suitable for modeling suture properties mentioned above. In this paper, Lennard-Jones bi-reciprocal function is implemented to calculate the potentials,

$$\phi(r) = \frac{-e_0}{m-n}\left(m\left(\frac{r_0}{r}\right)^n\right) - n\left(\frac{r_0}{r}\right)^m)), \tag{3}$$

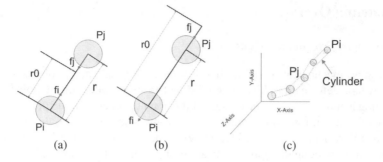

(a)   (b)   (c)

Fig. 1. Potential model parameters for suture simulation, (a) When the distance r between two particles is larger than the nominal distance r_0, potential force act as attraction force; (b)When the distance r between two particles is less than equilibrium distance r_0, potential force act as repulsion force; (c) the suture model, where the cylinders between particles are for visualization rendering

where m and n are two tunable parameters which affect the rate of change of the potential in terms of r, and e_0 is the balance potential when distance r between two points reaches the balance distance r_0. Finally, the overall force on each point is calculated as,

$$f_i = -\nabla_{r_i}\phi_i; \qquad (4)$$

One drawback of Lennard-Jones potential field is that when the distance between two neighboring suture points is larger than r_0, the magnitude of the attraction force is not sufficient to generate the effect that the suture thread is hard to be stretched when it reaches its full length. A modified expression for equation (4) is introduced with the added term $\frac{r}{|r|}e^{\alpha\frac{r-r_0}{r_0}}$ where the parameter α can be adjusted.

$$f_i = -\nabla_{r_i}\phi_i + \frac{r}{|r|}e^{\alpha\frac{r-r_0}{r_0}}; \qquad (5)$$

Figure 1(a) to 1(c) illustrate the notions used in potential field definition of suture model. Another key advantage of the potential field model is that it is easy to be stabilized when the internal structure (internal points) of the object are adaptively modified. The only adjustment that needs to be made is the distance r_0 for various modified points. Using this feature, in the next section we have proposed the adaptive suture model.

Table 1. Initial conditions for fluid flow simulation. The solid lines are the original suture segment shapes; The dotted lines are the trajectory of the fluid particles. Through tuning the initial conditions such as the artificial gravity force and initial velocity, we can obtain various fluid particle trajectory and the corresponding sample points.

Tuning fluid flow$(v(cm/s),g(N/s^2))$			
case 1 $v=0.2$, $g=9.8$	case 2 $v=1.0$, $g=9.8$	case 3 $v=0.5$, $g=9.8$	case 4 $v=0.2$, $g=2.6$
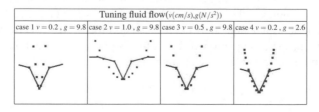			

2.2   Adaptive Suture Thread Model

The main motivation for developing an adaptive suture model is to increase the sense of realism in computational mechanics model, graphical visualization and the haptic interaction. In order to establish such model, we utilize the curvature evaluation technique [16]. Here we define $c_i = \frac{1}{2}(P_iP_{i-1} \cdot P_iP_{i+1})$ where P_iP_{i-1} and P_iP_{i+1} are two suture segments between the consecutive i^{th} suture points, respectively. Our adaptive suture simulation is inspired by the smooth representation of the fluid particle motion in a laminar flow. The upsampling along the 1D suture direction is achieved by initializing the fluid flow at a location of high curvature region of the suture and adding fluid particles along the desired path of the suture (Figure 2).

The motion of the fluid is governed by the the the following equation [17],

$$\dot{v} = \frac{f_{pressure}}{\rho} + \frac{f_{viscous}}{\rho} + \frac{f_{external}}{\rho} \tag{6}$$

Where ρ is density, $\dot{v}$ is the acceleration of a fluid particle along a streamline. Force created by the change in pressure can be calculated as the negative pressure differences $f_{pressure} = -\nabla P$. Here pressure P is computed as $P = k((\frac{\rho}{\rho_0})^\gamma - 1)$ [14], where ρ_0 is the standard density of the fluid under the standard atmosphere pressure, k is a constant

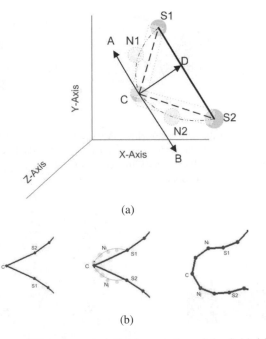

(a)

(b)

Fig. 2. LOD in suture modeling concept. (a)Implementation of the fluid driven LOD based on practical fluid flow simulation. Fluid flow simulation will start at point C when the curvature at C is larger than a pre-set threshold. CA and CB are the initial velocity vectors of the fluid particles starting at C. The two arc lines represent the trajectory of the fluid flow, and the semi-transparent points are the new particles, (ie. Ni and Nj are sampled points from the generated fluid particle points). (b) examples of adaptive suture model.

through which we can modify the incompressibility of the fluid, γ is a constant which also affects the compressibility. Low value of γ models the fluid particles to be more compressible. Acceleration caused by viscosity effect is defined as $\frac{f_{viscous}}{\rho} = \mu \Delta v$ [15]. The external force $f_{external}$ in equation (6) can be an artificial gravity force, of which the direction can be changed depending on the different shape of the high curvature. In order to compute the continuous function (equation (6)) on each discretized fluid particle, a computational tool is needed. SPH (Smoothed Particle Hydrodynamics) is introduced for this purpose since it can perform continuous calculation such as differentiation of a discretized function[13].

Figure 2(a) illustrates the actual computations carried out when the fluid flow model is implemented in the actual adaptive suture model simulation. Here, the artificial gravity force vector is defined with the direction given by $CD = S_1 S_2 \times (CS_1 \times CS_2)$. As a result, through tuning the magnitudes of the initial velocity vectors and the gravity force vector, different fluid flow can be obtained (Table 1).

We have implemented a binary search tree hierarchy for a fixed segment model of suture and detect the collisions between the suture segments using a binary search algorithm, figure 3(a) and 3(b). In the adaptive multi-resolution model, we add the newly defined particle points dynamically into the binary search tree, and update the collision detection hierarchy immediately figure 3(c) and 3(d).

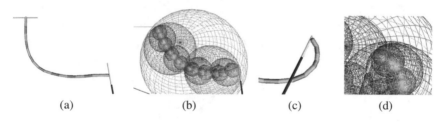

(a)   (b)   (c)   (d)

Fig. 3. Collision detection for the suture model. (a) A fixed resolution suture model. (b) A binary search tree collision detection hierarchy for the suture model. (c)Adaptive suture model, where newly created points are added. (d)The binary tree collision detection hierarchy is also adaptive and is updated when new points are added.

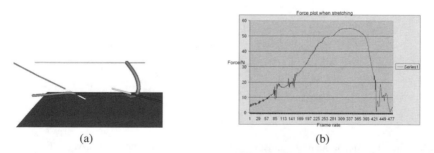

(a)   (b)

Fig. 4. Haptic Suture interaction based on Point-based Potential field mechanical model, (a) User interaction while stretching, when the suture is stretched to its full length, and can not be stretched any further; (b) The plot of corresponding to uncalibrated computed haptic reaction force when stretching.

3   A Case Study

Our simulation was implemented on a PC with Intel(R) Pentium(R) 4 3.00GHz CPU, 1.00 GB RAM, and Geforce 9500GT graphic card. We first present several results of the fixed resolution suture model based on potential field mechanics. In this study, the resolution is set to be 30 suture points. Figure 4 displays the stretching manipulation and the corresponding haptic force feedback plot. Figure 5(a) to 5(d) demonstrate the adaptive suture model under user interaction involving in tying a knot. As can be

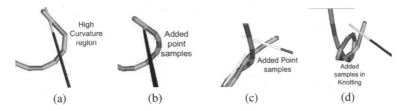

(a)   (b)   (c)   (d)

Fig. 5. Illustration of the adaptive suture model, (a) high curvature is about to occur in the specified region; (b) New sample points generated by fluid flow simulation are added to the highly curved region to smoothen both graphic and haptic rendering results; (c) The user is pulling one end of the suture and try to bend it across the knot; (d)The knot is tied.

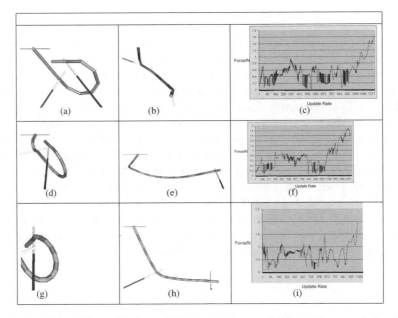

Fig. 6. LOD model stability validation, which is carried out on 3 different base resolution. We perform bending and stretching as test experiments. The results include the action scenes and force plot. (a)-(c): Base resolution 1 (5 suture segments). The number of suture segments increased to 9; (d)-(f): Base resolution 2(10 suture segments). The number of suture segments increased to 18; (g)-(i): Base resolution 3(15 suture segments). The number of suture segments increased to 21.

observed when two suture segments collide, they won't penetrate each other. This is due to the fact that according to equation (2), the potential field model of a suture at a point is only affected by its two closest neighbors. In addition, when two suture segments collide, we also introduce additional repulsive force field between the segments. As a results the two suture segments do not penetrate each other.

To illustrate the stability of model, an experimental study is performed by bending and stretching for different suture resolution. Figures 6(a) to 6(i) display the comparative experimental study. The results are categorized into 3 cases whose base resolutions are 5, 10 and 15 suture segments respectively. Base resolutions are the original fixed resolution of the suture. After performing bending, additional points are added into the original suture model and this modified model is used for further stretching. Based on the feedback force plot, we can observe that the LOD adaptive suture model did not cause any instability [18].

4   Discussion and Conclusions

There are mainly two key constants which can significantly change the material property of the suture: the stiffness constant and the number of neighborhood pairs of points. Larger values of stiffness constant result in larger body stiffness which can cause the suture to be difficult to bend. The exponential parameter α in equation (5) can affect the elasticity of the suture body. Large value of α results in less stretchability of the suture. As a results, it can be possible to tune these parameters for creating more realistic suture model.

The initial conditions(combinations of initial velocity and artificial gravity force) of the fluid flow simulation for upsampling are also critical. As discussed in table 1, different values of initial conditions can affect the upsampling technique.

Based on the point based mechanical framework, we developed an efficient LOD(Level of Detail) adaptive suture model. Compared with other existing LOD techniques for both 3D and 1D objects, our proposed method is based on the fluid flow model. The smooth laminar fluid particle flow can be used to ensure both smooth graphical visualization and haptic force feedback. The real-time experimental implementation of the proposed approach for LOD has shown the stable increase in both the effective haptic feedback rate and the level of realism when needed (e.g. closed-loop haptic feedback rate of about 800Hz). However it was observed that when new point samples are being added, there exist a sudden but small decaying oscillatory in haptic force feedback. As a part of the future work, one can investigate an implement of a low-pass filter for negating such unwanted oscillations.

References

1. Brown, J., Montgomery, K., Latombe, J.-C., Stephanides, M.: A microsurgery simulation system. In: Niessen, W.J., Viergever, M.A. (eds.) MICCAI 2001. LNCS, vol. 2208, p. 137. Springer, Heidelberg (2001)
2. LeDuc, M., Payandeh, S., Dill, J.: Toward modeling of a suture task. In: Graphics Interface (GI), Halifax, Nova Scotia, pp. 273–279 (2003)

3. Shi, H.F., Payandeh, S.: Real-Time Knotting and Unknotting. In: IEEE International Conference on Robotic Automation (ICRA 2007), April 10-14, pp. 2570–2575 (2007)
4. Theetten, A., Grisoni, L., Andriot, C., Barsky, B.: Geometrically exact dynamic splines. Computer-Aided Design 40, 35–48 (2008)
5. Lenoir, J., Meseure, P., Grisoni, L., Chaillou, C.: Surgical thread simulation. In: Modelling and Simulation for Computer-aided Medecine and Surgery (MS4CMS), Rocquencourt, INRIA, EDP Sciences, vol. 12, pp. 102–107 (November 2002)
6. Lenoir, J., Grisoni, l., Meseure, P.: Adaptive resolution of 1D mechanical B-spline. In: Proceedings of the 3rd International Conference on Computer Graphics and Interactive Techniques in Australasia and South East Asia, pp. 395–403 (2005)
7. Pai, D.: Strands: Interactive simulation of thin solids using cosserat models. In: Proceedings of EUROGRAPHICS 2002, Computer Graphics Forum, vol. 21(3) (September 2002)
8. Bertails, F., Audoly, B., Cani, M.-P., Querleux, B., Leroy, F., Lvque, J.-L.: Super-Helices for Predicting the Dynamics of Natural Hair. ACM Transactions on Graphics, Proceedings of the SIGGRAPH Conference (August 2006)
9. Bertails, F., Audoly, B., Querleux, B., Leroy, F., Lvque, J.-L., Cani, M.-P.: Predicting Natural Hair Shapes by Solving the Statics of Flexible Rods. In: EUROGRAPHICS 2005 (2005)
10. Grinspun, E., Krysl, P., Schroder, P.: CHARMS: A Simple Framework for Adaptive Simulation. In: Proceedings of the 29th Annual Conference on Computer Graphics and Interactive Techniques, pp. 281–290 (2002)
11. Spillmann, J., Teschner, M.: An Adaptive Contact Model for the Robust Simulation of Knots. In: EUROGRAPHICS 2008, vol. 27(2) (2008)
12. Tonnesen, D.: Spatially coupled particle system. In: SIGGRAPH 1992 Course 16 Notes: Particle System Modeling, Animation, and Physically Based Techniques, pp. 4.1–4.21 (1992)
13. Monaghan, J.J.: Smoothed Particle hydrodynamics. Annu. Rev. Astron. Physics 30, 543 (1992)
14. Monaghan, J.J.: Simulating free surface flows with SPH. J. Comput. Phys. 110(2), 399–406 (1994)
15. Muller, M., Charypa, D., Gross, M.: Particle-based fluid simulation for interactive application. In: Eurographics/SIGGRAPH Symposium on Computer Animation, pp. 154–159 (2003)
16. Grisoni, L., Marchal, D.: High Performance generalized cylinders visualization. In: Proceedings of the Shape Modeling International 2003, SMI 2003 (2003)
17. Crowe, C.T., Roberson, J.A.: Engineering Fluid Mechanics. Houghton Mifflin Co., Boston (1975)
18. Shi, W.: Point-Based suture simulation demo, http://www.sfu.ca/~wsa18

Study of Performances of "Haptic Walls" Modalities for a 3D Menu

Antonio Capobianco[1] and Caroline Essert[1,2]

[1] Université de Strasbourg / LSIIT, F-67412 Illkirch Cedex, France
[2] INRIA, Campus de Beaulieu, F-35042 Rennes, France
a.capobianco@unistra.fr, essert@unistra.fr

Abstract. We introduce a new technique of haptic guidance for item selection in 3D menus for VR applications called "haptic walls". It consists in haptically rendering a solid funnel to guide the pointer towards a target located in the angle. We designed a 3D haptic menu using this approach: a thin polyhedral shape with the items at the corners. The "haptic walls" are experimented with 2 different shapes of polyhedra, and compared to 2 reference conditions. We propose the results of our first empirical evaluation of this technique.

Keywords: Computer-Human interfaces, Haptic I/O, Menus, Interaction techniques, Performance evaluation.

1 Introduction

Haptically enhanced interaction for guidance (in the sense of Miller and Zeleznik, [7]) mainly relies on "snap-to" effects. They can be local magnetic effects around a target that actively captures the pointer if it enters a specific area [8], or can behave as a gradient force all over the environment [11] to draw the pointer towards points of interest. For object selection, magnetic targets can help by reducing selection times and error rates [1]. However some studies report benefits from magnetic widgets to precision but not to selection times [12]. Moreover, these techniques seem to lead to higher selection times and to a significantly higher overall cognitive load when multi-target selection is considered [9,4].

As we can see, "snap-to" effects can have contradictory consequences. We propose a technique able to reduce these drawbacks, and apply it in the context of item selection in 3D menus. Our approach called "haptic walls" consists in haptically rendering solid walls shaped like a funnel, leading to a target located at the intersection of the 2 walls. The walls act as virtual fixtures: the targets are accessible while slipping along the interior faces and edges of the convex polyhedron that connects them. This approach differs from a magnetic grid [13] since the edges of our haptic shape are not attracting the pointer towards them. This technique can be adapted to any configuration of targets able to be represented as a convex polyhedron.

We presented in [3] some first results on only one haptic wall modality. In the present paper, we extend this study by experimenting several shapes and combinations of haptic modalities, and 2 different selection techniques.

A.M.L. Kappers et al. (Eds.): EuroHaptics 2010, Part II, LNCS 6192, pp. 152–159, 2010.

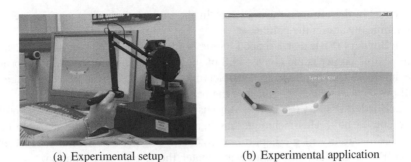

(a) Experimental setup   (b) Experimental application

Fig. 1. Experimental setup and application designed for haptic menu tests

2   3D Menu: Haptic and Selection Techniques

The present study has been restricted to the experimentation of the haptic walls techniques on a 1-level 3D menu, represented as a regular polyhedron (extruded polygon, see Fig.1(b)). The 8 items of the menu, represented as gray spheres, are located on the vertices of the polyhedron. This design is very similar to pie or marking menus which are known to allow precise and rapid interaction for menu selection tasks [2]. Moreover, pie menus are more appropriated to 3D interaction than linear menus [5]. The number of items was selected according to the design recommendations for the conception of marking menus [6]. The polyhedron is lying on a haptic 3D plane to guide the user and help with the perception of depth [5]. The menu presents a 20° tilt from the (x,z) plane. This was chosen to force the use of the in-depth dimension, and assess its impact on the performances. The diameter of the menu was set to 8 cm and each sphere representing an item had a 0.4 cm radius. All these parameters were set after an empirical preliminary evaluation involving 6 participants.

Using this configuration, we compared 6 haptic conditions, among which HB, MH, SB, and SBD are different implementations of the haptic walls approach:

- **NoHaptics (NH):** the only force feedback guidance is the 3D plane the pointer relies on. This technique was designed to have a reference situation with no haptic guidance to help selecting the targets.
- **Magnet (M):** the device pointer is attracted towards the target when it arrives inside the radius of influence (fixed to 5 times the radius of the spheres representing the items), as illustrated on Fig.2(a). The attraction is increasing while the distance to the target decreases, until a threshold of 80% of the distance, then it decreases to avoid oscillations.
- **HardBorders (HB):** the external faces of the menu are made haptically solid and slippery, to guide the pointer towards the corners (see Fig.2(b)), like a funnel with obtuse angles.
- **MagnetHard (MH):** this technique is the combination of the HardBorders and Magnet techniques (see Fig. 2(c)). It was designed to know if the association of 2 haptic guidances could take advantage of the best of each one. Hardborder could provide a smooth guidance in the first phase of the selection by helping the user

to enter in the attraction area, while in the end of the movement magnet could dynamically attract the pointer.

- **StarBorders (SB):** a star-shaped haptic border is felt, as shown on Fig. 2(d), but the visible border is the convex hull of the polyhedral menu, as with the previous techniques. This haptic shape also acts like a funnel, with more acute angles : it allows us to evaluate the impact of the parameters of the shape.
- **StarBordersDisplay (SBD):** the star-shaped border is felt and visible, and replaces the convex hull. This technique has been added to quantify the possible effects of the invisibility of the haptic border in the StarBorders modality, since in the HardBorder modality the haptic walls match the visual representation.

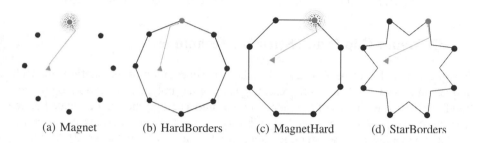

(a) Magnet   (b) HardBorders   (c) MagnetHard   (d) StarBorders

Fig. 2. Haptic modalities (2D projection): the target is in red, and the initial pointer position and its trajectory are represented in green

We also wanted to know if the most appropriate selection technique was depending on the haptic modality. We chose to test 2 different selection modalities. The first one, **"ReleaseButton"**, is very common. It requires the user to validate his selection with a button when pointing at the chosen item. The other one, similar to the **"ExceedBorder"** technique used in [5], requires the user to simply enter in the accessible volume of a menu item (*i.e.* a conical area inside the polyhedron). The selection is then automatically validated.

3   Experimental Setup and Results

We performed all our experiments using a quadro processor PC at 2,60 GHz, equipped with a 17 inch 2D screen with a resolution of 1280*1024. The haptic device was a PHANToM Premium (Sensable) with 6 degrees of freedom (dof), even if this specific application only uses 3 dof (see Fig.1(a)).

For each of the 6 haptic and the 2 selection conditions presented above, after a short training session, we asked 24 subjects to realize a series of 10 tasks, each task composed of 2 successive selections. This makes a total of 6*2*10*2=240 selections for each subject. The ordering of the tested combinations has been balanced in order to avoid a learning phenomenon.

For each task, the menu appears centered at the point where the button was pressed. One of the spheres, randomly chosen as the target, is displayed in red, and has to be selected by the user. Then a second target is randomly chosen among the remaining spheres, displayed in red, and selected by the user. The 2 successive selections were asked in this protocol to place the user in the situation of hesitation, and test the ergonomics of the modalities in this case. An item is considered as selected even if it was not the required target. In this case, it is considered as a wrong selection.

We present below the experimental datas collected during the experiment. We ran a One-Way ANOVA (ANalysis Of VAriance) on the collected values and a post-hoc Tukey HSD test to compute the relevancy of the differences between the different techniques.

- **Precision (PRE):** distance between the center of the target and the location of the pointer at the moment of the selection. The haptic modality as a significant impact on precision ($F(5, 138)=340.3$, $p<.0001$). The techniques can be grouped as follows: SB and SBD perform significantly better than HB and MH, which are significantly more precise modalities than M and NH (see Tab. 1).

Table 1. Mean values for the precision (PRE, in mm)

Modality	Mean PRE	Standard deviation	Pairwise comparison (p-value)					
			NH	M	MH	HB	SBD	SB
NH	0.501	0.16	-	0.206	<.001	<.001	<.001	<.001
M	0.488	0.17		-	0.014	<.001	<.001	<.001
MH	0.470	0.18			-	0.887	<.001	<.001
HB	0.464	0.19				-	<.001	0.001
SBD	0.427	0.2					-	0.974
SB	0.423	0.2						-

- **Task Completion Time (TCT):** time necessary to select the item. The haptic modality as a significant effect ($F(5, 138)=41.7$, $p<.0001$) on task completion times. The HB modality leads to significantly better results than all other techniques except MH (see Tab. 2). We also looked if there was an interaction between the haptic modality and the position of the target. We found no such statistical result: the time necessary to reach a particular target is statistically independent from the haptic modality. However, the targets can be gathered in two statistically different ($p<.0001$) clusters regarding TCT: targets $\{0, 4, 1, 5\}$ obtain the worst results, whereas targets $\{2, 6, 7, 3\}$ obtain the best results (see Fig.3(a)).
- **Number of Target Re-Entry (TRE):** number of times the pointer goes out the accessible volume of the target and then goes again inside the target before selection. The haptic condition significantly influences the number of target re-entry ($F(5, 138)=14.451$, $p<.0001$). The M modality performed significantly worst than all the other techniques except NH (see Tab. 3). On the other hand, SBD performed significantly better than MH and HB.
- **Extra Distance (ED):** difference between the shortest path authorized by the haptic modality from starting point to target, and the actual covered distance. The haptic modality has a significant effect on extra distance ($F(5, 138)=38.13$, $p<.0001$). HB performed significantly better than all other techniques (see Tab. 4).

Table 2. Mean task completion times (TCT, in sec.)

Modality	Mean TCT	Standard deviation	NH	SB	M	SBD	MH	HB
NH	1.429	0.72	-	0.884	0.870	0.194	<.001	<.001
SB	1.390	0.94		-	0.999	0.833	0.002	<.001
M	1.389	0.72			-	0.85	0.002	<.001
SBD	1.347	1.1				-	0.086	0.001
MH	1.253	0.67					-	0.738
HB	1.204	0.59						-

Table 3. Mean number of target re-entry (TRE)

Modality	Mean TRE	Standard deviation	M	NH	MH	HB	SB	SBD
M	0.664	0.79	-	0.440	0.002	0.002	<.001	<.001
NH	0.632	0.75		-	0.364	0.329	<.001	<.001
MH	0.599	0.71			-	0.999	0.138	0.008
HB	0.598	0.72				-	0.159	0.01
SB	0.557	0.63					-	0.924
SBD	0.541	0.59						-

Table 4. Mean extra-distance (ED, in mm)

Modality	Mean ED	Standard deviation	SB	SBD	NH	MH	M	HB
SB	1.4	2.76	-	1	0.48	0.088	0.061	<.001
SBD	1.4	3.54		-	0.62	0.147	0.106	<.001
NH	1.3	1.95			-	0.955	0.918	<.001
MH	1.2	1.49				-	1	<.001
M	1.2	1.21					-	<.001
HB	0.3	0.98						-

Table 5. Comparison of target placement according to TCT and ERR

Target	#0	#4	#1	#5	#3	#7	#6	#2
TCT	1.524	1.431	1.429	1.403	1.305	1.255	1.182	1.161
ERR (%)	0.14	1.00	0.69	0.59	0.27	0.14	0.40	0.42

- **Error rates (ERR):** the percentage of wrong selections for a given condition. ERR is globally low (average 0.45%). We found no significant influence of the haptic modality regarding ERR. However, it was influenced by the position of the target. The results showed two statistically different (p=.008) clusters {1, 4, 5} and {0, 2, 3, 6, 7} (see Fig.3(b) and Tab. 5).

We also analyzed the influence of the selection modality and the order of the selection (first or second) on TCT. There is a statistically significant difference between both selection modalities (p<.0001): ExceedBorder is significantly faster than ReleaseButton.

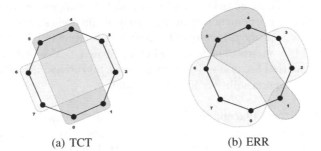

(a) TCT   (b) ERR

Fig. 3. Influence of targets position on TCT and ERR. In red the worst results, and in green the best results.

The order of the selection also influenced TCT (p<.0001): first selections are significantly faster than second ones (see Tab. 6).

4 Discussion

Influence of the Interaction Technique. The overall results suggest that for any of the measurements, 2 techniques detach as those having the worst results: NH and M. We think that the bad results of M rely on the "snap-to" paradigm. This haptic modality induces unexpected drifts in the trajectory of the pointer that the users cannot anticipate, as the area of effect is not visible. This can lead to an unwanted resistance from the users that may try for a while to continue their initial movement. This should explain the low performances of M regarding PRE, TCT and TRE. On the contrary the "haptic wall" techniques, especially HB and SBD, can be more easily anticipated.

Table 6. Comparison of TCT according to selection modality and selection order

	Overall	HB	SB	SBD	MH	M	NH
ReleaseButton	1.553	**1.421**	1.619	1.522	1.499	1.615	1.640
ExceedBorder	1.118	**0.987**	1.161	1.173	1.007	1.162	1.218
First selection	1.286	**1.182**	1.328	1.240	1.234	1.355	1.379
Second selection	1.384	**1.226**	1.452	1.454	1.272	1.423	1.479

Of course, setting larger areas of attraction for M might have changed the results of TCT, but would probably have harmed the control of the pointer, leading to increased error rates.

The results also suggest that among haptic walls modalities, a more constraining technique such as SB or SBD leads to an increased precision, but also increases significantly the selection time, especially for the second selections (see Tab. 6). In fact, for first selections the pointer starts from the center whereas for second selections, the pointer starts from the previously selected target. This implies in average a longer path towards the next target, increasing inevitably the TCT. But the star-shaped haptic walls may also have been experienced as an obstacle while users tried to follow the shortest path between 2 successive items. This could also account for the results observed concerning the Extra Distance (ED), with SB and SBD leading to the worst results. To better understand this phenomenon, a further analysis, involving acute control of the direction of the selection and difficulty of the path will be necessary [10].

MH and SB led to intermediate results when compared to M or HB and SBD. We think MH was penalized because of its magnetic attraction component while SB might have suffered from the invisibility of its haptic guidance.

Influence of the Targets Placement. The clusters configurations according to targets numbering (see Fig.3) suggest the existence of an "accessibility axis" corresponding to the "left-right" direction. We think that this could be explained by an increased difficulty of the selection task in the in-depth direction. A lower muscular requirement may also explain this phenomenon, since when performing a "left-right" movement, users used a wrist movement, while "in-depth" movements involved the whole arm. We think that the slight rotation to the left that can be observed appeared because all participants were right-handed, and the axis is rotated in the direction of their forearm.

Influence of the Selection Modality. ExceedBorder is faster than ReleaseButton whatever the haptic modality used for the guidance. However, there is no significant influence of the selection modality on the error rate (p = 0.238). The best results are obtained with the HB technique. We think that the combination of HB and Exceed-Border is probably the most appropriate modality for menu selections. It allows good overall performances regarding TCT, PRE and ED with successive selections.

5   Conclusion

In this paper we reported our experiments on several "haptic walls" modalities for 3D menu, *i.e.* haptic techniques acting like a funnel. These results are very encouraging, especially for HardBorders. These techniques seem to provide a better control over the movement of the pointer, that can be more easily anticipated than with magnetic techniques. We will continue our study by refining the parameters of the menu (diameter, max. number of items, angle of tilt, etc.). We also intend to extend this single-level menu to a complete hierarchical menu.

Acknowledgments

The authors wish to thank Alex Ocampo for his participation to this work, and all the participants of our evaluation.

References

1. Akamatsu, M., Sato, S.: A multi-modal mouse with tactile and force feedback. Int. J. Hum.-Comput. Stud. 40(3), 443–453 (1994)
2. Callahan, J., Hopkins, D., Weiser, M., Shneiderman, B.: An empirical comparison of pie vs. linear menus. In: CHI 1988: Proceedings of the SIGCHI Conference on Human Factors in Computing Systems, pp. 95–100 (1988)

3. Essert-Villard, C., Capobianco, A.: HardBorders: a New Haptic Approach for Selection Tasks in 3D Menus. In: Proceedings of ACM VRST 2009, pp. 243–244 (2009)
4. Hwang, F., Keates, S., Langdon, P., Clarkson, P.J.: Multiple haptic targets for motion-impaired computer users. In: Proceedings of the ACM CHI 2003, pp. 41–48 (2003)
5. Komerska, R., Ware, C.: A Study of Haptic Linear and Pie Menus in a 3D Fish Tank VR Environment. In: Proceedings of International Symposium on Haptic Interfaces for Virtual Environment and Teleoperator Systems, pp. 224–231 (2004)
6. Kurtenbach, G.P.: The Design and Evaluation of Marking Menus. Doctoral Thesis, University of Toronto (1993)
7. Miller, T., Zeleznik, R.: The design of 3D haptic widgets. In: Proceedings of the 1999 Symposium on interactive 3D Graphics, pp. 97–102 (1999)
8. Oakley, I., McGee, M.R., Brewster, S., Gray, P.: Putting the feel in "look and feel". In: Proceedings of ACM CHI 2000, pp. 415–422 (2000)
9. Oakley, I., Brewster, S., Gray, P.: Solving multi-target haptic problems in menu interaction. In: Proceedings of ACM CHI 2001: extended abstracts, pp. 357–358 (2001)
10. Soukoreff, W., MacKenzie, S.I.: Towards a standard for pointing device evaluation, perspectives on 27 years of Fitts' law research in HCI. International Journal of Human-Computer Studies 61(6), 751–789 (2004)
11. Vidholm, E., Nystrom, I.: A Haptic Interaction Technique for Volume Images Based on Gradient Diffusion. In: Proceedings of WHC 2005, pp. 336–341 (2005)
12. Wall, S.A., Paynter, K., Shillito, A.M., Wright, M., Scali, S.: The Effect of Haptic Feedback and Stereo Graphics in a 3D Target Acquision Task. In: Proc. Eurohaptics 2002, pp. 23–29 (2002)
13. Yamada, T., Ogi, T., Tsubouchi, D., Hirose, M.: Desk-sized immersive workplace using force feedback grid interface. In: Proceedings of IEEE VR, pp. 135–142 (2002)

Spherical MR-Brake with Nintendo Wii Sensors for Haptics

Doruk Senkal and Hakan Gurocak

School of Engineering and Computer Science
Washington State University
14204 NE Salmon Creek Ave., Vancouver, WA 98686, USA
doruksenkal@yahoo.com, hgurocak@vancouver.wsu.edu

Abstract. This research improves the position measurement system of a magnetorheological (MR) spherical brake we recently designed. The brake is a multi-DOF actuator. The initial design had a position measurement system with infrared (IR) sensors. Although the IR sensors gave good results, there were some performance degradations in the brake due to the noise in the sensors. In this research we implemented a new position measurement system using accelerometers and gyroscopes from a Nintendo Wii. Much better haptic feedback could be obtained in virtual wall collisions and in a virtual gear shifter simulation that used the brake as a joystick.

Keywords: Haptics, inertial sensor, magnetorheological brake, multi-DOF actuator, force feedback.

1 Introduction

MR actuators are quite promising since they provide high torque or force output in a relatively compact volume. But all of these actuators are single degree-of-freedom (DOF). Using two or four single-DOF MR disc brakes and gimbal mechanisms, multi-DOF haptic joysticks have been built [1,2]. The overall size of all of these devices is fairly large. We recently designed a spherical MR-Brake as a multi-DOF actuator [3]. When it is activated, it can restrict or lock all three DOFs simultaneously. To the best of our knowledge, our design is the first ever multi-DOF spherical brake using MR fluid. MR actuators with multi-DOF could find applications in minimal invasive robotic surgery, prosthetics, haptics and in computer games.

Our spherical MR-Brake uses the serpentine flux path concept [4,5] to minimize the size of the brake while improving the torque output. The resulting brake has a diameter of 76.2 mm and can apply up to 3.7 Nm braking torque. The initial design had an optical position measurement with infrared (IR) sensors for position measurement. Although the IR sensors gave good results, there were some performance degradations in the brake due to the noise in the sensors. In this research we implemented a new position measurement system using accelerometers and gyroscopes from a Nintendo Wii.

A.M.L. Kappers et al. (Eds.): EuroHaptics 2010, Part II, LNCS 6192, pp. 160–165, 2010.

2   Overview of Spherical MR-Brake

Previously we designed single DOF rotary, compact and powerful MR-Brakes using a serpentine flux path concept [4,5]. In this approach, aluminum and steel rings were employed to weave the magnetic flux path through the MR fluid gap. The same concept was adapted in the design of the spherical MR-Brake. Since the aluminum ring (Figure 1) is magnetically non-conductive, it prevents the magnetic circuit from shorting around the coil and forces it to go through the MR fluid gap [3].

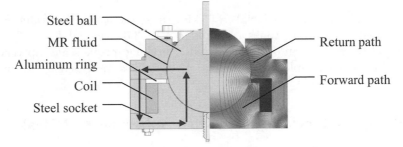

Fig. 1. Spherical MR-Brake flux path with finite element model

The MR fluid needs to be activated with a strong, homogeneous magnetic field to develop a compact actuator with high torque output. For this reason, the position of the aluminum ring is critical (Figure 2). For homogeneity, the ring must be placed at a location such that the forward and return cross-sectional areas are equal [3]:

$$\int_0^\beta 2\pi \cdot r^2 \cdot \sin \sigma \, d\sigma = \int_\beta^\alpha 2\pi \cdot r^2 \cdot \sin \sigma \, d\sigma \implies \beta = \cos^{-1}\left(\frac{1+\cos\alpha}{2}\right) \ . \ (1)$$

where β is the angle at which the aluminum ring is placed, α is the angle where the MR Fluid gap ends and r is the radius of the sphere (Figure 2). A moderate

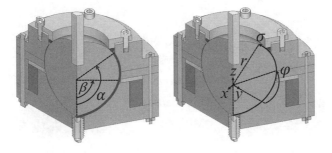

Fig. 2. Cross-sectional area for the forward and return paths (Left). Torque calculation about the x and z axes. α is the azimuth angle, φ is in the horizontal x-y plane.

socket size of $\alpha = 120°$ was selected. Then, the location for the aluminum ring was computed as $\beta = 75.5°$. The torque about the z-axis is:

$$T_z = \int_0^\alpha (r \cdot \sin \sigma) \cdot (\tau \cdot 2\pi \cdot r^2 \cdot \sin \sigma) \, d\sigma \ . \tag{2}$$

here τ is the shear stress in the MR fluid. Torque along the x and y axes can be calculated as [3]:

$$T_{x,y} = \tau \cdot \pi^2 \cdot r^3 - \int_0^{\pi-\alpha} 2 \int_0^\pi \tau \cdot r^3 \cdot \sin \sigma \cdot \sqrt{(\cos \sigma)^2 + (\sin \sigma \cdot \sin \varphi)^2} \, d\varphi \, d\sigma \ . \tag{3}$$

For $r = 20.32$ mm and $\tau (1\,\text{Tesla}) = 55$ kPa (near the saturation value for the fluid we used), the torque values are found as $T_z = 3.66$ Nm and $T_{x,y} = 3.28$ Nm. Because of the r^3 term in equations 2 and 3, braking torque scales up very well with radius. For example, if the radius of the ball is increased to 30 mm, the brake will output about 12 Nm torque.

3   Force Feedback Joystick with Spherical MR-Brake

3.1   Using IR Sensors for Position Measurement

Conventional spherical joints use encoders attached to three different axes of the joint through a gimbal mechanism to measure the orientation. Although this is a viable approach, we explored another approach to meet the design goal of building a compact system. Three IR sensors by Sharp, Inc. (Model No. GP2D120XJ00F) were used to build an optical triangulation system to measure the position of the joystick handle (Figure 3, left). The sensors measured distance by sending an infrared signal and receiving the signal that bounced back from the surface below the joystick. Although this system gave good results as shown later, this approach had some issues. First the performance of the brake in VR simulations was degraded due to the noise in the sensor signals. The noise was filtered in the software layer, but this induced lag. Second, the sensors measure the position with respect to a flat surface (such as a table-top), hence these sensors cannot be used in applications without such a surface [6].

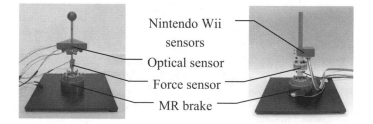

Nintendo Wii sensors

Optical sensor

Force sensor

MR brake

Fig. 3. (Left) Initial design of the force feedback joystick. (Right) New design with the Wii Components. (Design uses ATI Mini45 Force sensor.)

3.2   Using Nintendo Wii Components for Position Measurement

Our objective was to improve over the existing positioning system, while still avoiding an encoder or gimbal based solution to keep the device compact. Laser mouse sensors were considered as one of the alternatives. However, since they are relative sensors, any error in sensor readings results in unbounded positioning errors. For that reason, we used accelerometers and rate gyroscopes from Nintendo Wii components. Circuit boards from the Nintendo Wii Nunchuk for the accelerometers and from the Nintendo Wii MotionPlus for the rate gyroscopes were used as a low-cost solution (Figure 3, right).

We connected the circuit boards for Nunchuk and MotionPlus to two Wii Remotes which are interfaced with a PC via Bluetooth. The gyroscope and accelerometer axes were arranged in a perpendicular fashion.

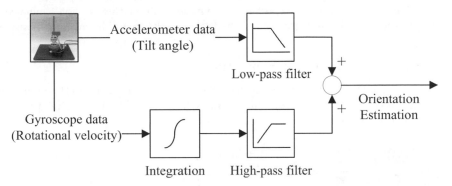

Fig. 4. Complementary filter for orientation estimation (Corner frequency at 0.13 Hz)

The accelerometers sense tilt angle, but also any acceleration along the sensor axis. The gyros drift over time. As a haptic joystick requires the measurement of absolute tilt angle and must perform dynamic motions, accelerometers and rate gyroscopes had to be used together to complement each other's shortcomings [7]. Figure 4 shows this complementary filter approach. The low pass-filters on the accelerometers dampen out errors introduced to the tilt estimate by sudden accelerations, while sacrificing response time. The high pass filters on the gyroscopes cause the orientation estimate of the gyroscope to decay back to zero, effectively removing the growth due to drift, at the same time making the signal only valid for dynamic motions. When these two signals are added together an absolute orientation sensor is created which can also measure dynamic motions thanks to the gyroscopes.

4   Experiments and Results

4.1   Wall Collision

The VR simulation environment was built using the H3DAPI by SenseGraphics. A virtual wall was placed into the simulation to assess how well the brake could simulate collision with a virtual surface (Figure 5).

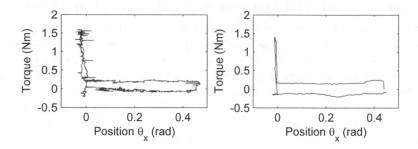

Fig. 5. Simulation of collision with a virtual wall at position $\theta_x = 0°$. (Left) using the IR sensors, (Right) using the new Wii components for position measurement. The joystick handle is first pulled away from position zero through approximately 0.45 radians. Then, it is pushed back towards the virtual wall for the collision simulation. Hysteresis due to residual magnetism in the brake results in a different return path.

4.2   Virtual Environment Simulation

A virtual manual gear shifter was constructed. User's goal was to go through each gear and then return to the starting point, which was the straight up position of the joystick (Figure 6).

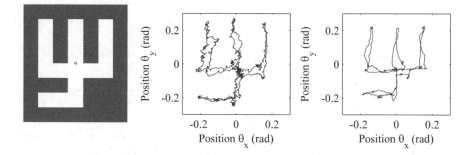

Fig. 6. (Left) VR simulation for a manual gear shifter in an automobile. Recorded joystick positions as a user tries to shift gears with haptic feedback from the joystick (Middle: with IR sensors, Right: with Wii components).

5   Discussion and Conclusions

In this paper, we presented a compact multi-DOF spherical brake using MR fluid. To the best of our knowledge, our design is the first ever multi-DOF spherical brake using MR fluid. The brake was used in the design of a haptic joystick, where position measurement turned out to be challenging. In this research we implemented a new position measurement system using accelerometers and gyroscopes from a Nintendo Wii. We also implemented a complimentary filter approach which enabled us to add the filtered accelerometer and gyroscope signals to create essentially an absolute orientation sensor.

Results of the virtual wall collision experiments with the new system were much crisper and cleaner. High friction on the virtual surfaces was observed. Since passive devices can only create forces against the user's direction of motion, it is impossible to create frictionless wall surfaces with them.

In general, the new position measurement system has considerably less noise and it is very compact. Therefore, it can be a viable low cost option in haptic device design.

References

1. Li, W.H., Liu, B., Kosasih, P.B., Zhang, X.Z.: A 2-DOF MR actuator joystick for virtual reality applications. Sensors and actuators. A, Physical 137(2), 308–320 (2007)
2. Yamaguchi, Y., Furusho, J., Kimura, S., Koyanagi, K.: Development of High-Performance MR Actuator and its Application to 2-D Force Display. International Journal of Modern Physics B 19, 1485–1491 (2005)
3. Senkal, D., Gurocak, H.: Spherical Brake with MR Fluid as Multi Degree of Freedom Actuator for Haptics. Journal of Intelligent Material Systems and Structures 20(18), 2149–2160 (2009)
4. Blake, J., Gurocak, H.: Haptic Glove With MR Brakes for Virtual Reality. IEEE/ASME Transactions on Mechatronics 14(5), 606–615 (2009)
5. Senkal, D., Gurocak, H.: Compact MR-brake with serpentine flux path for haptics applications. In: WHC 2009: Proceedings of the World Haptics 2009 - Third Joint EuroHaptics Conference and Symposium on Haptic Interfaces for Virtual Environment and Teleoperator Systems, Washington, DC, USA, pp. 91–96. IEEE Computer Society, Los Alamitos (2009)
6. Senkal, D., Gurocak, H., Konukseven, E.I.: Passive Haptic Interface with MR-Brakes for Dental Implant Surgery. Presence: Teleoperators & Virtual Environments (2009) (submitted)
7. Gallagher, A., Matsuoka, Y., Ang, W.T.: An efficient real-time human posture tracking algorithm using low-cost inertial and magnetic sensors. In: Proceedings of 2004 IEEE/RSJ International Conference on Intelligent Robots and Systems, IROS 2004, September 28-October 2, vol. 3, pp. 2967–2972 (2004)

FlexTorque: Exoskeleton Interface for Haptic Interaction with the Digital World

Dzmitry Tsetserukou[1], Katsunari Sato[2], and Susumu Tachi[3]

[1] Toyohashi University of Technology, 1-1 Hibarigaoka, Tempaku-cho, Toyohashi, Aichi,
441-8580 Japan
tsetserukou@erc.tut.ac.jp
[2] University of Tokyo, 7-3-1 Hongo, Bunkyo-ku, Tokyo, 113-8656 Japan
Katsunari_Sato@ipc.i.u-tokyo.ac.jp
[3] Keio University, 4-1-1 Hiyoshi, Kohoku-ku, Yokohama, 223-8526 Japan
tachi@tachilab.org

Abstract. We developed a novel haptic interface FlexTorque that enables realistic physical interaction with real (through teleoperation system) and Virtual Environments. The idea behind FlexTorque is to reproduce human muscle structure, which allows us to perform dexterous manipulation and safe interaction with environment in daily life. FlexTorque suggests new possibilities for highly realistic, very natural physical interaction in virtual environments. There are no restrictions on the arm movement, and it is not necessary to hold a physical object during interaction with objects in virtual reality. Because the system can generate strong forces, even though it is light-weight, easily wearable, and intuitive, users experience a new level of realism as they interact with virtual environments.

Keywords: Exoskeleton, haptic display, haptic interface, force feedback, Virtual Reality, game controller.

1 Introduction

In order to realize haptic interaction (e.g., holding, pushing, and contacting the object) in virtual environment and mediated haptic communication with human beings (e.g., handshaking), the force feedback is required. Recently there has been a substantial need and interest in haptic displays, which can provide realistic and high fidelity physical interaction in virtual environment. The aim of our research is to implement a wearable haptic display for presentation of realistic feedback (kinesthetic stimulus) to the human arm. We developed a wearable device FlexTorque that induces forces to the human arm and does not require holding any additional haptic interfaces in the human hand. It is completely new technology for virtual and augmented environments that allows user to explore surroundings freely. The concept of Karate (empty hand) Haptics proposed by us is opposite to conventional interfaces (e.g., Wii Remote [1], SensAble's PHANTOM [2]) that require holding haptic interface in the hand, restricting thus the motion of the fingers in midair.

A.M.L. Kappers et al. (Eds.): EuroHaptics 2010, Part II, LNCS 6192, pp. 166–171, 2010.

The powered exoskeleton robots, such as HAL [3] (weight of 23 kg) and Raytheon Sarcos [4] (weight of about 60 kg) intended for the power amplification of the wearer can be used for the force presentation as well. However, they are heavy, require high power consumption, and pose danger for user due to the powerful actuators.

The compact string-based haptic device for bimanual interaction in virtual environment was described in [5]. The users of SPIDAR can intuitively manipulate the object and experience 6-DOF force feedback. The human-scale SPIDAR allowing enlargement of working space was designed [6]. However, the wires moving in front of the user present the obstacle for the human vision. They also restrict the human arm motion in several directions and user has to pay attention to not injure himself. Moreover, user grasps the ball-shaped grip in such a way that fingers cannot move.

2   Development of Haptic Interface FlexTorque

In order to achieve human-friendly and wearable design of haptic display, we analyzed the amount of torque to be presented to the operator arm. Generally, there are three cases when torque feedback is needed. The first case takes place when haptic communication with remote human needs to be realized. For example, the person handshakes the slave robot and joint torques are presented to the operator. Such interaction results in very small torque magnitude (in the range of 0-1.5 Nm). The second situation takes place when slave robot transports heavy object. Here, the torque values are much higher than in previous case and torque magnitude depends on the load weight. However, continuous presentation of high torques to the operator will result in human muscle fatigue. We argue that downscaled torque indicating direction of the force would be informative enough. The third and the worst case of contact state in term of interactive force magnitude is collision. The result of collision with fixed object (as it is often the case) is immediate discontinuation of the operator's arm motion. Therefore, the power of torque display must be enough to only fixate the operator arm.

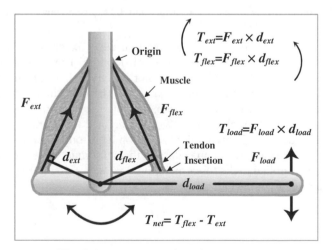

Fig. 1. Structure and action of a skeletal muscle

The idea behind novel torque display **FlexTorque** (haptic display that generates **Fl**exor and **ex**tensor **Torque**) is to reproduce human muscle structure, that allows us to perform dexterous manipulation and safe interaction with environment in daily life. Main functions of the muscles are contraction for locomotion and skeletal movement [7]. Muscle is connected to the periosteum through tendon (connective tissue in the shape of strap or band). The muscle with tendon in series acts like a rope pulling on a lever when pulling tendons to move the skeleton (Fig. 1).

Because muscles pull but cannot push, hinge joints (e.g. elbow) require at least two muscles pulling in opposite direction (antagonistic muscles). The torque produced by each muscle at a joint is the product of contractile force (F) and moment arm at that joint (d). The net torque T_{net} is the sum of the torques produces by each antagonistic muscle. Movement of human limbs is produced by coordinated work of muscles acting on skeletal joints. The structure of the developed torque display FlexTorque and the detailed view of the driving unit of haptic display are presented in Fig. 2.

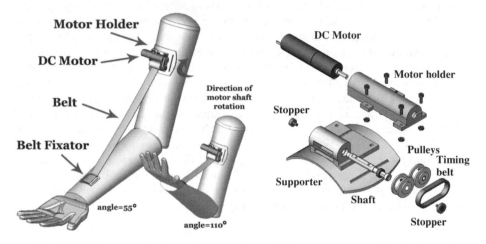

Fig. 2. FlexTorque on the human's arm surface and 3D exposed view of the driving unit

FlexTorque is made up of two DC motors (muscles) fixedly mounted into plastic Motor holder unit, Belts (tendons), and two Belt fixators. The operation principle of the haptic display is as follows. When DC motor is activated, it pulls the belt and produces force F_{flex} generating the flexor torque T_{flex}. The oppositely placed DC motor generates the extensor torque T_{ext}. Therefore, the couple of antagonistic actuators produce a net torque at operator elbow joint T_{net}. We defined the position of the Insertion point to be near to the wrist joint in order to develop large torque at the elbow joint.

Let us consider the calculation procedure of the net torque value. The layout of the forces and torques applied to the forearm during flexion is given in Fig. 3.

The tension force F_t of the belt can be derived from:

$$F_t = \frac{T_m i}{r},$$ (1)

where T_m is the motor torque, i is the gear ratio, and r is the shaft radius.

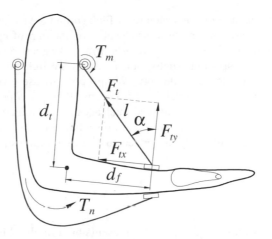

Fig. 3. Diagram of applied forces and torques

The net torque T_n acting at the elbow joint is:

$$T_n = F_{ty}d_f = F_t d_f \cos(\alpha),$$ (2)

where d_f is the moment arm.

The angle α varies according to the relative position of the forearm and upper arm. It can be found using the following equation:

$$\alpha = \cos^{-1}\left(\frac{l^2 + d_t^2 - d_f^2}{2ld_t}\right),$$ (3)

where d_t is the distance from the pivot to the Origin; l is the length of belt, it can be calculated from the rotation angle of the motor shaft.

The biceps actuator of FlexTorque is capable of producing the net torque at the elbow joint as high as 8.0 Nm (Maxon motor RE 13, Stall torque of 8.52 mNm, Gearhead reduction ratio of 17:1). Each unit is compact and extremely light weight (61 g). This was achieved due to the use of plastic and duralumin materials in manufacturing the main components. The Supporter surface has concave profile to match the curvature of human arm surface (Fig. 4).

Fig. 4. Manufactured driving unit of FlexTorque

The essential advantage of the structure of FlexTorque device is that heaviest elements (DC motors, shafts, and pulleys) are located on the part of upper arm, which is nearest to the shoulder. Therefore, operator's arm undergoes very small additional loading. The rest of components (belts, belt fixators) are light in weight and do not load the operator's muscles considerably. We propose to use term "Karate (empty hand) Haptics" to such kind of novel devices because they allow presenting the forces to the human arm without using additional interfaces in the human hands. The developed apparatus features extremely safe force presentation to the human's arm. While overloading, the belt is physically disconnected from the motor and the safety of the human is guaranteed.

3   Applications

The main features of FlexTorque are: (1) it presents high fidelity kinesthetic sensation to the user according to the interactive forces; (2) it does not restrict the motion of the human arm; (3) it has wearable design; (4) it is extremely safe in operation; (5) it does not require a lot of storage space. These advantages allow a wide range of applications in virtual and augmented reality systems and introduce a new way of game playing. A number of games for augmented sport experiences, which provide a natural, realistic, and intuitive feeling of immersion into virtual environment, can be implemented.

Haptic interface FlexTorque was demonstrated at SIGGRAPH ASIA 2009 [8]. We designed three games with haptic feedback. We developed the Gun Simulator game with the recoil imitation and Teapot Fishing game with haptic presentation of the rod tug when fish bites. The virtual biceps curl exercise machine was designed. With Virtual Gym game we can do the strength training exercise at home in a playful manner (Fig. 5). The belt tension creates the resistance force in the direction of the forearm motion. The user can adjust the weight easily.

Wii MotionPlus controller was used in order to capture the complex motion of the user arm. To maintain the alignment of the extensor belt on the elbow avoiding thus slippage, user wears specially designed pad equipped with guides. In total more than 100 persons had experienced novel haptic interface FlexTorque. We have a got very

Fig. 5. The Virtual Gym game

positive feedback from the users and companies. While discussing the possible useful applications with visitors, the games for physical sport exercises and rehabilitation were frequently mentioned. The majority of users reported that this device presented force feedback in a very realistic manner.

4 Conclusions and Future Research

Novel haptic interface FlexTorque suggests new possibilities for highly realistic, very natural physical interaction in virtual environments, augmented sport, augmented game applications, and teleoperation.

A number of new games for sport experiences, which provide a natural, realistic, and intuitive feeling of physical immersion into virtual environment, can be implemented (such as skiing, biathlon (skiing with rifle shooting), archery, tennis, sword dueling, etc.). FlexTorque will also enable the presentation of strong vibrations in driving simulator, muscle stiffness, and collision (contact) with a virtual object.

The future goal is to capture the complex movement and recognize the gesture of the user through accelerometers and MEMS gyroscopes integrated into the holder and fixator of the FlexTorque and optical full-body motion capture system. The new version of the FlexTorque (**ExoInterface**) will take advantages of the **Exo**skeletons (strong force feedback) and Wii Remote **Interface** (motion-sensing capabilities and simplicity of usage).

We expect that FlexTorque will support future interactive techniques in the field of robotics, virtual reality, sport simulators, and rehabilitation.

References

1. Wii Remote. Nintendo Co. Ltd.,
   http://www.nintendo.com/wii/what/accessories
2. PHANTOM OMNI haptic device. SensAble Technologies,
   http://www.sensable.com/
3. Hayashi, T., Kawamoto, H., Sankai, Y.: Control Method of Robot Suit HAL Working as Operator's Muscle using Biological and Dynamical Information. In: IEEE/RSJ International Conference on Intelligent Robots and Systems, pp. 3063–3068. IEEE Press, New York (2005)
4. Raytheon Sarcos Exoskeleton, http://www.raytheon.com/
5. Murayama, J., Bougrila, L., Luo, Y., Akahane, K., Hasegawa, S., Hirsbrunner, B., Sato, M.: SPIDAR G&G: a Two-handed Haptic Interface for Bimanual VR Interaction. In: EuroHaptics, pp. 138–146. Springer, Heidelberg (2004)
6. Richard, P., Chamaret, D., Inglese, F.-X., Lucidarme, P., Ferrier, J.-L.: Human Scale Virtual Environment for Product Design: Effect of Sensory Substitution. The International Journal of Virtual Reality 5(2), 34–37 (2006)
7. Kandel, E.R.J., Schwartz, H., Jessell, T.M.: Principles of Neural Science. McGraw-Hill, New York (2000)
8. Tsetserukou, D., Sato, K., Neviarouskaya, A., Kawakami, N., Tachi, S.: FlexTorque: Innovative Haptic Interface for Realistic Physical Interaction in Virtual Reality. In: 2nd ACM SIGGRAPH Conference and Exhibition on Computer Graphics and Interactive Technologies in Asia, Emerging Technologies, p. 69. ACM Press, New York (2009)

Influence of Vision and Haptics on Plausibility of Social Interaction in Virtual Reality Scenarios

Zheng Wang, Ji Lu, Angelika Peer, and Martin Buss

Institute of Automatic Control Engineering
Technische Universität München, D-80290 Munich, Germany
zheng.wang@ieee.org, ji.lu@mytum.de, angelika.peer@tum.de, mb@tum.de,
http://www.lsr.ei.tum.de

Abstract. This paper focuses on the effects of visual and haptic feedback on the experienced plausibility of social interaction in a virtual reality scenario, where participants were asked to perform handshakes with a virtual, visually and haptically rendered partner. A 3D virtual environment was created and integrated with a handshaking robot, enabling the participant to see the virtual partner while shaking hands. To assess the effect of visual and haptic rendering strategies on plausibility, an experiment with human subjects was carried out. The results indicate that adding vision and improving the quality of haptics, both improve plausibility. Similar effect sizes further suggest that vision and haptics are equally important to the perceived plausibility of a virtual handshaking task.

Keywords: plausibility, social interaction, virtual reality.

1 Introduction

Adding haptic feedback to multimodal virtual reality (VR) systems enables users to not only see, but also physically interact with objects and characters in a virtual world. Knowledge about the influence of haptics and vision on plausibility of the interaction is an important factor when developing VR systems and is especially critical when assigning limited resources for system development. The work is focused on the plausibility of a social interaction task: handshaking.

Plausibility illusion refers to the perception that an event/object in the virtual world is actually occurring/existing, although knowing it is only computer mediated [10]. It is different from the illusion of "being there", often referred as *presence*. While the experience of sharing a room with a virtual character, e.g., can be achieved by visual feedback only, plausible handshaking with a virtual character not only requires rendered limb motions similar to a real handshake, but the physicality of interaction also calls for an adequate haptic feedback.

There are studies of the integration of haptics and vision in presence ([11], [6]) as well as human perception [7], and studies on social interaction that focus on the effect of haptics on performance ([2], [9], [5]) and the level of presence ([2], [9]). To the authors' knowledge, however, there is no report on the interaction of haptics and vision and their influences on plausibility when performing a social interaction task. Based on common findings it is expected that: i) enabling both, haptics and vision, improves

A.M.L. Kappers et al. (Eds.): EuroHaptics 2010, Part II, LNCS 6192, pp. 172–177, 2010.

plausibility compared to providing a single modality alone, ii) improving the quality of haptics improves plausibility.

2   Method

To assess the validity of these assumptions, an experiment was carried out, where subjects were asked to perform handshakes with a virtual character. Handshaking was selected as it represents a basic and common social interaction task relying on both vision and haptics.

2.1   Experimental Setup

An immersive VR system was used, see Fig. 2. The user wears a head-mounted display (HMD) that provides visual feedback. A motion tracker is mounted on the HMD that allows her/him to look around in the virtual environment just by turning her/his own head. To provide haptic feedback a haptic interface consisting of a 7 DOF robotic arm [8] with a rubber artificial hand mounted at the end-effector was used. A second motion tracker is mounted to the base of the robot platform to map the position and orientation of the end-effector to the world coordinate system for visual rendering. A 6 DOF force/torque sensor located between rubber hand and robot end-effector allows measuring interaction forces. The rubber hand is placed coincidentally with the hand of the virtual character such that it is waiting when the user reaches out to the virtual hand. The robot arm is registered with the virtual environment and measurement data is used to update position and orientation of the rubber hand in the virtual environment. Human hand posture is measured using a CyberGlove [4] worn by the participant. A third motion tracker is placed on the glove to provide the actual position and orientation of the user's wrist for the visual rendering engine. The overall structure of the experimental setup is shown in Fig. 1.

Haptic and visual rendering is handled by separate subsystems. After fine calibration, the two virtual hands touch each other then, when in the physical world the hand of the participant touches the rubber hand mounted on the robot. Because of the existence of the rubber hand, the hand of the participant does not move further and the two virtual hands do not penetrate.

Haptic Rendering: Control algorithms have been developed to render the haptic channel of handshaking, see [13]. To investigate whether the quality of haptic feedback has an effect on the experienced plausibility of interaction, two types of haptic feedback, basic and human-driven, were provided and compared with each other. The basic form (H) aims at providing a very poor resemblance of the real world. The robot implements a virtual impedance and acts as a passive mass-spring-damper model with mass 10 kg, damping 20 Ns/m, and stiffness 20 N/m. Thus, the human needs to continuously accelerate the robot, otherwise it stops quickly. The second, human-driven haptic feedback (Hm) uses a trained human expert to drive the robot arm and shake with the participant in real-time.

Visual Rendering: The virtual scene consists of an empty space with a floor of size 2 m by 4 m, a female virtual character, and the virtual representation of the participant's own forelimb. To achieve a high level of realness, fine details and vividness of the virtual character are expected. The detail-rich hand postures of both the virtual character and the participant are rendered by a realistic hand model with 24 degrees of freedom (DOF) [3]. The virtual handshake partner and the virtual body of the participant are created using commercially available virtual characters from Poser [12]. Poser is not capable of rendering the virtual characters online, therefore Open Inventor (OI) is employed in real-time visual rendering. From Poser to OI, color and texture information is lost, as well as the links between body parts. To solve this problem the virtual human model is first exported to 3Ds Max [1] to separate the necessary body parts and add color and texture information. The right hand is substituted by the 24 DOF hand model.

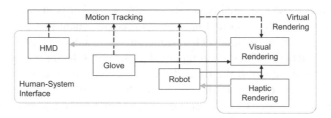

Fig. 1. Structure of the experimental system. Thick gray lines indicate feedback signals, solid black lines indicate the measurements from the devices, dashed black lines indicate the position and orientation measurements by the motion trackers on each device.

2.2   Experimental Design

In the experiment two different levels in vision, *without vision* (nV) and *with vision* (V) as well as three levels in haptics, *without haptics* (nH), *with basic haptics* (H), and *human driven* (Hm) were distinguished. This results into 6 different conditions to be compared: (C1) nV+nH, (C2) nV+H, (C3) nV+Hm, (C4) V+nH, (C5) V+H, and (C6) V+Hm.

A black screen is presented in nV, while the normal VR environment is provided in V, see Fig. 2b. The participant holds nothing and shakes air in nH, while holding the rubber hand and basic haptic feedback is provided in H, while the human drives the

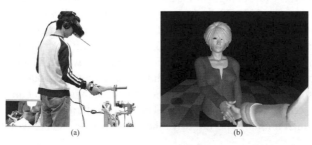

Fig. 2. (a) Experimental setup; (b) 3D virtual scenario

robot in Hm. Since only arm dynamics is considered and rendered in this work, the human condition is realized by letting the human partner drive the robot arm, so that the participant always grasps onto the same end-effector for all the presented conditions. Given the technical constraints, the best achievable condition C6 and the worst condition C1 are repeated in every handshake group to enforce the comparison boundaries. The participants are actually evaluating *how close* on the subjective scale of plausibility the handshake in question is with respect to the best case. A number of 13 (4 females, 9 males, averaged age 26.9) college students participated in the experiment.

Procedure: The experiment consists of three parts: pre-experiment briefing, training, and the main experiment. The training session is crucial for getting the participant naive to the experiment familiar to the system, and to focus them to the plausibility of haptic/vision rendering instead of other factors. An experimenter guides the participant through the entire procedure.

1. Pre-experiment briefing. The expert first introduces the experiment to the participant outside the experiment room and then blind-folds and guides the participant into the room. The participant puts on the HMD with sound-proof headphones as well as the CyberGlove. Then calibration of the data glove is performed.
2. Training session. The training session was introduced to get the participant familiar to the system and to present all possible handshakes to the participant. In the first step, the participant shakes hands with the most unrealistic handshake C1 and the most realistic handshake C6 to define the upper and lower limit of the plausibility scale. A seven point plausibility scale is introduced, with 1 being *most unrealistic*, and 7 being *most plausible*. C1 was assigned the score 1 as the worst condition with "seeing nothing while shaking air". C6 with visual feedback and a trained human driving the robot was the best achievable condition, hence assigned score 7.
   Then the participant performed 6 groups of handshakes, each group consisting of three handshakes arranged in the following order: C1, C6, and C(x), where C(x) is one of the conditions C1-C6 to be evaluated. In each handshake group C1 and C6 were carried out to remind the participant of the worst and best handshakes before C(x) was presented to standardize the latent scale of plausibility. Finally, the participant evaluates plausibility of social interaction for the condition C(x) and gives an integer score between 1 and 7.
3. Main experiment. After training, the main experiment took place which was performed in exactly the same way as the training. Again the participant performed 6 groups of handshakes, giving a score for the actual presented C(x). The order of presented handshake groups was randomized between participants.

3   Results and Discussion

In the following only data of the main experiment is analyzed. Descriptive results of the effect of the six conditions on the experienced plausibility of social interaction are depicted in Fig. 3. As can be seen the two extreme conditions C1 and C6 could be clearly identified and categorized compared to the other conditions. Since the two extreme conditions C1 and C6 have zero variance, no ANOVA (analysis of variance) could be calculated because of the violation of its assumptions. To analyze effects of the single modalities, conditions in vision (nV,V) and haptics (nH, H, Hm) were grouped and single t-tests were calculated to analyze whether adding the visual modality or adding/improving the haptic modality has a significant effect on plausibility. To keep the overall alpha error on a 5% level, the significance level for the individual tests was adjusted to 0.0125 according to Bonferroni (α/n, where n is the number of performed tests). Results show significant differences between the two conditions in vision ($t(12)= 9.54$; $p<.0125$; $r= .940$) and between the three conditions in haptics (nH-H: $t(12)= 7.584$; $p<.0125$; $r= .909$; nH-Hm: $t(12)= 12.660$; $p<.0125$; $r= 0.965$; H-Hm: $t(12)= 3.926$; $p<.0125$; $r= .752$).

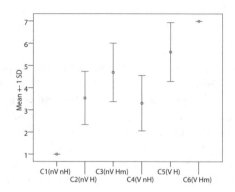

Fig. 3. Mean values and standard deviation among different conditions

Thus, it can be concluded that adding vision as well as adding and improving haptic feedback to the studied social interaction scenario "handshaking" can all improve the plausibility of interaction. Similar effect sizes for the conducted tests indicate further that the two components vision and haptics are equally important for the experienced handshake plausibility and thus, both need to be taken into account for system design.

4   Conclusions

The influence of visual and haptic feedback on plausibility of social interaction was investigated. To this end, an experimental approach was employed, where human participants were invited to perform handshakes with a virtual character while experiencing different visual and haptic rendering strategies. The results suggest that adding vision as well as improving haptics have a positive effect on experienced plausibility of a handshake and that the two modalities both contribute to this illusion.

Future directions include improving the information richness of the visual scenario to provide different levels of vision conditions, as well as introducing new haptic rendering algorithms into the comparison.

Acknowledgements

This work is supported by the ImmerSence project within the 6th Framework Programme of the European Union, FET- Presence Initiative, contract number IST-2006-027141.

References

1. Autodesk. 3ds Max. http://www.autodesk.com
2. Basdogan, C., Ho, C.H., Srinivasan, M.A., Slater, M.: An experimental study on the role of touch in shared virtual environments. ACM Transactions on Computer-Human Interaction (TOCHI) 7(4), 443–460 (2000)
3. Cobos, S., Ferre, M., Ortego, J., Sanchez-Uran, M.: Simplified hand configuration for object manipulation. In: Ferre, M. (ed.) EuroHaptics 2008. LNCS, vol. 5024, pp. 730–735. Springer, Heidelberg (2008)
4. CyberGlove, http://www.cyberglovesystems.com/
5. Giannopoulos, E., Eslava, V., Oyarzabal, M., Hierro, T., González, L., Ferre, M., Slater, M.: The effect of haptic feedback on basic social interaction within shared virtual environments. In: Proceedings of Euro Haptics 2008, Madrid, Spain, pp. 301–307 (2008)
6. Hoffman, H.: Physically touching virtual objects using tactil augmentation enhances the realism of virtual environments. In: Proceedings of the IEEE Virtual Reality Annual International Symposium, USA, pp. 59–63 (1998)
7. Lederman, S., Thorne, G., Jones, B.: Perception of texture by vision and touch: Multidimensionality and intersensory integration. Journal of Experimental Psychology: Human Perception and Performance 12(2), 169–180 (1986)
8. Peer, A., Buss, M.: A New Admittance Type Haptic Interface for Bimanual Manipulations. IEEE/ASME Transactions on Mechatronics 13(4), 416–428 (2008)
9. Sallnäs, E., Rassmus-Gröhn, K., Sjöström, C.: Supporting presence in collaborative environments by haptic force feedback. ACM Transactions on Computer-Human Interaction 7, 461–476 (2000)
10. Slater, M.: Place illusion and plausibility can lead to realistic behaviour in immersive virtual environments. Philosophical Transactions of the Royal Society of London B (in Press), http://www.cs.ucl.ac.uk/staff/m.slater/Papers/rss-prepublication.pdf/
11. Slater, M., Marcos, D., Ehrsson, H., Sanchez-Vives, M.: Inducing illusory ownership of a virtual body. Frontiers in Neuroscience 3(2), 214–220 (2009)
12. SmithMicro. Poser, http://www.smithmicro.com/poser
13. Wang, Z., Peer, A., Buss, M.: An HMM approach to realistic haptic human-robot interaction. In: Proceedings of World Haptics, USA, pp. 374–379 (2009)

Haptic Feedback Increases Perceived Social Presence

Eva-Lotta Sallnäs

Dept of Human-Computer Interaction
Royal Institute of Technology, S-100 44 Stockholm, Sweden
evalotta@csc.kth.se

Abstract. Passing an object between two people is a common event that happens in various forms for example when giving someone a cup of coffee. An experimental study is presented where passing objects between two people in a virtual environment with haptic feedback was compared to passing objects in a nonhaptic virtual environment. The aim of the experiment was to investigate if and how added haptic feedback in such an environment affects perceived virtual presence, perceived social presence and perceived task performance. A within subject design was used, were nine pairs of subjects performed a hand off task with six differently sized cubes without audio communication. Results showed that haptic force feedback significantly improved perceived virtual presence, perceived social presence and perceived performance in this experiment.

Keywords: Haptic, Presence, Social presence, Collaborative.

1 Introduction

In face-to-face communication and collaboration people are used to being able to both see and hear other persons. People also take for granted the possibility to give objects to each other, to shake hands or to get someone's attention by a pat on the shoulder. However, current systems for mediated collaboration usually do not take physicality into account but are for example shared editors that are just extensions of the single user GUI. Now emerging media space technologies like three-dimensional haptic interfaces makes it possible to interact physically in shared haptic object spaces. Many questions then arise about the effects of these modalities on communication and collaboration. Theories of social presence [27, 20] have argued that the more modalities used for mediated communication the more socially rich the interaction is perceived to be. It has also been argued that the more modalities used the more present and immersed a person perceives himself to be in a remote or distributed environment when he in fact is physically in another environment [30].

Haptic sensing is defined as the use of motor behaviors in combination with touch to identify objects [1]. In a shared haptic object-space people can coordinate joint movement of objects by signaling direction through haptic force and they can give objects to each other almost without verbal communication. Also, the bilateral [4] qualities of haptic perception makes it possible to both move an object and getting information from it at the same time. In a collaborative situation these aspects of haptic sensing can facilitate the joint understanding of complex information. In this paper

A.M.L. Kappers et al. (Eds.): EuroHaptics 2010, Part II, LNCS 6192, pp. 178–185, 2010.

an experimental study is presented with the aim of investigating the effects of haptic feedback on subject's perceived social presence, virtual presence and perceived performance when collaborating in an environment. In an earlier experiment it was shown that if people could communicate through audio (telephone), haptic feedback did not improve subject's perceived social presence but indeed the perceived virtual presence and perceived performance [21, 22]. In the experiment presented here subjects did not have audio communication that in the earlier study might have overshadowed the effects of haptic feedback on perceived social presence. In the study presented in this paper not only perceived virtual presence and performance was significantly improved but also perceived social presence.

2 Background

2.1 Perceived Presence

Ever since people started to communicate and collaborate with media, the notion that media differ regarding how well people could communicate what they intended has been of interest. Social presence theory [27] evolved through research about efficiency and satisfaction in the use of different telecommunications media. Social presence refers to the feeling of being socially present with another person at a remote location. Short et al. [27] regard social presence as a single dimension that represents a cognitive synthesis of several factors that are naturally occurring in face-to-face communication. Among these are the capacity to transmit information about tone of voice, gestures, facial expression, direction of gaze, posture, touch and non-verbal cues as they are perceived by the individual to enhance presence in the medium. People are more or less aware of the degree of social capacity of a medium, and they choose to use a medium that is perceived to be appropriate for a given task or purpose [8, 20, 27]. In relation to virtual reality, it has increasingly become recognized that it is important to investigate the social dimension of perceived presence. In virtual reality contexts, the concepts of togetherness, co-presence and also social presence are used in order to address issues of social interaction [10, 13]. The notion of togetherness has been investigated as a sense of people being together in a shared virtual space [10]. Modes of interaction are claimed to be important for enhancing the sense of togetherness. In contrast to the notion of social presence, there is also the notion of presence, or of feeling as if being more or less physically inside a computer-generated environment that feels like reality. The notion of presence is linked here to a state of consciousness, the psychological state of being there in a virtual environment (VE) [28]. Similarly, Witmer and Singer [30] define presence as the subjective experience of being in a place or environment, even when one is physically situated in another. This notion of being present in locations that are not physical has also been called virtual presence [9]. Factors that affect immersion include isolation from the physical environment, perception of self-inclusion in the VE, natural modes of interaction, and control of ones own interaction and the perception of self-movement. For an extensive review of definitions and measures of presence see Sanchez-Vives and Slater [26].

A number of projects have explored haptic interpersonal communication interfaces or devices and a lot of interesting aspects of haptic communication have been addressed [5, 12, 29]. The positive effect of haptic feedback on collaboration has also been shown in a number of studies (2, 6, 7, 14, 15, 16, 18). In one experiment, results showed that haptic feedback enhanced perceived togetherness and improved task performance when pairs of people worked together VE [3]. In another study the use of haptic cursor communication mechanisms was investigated in a two-dimensional multiuser haptic interface [19]. Results showed that haptic feedback significantly increased presence (ITC Presence Questionnaire), and that the usability was significantly improved in the haptic condition measured by a usability questionnaire. The aimed movement paradigm of Fitts [11] has been widely applied in human computer research. Traditionally, Fitts' law has been applied to the paradigm that one person is asked to move a pointer to a stationary target. It has been shown however, that Fitts' law could also apply to a collaboratively performed Fitts' law task [17, 23]. Intuitively, haptic feedback plays a critical role in object hand off. The giver has to sense that the recipient has firmly grasped the object before releasing it. The recipient has to feel that the giver is releasing it before taking it towards oneself. Object hand off is a type of joint haptic event between two people that requires coordinated action to accomplish.

3   Method

The main aim of this study was to test the hypothesis that a three-dimensional collaborative VE supporting the touch modality will increase the perceived virtual presence, perceived social presence and perceived task performance.

(H1)   Haptic force feedback increases perceived social presence
(H2)   Haptic force feedback increases perceived virtual presence
(H3)   Haptic force feedback increases perceived performance

3.1 Design and Task

Eighteen subjects participated in this experiment with the mean age of 29. There were nine dyads - each consisting of one woman and one man except one dyad with two men. The subjects were students from Stockholm University and Royal Institute of Technology in Sweden and a few administrative staff.

A within subject design was used in the experiment presented here. Each subject was seated in front of a haptic display system in separate rooms (Figure 1.). Subjects used their dominant hand for the hand off task. Subjects were not able to communicate verbally with each other during the experiment. To begin the task, the experimenter took a cube from the upper shelves and placed the cube on one of the target shelves. Subjects were instructed to alternately grasp that cube with the haptic devise, lift it and hand it to the other subject who tapped the second target shelf with the cube. Subsequently, the second subject returned the cube to the first subject who then proceeded to tap the first shelf and so on. Subjects were asked to do the hand off task over a period of 60 seconds. The subjects were told when to start and when to stop doing the task. The experimenter then placed the next cube at a target shelf and the subjects proceeded with the hand off task. Task difficulty was manipulated by changing cube sizes in randomized order.

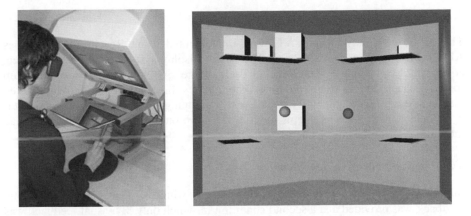

Fig. 1. The left picture shows the experimental setting for one of the two subjects and the picture on the right shows the two subjects represented by a blue and a green sphere respectively performing a hand off task in the collaborative VE

The definition of social presence in this experimental study was "feeling that one is present with another person in a mediated environment". The social presence questionnaire was based on dimensions argued to be important in the Social presence theory [27]. A bipolar seven point Likert-type scale was used. The questionnaire consisted of 34 questions. The items in the questionnaire can be found in Sallnäs's thesis [24]. In this study presence will be referred to as virtual presence and was defined as, "feeling as if being in a mediated environment". Virtual presence was measured using the Witmer and Singers Presence questionnaire (PQ) with Likert-type seven-point scales. In their article, Witmer and Singer [30] describe the specific questions in great detail. Aspects measured are according to Witmer and Singer the feeling of being able to control events, whether the VE seems responsive to actions and how involved the subject became in the experience. Furthermore, how natural the interaction felt, how consistent the VE was with reality, and how natural the movement control was. Finally, whether the controls or the display interfere or distract from task performance, and the extent to which they felt able to concentrate on the task. The PQ was translated into Swedish, three questions about audio were excluded and one very complex question was reformulated into two questions. The questionnaire used in this study finally consisted of 30 questions. Perceived task performance was measured by a questionnaire using bipolar Likert-type seven-point scales. The questionnaire focused on the users' evaluation of their own task performance when using the system, how well they understood the system and to what degree they felt that they learned how to use the system and also their skill level in using specific features in the system. The questionnaire consisted of 14 questions. The items in the questionnaire can be found in Sallnäs's thesis [24].

The validity of the three questionnaires used in the study presented here has been validated in a principal component and a factor analysis performed in a study by Sallnäs [25]. In that study it was shown that especially the items in the social presence questionnaire formed a very distinct cluster.

3.2 Apparatus

The haptic and the nonhaptic VE were implemented using Reachin Technologies AB's API on a Windows 2000 PC. The haptic display systems used in this project consisted of two displays from Reachin Technologies AB with two Desktop Phantom force feedback devices from SensAble Technologies, Inc. This system provides stereo vision through Stereographics CrystalEyes 3 shutter glasses. In order to avoid network delays and related problems, both devices ran on the same PC. Both users had the same view of the environment.

3.3 The Collaborative Interfaces

In the experiment there were two conditions, one in which 3D visual and 3DOF haptic feedback was provided and a second condition in which only 3D visual feedback was provided but where the same haptic devise was used. It then functioned as a 3D computer mouse. The three-dimensional haptic collaborative interface was designed as a room with two larger shelves, on top of which six cubes were placed, three on each side (Figure 1.). The room also contained two smaller shelves that served as target areas, underneath the two larger shelves. Two cursors, colored green and blue, corresponded to the tip positions of the two Phantom probes.

In both the haptic and the nonhaptic environment it was possible to grasp a cube by touching the cube with a cursor and then pressing the button on the haptic device. Once grasped, the cube could be moved in the environment. The haptic user interface was developed so that all surfaces in the environment were touchable and thus provided haptic force feedback. It was also possible to "feel" gravity, and collisions between cubes. Finally, if two subjects grasped the same object by pushing a button on at the haptic pen-like devise they could feel the forces applied to that object by the other person, as a rigid virtual connection was implemented in this interface. The haptic properties of the cubes were texture, size, weight and stiffness. All other surfaces in the environment were also haptic with a certain friction and stiffness.

In the condition without haptic force feedback, the user could neither feel the cubes, walls, floor nor the shelves in the environment. In that case, the Phantom functioned solely as a 3D mouse without force feedback.

4 Results

The analysis of the data, using repeated measures ANOVA, showed three significant differences between the three-dimensional visual/haptic condition and the three-dimensional visual only condition. The three significant results were perceived virtual presence, perceived social presence and perceived task performance. The significance level chosen was $p \leq 0.05$.

Perceived virtual presence improved significantly ($F=5.11$ $p=0.037$) in the haptic feedback condition (Table 1.). As there were 30 questions the mean value on a seven point Likert type scale was 5.7 for the haptic condition and 5.2 in the nonhaptic condition.

Perceived social presence improved significantly ($F=10.76$ $p=0.004$) in the haptic feedback condition compared to the nonhaptic condition (Table 1.). As this questionnaire had 34 questions the mean value on a seven point Likert type scale was 5.2 for the haptic condition and 4.6 in the nonhaptic condition.

Perceived performance also improved significantly (F=4.80 p=0.043) in the haptic compared to the nonhaptic condition (Table 1.). The mean value as this questionnaire had 14 questions was 6.1 in the haptic and 5.5 in the nonhaptic condition.

Table 1. Experimental results regarding perceived social presence, virtual presence and perceived performance for the 18 subjects, the unit of analysis are the 9 dyads

(n=9)		Haptic feedback	No haptic feedback
Virtual presence	F=5.11 p=0.037*	M=171, sd=20	M=156, sd=25
Perceived Performance	F=4.80 p=0.043*	M=85, sd=11	M=77, sd=13
Social presence	F=10.76 p=0.004*	M=178, sd=27	M=158, sd=34

* = significant at 5 % level

Reliability analyses were performed on the questionnaires and the internal consistency measures of reliability (Cronbach´s Alpha) were 0.95 for the social presence questionnaire, 0.91 for the virtual presence questionnaire and 0.91 for the perceived performance questionnaire. This is well beyond 0.80 that is used as a limit for what is considered acceptable in social science studies. Cronbach's alpha measures how well a set of items measures a single unidimensional latent construct.

5   Conclusions

Results from this study showed that haptic feedback increased subject's perceived virtual presence significantly. This result is consistent with the study performed by Oakley et al. [19] where feelings of presence in a collaborative VE were improved measured by the ITC Presence Questionnaire. It thus seams as if haptic feedback makes the impression that one is actually there in a mediated environment much stronger than if one does not have haptic feedback. The results from this study also show a significant difference in how well subjects perceived that they performed in the haptic VE compared to a nonhaptic environment. Subjects commented, after experimental sessions in this study, on the fact that they felt more secure in handing off cubes in the haptic environment. This result validates the results from the quantitative results from this study [23] that showed that the hand off task was performed with significantly improved precision in the condition with haptic feedback. The most interesting result was that haptic feedback increased the perceived social presence, which means that people perceived that the interaction with the other person was socially rich to a larger extent in the haptic environment. Following from the topics in the social presence questionnaire people perceive that the interaction was more personal, social and that they understood and could express feelings and intentions to a larger extent and that they perceived the other person as more real and socially present. In Basdogan et al. [3] study they also showed that the feeling of togetherness was significantly improved by haptic feedback. However, results from an earlier study [21] were audio communication (telephone) was provided showed, no significant differences regarding social presence between a haptic and a nonhaptic condition. One plausible interpretation is that audio (telephone) communication overshadows the effect of haptic feedback on perceived social presence.

References

1. Appelle, S.: Haptic perception of form: Activity and stimulus attributes. In: Heller, M., Schiff, W. (eds.) The Psychology of Touch, pp. 169–188. Lawrence Erlbaum Associates, Inc., New Jersey (1991)
2. Bailenson, J.N., Yee, N.: Virtual interpersonal touch: Haptic interaction and copresence in collaborative virtual environments. International Journal of Multimedia Tools and Applications 37(1), 5–14 (2008)
3. Basdogan, C., Ho, C., Srinivasan, M.A., Slater, M.: An experimental study on the role of touch in shared virtual environments. ACM Transactions on Computer-Human Interaction 7(4), 443–460 (2000)
4. Biggs, J., Srinivasan, M.A.: Haptic Interfaces. In: Stanney, K.M. (ed.) Handbook of Virtual Environment Technology. Lawrence Erlbaum Associates, Inc., Mahwah (2002)
5. Brave, S., Ishii, H., Dahley, A.: Tangible interfaces for remote collaboration and communication. In: Proceedings of CSCW 1998, Seattle, pp. 169–178 (1997)
6. Burke, J., Prewett, M.S., Gray, A.A., Yang, L., Stilson, F.R.B., Coovert, M.D., Elliot, L.R., Redden, E.: Comparing the Effects of Visual-Auditory and Visual-Tactile Feedback on User Performance: A Meta-analysis. In: Proceedings of the 8th International Conference on Multimodal Interfaces, Banff, Alberta, Canada, November 2-4, pp. 108–117 (2006)
7. Crossan, A., Brewster, S.: Multimodal Trajectory Playback for Teaching Shape Information and Trajectories to Visually Impaired Computer Users. ACM Transactions on Accessible Computing, article 12, 1(2) (2008)
8. Daft, R.L., Lengel, R.: Organizational information requirements, media richness, and structural design. Management Science 32, 554–571 (1986)
9. Ditlea, S.: Another world: Inside artificial reality. PC Computing 2(11), 95–102 (1989)
10. Durlach, N., Slater, M.: Presence in shared virtual environments and virtual togetherness. Presence: Teleoperators and virtual environments 9(2), 214–217 (2000)
11. Fitts, P.M.: The information capacity of the human motor system in controlling the amplitude of movement. Journal of Experimental Psychology 47(6), 381–391 (1954)
12. Fogg, B.J., Cutler, L., Arnold, P., Eisback, C.: HandJive: a device for interpersonal haptic entertainment. In: Proceedings of CHI 1998, Los Angeles, pp. 57–64 (1998)
13. Heeter, C.: Being there: The subjective experience of presence. Presence: Teleoperators and virtual Environments 1(2), 262–271 (1992)
14. Lee, S., Kim, G.J.: Effects of haptic feedback, stereoscopy, and image resolution on performance and presence in remote navigation. International Journal of Human-Computer Studies 66(10), 701–717 (2008)

15. McGookin, D., Brewster, S.: An initial investigation into non-visual computer supported collaboration. In: Conference on Human Factors in Computing Systems, San Jose, California, April 28-May 3, pp. 2573–2578 (2007)
16. Moll, J., Sallnäs, E.-L.: Communicative Functions of Haptic Feedback. In: Proceedings of the 4th International Conference on Haptic and Audio Interaction Design (HAID 2009), Dresden, Germany, September 10-11, pp. 1–10 (2009)
17. Mottet, D., Guiard, Y., Ferrand, T., Bootsma, R.J.: Two-handed performance of a rhythmical Fitts task by individuals and dyads. Journal of Experimental Psychology: Human Perception and Performance 27(6) (2001)
18. Nam, C.S., Shu, J., Chung, D.: The roles of sensory modalities in collaborative VEs (CVEs). Computers in Human Behavior 24, 1404–1417 (2008)
19. Oakley, I., Brewster, S., Gray, P.: Can you feel the force? An investigation of Haptic Collaboration in Shared Editors. In: Proceedings of Eurohaptics 2001, pp. 54–59 (2001)
20. Rice, R.E.: Media appropriateness: Using social presence theory to compare traditional and new organizational media. Human Communication Research 19(4), 451–484 (1993)
21. Sallnäs, E.-L., Rassmus-Gröhn, K., Sjöström, C.: Supporting presence in collaborative environments by haptic force feedback. ACM Transactions on Computer-Human Interaction 7(4), 461–476 (2000)
22. Sallnäs, E.-L.: Improved precision in mediated collaborative manipulation of objects by haptic force feedback. In: Brewster, S., Murray-Smith, R. (eds.) Haptic HCI 2000. LNCS, vol. 2058, pp. 69–75. Springer, Heidelberg (2001)
23. Sallnäs, E.-L., Zhai, S.: Collaboration meets Fitts' law: Passing virtual objects with and without haptic force feedback. In: Rauterberg, M., Menozzi, M., Wesson, J. (eds.) Proceedings of INTERACT 2003, pp. 97–104. IOS Press, Amsterdam (2003)
24. Sallnäs, E.-L.: The effect of modality on social presence, presence and performance in collaborative VEs. Ph.D. thesis, TRITA-NA-0404. NADA, KTH, Sweden (2004)
25. Sallnäs, E.-L.: Effects of communication mode on social presence, presence and performance in collaborative virtual environments. Journal of Presence: Teleoperators and virtual environments 14(4), 434–449 (2005)
26. Sanchez-Vives, M.V., Slater, M.: From presence to consciousness through virtual reality. Nature Reviews Neuroscience 6, 332–339 (2005)
27. Short, J., Williams, E., Christie, B.: The Social Psychology of Telecommunications. Wiley, London (1976)
28. Slater, M., Wilbur, S.A.: framework for immersive virtual environments (FIVE): Speculations on the role of presence in virtual environments. Presence: Teleoperators and virtual environments 6(6), 603–616 (1997)
29. Strong, R., Gaver, B.: Feather, Scent and Shaker: Supporting simple intimacy. In: Videos, Demonstrations and Short Papers of CSCW 1996, Boston, pp. 29–30 (1998)
30. Witmer, B.G., Singer, M.J.: Measuring presence in virtual environments: A presence questionnaire. Presence: Teleoperators and virtual environments 7(3), 225–240 (1998)

Haptic/VR Assessment Tool for Fine Motor Control

Christophe Emery[1], Evren Samur[1], Olivier Lambercy[2],
Hannes Bleuler[1] and Roger Gassert[2]

[1] Ecole Polytechnique Fédérale de Lausanne, Robotic Systems Lab, Switzerland
[2] ETH Zurich, Rehabilitation Engineering Lab, Switzerland
{christophe.emery,evren.samur,hannes.bleuler}@epfl.ch,
{olambercy,gassertr}@ethz.ch

Abstract. The Nine Hole Peg Test (NHPT) is routinely used in clinical environments to evaluate a patient's fine hand control. A physician measures the total time required to insert nine pegs into nine holes and obtains information on the dexterity of the patient. Even though this method is simple and known to be reliable, using a virtual environment with haptic feedback instead of the classical device could give a more complete diagnosis which would isolate different constituting components of a pathology and objectively assess motor ability. Haptic devices enable extracting a large quantity of information by recording the position and the exerted forces at high frequency (1kHz). In addition to the creation of a realistic virtual counterpart of the NHPT, the present work also includes the implementation of real-time data analysis in order to extract meaningful and objective scores for the physician and the patient. A healthy group of volunteers performed the real and virtual tests which yielded a baseline for the scores of the different measured mobility parameters. Once calibrated, the virtual test successfully discriminates different mobility dysfunctions simulated by a healthy subject.

Keywords: haptics, virtual reality, clinical, assessment, dexterity.

1 Introduction

Robotics is widely used in industry because of its ability to precisely and repetitively control positions and interaction forces, and provide objective measures of various parameters, which has not only motivated its use in physical therapy, but also in clinical diagnostics. A haptic rendering system consisting of a screen (for visual feedback) and a haptic interface (for force feedback) allows immersing the user into a virtual scene [5] and tracking the movements of the user at a high frequency. A growing number of studies demonstrate that these systems give quite reliable information on the user's dexterity, for instance precision and stability [3]. Nevertheless, there are major issues that can interfere with these measures, such as the quality of the visual or force feedback, the limited workspace or the user's inability to link the scene on the screen to a displacement of the interface. However, this field is progressing quickly and these issues tend to disappear as the realism increases and the technologies evolve. Using a haptic rendering system to provide a recognized, objective measure of the dexterity of a human could soon be a reality.

A.M.L. Kappers et al. (Eds.): EuroHaptics 2010, Part II, LNCS 6192, pp. 186–193, 2010.

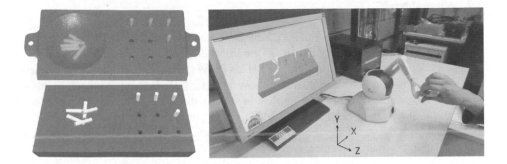

Fig. 1. Left: Conventional Nine Hole Peg Test (top) and its virtual counterpart (bottom). Right: Virtual NHPT setup.

The Nine Hole Peg Test (NHPT) is a common clinical tool to assess the dexterity of a subject with impaired mobility, and consists of the insertion and removal of nine pegs in nine holes (Fig. 1) with one hand as fast as possible. The total time is measured and allows the physician to evaluate the dexterity of the patient. However, this measure gives no information on specific parameters such as reaction time, stability or speed. Knowing that an insertion task requires a wide range of abilities such as upper limb mobility, movement coordination, precision and stability, a test that could extract more parameters than only the total execution time, but with the simplicity of the NHPT, would be of great benefit to obtain a better assessment of dexterity.

The goal of this study is to develop an experimental setup that takes advantage of the classical NHPT (easy to administer, standardized, established) and of a virtual environment (controlled environment, adjustable parameters, quantitative and objective measures), while trying to reduce the drawbacks of the haptic rendering system (vibrations, contact instabilities and realism) [2,9]. Previous studies suggested the potential of combining the NHPT with haptics technology [1,10]. However, these studies did not extract parameters related to orientation (important during grasping and insertion of pegs) or simulate active grasping of the pegs (e.g. over an integrated switch). Here, we propose a novel method to determine dexterity parameters based on the measurements extracted from the haptic device in order to provide objective information in an intuitive manner to physicians and patients.

2   Materials and Methods

2.1   Nine Hole Peg Test

The apparatus used in this study is the Rolyan© 9-Hole Peg Test consisting of a blue plastic board with nine holes on one side and a round container on the other, and nine white plastic pegs placed in the round container (Fig. 1). The board is 255 mm long, the pegs are 31.9 mm long and 6.2 mm in diameter and the holes are 7.2 mm in diameter and 12.8 mm deep. The test is sold for around 80$ and the validity and reliability of this test to evaluate dexterity have been demonstrated by clinical trials [6,8].

2.2   Virtual NHPT

The experimental setup consists of a PC (Intel Core 2 Duo with 3 GHz CPU) to run the tests, an LCD screen to display the virtual environment, and a force-feedback device to simulate haptic interactions (Fig. 1). The PHANTOM OMNI® from SensAble Technologies, Inc., which has 6-DOF positional sensing and 3-DOF force feedback, is used for this study as it has already been applied in similar studies [3,4] and is affordable for clinical use. It's workspace (160 W x 120 H x 70 D mm^3) is just wide enough to allow a 1:1 scale with the real setup and it's resolution of 55 μm is good enough to obtain a fine measure of human movements.

A dual-thread software package is developed to realize the virtual version of the NHPT. The graphic rendering is set up with OpenGL and GLu libraries. The low-level foundational API (hd and hdu) provided by the PHANTOM vendor is used for the interaction with the haptic interface. The haptic and visual loops are updated at a rate of 1000 and 60 Hz, respectively. The coordinate system was set in a way that the X-axis points right and the Y -axis points up.

The objects in the entire virtual scene are modeled as rigid bodies. These include ten cylinders (nine as the pegs (opaque white) and one as the cursor (transparent grey) representing the PHANTOM stylus), nine holes, the board and the ground. The distance between the cursor (or a peg) and the other objects is calculated for collision detection. A linear spring model with a stiffness value of 0.4 N/mm is implemented to render the force given by the device when there is a collision. The weight of the pegs is not considered in the simulation. During the peg insertion, the total force corresponds to the vectorial sum of a vertical force due to the penetration into the surface and an inward horizontal force due to penetration into the wall of the hole. This horizontal force is decreased by a factor of 0.15 in order to avoid instabilities (the diameter of the holes is only slightly larger than that of the pegs). Collisions between the pegs are not considered in the simulation. When the user presses one of the two buttons on the stylus, the grip is active and the cursor turns from transparent grey to transparent blue. When the cursor is precisely superimposed with a peg and the grip is active, the cursor becomes opaque red and the peg can then be manipulated. If the button is released, the peg falls from the cursor and its color turns back to opaque white. If the peg is correctly inserted into a hole, it becomes green, the cursor is ejected from the hole and the inserted peg cannot be moved any more.

Subjects and Procedure. Ten healthy volunteers aged between 23 and 38 (mean 26.8 $\pm$ 3.2) participated to the evaluation of the virtual NHPT. Two of them were left-handed and eight of them were not familiar with haptic interfaces. The goal of this study was to compare the real and virtual test, and determine baseline parameters to assess dexterity in healthy subjects.

The experiment consisted of two experimental conditions (real and virtual) performed with both hands (dominant and non-dominant). The tasks were crossed between subjects and randomly assigned in order to minimize the effect of learning. A task with the real test consisted of two training sessions followed by three recorded sessions where subjects were told to insert the 9 pegs, one at a time, as fast as possible, only with the tested hand. The test was completed once the nine pegs were inserted into the nine holes. Unlike the normal NHPT procedure, subjects were not told to remove the pegs after inserting them. Completion times of the three trials were averaged for the analysis. For the virtual test, the PHANTOM was placed on the side of the tested hand and the subject had to hold the stylus like a pen, with the thumb on the buttons. Raw data including elapsed time (t), positions (x,y,z), orientations in polar coordinates (ϕ,θ), forces (F_x,F_y,F_z) and order of peg manipulation (P), was recorded at 1 kHz.

3   Data Analysis

The analysis consists of two steps (Fig. 2): first the raw data is divided into sequences using position thresholds [7] to extract raw parameters (velocities, accelerations etc.), then each of these raw parameters is compared to its baseline and contributes to a calculated score that has meaning for both patients and physicians, such as precision, stability or flexibility.

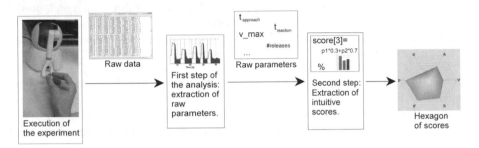

Fig. 2. Schematic representation of the data extraction process

Extraction of the Raw Parameters. For each movement (i.e. movement from a peg to a hole and then to a peg again), we extract nine raw parameters: the reaction time (t_{reac}), approach time (t_{appro}), mean velocity $(\bar{v})$, maximum velocity (v_{max}), maximum acceleration (a_{max}), sensitivity to orientation (σ_{ori}/μ_{ori}), number of zero-crossings of the acceleration signal $(\sharp_{jerks})$, number of drops $(\sharp_{drops})$, and root mean square of the forces $(\sqrt{\sum F^2})$. These values are averaged over the different movements within a trial to obtain raw parameters.

Extraction of the Scores. In order to give the physician more intuitive information, the six scores (representing different axes of mobility) were calculated using the raw parameters:

1. Velocity: indication of the displacement speed from one point to another. A low velocity could reveal muscle weakness or abnormal muscle tone.
2. Acceleration: indication of the capacity to reach a displacement speed in a short time. A lack of force could be the cause of a weak acceleration.
3. Stability: if the patient trembles (repeated inversion of the acceleration sign), encounters difficulties to keep the buttons pressed or often collides with virtual elements, this is interpreted as a lack of stability.

Table 1. The raw parameters and their weights to compute the scores

Weights	t_{reac}	t_{appro}	$\bar{v}$	v_{max}	a_{max}	$\sqrt{\sum F^2}$	$\#_{drops}$	$\#_{jerks}$	σ_{ori}/μ_{ori}
Velocity	0	0	0.5	0.5	0	0	0	0	0
Acceleration	0	0	0	0	1	0	0	0	0
Stability	0	0	0	0	0	0.2	0.3	0.5	0
Precision	0	0.7	0	0	0	0.3	0	0	0
Flexibility	0	0.5	0	0	0	0	0	0	0.5
Reactivity	1	0	0	0	0	0	0	0	0

4. Precision: highlights the patient's ability to align his/her hand quickly and precisely with a peg or hole (without pushing too much into the walls).
5. Flexibility: the patient's ability to move his/her wrist in order to access complex orientations with the stylus; this is revealed, on one hand, by the differences between the approach times of the pegs depending on their orientation and, on the other hand, by the approach speed of the pegs in general.
6. Reactivity: measure based on the time required to initiate a movement once a peg is grasped or inserted.

Each raw parameter is rated between 0 (very bad) and 100 (excellent) using an *arctan* function and two baselines. The baseline for a good result is set by the mean of all healthy subjects (corresponding to a score of 80) and the one for a bad result is arbitrarily set (corresponding to 20). Then the scores are calculated with weighted averages as shown in Table 1.

4   Results and Discussion

Comprehensibility. Healthy subjects who participated in this study quickly understood the principle and carried out the virtual test with a relative ease. The main issue that was encountered is the necessity to precisely superimpose the cursor to the pegs. Indeed, there is no force feedback between the cursor and the peg and the only feedback is visual, which was not sufficient for some users. A learning effect was visible even after the training sessions (for each subject, last session is around 12 % faster than the first one). Another issue was due to the limited workspace of the haptic device, which prevented some orientations of the stylus. Some pegs were thus only accessible with one specific orientation of the stylus, resulting in additional time to grab the virtual peg. This was countered by taking into account these limitations when setting the initial orientation of the virtual pegs.

General Trends. The recorded trajectories and forces clearly showed a repeatable pattern that was observed for every peg and each user. First, the cursor followed a coarse displacement to approach a peg, followed by a fine and slow move to precisely align with the peg. Subjects then performed another coarse movement up to a hole followed by a slow movement to insert the peg (Fig. 3).

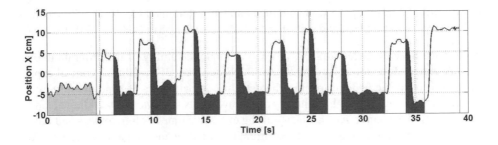

Fig. 3. X position in function of time in a typical session. Light grey: start phase; white: from peg to hole; and dark grey: from hole to peg.

Comparison between Real and Virtual Tests. When the total completion times of the real and virtual tests are compared, it appears that the virtual one is around three times longer than the real one. This is essentially due to the time required to align the cursor with the pegs. While in the real task the fingers allow grasping pegs in different orientations without turning the hand, this is not possible in the virtual task where the stylus needs to be aligned with the peg. Nevertheless, there is a good correlation between average completion times for the real and virtual test (R=0.77). This suggest that the virtual test gives results that are similar to the real NHPT, and validates its use as a tool to assess dexterity. In addition to the completion time, the virtual test offers the possibility of extracting additional values to quantitatively and objectively assess fine hand function.

Effect of Hand Dominance on Virtual Tests. An ANOVA was performed on total completion times depending on used hand and hand dominance (Table 2) and showed

Table 2. Mean and standard deviation of the completion time for the real and the virtual NHPT (a) and effect of hand dominance and used hand on the virtual test(b)

(a)

Test	Hand	N	Mean [s]	SD [s]
Real	Dominant hand	30	12.01	1.39
	Non-dominant hand	30	12.69	1.29
Virtual	Dominant hand	30	32.69	9.6
	Non-dominant hand	30	35.29	11.43

(b)

Dominance	Tested hand	N	Mean [s]	SD [s]
Right Hand	Right	24	33.68	10.45
	Left	24	36.54	12.45
Left Hand	Right	6	30.3	1.63
	Left	6	28.74	2.16

no significant differences between dominant and non-dominant hands (F(1;58)=0.88, p ≫ 0.05) and between left- and right-handed subjects (F(1;58)=2.68, p > 0.05).

Tests with Specific Behaviors. In order to evaluate the ability of the program to discriminate hand function according to the six chosen axes of mobility, a control experiment was conducted where specific characteristic impairments of hand mobility were simulated: *tremor*, with high frequency arm movements; *weakness*, by adding an additional mass to the hand; *inaccurate*, requiring excessive time to align to pegs and holes; *rough*, exerting high forces against the virtual board; *slow*, moving at low velocity. Results were compared to an optimal performance session by computing scores based on the raw parameters. Figure 4 presents the visual representation of scores, and demonstrates that the selected parameters could be used to detect specific impairments. For instance, the inaccurate behavior gave a low score on the precision axis, and the slow behavior resulted in a low velocity score and a low acceleration score.

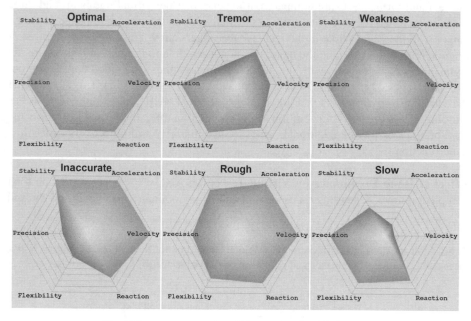

Fig. 4. Scores representing different simulated behaviors

5   Conclusion

A virtual counterpart of the established NHPT has been designed, implemented on a low-cost PHANTOM Omni device, and validated as a powerful VR tool for the assessment of dexterity and related impairments. This virtual test is easy to understand and perform. The main features of the hand movement can easily be detected and are found in every trial among all healthy subjects, which allows to analyze the raw data with a generalized algorithm and to fix baselines representing a healthy user's scores. In addition, the axes of mobility defined in this study reflect the fine hand motor functions of the user and successfully reveal the simulated impairments. As the current test group only involved subjects aged less than 38 years, it is possible that the results might not be generalized for subjects that are not used to virtual reality environments. Future work will focus on establishing a baseline for different age groups as well as with subjects suffering from impaired hand function, e.g., after stroke.

Acknowledgments. Olivier Lambercy and Roger Gassert are supported by the NCCR Neural Plasticity and Repair, Swiss National Science Foundation.

References

1. Amirabdollahian, F., Gomes, G.T., Johnson, G.R.: The Peg-in-Hole: A VR-Based Haptic Assessment for Quantifying Upper Limb Performance and Skills. In: IEEE 9th International Conference on Rehabilitation Robotics (2005)
2. Choi, S., Tan, H.Z.: Discrimination of Virtual Haptic Textures Rendered with Different Update Rates. In: Proc. of the 1st Joint Eurohaptics Conference and Symp. on Haptic Interfaces for Virtual Environment and Teleoperator Systems (2005)
3. Feys, P., et al.: Arm training in Multiple Sclerosis using Phantom: clinical relevance of robotic outcome measures. In: IEEE 11th Int. Conf. on Rehabilitation Robotics (2009)
4. Gomes, G.T., Amirabdollahian, F., Johnson, G.R.: Quantifying upper limb motor control: the Peg in Hole test. In: ISB XXth Congress - ASB 29th Annual Meeting (2005)
5. Hannaford, B., Wood, L., McAffee, D.A., Zak, H.: Performance Evaluation of a Six-Axis Generalized Force-Reflecting Teleoperator. IEEE Transactions on Systems, Man, and Cybernetics 21(3) (1991)
6. Mathiowetz, V., Weber, K., Kashman, N., Volland, G.: Adult norms for the Nine Hole Peg Test of finger dexterity. Occup. Ther. J. of R 5(1), 24–38 (1985)
7. Milner, T.E.: A model for the generation of movements requiring endpoint precision. Neuroscience 49(2), 487–496 (1992)
8. Oxford Grice, K., Vogel, K., Le, V., Mitchell, A., Muniz, S., Vollmer, M.: Adult norms for a commercially available Nine Hole Peg Test for finger dexterity. Am. J. Occup. Ther. 57(5), 570–573 (2003)
9. Unger, B.J., Nicolaidis, A., Berkelman, P.J., Thompson, A., Klatzky, R.L., Hollis, R.L.: Comparison of 3-D haptic peg-in-hole tasks in real and virtual environments. In: IEEE/RSJ, IROS, pp. 1751–1756 (2001)
10. Xydas, E.G., Louca, L.S.: Design and Development of a Haptic Peg-Board Exercise for the Rehabilitation of People with Multiple Sclerosis. In: IEEE 10th International Conference on Rehabilitation Robotics (2007)

Hand and Arm Ownership Illusion through Virtual Reality Physical Interaction and Vibrotactile Stimulations

Miguel A. Padilla, Silvia Pabon, Antonio Frisoli, Edoardo Sotgiu, Claudio Loconsole, and Massimo Bergamasco

Perceptual Robotics Lab (PERCRO), Scuola Superiore Sant'Anna,
Via Rinaldo Piaggio, 34, Pontedera(PI) 56025, Italy
{m.padillacastaneda,s.pabon,a.frisoli}@sssup.it
http://www.percro.org

Abstract. Body awareness has important implications for the use of virtual reality (VR) and its effectiveness. This involves the senses of agency and body ownership, studied in the past by producing the Rubber Hand Illusion (RHI). Recent studies reported the RHI on virtual environments (VE) by giving the participant synchronous 3D visual stimulation and passive tactile stimulation manually on the hidden real hand placed on a static position. In this paper we present a novel study of the RHI within highly dynamic VE sessions with synchronous pure virtual vibrotactile stimulation of the fingers. The hand/arm participant's movements are realistically reproduced on the VE and tactile stimulations are self-inflicted by the participant through actively touching the virtual objects. The results revealed that the RHI is possible in active, dynamic and fully multisensored VE sessions.

Keywords: Vibrotactile stimulations, Rubber Hand Illusion, Body awareness.

1 Introduction

It is considered that the effectiveness of a virtual environment (VE) relies on the sense of the user, or part of one's self to be there in the virtual environment, rather than on the current real place. Known as *Presence*, this is a subjective experience that requires the ability to focus on a meaningful coherent and correlated set of stimuli provided by the VE [1]. Such body awareness (the sense of one's own body), involves two important aspects: the sense of agency and the sense of body ownership. Agency is the sense of intending, executing actions and controlling one's own body movements. Body ownership refers to the sense that one's own body is the source of sensations [2]. Botvinick and Cohen in [4] introduced the Rubber Hand Illusion (RHI) that means the sense of feeling a fake virtual body part seems like the one's own body part, as a method for study body awareness. The RHI consisted on watching a rubber hand being stroked synchronously with one's own unseen hand causing the rubber hand to be attributed to one's own body. The illusion of ownership was evident by the displacement of sensation of feeling towards the rubber arm (proprioceptive awareness). The RHI has been replicated in the past [2,7,8]. For example, Tsakiris et al. [2] showed that active and passive

A.M.L. Kappers et al. (Eds.): EuroHaptics 2010, Part II, LNCS 6192, pp. 194–199, 2010.

movements, rather than tactile stimulation, would lead to body awareness when induced changes in body awareness are local and fragmented. Virtual reality and teleoperation systems have proven to be important tools for studying body self-identification [5,6,7]. Slater et al. [7] demonstrated that the illusion can be produced on a complete virtual limb, through passive tactile stimulation (manually controlled by the experimenter) on a persons hidden real right hand placed in a static position, with synchronous visual stimulation of the virtual arm.

In this paper we present a VR system for study presence and body ownership in VR and a novel study of the RHI within highly dynamic VE sessions with pure virtual vibrotactile stimulation of the fingers. During the sessions, the participant's own hand/arm movements are mapped on the virtual arm/hand at the time that tactile stimulations are self-inflicted by the participant through actively touching the virtual objects, thereby allowing the central nervous system to establish both visuotactile and visuomotor contingencies. The results of the proprioceptive drift and the response ratings over the questionnaire applied revealed that the RHI is possible in active, dynamic and fully multisensored VE sessions.

2   Virtual Reality System

The low cost PERCRO Data–Glove has some purely goniometric sensors (not sensitive to dimensions of the user hand) for measuring the relative angular displacement between two consecutive phalanxes of the hand. The vibrotactile feedback system consists of small motors commonly used as vibrational alarms in mobile devices. The motors are attached on the palm-side of the fingertips and can rotate at different speeds for setting up the vibration level. When there exists a collision between a virtual object and the hand inside the VE, a vibration arises and its intensity is controlled by varying the voltage delivered to each tactor. The hardware control architecture acquires the analogue signals from the goniometric sensors, and converts them to digital signals; afterwards the digital data are sent to a host computer via wireless bluetooth communications. For further information of the Percro data/glove communications system, see [9].

The human upper extremities model consists on three basic parts: 1) a kinematic model of the arm for movements tracking; 2) a dynamic model of the arm-hand for VR physical interaction; 3) a graphic model for visual feedback.

The kinematic model of the human arm was modeled as a 7 degrees of freedom (DoF) mechanism, consisting on three rotational joints: 3-DoFs between the shoulder and the upperarm (abduction-adduction, flexion-extension and pronation-supination of the upperarm); 2-DoFs at the elbow (flexion-extension, and pronation-supination of the forearm); 2-DoFs at the wrist with 2-DoFs (abduction-adduction and flexion-extension of the hand) [10]. A 3D fast and robust tracking system (Polhemus Liberty) with electromagnetic sensors were used to estimate in real-time the hand/arm user's poses; with an inverse kinematics closed solution the seven joints angles were estimated in real-time. The dynamic model consist on a multibody rigid dynamic system, where each rigid body has its own collision geometry, dynamic properties, and are serially interconnected with spring-dampers constrained rotational joints: 3-DoFs for the proximal, intermedial and distal articulations of the fingers; 4-DoFs for the thumb (including the limb articulation); 3-DoFs for the shoulder-upperarm and forearm-hand linkages and another 1-DoF for the elbow. The moded was implemented in C++ using the NVIDIA PhysX simulation engine and the VRMedia XVR programming system for VR.

3   Experimental Methods

The sessions were performed on a VR Cave of 2 x 2.5 m under the following conditions (figure 1): the participant wears stereovision glasses; wears the data-glove with the electronic system attached to the forearm; wears two sensors for tracking the right arm movements (at the wrist and elbow) and one sensor at the left hand's index finger for indicating the right arm position. The participant stood up in front of the display and had the perspective as looking its own right arm; the participant's real arm was hidden all the time inside a platform; the experiments were performed in a light-off room.

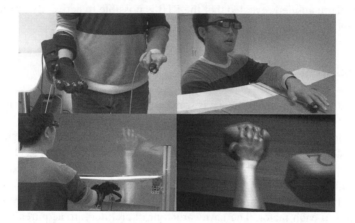

Fig. 1. VE for study the body ownership illusion of a virtual hand/arm with vibrotactile stimulations

Twenty healthy participants were recruited for the experiment, among students and personnel of the staff, nobody involved on the details of the experiments. The experiments were divided in two modalities: in synchronous and asynchronous modes, as is explained later in the text.

At the beginning of the session the participant moved and put their right arm on the platform at the starting pose. Immediately, with the Cave display in black, the participant pointed the position were he/she toughs his/her right hand was by using the sensor in his left hand's index finger. The system showed again the virtual arm and placed for some seconds three virtual cubes at random position on a virtual table. Then, the participant was motivated to move his real arm hand-fingers and to touch the yellow block at the time that received vibrotactile stimulations on the fingers and visuomotor stimulation of the virtual arm/hand/fingers postures. During the sessions the participant repeatedly performed the active tapping exercises for 4 minutes. From the beginning of the session, an unnoticeable and incremental drift on the virtual right arm towards the left of the display was applied, by introducing progressive medial rotation in total of 40°

with the elbow joint extended (by contribution of the abduction-adduction, shoulder's pronation-supination and elbow's pronation-supination movements). At the end of the session the system turned off the scene and next the participants quickly indicated again with their left index finger the position where they thought their right hand was. This allowed to measure the proprioceptive drift by computing the difference between the felt positions of the hand before and after the experiments. The asynchronous condition consisted on a vibratory and visual discrepancy introduced by a time delay on the user movements of approximately 4 seconds, a sufficient delay to reduce the RHI [3].

At the end of both sessions the participant answered a questionnaire of 13 questions, similar to the one used in [7] but extended to the particularities of this method and translated into Italian. Each question was rated by the participants using a 7-point Likert scale (1 means totally disagree and 7 totally agree); five questions were considered as indicators of the RHI and 8 questions were considered as control questions. The illusion questions were:

1) *Sometimes I had the sensation that my own arm was where the virtual hand was*;
2) *Sometimes I had the sensation that the vibration I felt on my hand was on the same point where the virtual hand was in contact with the objects*;
3) *Sometimes I had the sensation that the vibration I felt on my hand was caused by the contact of the objects in contact with the virtual hand*;
4) *Sometimes I had the sensation that the virtual hand was my own hand*;
12) *The movements of the virtual hand and fingers were caused by my own movements.*

Question 1 asses the proprioception; question 2 and 3 asses the tactile sensation; question 4 asses the ownership illusion; and question 12 asses the sense of agency.

4   Results

For the proprioceptive drift evaluation, we calculated the relative differences between the signed horizontal distance between the real and thought positions of the participant's hand, both before and after the experiment. Then we obtained the drift by subtracting these two relative differences. After discarding 5 cases (due to measuring errors done by the practitioners), we observed a significant drift for the synchronous condition: a mean drift of 1.60 cm with a range from -1.2 to 6.36 cm and a standard deviation of 2.24 cm (with significant $p=0.03010$ on t-test). We found on that a significant drift does not hold for the asynchronous condition: a mean drift of 0.31 cm for with a range from -4.99 cm to 7.40 cm with a standard deviation of 2.94 cm (with no significant p value on t-test).

Figure 2 shows the questionnaire responses. For the synchronous condition the results of Q1,Q2,Q3,Q4 and Q12 have higher scores than the control questions. For the asynchronous condition the results for the same questions are not much higher than the other ones, with exception of Q3, Q11 and Q12. Q3 could have a vague interpretation (feeling vibrations at contact even if the virtual hand follows the real hand or not). For question Q2 this can be explained because the participants learned to predict the imposed time delay and anticipate their movements. Control question Q11 (*The hand and fingers seemed to move by themselves*) had a high score as expected, due to the visual discrepancy introduced by the time delay. Comparing the scores on both conditions,

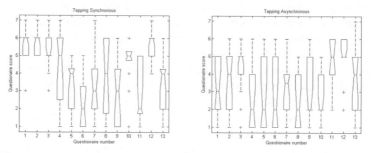

Fig. 2. Questionnaire responses. a) Synchronous condition. b) Asynchronous condition. Questions 1,2,3,4,12 address the RHI illusion. The medians are shown in red lines, the cones are the interquartile ranges (IQR), the whiskers indicates the extreme data points, and the + represents the outliers.

could be observed that in questions Q1,Q2,Q4 and Q12 that indicate the illusion, the median scores are greater and significantly different for the synchronous condition (with $p < 0.05$ for all Q1,Q2,Q4 and Q12, by comparing both conditions by using Wilcoxon rank sum tests). In particular, Q4 that directly evaluates if the participant experienced the ownership illusion has a low score on the asynchronous condition as expected, and a greater score or "agree" response on the synchronous condition.

5   Conclusions

In this paper we presented a VR system of the human arm/hand for doing studies on presence and body ownership in VE. The system consists on a data-glove with fully actuated vibrotactile stimulation capabilities and a virtual hand/arm model for visual stimulation. We studied the sense of ownership and agency in virtual environments by studying the effect of multiple sensory-motor correlations (synchronous or asynchronous), in particular visual, proprioceptive (arm, wrist, fingers) and vibrotactile sensory stimulation. We also evaluated the existence of proprioceptive drift in non static and high dynamic conditions and applied the ownership illusion by the application of a questionnaire. Both, the proprioceptive drift and the questionnaires revealed that there is a significant difference between synchronous and the asynchronous conditions. In fact, greater responses are found for the synchronous conditions. As a consequence, the results revealed that the RHI, it means ownership illusion, is possible in very active and fully multisensored VE sessions. Future work includes to extend the study to other conditions: varying the vibrotactile intensity, including stimulations to the palm and the arm, using an arm/hand model with a complete non-human synthetic appearance, among others.

Acknowledgments

This work is funded under the European Union FET project PRESENCCIA Contract Number 27731.

References

1. Witmer, B.G., Singer, M.J.: Measuring Presence in Virtual Environments: A Presence Questionnaire. Presence 7(3), 225–240 (1998)
2. Tsakiris, M., Prabhu, G., Haggard, P.: Having a body versus moving your body: How agency structures body-ownership Consciousness and Cognition 15, 423–432 (2006)
3. Tsakiris, M., Hesse, M.D., Boy, C., Haggard, P., Fink, G.R.: Neural signatures of body ownership: a sensory network for bodily self-consciousness. Cerebral Cortex 17, 2235–2244 (2007)
4. Botvinick, M., Cohen, J.: Rubber hands feel touch that eyes see. Nature 391, 756 (1998)
5. Haans, A., IJsselsteijn, W.A.: Self-Attribution and Telepresence. In: Procs. of the 10th Annual Int. Workshop on Presence, Barcelona, Spain, pp. 51–58 (2007)
6. Raz, L., Weiss, P.L., Reiner, M.: The Virtual Hand Illusion and Body Ownership. In: Ferre, M. (ed.) EuroHaptics 2008. LNCS, vol. 5024, pp. 367–372. Springer, Heidelberg (2008)
7. Slater, M., Perez-Marcos, D., Ehrsson, H.H., Sanchez-Vives, M.V.: Towards a digital body: the virtual arm illusion. Frontiers in Human Neurosciences, Article 6, 2, 1–8 (2008)
8. Kammers, M.P.M., Longo, M.R., Tsakiris, M., Dijkerman, H.C., Haggard, P.: Specificity and coherence of body representations. Perception 38(12), 1804–1820 (2009)
9. Portillo-Rodriguez, O., Avizzano, C., Sotgiu, E., Pabon, S., Frisoli, A., Ortiz, J., Bergamasco, M.: A wireless bluetooth dataglove based on a novel goniometric sensors. In: Procs. of the IEEE RO-MAN 2007, 16th IEEE International Symposium on Robot & Human Interactive Communication, pp. 1185–1190 (2007)
10. Mihelj, M.: Human arm kinematics for robot based rehabilitation. Robotica 24, 377–383 (2006)

Part III
Grasping and Moving

Animating a Synergy-Based Deformable Hand Avatar for Haptic Grasping

Sara Mulatto[1], Alessandro Formaglio[1], Monica Malvezzi[1],
and Domenico Prattichizzo[1,2]

[1] Department of Information Engineering, University of Siena
[2] Italian Institute of Technology, Genova, Italy
mulatto@dii.unisi.it, formaglio@dii.unisi.it, malvezzi@dii.unisi.it,
prattichizzo@dii.unisi.it

Abstract. A 3D deformable hand avatar for virtual grasping using multiple single-contact-point haptic devices is introduced. The proposed technique has two main advantages. First, the whole hand motion is reconstructed by measuring only fingertips positions and using a biomechanical model of the hand along with the postural synergies characterizing grasping actions. Secondly, this technique requires only simple algebraic computations.

Keywords: hand, grasping, multicontact, synergies, animation.

1 Introduction

Haptically enabled applications are getting widespread also for end users that are not very familiar with virtual reality. In spite of the great deal of development, often users complain they cannot see an avatar of their hands in the virtual simulation scenario, thus losing a relevant visual feedback commonly available in reality. To provide for this lack, two main approaches can be found in the literature: the first consists in representing a low-detail avatars using sets of geometrical primitives (cylinders and spheres), whose computational complexity allows real-time simulations [1]. The second is based on pre-computing several deformation patterns for a 3D hand model and interpolating them to perform data-driven real-time animation [2]. Anyway, both approaches are characterized by the use of multifingered devices or gloves featuring high number of sensors to capture the real hand motion.

Our approach consists of realizing a high-realism hand avatar that can be animated in virtual grasping applications using some single-contact-point haptic devices. Such devices allow to capture only fingertips motion, therefore the movement of the whole hand is reconstructed using a biomechanics-based kinematical model and exploiting a neuroscience-based technique to reduce the number of degrees of freedom (DoFs). In particular, recent studies in [3, 4] demonstrated that, notwithstanding the complexity of the human hand, a few input control variables, named *postural synergies*, are able to account for most of the variance in the patterns of hand movements and configurations in manipulation and grasping tasks. These conclusions were based on the results of experimental tests in which subjects were asked to perform grasping actions on a wide

A.M.L. Kappers et al. (Eds.): EuroHaptics 2010, Part II, LNCS 6192, pp. 203–210, 2010.

variety of objects. Data were recorded by means of data gloves and were analyzed with the Principal Component Analysis (PCA) technique. Our assumption is that the *postural synergies* can be represented as a joint displacement aggregation corresponding to a reduced dimension representation of hand movements. In other words, the synergies are a set of dependencies among the hand joints angles that allow to accurately approximate the hand shape in grasping tasks reducing the number of DoFs. Their main advantage is that just few synergies are sufficient to reasonably approximate the general shape of the hand during a grasp, while higher-order synergies account for finer and subtle adjustments of fingers depending on the target object shape.

Hence, the key idea of the proposed technique consists in capturing only the motion of some fingertips, e.g. index and thumb, transforming measures in the related joint-space trajectories and using synergies to suitably distribute such trajectories to the whole hand joints. Once the current kinematic configuration of the hand skeleton has been computed, the consequent skin deformation is achieved using a smooth skinning technique. This solution involves only algebraic computation for kinematic inversion, and requires no time-consuming optimization neither the online solution of dynamic equations.

This work presents an application of the proposed technique in a virtual pinch grasping simulation, involving the index and the thumb fingers. The remainder of this paper is structured as follows: in Section 2 the design of the 3D model is discussed; Section 3 reports the animation controller; Section 4 presents the implementation; finally, in Section 5 the concluding remarks are drawn and the future research perspectives are discussed.

2   Modeling the Deformable Hand Avatar

The deformable hand avatar has been realized using a 3D skinned mesh. A hierarchical skeleton has been bound to a static hand mesh, according to hand biomechanical

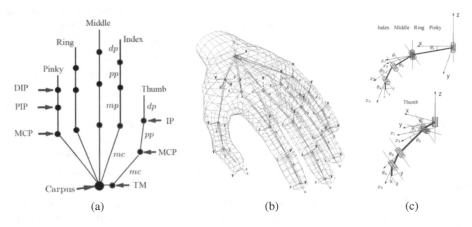

(a)   (b)   (c)

Fig. 1. (a) Bone-joint structure of the hand skeleton. (b) 3D avatar. (c) The DH representation for the index and the thumb fingers.

Table 1. Table of bone-to-bone length ratios, and Denavit-Hartemberg parameters for the thumb and the index

Finger		mp/dp	pp/dp	mc/dp
Thumb	right	–	1.37	2.09
	left	–	1.36	2.08
Index	right	1.41	2.45	4.17
	left	1.41	2.44	4.10
Middle	right	1.60	2.54	3.71
	left	1.59	2.54	3.71
Ring	right	1.50	2.33	3.25
	left	1.49	2.31	3.22
Pinky	right	1.15	2.04	3.32
	left	1.16	2.04	3.32

Thumb				Index			
a_i	α_i	d_i	q_i	a_i	α_i	d_i	q_i
a_o	0	d_1	-51°	mc_I	0	0	-22°
0	90°	0	q_0	0	-90°	0	q_4
mc_T	90°	0	q_1	pp_I	0	0	q_5
pp_T	0	0	q_2	mp_I	0	0	q_6
dp_T	0	0	q_3	dp_I	0	0	q_7

$$[q_0\ q_1\ q_2\ q_3]^T = \mathbf{q}_T^T \quad [q_4\ q_5\ q_6\ q_7]^T = \mathbf{q}_I^T$$

models available in the literature [5, 6, 7]. Referring to the Figure 1.a, each finger has the metacarpal (mc) bone fixed with respect to the hand frame, and features four degrees of freedom (DoFs), hence the mesh skeleton globally features 20 DoFs. The TM joint of the thumb as well as the MCP joint of the index, middle, ring and pinky fingers have two DoFs each (one for adduction/abduction and another flexion/extension). The MCP and IP joints of the thumb, as well as the PIP and DIP joints of the other fingers have one DoF each (joint names acronyms: metacarpophalangeal(MCP), proximal interphalangeal (PIP), distal interphalangeal (DIP), trapeziometacarpal (TM), interphalangeal (IP); bone names acronyms: metacarpal (mc), proximal phalanx (pp), middle phalanx (mp), and distal phalanx (dp)).

As shown in Figure 1.b, we assume that the hand reference frame is attached to the carpus. Each finger is modeled as a kinematic chain whose joints are displaced accordingly to the main degrees of freedom of a real hand. The kinematics of each finger have been modeled using the Denavit-Hartenberg (DH) representation [8] (see Figure 1.c), hence the hand configuration can be represented by the joint variables vector $\mathbf{q}$ defined as:

$$\mathbf{q} = [\mathbf{q}_T^T\ \mathbf{q}_I^T\ \mathbf{q}_M^T\ \mathbf{q}_R^T\ \mathbf{q}_P^T]^T \in \mathbf{R}^{20 \times 1} \tag{1}$$

The bone lengths have been chosen according to the anatomy of the real hand skeleton. In absence of disabilities or handicaps, the ratios between the bones lengths of each finger are almost constant [9]. Hence, in Table 1 we report the bone length ratios defined with respect to the length of the distal phalange of each finger [10]. Besides, we report also the DH parameters of the fingers, for the sake of simplicity only for the index and the thumb [7].

To easily achieve deformable avatar skin, a set of influencing skeleton joints is assigned to each vertex of the mesh, along with a weight factor per influence (*blending weights*). With this strategy, the current position $\mathbf{v}_i^c$ of the ith vertex can be achieved as a linear combination of the bone rigid transformations, taking the weights into account:

$$\mathbf{v}_i^c = \sum_{j=1}^{m} w_{ij} \mathbf{H}_j(\mathbf{q}) \mathbf{v}_i^0 \quad (\sum_{j=1}^{m} w_{ij} = 1, \ i = 1, ..., n) \tag{2}$$

where w_{ij} is the weight of the jth joint assigned to the ith vertex; $\mathbf{H}_j(\mathbf{q})$ is the current global transformation of the jth bone; $\mathbf{v}_i^0$ is the ith vertex rest pose; m is the number of influencing bones; n is the number of mesh vertices [11].

3   Animation Control

A large number of degrees of freedom characterizes the problem of animating the hand avatar. The biomechanical model we use to define the mesh skeleton globally features 20 degrees of freedom (DoFs). In this preliminary study, we decided to not to include the wrist motion in the synergy-based animation control, leaving it to future developments. The test application consists of a pinch grasping task, involving only two haptically-enabled contact points for the thumb and for the index, respectively. This yields 6 measured DoFs. The measured DoFs are less than those of the hand skeleton, hence the animation controller is expected to solve the kinematical redundancy relying on the hand model, using the postural synergies to propagate the motion also to the other fingers that are not directly captured by the haptic devices.

The postural synergies represent a set of linear dependencies between the joint variables of the whole hand, therefore they allow to univocally define the hand posture through a number of degrees of freedom lower than 20. In this work, the mathematical definition of synergies is a simplification of the one proposed in [12] for the control of robotic hands, hence:

$$\mathbf{q} = \mathbf{S}z \qquad (3)$$

where $z \in \mathbf{R}^{n_z}$ is the vector of synergy variables, n_z is the number of the involved synergies, $\mathbf{S} \in \mathbf{R}^{20 \times n_z}$ is the synergy matrix, whose columns describe the shape of each linear dependency.

In the application of interest, the key idea consists of evaluating the postural synergy variables using an inverse kinematics algorithm based on transpose jacobian matrices [13]. Since only real thumb and index are captured by the haptic devices, only the jacobian matrices of these fingers are taken into account along with the related $m = 8$ joint variables $\bar{\mathbf{q}}^T = [\mathbf{q}_T^T \ \mathbf{q}_I^T]$, yielding:

$$\mathbf{J}(\bar{\mathbf{q}}) = diag\{\mathbf{J}_T(\mathbf{q}_T), \mathbf{J}_I(\mathbf{q}_I)\} \ \in \mathbf{R}^{6 \times m} \qquad (4)$$

Now let $\mathbf{x}_I(t)$ and $\mathbf{x}_T(t)$ be the real fingertip positions of operator's index and thumb, respectively. Similarly, let $\hat{\mathbf{x}}_I(t)$ and $\hat{\mathbf{x}}_T(t)$ be the fingertip positions of the avatar index and thumb, respectively. The avatar tips are coupled to the corresponding operator's tips through a virtual spring, hence at each time instant t, $\mathbf{F}_I(t) = k_{vc}(\mathbf{x}_I(t) - \hat{\mathbf{x}}_I(t))$ and $\mathbf{F}_T(t) = k_{vc}(\mathbf{x}_T(t) - \hat{\mathbf{x}}_T(t))$ are the force required for the avatar fingertips to track the real fingertip trajectories measured by the haptic devices.

The forces $\mathbf{F}(t) = [\mathbf{F}_T^T(t), \mathbf{F}_I^T(t)]^T \in \mathbf{R}^{6 \times 1}$ reflect on the synergy-space generalized forces $\sigma(t)$, defined as:

$$\sigma(t) = \bar{\mathbf{S}}^T \mathbf{J}^T(\mathbf{q})\mathbf{F}(t)$$

where $\bar{\mathbf{S}} \in \mathbf{R}^{m \times n_z}$ has the first m rows of $\mathbf{S}$, i.e. those related to thumb and index. Now the new kinematic configuration in the synergy-space can be updated as:

$$z(t+1) = z(t) + k_\sigma \, \sigma(t)$$

where k_σ is a constant factor determining the responsiveness of the animation. Finally, the joint-space configuration $\mathbf{q}(t+1)$ required to give the 3D avatar the desired shape at time $t+1$ is computed according to the (3):

$$\mathbf{q}(t+1) = \mathbf{S}z(t+1)$$

In order to avoid unnatural finger positions, the equation above has been combined with the following set of angle constraints [14]:

Table 2. Allowed ranges for the joint angle variables

Finger	q_1	q_2	q_3	q_4
Thumb	$-10^o,\ 80^o$	$0^o,\ -55^o$	$0^o,\ -55^o$	$0^o,\ -40^o$
Index	$0^o,\ 90^o$	$-15^o,\ 15^o$	$0^o,\ 110^o$	$0^o,\ 90^o$
Middle	$0^o,\ 90^o$	$-12^o,\ 12^o$	$0^o,\ 110^o$	$0^o,\ 90^o$
Ring	$0^o,\ 90^o$	$-10^o,\ 10^o$	$0^o,\ 110^o$	$0^o,\ 90^o$
Pinky	$0^o,\ 90^o$	$-12^o,\ 12^o$	$0^o,\ 110^o$	$0^o,\ 90^o$

Once the current kinematic configuration $\mathbf{q}$ of the skeleton has been determined, the skin deformation is finally achieved by computing the resultant transformation of all the mesh vertices using the equation (2).

In summary, the proposed animation controller is able to approximate the principal motion components of all the avatar fingers taking only the real index and thumb fingertip trajectories as inputs. Note that the equations discussed so far involve only simple algebraic computations.

4   Implementation

A demonstrative application has been developed to evaluate the avatar animation controller in a virtual pinch grasp involving the thumb and the index. The attention was mainly addressed to evaluate the realism of animation for the other fingers, determined by the use of postural synergies.

As already mentioned in the previous section, the proposed technique still cannot account for the wrist motion. In this demo application, wrist rotation is neglected as well, but a simple strategy has been studied for wrist translation according to the measured fingertip trajectories. Let $\mathbf{P}_w$ be the position of the wrist reference frame with respect to the base frame. At each time instant, the average force $\mathbf{F}_w$ between the virtual coupling forces at index and thumb fingers is computed. Then, $\mathbf{F}_w$ is used to assign a desired velocity $\dot{\mathbf{P}}_w$. The discrete-time wrist update rule can be written as:

$$\mathbf{P}_w(t+1) = \mathbf{P}_w(t) + k_w \mathbf{F}_w \qquad (5)$$

The hand skinned mesh as well as the skeleton design have been realized using Autodesk Maya 2008. The demo application has been coded in C++ on Win32 API for WindowsXP, using DirectX and HLSL shaders for graphic rendering on the GPU. Haptik Library for the low-level access to haptic devices [15], Libralis Library [16] for gravity compensation, nVidia PhysX SDK for the physics engine on GPU. The haptic rendering

Fig. 2. The experimental setup

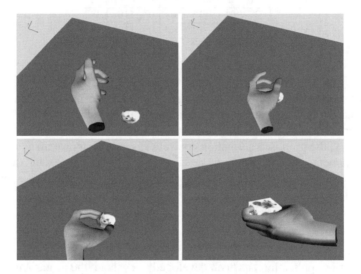

Fig. 3. Some screenshots from the pinch-grasping demo application

has been performed via a classic visco-elastic contact model to feed forces back, using the Friction Cone [17] and Soft-Finger [18] algorithms to simulate contact friction. Clearly, the haptic feedback can be rendered only to the index and the thumb, currently the other fingers are only animated to improve the simulation realism. The following parameters were used to set up the hand model and the animation controller: $k_{vc} = 0.05$, $k_\sigma = 0.004$, $dp_I = 19$mm, $dp_T = 22$mm. In Figure 2 we reported a picture of the experimental setup, consisting of two Omega Haptic Devices featuring a finger-thimble end-effector. The Figure 3 shows some screenshots taken from the running application, where virtual objects (a sphere or a cube) are grasped by a left-handed operator.

5   Conclusion and Future Works

The work discussed in this paper consists of developing a deformable hand avatar and its animation control to be employed in virtual reality using commercial single-contact-point haptic devices such as the Omega or the PHANToM. A kinematic skeleton featuring 20 DoFs has been designed according to the biomechanics of the hand. Besides we took advantage from the postural synergies, i.e. a set of dependencies among the hand joints angles that allow to accurately approximate the hand shape in grasping tasks reducing the number of DoFs. Therefore, the proposed animation technique consists in capturing the motion of some fingertips, transforming measures in the related joint-space trajectories according to the biomechanics-based kinematical model, and finally using postural synergies to distribute the angular displacements to the whole hand joints. Once the current kinematic configuration of the hand skeleton is available, the consequent skin deformation is computed using a smooth skinning technique. This algorithm involves only algebraic computation for kinematic inversion, and requires no time-consuming optimization neither the online solution of dynamic equations. This solution has been applied in a demo application to simulate pinch grasping with the index and the thumb. Given the low computational load of this technique, it does not affect the realism of haptic rendering.

In our future perspectives, we plan to carry out several experiments to numerically evaluate the motion approximation performance with respect to the number of employed synergies. Besides we aim at improving the animation controller including also the wrist motion.

Acknowledgments

This work has been partially supported by the European Commission with the Collaborative Project no. 248587, "THE Hand Embodied", within the FP7-ICT-2009-4-2-1 program "Cognitive Systems and Robotics" and by the Ministero dell'Università e della Ricerca with the PRIN 2008 project "Attuatori innovativi per sistemi avanzati di manipolazione e di interazione aptica".

References

1. Popescu, V., Burdea, G., Bouzit, M.: Virtual Reality Simulation Modeling for a Haptic Glove, pp. 195–200 (1999)
2. Kry, P., James, D., Pai, D.: EigenSkin: real time large deformation character skinning in hardware, pp. 153–159 (2002)
3. Santello, M., Flanders, M., Soechting, J.F.: Gradual molding of the hand to object contours. The Journal of Neuroscience 79(3), 1307–1320 (1998)
4. Santello, M., Soechting, J.F.: Force synergies for multifingered grasping. Experimental Brain Research 133(4), 457–467 (2000)
5. Lee, J., Kunii, T.: Model-based analysis of hand posture. IEEE Computer Graphics and Applications 15(5), 77–86 (1995)
6. Lin, J., Wu, T.: Modeling the Constraints of Human Hand Motion. Urbana 51(61), 801 (2000)
7. Baud-Bovy, G., Prattichizzo, D., Brogi, N.: Does torque minimization yield a stable human grasp? In: STAR, Springer Tracks in Advanced Robotics. Springer, Heidelberg (2005)
8. Hartenberg, R., Denavit, J.: Kinematic synthesis of linkages. McGraw-Hill, New York (1964)
9. Kim, K., Youm, Y., Chung, W.: Human kinematic factor for haptic manipulation: The wrist to thumb. In: 10th Symposium on Haptic Interfaces for Virtual Environment and Teleoperator Systems, HAPTICS 2002, Proceedings, pp. 319–326 (2002)

10. Youm, Y., Holden, M., Dohrmann, K.: Finger Ray Ratio Study. Technical report (Technical Report on Wrist Project)
11. Kavan, L.: Real-time Skeletal Animation. PhD thesis, Faculty of Electrical Engineering Department of Computer Science and Engineering. Czech Technical University (2007)
12. Prattichizzo, D., Malvezzi, M., Bicchi, A.: On motion and force control of grasping hands with postural synergies. In: 2010 Robotics: Science and Systems Conference, Zaragoza (2010)
13. Sciavicco, L., Siciliano, B.: Modelling and control of robot manipulators. Springer, Heidelberg (2000)
14. Chao, E.: Biomechanics of the hand: a basic research study. World Scientific Publishing Company, Singapore (1989)
15. de Pascale, M., Prattichizzo, D.: The Haptik Library: a component based architecture for uniform access to haptic devices. IEEE Robotics and Automation Magazine 14(4), 64–75 (2007)
16. Formaglio, A., Fei, M., Mulatto, S., de Pascale, M., Prattichizzo, D.: Autocalibrated gravity compensation for 3DoF impedance haptic devices. In: Ferre, M. (ed.) EuroHaptics 2008. LNCS, vol. 5024, pp. 43–52. Springer, Heidelberg (2008)
17. Harwin, W., Melder, N.: Improved Haptic Rendering for Multi-Finger Manipulation Using Friction Cone based God-Objects. In: Proceedings of Eurohaptics Conference, Citeseer, pp. 82–85 (2002)
18. Barbagli, F., Frisoli, A., Salisbury, K., Bergamasco, M.: Simulating human fingers: a soft finger proxy model and algorithm. In: Proceedings of 12th International Symposium on Haptic Interfaces for Virtual Environment and Teleoperator Systems, HAPTICS 2004, pp. 9–17 (2004)

Development of a 3 DoF MR-Compatible Haptic Interface for Pointing and Reaching Movements

Stefan Klare, Angelika Peer, and Martin Buss

Technische Universität München, 80290 Munich, Germany
{stefan.klare,angelika.peer,mb}@tum.de
http://www.lsr.ei.tum.de/

Abstract. This paper describes a 3 DoF MR-compatible haptic interface which can be used to investigate human brain mechanisms of voluntary finger movements. The newly developed device is built of non-ferromagnetic materials to avoid safety hazards and uses MR-compatible sensors and actuators to not disturb the image quality. The selected parallel kinematics not only guarantees a stiff construction and reduces inertia of moving parts, but also avoids time-varying motion artifacts originating from moving active components. Geometric parameters of the device are selected to optimize manipulability and to cover the workspace of pointing movements using the index finger up to small reaching movements with the arm. Finally, performance indices like transmission-quality, force, velocity, and acceleration capability are evaluated for the presented device.

Keywords: fMRI, haptic, interface, parallel kinematics.

1   Introduction

Functional Magnetic Resonance Imaging (fMRI) is an often adopted tool in neuroscience to study human brain mechanisms involved in human motor control. Highly controllable arm and finger movements, which can be achieved by linking the human arm or finger to a haptic interface, are prerequisites for the analysis and interpretation of fMRI data. The benefit of using a haptic interface is twofold: On the one hand it provides the operator with highly standardized and easily configurable force/torque information, and on the other hand it reads the operator's motion/force input, required for the statistical analysis. In this paper, we present a newly developed MR compatible haptic interface with 3 translational degrees of freedom (DoF) that can be used to study human brain mechanisms of voluntary pointing and reaching movements.

Mechatronic devices to be used in an MR scanner must fulfill a variety of requirements and, thus, conventional haptic interfaces cannot be used in a typical MR environment. First, every device brought into the scanner room is exposed to a strong static magnetic field, which inevitably leads to high accelerating forces acting on any ferromagnetic part used in the construction. To avoid safety hazards resulting from such components, devices need to be engineered from materials with low magnetic susceptibility. Second, used materials, actuators, and sensors should not disturb the MR acquisition. Conventional components often emit radio frequencies and thus produce artifacts in MR images. They need to be substituted by MR-compatible components. Third, the

A.M.L. Kappers et al. (Eds.): EuroHaptics 2010, Part II, LNCS 6192, pp. 211–218, 2010.

functionality and performance of the device should be unaffected by the MR environment, i.e. the high static magnetic field of typically 1.5 to 3 Tesla, the time-varying gradient fields, and the radio frequency pulses. All these requirements are covered by the active terms MR-safe and MR-conditional defined in the ASTM standard F2503 [1].

Further, to guarantee generalizability of obtained results, the haptic interface should not restrict typical human arm and finger movements and allow a very natural form of interaction. Thus, in contrast to state-of-the-art MR compatible haptic interfaces, we aim for developing a haptic interface with a large number of degrees of freedom (DoF). Existing MR-compatible haptic interfaces with only 1 DoF can be found in [2,3,4,5], while haptic interfaces with 2 DoF are presented in [6,7,8,9]. In [10] drawings of a 3 DoF interface are presented, but the device has not been built. Thus, we conclude that MR-compatible haptic devices with more DoF still do not exist.

2   Design Issues

Specifications: The main aim of this work is to develop a haptic interface which allows studying human brain mechanisms of voluntary finger movements. On this account, the biomechanical properties of a human finger need to be taken into account before designing an appropriate haptic interface: In [11] the maximum force that can be exerted by an index finger was determined to 50 N, while [12] showed that only 15% of the maximum force should be exerted in order to avoid fatigue and discomfort. Beside guidelines for the maximum force, also guidelines concerning the required bandwidth exist. In [13] it was shown that humans can output force commands up to 10 Hz and can feel forces up to $\sim$ 10 Hz for compressive stress. The required workspace of the device can be derived from [14], which analyzed the workspace of a typical human index finger that fits into a 38 mm x 116 mm x 127 mm cuboid. The workspace of the device must be slightly bigger than the workspace of the index finger. In [15] the maximum velocity and acceleration of human fingertips was determined to 1 m/s and 300 m/s^2, respectively. The analysis of human grasping studies, however, indicates that the maximum finger velocity is considerably lower than 1 m/s, see [16].

Following these design criteria and taking into account general guidelines for the design of haptic interfaces, see [17], [18], and [19], as well as considering the application field, the device to be designed should satisfy the following specifications: Bandwidth of 10 Hz; Volume of operation of 190 mm x 190 mm x 140 mm; Maximum force: about 10 N; Maximum velocity: 1 m/s; Maximum acceleration: 300 m/s^2; Backdriveability; Low inertia; Low backlash; Stiff construction; Low friction; MR-safety and compatibility.

Kinematical Design: In robotics two main types of kinematics are distinguished, serial and parallel kinematics. Robots with serial kinematics have the advantage of a comparatively larger workspace compared to parallel robots with similar link length. Parallel robots, on the other hand, are very rigid and fast at the same time. When deciding for the kinematics of the newly developed MR-compatible haptic interface, the following considerations have been made: i) the usage of the device in an MR environment limits the choice of permissible materials to realize a rigid construction, and ii) a parallel

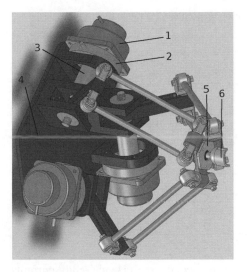

Workspace, L_F=0.14m, L_A=0.08m, R=0.04m

Fig. 1. CAD-drawing of the newly developed haptic interface (1: motor, 2: sensor, 3: coupling, 4: base plate, 5: end-effector plate, 6: end-effector)

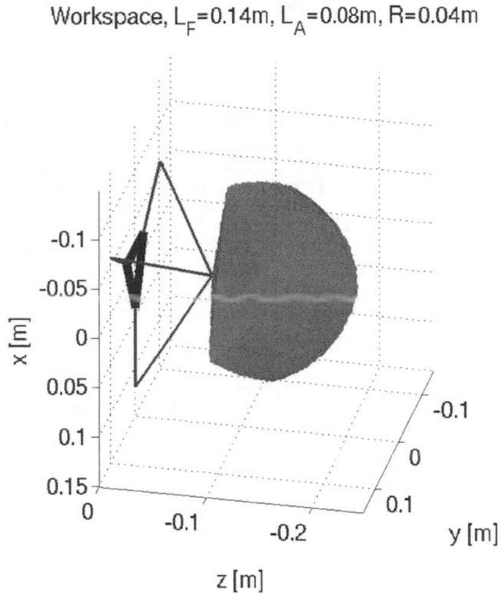

Fig. 2. Workspace (red) of the interface with links (blue) and base plate (black) ($\varphi_i = 0$)

kinematics allows to have fixed actuators and sensors and, thus, reduces inertia of the moving parts as well as time-varying motion artifacts originating from actuator and sensor radio frequencies. Taking these considerations into account, the delta kinematics by Clavel [20], a well investigated parallel kinematics, was chosen.

Sketch of New MR-compatible Haptic Interface: Fig. 1 shows a CAD-drawing of the newly developed haptic interface. The index finger is fixed at the end-effector (6) which is connected to the end-effector plate (5) via a ball-joint. The rotational DoF of the ball joint are unactuated, but allow arbitrary rotations of the finger and thus guarantee naturalness of interaction. The ball joints' angles are not sensed. The end-effector plate of the device is actuated by 3 ultrasonic motors (1) which are connected to the end-effector plate via rods. Torque sensors (2) are used to measure the reaction torque of the motors.

Materials: The choice of materials is an important issue when building an MR-compatible haptic interface. Ferromagnetic materials are generally prohibited because they produce artifacts in the image and can hurt people if accelerated by the magnetic field of the scanner. Exceptions can be made for very small parts in the fringe field of the scanner. The design of the newly developed haptic interface does not use ferromagnetics at all. Used materials are: rigid PVC, fiber-glass, ABS+ (Acrylnitril-Butadien-Styrol), nylon, aluminum, and brass. MR-compatible plastic bearings with glass-balls were selected and arranged in an o-arrangement to guarantee backlash-free interaction. Using plastics and composite materials guarantees a lightweight design and thus minimizes inertia of moving parts. To obtain a rigid base plate, aluminum was

Table 1. MR-compatible actuation principles [21] [22] [23]

Principle	Pros	Cons
Pneumatic Transmission	clean	low frequencies, hard to control, no precise motion
Hydrostatic Transmission	high forces	leaking
Electrostatic Motor		high voltage
Piezoelectric Actuator	high forces, highly stable, precise actuation, compact	high voltage, short expansions
Piezoelectric Stepping Motor	compact	incremental transmission
Ultrasonic Motor	high torque at low speed compact, high response good speed controllability	difficult to control torque
Electroactive Polymers	compact	high voltage

used. Aluminum is non-ferromagnetic, but electric conductive. Hence, eddy-currents induced in the base plate can heat the material. As the base plate is a static part located in the fringe field of the scanner, this problem, however, is of minor importance.

Sensors and Actuators: The choice and collocation of sensors and actuators is a critical point in the design-process. Components like sensors and actuators, which include electric circuits, can produce artifacts, especially, when moved in the MR-environment. The electrical connections are commonly made of ferromagnetics and thus electromagnetic shielding is necessary. When using a DELTA kinematics, sensors and actuators are fixed to the base-plate and not moved in space. This, on the one hand, reduces artifacts in the image, and on the other hand, has positive effects on the inertia of the device.

There are only few MR-compatible principles which can be used to actuate the device. Table 1 summarizes different MR-compatible actuation principles reviewed in [21], [22] and [23] and itemizes some of the most prominent pros and cons of each actuation principle. A perfect actuation principle does not exist and thus the optimal principle for the application has to be chosen. Major aspects are controllability, speed-force characteristics, and compactness.

For the newly developed device, ultrasonic motors of type Shinsei USR-60 were chosen due to their good (speed)-controllability, high response combined with high torques and compact design compared to other actuation principles. Although these motors can principally affect the image-quality of the scanner, this effect goes to zero when they are located in the fringe field of the scanner as shown in [24]. Ultrasonic motors have the advantage of distributing high torque at low speed, and thus no gearing is necessary. A non-ferromagnetic variant of the USR-60 equipped with an optical encoder is available on the market.

When controlling haptic devices, position and/or force sensors are necessary. Table 2 lists a variety of measurement principles which can be used in MR-environments, see [23] for details.

Since strain-gauge-based torque sensors are standard components in industry, sensors of type ME-Systeme TS-70 have been selected to measure the reaction torque of

Table 2. MR-compatible sensing principles

Data 2 sense	Principle	Pros	Cons
Position	Optical (encoder)	no EMI	incremental data
Position	Optical (tracking system)		very complex setup
Position	Optical (intensity measurement)	no EMI	high current supply
Force	Optical (intensity measurement)	no EMI	high current supply
Force	Piezoresistive	low current supply	shielding and filtering
Force	Strain gage	low current supply	shielding and filtering

the motors with a full-bridge design. The sensor-frame is machined of aluminum and the amplifying circuit is shielded with a copper housing. Shielded twisted-pair cables are used for supply. Position measurement of the motor angle is performed by optical encoders with a pulse count of 1000 pulses/round, which are built-in with the ultrasonic motors.

3   Kinematic and Dynamic Model

In [25] the forward-kinematics problem of a delta kinematics was solved by adopting a closed-vector loop method and the reduced dynamic model of the interface was calculated according to

$$\tau = I_{bt}\ddot{\varphi} + J^T m_{nt}\ddot{x}_T - J^T m_{ng} \begin{bmatrix} g \\ 0 \\ 0 \end{bmatrix} - G_{bg} - J^T f_H. \tag{1}$$

Compared to [25] in (1) the human force at the end-effector f_H was added and the direction of gravitation was modified. Motor torques, end-effector position, and moving angles of the motors relating to the base plate are constituted by vectors τ, x_T, and φ. For details about the meaning of parameters please refer to the original publication.

In the next section the kinematic and dynamical model will be used to derive typical performance measure of the device.

4   Performance

In this section performance indices of the newly developed haptic interface are presented. To achieve good performance, a high transmission-quality as well as a high acceleration and velocity capability (available over the whole workspace) are required. In the following paragraphs, these performance indices are determined.

Workspace: Since the device is supposed to allow natural pointing and reaching movements, its desired workspace expansion was set to 190 mm x 190 mm x 140 mm in x-, y-, and z-direction. During the design process the angle between the 3 motors was defined to be $\theta = 120$ and the moving angle of the motors to range from $\varphi_i = 0\cdots90$. Thus, remaining varying parameters are arm length L_A, forearm length L_F, and the distance of motors from the origin R. To avoid singularities in the workspace $L_F > L_A + R$

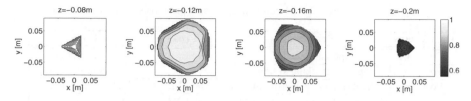

Fig. 3. Transmission-quality in different z-planes

has to be further satisfied. Optimal link length parameters were found by searching the parameter space in steps of 10 mm for an optimal conditioning number C_s:

$$C_s = \frac{C_x + C_y + C_z}{3} \tag{2}$$

$$C_x = 1 - \left| \frac{190mm - \Delta x}{190mm + \Delta x} \right|, \quad C_y = 1 - \left| \frac{190mm - \Delta y}{190mm + \Delta y} \right|, \quad C_z = 1 - \left| \frac{140mm - \Delta z}{140mm + \Delta z} \right|.$$

The conditioning number C_s, consisting of numbers (C_x, C_y, C_z) for the x-, y-, and z-direction of the workspace, is shown in (2). After varying $R = 20$ mm$\cdots 80$ mm, $L_F = 80$ mm$\cdots 200$ mm, and $L_A = 20$ mm$\cdots (L_F - R - 10$ mm$)$, conditioning number optimizing design parameters were found to be $\hat{R} = 40$ mm, $\hat{L}_F = 140$ mm, and $\hat{L}_A = 80$ mm. The visualization of the obtained workspace with $1.835 \cdot 10^6$ mm^3 is shown in Fig. 2.

Transmission-Quality: Transmission quality considers velocity-transmission M and force-transmission F and its maximization is a goal when developing parallel kinematics. Following [26] transmission quality is defined as follows, with index matrix E and Jacobian J:

$$T = F \cdot M = \frac{||E||^2}{||J^{-1}|| \cdot ||J||} \leq 1 \tag{3}$$

Note: The notation $|| \cdot ||$ means the Euclidean norm of the matrix.
Fig. 3 shows the transmission quality of the device in different z-planes. As can be seen, for the developed device the transmission-quality is always greater than 0.5 and small values only appear in the boundary area of the workspace.

Force: For stationary loads a maximum force of 10 N can be guaranteed over the whole workspace. This was assured by simulating a force of 10 N at the end-effector and calculating necessary motor torques by using $\tau = J^T f$ while varying the direction of force f acting at the end-effector and the end-effector position. The motor torque remained always below 1 N which is the maximum torque of the ultrasonic motors.

Velocity: With no load at the end-effector the motors can achieve a maximum velocity of 15.7 rad/s. When simulating a velocity of 1 m/s at the end-effector a required motor velocity of about 15 rad/s is obtained in the center of the workspace by adopting $\dot{\varphi} = J^{-1}\dot{x}_T$. This value increases up to about 30 rad/s in the border area.

Acceleration: Considering (1) the required motor torque to achieve an end-effector acceleration of 300 m/s^2 can be calculated. Maximum acceleration was calculated in the resting state ($\dot{x}_T = 0$). To achieve an acceleration of 300 m/s^2 a motor torque of 3 Nm is required which is higher than the torque supplied by the ultrasonic motors. Using the previously selected ultrasonic motors, however, still an end-effector acceleration of 100 m/s^2 can be realized over the entire workspace, which is nevertheless fairly high.

5   Conclusions and Future Work

This paper presented the design of a MR-compatible 3-DoF haptic interface for usage in fMRI-studies to investigate the human brain mechanism of voluntary pointing and reaching movements. Based on biomechanical properties of the human index-finger desired specifications for the haptic interface were defined and taken into account in the design process. Components, materials, actuators, and sensors were selected to meet these requirements. Conditioning number optimizing geometric parameters of the device were selected and transmission-quality, force, velocity, and acceleration capability were determined. To the best of the authors knowledge, this is the first time an MR-compatible haptic interface with 3-DoF was built.

In future work, an admittance control strategy will be implemented for the device and experiments will be conducted to determine controller-dependent performance measures. In addition, MR-compatibility will be tested in an MR scanner (Siemens 3T TIM Trio). Finally, the presented kinematics will be extended by a gripping mechanism to allow simultaneous 2-finger grasping and manipulation.

Acknowledgements. The help of Axel Thielscher and Alexandra Reichenbach from the Max-Planck Institute for Biological Cybernetics is thankfully appreciated.

References

1. ASTM, Standard test method for measurement of magnetically induced displacement force on medical devices in the magnetic resonance environment (2002), http://www.astm.org
2. Flueckinger, M., Bullo, M., Chapuis, D., Gassert, R., Perriard, Y.: fMRI compatible haptic interface actuated with traveling wave ultrasonic motor. In: Industry Applications Conference, vol. 3, pp. 2075–2082 (2005)
3. Riener, R., Villgrattner, T., Kleiser, R., Nef, T., Kollias, S.: fMRI-compatible electromagnetic haptic interface. In: 27th Annual International Conference of the Engineering in Medicine and Biology Society, pp. 7024–7027 (2005)
4. Gassert, R., Dovat, L., Lambercy, O., Ruffieux, Y., Chapuis, D., Ganesh, G., Burdet, E., Bleuler, H.: A 2-DoF fMRI compatible haptic interface to investigate the neural control of arm movements. In: IEEE International Conference on Robotics and Automation, pp. 3825–3831 (2006)
5. Yu, N., Hollnagel, C., Blickenstorfer, A., Kollias, S., Riener, R.: fMRI-compatible robotic interfaces with fluidic actuation. In: Proceedings of Robotics: Science and Systems IV, Zurich, Switzerland (June 2008)
6. Gassert, R., Moser, R., Burdet, E., Bleuler, H.: MRI/fMRI-compatible robotic system with force feedback for interaction with human motion. IEEE/ASME Transactions on Mechatronics 11(2), 216–224 (2006)

7. Izawa, J., Shimizu, T., Gomi, H., Toyama, S., Ito, K.: MR compatible manipulandum with ultrasonic motor for fMRI studies. In: IEEE International Conference on Robotics and Automation, pp. 3850–3854 (2006)
8. Hara, M., Matthey, G., Yamamoto, A., Chapuis, D., Gassert, R., Bleuler, H., Higuchi, T.: Development of a 2-dof electrostatic haptic joystick for MRI/fMRI applications. In: IEEE International Conference on Robotics and Automation, pp. 1479–1484 (2009)
9. Dietrichsen, J., Hashambhoy, Y., Rane, T., Shadmehr, R.: Neural correlates of reach errors. The Journal of Neuroscience 25, 9919–9931 (2005)
10. Li, S., Frisoli, A., Borelli, L., Bergamasco, M., Raabe, M., Greenlee, M.: Design of a new fMRI compatible haptic interface. In: Proceedings of the World Haptics 2009-Third Joint EuroHaptics Conference and Symposium on Haptic Interfaces for Virtual Environment and Teleoperator Systems, pp. 535–540. IEEE Computer Society, Washington (2009)
11. Sutter, P., Iatridis, J., Thakor, N.: Response to Reflected-Force Feedback to Fingers in Teleoperations. In: Proc. of the NASA Conference on Space Telerobotics,
12. Wiker, S., Hershkowitz, E., Zik, J.: Teleoperator comfort and psychometric stability: Criteria for limiting master-controller forces of operation and feedback during telemanipulation. In: JPL, California Inst. of Tech., Proceedings of the NASA Conference on Space Telerobotics, vol. 1 (1989)
13. Brooks, T., Robotics, S., Lanham, M.: Telerobotic response requirements. In: IEEE International Conference on Systems, Man and Cybernetics, pp. 113–120 (1990)
14. Abdel-Malek, K., Yang, J., Brand, R., Tanbour, E.: Towards understanding the workspace of human limbs. Ergonomics 47(13), 1386–1405 (2004)
15. Nakagawara, S., Kajimoto, H., Kawakami, N., Tachi, S., Kawabuchi, I.: An encounter-type multi-fingered master hand using circuitous joints. In: IEEE International Conference on Robotics and Automation, vol. 3, p. 2667. IEEE, Los Alamitos (1999/2005)
16. Gentilucci, M., Benuzzi, F., Gangitano, M., Grimaldi, S.: Grasp with hand and mouth: A kinematic study on healthy subjects. Journal of Neurophysiology 86, 1685 (2001)
17. Fischer, P., Daniel, R., Siva, K.: Specification and design of input devices for teleoperation. In: IEEE International Conference on Robotics and Automation, pp. 540–545 (1990)
18. McAffee, D., Fiorini, P.: Hand controller design requirements and performance issues in telerobotics. In: Fifth International Conference on Advanced Robotics, Robots in Unstructured Environments, pp. 186–192 (1991)
19. Hayward, V., Astley, O.: Performance measures for haptic interfaces. In: Robotics Research-International Symposium, Citeseer, vol. 7, pp. 195–206 (1996)
20. Clavel, R.: Conception d'un robot parallele rapide a 4 degres de liberte. PhD thesis, Ecole Polytechnique Federal de Lausanne (1991)
21. Uffmann, K., Ladd, M.: Actuation Systems for MR Elastography. IEEE Engineering in medicine and biology magazine 739, 28–34 (2008)
22. Elhawary, H., Zivanovic, A., Rea, M., Davies, B., Besant, C., Young, I., Lamperth, M.: A modular approach to MRI-compatible robotics. IEEE Engineering in medicine and biology magazine 739, 35–41 (2008)
23. Gassert, R., Burdet, E., Chinzei, K.: Opportunities and challenges in MR-compatible robotics. IEEE Engineering in medicine and biology magazine 27, 15–22 (2008)
24. Chinzei, K., Kikinis, R., Jolesz, F.: MR compatibility of mechatronic devices: design criteria. In: Taylor, C., Colchester, A. (eds.) MICCAI 1999. LNCS, vol. 1679, pp. 1020–1030. Springer, Heidelberg (1999)
25. Codourey, A.: Dynamic modeling of parallel robots for computed-torque control implementation. The International Journal of Robotics Research 17(12), 1325 (1998)
26. Neugebauer, R.: Parallelkinematische Maschinen. Springer, Heidelberg (2006) (in German)

Cold Objects Pop Out!

Myrthe A. Plaisier[1,2] and Astrid M.L. Kappers[1]

[1] Helmholtz Institute, Utrecht University, The Netherlands
[2] Faculty of human movement science, VU University Amsterdam,
The Netherlands
m.plaisier@fbw.vu.nl, A.M.L.Kappers@uu.nl

Abstract. We can haptically extract thermal properties of different material, but we can also sense object temperature. It has been shown that thermal properties of materials are not very salient features. In this study, we investigate saliency of actual temperature differences. To this end we let subjects grasp varying numbers of spheres in the hand. These spheres were warmer ($38°C$) than the hand temperature, but in half of the trials there was one sphere colder ($22°C$) than the hand temperature. Subjects had to indicate whether the cold sphere was present and response times were measured as a function of the number of spheres. This yielded a target present slope as small as 32 ms/item. This is comparable to slopes found earlier for search for a tetrahedron among spheres and indicates that there is pop-out effect for a cold sphere among warm spheres.

Keywords: Haptic search, Temperature perception, Psychophysics.

1   Introduction

Haptic object recognition relies on cues like shape, size and material properties. Some properties like the presence of edges or rough materials [1,2,3] have been shown to be very salient properties that make an object stand out among others. Also thermal properties can play a role in object identification. It has been shown that for large differences in thermal properties, materials can be reliably discriminated using these properties [4].

Saliency of object properties can be investigated using haptic search tasks. These tasks have been adapted from visual search tasks, in which subjects generally have to search for a certain 'target' item (e.g. a green dot) among varying numbers of 'distractor' items (e.g. red dots). Response times are then measured as a function of the number of items and the slope of this function is interpreted as a measure of the efficiency at which the search task was performed. Small slopes mean that the number of distractor items did not increase response times much and indicate that the search was performed 'in parallel' over all presented items [5,6]. In this case, the target differs from the distractors in terms of a salient feature and this feature is said to 'pop out'.

Lederman and Klatzky performed a haptic search task in which subjects had to search for a target material (copper) that felt cooler than the distractor material (wood) [1]. In that study all materials were at room temperature, meaning that both materials felt cold. Saliency of actual temperature differences may be quite different. In the present study,

A.M.L. Kappers et al. (Eds.): EuroHaptics 2010, Part II, LNCS 6192, pp. 219–224, 2010.

we set out to investigate saliency of a cold object among warm objects. In this case, the material of the target and distractor items was the same, but the target item had a temperature below skin temperature, while the distractor items were warmer than the skin. Knowledge about saliency of temperature differences could be useful for design of haptic interfaces in which temperature is used to present abstract information such as proximity or direction (see [7] for an overview of such applications).

2   Experimental Design and Setup

2.1   Participants

Ten paid subjects participated in the experiment (mean age 24 ± 3 years). Two of them were left handed, while all others were right handed according to Coren's test [8]. None of them reported any known hand deficits.

2.2   Stimuli and Setup

The items consisted of brass spheres (radius 0.93 cm) which were suspended from flexible wires. The thermal conductivity of brass is 119 W/mK, the specific heat is 380 J/kgK and the density is 8800 kg/m^3 . This means that the spheres exchange heat with the surroundings relatively fast. Sets of 3, 4, 5 or 6 spheres were presented and in half of the trials a target item was present. The target item was a sphere with a temperature of 22°C, while the other spheres (distractor items) had a temperature of 38°C. The items as well as the hand of the subject were temperature controlled by placing them in water baths with a piece of plastic on the water surface to prevent contact with the water underneath. Room temperature was 21 ± 1°C (SD). The water bath for the target items as well as that for the hand of the subject were temperature controlled using aquarium heaters (Tetratec 25 and Tetratec 200). The water bath for the distractor items was controlled by adding hot water during the experiment and was maintained at a temperature of 41 ± 2°C (SD). Because the distractors had to be much warmer than room temperature it was necessary for the water bath to be about 41°C in order to heat the distractor items to 38 ± 1°C (SD). Temperature of the spheres was measured prior to the experiments using a temperature sensor (Dallas semiconductor DS600) placed on the surface of a sphere, recording at 1 Hz. During the experiments only the temperature of the water baths was monitored. Figure 1a shows the temperature over time of an item at room temperature that was placed on the water bath. It can be seen that it heated to 38°C in approximately 9 min. The spheres were placed in the water bath at least 30 minutes prior to the start of the experiment. Figure 1b shows the temperature of a distractor sphere that was removed from the water bath and placed back again. The temperature decrease and increase were approximated using a linear model and slope values are indicated. In half a second the temperature of the distractors decreased by $(0.0035°C/s \times 30s =)$ 1°C. The spheres were taken out of the water bath only a few seconds before a trial was started and were placed back immediately after the trial. Therefore, it is reasonable to assume that the initial temperature of the distractors was always in between 37°C and 39°C. Five sets of target and distractor spheres were used

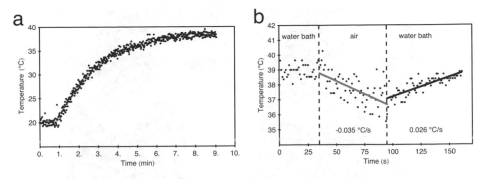

Fig. 1. Temperature recorded in time a) for a sphere at room temperature placed in a water bath of 42°C and b) a sphere in a water bath of 42°C removed to be suspended in air and placed back again in the water bath. The solid lines represent linear regression and the slope values are indicated in the figure.

subsequently so that there was time for the items to regain their temperature after each trial.

Upon arrival subjects were asked to place their dominant hand on the plastic covering a water bath of 30°C for 5 minutes. After every ten trials the subject was asked to place his or her hand back onto the water bath for 1 minute. Hand temperature was measured before the experiment was started and after the experiment. Hand temperatures ranged from 28°C to 33°C. This means that for all subjects the target sphere was below skin temperature and the distractor spheres were above skin temperature.

Response times were measured using a custom built device (see [9] for details about this set-up). Time measurement was started automatically when the subject touched the stimuli and was terminated with a vocal response.

2.3 Experimental Design

Subjects placed their hand palm upwards below the spheres. They were instructed to grasp the spheres and respond as fast as possible whether the target item was present (Figure 2). After each trial, feedback was provided on whether the answer was correct. There were no restrictions on hand movements other than having to initially grasp all items simultaneously. After grasping all items, they were allowed to release items from the hand and the experimenter scored whether items were released during the the trial. All numbers of spheres were presented 20 times, 10 times target present and 10 times target absent. Error trials were not included in the analysis and repeated at the end of the experiment to ensure an equal number of trials for each numerosity. Prior to the experiment, at least 20 practice trials were performed in order to let to subject become acquainted with the task. Practice trials were continued until 10 trials in a row were performed correctly, but it was never necessary to exceed 20 practice trials for any of the subjects. The experiment was run in a single one hour block of trials per subject.

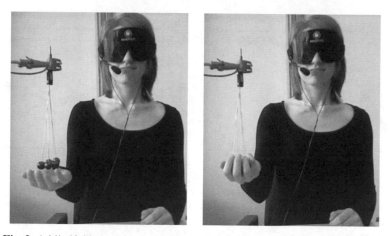

Fig. 2. A blindfolded subject grasping a set of spheres suspended above the hand

3   Results

Error rates were overall low (2.3 %) and the highest error rate of 5 % was reached for five items in the target present case. Subjects never released spheres from the hand. Generally they only grasped them in the hand and did not move them around much.

The response times as a function of the number of items averaged over all subjects are shown for the target present trials in Figure 3a and for the target absent trials in Figure 3b. The solid lines represent linear regression weighted according to the inverse squared standard error. This yielded a target present slope of 32 ± 7 ms/item and a target absent slope of 72 ± 1 ms/item. In this case the reported uncertainty in the slope values is the standard error that resulted directly from the regression procedure. Linear regression was also performed on the single subject data. Averaged over subjects this resulted in a target present slope of 22 ± 46 ms/item and target absent slope of 79 ± 73

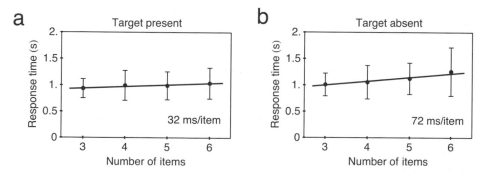

Fig. 3. Response times as a function of the number of items averaged over all subjects for the a) target present trials and b) target absent trials. Error bars indicate the standard deviation of the single subject means. The solid lines represent linear regression to the response times. Slope values are indicated in the figure.

ms/item. None of the single subject's target present slopes were significantly different from zero and for only three subjects the target absent slope was significantly different from zero at the 0.05 significance level.

A 2×2 (target presence $\times$ measure) repeated measures ANCOVA (Analysis Of Co-Variance) was performed on the slopes and the axis-intersections, with skin temperature (averaged over begin and end temperature) as co-variate. This analysis did not show any effects ($F(1,8) \leq 2, p \geq 0.2$).

4   Discussion and Conclusions

In a previous study we have shown that there is a whole range of possible response time slopes when searching for a certain target-distractor combination differing in shape [3]. In that study it was found that search for a tetrahedron among spheres(25 ms/item) was performed in parallel, while search for a tetrahedron among cubes (703 ms/item) was performed serially. In both cases the target present slope is indicated. The slope value (32 ms/item) from the present study indicates parallel search. Also the item release rate of 0% suggests parallel search, because in serial search generally items are released from the hand [3]. Therefore, the results clearly indicate that there is a pop-out effect for a cold object among warm objects.

The present results show that a cold object among warm objects is roughly equally salient as an object with edges among objects without edges. Lederman and Klatzky found that a copper target among wooden distractors is much less salient than the presence of an edge [1]. This shows that temperature differences are more salient than thermal properties of materials.

An explanation for this difference between saliency of thermal properties and saliency of temperature differences is the fact that two objects at room temperature differing in thermal properties normally both cause heat flow out of the skin, but at different rates. Therefore, both objects activate the same population of receptors and nerve endings in that case. On the other hand, a warm object causes heat flow into the skin, while a cold object causes heat flow out of the skin. In this case the cold objects are detected by a system of nerve fibres and receptors dedicated to cold perception, while the warm objects activate nerve fibres and receptors dedicated to warmth perception. Consequently, there is a categorical difference between an object below skin temperature and an object above skin temperature. Whether such a categorical difference is necessary for pop-out effect remains to be investigated.

Summarising, our results show that a cold object pops out among warm objects. Furthermore, slight variations in hand temperature among subjects did not affect the search slopes, which is practical for applications. The high saliency of a cold item among warm items make temperature differences useful as encoding variables in haptic interfaces.

Acknowledgments. This work was financed by the European Union as part of a CP-Large-Scale integrating project The Hand Embodied (consortium agreement: ICT-248587-THE).

References

1. Lederman, S.J., Klatzky, R.L.: Relative availability of surface and object properties during early haptic processing. Journal of Experimental Psychology: Human Perception and Performance 23, 1680–1707 (1997)
2. Plaisier, M.A., Bergmann Tiest, W.M., Kappers, A.M.L.: Haptic pop-out in a hand sweep. Acta Psychologica 128, 368–377 (2008)
3. Plaisier, M.A., Bergmann Tiest, W.M., Kappers, A.M.L.: Salient features in three-dimensional haptic shape perception. Attention, Perception & Psychophysics 71(2), 421–430 (2009)
4. Ho, H.N., Jones, L.A.: Contribution of thermal cues to material discrimination and localization. Perception & Psychophysics 68, 118–128 (2006)
5. Treisman, A., Gelade, G.: A feature-integration theory of attention. Cognitive Psychology 12, 97–136 (1980)
6. Wolfe, J.M., Cave, K.R., Franzel, S.L.: Guided search: an alternative to the feature integration model for visual search. Journal of Experimental Psychology: Human Perception and Performance 15, 419–433 (1989)
7. Jones, L.A., Ho, H.N.: Warm or cool, large or small? The challenge of thermal displays. IEEE Transactions on Haptics 1, 53–70 (2008)
8. Coren, S.: The left-hander syndrome: The causes and consequences of left-handedness. Vintage Books, New York (1993)
9. Plaisier, M.A., Bergmann Tiest, W.M., Kappers, A.M.L.: Haptic search for spheres and cubes. In: Ferre, M. (ed.) EuroHaptics 2008. LNCS, vol. 5024, pp. 275–282. Springer, Heidelberg (2008)

Using Haptic-Based Trajectory Following in 3D Space to Distinguish between Men and Women

Eleni Zarogianni, Ioannis Marras, and Nikos Nikolaidis

Department of Informatics, Aristotle University of Thessaloniki, Greece
{ezarogianni,imarras,nikolaid}@aiia.csd.auth.gr

Abstract. Gender differences in spatial abilities are widely acknowledged and scientifically proved. In this paper, we explore the feasibility of implementing a behavioral biometrics system capable of distinguishing between men and women, based on a 3D trajectory following test that examines abilities in a spatial context. Haptics were used in order to capture and record various behavioral biometric characteristics such as exerted force, distance from the target trajectory etc. A 83.11% accuracy was observed, suggesting that this novel use of haptics is suitable for this purpose.

Keywords: haptics, behavioral biometrics, spatial abilities, gender recognition, support vector machines.

1 Introduction

The term "spatial abilities" is used to address several skills concerning space. Although an unanimously accepted definition of the term does not exist, it includes, in general, one's ability to explore his/her optical field, perceive shapes, objects and relative distances between them and form mental representations of these shapes and objects which can subsequently be mentally processed. Sex differences associated with space perception have been a subject of research for the past few years. The majority of the studies indicate a substantial lead of men versus women [1] in various aspects related to spatial processing, ranging from learning the spatial route through an unfamiliar environment [4,6] to mental rotation ability [7]. Experiments conducted have shown that men outperform women in the majority of these tests, performing faster, more accurately and making less mistakes [2,3]. In contrast to the above mentioned studies that involve visual processing of spatial information, studies that involved haptic manipulation and perception revealed once again the superiority of men over women in tests where the subjects had to haptically interact with objects in order to perceive orientation and other spatial features [5], suggesting gender differences in haptic orientation perception.

In this paper, our goal is to distinguish men and women on the basis of how they follow a pre-specified trajectory in the three-dimensional space, using haptic technology. To do so, we implemented a series of experiments, the conception of which was based upon the above mentioned scientifically proven gender differences in spatial contexts. The experiments we created are related to spatial abilities as they require one's judgement of orientation in space and examine one's ability to perceive space geometry and analyze depth information. In essence, our system can be considered as a behavioral

A.M.L. Kappers et al. (Eds.): EuroHaptics 2010, Part II, LNCS 6192, pp. 225–230, 2010.

biometrics one. The idea of using haptics in order to capture biometric traits is relatively new and provides the possibility of capturing behavioral features such as velocity, force, angular orientation and time that conventional devices (e.g. mouse or keyboard) cannot.

Indeed, haptic-based behavioral biometrics related to spatial ability have been used in the development of both identity recognition and verification systems [8,9,10,11]. In [8] the authors develop a system that enables continuous identification in a virtual environment using haptics. To do so, they implemented a test in which participants had to wander in a 2D flat "elastic" maze that has only one correct path through it. User paths within the maze are compared either in the spatial domain through the matching score evaluated after dynamic time warping or in the Fourier domain after first matching the time scales. The latter approach provided the best results, with an Equal Error Rate of 22.3%. In the verification system described in [9], the data recorded during trials of users on the same elastic maze setup included velocity, force, torque, and angular orientation of the haptic end effector. Windowed Fourier transform was applied on each of these quantities (separately on each dimension) and Kullback- Leibler divergence was used to evaluate the most information rich subset of measurements. Experiments showed that 3D force and torque are the more discriminant features for verification purposes. Using this feature set along with the maze solving time led to a 95.4% successful verification rate at 16% false acceptance rate (FAR). A similar recognition and verification approach is detailed in [10]. In [11], the authors develop a test in which users were asked to trace using a haptic device the outer line of a 2D circle. The recorded data included the force exerted in particular positions, the Euclidean distances from the circle, the test's completion time and the angular momentum on several positions. Principal Component Analysis (PCA) was used to select those features that showed the least correlation. The classifier design included the development of a fuzzy controller. The system achieved a 82.22% subject (client) verification rate and 94.7% impostor identification rate.

2   Method Description

As already mentioned, our goal is to design a system capable of distinguishing men and women, by capturing behavioral biometric features related to spatial tasks with the aid of a haptic device. A series of tests in which participants were asked to follow a trajectory, designed on a surface in the 3D space were conducted. In the sections below, we provide an overview of our system and the methodology used.

2.1   Haptic Device, API and Data Capture

For our experiments, we used the Phantom Desktop haptic device [12] by Sensable Inc. The haptic application was developed using the CHAI 3D API [13]. For our tests, we designed two surfaces of different complexity. The complexity difference lies in the number of concave and convex areas created in each 3D surface. The concave and convex areas add a factor of difficulty in the sense that they require one's judgement of their depth and height accordingly and test one's ability to estimate the direction of the superimposed path. In addition, we designed two trajectories that the user had to follow,

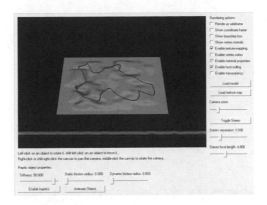

(a)

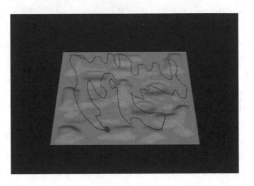

(b)

Fig. 1. The first and the fourth test that the users had to perform. The application interface is shown in (a).

a simple one and a more difficult one in the sense that it consists of multiple turns that make the tracing process more difficult.

Thus, by combining these surfaces and trajectories, we produced 4 tests of increasing difficulty (Fig. 1). It should be noted that the view angle (orientation) of the 3D surface was kept fixed for those 4 tests and could not be altered by the user.

A total of N=37 volunteers, with no previous experience in handling a haptic device, took part in the experiments, 20 men and 17 women. Participants were asked to follow the trajectory on each surface, starting from a black dot that stands as a starting point and returning back at it, paying attention first in being as close to the original trajectory as they can and secondly in performing the tests as fast as they can. Each individual was given the opportunity to familiarize himself with the haptic device and the procedure before the experiments were actually recorded in order to eliminate the "training effect". Participants performed the series of 4 tests, one after the other, four times, with an interval of at least 4 to 5 hours between two consecutive batches. The purpose of these

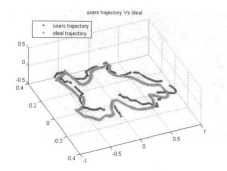

Fig. 2. Graphical representation of a user's trajectory compared to the ideal trajectory he was asked to follow in the first test

intervals was to exclude the possibility that the user repeats the same path by recalling his previous trial.

Our system begins to record data as soon as the user handling the stylus of the haptic device makes contact with the 3D surface near the starting point. From that point on, our system records data both when the user touches the surface and when he deviates from his course and looses touch, at a rate of 100 samples per second. The behavioral traits captured or evaluated throughout the experiments include the x,y,z coordinates of the user's trajectory $[P_x, P_y, P_z]$, the total time during which the subject remains at the same x,y,z position, the force vector $[F_x, F_y, F_z]$ that is exerted to the user (only in instances when his trajectory is in contact with the surface), the velocity $[V_x, V_y, V_z]$ in which he/she proceeds and the total time t in which the subject completes each trial. The data recording phase stops as soon as the user returns to the starting point.

2.2 Preprocessing and Feature Selection

Data Preprocessing. This step includes preprocessing of the raw data we recorded during the experiments in order to evaluate additional features. This involves calculation of variance and mean values for each component of velocity and force vectors, per user and per trial. In addition, in order to estimate the deviation of each user's trajectory from the ideal (Fig. 2), we calculated a vector that contains, for each point of the ideal (target) trajectory, the Euclidean distance from the nearest point of the user's trajectory. In addition, before the calculation of the vector of minimum Euclidean distances, we performed a point interpolation procedure, on each user trajectory so that the number of points on this trajectory becomes equal to the number of points of the ideal trajectory. The same process was also applied on the velocity and force vectors. Moreover, a normalization procedure (conversion to the [0 1] range) was performed on the elements of the vectors of minimum Euclidean distances in order to facilitate the classifier later on.

Principal Component Analysis. PCA was used in order to reduce the dimensionality of our data set. In our implementation, PCA was applied in two cases. The first case involves the vectors that contain the minimum Euclidean distances between the user and the ideal trajectory whereas the second case involves the force vectors, separately in each component (x,y,z). The decision on how many dimensions to keep was taken by exploring the eigenvalue spectrum of the corresponding data set, with the aim to retain approximately 95% of the signal energy. For example, for the fourth test, we reduced the dimensions of the vector of minimum distances from 23523 to 65.

2.3   Classifier Design

In this work, we have chosen Support Vector Machines (SVM) [14] as our classification method. SVMs are widely considered as one of the best performing classifiers, and have been successfully used in a wide range of applications. When the classes are not linearly separable, as in our case, kernels can be introduced so as to map the original data into a new feature space where classes are linearly separable. Polynomial and Radial Basis Functions (RBF) kernels were used in our implementation. Performance evaluation was done using the leave-one-out cross validation method [15]. This method uses the entire data set minus one instance for the SVM training phase and tests the trained SVM with the remaining instance. The procedure is repeated until all samples/instances have been used as test samples and the average performance over all runs is calculated. In our case the leave-one-out method was applied as follows. As it was mentioned before, each participant was asked to repeat each test four times. Since we want our system to distinguish between men and women, in each run we leave a man's set of four trials and a woman's set of four trials (each trial is an instance) outside the training set and use it for testing. The procedure is repeated 20 times so that every man and every woman is used at the testing phase. The method is applied separately for each of the 4 tests, that users performed. In addition, an experiment where we used 2/3 of the subjects (both male and female) for training and the remaining 1/3 for testing was performed.

3   Results

We performed a significant number of trials with different combinations of SVM kernels and features in order to find the one that provides the highest level of accuracy (correct classification rate). The system achieved an accuracy of 83.11% in distinguishing men and women (85% for men and 80.88% for women), on the fourth test using the LOOCV method and an accuracy of 81.03% when the 2/3 - 1/3 setup was used. The feature vector we used involved (a) the [0 1] normalized vector of minimum Euclidean distances, after having applied the point interpolation technique and PCA to reduce dimensions, (b) the variance of force in the x dimension, (c) the mean value of force in y and (d) the mean value of force in the z dimension. This level of accuracy was achieved using a second degree polynomial kernel in the SVM. The same accuracy was achieved with the use of a first degree RBF kernel, too.

We observed that as the difficulty level of the tests increased from tests 1 to 4, so did the discrimination accuracy of our system. This may be attributed to the fact that the differences in spatial abilities between men and women become more prominent as the spatial tasks become more complex.

4   Conclusions and Future Work

In this paper, we investigated the possibility of implementing a haptics-based system capable of distinguishing men and women. We used haptic technology in order to capture the behavioral features that men and women exhibit, as they perform a path following task on a surface. It has been shown that such an approach can achieve satisfactory levels of accuracy. This gender distinction information could be applied as a preprocessing stage in a user identification or verification system, which utilizes haptic-based behavioral biometric traits. More specifically, the proposed system could classify the unknown person as man or woman so that the subsequent recognition or verification stage can be applied on the men or women subset only, thus potentially increasing the recognition accuracy. In the future, the application of more refined techniques for feature selection will be attempted.

References

1. Voyer, D., Voyer, S., Bryden, M.: Magnitude of sex differences in spatial abilities: a meta-analysis and consideration of critical variables. Psychological Bulletin 117 (1995)
2. Scali, R.M.: Gender differences in spatial task performance as a function of speed or accuracy orientation. Sex Roles 43(5-6), 359–376 (2000)
3. Osin, P.P., Lee, S., Lee, J.: Gender differences in spatial navigation. In: Proceedings of World Academy of Science, Engineering and Technology, vol. 31 (2007)
4. Moffat, S.D., Hampson, E., Hatzipantelis, M.: Navigation in a virtual maze: Sex differences and correlation with psychometric measures of spatial ability in humans. Evolution and Human Behavior (1998)
5. Zuidhoek, S., Kappers, A.M.L., Postma, A.: Haptic orientation perception: Sex differences and lateralization of functions. Neuropsychologia (2007)
6. Galea, L.A., Kimura, D.: Sex differences in route learning. In: Personality and individual differences (1993)
7. Linn, M.C., Petersen, A.C.: Emergence and characterization of sex differences in spatial ability: A meta-Analysis. Child Development (1985)
8. Orozco, M., Asfaw, A., Adler, A., Shirmohammadi, S., El Saddik, A.: Automatic Identification of participants in haptic systems. In: IEEE Instrument and Measurement Technology Conference, vol. 12, pp. 888–892 (2005)
9. Orozco, M., Graydon, M., Shirmohammadi, S., El Saddik, A.: Using haptic interfaces for user verification in virtual environments. In: IEEE International Conference on Virtual Environments, Human-Computer Interfaces and Measurement Systems, pp. 25–30 (2006)
10. El Saddik, A., Orozco, M., Asfaw, Y., Shirmohammadi, S., Adler, A.: A novel biometric system for identification and verification of haptic users. IEEE Transactions on Instrumentation and Measurement 56(3), 895–906 (2007)
11. Kanneh, A., Sakr, Z.: Biometric user verification using haptics and fuzzy logic. In: Proceedings of the 16th ACM International Conference on Multimedia, pp. 937–940 (2008)
12. SensAble Technologies, http://www.sensable.com
13. CHAI 3D, http://www.chai3d.org
14. Vapnik, V.: The Nature of statistical learning theory. Springer, New York (1995)
15. Geisser, S.: Predictive inference: An introduction. Chapman and Hall, New York (1993)

Hand-Held Object Force Direction Identification Thresholds at Rest and during Movement

Gabriel Baud-Bovy[1,2] and Elia Gatti[1]

[1] Vita-Salute San Raffaele University, Milan, Italy
[2] IIT Network Research
Unit of Molecular Neuroscience, San Raffaele Foundation, Milan, Italy
baud-bovy.gabriel@hsr.it, e.gatti1@studenti.hsr.it

Abstract. This study measured the minimum amount of force necessary to identify its direction. The force was produced by a robot and transmitted to a small spherical handle held between the thumb and index finger. We also examined whether this threshold changed during movement. We found that the force threshold was lower when it was possible to move the arm (5 g) than when it was immobile (10 g).

Keywords: force perception; kinesthesia; touch; grasping.

1 Introduction

Starting from the earliest days of Psychophysics [1], force perception has been in large part the study of the perception of weights although more recent studies have also investigated the perception of elastic, viscous and inertial force fields [e.g., 2]. With respect to force, previous studies have generally measured the capacity of the arm to discriminate weights of hand-held objects (Weber fractions typically range between 8% and 15%, [3]). In contrast, little is known about the lightest hand-held weight that can be detected. One reason might be that the detection of a very small force seems to belong to the realm of the sense of touch rather than that of the sense of force. As a matter of fact, thresholds as low as 0.01 g for point pressure detection and 0.1 g point pressure localization at the finger pad have been reported [4].

In this study, subjects had to identify the direction of a weak force. The force was produced by a robot and transmitted to a small spherical handle held between the thumb and index finger. It is important to note that we did not aim at measuring the minimum amount of force applied to the skin that could be detected but the minimum force transmitted by a hand-held object that could be detected in a task where participants grasped the object with a force much larger than the one that they had to perceive. Also, our task involved the identification of the direction of this force, which might be more difficult than a simple detection task. Various studies have shown that movement can influence the sensitivity of the tactile and kinesthetic senses (e.g., [3][5]). A second objective of our study is therefore to examine whether this threshold would increase or decrease during movement.

A.M.L. Kappers et al. (Eds.): EuroHaptics 2010, Part II, LNCS 6192, pp. 231–236, 2010.

2 Material and Methods

2.1 Subjects

10 right-handed participants (2 males) aged between 19 and 27 years (mean 24) with no known neuromuscular disorders and naïve to the task, participated in the experiment. All participants gave their informed consent prior to testing.

2.2 Experimental Setup

The experimental setup consisted of an impedance-controlled 3-DOF haptic device (Omega, Force Dimension). A small force torque transducer (Nano-17, ATI Technologies) was mounted between the spherical handle (diameter 1.5 cm) and a custom-made nacelle to measure the interaction force. The software ran on a AMD Sempron processor under Windows XP and was developed in C++ using Force Dimension DHD API to interface with the device and National Instrument NIDAQmx API to interface with the force sensor via a NI-2634E DAC card.

The haptic loop computing the force ran at 1 kHz. The device produced a strong visco-elastic force field (stiffness = 1000 N/m, damping = 20 N/m/s) that constrained hand movements along a horizontal laterally oriented line (length = 20cm.). During the presentation of the stimulus (see below), a proportional force feedback was included in the control law to compensate for the inertia and friction of the device along the unconstrained direction. To avoid instabilities, the gain of the force feedback decreased when the end-effector distance from the workspace center exceeded 6 cm. The control law also included a simple model of the Coulomb friction force (circa 0.25 N). The velocity was computed from two consecutive samples and filtered using a simple exponential filter (time constant = 1.5 ms).

To reduce the sensory noise, the force was sampled continuously at 33kHz and the last 33 samples (about 1 ms) were used in the haptic loop to compute the sensed force. In addition, the sensed force was filtered on-line with an exponential filter (time-constant 4 ms). DHD antigravity compensation scheme was activated throughout the experiment (end-effector mass parameter = 0.06 kg). Position and force information was saved in memory at 200 Hz and saved in a file at the end of each trial for off-line analyses.

2.3 Experimental Protocol

Participants grasped the spherical handle mounted on the device's nacelle using a key grasp with the thumb placed on the top. The height and position of the seat were adjusted to align the elbow with the center of the workspace. A brief familiarization period was offered at the beginning of the experiment. After the familiarization, participants were blindfolded and a double face tape was put on the handle to insure that participants would not release the handle during the experiment.

Each trial started with the device that brought subject's hand to the center of the workspace. Haptic guidance was obtained by increasing progressively the stiffness of a centered elastic force field (max stiffness = 1000 N/m). The stiffness was then progressively released to zero to avoid discontinuity with the following 2.5 s long loading phase where the force magnitude would increase up to the desired level. Then the force remained constant until the end of the trial (see Fig. 1).

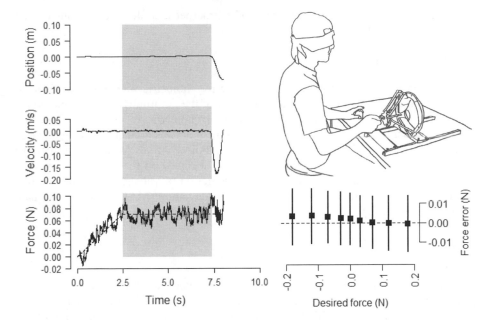

Fig. 1. Left: Typical trial in the static condition. The dashed line in the bottom panel corresponds to the desired force (0.07 N) while the noisy curve represents the actual force measured by the force sensor. The first 2.5 s correspond to the *loading phase*. The grey area denotes the *holding phase* used by the participant to make a decision about the direction of the force in the static condition. The last part of the record corresponds to the response movement. The final hand position (in the left hemispace) indicates that the subject felt (correctly) that force was oriented toward the right. **Top right:** View of the experimental setup. **Bottom right:** Force rendering accuracy: Average force error ± average standard deviation of the force measured during each trial.

The task consisted in identifying the direction of the force. To give the response, the participant moved the end-effector against the perceived force direction and pushed a button held with the other hand. The response was recovered from the final hand position (the button was used only to stop the trial). The stimuli consisted of a force of 0, 0.03, 0.07, 0.12, or 0.18 N in one of the two possible directions. Note that the actual force differed by less than 1.5 g for the desired force in both conditions (average RMS force error ± SD = 0.015 ± 0.005 N; see also Fig. 1). The experiment included a *static condition* where the participants were instructed to keep their hand immobile until they had decided how to respond and a *dynamic condition*, where they were free to move the end-effector to feel better the force before giving the response. The condition changed every 10 trials, and the participants switched hands every 40 trials. The order of the 10 possible force stimuli was randomized within the 10-trial blocks (the 0 force was presented twice). The experiment comprised 12 blocks in each condition, which included 6 blocks with the left hand and 6 blocks with the right hand (240 trials per subject). Starting condition and starting hand were counterbalanced across subjects. The experiment was divided into two 1-hour long sessions: the first session included the task familiarization plus 80 trials while the second session included the 160 remaining trials. The time between the two sessions ranged from 3 hours to 4 days.

2.4 Data Analysis

The location and scale parameters of a logistic psychometric function were fitted to the percentage of correct responses as a function of the (non-null) force magnitude for each subject and condition. The range of the psychometric function was fixed between 0.5 (chance level) and 1. The detection threshold was defined as the force magnitude that yielded 75% of correct responses. For the trials with zero force, we computed the percentage of responses indicating a rightward force. Unless indicated otherwise, we report the mean and standard deviation of values. The median, when reported, is accompanied by the median absolute deviation (MAD), a robust estimate of the standard deviation.

3 Results

In the static condition, participants held the end-effector fixed for 1.7 ± 1.14 s (holding phase). The average displacement was 3.1 ± 2.7 mm, which indicates that subject maintain well the initial position during the holding phase. The median length of the response movements in the static condition was 7.3 ± 2.7 cm. In the dynamic condition, the number of exploratory movements varied from trial to trial as well as across participants. The median number of movements ranged from 1 to 4 depending on the participant. The total movement length was 14.6 ± 6.4 cm (including the response). In general, participants produced more to-and-fro movements and took slightly more time to respond when the force was weak.

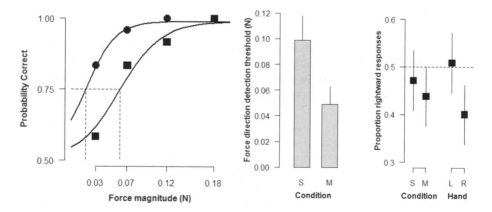

Fig. 2. Left: Psychometric functions of one subject in the static (squares) and dynamic (circles) conditions. The vertical dashed lines indicate the thresholds. Zero-force trials are analyzed separately because the correct response is not defined for these trials. **Center:** Average force direction identification thresholds in the static (S) and dynamic (M) conditions. Vertical bars denote 95% confidence intervals. **Right:** Proportion of responses indicating a rightward force in absence of any signal (zero force trials).

Figure 2 shows the value of the psychometric functions fitted to the responses of a subject in the static and dynamic conditions. This participant was able to identify the direction of the force better in the moving condition. This observation holds true for all subjects who participated to the experiment. The average (±SD) values of the thresholds were 0.099±0.031 N in the static condition and 0.049±0.022 N in the dynamic condition. The difference between the two conditions was highly statistically significant (paired t-test, t_9 = 5.55, p < 0.001). Finally, we examined the presence of eventual biases in the perception of the force direction analyzing responses in absence of any force. When the left hand was used, There was a tendency to respond toward the right and thus to indicate a left-oriented force field ($\chi^2(1)$=5.21, p = 0.02).

4 Discussion

This study measured the minimum amount of force transmitted by a hand-held object required to identify its direction. The main finding was that the force direction is more easily identifiable when it is possible to move the arm (5 g) than when it is at rest (10 g). The order of magnitude of these thresholds is in line with the results of the only other study to our knowledge that measured the minimum amount of assistive or resistive force that could be detected during a movement (7 g, [7]). It also agrees with an indirect measurement of the absolute force threshold obtained in a task involving the localization of the center of a weak elastic force field [8]. The estimates obtained here are however much more precise than those obtained in [7] where the force effectively produced by the haptic device was not precisely controlled.

While any variation of afferent activity might be interpreted directly as the result of the external force in the static condition, the haptic system must tear apart the information that is related to the movement and the information about the external force from afferent signals that mix both in the dynamic condition. It is important to note that the movements in the dynamic condition did provide any additional cues (such as inertial cues when jiggling lifted weights [6]) about the magnitude or direction of the force because the force remained constant. Therefore, this improvement must reflect some movement-related change of the haptic system sensitivity at the peripheral or central level.

Mechanoreceptors in the skin in contact with the handle can provide information about the force direction. Directionally dependent responses have been evidenced by moving slowly a light stimulus on the skin (normal force < 8 g, [9]) and during the application of forces typical of the manipulation of objects [10]. Our results are compatible with the observation that subjects can scale appropriately a tangential force applied to the fingerpad [11]. However, it is unlikely that the performance improvement in the dynamic condition can be related to the sense of touch since directional tactile sensibility decreases during movement [5].

Golgi organs are usually retained to be the main source of information for the sense of force [12] but the difference between the static and dynamic conditions suggests that muscles spindles might have contributed to the perception of the force direction in our task since muscle spindles are the only sensory organs the sensitivity of which can be directly controlled by the central nervous system [13]. Moreover, the better performance observed in the dynamic condition is in line with the commonly accepted view is that proprioception is better during active than passive movements although this point of view has been recently questioned [14].

Finally, it is important to mention the possible role of corollary discharges, which contribute not only to the decoding of muscle spindle activity but also to the so-called sense of effort or innervation [15]. It is possible that the participants perceived the differences between the efferent signals associated with the two movement directions due the directional force. Recent studies have indeed reemphasized the contribution of efferent signals to the kinesthetic senses [14].

References

1. Weber, E.H.: The sense of touch. Academic Press, London (1834/1978)
2. Baud-Bovy, G., Schochia, L.: Is mass invariant? Effects of movement amplitude and duration. In: Proc. 25th Meeting of the International Society for Psychophysics, Galway, Ireland, pp. 369–374 (2009)
3. Jones, L.A.: Perception of Force and Weight: Theory and Research. Psychological Bulletin 100(1), 29–42 (1986)
4. Voerman, V.F., van Egmond, J., Crul, B.J.: Normal values for sensory thresholds in the cervical dermatomes: a critical note on the use of Semmes–Weinstein monofilaments. Am. J. Phys. Med. Rehabil. 78, 24–29 (1999)
5. Vitello, M.P., Ernst, M.O., Fritschi, M.: An instance of tactile suppression: Active exploration impairs tactile sensitivity for the direction of lateral movement. In: Proc. EuroHaptics 2006, vol. 351, p. 355 (2006)
6. Brodie, E.E., Ross, H.E.: Jiggling a lifted weight does aid discrimination. The American Journal of Psychology 98, 469–471 (1985)
7. Zadeh, M.H., Wang, D., Kubica, E.: Perception-based lossy haptic compression considerations for velocity-based interactions. Multimedia Systems 13, 275–282 (2008)
8. Bocca, F., Baud-Bovy, G.: A model of perception of the central point of elastic force fields. In: 3rd Joint EuroHaptics Conf. and Symp. on Haptic Interfaces for Virtual Environment and Teleoperator Systems, Salt-Lake City, USA, pp. 576–581 (2009)
9. Olausson, H., Wessberg, J., Kakuda, N.: Tactile directional sensibility: peripheral neural mechanisms in man. Brain Research 866, 178–187 (2000)
10. Birznieks, I., Jenmalm, P., Goodwin, A.W., Johansson, R.S.: Encoding of Direction of Fingertip Forces by Human Tactile Afferents. Journal of Neuroscience 21(20), 8222–8237 (2001)
11. Pare, M., Carnahan, H., Smith, A.M.: Magnitude estimation of tangential force applied to the fingerpad. Experimental Brain Research 142, 342–348 (2002)
12. Jami, L.: Golgi tendon organs in mammalian skeletal muscle: functional properties and central actions. Psychological Review 72(3), 623–666 (1992)
13. Matthews, P.B.C.: Where does Sherrington's "Muscular Sense" originate? Muscles, joints, corollary discharges? Annual Review of Neuroscience 5, 189–218 (1982)
14. Proske, U., Gandevia, S.C.: The kinaesthetic senses. J. Physiol. 587(17), 4139–4146 (2009)
15. McCloskey, D.I.: Corollary discharges and motor commands. In: Handbook of Physiology The Nervous System III, Motor Control, Bethesda, pp. 1415–1448 (1981)

A New Planar 4-DOF Spring and Cable Driven Force Feedback Device

Yi Yang[1], Yuru Zhang[1], and Betty Lemaire-Semail[2]

[1] State Key Laboratory of Virtual Reality Technology and Systems, Beihang University,
37 Xueyuan Road, Haidian District, 100191 Beijing, China
eyang@me.buaa.edu.cn, yuru@buaa.edu.cn
[2] L2EP-IRCICA, University Lille 1, 50, Avenue Halley,
Parc Scientifique de la Haute Borne, 59650 Villeneuve d'Ascq, France
betty.semail@polytech-lille.fr

Abstract. This paper presents a new planar Spring & Cable driven Force feedback Device (SCAFD). The new device uses fewer cables to realize multi-finger grasp and manipulation feedback. The principle and cable tension calculation of the planar SCAFD are explained. The result of an example of virtual grasp task shows that the device can realize 1-DOF grasp and 3-DOF manipulation force feedback on a plane with only four cables and a spring.

Keywords: Spring and cable driven, grasp, haptic device.

1 Introduction

Grasping objects and operating them with our fingers is one of the most common actions we undertake on a daily basis. To simulate the sense of touch and manipulation, many single-point haptic devices have been developed. But they do not provide the natural grasp and manipulation found in the real world, as afforded by multi-fingered haptics [1]. Furthermore single-point haptic interfaces severely limit or slow down the user's ability to determine characteristics of objects such as shape, mass, stiffness and size [2].

The simulation of multi-finger grasp and operation is attracting researchers' interest. One degree of freedom grasp with two fingers is the most basic model of multi-finger grasp and operation. The experience and knowledge gained from 1-DOF grasp can be duplicated and improved to develop multi-finger interface. Conventional force feedback devices are driven by links. However, link type haptic interfaces have the drawbacks of backlash, back-drive friction and inertia, and limited workspace. When two PHANToMs are used to grasp virtual objects, only two fingers are displayed in the virtual environment (the thumb and the index finger). This setup also suffers from limited workspace, due to the effects of inertia [3]. Compared with link-driven devices, cable-driven (tension based) haptic interfaces have the advantages of fast reaction speed, simple structure, smooth manipulation, and scalable workspace.

The SPIDAR II [4] enables pick-and-place tasks with two fingers. The operator wears two caps on his/her thumb and forefinger. Each cap is held by four cables. This device can be considered as a combination of two simple SPIDARs [5]. The other example is the SPIDAR-G [3, 6]. This device enables a cross-type grip which is a

A.M.L. Kappers et al. (Eds.): EuroHaptics 2010, Part II, LNCS 6192, pp. 237–242, 2010.

1-DOF grasp related to the centre of the cross. Each tip of the cross is tensed with two cables. So both the SPIDAR II and the SPIDAR-G need eight cables.

Each cable needs an actuating module to keep the cable tensed and rolled on the pulley. More cables increase the cost of the device, make it complex to control and cause more interference between cables during operation. We propose a new type of device which can decrease the number of cables and realize the same function in a simple way. The device is named as Spring & Cable driven Force Feedback Device (SCAFD). In this paper, a planar 4-DOF SCAFD is presented to prove the validity of the idea. The principle of the planar SCAFD is introduced in Section 2. The cable tension calculation algorithm is presented in Section 3. Section 4 presents an example of a virtual grasp task. Section 5 is the conclusion of the paper.

2 Principle of the Planar SCAFD

In a virtual grasp task in a plane, there are three conditions to be simulated:

1. In free space, when the fingers do not collide with virtual objects, the fingers should be able to move freely without feeling any restriction.
2. When the user grasps a virtual object, the grasp force should be simulated.
3. When moving the grasped virtual object to collide with other virtual objects, both the grasp force and the collision force should be simulated.

Figure 1 presents two configurations of the planar Spring & Cable driven Force Feed-back Device (SCAFD). The grasp points D_1 and D_2 are connected with two cables respectively. A spring links D_1 and D_2. In Fig. 1(a) the spring is a draught spring while in Fig. 1(b) the spring is a compression spring. The configuration in Fig. 1(a) can realize grasp from the external side of an object. The configuration in Fig. 1(b) can realize grasp from the internal side of an object.

Since cables cannot exert stress but only tensions, cable tensions should maintain positive all the time. Therefore there will always be resultant force of cable tensions exerted on the fingers when the user operates the device at D_1 and D_2. The springs are used to balance the resultant force of cable tensions in free space. Thus when moving the fingers in free space, the user will not feel any restriction.

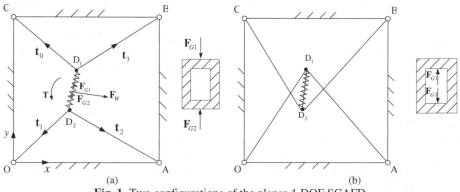

(a)   (b)

Fig. 1. Two configurations of the planar 4-DOF SCAFD

Treating the spring as a rigid body, it has three DOFs on a plane (two translations and one rotation). This 3-DOF planar device can exert a wrench (two dimensional force and one dimensional torque) to simulate 3-DOF manipulation force feedback [7]. Meanwhile the spring can stretch and shrink along its axis ($\overline{D_1D_2}$). So there is an extra DOF of the device. The grasp force $\mathbf{F}_{G1}$ and $\mathbf{F}_{G2}$ are along the spring axis ($\overline{D_1D_2}$). The spring force, the grasp force and the wrench are independent. Each of them can be balanced by the four cables separately. The ultimate tension of each cable is the sum of its components. The calculation model of the cable tensions will be introduced in section 3.

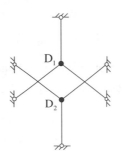

Fig. 2. A configuration combining two 2-DOF planar cable-driven devices

It may be noted that a combination of two 2-DOF planar cable-driven devices can also realize 1-DOF grasp and 3-DOF manipulation. Figure 2 presents a configuration of the combination. However, the combination needs six cables [8]. As the planar SCAFD only needs four cables and a spring, it will decrease the cost, simplify the means of control and avoid interference between cables during operation. We think this principle of simulating 1-DOF grasp and 3-DOF manipulation force feedback can also be extended to simulate multi-finger grasp and 6-DOF manipulation in space.

3 Cable Tension Calculation

Cable-driven haptic devices use controlled cable tensions to exert force feedback. According to the principle of the planar SCAFD, the cable tensions are composed of three parts: tensions to equilibrate the spring force, tensions to balance the grasp force and tensions to balance the manipulation force. Here we explain how the cable tensions are calculated with the configuration in Fig. 1(a) as an example.

Figure 1(a) also presents the statics diagram of the configuration. The spring exerts tension when it is stretched. The magnitude of spring tension is calculated by Hook's Law:

$$F_S = k(d - d_0) \tag{1}$$

where F_S is the magnitude of the spring tension, k is the spring constant, d_0 is the original length of the spring, d is the distance between D_1 and D_2. The coordinates of

D_1 and D_2 can be obtained from the forward kinematics of a 3-DOF planar force feedback device. More details of the kinematics can be found in [7].

The spring force is balanced by cable tensions to enable the user to move freely in the free space. The static equilibriums are set up at D_1 and D_2 respectively

$$\mathbf{t}_{S0} + \mathbf{t}_{S3} = \mathbf{F}_S, \mathbf{t}_{S1} + \mathbf{t}_{S2} = \mathbf{F}_S' = -\mathbf{F}_S \tag{2}$$

where $\mathbf{t}_{si}$ ($i = 0,1,2,3$) is the cable tension to balance the spring tension, $\mathbf{F}_s$ is the spring tension at D_1, $\mathbf{F}_S'$ is the spring tension at D_2 and $\|\mathbf{F}_S\| = \|\mathbf{F}_S'\| = F_S$.

When the fingers grasp a virtual object, the grasp force is balanced by the cable tensions. The static equilibriums are set up at D_1 and D_2 respectively

$$\mathbf{t}_{G0} + \mathbf{t}_{G3} = \mathbf{F}_{G1}, \mathbf{t}_{G1} + \mathbf{t}_{G2} = \mathbf{F}_{G2} \tag{3}$$

where $\mathbf{t}_{Gi}$ ($i = 0,1,2,3$) is the cable tension to balance the grasp force, $\mathbf{F}_{G1}$ is the grasp force at D_1, $\mathbf{F}_{G2}$ is the grasp force at D_2. The grasp force equals to each other when the grasp is stable.

To simulate the manipulation force solely, the grasped object and the two fingers are considered as a whole. The resultant force of four cable tensions will balance the wrench of manipulation

$$\mathbf{\$}^w = \mathbf{A}\mathbf{t}_W \tag{4}$$

where $\mathbf{\$}^w = \begin{bmatrix} F_{Wx} & F_{Wy} & T \end{bmatrix}^T$ is the wrench of the grasped object, $\mathbf{A}$ is the static Jacobian matrix, and $\mathbf{t}_W = \begin{bmatrix} \mathbf{t}_{W0} & \mathbf{t}_{W1} & \mathbf{t}_{W2} & \mathbf{t}_{W3} \end{bmatrix}^T$ is the cable tension vector to balance the wrench. More details about how to obtain $\mathbf{A}$ can also be found in [7].

Therefore the total cable tension of each cable is the sum of the three components that balance different force

$$\mathbf{t}_i = \mathbf{t}_{Si} + \mathbf{t}_{Gi} + \mathbf{t}_{Wi}, i = 0,1,2,3 \tag{5}$$

where $\mathbf{t}_i$ is the ultimate cable tension. The components of $\mathbf{t}_i$ are calculated from equations (2)(3) and(4). The magnitude of $\mathbf{t}_i$ is then used to control the motor current.

4   Example

This example is provided in order to simulate the virtual grasp task mentioned in section 2. Figure 3(a) presents the device. The user wears two rings which represent the grasp points D_1 and D_2 in Fig. 1(a). Each ring is connected by two cables and the two rings are connected by a draught spring. Figure 3(b) presents the three stages of the virtual grasp task. The movement of the two balls corresponds with the two fingers. The user moves the fingers to grasp the rectangular box (Stage 1), then he grasps the box and moves it (Stage 2), finally he manipulates the box to collide with the cylinder (Stage 3).

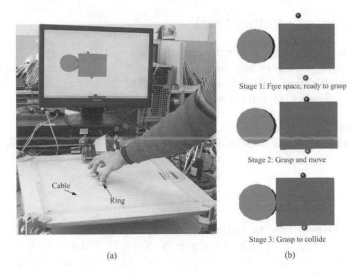

Stage 1: Free space, ready to grasp

Stage 2: Grasp and move

Stage 3: Grasp to collide

(a)   (b)

Fig. 3. The device and stages of the virtual grasp task

Figure 4(a) presents the force exerted in the virtual grasp experiment. In Stage 1, the user attempts to grasp the box. The distance between his fingers is shortened. Therefore the spring force decreases. In Stage 2 and Stage 3, the user grasps the box. He experiences the grasp force clearly with a maximum force of about $5.1N$. In Stage 3, the user moves the box to collide with the cylinder. He feels the collision force, with a maximum value of about $5.6N$. Stage 4 in Fig. 4 presents the reverse procedure. In this stage, the user releases the box and moves the fingers in free space.

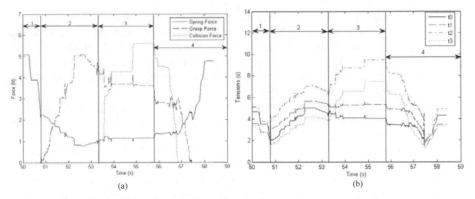

(a)   (b)

Fig. 4. Force and cable tensions in the virtual grasp experiment

During the process of the virtual grasp task, all cable tensions remain positive, as presented in Fig. 4(b). The user is able to feel the grasp force and the collision force clearly when he manipulates the grasped object. In free space, the resultant force of cable tensions is balanced by the spring force. The user can move his fingers freely.

5 Conclusion and Future Work

We present a new Spring & Cable driven Force feedback Device (SCAFD) to realize multi-finger grasp and manipulation. A planar SCAFD is introduced, including its principle and cable tension calculation algorithm. The device can realize 1-DOF grasp and 3-DOF manipulation force feedback on a plane with only four cables and a spring. This new device can decrease the cost, simplify the means of control and avoid interference between cables during operation. Future work includes extending the principle of the planar 4-DOF device to multi-finger and 6-DOF manipulation in space.

Acknowledgments

This work is supported by the National High Technology Research and Development Program ("863" Program) of China under grant No. 2008AA04Z206. It has also been carried out within the framework of the INRIA Alcove project and is supported by the IRCICA and The European Commission (FEDER). Their support is greatly appreciated.

References

1. McKnight, S., Melder, N., Barrow, A.L., Harwin, W.S., Wann, J.P.: Perceptual cues for orientation in a two finger haptic grasp task. In: First Joint Eurohaptics Conference and Symposium on Haptic Interfaces for Virtual Environment and Teleoperator Systems, pp. 549–550. IEEE Press, New York (2005)
2. Barbagli, F., Salisbry Jr., K., Devengenzo, R.: Enabling multi-finger, multi-hand virtualized grasping. In: 2003 IEEE International Conference on Robotics and Automation, vol. 1, pp. 809–815. IEEE Press, New York (2003)
3. Kim, S., Hasegawa, S., Koike, Y., Sato, M.: Development of tension based haptic interface and possibility of its application to virtual reality. In: 2002 ACM Symposium on Virtual Reality Software and Technology, pp. 199–205. ACM Press, New York (2000)
4. Ishii, M., Sato, M.: A 3D interface device with force feedback: a virtual work space for pick-and-place tasks. In: IEEE Annual International Symposium on Virtual Reality, pp. 331–335. IEEE Press, New York (1993)
5. Hirata, Y., Sato, M.: 3-dimensional Interface Device For Virtual Work Space. In: 1992 IEEE/RSJ International Conference on Intelligent Robots and Systems, vol. 2, pp. 889–896. IEEE Press, New York (1992)
6. Kim, S., Hasegawa, S., Koike, Y., Sato, M.: Tension based 7-DOF force feedback device: SPIDAR-G. In: 2002 IEEE Virtual Reality, pp. 283–284. IEEE Press, New York (2002)
7. Yang, Y., Zhang, Y.: A new cable-driven haptic device for integrating kinesthetic and cutaneous display. In: 2009 ASME/IFToMM International Conference on Reconfigurable Mechanisms and Robots, pp. 386–391. IEEE Press, New York (2009)
8. Kawamura, S., Ito, K.: A new type of master robot for teleoperation using a radial wire drive system. In: 1993 IEEE/RSJ International Conference on Intelligent Robots and Systems, vol. 1, pp. 55–60. IEEE Press, New York (1993)

A Laparoscopic Grasper Handle with Integrated Augmented Tactile Feedback, Designed for Training Grasp Control

Eleonora Westebring-van der Putten, Mostafa Hajian, Richard Goossens, John van den Dobbelsteen, and Jack Jakimowicz

TU Delft, faculty of Industrial Design Engineering, Landbergstraat 15, 2628CM, Delft, Netherlands
{E.P.Westebring-vanderPutten,M.Hajian,R.H.M.Goossens,
J.J.vandenDobbelsteen,J.Jakimowicz}@TUDelft.nl

Abstract. During laparoscopic grasping, excessive grasp forces and tissue slippage may well lead to tissue damage. Because surgeons have difficulty gauging the force exerted on the grasped tissue, it is desirable to train them in applying the right degree of force in order to prevent tissue damage. Previously it was demonstrated that grasp force control can be learned when augmented tactile feedback is provided in a training task. The present paper discusses the design of a new laparoscopic grasper with augmented tactile feedback. Two grasper handles were developed and tested. Each of them contained augmented tactile feedback actuators.

Keywords: Tactile feedback, Haptic feedback, Sensor, Actuator, Grasper, Laparoscopy.

1 Introduction

Laparoscopic surgery, a Minimally Invasive Surgery (MIS) technique performed in the belly alcove, is a very efficient operating technique. Laparoscopy is performed via small incisions with the help of long thin instruments. An endoscope (camera) is used to follow the surgeon's activities on a screen. When compared to open surgery the procedure has certain advantages and disadvantages. The advantages are mostly for the patient who experiences less trauma and is therefore in hospital for a shorter period and makes a speedier recovery. However, this technique brings with it difficulties for the surgeon because visually everything is indirect in much the same way that the tissue contact is indirect [1]. This can endanger the patient's health if, for instance, tissue is damaged [2].

In laparoscopic surgery, the surgeon's hands manipulate tissue indirectly using instruments. As a result, it is difficult for the surgeon to estimate just how much force needs to be applied to grasp tissue without exerting excessive force giving rise to slippage since haptic perception is distorted [3] by the interference caused by the instrument. Haptic perception provides feedback on the grasped tissue and is defined as a combination of tactile perception and kinesthetic perception. In an endeavor to

A.M.L. Kappers et al. (Eds.): EuroHaptics 2010, Part II, LNCS 6192, pp. 243–250, 2010.

find solutions to distorted haptic perception during MIS, a research project was initiated at Delft University of Technology in cooperation with the Catharina Hospital in Eindhoven. In our previous study we demonstrated that augmented tactile feedback can aid grasp control and shorten the laparoscopic grasping learning curve [4] when an object is being lifted. Surgeons can and in fact need to be taught and trained, before they practice actual surgery, to maintain a safe grasp faster and with greater accuracy. Ultimately this will improve patient safety and reduce training costs.

In the previous study, tactile-actuators were used to provide feedback on slippage and excessive pinch force. However, these actuators were not integrated into the grasper-handle itself, but where attached instead to the surgeon's hand and to the handle. This resulted in a bulky and less user-friendly system (handle A in Fig. 1)(see [5] for details of the design). Moreover, from the ergonomic point of view, the grasper-handle needed to be improved. Although much research has been done in recent decades into haptic feedback in MIS, no specific research data could be found that provided evidence of augmented tactile feedback on grasp forces for the purposes of learning grasp control (for reviews see [6, 7]). There is, however, one Patent that claims credit for inventing a minimally invasive surgical tool comprising a sensor that generates a signal in response to interaction with the tool and a haptic feedback system that generates a haptic effect in response to the signal [8]. However, no research data could be found for this specific tool.

This paper describes in detail the design of an optimized grasper-handle, including the integration and miniaturization of actuators. The box-trainer set-up is explained as well, as this grasper handle is intended for use in training situations where grasp control can be learned. The main objective of the whole grasp-control-training device is to measure the effect of augmented tactile feedback during a grasping task with the aid of a laparoscopic handle both during and after having learnt to control the laparoscopic grasp.

2 Handle Design and Ergonomics

The ergonomic characteristics of the new handle design, incorporating the feedback actuators of handle A, are based on the action guidelines for laparoscopic graspers [9]. The final design is based on the handle designed by M.A. van Veelen [9] (handle B) since, as was established during interviews with surgeons, its ergonomic shape was preferred to the shapes of other commercial graspers. The final prototype is shown in Fig. 1, together with handle B and another commonly used handle (Storz, Tutlingen, Germany). The shape of the product is the result of an evaluation of alternative options for each part of the handle. The prototype was divided into three main sections: a back hinge, a front hinge and the body part. Different alternatives were designed for each part (a total of 10 alternatives), based on a Quality Function Deployment type of analysis [10], in which the ergonomic attributes of the handle were identified and classified according to level of importance. User tests with foam models were performed in order to choose the most comfortable alternative design for each part. Fig. 2 shows one of the 36 different foam handles used in the user tests.

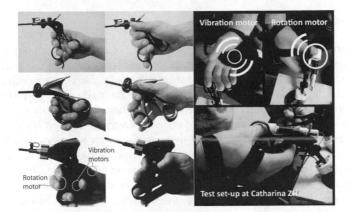

Fig. 1. Left: Top panel: the commonly used handle (Storz), Middle panel: Handle B. Lower panel: final prototype. Right: actuators used in the first prototype (handle A) with tactile feedback.

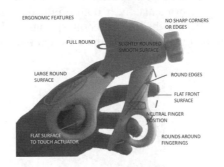

Fig. 2. One of the foam models used in the user tests

The new handle can be used with both hands as it incorporates optimized versions of the actuators developed by E. Westebring. The actuators from the first prototype are shown in the center of Figure 1 (see Section 3.2), and are thus in contact with the fingers and/or palm during use. As with handle B, our design incorporates elements such as the rotating back hinge, the large curves and the smooth surfaces, thereby preventing extreme bending of the wrist joint and minimizing the pressure points. However, the overall dimensions were adjusted to fit smaller hands, as handle B was too large for most users and the rotating knob was difficult to reach when precision gripping was required. A support was added for the little finger as this feature is more comfortable than the original design in handle B. The main body of the handle is fabricated from Acrylonitrile Butadiene Styrene (ABS) created by means of Fused Deposition Modeling (FDM). In previous prototyping of handle B it was the Stereo Lithography (SL) technique that was used in combination with an epoxy resin. This resulted in a handle B prototype that was very fragile, causing parts of it break when dropped on the ground.

3 The Box- Trainer Set-Up

When manipulating tissue, surgeons exert a combination of pinching and pulling forces. Depending on the relative magnitude of the forces exerted, the tissue can slip, be damaged, or be grasped safely. Fig 3 shows the safe, damage and slip region as a function of the degree of pinch and pull force. When the pull force is high compared to the pinch force, the tissue slips out of the grasper, whereas when both the pull and the pinch forces are high, the tissue can be damaged. Even high pinch force without pull force can be detrimental. Every type of tissue grasped by an instrument has its own profile, as each tissue and grasper jaw has different properties [11]. The boundaries of what is known as the safe area are called the slip-line and the damage-line [3, 12].

In order to teach the surgeon how to control his grasp forces we developed a special box trainer. In the box-trainer there are 4 objects that simulate different tissue types and can be grasped by the surgeon/trainee. The objects are each equipped with two sensors so that the pull and pinch forces applied can be measured. The sensors were designed to measure forces applied between 0 and 15 N of the pinch force and between 0 and 7 N of the pull force. These forces where the applied range of forces measured in our former experiments under both non and augmented feedback conditions [4]. The objects are attached to different springs, each with different spring constants and are built to virtually simulate the different types of tissues.

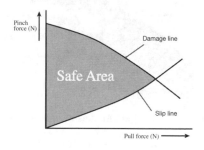

Fig. 3. Safe area

Each of the grasper handles has 3 actuators to provide the user with augmented tactile feedback in relation to the grasp force; two vibrating patches, to record excessive force and a rotating cylinder to monitor slippage (as discussed in Section 3.2). A special situation arises when one of the actuators is not working optimally or is damaged. The controller measures the voltage across the actuators. If this is less than the optimal voltage then a red LED on top of the handle will be turned off. The sensors and actuators are discussed in more detail in the next section. The control process in brief is; the user grasps, with one of the two laparoscopic graspers, one of the objects. The sensors measure the pressure applied and the pull forces. Sensors send out data on the amount of pinch and pull force to a microprocessor. Data is read by the microprocessor and sent to a PC. The data is processed using our own software. Decisions are taken on the basis of the programmable slip and damage profiles of each object and the necessary data is transmitted back to the microprocessor for further action. The microprocessor sends independent signals to activate the actuators of the corresponding grasper handle. The user feels the feedback signals and is able to act accordingly

Sensors: Several different objects integrated with pinch and pull sensors were built and tested. The final objects to be grasped are made of a curved steel plate (10 x 80mm) forming a 15-degree wedge covered with 0.5 mm rubber. A miniature round force sensor measuring 9.8 x 4 mm (type KM10, ME-meßsysteme GmbH, Henningdorf, Germany) was placed underneath the steel plate. The sensor measures the pinch force applied to the surface of the object. The output signal of the sensor is fed into a custom-made amplifier. The responsiveness of the sensor to forces that were applied to the surface was determined with standardized weights. Fig. 4 shows the test set-up.

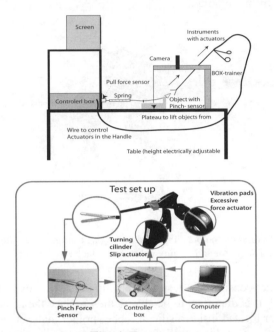

Fig. 4. Test set up

Because different tissues may have different elasticity profiles, we attached each object to different springs with a wire in order to simulate the different tissue types. Each spring is attached to a pull sensor (type KD40S ME-meßsysteme GmbH, Henningdorf, Germany) to measure the pull force exerted on the object by the grasper. Slip is measured by comparing the applied pinch force with the object's actual slip-force. This slip-force was measured for each block beforehand and the resulting slip-lines were integrated into the software.

Actuators: Three miniature actuators are implanted in the grasper handle. One indicates whether tissue is slipping from the tip and the other two indicate if too much force is being applied. Fig. 5 depicts the inside of the laparoscopic handle. In the front hinge, a rotating motor is integrated into the handle to provide feedback on slippage while two vibrating coin motors are located in the back hinge to provide feedback on excessive force. The two actuators that provide feedback on excessive force are positioned in such a way that both in the case of force and precision grip the user's hand touches one of them.

The actuators that provide feedback when excessive force is applied are 8mm vibrating coin motors operating at 3V. The coin motor choice was based on size and vibration strength. Due to the limited space in the back hinge, they had to be as small as possible. The vibration intensity should be great enough to be felt by a hand through a glove but also as low as possible to minimize vibration in the handle. The intensity that can be optimally felt with a minimum amount of vibration in the whole handle was determined by a process of trial and error. The motors were situated perpendicular to the skin and damping material was placed around the motor to prevent the whole handle from vibrating.

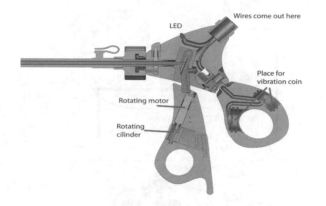

Fig. 5. Miniaturized vibration motors are placed in the back hinge where the holes for the vibration caps are visible. The motor and turning cylinder is placed in the front hinge.

Since the product consists of a test device, it is likely that over the course of time the motor will fail. It is important to be able to then replace the actuator. Fig. 4 shows the vibration motor located inside a silicon rubber holder that can be placed inside the available hole in the back hinge and fixed by means of ribs that fall into the same shape in the hole. In addition, the rubber cap has space inside for isolation material, which does not affect the motor's performance but it confines the vibrations mostly to the back hinge. The motor that rotates the cylinder when slippage occurs is a 6 mm round brushed precious metal 0.3 watt Maxon DC motor with a GP 6A gear-head. The motor plus gear-head have a nominal torque of 0,03 Nm, turn at a maximum speed of 84rpm and operate with a 4.5V power source.

The whole motor is located in the front hinge. The cylinder attached to the motor has a diameter of 15 mm and a length of 15 mm and is made out of PVC. The dimensions of the cylinder were based on research conducted by Murphy et al. [13]. As the sensitivity to the perception of slip at the fingertip very much depends on surface texture the surface of the cylinder should not be homogenous. Small features evoke more accurate perceptions than homogenously textured surfaces [14]. The surface is therefore made rough by arbitrarily puncturing it with a hot needle. The research furthermore showed that the angle between the fingertip and the feedback did not seem to be relevant [15]. Therefore, it was justifiable to place the cylinder in the front hinge so that it would tangentially touch the inner side of the user's second or third finger.

Data Acquisition. The analog signals from the force sensors were captured at a rate of 200 Hz using an AD-converter (LabJack UE9) connected to a laptop via USB. Custom-made software, written in C++, was used to activate the actuators in the handle on the basis of the output of the force sensors via the digital output channels of the LabJack. Four digital LabJack outputs are used as input sources for the vibrating and slippage motors and two for the LEDs (i.e. for the two graspers). The digital output channels of the LabJack have a DC voltage of 3.3V, which is sufficient to drive the actuators and the LED. For each block, the slip-line and damage-line can be set according to the spring properties and the desired behavior of the user. For example, by adjusting the damage and the slip-line the safe area can be enlarged for inexperienced surgeons and decreased when more skilled surgeons are practising. In this way, grasp control can be trained at each level of expertise. In order to be able to further analyze the performance of the user, the data of the force sensors is saved in a data file and stored on the PC.

4   Discussion and Conclusions

The concept and analysis of an optimized laparoscopic grasper for the training of grasp control is addressed. The box trainer was equipped with sensors to measure pull and slippage forces, and miniature actuators that are integrated into the handle of the grasper provide augmented tactile feedback for the surgeon if the grasp forces are not in the safe area. Extensive user tests were carried out to demonstrate and to validate the proposed concept. It was shown that the grasper functions properly. We showed that when using handle A for one-handed grasping tasks[4], grasp control and the learning of it improved significantly with the aid of augmented tactile feedback (even when attention was distracted from the grasping hand). Therefore, the goal in our further research is to investigate whether grasp control performance improves when one has to learn a two-handed grasping task with the new handle presented in this article. As a two-handed grasping task is a realistic surgical task (it is used, for example, in bowel surgery when one performs bowel translocation) it is of interest to be able to deal with augmented feedback input from two hands at the same time. If a surgeon in training can learn to control his/her grasp forces with this device and does not become dependant on the augmented feedback this box trainer could be integrated into the curriculum for resident surgeons. The relevant research is in progress and data gathering will continue in the near future.

Acknowledgments. The authors would like to thank all the students who helped to accomplish and perfect the design: Phil van den Eerenbeemt, Albertien Greijdanus, Toon Jacobse, Geert Koemans, Antonio Recamier Elvira and Jan Schets.

References

1. Stassen, H.G., Dankelman, J., Grimbergen, C.A., Meijer, D.W.: Man-machine aspects of minimally invasive surgery. Annual Reviews in Control 25, 111–122 (2001)
2. Dankelman, J., Wentink, M., Stassen, H.G., Gouma, D.J.: Human reliability and training in minimally invasive surgery. Minimally Invasive Therapy and Allied Technologies 12, 129–135 (2003)

3. Westebring-van der Putten, E.P., van den Dobbelsteen, J.J., Goossens, R.H., Jakimowicz, J.J., Dankelman, J.: Force feedback requirements for efficient laparoscopic grasp control. Ergonomics 52, 1055–1066 (2009)
4. Westebring - van der Putten, E.P., van den Dobbelsteen, J.J., Goossens, R.H.M., Jakimowicz, J.J., Dankelman, J.: The Effect of augmented feedback on grasp force in laparoscopic grasp control. IEEE Transactions on Haptics (accepted 2010)
5. Westebring-van der Putten, E.P., Lysen, W.W., Henssen, V.D., Koopmans, N., Goossens, R.H., van den Dobbelsteen, J.J., Dankelman, J., Jakimowcz, J.: Tactile feedback exceeds visual feedback to display tissue slippage in a laparoscopic grasper. Studies in Health Technology and Informatics 142, 420–425 (2009)
6. Westebring-van der Putten, E.P., Goossens, R.H.M., Jakimowicz, J.J., Dankelman, J.: Haptics in minimally invasive surgery - a review. Minimally Invasive Therapy and Allied Technologies 17, 3–16 (2008)
7. Schostek, S., Schurr, M.O., Buess, G.F.: Review on aspects of artificial tactile feedback in laparoscopic surgery. Medical Engineering & Physics 31, 887–898 (2009)
8. Ramstein, C., Ullrich, C.J., Degeest, A.: Minimally invasive surgical tools with haptic feedback. In: Corporation, I. (ed.) PCT, WO, pp. 1–11 (2009)
9. van Veelen, M.A., Meijer, D.W., Goossen, R.H.M., Snijders, C.J., Jakimowcz, J.: Improved usability of a new handle design for laparoscopic dissection forceps. Surgical Endoscopy 16, 201–207 (2002)
10. Chan, L.-K., Wu, M.-L.: Quality function deployment: A literature review. European Journal of Operational Research 143, 463–497 (2002)
11. Heijnsdijk, E.A.M., de Visser, H., Dankelman, J., Gouma, D.J.: Slip and damage properties of jaws of laparoscopic graspers. Surgical Endoscopy 18, 974–979 (2004)
12. de Visser, H.: Grasping Safely: Instruments for bowel manipulation investigated. Faculty Mechanical Maritime and Materials Engineering, Vol. PhD. Delft University Press, Delft (2003)
13. Murphy, T.P., Webster, R.J., Okamura, A.M.: Design and performance of a two-dimensional tactile slip display. In: EuroHaptics 2004, pp. 130–137 (2004)
14. Salada, M., Vishton, P., Colgate, J.E., Frankel, E.: Two experiments on the perception of slip at the fingertip. In: 12th International Symposium on Haptic Interfaces for Virtual Environment and Teleoperator Systems, pp. 146–153 (2004)
15. Webster, R.J., Murphy, T.E., Verner, L.N., Okamura, A.M.: A novel two-dimensional tactile slip display: design, kinematics and perceptual experiments. ACM Trans. Appl. Percept. 2, 150–165 (2005)

Collision Avoidance Control for a Multi-fingered Bimanual Haptic Interface

Takahiro Endo, Takashi Yoshikawa, and Haruhisa Kawasaki

Department of Human and Information Systems, Gifu University,
1-1 Yanagido Gifu 501-1193, Japan
tendo@gifu-u.ac.jp, o3128035@edu.gifu-u.ac.jp,
h_kawasa@gifu-u.ac.jp

Abstract. To present three-directional force at ten fingertips of both human hands, we previously developed a multi-fingered bimanual haptic interface consisting of two five-fingered haptic hands and two interface arms. However, there is a risk that haptic hands and interface arms will collide while a user is manipulating the haptic interface. To alleviate this risk, we propose a collision avoidance control for the multi-fingered bimanual haptic interface. In particular, by constructing the collision avoidance using a penalty method, we hope to reduce the user's feeling of collision insecurity. Through an experiment, we investigated the validity of the proposed control law.

Keywords: bimanual haptic interface, collision avoidance, virtual reality.

1 Introduction

In dangerous situations such as maintenance work in nuclear facilities, mine removal in mine fields and various tasks at disaster sites, robots are operated remotely. In addition, the application of robots to more advanced, more complex work is desired as a recent social need, and the teleoperation of dual-arm robots has been researched aggressively. When performing activities in our daily lives, we usually use both hands, so it is important to exert force on both hands to make the sensation of robot operation highly realistic. Thus, from the standpoints of the telexistence/telepresence [1] and the teleoperation of dual-arm robots [2,3], research and development of bimanual haptic interfaces continue [4-6].

The existing bimanual haptic interfaces [4,5] can exert forces at multiple fingertips, but the presented force is only a one-directional force. For example, when the haptic interface generates force by using a wire, the presented force is only exerted in the direction that the wire pulls. Even if the interfaces can present three-directional force, the location at which the force is exerted is only one point [2,3,6]. Thus, the existing bimanual haptic interfaces cannot present three-directional force at all of the fingertips, and it is difficult to produce a delicate force. The user of the existing bimanual haptic interfaces can grasp a virtual object via a simple open-close movement, but the user cannot grasp/manipulate an arbitrarily shaped virtual object (see the literature of robotics [7] for details). Also, it is difficult to create a highly realistic sensation. To perform elaborate tasks with both hands in the VR space, it is necessary to present three-directional forces at all of the fingertips of both hands.

A.M.L. Kappers et al. (Eds.): EuroHaptics 2010, Part II, LNCS 6192, pp. 251–256, 2010.

With these issues in mind, we developed a bimanual haptic interface, named bimanual HIRO ("Haptic Interface Robot"), which can present three-directional forces at all of the fingertips of both hands [8]. To construct this interface, we used two multi-fingered haptic interface HIRO III units [9], each of which consists of a five-fingered haptic hand and an interface arm and can present three-directional force to five human fingertips. However, since we used two unimanual HIRO III units without modification, the collision avoidance that was a problem peculiar to the bimanual interface was not investigated. Namely, there is a risk that the haptic hands and arms will collide while a user is operating the haptic interface. The potential for collision makes the user anxious, and thus collision avoidance is very important.

Our goals in this paper were to propose a control law that considers collision avoidance during use of the bimanual haptic interface and to investigate the control law experimentally. In particular, we propose the collision avoidance control law using a penalty method. The penalty method has been used in various fields including the animation [10], the haptic rendering [11], and it is not new method. However, we apply the penalty method to the collision avoidance control law, and it is applied on a new and advanced bimanual HIRO system. The paper is organized as follows: In the next section, we introduce the bimanual HIRO. Section 3 presents the control law for collision avoidance. We then investigate the control law experimentally, as described in Section 4. Finally, Section 5 presents our conclusions.

2 Bimanual HIRO

The authors have developed a multi-fingered bimanual haptic interface, named bimanual HIRO, which is shown in Fig. 1. The bimanual HIRO consists of two multi-fingered haptic interface HIRO III units [9], and can present three-directional force at all of the fingertips of both hands. Here note that the haptic interface connected to the user's left hand is an uncovered HIRO III in Fig. 1. HIRO III and its specifications are shown in Fig. 2 and Table 1, respectively.

HIRO III consists of an interface arm and a five-fingered haptic hand. The arm has 6 DOF, and the haptic finger has 3 DOF. HIRO III has a total of 21 DOF, and its

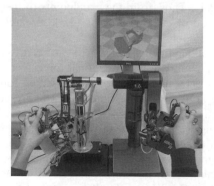

Fig. 1. Bimanual HIRO. A user can interact with a virtual environment through ten fingertips.

(a) The five-fingered haptic interface robot, HIRO III.   (b) Finger holder.

Fig. 2. HIRO III and Finger holder

work space covers VR manipulation on the space of a desktop. A force sensor is installed at the top of each finger. To manipulate HIRO III, the user wears a finger holder (Fig.2 (b)) on his/her fingertips. The finger holder has a sphere which, when attached to the permanent magnet at the force sensor tip, forms a passive spherical joint. Its role is to adjust for differences between the human and haptic finger orientations. To ensure enough working space of bimanual HIRO for a task on a desktop, the distance between the left- and right-HIRO III was set to be the same as the Japanese adult biacromial breadth [8].

By using two HIRO III units, a user can manipulate the virtual objects with both hands, as shown in Fig. 1. In addition, the striking point is that bimanual HIRO and the user are connected only at the user's fingertips. This means that the bimanual HIRO does not cause an oppressive feeling when it is attached to the user and does not represent its own weight.

3 Control Law for the Bimanual HIRO System

Although the bimanual HIRO has the advantages offered by the connection between the haptic interface and the user being accomplished by only fingertips, this setup does make it difficult to control the haptic interface. We proposed redundant force control to be the control law of HIRO III [12]. First we introduce the redundant force control, and then we propose the redundant force control while considering collision avoidance.

Table 1. Specifications of HIRO III

Hand	Number of fingers		5
	Weight		0.78 [kg]
Finger	Degree of freedom		3 [DOF]
	Weight		0.12 [kg]
	Output force		3.6 [N]
	Operating angle of joints	1st	(Thumb) -36~36[rad] (Other) -30~30[rad]
		2nd/3rd	-35~90 / 0~112 [rad]
Arm	Degree of freedom		6 [DOF]
	Weight		3.0 [kg]
	Output force		56 [N]
	Operating angle of joints	1st/2nd	-110~110 / -125~0 [rad]
		3rd/4th	0~145 / -90~90 [rad]
		5th/6th	-45~45 / -60~60 [rad]

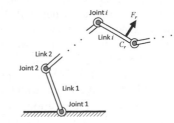

Fig. 3. n-link robot with the reaction force on link i

The redundant force control consists of the force control of the haptic finger and the interface arm. The control of the haptic finger is given by $\tau(t)=K_1J^TF_e(t)$ $+K_2J^T\int F_e(s)\mathrm{d}s - K_3\dot{q}_f + J^TF_d$ where $\tau=[\tau_1^T,\cdots,\tau_5^T]^T\in\mathrm{R}^{15}$ is the joint torque of a haptic finger, J is a Jacobian, $F=[F_1^T,\cdots,F_5^T]^T\in\mathrm{R}^{15}$ is a force at the fingertip, $F_d\in\mathrm{R}^{15}$ is the desired force, $F_e=F_d-F$, $q_f=[q_{f1}^T,\cdots,q_{f5}^T]^T\in\mathrm{R}^{15}$ is the joint angle of the haptic finger and K_i is the feedback gain matrix. In the control, a haptic finger that reaches the limit of the movable range is switched to a position control to keep the joint angle in the movable range, and the rest of the haptic fingers are controlled by the redundant force control. After reaching the limit of the movable range, the control is switched back to the redundant force control when the direction of the joint toque input is in the same direction as that of the joint angle apart from the limit of the movable range. On the other hand, the control of the interface arm is given by

$$\tau_a(t)=K_{a1}\tau_e(t)+K_{a2}\int\tau_e(s)\mathrm{d}s-K_{a3}\dot{q}_a(t)+J_a^T\begin{pmatrix}\sum_{i=1}^{5}F_{di}\\\sum_{i=1}^{5}(p_i-p_{hb})\times F_{di}\end{pmatrix}, \tag{1}$$

where K_{ai} is the feedback gain matrix, $q_a\in\mathrm{R}^6$ is the joint angle, J_a is a Jacobian, $p_i\in\mathrm{R}^3$ is the i-th fingertip position, $p_{hb}\in\mathrm{R}^3$ is the tip of the interface arm, F_{di} is the desired force of the i-th fingertip and τ_e is an equivalent joint torque to the offset forces at the five fingertips. The arm that reaches the limit of the movable range is switched to a position control, as when controlling the fingers. Next, by applying the collision detection that is well known in computational geometry and robotics, we propose the control law while considering collision avoidance.

The proposed control law addresses collision detection and collision avoidance. Considering collision detection first, let us approximate each link of the fingers and arm of both HIRO III units by a cylinder, and we will consider each cylinder as one that made a line segment thick. Here note that we set the cylinder so that it covers the arm and fingers. That is, we choose the radius of the cylinders through a traial and error process. And then, for all pairs of lines, we derive the minimum distance L between two lines in the pair. Further, by using the minimum distance $L_{\min}$, that is the minimum in all of L, and the radius r_1 and r_2 of the corresponding cylinders, we carry out the collision detection. When the collision of the cylinders is detected (namely, when $r_1+r_2>L_{\min}$), we derive the penetration depth $d=r_1+r_2-L_{\min}$. Since the collision detection is carried out within 0.5 [ms], we can control the haptic interface at a sufficient control rate (1 [kHz]).

Next, we consider collision avoidance by making the reaction force F_r that corresponds to the penetration depth d. In particular, the virtual spring and damper are connected at point C_r where the collision is detected, and the reaction force F_r $=Kd+Dv$ is generated when the arm or finger moves in the direction where d becomes large, where K is the stiffness of the virtual spring, D is the damping coefficient of the damper and v is the relative speed. For example, in the n-link robot shown in Fig. 3, let us consider the situation in which the reaction force F_r is generated at C_r on link i. In this case, by using the position vector P_r of C_r and the joint angle $\theta=[\theta_1,\cdots,\theta_i]^T$ from link 1 to i, a Jacobian $J_r=\partial P_r/\partial\theta$ is calculated. And then, the joints 1 to i are controlled by the torque $\tau_r=-J_r^TF_r$, and the rest of the joints (joint $i+1$ to n) are controlled by the redundant force control. In other words, to create F_r at C_r, F_r is transformed into the joint torque $\boldsymbol{\tau}_r$ and the joints until C_r are controlled by $\boldsymbol{\tau}_r$, and the rest of the joints are controlled by the redundant force control. Here note that all of the joints are controlled by the redundant force control when the collision is not detected. Further, when $\boldsymbol{F}_r$ is created at link j of the i-th haptic finger, $\boldsymbol{\tau}_r$ is created at joint 1 to j of the i-th haptic finger, and the rest of the joints of the haptic fingers and the interface arm are controlled by the redundant force control. By achieving collision avoidance with the virtual spring and damper method (penalty method), the sudden stop of the haptic interface by collision does not occur, and the avoided collision's influence on the user's fingertips is minimal.

4 Experiment

To investigate the control law, we carried out an experiment in which a user manipulated virtual objects by two hands in VR. In particular, the user intentionally manipulated the haptic interface so that the haptic fingers and arms would collide. We used the same experimental environment as that described in a previous work [8].

As an example, we show the joint torque, norm of fingertip position and fingertip force of the thumb of the right-handed HIRO III in Fig. 4. The data are measured in the case in which the corresponding cylinders of the thumbs of the right- and left-HIRO III collide. In the figure, the zone enclosed by the dotted lines is the interval where the collision of the two thumbs' cylinders is detected. From (c), the force is added to the tip of the thumb in the interval, but the fingertip position in the interval is constant from (b). So, we found that neither thumb could penetrate the inside of the cylinders, even if the user added force. Further, from (a), we see that the joint torque in the interval, where the collision of the two thumbs' cylinders is detected, is constant, which is different from the joint torque in the interval when a collision does not occur. This indicates that the fingertip position after the averted collision becomes constant, and thus the penetration depth does not change. So, the reaction force $\boldsymbol{F}_r$ becomes constant and thus the reaction torque $\boldsymbol{\tau}_r$ also becomes constant. From the experimental results, it is clear that collision avoidance was accomplished. Here note

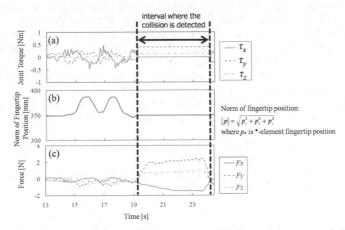

Fig. 4. Experimental results: (a), (b) and (c) show the joint torque, the norm of the fingertip position and the fingertip force of the thumb of the right-handed HIRO III.

that the collision avoidance under the situation, where the left-HIRO III collides with both a virtual object and the right-HIRO III, was also accomplished through another experiment. In addition, the participants felt that the collision avoidance worked well.

5 Conclusions

In this paper, we proposed the collision avoidance control law for the multi-fingered bimanual haptic interface and considered the validity of the proposed control law experimentally. The collision avoidance control law was based on the penalty method, and it was applied on a new and advanced bimanual HIRO system. The computational time of the proposed control law is within 0.5 [ms], and thus we can control the haptic interface at a sufficient control rate. In the control law, the collision avoidance is accomplished by the virtual spring-damper, and thus the sudden stop of the haptic interface by collision does not occur, with little effect on the fingertips of the user. Collision avoidance with the virtual spring damper reduces the user's feeling of insecurity about collisions. On the other hand, to manipulate the haptic interface at high speed, the design of the dynamic control considering inertia, viscosity and friction is another crucial task that awaits us.

Acknowledgments. This paper was supported by the Ministry of Internal Affairs and Communication R & D Promotion Programme (SCOPE).

References

1. Tachi, S.: Telexistence. World Scientific Publishing Co. Pte. Ltd., Singapore (2010)
2. Ishii, A.: Operation System of a Double-front Work Machine for Simultaneous Operation. In: 23rd Int. Symp. Automation and Robotics in Construction, pp. 539–542 (2006)
3. Hayakawa, M., Hara, K., Sato, D., et al.: Singularity Avoidance by Inputting Angular Velocity to a Redundant Axis During Cooperative Control of a Teleoperated Dual-Arm Robot. In: IEEE ICRA, pp. 2013–2018 (2008)
4. SyberGlove Systems: Haptic Workstation,
   http://www.cyberglovesystems.com/products/hardware/hapticworkstation.php
5. Kron, A., Schmidt, G., Petzold, B., et al.: Disposal of Explosive Ordnances by Use of a Bimanual Haptic Telepresence System. In: IEEE ICRA, pp. 1968–1973 (2004)
6. Peer, A., Buss, M.: A New Admittance-Type Haptic Interface for Bimanual Manipulations. IEEE/ASME Trans. on Mechatronics 13, 416–428 (2008)
7. Murray, R., Li, Z., Sastry, S.: A Mathematical Introduction to Robotic Manipulation. CRC Press, Boca Raton (1994)
8. Yoshikawa, T., Endo, T., Maeno, T., Kawasaki, H.: Multi-Fingered Bimanual Haptic Interface with Three-Dimensional Force Presentation. In: 9th IFAC Symp. Robot Control, pp. 811–816 (2009)
9. Endo, T., Kawasaki, H., Mouri, T., et al.: Five-Fingered Haptic Interface Robot: HIRO III. In: WorldHaptics 2009, pp. 458–463 (2009)
10. Moore, M., Wilhelms, J.: Collision Detection and Response for Computer Animation. Computer Graphics 22, 289–298 (1988)
11. Hasegawa, S., Sato, M.: Real-time Rigid Body Simulation for Haptic Interactions Based on Contact Volume of Polygonal Objects. Computer Graphics Forum 23, 529–538 (2004)
12. Mouri, T., Kawasaki, H., Kigaku, K., Ohtsuka, Y.: Novel Control Methods for Multi-fingered Haptic Interface Robot. In: IROS 2006, 1576–1581 (2006)

Optimization Criteria for Human Trajectory Formation in Dynamic Virtual Environments

Sebastian Albrecht[1], Carolina Passenberg[2], Marion Sobotka[2], Angelika Peer[2], Martin Buss[2], and Michael Ulbrich[1]

[1] Institute for Mathematical Optimization
[2] Institute of Automatic Control Engineering,
Technische Universität München, Germany
{albrecht,mulbrich}@ma.tum.de, cpassenberg@lsr.ei.tum.de,
{marion.sobotka,angelika.peer,mb}@tum.de

Abstract. Which criteria determine the formation of rest-to-rest arm movements when interacting with virtual mass-damper dynamics? A novel bilevel optimization approach is used to find the optimal linear combination of common optimization criteria for human trajectory formation such that the resulting trajectory comes closest to the human-performed one. The goal is to utilize this optimal combination to predict human motions in robot control. Experimental results show that subject-dependent criteria combinations can be found for different dynamics.

Keywords: Human trajectory formation, Bilevel optimization.

1 Introduction

The question how humans form a rest-to-rest arm trajectory has attracted much attention in behavioral science. This knowledge is used, for example, for path planning algorithms of robot assistants in human-robot collaborative manipulation (HRCM) or for predictive control algorithms in teleoperation systems. The goal is in both cases to adapt the planning/control algorithms to the movements of the human by predicting his/her trajectory [2,5,7,12].

Various research groups report invariant features for rest-to-rest movements, e.g. a bell-shaped velocity profile. To account for these invariant features, different optimization criteria were presented (see Sec. 2). Only little is known about the influence of external mass-damper dynamics on the arm trajectory formation. Many tasks, however, are performed under the influence of these dynamics, e.g. a common task in HRCM is to collaboratively carry an object. The influence of external dynamics was investigated, for example, by Luo *et al.* [4] for a constrained rotating crank experiment and by Svinin *et al.* [9] for flexible objects. Luo *et al.* explained the data as a combination of two cost functions, Svinin *et al.* used an optimization criterion for unconstrained motions.

In this paper we analyze rest-to-rest arm movements for different mass-damper dynamics acting on the human hand. Our approach is based on two steps: first, arm trajectories are recorded, and second, a linear combination of four common optimization

A.M.L. Kappers et al. (Eds.): EuroHaptics 2010, Part II, LNCS 6192, pp. 257–262, 2010.

criteria is computed that approximates the recorded trajectories best. A novel bilevel optimization approach [1], see Sec. 3, is used to find the linear combination of optimization criteria which yields a trajectory with minimal costs. Thus, arm trajectories can be predicted, such that a planning/prediction algorithm of an autonomous/teleoperated robot can be adapted accordingly. A basic assumption is that the end point of the movement is known or can be predicted. The experimental setup, procedure and results are given in Sec. 4. The paper concludes with a summary and outlook in Sec. 5.

2 Models of Arm Motion

Arm and Muscle Dynamics. The biomechanical dynamics of the human arm is modeled to analyze human arm motion. Thus, the rigid-body dynamics describing the properties of the human skeleton is combined with an ODE-model approximating the dynamical behavior of human muscles.

Following the line of [8], standard rigid body dynamics is used to model a planar two-link human arm. Joint torques τ result from muscles forces f_m, joint damping and external forces. In our experiment these external forces are created by the virtual dynamics.

The arm model allows to include muscle dynamics where models of different complexity can be utilized, e.g. [8,13]. The complete system of the human arm dynamics can be denoted by the first-order ODE $\dot{x} = h(x, u)$, where u is the control input and x the state that includes the joint angles q.

Optimization Principles. The approach is based on the assumption that human trajectories can be described as the result of minimizing an unknown cost function while accomplishing a predefined task. Since one criterion often does not reproduce all different trajectories well enough, we extend this assumption to the minimization of a linear combination of cost functions. As will be shown in the following, the linear combination of four common optimization criteria delivers an accurate description of our experimental data. Flash & Hogan [3] introduced the *Minimum Hand Jerk* cost function f_{HJ} using the Cartesian coordinates of the hand position $p(t)$. The resulting hand paths are fairly straight. A variation of this cost function is the *Minimum Joint Jerk* criterion f_{JJ} which yields slightly curved hand paths by directly utilizing the kinematics of the human arm

$$f_{HJ} = \int_{t_0}^{t_f} \left\| \frac{d^3}{dt^3} p(t) \right\|^2 dt, \quad f_{JJ} = \int_{t_0}^{t_f} \left\| \frac{d^3}{dt^3} q(t) \right\|^2 dt.$$

The *Minimum Torque Change* criterion f_{TC} proposed by Uno *et al.* [10] is the integral over the squared norm of the first time derivative of the torques τ in the joints. As a variation we additionally consider the *Minimum Muscle Force Change* criterion f_{MC} utilizing the muscle dynamics directly. Note that the torques τ are the sum of the torques resulting from joint damping and external forces in addition to the torques caused by muscle forces f_m.

$$f_{TC} = \int_{t_0}^{t_f} \left\| \frac{d}{dt} \tau(t) \right\|^2 dt, \quad f_{MC} = \int_{t_0}^{t_f} \left\| \frac{d}{dt} f_m(t) \right\|^2 dt.$$

3   Optimization Problem

Mathematical Problem Formulation. The combination of the dynamics of the human arm and a cost function (cp. Sec. 2) yields a nonlinear optimization problem, *the lower level program*. Another problem, *the upper level program*, is to find the cost function f out of a family of considered cost functions minimizing the distance d between the recorded human arm data p_{rec} and the computed arm data $p_{comp}(f)$ obtained by solving the respective lower level program. Only linear combinations with the weights $w_i \geq 0$ are considered here: $f = \sum w_i f_i$. The combination of the lower and upper level program is a *bilevel program*.

Solution of Bilevel Program. The chosen direct optimization approach is based on discretization of the ODE $\dot{x}(t) = h(x(t), u(t))$, i.e. the ODE is transformed into the equation $H(\bar{x}, \bar{u}) = 0$ with the time-discretized state $\bar{x}$ and control $\bar{u}$, such that the lower level program can be rewritten as $\min F(\bar{x}, \bar{u} | w_i = const.)$ subject to $H(\bar{x}, \bar{u}) = 0$. Then the Kuhn-Tucker-conditions of the lower level program are utilized to transform the bilevel problem into a standard nonlinear optimization problem of the type $\min D(\bar{z})$ subject to $\bar{z} \geq 0$ and $C(\bar{z}) = 0$.

Here the interior-point algorithm IPOPT [11] is used to solve the problem. In [1] we analyze the performance of this approach and show that the results of the algorithm are reasonably close to the optimum.

4   Experimental Results

In this section an experimental setup is presented to record human rest-to-rest movements under the influence of external mass-damper dynamics. For each recorded trajectory an optimal combination of optimization criteria is determined and the variations of the combinations are analyzed with respect to the different subjects and different external influences.

Experimental Setup. A 2 DoF haptic interface consisting of two linear actuators, where a Thrusttube module 2504 from Copley Controls Corp. is mounted at a right angle on top of a second Thrusttube module 2510, is used for the experiments. Each of the actuators is equipped with an optical position encoder (resolution 1 μm). A 6 DoF JR3 force sensor together with a handle is mounted on the upper actuator (Fig. 1). The haptic interface is controlled using a position-based admittance controller with force input, see [6] for details. Thus, the desired behavior of the device is obtained through the choice of the admittance gains virtual mass m_v and damping b_v. The task consisted of rest-to-rest movements between two targets A and B, see Fig. 1. The workspace of the task was 0.29 m x 0.16 m. The targets and hand position were visualized in a virtual scene, which was presented to the subject via a head-mounted display. To decrease the coupling effects between task completion time and accuracy described by Fitt's law a deviation of ± 1.5 cm from the target was allowed.

Eight mass-damper combinations ($m_v \in \{2, 4, 8, 12\}$ kg, $b_v \in \{0, 5, 10, 20\}$ Ns/m) were implemented and presented to the subjects in a randomized order. With each stimulus, 10 trials in a row were performed.

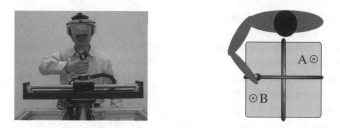

Fig. 1. Experimental setup: Photo and sketch of 2 DoF device

Position and force data were recorded at a frequency of 1 kHz. Three male and one female subject, all right-handed and aged between 23 and 27, took part in the experiment. The subjects' chair was adjusted such that the handle was grasped at the height of the subject's shoulder. The subjects were asked to make rest-to-rest movements as *naturally* (not as fast or as straight) as possible between the targets.

Results. For a proper analysis, the first trial of each stimulus was discarded to avoid after-effects of the previous one. Of the remaining ones, the two-thirds closest to the median of all 10 trials were selected for the analysis. The left plot of Fig. 2 shows one example of six selected trials.

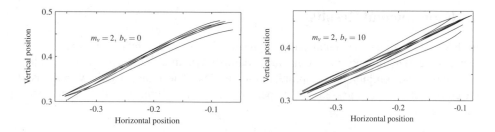

Fig. 2. Recorded human trajectories for different stimuli: Common structure for low relative damping (left) and no apparent scheme for high relative damping (right)

For our analysis the mean of the weight distributions (cp. Sec. 3) was calculated for each stimulus and subject. Our experiments show that the weight distributions differ between subjects with the same stimulus, but all by themselves are quite stable, i.e. the standard deviation is small compared to the general distribution of weights (cp. Fig. 3). Consequently, the one or two dominant criteria are found to be dominant in all considered trials. The differences between subjects can be attributed to human variability. Although the task of performing natural arm movements was the same for all subjects, one subject may still focus more on making lines as straight as possible, while another subject may try to move with minimal effort. Also, biological parameters such as emotional state, time of the day, motor skills etc. can lead to variations between subjects. This finding implies, that an optimal weight distribution can only be used for a specific subject, but then we obtain a high prediction accuracy.

Furthermore, the trajectories can be explained for some stimuli as a combination of only two optimization criteria (cp. Fig. 3). The computations also reveal that the distances between the selected human trajectories and the computed optimal ones are smaller than 1 cm. This accuracy in combination with the small variation will be useful to predict short-term future movements of a subject in his current state, such that the behavior of an autonomous/teleoperated robot can be adapted accordingly. Note that only a few test-trials are needed for self-calibration of such a control approach.

An increase of relative damping $\frac{b_v}{m_v}$ raises the variance of the trajectories of all subjects, compare Fig. 2 (left: small relative damping, right: large relative damping), such that for a high relative damping, e.g. $\frac{b_v}{m_v} = 5$, the weights seem to become random, compare Fig. 4 (left) with Fig. 3. Consequently, the selected trajectories cannot be explained soundly using one weight distribution.

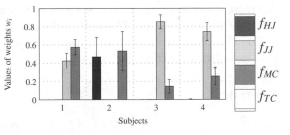

Fig. 3. Mean values with standard deviations for each subject $[m_v = 2, b_v = 0]$

A strong correlation between external dynamics and the resulting weight distribution for a specific subject could not be found. An increase in virtual mass m_v for constant virtual damping b_v, however, tends to correlate with a larger weight corresponding to f_{MC} (e.g. Fig. 4 (right)). A possible interpretation is that for larger m_v the physically more demanding task results in taking muscle forces more into consideration.

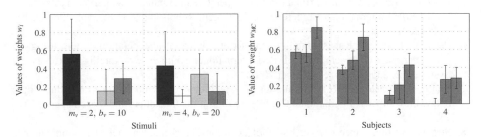

Fig. 4. Weight distributions of one subject for high relative damping with large deviations (left) and weights corresponding to f_{MC} for all subjects where $b_v = 5$ and $m_v \in \{2,4,8\}$ (right) [see Fig. 3 for color coding]

5   Conclusion

We investigated rest-to-rest arm movements for different external dynamics. Utilizing the bilevel optimization approach the optimal combinations of cost functions were found to reproduce the recorded hand paths. Variation of the respective weights within a series of trials for one stimulus was found to be small if the trajectories exhibit similarities. Thus, for given mass-damper dynamics, a subject-specific weight distribution can be determined, which can be used to predict the next movement of this subject. A strong general correlation between mass-damper dynamics and weight distribution has not been observed.

Future work consists in a larger behavioral study to confirm the results and in the implementation of path planning algorithms based on the found criteria.

Acknowledgments

This work is supported in part by the German Research Foundation (DFG) within the collaborative research center SFB453 "High-Fidelity Telepresence and Teleaction" and the CoTeSys cluster of excellence "Cognition for Technical Systems" within the Excellence Initiative of the DFG.

References

1. Albrecht, S., Sobotka, M., Ulbrich, M.: A bilevel optimization approach to obtain optimal cost functions for human arm-movements. Preprint in preparation, Fakultät für Mathematik, TU München (2010)
2. Corteville, B., Aertbelien, E., Bruyninckx, H., De Schutter, J., Van Brussel, H.: Human-inspired robot assistant for fast point-to-point movements. In: IEEE International Conference on Robotics and Automation, pp. 3639–3644 (2007)
3. Flash, T., Hogan, N.: The coordination of arm movements: An experimentally confirmed mathematical model. The Journal of Neuroscience 5, 1688–1703 (1985)
4. Luo, Z., Svinin, M., Ohta, K., Odashima, T., Hosoe, S.: On optimality of human arm movements. In: IEEE International Conference on Robotics and Biomimetics, ROBIO 2004, pp. 256–261 (August 2004)
5. Maeda, Y., Hara, T., Arai, T.: Human-robot cooperative manipulation with motion estimation. In: IEEE/RSJ International Conference on Intelligent Robots and Systems, vol. 4, pp. 2240–2245 (2001)
6. Peer, A., Buss, M.: Robust stability analysis of a bilateral teleoperation system using the parameter space approach. In: IEEE/RSJ International Conference on Intelligent Robots and Systems, pp. 2350–2356 (September 2008)
7. Smith, C., Christensen, H.I.: A minimum jerk predictor for teleoperation with variable time delay. In: IEEE/RSJ International Conference on Intelligent Robots and Systems, pp. 5621–5627 (2009)
8. Stroeve, S.: Impedance characteristics of neuromusculoskeletal model of the human arm. Biological Cybernetics 81, 475–494 (1999)
9. Svinin, M., Goncharenko, I., Luo, Z., Hosoe, S.: Modeling of human-like reaching movements in the manipulation of flexible objects. In: IEEE/RSJ International Conference on Intelligent Robots and Systems, pp. 549–555 (2006)
10. Uno, Y., Kawato, M., Suzuki, R.: Formation and control of optimal trajectory in human mulitjoint arm movements. Biological Cybernetics 61, 89–101 (1989)
11. Wächter, A., Biegler, L.T.: Line search filter methods for nonlinear programming: Local convergence. SIAM Journal on Optimization 16(1), 32–48 (2005)
12. Weber, C., Nitsch, V., Unterhinninghofen, U., Färber, B., Buss, M.: Position and force augmentation in a telepresence system and their effects on perceived realism. In: WorldHaptics, pp. 226–231 (2009)
13. Winter, D.: Biomechanics and motor control of human movement. Wiley, Chichester (2005)

Bodily Self-attribution Caused by Seeing External Body-Resembling Objects and the Control of Grasp Forces

Eleonora Westebring-van der Putten, Richard Goossens,
Jenny Dankelman, and Jack Jakimowicz

TU Delft, faculty of Industrial design engineering, Delft, Netherlands
{E.P.Westebring-vanderPutten,R.H.M.Goossens,
J.Dankelman,J.Jakimowicz}@TUDelft.nl

Abstract. The brain localizes body parts in their perceived visual locations. The brain can, however, be easily fooled. By making use of the Rubber Hand Illusion (RHI), a feeling of ownership of the rubber hand can be evoked. The influence of this illusion on grasp force has not yet been researched, but it might well prove promising for grasp control during tool usage. This study explores whether the RHI can be used to give a person better control over grasp force when manipulating an instrument that makes use of the RHI than when using an instrument that does not. Ten participants performed grasp and pull tasks under three different conditions. They were required to grasp an object with their bare hands, with a rubber-hand, and with an instrument. After analyzing grasp forces during maximal pulling loads (4.95 N barehanded, 6.45 N rubber-handed and 7.9 N using an instrument), it may be concluded that the RHI can contribute to improved grasp control.

Keywords: bodily self, touch, vision, sense, rubber hand illusion, perception.

1 Introduction

During daily life we can simply feel and manipulate objects with our bare hands. We can rely on the tactile and proprioceptive feedback that the body provides, to control grasp forces. Differences in applied force and slipperiness can be naturally corrected without damaging the grasped object or having slippage. We do not have conscious control over grip force modulations [1]. It is when we start to use tools to grasp objects that problems can occur as we do not touch the objects directly which means that cutaneous receptors are not in direct contact with the objects in question. Objects can therefore be damaged or broken due to excessive pinch force or slippage.

The literature suggests e.g. [2-6] that the brain constructs a sense of the body by combining the information received from sight, proprioception and touch. Vision is the most dominant modality in creating such body images. Proprioception is the perception of movement and body part spatial orientation derived from stimuli (detected by mechanoreceptors in muscle tendons and joints, the vestibular system and the cutaneous sense) within the body itself [3, 7]. In this way, the brain constructs a sense

A.M.L. Kappers et al. (Eds.): EuroHaptics 2010, Part II, LNCS 6192, pp. 263–270, 2010.
© Springer-Verlag Berlin Heidelberg 2010

of the body by combining influences and information gained from sight, touch and proprioception, rather than just passively receiving it [8, 9]. Modalities are weighted by the brain on the basis of the estimated reliability of the information [9]. In cases where vision does not correspond with proprioception and touch the brain often gives more weight to visual information than to proprioception and touch because vision is more reliable and spatial acuity is greater [5, 10]. Body parts are traced to the apparent visual location, particularly when the visible location corresponds to the possible range dictated by proprioception [5]. Even non-informative vision can improve the spatial resolution of touch; during non visible passive touching of a body, gazing in the direction of the touched body part (but not seeing the actual touching) enhances the spatial resolution of touch [11].

The Rubber Hand Illusion (RHI) reported in the relevant literature amounts to a multisensory conflict between sight and touch. Touch is seen on the rubber hand, but felt at a different location (in the own hand). The spot and the way in which both hands are touched should be similar though if this effect to be optimally present. The body can resolve the conflict by representing the rubber hand as one's own hand (and part of the so-called bodily-self) and picturing the real hand being in the rubber hand's position [12-14]. With RHI there is a drift of bodily awareness towards the rubber hand. An external object can be perceived as a body part thanks to the visual capturing of proprioceptive information. Due to the rapid decrease in proprioception when there is no direct view of the touched object, the body automatically allows the visual information to replace the lack of visually supported proprioception [13, 14]. The key to all of this lies in touch, synchrony between the stimulation of the rubber and the real hand, and the hands being equally postured and laterally similar.

The rubber hand illusion is mainly allied to the 'Bayesian logic' underlying all perception. When two perceptions from different modalities co-occur with high probability, they are connected to each other. With the RHI the seen and the felt touching are connected because they occur synchronously [5]. The illusion is not significantly influenced by differences in skin tone, hand size, or specific characteristics of the participant's hand that are not visible on the rubber hand [5]. Holmes et al. [15] concluded that the visual information from the rubber hand only needs to approximately resemble aspects of the real hand.

The RHI also influenced the felt position of one's own hand. This derives from three-way interaction between sight, touch and proprioception (sensory information coming from the skin, joints, muscles, eyes and even from the ears [16]); the visually captured touch results in the mis-localisation of one's own (unseen) hand towards the position of the (visible) rubber hand. It is in combination with the misinterpretation of visually captured proprioception that RHI occurs [12, 14]. During the RHI the peri-hand space is shifted from the own hand to the rubber hand[17]. The peri-personal space is the space closely surrounding the different body parts. It represents the separation zone between the external environment and the body. The neurons, which code this peri-personal space, combine the visual and proprioceptive information of the hand to estimate the hand's position. If this information conflicts the movement of the hands can be disrupted [4].

With the RHI, when the rubber hand is placed outside the original peri-hand space the visual information near the hand is not represented by the peri-hand mechanism [18]. That is why the strength of the illusion decreases when the rubber hand is placed further away from the real hand. A rubber hand can be assimilated, with simultaneous touch, into both the real hand and the rubber hand up to a distance of 91cm [5]. This shows that the brain is able to assimilate a rubber hand to anatomically impossible distances. The strength of the illusion decreases though when the distance between the real and the rubber hand is greater than 27.5 cm. [18]

In this article, we investigate whether bodily self-attribution caused by the seeing of external body-resembling objects can improve the control of grasp forces in tool usage. In other words whether, for instance, visual feedback obtained from a dummy hand implemented with the instrument used, can sufficiently stimulate bodily self-attribution to create greater control of the instrument and to thus allow the user to apply force in a more controlled way. This is a field that has not yet been investigated in this setting, though it is interesting and full of opportunities, for instance for the medical design industry, especially in circumstances where indirect grasping instruments are used, like in the case of Minimally Invasive Surgery (MIS; surgery through small incisions, using elongated instruments).

With the information given above it is hypothesized that a human using a tool to grasp something, can mentally override the lack of direct touch when the grasper tip looks like a real hand. There is currently no instrument or system that uses the effects of RHI. Before actually performing research in a complete MIS setting we test to see if the RHI can aid grasp control during tool usage by actually allowing subjects to see the tool-tip via a screen. It is hypothesized that participants will view the Rubber Hand as their own and therefore it is hypothesized that grasp forces will be better controlled (less force, less slippage) with the tool that makes use of the RHI than with the normal tool.

2 Method

Participants: Ten right-handed participants, three male and seven female, aged between 19 and 23 years participated in this study. The participants were unaware of the purpose of the experiment. The task of the participants was to grasp an object in three states: with their Bare Hand, between their thumb and index finger (1), with a Rubber Hand (2) or with an Instrument (3). The object had to be grasped from an elevation and pulled in a straight line towards the participant until out of range of the camera. Afterwards it had to be put back on the elevation.

Experimental set-up. The object used was a cube (ten mm3, weighing 1.2 grams). To measure the pinch forces, a load cell (Futek WC1 USA, 245108-10LB) was attached to the top of the object. The pins of the load cell were the points where the object had to be grasped. The object was placed on an elevation that was 100 mm high. This was done to make the grasping of the object easier and to prevent the Instrument, the Rubber Hand and the real hand from touching the table and to thus, in that way, make it more difficult to successfully grasp the object.

In order to measure pull forces and ensure that the participants applied more grasp force than just the force needed to overcome gravity, a rubber band was attached to the object which, in turn, was attached to a second load cell (50 N, 57250 type LCV-U). This second load cell was then attached to a fixed point.

In order to generate similar visual feedback in all three circumstances, a box was used to prevent the participant from directly seeing the object and hands. A camera (ELMO CCD AC-E31ZW) that was attached to the top of the box (see Fig 1), provided visual feedback on the object and Instrument/hands. The camera images were presented on a television screen that was positioned at eye level.

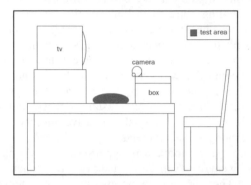

Fig. 1. Schematic illustration of the experimental setup

Two pairs of tongs (IKEA 365+ baking pincers) were used as instruments. One of the instruments was equipped with a fake rubber hand. We will refer to this instrument as the Rubber Hand. The other instrument was also equipped with a similar fake rubber hand, however it was painted and taped to make sure that, apart from its shape, it did not look like a real hand (see Fig 2). The object-contact places of the Instrument were not covered with paint or tape so that the material properties were similar to those of the Rubber Hand. We will refer to this as the 'Instrument'. The Instrument and Rubber Hand had to be similar in terms of shape and stiffness for the test results to be compared. A Left hand was used as no right Rubber Hands where available.

Fig. 2. The Instrument, Rubber Hand, Real hand

Procedure: The participants sat in front of the experimental set-up that was placed on a table in a well-lit up room. The non-dominant hand of the participant was placed in the box while their other hand rested on their lap or on the table. The participants were instructed to grasp the object with the minimal degree of force required to prevent slippage.

In each situation (1,2,3) the participant had to perform ten lifts. Before each new test, the participants were allowed to practice five times to be sure that they could perform the task that was required of them and to discover how to apply as little force as possible to prevent slippage. In total each participant performed fifteen practice lifts and thirty lifts in the three different situations. If slip occurred the lift had to be repeated. In between the different tests there was a break so that the procedure for the next test could be explained and the subjects had the chance to practice.

To prevent and exclude learning effects, the order of the tasks varied from participant to participant. There were six different orders, which were randomly assigned to the participants. The participant was provided with visual feedback through the screen about the movement made during the task. No feedback was given on the pinch and pull forces applied. After the experiment the participants were asked to rank the extent to which they agreed with three statements relating to their experiences during each of the tests. The following three statements were read aloud by the experimenter:

- "I had the feeling that the force I had to apply to the object with my own hand matched the force that I had to apply with the Rubber Hand and the Instrument."
- "I had the feeling that the Rubber Hand resembled my own hand when I looked at the television screen."
- 'I had the feeling that the Silver Hand resembled my own hand when looking at the television screen."

The statements were translated into Dutch and the participants responded verbally using a ten-point scale with a score of 1 to show that they "strongly disagreed" and a score of 10 to indicate that they "very much agreed".

Data acquisition and analysis. A descriptive analysis was used for the data obtained from the questionnaires to indicate whether the participants experienced the Rubber Hand as part of their own body. Further analysis of the data will reveal whether this feeling of the Rubber Hand belonging to one's self (the so-called Rubber Hand Illusion), gives the participant better control over his grasp force while using the Rubber Hand. The data acquired from the pull and pinch sensors was then processed in Mat-Lab 2007b. The mean and standard deviation of pinch forces during the extreme pull, (mean pinch force at maximum pull forces) and maximum pinch force values during the movement were calculated. In this way it is possible to see if the forces using the Rubber Hand come closer to the forces used during a barehanded grasp than during a grasp with an Instrument. The number of times that slip occurred were counted during each condition.

To ascertain if the data from the various conditions differed, a repeated measure ANOVA (SPSS 16) was carried out for all pinch force data. The number of times slip occurred was tested using the Wilcoxon Signed Rank Test. Posthoc tests were performed to see which condition differed. Significance levels were set at $p < 0.05$.

3   Results

For technical reasons 36 out of 300 grasps contained incomplete data and were not therefore analyzed. The score on the first question showed that (average 4.6) that the participants did not have the feeling that the force they had to apply with their own hands matched the force that they had to apply with the Rubber Hand or the Instrument. The scores on the second question showed (average 7.3) that the participants had the feeling that the Rubber Hand resembled their own hand. The score on the third question showed that (average 4.9) that the participants did not have the feeling that the Instrument resembled their own hand.

Table 1. Mean of the measured maximal pinch forces

	Bare hand	Rubber hand	Instrument
Maximal pinch force during maximal pull force (N)	4.95	6.45	7.90
p		0.003*	
			0.006*
		<0.000*	
Standard deviation of pinch force during maximal pull force (N)	0.22	0.15	0.09
p		0.35	
			0.48
		0.006*	
Maximal pinch force during the whole movement. (N)	5.88	7.74	8.58
p		0.001*	
			0.288
		<0.000*	

Table 1 shows the means of the maximal pinch forces for the three different situations. As expected, the mean maximal pinch force during the highest pull forces exerted with the Rubber Hand were significantly different when compared to the mean force exerted with the Instrument and the mean pinch force applied with the Bare Hand. The participants needed less pinch force to hold the object, while pulling hardest, with the Rubber Hand than with the Instrument. In addition, during the last pull phase there was no pinch force variation between the Bare Hands and the Rubber Hand whereas there was a difference between the Bare Hand and Instrument usage. If we look at the whole picture the Bare Hand circumstances demanded lower maximum pinch forces compared to both the other situations. The degree of slippage was significantly lower between the Bare Hand (median of zero times) and the Rubber Hand (median of two times) (p=0,02). The slippage shown while using the Instrument (median of one time) did not differ from the two other conditions.

4 Discussion

The purpose of this study was to establish whether bodily self-attribution caused by the sight of external body-resembling objects, improves the control of grasp forces during tool usage. The results of the questionnaire suggest that people do experience bodily self-attribution while using a Rubber Hand while that is not the case when using the Instrument. This was the expected outcome as the Instrument has the same form as a normal hand but not the same general appearance or skin color resemblance.

It was expected that when using the Rubber Hand the participant would have a better control of his grasp forces than with the Instrument. The force applied when using the Rubber Hand would also be closer to what was exerted when using an own hand than the force exerted while using the Instrument. The participants needed less pinch force to pull the object with the Rubber Hand than with the Instrument. This could indicate that the Rubber Hand illusion was evoked and that the Rubber Hand was thus perceived as part of the participant's own body.

The participants used less force during the Rubber Hand experiment, especially during the high pull force phase of the movement, than when using the Instrument. They therefore used forces closer to slip forces (smaller safety margin) and as their own skin did not touch the object their cutaneous receptors are not able to detect slippage. With the Instrument they had a large safety margin, which was why slippage did not occur very often. Conversely, the results also showed that during the whole procedure the maximal pinch force exerted was lower, but not significantly lower when Rubber Hand use was compared to Instrument use. As the phase of the movement when this pinch force was exerted was not investigated it is difficult to compare the three conditions for this value. Part of the difference in force control between the conditions lies in the grip type that was used. Although the instruction was to hold the backing pincers with a precision grip they were grasped with a grip that looked more like a power grip (instead of the thumb and the tip of the index finger, the thumb and the side of the index finger where used) while the bare hand displayed a real precision grip. These grip types involve different neural structures with probably less fine control of force in the power grip.

The ideal situation during tool use would be for the user to feel as though he/she is actually touching the object with his/her barehands. It is not always possible to touch objects with one's bare hands, for example, during MIS. Our research showed that it might be possible for the sight of a hand touching tissue to evoke the RHI and a feeling of ownership over the Rubber Hand. Ideally the distance between the real hand and the Rubber Hand should not be greater than 27.5 cm [18] because beyond that the illusion decreases significantly. The closer to the body the information is, the stronger the illusion will be. The relevant literature suggests that tool use can extend the peripersonal space [19, 20]. This means that distance would not be an obstacle.

Making use of the Rubber Hand Illusion to innovate grasping tools may prove useful, since it will improve a users grasp force control by creating bodily self-attribution with his/her tools. If we look beyond the field of surgery, though, enhanced bodily sense would prove useful in generally evoking greater control over objects, for instance, in such areas as archaeology, production industries, the construction business, repairs, robotics and artificial limb creation.

Acknowledgements. We would like to thank the following students: Jael Nanarjain, Stephanie Kool, Mischa Meekes and Ingrid Verhoef for contributing to this research.

References

1. Johansson, R.S.: Sensory input and control of grip. Novartis Found Symp. 218, 45–59 (1998) (discussion 59-63)
2. Longo, M.R., Cardozo, S., Haggard, P.: Visual enhancement of touch and the bodily self. Consciousness and Cognition 17, 1181–1191 (2008)

3. Makin, T.R., Holmes, N.P., Zohary, E.: Is that near my hand? Multisensory representation of peripersonal space in human intraparietal sulcus. J. Neurosci. 27, 731–740 (2007)
4. Makin, T.R., Holmes, N.P., Ehrsson, H.H.: On the other hand: dummy hands and periperpersonal space. Behav. Brain Res. 191, 1–10 (2008)
5. Armel, K.C., Ramachandran, V.S.: Projecting sensations to external objects: evidence from skin conductance response. Proc. Biol. Sci. 270, 1499–1506 (2003)
6. Ijsselsteijn, W.A., De Kort, Y.A.W., Haans, A.: Is this my hand I see before me? The rubber hand illusion in reality, virtual reality, and mixed reality. Presence: Teleoperators and Virtual Environments 15, 455–464 (2006)
7. Westebring-van der Putten, E.P., Goossens, R.H.M., Jakimowicz, J.J., Dankelman, J.: Haptics in minimally invasive surgery - a review. Minimally Invasive Therapy and Allied Technologies 17, 3–16 (2008)
8. Haggard, P., Taylor-Clarke, M., Kennett, S.: Tactile perception, cortical representation and the bodily self. Curr. Biol. 13, 170–173 (2003)
9. Ernst, M.O., Banks, M.S.: Humans integrate visual and haptic information in a statistically optimal fashion. Nature 415, 429–433 (2002)
10. Lee, D.N., Aronson, E.: Visual proprioceptive control of standing in human infants. Perception and Psychophysics 15, 529–532 (1974)
11. Kennett, S., Taylor-Clarke, M., Haggard, P.: Noninformative vision improves the spatial resolution of touch in humans. Curr. Biol. 11, 1188–1191 (2001)
12. Costantini, M., Haggard, P.: The rubber hand illusion: Sensitivity and reference frame for body ownership. Consciousness and Cognition 16, 229–240 (2007)
13. Botvinick, M., Cohen, J.: Rubber hands 'feel' touch that eyes see [8]. Nature 391, 756 (1998)
14. Tsakiris, M., Haggard, P.: The rubber hand illusion revisited: Visuotactile integration and self-attribution. Journal of Experimental Psychology: Human Perception and Performance 31, 80–91 (2005)
15. Holmes, N.P., Snijders, H.J., Spence, C.: Reaching with alien limbs: Visual exposure to prosthetic hands in a mirror biases proprioception without accompanying illusions of ownership. Perception and Psychophysics 68, 685–701 (2006)
16. Makin, T.R., Holmes, N.P., Ehrsson, H.H.: On the other hand: Dummy hands and periperpersonal space. Behavioural Brain Research 191, 1–10 (2008)
17. Graziano, M.S.: Where is my arm? The relative role of vision and proprioception in the neuronal representation of limb position. Proc. Natl. Acad. Sci. USA 96, 10418–10421 (1999)
18. Lloyd, D.M.: Spatial limits on referred touch to an alien limb may reflect boundaries of visuo-tactile peripersonal space surrounding the hand. Brain and Cognition 64, 104–109 (2007)
19. Serino, A., Bassolino, M., Farne, A., Ladavas, E.: Extended multisensory space in blind cane users. Psychol. Sci. 18, 642–648 (2007)
20. Tlauka, M.: Display-control compatibility: the relationship between performance and judgments of performance. Ergonomics 47, 281–295 (2004)

Do Changes in Movements after Tool Use Depend on Body Schema or Motor Learning?

Raoul M. Bongers

Center for Human Movement Sciences, University of Groningen
UMCG, sector F, P.O. Box 196, NL-9700 AD Groningen, The Netherlands
R.M.Bongers@rug.nl

Abstract. In a recent study, Cardinali et al. (2009) showed that training the use of a tool affected kinematic characteristics of subsequent free movements (i.e., movement were slower, for instance), which they interpreted as that the use of a tool affects the body schema. The current study examined whether these results can also be explained in terms of motor learning where movement characteristics during tool use persist in the free movements. Using a different tool we replicated parts of the study of Cardinali et al: As did Cardinali et al. we found that tool use after-effects can be found in subsequent free movements. Importantly, we showed that the tooling movement was very slow compared to the free hand movement. We concluded that it can not be ruled out yet that after-effects of tool use originate from a general slowing down of movement speed that persists in free hand movements.

Keywords: Body Schema, Tool Use, Motor Learning, Motor Control, Prehension, Kinematics.

1 Introduction

To arrive at a goal in space, the neuromotor system should not only use the position and orientation of the goal-object but also the position and orientation of its own body parts. It is generally acknowledged that to do this the neuromotor system relies on the body schema, a somatosensory representation of the body based on proprioception, kinesthesia and touch (for an overview see Berlucchi and Aglioti, 2010). Interestingly, it is assumed that a tool in use is incorporated in this body schema, implying that a tool is integrated in the sensory-motor map of the body-part holding the tool. Neural evidence for this incorporation comes from, for instance, a study of Iriki et al. (1996) showing that the size of visual receptive fields in bimodal neurons in the intraparietal cortex, coding the schema of the hand, enlarge to include the length of the tool in use.

Although a series of studies show an effect of tool use on the perceptual representation of the body (see Maravita and Iriki, 2004), it is unclear whether this adapted body schema is used to control bodily movements. Therefore, Cardinali, et al. (2009) studied whether tool use affected movements of the body. In a pretest-posttest design they showed that kinematic characteristics of pointing and grasping changed after participants had used a mechanical grabber to pick up an object. More specifically, the reaching movements after the use of the tool were slower, indicated by a later peak acceleration, peak velocity and peak deceleration and smaller magnitude of these peaks.

A.M.L. Kappers et al. (Eds.): EuroHaptics 2010, Part II, LNCS 6192, pp. 271–276, 2010.

Cardinali et al. argued that these changes in kinematics were in agreement with changes in kinematics for longer arms. In an additional experiment participants had to locate the positions of anatomical landmarks of their own arm on a cover placed over this arm. Results showed that after tool learning the positions indicated on the cover corresponded to a longer arm. Based on these results Cardinali et al. argued that tool use modifies the body schema.

Interestingly, Cardinali et al. (2009) hardly presented analyses on the characteristics of the tooling movements. This is peculiar because it is known that grasping movements with a mechanical grabber, when compared to a movement without a grabber, show a prolonged movement duration and affect the kinematic profile of the grasp (Gentilucci, et al. 2004). If movements with a mechanical grabber are prolonged, compared to free movements, then it could be that the effects of the tool training on the kinematic profiles of free movements do not originate from adaptation of the body schema, but stem from a tendency to move slower because the movement speed had been slower with the tool. In other words, the slower moving with a tool might continue in the subsequent free hand movements, which would give an alternative explanation to the body schema explanation of the results of Cardinali et al.

The current study sets the first steps in investigating this alternative hypothesis, using a design similar to that of Cardinali et al. (2009) but with a different tool. We used a pair of pliers attached to the thumb and index finger (see Figure 1). With this pair of pliers the tip of the thumb and the tip of the index finger were displaced to the beaks of the pair of pliers. This is a tool that comes very close to a functional displacement of the tip of the thumb and index finger to the tip of the tool. In this way we aimed to maximize the chance that we changed the body schema in our study. In the pretest and the posttest participants picked up an object with a precision grip and in the training phase with the pair of pliers.

Fig. 1. Three stages in the unfolding of a tool trial

2   Methods

Participants were 8 females and 7 males ranging in age from 18-19 years. All participants were right-handed, had normal or corrected to normal sight and no known neurological disorders. All signed an informed consent before the start of the experiment.

The pair of pliers (Figure 1) had a length of 40 cm; this was the distance from the hinge at the tip of the thumb and index finger to the middle of the beak. The hinge of the pair of pliers was located in the middle, so that movements of the hand corresponded 1:1 to movements of the beaks of the pliers. The pair of pliers was attached to the hand with tape. The beaks of the pliers were covered with silicone to provide for grip on the object.

We used two cylindrical objects with diameters of 3 cm and of 5 cm, both with a height of 2.5 cm. Objects were located at 35 cm from the edge of the table. The same starting position for the thumb and index finger and the beaks of the pair of pliers was used, which was indicated at the edge of the table. The position of the chair did not change inbetween conditions. Hand and pair of pliers were closed at the start of each trial.

Movements were measured with an Optotrak 3020 system (Northern Digital, Waterloo, Canada). This system sampled (frequency of 100 Hz) four LEDs that were placed at each beak of the pair of pliers and at the medial part of the tip of the thumb and the lateral part of the tip of the index finger. The experiment consisted of 6 blocks of 12 trials. In each block each object was picked up 6 times in a randomized order. The first block was the pretest and the last block the posttest. In the test phases participants picked up the object with a precision grip, while in the intermediate learning phase (48 trials) participants picked up the object with the pair of pliers. At the start of the experiment participants were instructed to perform the movement as fast and accurate as possible.

The position data of the individual markers were filtered with a 15 Hz cut-off frequency using a second order recursive Butterworth filter. The average position of the thumb marker and the marker of the index finger, and the average position of the markers on the beaks of the pair of pliers represented the reach component in the free hand trials and the tool trials, respectively. The hand aperture, representing the grasp component, was computed as the three-dimensional distance between the finger and thumb marker in the free hand trials and as this distance between the markers on the beaks of the pair of pliers in the tool trials. The time series of the reach component and the grasp component were differentiated with a three-point difference algorithm to obtain the velocities. These velocities were again differentiated to obtain acceleration. The beginning and end of the reach were determined with a threshold of 5 cm/s and the beginning and end of the grasp with a threshold of 3 cm/s. For determining the end of opening and the beginning of closing of the grasp component also a threshold of 3 cm/s was used. The plateau time was computed as the time difference between these moments. We conducted univariate ANOVAs with test (pretest vs posttest) and object size (3 vs 5 cm) as within-subject factors.

3   Results

We commenced our analyses with examining whether our results were comparable to the results of Cardinali et al. (2009). Figure 2 presents the changes over the trials of the experiment for the movement time and the peak velocity. It clearly shows differences between the test phases and the learning phase; a strong learning curve is shown at the beginning of the experiment and at the beginning of the posttest. A gradual adaptation can be seen over the learning phase.

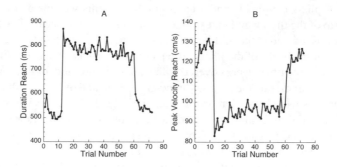

Fig. 2. The duration of the reach (A) and the peak velocity (B) for all the trials, averaged over participants

To examine whether the movements before and after the learning differed, we analyzed the movement time (MT), latency of peak velocity (LV), latency of peak acceleration (LA), latency of peak deceleration (LD), peak velocity (PV), peak acceleration (PA), and peak deceleration (PD) of the reach component over the 2 blocks of trials of the test phases. These analyses revealed that none of the effects were significant, with the exception of one interaction that just reached significance. We wanted to make sure that these results were not biased by the effect that participants had to get used to the experimental situation, which might have resulted in relatively slow movements at the beginning of the experiment. Therefore, we performed the same analyses but now on the averages of the last 6 trials of the pretest and the first 6 trials of the posttest. These analyses showed that the movement was indeed slower in the posttest than in the pretest (MT: $F(1,14)=13.11$, $p<0.005$, pre=506 ms, post=544 ms; LV: $F(1,14)=5.17$, $p<0.05$, pre=219 ms, post=227ms; LD: $F(1,14)=9.05$, $p<0.010$, pre=349 ms, post=361ms; PV: $F(1,14)=7.41$, $p<0.05$, pre=129 cm/s, post=123 cm/s; PD: $F(1,14)= 4.68$, $p<0.05$, pre=811 cm/s^2, post=725 cm/s^2).

To get an understanding of the possible origins of these changes in kinematics after the use of the tool, we now turn to the kinematics of the grasp component. In Figure 3A we plotted the grasp component for one trial of the pretest and one trial of the tool training

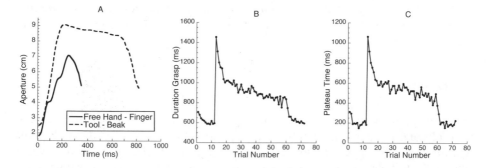

Fig. 3. Examples of a the tip aperture for a free hand trial and a tool trial (A). The duration of the grasp (B) and the plateau time (C) for all the trials, averaged over participants.

phase. It can be readily observed that the tooling movement has a longer duration and that there is a clear plateau in the aperture of the pair of pliers, which is not present in the free hand grasping. Moreover, the hand opened farther in the tool condition (averages: free hand: 8.3 cm vs. pair of pliers: 8.7 cm) and for the tool the grasp ended much later than the reach (198 ms) than for the free hand (75 ms) trials.

Figure 3 (B and C) shows the changes in the movement time of the grasp and the plateau time over the trials of the experiment. The analyses for each of these two variables showed no significant effects for the test phases, when using all 12 trials in the blocks. When we analyzed the last 6 trials of the pretest and the first 6 trials of the posttest, the analyses on the duration of the grasp showed an effect of test phase, $F(1,14)=7.53$, $p<0.05$, whereas the plateau time showed no effect.

4 Discussion

In this study we replicated the experiment of Cardinali et al. (2009), albeit with a different type of grabbing tool, to further test their conclusion whether a tool in use changes the body schema. The key question of this study was whether the reported change in kinematics of the reach component after training of tool use originates from the hypothesized change of the body schema or whether it is merely a result of the motor adaptation processes. We replicated the main results of the study of Cardinali et al. but the effects of the training seemed less strong than those of Cardinali et al. That is to say, we found the effect only when analyzing the difference of the trials closest to the training phase. It might be possible that this is due to the fact that we examined only one task in the test phases of this study and not two, as Cardinali et al. have done. In our study, the initial stage of the experiment, where participants got used to the setup, showed relatively slow movements. Because slowing of the movements is exactly what one expects to happen after the tool training, this might have resulted in finding a weaker effect. An other possibility for the weaker effect is of course the differences in tool that we used. However, our knowledge on how tools affect actions is too sparse to understand how different tools affect the kinematics in the posttest differently.

As did Cardinali et al. (2009), we found that free hand movements are slower after tool training. To explain the origins of this effect we examined the grasp component of the movement. The hand opened farther when using a tool. As was shown by Gentilucci et al. (2004) for a mechanical grabber, we showed that when grasping with a pair of pliers the aperture showed a plateau phase, implying that in grasping with a tool, hand opening and hand closing are decoupled. This is supported by the longer duration of the grasp than that of the reach during use of the pair of pliers; the grasp ended later than the reach indicating that the closing was started only after the beaks of the pair of pliers had arrived at the object. This decoupling is normally not found with free hand grasping. We assume that the longer durations of the grasp with tools originate from this decoupling of hand opening and hand closing. However, we did not find that the hand opening and hand closing of the free grasping in the posttest were more decoupled than those in the pretest. Hence, it is not the case that the effect of slower movements after tool learning is due to a decoupling of movements within the grasp. It seems that it is the general slowing down of the movement in the tool phase is persevered in the posttest.

The current findings suggest that the slowing of movements during training of tool use continues in subsequent free hand movements after the tool use. The slowing of the tooling movements seems to stem from a decoupling of hand opening and hand closing. It is important to note that we do not see how this decoupling with tool grasping is related to a change in the body schema. Hence, we propose that the change in kinematics after tool learning might stem from a general slowing down of the movement in the tool learning stage. However, our results are too premature to make this our definite conclusion. Future experiments, such as testing more tasks with our pair of pliers, are needed to strengthen our argument.

References

1. Berlucchi, G., Aglioti, S.M.: The body in the brain revisited. Exp. Brain. Res. 200, 25–35 (2010)
2. Cardinali, L., Frassinetti, F., Brozzoli, C., Urquizar, C., Roy, A.C., Farn, A.: Tool-use induces morphological updating of the body schema. Curr. Biol. 19, 478–479 (2009)
3. Gentilucci, M., Roy, A.C., Stefanini, S.: Grasping an object naturally or with a tool: are these tasks guided by a common motor representation. Exp. Brain. Res. 157, 496–506 (2004)
4. Iriki, A., Tanaka, M., Iwamura, Y.: Coding of modified body schema during tool use by macaque postcentral neurones. Brain 7, 2325–2330 (1996)

A Motion-Based Handheld Haptic Interface

Ki-Uk Kyung and Junseok Park

POST-PC Research Group, Electronics and Telecommunications Research Inssitute
161 Gajeong-dong, Yuseong-gu, Daejeon, 305-700, Korea
kyungku@gmail.com, parkjs@etri.re.kr

Abstract. This paper deals with a motion-based handheld haptic interface. A 6 DOF motion sensor and hybrid vibrators are embedded into the device. With wrist motion, a user controls the position of the pointer on the screen. Haptic feedback is provided in response to the manipulation of a GUI element. Gyroscope-based motion sensing and the rapid response of a hybrid actuator improve the usability of a remote control for a GUI.

Keywords: haptic, handheld, remote control, motion, presenter.

1 Introduction

Figure 1 shows the structure of a motion-based haptic remote controller, which is a handheld-type stand-alone system. The controller measures the motion of a human hand and wrist and generates haptic cues to stimulate the user's hand.

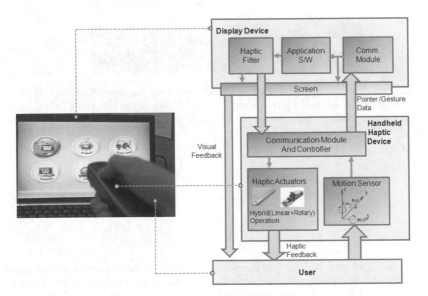

Fig. 1. Motion-based handheld interface. This device is a kind of remote control. It is composed of hybrid actuators, a motion sensor and a communication module. It communicates with a display device.

A.M.L. Kappers et al. (Eds.): EuroHaptics 2010, Part II, LNCS 6192, pp. 277–282, 2010.
© Springer-Verlag Berlin Heidelberg 2010

Haptic techniques are expected to be a useful tool for improving the usability of media devices [1]. One useful application is a gaming interface that interacts with motion [2][3][6][7]. The interface measures human motion. Users often find this type of interface more intuitive than conventional buttons; they enjoy the haptic feedback function and soon gain confidence in manipulating the device. Unfortunately, the haptic feedback functions do little to improve the usability of such devices. For more precise control of a GUI with haptic feedback, several studies have focused on providing haptic cues for the touch screens of mobile devices [4][5][8].

The motion-based haptic interface described in this paper takes advantage of motion sensing and precise haptic feedback control. The proposed device can be applied to various devices other than game equipment, particularly those that depend on a GUI and media control.

2 Implementation

The design of the motion-based haptic interface is based on two main factors: intuitive pointer control and effective haptic feedback.

2.1 Principle

Figure 2 shows the controller hardware of the motion-based haptic interface. The controller is composed of vibrators, a motion sensor and a wireless communication module.

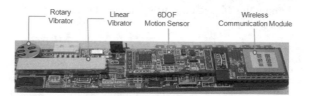

Fig. 2. Controller of the motion-based handheld interface. The controller provides control signals to a rotary vibrator and a linear vibrator. A 3 DOF accelerometer and a DOF gyroscope are installed on the board. The controller also has a wireless communication module and a battery.

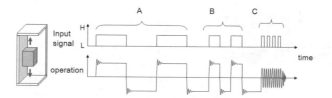

Fig. 3. Control of a linear vibrator. The operation of the mass in the linear actuator is controlled by a digital signal. The linear actuatorcreates discrete impacts as in case A. When two or three pulses are provided for 50 ms, the repetition of bilateral impacts resembles the short trembling shown in case B. If the pulse frequency is higher than 150 Hz, the actuator generates the type of concentrated vibration shown in case C.

The hybrid vibrator is composed of a rotary vibrator and a linear vibrator. The rotary vibrator generates an intense vibration diffused over the whole body of the hand-held device. The linear vibrator generates a concentrated vibration. In general, a linear vibrator has more precise control and provides information more often than a rotary vibrator [8]. Figure 3 shows the control of the linear vibrator (Force Reactor, ALPS) used for this paper. Depending on the control signal, the linear vibrator can produce vibration, short trembling or impact.

Figure 4 shows the concept of the pointer control which is based on hand motion. The 6 DOF motion sensor is composed of a 3 DOF accelerometer and a 3 DOF gyroscope. The yaw and pitch motion are measured by the gyroscope; the change of angle induced by wrist motion is converted into the position of the pointer on a remote screen. Note that the angle is measured in a ground coordinate frame because the posture measurement of the accelerometer compensates for the moving coordinate of the device itself. The counterclockwise rolling and clockwise rolling correspond to the *previous* and *next* commands, respectively. Additionally, the shaking of the device elicits commands such as *cancel, close* or *exit.*

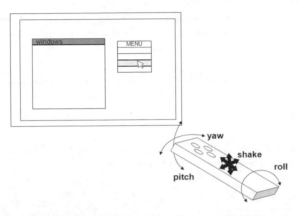

Fig. 4. Pointer control with the handheld interface. The yaw and pitch motion correspond to the horizontal and vertical movement of the pointer on the screen. The user can use shake and rolling motions for other commands.

2.2 Performance

The resolution of the gyroscope is 0.1 deg/s, and the data is measured with an 8 bit resolution. The resolution of the camera-based position measurement depends strongly on the distance between the screen and the user [7]; in addition, the accelerometer-based position measurement does not guarantee coincidence of the hand motion and position movement [2]. However, the gyroscope-based measurement depends slightly on the distance and produces greater coincidence of the hand motion and position movement [6].

The motion-based handheld interface with vibration was used in a TV remote control [6]. However, the vibration provided by the rotary vibrator is used exclusively for menu selection or game effects; it is not used for precise manipulation tasks, such as scrolling, text highlighting, and small menu selections. The response time of the actuator is a significant factor for rapid and precise manipulation [8]. We use a linear vibrator that responds at a rate of more than 50 times per second. Table 1 shows how the proposed device compares with other popular devices.

Table 1. Performance comparison of motion-based handheld interfaces. The proposed device has a higher position resolution, a fast response time, and more types of haptic output.

	Proposed device	Wii controller [7]	Magic remote [6]
Motion sensing method	Gyroscope, accelerometer	Vision, accelerometer	Gyroscope, accelerometer
Pointer position resolution (min. disp./1 m screen width)	< 1/100	> 1/50	< 1/100
Haptic output type	Diffused vibration, concentrated vibration, impact	Diffused vibration	Diffused vibration
Haptic out speed (times per second)	> 50	< 10	< 10
Application	Menu selection, scroll/resize, Web exploration, game effect, educational content	Menu selection, game effect	Menu selection, game effect

3 Application

We developed the software application shown in Figure 5. All the UI elements and content interact with motion control with haptic cues.

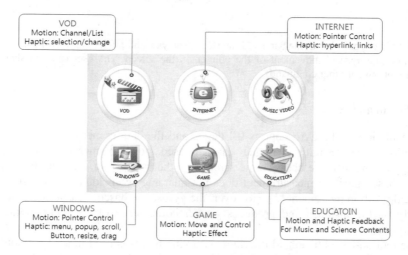

Fig. 5. UI of the IPTV application for a handheld interface. The handheld interface provides haptic feedback when the pointer moves into a menu.

Figure 6 and 7 show examples of haptic feedback for media control and music education. The techniques in Figure 6 are applied to Web exploration and a media player. The user places the pointer accurately in a Web site with more than 50 lines in a page.

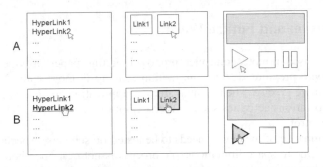

Fig. 6. Links and haptic feedback. When the position of the pointer is changed from state A to state B, the handheld haptic interface provides haptic cues. For example, the impact or short vibration function is applied at the moment when the pointer is on a hyperlink text or image or graphical button.

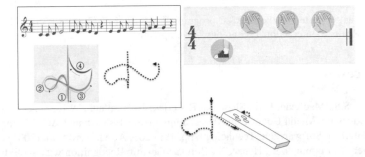

Fig. 7. Music education and motion-based haptic interface. Because the motion of a handheld interface corresponds to the movement of a baton, the device can be used for teaching conducting techniques with a visual display. For children, the haptic feedback is used in a similar manner to a beat meter. For example, in the case of four-four time, an intense diffused vibration is provided for a kicking beat and a short trembling is provided for clapping beats.

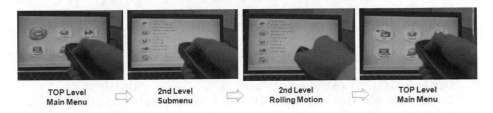

Fig. 8. Application of rolling motion. The combination of 90° counterclockwise rolling and clockwise rolling can used as a command. For example, the rolling motion can switch to a previous scene in an IPTV application.

Figure 8 shows an example of the rolling motion command. Wrist motion elicits commands for the volume control or transitions to the previous or next scene. A proportional increase or decrease in vibration triggers a short vibration or impact in accordance with the control state.

4   Conclusion and Future Work

The motion-based remote controller proposed in this paper provides haptic cues. Compared with previous devices, its motion sensing is more natural and its haptic feedback is more precise. The potential areas of application go beyond menu selection and games to various activities such as Web exploration, Windows GUI manipulation, and media control.

The performance of the device needs to be tested on subjects, especially in terms of its usability. Due to space limitations, the process is not described here in detail. The primary results confirm that the workload of our device in handling GUI manipulation tasks is less than that of other devices.

Acknowledgment

This work was supported by the IT R&D program of MKE/KEIT [2009-S-035-01, Contact-free Multipoint Realistic Interaction Technology Development].

References

1. Snibbe, S.S., MacLean, K.E., Shaw, R., Roderick, J., Verplank, W.L., Scheeff, M.: Haptic Techniques for Media Control. In: Proceedings of the 14th Annual ACM Symposium on User Interface Software and Technology, pp. 199–208. ACM, New York (2001)
2. Schlmer, T., Poppinga, B., Henze, N., Boll, S.: Gesture Recognition with a Wii Controller. In: Proceedings of the Second International Conference on Tangible and Embedded Interaction (TEI 2008), pp. 11–14. ACM, New York (2008)
3. Schou, T., Gardner, H.J.: Using a Mobile Phone as a "Wii-like" Controller for Playing Games on a Large Public Display. International Journal of Computer Games Technology, Article ID 539078, 2008 (2008)
4. Poupyrev, I., Shigeaki, M., Rekimoto, J.: TouchEngine: A Tactile Display for Handheld Devices. In: Proceedings of the SIGCHI Conference on Human Factors in Computing Systems (CHI 2002), pp. 644–645. ACM, New York (2002)
5. Luk, J., Pasquero, J., Little, S., Maclean, K., Levesque, V., Hayward, V.: A Role for Haptics in Mobile Interaction: Initial Design Using a Handheld Tactile Display Prototype. In: Proceedings of the SIGCHI Conference on Human Factors in Computing Systems (CHI 2006), pp. 171–180. ACM, New York (2006)
6. LG UK Blog, Why Have a Confusing TV Remote When You Can Have a Magic Wand?, http://www.lgblog.co.uk/2010/01/08/
7. Wii at Nintendo, http://www.nintendo.com/wii
8. Kyung, K.U., Lee, J.Y., Srinivasan, M.A.: Precise Manipulation of GUI on a Touch Screen with Haptic Cues. In: Proceedings of the World Haptics 2009, pp. 202–207. IEEE Computer Society, Los Alamitos (2009)

A Multi-functional Rehabilitation Device to Assist Forearm/Wrist and Grasp Therapies

Ismail Hakan Ertas and Volkan Patoglu

Faculty of Engineering and Natural Sciences
Sabancı University, Istanbul, Turkey
hertas@su.sabanciuniv.edu, vpatoglu@sabanciuniv.edu

Abstract. We present a novel rehabilitation device for forearm/wrist and grasp therapy of a neurologically injured human arm and hand. Emphasizing the importance of coordinated movements of the wrist and hand while performing activities of daily living (ADL) tasks, the device is designed to assist abduction/adduction and palmar/dorsal flexion of the wrist and pronation/supination of the forearm, concurrently with grasping and releasing movements of hand. Thanks to its modular, interchangeable end-effectors, the device supports ADL exercises, such as door opening. It can also be used as a measurement device, to characterize the range of motion and the isometric strength of the injured forearm/wrist and hand. Usability studies have been conducted and accuracy of the measurements provided with the device has been characterized.

Keywords: rehabilitation robotics, wrist therapy, hand grasp, virtual reality.

1 Introduction

Neurological injuries are the leading cause of serious, long-term disability in developed countries according to statistics by World Health Organization and physical rehabilitation therapy is responsible for most of the recovery experienced by patients with disabilities secondary to neurological injuries [1]. Using robotic devices in repetitive and physically involved rehabilitation exercises helps to eliminate the physical burden of movement therapy for the therapists, and enables safe and versatile training with increased intensity.

Many robotic devices have been proposed in the literature to assist rehabilitation exercises of wrist and hand after neurological injuries. These rehabilitation robots can be loosely categorized as exoskeleton-type and endpoint devices. The exoskeleton-type rehabilitation devices are advantageous in that, they can precisely impose/measure individual joint movements. HWARD [2] and PERCRO [3] are two exoskeleton type systems that can assist both grasping and wrist motions. Exoskeleton-type devices share the common disadvantage of being relatively complex and expensive to be employed as home therapy devices.

Endpoint rehabilitation devices, on the other hand, are generally more practical, since they are simpler to implement with lower costs. For instance, the wrist module of the MIT-Manus system allows assistance and measurement of 3 DoF forearm-wrist movements [4]. Another wrist module, which is proposed as a part of the Robotherapist can

A.M.L. Kappers et al. (Eds.): EuroHaptics 2010, Part II, LNCS 6192, pp. 283–290, 2010.

apply 1 Nm torque to assist forearm-wrist rotations [5]. Even though these systems are simple and practical, they lack in supporting the vital grasp functionality for the hand. 9 DoF Gentle/G [6] and 18 DoF GiHapIn [7] are other examples of endpoint based neuro-rehabilitation systems with torque capabilities of 0.72 Nm and 1.3 Nm respectively. Both of these systems can deliver full-arm therapy including forearm/wrist and grasp exercises. Unfortunately, both of these devices are very complex and high-cost. Dovat *et al.* has proposed another endpoint rehabilitation device, the 2 DoF Haptic Knob, that specifically targets combined wrist-grasp therapy exercises [8]. This simple yet elegant device can deliver combined wrist and grasp therapies with 1.5 Nm assistance, but is limited to single wrist rotations at a time.

Emphasizing the importance of coordinated movement of wrist and hand grasp while performing ADL tasks, we propose a novel endpoint oriented physical rehabilitation device for forearm/wrist and grasp therapy. The device possesses 3 DoF, allows for individual and coupled abduction/adduction and palmar/dorsal flexion of the wrist or pronation/supination of the forearm, concurrently with functional grasping movements of the hand. With the help of its modular interchangeable end-effectors, the device can be used to exercise ADL tasks. It can also be used as a measurement device, to characterize the range of motion and the isometric strength of the injured forearm/wrist and the hand.

2 Human Hand and Device Requirements

Simplified kinematics of the forearm and wrist can be modeled as a 3 DoF kinematic chain that allows supination/pronation of the forearm and palmar/dorsal flexion and abduction/adduction of the wrist joint. Although hand has many DoF, hand therapies after neurological injuries mostly focus on the grasp and release movements of the hand, rather than its fine movements. However, human hand and forearm/wrist almost always work in coordination while performing ADL tasks. For instance, successful competition of the simple task of door opening requires a coordinated motion of the wrist and hand grasp. Along these lines, medical experts advocate for the rehabilitation procedures that contain ADL tasks necessitating coordinated motion of the forearm/wrist and the hand grasp.

Safety and ergonomics are two imperative design requirements every rehabilitation device must satisfy [9]. In our device, safety is assured by high back-drivability and force/torque limits implemented in software, while the ergonomy is considered at the kinematic synthesis level by selecting a device that complies with human joint rotations. The performance requirements for the rehabilitation device are set as the span of the singularity-free workspace and the force/torque limits that can be provided at end-effector. In particular, our device is designed to concurrently span whole of the natural human wrist/forearm workspace and the full extend of human grasp, and to provide enough forces/torques to impose motions to patients. Compactness, portability and manufacturing costs of the device are set as the primary design requirements. The secondary requirements are high motion resolution and low parasitic dynamics (friction and backlash), so that the device can be effectively employed as a measurement tool.

3 Wrist/Forearm and Grasp Rehabilitation System

3.1 Kinematics of the Device

Kinematics of the device is selected to allow rotations of the wrist/forearm, concurrently with the hand grasp/release action within the natural workspace of these joints. In particular, a planar parallel 3-CRP (circular-revolute-prismatic) robot is selected as the main kinematic structure of the rehabilitation system (see Figure 1-A). The 3-CRP mechanism has 3 DoF on the plane: two translations and one rotation of its end-effector. Mechanism is dimensioned such that its end-effector can span a circular workspace of 130 mm diameter. More importantly, the device end-effector can rotate more than 360 degrees at any point within the workspace of the device. The kinematics of 3-CRP mechanism allows concurrent rotations of the wrist joint through its translations, while the rotation of the device end-effector can accommodate, either the forearm rotations, or the grasp/release actions of the hand, thanks to specially designed modular end-effectors. The workspace of the device is set large enough to fit various hand sizes and set to be symmetric to allow for both right-handed or left-handed use.

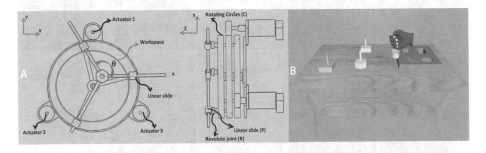

Fig. 1. A: Kinematics and workspace (130 mm diameter) of the 3-CRP mechanism. B: A screen shot of the sample VR animation of a hold, rotate, place and drop scenario.

3.2 Modular End-Effectors

One of the unique features of the wrist/forearm and grasp rehabilitation system is the possibility of enabling different exercises by simply altering its modular end-effectors. In particular, three different types of end-effectors are designed for the device: specified motion imposing end-effectors, the external hand module, and task oriented attachments.

Specified motion imposing end-effectors target concurrent and coordinated motion of hand grasp with wrist rotations (palmar/dorsal flexion and abduction/adduction). Two examples of such end-effectors are illustrated in Figure 2 A-B. In particular, the end-effector illustrated in Figure 2 A relies on a slider-crank mechanism to convert rotational motion of the 3-CRP end-effector into the linear opening and closing motion of the hand attached to a handle pair. With this mechanism in place, the translational motion of the 3-CRP can be employed to exercise palmar-dorsal flexion of the wrist, while grasp/release motions are being concurrently imposed to the hand. The end-effector pictured in Figure 2 B is based on a cam mechanism and is designed to impose grasping/releasing motions to the hand concurrently with the wrist abduction/adduction movements. When this end-effector is used, the rotation of the 3-CRP end-effector enforces opening and closing of the hand. While using this end-effector each finger is covered with a silicon ring and is attached to the device by the means of rings constrained to slide on the cam profile. The aperture amount can be adjusted with this design, by simply selecting from several cam surface alternatives.

The external hand module (Figure 2 K) is an independently actuated end-effector and appends system with one extra DoF. With this end-effector, combined motion of palmar/dorsal flexion of wrist with hand grasp can be exercised, while grasp/release of hand can be controlled independent from wrist/forearm motions. The finger exoskeleton developed in [10] can also be attached to the 3-CRP device to act as an alternative external module, targeting individual finger movements (for example, to exercise pinch grasps).

Fig. 2. End-effectors for different modes of therapy; A: Slider-crank based end-effector (palm/dors flex of wrist + hand open/close, power grasp) B: Cam based end-effector (abd/add of wrist or pro/sup of forearm + hand open/close, power grasp) C-J: Task oriented end-effectors— key (pro/sup of forearm, lateral pinch), door handle (pro/sup of forearm, power grasp), horizontal knob (pro/sup of forearm, precision grasp), tooth brush (palm/dors flex and abd/add of wrist, power grasp), vertical knob (pro/sup of forearm, precision grasp), card (palm/dors flex and abd/add of wrist, lateral pinch), pen (palm/dors flex and abd/add of wrist, lateral pinch) K: external hand module (palm/dors flex of wrist + hand open/close, power grasp)

Task oriented attachments are end-effectors used to simulate ADL tasks. Since ADL exercises have been considered to be very effective for stroke rehabilitation, a simple coupling mechanism is designed to allow regular objects to be attached to the 3-CRP end-effector (Figure 2 C-J). With this coupling mechanism, lightweight everyday items, such as pens, cards, jar lids, door handles, knobs, keys, or toothbrushes can be attached to the rehabilitation device to exercise ADL scenarios in a robot-assisted rehabilitation setting with force feedback and VR simulations, to provide immersion and to increase motivation.

3.3   Implementation Details

Direct drive DC motors are chosen to actuate the 3-CRP mechanism. The power transmission is fulfilled using capstan mechanism with a 1:6 transmission ratio. The motor selection is performed such that the maximal continuous torque that can be applied to the patients wrist is over 2 Nm. The motors are equipped with optical encoders with 500 counts per revolution. The position resolution of the system is 0.0559 mm for the translation and 0.03 degrees for the rotation DoF of the end-effector. Back-drivability of the system is characterized as 0.14 N in translational, 0.039 Nm in rotational directions.

The moving and base platforms, as well as all the linkages are manufactured from 6061 aluminium. Task based attachments are rapid prototyped using ABS plastic. The robotic interface is 21 x 24 x 24 cm^3 in size and weights about 2700 gr. Complying with the ergonomics and phycological confidence, the end-effectors are designed to be comfortable such that the patients can be attached to and de-attached from the device easily. To maximize comfort and hygiene, critical surfaces are covered with a silicon and disposable medical bands.

3.4   Therapy Modes and Control

The rehabilitation system supports a measurement mode and three distinct therapy modes: passive, assistive and resistive.

In the measurement mode, the device actuators are disabled and patient movements are recorded. These recordings are used to determine the RoM of the forearm/wrist DoFs and hand aperture. Furthermore, in the passive mode, these recordings are repetitively imposed to the patients as pre-recorded exercises.

In the passive mode, the robotic device is controlled by a disturbance observer based position controller. This controller views human as a disturbance and imposes pre-recorded movements to the patient. Note that, along with a disturbance torque observer, this mode can also be used to measure isometric strength of the joints by detecting the force thresholds of the patient.

Impedance controller is utilized for both assistive and resistive modes. To faithfully assign desired decoupled impedance values along each separate DoF of the device, model-based dynamics compensation is utilized. In assistive and resistive modes, patients are also motivated with force-feedback VR games presented on the visual display. In these modes, the robot supports/ressists the motion of the patient with the proper amount of force feedback.

3.5   Virtual Reality Integration and Graphical User Interface

The rehabilitation therapies feature force feedback and are supported by VR animation scenarios, such as door opening, key turning, tooth brushing, writing, and jar opening. While performing these exercises, real objects or lightweight replicas of the real objects are used. Figure 1-B presents a screen shot of a sample VR animation of a hold, rotate, place and drop scenario, applied with the external hand module. Other VR exercises include simple games that provide frequent feedback about the success of the actions, as well as the quality of the performance, to encourage participation and to promote concentration.

A graphical user interface (GUI) is designed to help the therapist to choose the type of the attached end-effector, the amount and speed of the wrist/hand movement, the amount and direction of the assistance/resistance. The GUI can also reproduce and display pre-recorded 3-D motions of the patient.

4   Usability Tests and Measurements

4.1   Test Setup

Human subject experiments with healthy volunteers have been conducted to examine the usability of the rehabilitation system, the effectiveness of the device to deliver various rehabilitation exercises to hand, wrist and forearm, and its applicability as a measurement device.

The experimental setup consisted of a desktop computer, a monitor screen, a wristband, and the rehabilitation system. Participants sat in front of the monitor and one hand of the participant was attached to the device. The elbow of the participant was supported to ensure a natural and comfortable posture.

4.2   Testing the Therapy Modes and the Measurement Mode

The device was tested both as a rehabilitation device and as a measurement tool. As a part of the usability tests, all types of exercises including concurrent movements of the hand opening/closing with the wrist palmar/dorsal flexion, abduction/adduction and the forearm pronation/supination were also tested by utilizing different end-effectors and orienting the device in various configurations. Moreover, ADL tasks were exercised using the task oriented attachments.

To test the efficacy of the device as a measurement tool, the forearm/wrist rotations collected through the 3-CRP mechanism is compared to a wrist exoskeleton, SUkorpion WR [11] which has high measurement accuracy, since its axes can be perfectly aligned with the human joint axes and the measurement of individual joint angles is possible with the device. For the comparison, typical wrist and forearm movements were performed when the subject was simultaneously attached to both devices and position data were recorded.

4.3   Results

Feasibility of using the device in different orientations to exercise various complex motions have been carried out. In general, the participants were satisfied with the ergonomy of the device and its practical use. They expressed that the ADL tasks integrated with force-feedback VR simulations were immersive and motivating.

Figure 3 presents the plots of the position data collected during the measurement experiments. In particular, the wrist abduction/adduction, palmar/dorsal flexion and the forearm pronation/supination measurements taken using both the 3-CRP mechanism and the SUkorpion WR exoskeleton are plotted on this figure. It can be observed

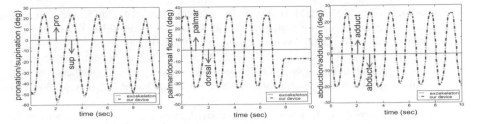

Fig. 3. Comparison of wrist motion measurements recorded concurrently using the 3-CRP rehabilitation system and the SUkorpion exoskeleton

that the measurements with the 3-CRP mechanism closely follows the measurements with the exoskeleton. The RMS values of the errors between the data measured by 3-CRP device and the exoskeleton are found as: $error_{abd-add} = 1.69^o$, $error_{palm-dors} = 1.64^o$, $error_{pro-sup} = 2.09^o$.

The measurement errors in the range of 2.09^o are acceptably low for quantification of the daily patient progress, and qualifies the device as a practical measurement tool for in-home use. A repeated measures ANOVA (with therapy modes as between-subject factor, session as within subject factor) was carried out to determine significant effects. The results revealed a significant main effect of therapy modes ($F(2,23)=218.66$, $p=0$) and no significant effects of devices ($F(1,23)=0.06$, $p=0.8096$) or interaction ($F(2,23)=0.46$, $p=0.6399$).

5   Conclusion

An endpoint oriented, impedance type, 3-DoF, portable haptic interface has been developed to deliver rehabilitation therapies and to administer RoM/strength measurements for the upper extremity, including forearm, wrist and hand. Usability studies have been conducted and the efficacy of the device on performing concurrent, coordinated motions of the hand and the forearm/wrist has been shown. Results indicate that the device is ergonomic. The measurement accuracy of the device has been characterized through a comparison test with a forearm/wrist exoskeleton. There is no statistically significance between measurement error of 3-CRP and an exoskeleton.

Future works include human subject studies with chronic stroke patients to test the therapeutic efficacy of the device and implementation of embedded controls for home use.

References

1. WHO, http://www.who.int/mediacentre/news/releases/2004/pr68/en/
2. Takahashi, C., Der-Yeghiaian, L., Le, V., Cramer, S.: A robotic device for hand motor therapy after stroke. In: IEEE International Conference on Rehabilitation and Robotics, pp. 17–20 (2005)
3. Frisoli, A., Rocchi, F., Marcheschi, S., Dettori, A., Salsedo, F., Bergamasco, M.: A new force-feedback arm exoskeleton for haptic interaction in virtual environments. In: IEEE Eurohaptics, pp. 195–201 (2005)

4. Palazzolo, J., Ferraro, M., Krebs, H., Lynch, D., Volpe, B., Hogan, N.: Stochastic estimation of arm mechanical impedance during robotic stroke rehabilitation. IEEE Transactions on Neural Systems and Rehabilitation Engineering 15(1), 94–103 (2007)
5. Furusho, J., Kikuchi, T., Oda, K., Ohyama, Y., Morita, T., Shichi, N., Jin, Y., Inoue, A.: A 6-dof rehabilitation support system for upper limbs including wrists "robotherapist" with physical therapy. In: IEEE International Conference on Rehabilitation Robotics, pp. 304–309 (2007)
6. Loureiro, R., Harwin, W.: Reach and grasp therapy: Design and control of a 9-dof robotic neuro-rehabilitation system. In: IEEE International Conference on Rehabilitation Robotics, pp. 757–763 (2007)
7. Mrad, C., Kawasaki, H., Takai, J., Tanaka, Y., Mouri, T.: Development of a multifingered robotic human upper limb as an inverse haptic interface. In: IEEE International Conference on Systems, Man and Cybernetics, vol. 4 (2002)
8. Dovat, L., Lambercy, O., Ruffieux, Y., Chapuis, D., Gassert, R., Bleuler, H., Teo, C., Burdet, E.: A haptic knob for rehabilitation of stroke patients. In: IEEE International Conference on Intelligent Robots and Systems, pp. 977–982 (2006)
9. Unal, R., Patoglu, V.: Optimal dimensional synthesis of force feedback lower arm exoskeletons. In: IEEE International Conference on Biomedical Robotics and Biomechatronics, pp. 329–334 (2008)
10. Ertas, I., Hocaoglu, E., Barkana, D., Patoglu, V.: Finger exoskeleton for treatment of tendon injuries. In: IEEE International Conference on Rehabilitation Robotics, pp. 194–201 (2009)
11. Erdogan, A., Satici, A., Patoglu, V.: Design of a reconfigurable force feedback ankle exoskeleton for physical therapy. In: ASME/IFToMM International Conference on Reconfigurable Mechanisms and Robots, pp. 400–408 (2009)

Virtual Surface Discrimination via an
Anisotropic-Stiffness Contact Model

Alessandro Formaglio[1], Gabriel Baud-Bovy[2], and Domenico Prattichizzo[1,3]

[1] Department of Information Engineering, University of Siena
[2] Vita-Salute San Raffaele University and IIT Network Research Unit of Molecular
Neuroscience, San-Raffaele Foundation, Milan, Italy
[3] Italian Institute of Technology, Genova, Italy
formaglio@dii.unisi.it, baud-bovy.gabriel@hsr.it, prattichizzo@dii.unisi.it

Abstract. In haptically enabled virtual reality, most existing devices render kinesthetic feedback via one 3DoF single-contact-point, thus they cannot stimulate tactily teh fingertip skin. This lack of information prevents the perception of contact surface orientation in absence of vision and of free exploratory movements. In this work we experimentally investigate the rendering performance of a contact model which exploits anisotropic contact stiffness to convey such information.

Keywords: perception, grasping, tactile, contact.

1 Introduction

The combination of tactile and kinesthetic flow of information commonly available in reality cannot always be rendered in haptically enabled virtual reality, mainly due to technological limitations of force feedback interfaces. The force feedback is usually mediated by tools like finger thimbles that convey kinesthetic information but prevent the transmission of tactile information about the surface properties. As a result, in absence of vision, the only way to gain information about virtual shapes is usually actively moving the fingers along their surfaces. This can be a relevant limitation in case of virtual grasping simulation: performing a stable grasp requires the contact points not to slip, but this prevents the correct perception of contact surfaces orientation, crucial to regulate both grip and load forces. The model discussed in this paper has been already addressed in our previous research [1, 2]. It consists in augmenting the kinesthetic feedback provided by 3DoF single-contact-point devices in order to convey information about the virtual surface orientation in absence of vision and of free exploratory movements. To that end, the adopted contact model features anisotropic stiffness. This is achieved by generating an ellipsoidal force field centered at the contact point, in order to influence the behavior of the finger during the contact, and to augment the kinesthetic stimulation fed back by the devices in multi-finger haptic interaction. To evaluate the impact of the proposed model we carried out a perceptual experiment based on a simplified virtual pinch-grasping task. The target consisted of verifying whether and to which

A.M.L. Kappers et al. (Eds.): EuroHaptics 2010, Part II, LNCS 6192, pp. 291–296, 2010.

extent the anisotropic stiffness allows users to discriminate four virtual surfaces with different orientations from one another, in absence of vision and of free explorations.

The remainder of this paper is structured as follows. Section 2 reports the formalization of the contact model. Section 3 describes general methods of the psychophysical experiment. Finally, in Section 4 concluding remarks are given.

2   The Anisotropic-Stiffness Contact Model

Before discussing the experimental study, we will briefly recall the basic principles of the anisotropic-stiffness contact model already introduced in [1, 2]. The most common penalty-based algorithms to render virtual contacts are the God-Object [3] and Friction Cone algorithm [4]. Let us suppose the friction cone constraint is satisfied, i.e. the contact point does not slip. Actually, the penalty-based contact model still allows small fingertip movements bounded within the friction cone, but the direction of the rendered force is the same as the virtual penetration vector (i.e. the penalty), and its magnitude depends only on the penetration depth. As a result, this model does not provide information about the contact surface orientation. Using the proposed contact model, the virtual stiffness is shaped as an ellipsoid centered at the contact point [1]. As a consequence, the force magnitude becomes a function also of the penalty direction, generating contact patterns that depend on the relative orientation between the penalty direction and the surface normal direction. Let us assume that the contact forces always lie within the friction cone, hence the contact point does not slip. Let $p_F = (x_F, y_F, z_F)$ be the position of the fingertip expressed in a local reference frame Σ, with origin at the god point p_G and the z−axis oriented as the the normal direction at p_G. Hence for each fingertip position p_F the contact force is computed as:

$$F = - \left\| \begin{bmatrix} k_1 & 0 & 0 \\ 0 & k_1 & 0 \\ 0 & 0 & k_2 \end{bmatrix} p_F \right\| \frac{p_F}{\|p_F\|} \qquad e = \frac{k_1}{k_2} \ (e \leq 1), \quad k = \sqrt{\frac{2k_1^2 + k_2^2}{3}} \qquad (1)$$

where k_1 is the stiffness along any direction of the tangential plane (x, y), and k_2 is the stiffness along the normal direction at the contact point, e and k are the *eccentricity* and the *total stiffness* of the ellipsoid. The force F has the same direction as the penalty vector, while its magnitude depends on both the depth and the direction of the penalty vector (see Figure 1).

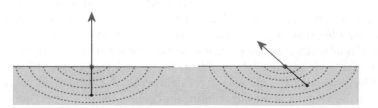

Fig. 1. Two penetration vectors with the same depth but two different orientations yield two forces F with different magnitude, depending on the stiffness ellipsoid

3   Experiments

The perceptual experiment consisted of a simplified pinch-grasp task. The setup was built up with a customized 3DoF Omega haptic device, equipped with a thimble end-effector for the index, and a passive thimble grounded to the desktop for the thumb (see Figure 2). The set of varying parameters adopted during experiments involved the surface orientation, the eccentricity and the global stiffness of the ellipsoid. We carried out preliminary experiments in our previous studies to evaluate the probability of correctly discriminating two different surfaces from one another [2]. The eccentricity revealed to have a key role: as e decreases, the probability increases as well. On the other hand, other factors such as the stiffness, the posture of the hand, the orientation of the virtual surfaces with respect to the hand did not reveal significant influences on the rendering performance.

In this study, we decided to perform a new experiment to evaluate the probability to discriminate four possible shapes (depicted in Figure 2) from one another, instead of only two as in our previous experiment. After a pilot-test session, three stiffness values ($k = 1.25$, 1.50 and 1.75N/mm) and three eccentricity values ($e = 0.20$, $e = 0.40$ and $e = 0.60$) were adopted for each orientation, yielding a total set of 36 different combinations of parameters.

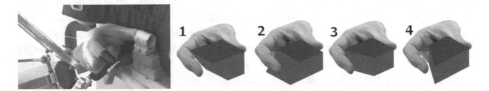

Fig. 2. The experimental setup and the 4 virtual shapes displayed during experiments

5 male subjects, aged 20-26 and right-handed, participated to the experiment. Their confidence with haptic interfaces has been qualitatively evaluated: subject 1 had never tried a device before; subjects $2 - 4$ had tried less than 10 times; subject 5 tried more than 10 times. Each participant performed 10 repetitions in which the 36 stimuli were presented in random order. Subjects performed 3 training repetitions, with the instruction of squeezing and maintaining the contact for a maximum duration of 3sec per trial (time events were announced by sound signals). The level of squeezing force was selected freely by the subject. No visual feedback was provided, the god-point could not slip during a contact, and the experimental setup was hid to the subjects' sight. As in previous studies, subjects associated the normal direction at the contact point to the direction of maximum stiffness of the force field [2]. Henceforth, we will define as "correct response" such an association. The left side of Figure 3 reports the correct responses percentages for all pairs (e, k). As we expected, the percentages were always greater than the chance value (25% in this experiment), hence the contact model was able to convey information about the surface orientation. The eccentricity e confirmed its key role, while no particular dependency on stiffness appeared. The global probabilities to perceive the correct shape were generally slightly lower than those in [2]. This

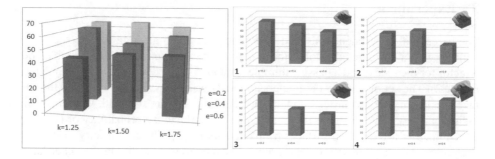

Fig. 3. Left: pooled percentages of correct responses over eccentricity and stiffness. Right: percentages over eccentricity for each shape, pooling stiffness values.

aspect is likely due to the four-alternative paradigm adopted in this experiment, which provided less information a-priori. On the other hand, the methods of previous studies did not reveal significant dependencies on the relative displacement between the shape and the hand, while in this case, combining the four shapes in the same experiment, it allowed us to notice slight differences in the percentages of correct responses among the shapes. Since the stiffness revealed no statistical significance, the percentages of correct responses have been averaged over all stiffness values. The rigth side of Figure 3 reports such percentages for each shape. In particular, the shapes 2 and 3 appear harder to be guessed for higher values of eccentricity. In other terms, not all surface orientations were haptically rendered with the same performance. We recall that the contact point could not slip, hence no free explorations were allowed. Anyway, we analyzed the fingertip penetration trajectories allowed by the penalty-based contact model, recorded for each experimental trial. We investigated eventual common trends that can be related to the probability to perceive the correct orientation. From the visual observation of some trajectory 3D plots, we noticed that the finger penetration is mainly extended towards the thumb, but other deviations from such a direction could be clearly observed. For each trajectory we computed the maximum extent of the penalty vector. Such amplitude values have been averaged over all trials and all repetitions, and grouped per subject. In the left side of Figure 4 we reported the mean of maximum penetration amplitudes and the related standard deviation per subject, setting apart the trials with correct responses from those with wrong responses.

No clear dependencies between the penetration extent and the probability to guess the shape can be identified. A Two-sample T-test at the 5% significance level between the correct-response values and the wrong-response values was performed per subject. It revealed that the two distributions are statistically different only for subject 4 and 5. Although no evident results stem from this statistics, an interesting observation can be drawn: subjects were able to guess the correct orientation independently from the penetration depth. This observation led us to investigate how the penetration direction can be related to the probability to perceive the correct orientation. In our expectations, the ellipsoidal force field would deviate the fingertip squeezing trajectory towards the direction where the surface gradient descends. Hence, four unit vectors v_1, v_2, v_3 and v_4 were associated to the gradient-descent direction for each shape. Then, for each

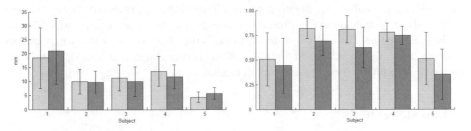

Fig. 4. Left: mean exploration amplitude and the related standard deviation per subject. Right: mean r and the related standard deviation per subject. (Light-grey bar: trials with correct responses. Dark-grey bar: trials with wrong responses.)

fingertip trajectory, we performed the Principal Component Analysis. The eigenvectors d_1, d_2, d_3 of the covariance matrix represent the directions of the principal components, while the related eigenvalues $\lambda_1, \lambda_2, \lambda_3$ quantify the principal component extent. For each trial i, we projected the first principal component on the related gradient-descent vector v_i. In mathematical terms, let λ_1 be the maximum eigenvalue, we computed the factor $r_i = < v_i, cd_1 >$, where $c = \lambda_1(\lambda_1 + \lambda_2 + \lambda_3)^{-1}$ and v_i depends on the shape displayed at the ith trial. The scale factor c quantifies how much the first principal component is greater than the others. The factor r_i ($0 < r_i < 1$) quantifies whether and to which extent the fingertip penetration trajectory tended to be aligned with the surface gradient-descent direction: as r_i is close to 1, then the fingertip trajectory was mainly spread along v_i. In the right side of Figure 4 we reported the mean r and the related standard deviation per subject, setting apart the trials with correct responses from those with wrong responses. For all subjects, in the trials with correct responses the factor r is greater than in trials with wrong responses. Again, a Two-sample T-test at the 5% level between the correct-response values and the wrong-response values was performed per subject. It revealed that the two distributions are statistically different, except for subject 1. Hence, a trend can be identified: as the fingertip penetration vector was aligned towards the gradient-descend direction, then subjects could better perceive the surface orientation, no matter the penetration depth.

4 Discussion and Conclusion

The experimental study discussed in this paper shows that the anisotropic-stiffness contact model can be applied to a simplified pinch grasp setup, and it generally allows users to perceive the orientation of the virtual surface even in absence of vision and of free exploratory movements. Experimental results showed that the factor mainly pertaining to the performance level was the eccentricity e, that is the ratio between the stiffness along the tangential and normal directions. In contrast, the global stiffness k revealed to have almost no effect throughout all the experiments we performed. Comparing the correct response percentages for each shape, the shapes 2 and 3 appeared harder to be guessed for higher values of eccentricity. This suggests that the ellipsoidal stiffness cannot render all possible surface orientations with the same performance. In our future works, we plan to investigate deeper this aspect to find its physical and/or cognitive motivation. The analysis of fingertip penetration trajectories revealed some common trends. All subjects had the clear trend to move their fingertip as far as it was allowed by the elastic contact model, in particular towards the direction where they expected to perceive the surface gradient. Statistical analysis revealed that this trend is significant for the probability to guess the correct orientation.

Acknowledgments

This work has been partially supported by the EC with the Collaborative Project FP7-ICT-2007-215190 "ROBOCAST" and by the Ministero dell'Università e della Ricerca with the PRIN 2008 project "Attuatori innovativi per sistemi avanzati di manipolazione e di interazione aptica".

References

1. Formaglio, A., Baud-bovy, G., Prattichizzo, D.: Is it possible to perceive the shape of an object without exploring it? In: Proceedings of Eurohaptics Conference, July 3-6, pp. 441–446 (2006)
2. Formaglio, A., Baud-Bovy, G., Prattichizzo, D.: Conveying virtual tactile feedback via augmented kinesthetic stimulation. In: Proceedings of International Conference on Robotics and Automation, ICRA, pp. 3995–4000 (2007)
3. Zilles, C.B., Salisbury, J.K.: A constraint-based god-object method for haptic display. In: Proc. IEE/RSJ International Conference on Intelligent Robots and Systems, Human Robot Interaction, and Cooperative Robots, vol. 3, pp. 146–151 (1995)
4. Harwin, W.S., Melder, N.: Improved Haptic Rendering for Multi-Finger Manipulation Using Friction Cone based God-Objects. In: Proceedings of Eurohaptics Conference, pp. 82–85 (2002)

Embedding Tactile Feedback into Handheld Devices: An Aperture-Based Restraint for the Finger or Thumb

Brian T. Gleeson and William R. Provancher

University of Utah, 50 S. Central Campus Dr., RM 2110, Salt Lake City, UT 84112-9208
brian.gleeson@gmail.com, wil@mech.utah.edu

Abstract. Tactile feedback has the potential to provide rich communication in a range of embedded applications, but this requires a finger restraint that is effective and practical for integration into a handheld device. This paper investigates an aperture-based restraint, a simple conical hole, used to prevent unwanted motion of the finger and to provide access to the tactile device. A range of aperture sizes were tested with both the index finger and thumb using a tactile display that applies tangential skin displacement. The aperture restraint was found to be effective, comparable to a traditional thimble-type restraint, with larger apertures performing better. There was no significant interaction between finger size and aperture size, meaning that the same aperture could be used for a wide range of fingers sizes.

Keywords: Haptic devices; finger restraint; haptic direction cues; tangential skin displacement; skin stretch.

1 Introduction and Background

In recent years there has been a growing interest in integrating haptic feedback into portable devices. Cell phones, music players and game systems featuring basic vibrotactile feedback have come to market. In the future, we hope to see more communicative haptic displays integrated into a variety of common devices. Haptic communication could be beneficial in situations where sight and vision are needed for safety-critical situational awareness, e.g., providing navigational cues to the driver of car or to a soldier in an urban setting. Alternately, communicative haptic feedback could be used to improve the user experience of common consumer electronics. If a greater variety of tactile devices are to be embedded into mobile phones or steering wheels, it will be necessary to design a finger restraint that maximizes the communication of the localized tactile stimulus, but does not inconvenience the user. This paper explores two aspects of tactile interface design relevant to the integration of haptic communication into everyday devices: the design of an aperture-based finger restraint and an evaluation of its use with the index finger and the thumb.

Researchers have developed portable, or potentially portable, tactile displays capable of communicating information using sensations of slip, stretch, shear force, and other skin deformations. The most common finger restraint in these devices is a thimble-type restraint. Gleeson et al. have investigated the use of tangential skin displacement for the communication of direction, represented schematically in Fig. 1a, using a

A.M.L. Kappers et al. (Eds.): EuroHaptics 2010, Part II, LNCS 6192, pp. 297–302, 2010.
© Springer-Verlag Berlin Heidelberg 2010

thimble-based restraint[1, 2]. A thimble-type interface was also used by Tsagarkis et al. in a miniature slip and stretch display [3] and by many researchers doing tactile interface development with a Phantom robot, e.g., [4] and [5]. While effective for lab use, a thimble-type interface would be inconvenient for handheld electronics and potentially unsafe on a moving device like a steering wheel.

Other researchers have introduced a simple finger restraint with potential for integration into handheld devices: a tapered, circular hole or aperture [6] [7]. We have adapted this concept for testing in our research. The user's finger rests on a flat surface surrounding the aperture while the flesh of the fingerpad presses down through the aperture to contact the haptic stimulator (Fig. 1b). Such an interface could be easily embedded into a device like a mobile phone or a steering wheel, would not inconvenience the user, and could be used with a variety of tactile display devices. In this paper, we study the effect of aperture size on performance and compare apertures to a traditional thimble-type restraint.

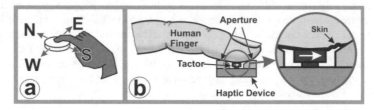

Fig. 1. a: A representation of direction communication using tangential skin displacement. b: An aperture-based finger restraint, as used in a tangential skin displacement display.

2 Haptic Device and Experimental Methods

While an aperture could be used to interface with a variety of haptic devices, we have chosen to use a display tangential skin displacement. In earlier work, tangential skin displacement has been shown to effectively communicate direction and could potential be used as a navigation aid [1]. A portable display has been built [2], but for this experiment a high precision, bench-top display was used. The test device consisted of a two-axis linear stage capable of positioning a tactor, the part of the device contacting the finger, in a plane to within 2.5 μm. The tactor used was a soft rubber IBM ThinkPad TrackPoint measuring approximately 7 mm in diameter with a sandpaper-like surface texture. The contact force between the tactor and the finger was monitored with a single-axis Omega LCEB-5 load cell, accurate to ±0.03%. The device and tactor are shown in Fig. 2. a. For more information on the device, see [1].

Test apertures were machined from aluminum in a range of sizes. See Fig. 2. for aperture geometry and dimensions. Apertures were rigidly attached to an armrest and suspended over the tactor so that the top of the tactor sat 0.5 mm below the upper surface of the aperture. The mounting bracket was designed so that users could comfortably interact with the tactor using either their index finger or thumb.

Experiments were conducted on 20 volunteer subjects, 10 of each gender, aged from 19 to 41 years (mean = 24.6). Fourteen subjects participated in the experiment for course credit, while the remaining subjects were uncompensated. Post-hoc analysis showed no significant effect from compensation [F(1,239)=0.01, p=0.938].

Subjects sat with their right arm on a padded armrest and their right index finger or thumb contacting the tactor through one of the experimental apertures (Fig. 2. a). The test device and right hand were covered with a cloth (not shown in the figure). The user wore headphones which played a tone to signal the start of each stimulus. External speakers played white noise to mask the noise of the test device.

Each stimulus consisted of a single 2.0 mm/s displacement of the tactor in one of four orthogonal directions in the plane of the fingerpad: proximal, distal, radial or ulnar. A range of displacement distances were tested. After a motionless pause of 300 msec, the tactor returned to center at 1.3 mm/s. When the tactor returned to center, a graphical interface on a PC prompted the subject respond with the direction of the stimulus by clicking on one of four arrow buttons. For more detailed information on the test setup or stimuli, see [1].

Specific test parameters were determined from prior work and from pilot testing. Pilot tests were conducted on 5 volunteer subjects to evaluate tactor displacement distance and aperture size. Displacements of 0.05, 0.10, 0.50 and 1.00 mm were tested using five apertures: the three described in Fig. 2. , plus two of intermediates sizes (inner diameters of 11 and 14 mm). The 11 and 14 mm apertures produced results very similar to the other apertures, and were thus not included in the main experiment. Larger apertures were not tested because they were deemed impractical for integration into small, handheld devices. An experimental ceiling effect was observed for 1 mm stimuli; subjects performed nearly perfectly, regardless of aperture.

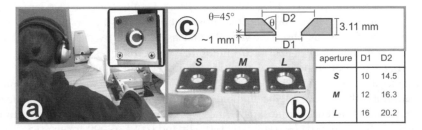

Fig. 2. Experimental equipment. a: The test setup, with the device cover removed. The inset shows the tactor and aperture *M*. b: The experimental apertures with an index finger, for scale. c: Cross-section drawing of an aperture, showing relevant dimensions. Table: Sizes of the three apertures, referring to the dimensions in cross-section drawing. All units are mm.

The main experiment was conducted using the three apertures described in Fig. 2. (*S M L*), using stimulus displacements of 0.05, 0.10, and 0.50 mm. Each test consisted of four sections evaluating different apertures on different fingers: index finger and *S*, index finger and *M*, thumb and *M*, thumb and *L*. The order of the sections was balanced between subjects using a Latin squares approach and subjects were given a rest period between each section. Each section included 10 repetitions of each direction and each displacement for a total of 120 stimuli per section (10 repetitions × 4 directions × 3 displacements = 120). Within each section, stimuli were presented in a pseudo-random order with the restriction that stimuli of the various directions and displacements were distributed approximately evenly throughout the section. The four sections required approximately 40 minutes to complete. A previous study using the same test protocols found no significant adaptation or learning effects in a test of this length [1]. Before the first section, the thickness, width, and length of the subject's index finger and thumb were measured using calipers. Measured width ranges were 12.8-17.1 mm (index) and 16.6-24.9 mm (thumb).

3 Results and Discussion

Response accuracy rates were computed for each stimulus type for each subject as $(N_{correct}/N_{stimuli})$, and then accuracy data were pooled between all subjects. These results are summarized in Fig. 3 along with data from a separate experiment [1] which tested the index finger in a thimble-type interface using the same test protocols. The various restraint types were compared using difference scores in order to remove the effects of subject baseline performance. Difference scores were calculated separately for each subject as (accuracy − mean accuracy). In an ANOVA, both aperture size and stimulus distance had main effects $[F(2,239)>5.28, p<0.006]$. For 0.5 mm stimuli, direction information was communicated with high accuracy under all test conditions, but the less salient stimuli showed more differentiation. Using the index finger, subjects performed better, on average, with aperture M than with S, although this difference was only statistically significant for 0.1 mm stimuli $[t(38)=2.56, p=0.015]$. Similarly, when stimuli were delivered to the thumb, subjects responded with higher accuracy when using the larger aperture. This effect was statistically significant for all three displacements $[t(38)>2.078, p<0.044]$. These results suggest that larger apertures are more effective, despite the observation that smaller apertures better restrained the finger (as observed visually and as reported by subjects). The likely explanation is that smaller apertures immobilize more of the skin of the fingerpad, preventing activation of peripheral afferents, as observed in prior work [8].

In general, the performance of the apertures was comparable to the performance of the traditional thimble, with the thimble producing slightly higher communication accuracy. The differences in accuracy rates between the index finger in aperture M and the thimble were 0.047±0.043, 0.094±0.075 and 0.081±0.090 for the 0.5, 0.1 and 0.05 mm stimuli, respectively. However, it should be noted that the thimble experiments were conducted on a separate subject pool and that these differences may also reflect a difference in baseline performance between pools.

The performances of the index finger and thumb were compared directly using data obtained with aperture M. An ANOVA revealed a main effect, with subjects performing with higher accuracy when using the index finger $[F(1,119)=16.4, p=0.0001]$. This difference is somewhat surprising, given the approximately equal mechanoreceptor densities on the index finger and thumb [9], along with observations of equal detection thresholds on the finger and thumb for a variety of stimuli [10, 11]. In our experiment, it is likely that differences in fingertip geometry affected how the two digits interfaced with the aperture and that this dominated over any differences in innate sensory acuity in determining performance. It is important to note, however, that the thumb can be just as effective as the index finger if a larger aperture is used; there was no significant difference between the Thumb L and Index M conditions $[t<0.51, p>0.612]$.

We conducted two analyses to measure the effect of finger size on accuracy: a simple test for correlation and an ANOCOVA to test for interactions between finger size and aperture size. In both tests, 0.50 mm stimuli were removed from the dataset as they exhibited a ceiling effect. The width of the finger at the base of the fingernail was used as the measure of finger size. Data from the index finger and thumb were analyzed separately, therefore this analysis does not address the size difference between the two digits. The correlation test suggested that subjects with smaller fingers generally performed better, with about 4% accuracy lost for each mm of finger width above the mean, although this correlation was not quite significant [Pearson's r = -0.30, p =0.059]. This trend is in agreement with prior work by Peters et al. who reported greater tactile sensitivity in smaller fingers, probably due to an increase in mechanoreceptor density [12]. We had expected to see some interaction between finger size and aperture size, e.g. small fingers performing relatively poorly with the largest apertures due to increased slipping of the finger in the aperture. No such interaction was observed when subjects were divided into two groups based on finger size [Index: F(1,36)=0.00, p=0.963, Thumb: F(1,36)=1.66, p=0.205], suggesting that the area of exposed skin dominates over other factors, such as variations in the degree of finger restraint, in determining communication accuracy. This result implies that apertures need not be adjusted to the size of the user's finger.

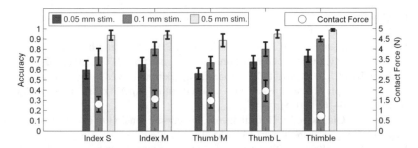

Fig. 3. Result of aperture experiment, along with data collected in a separate experiment [1] using a thimble-type interface on the index fingers of 16 subjects. All error bars represent 95% confidence intervals.

4   Conclusions and Future Work

The aperture restraint was effective in interfacing between a tactile display and both the index finger and thumb. Larger apertures resulted in better communication accuracy, but all tested apertures performed similarly well with 0.5 mm stimuli. Thus, if highly salient stimuli were used, a device could reasonably incorporate whichever aperture best fit its design requirements. Also important is the lack of interaction between finger size and aperture size, implying that one aperture could be used on fingers of all sizes. These results all recommend the aperture as an effective and practical means of interfacing with a tactile display in a handheld device. A forthcoming publication on this topic will include an analysis of the effects of stimulus direction on performance, the effects of contact force between the finger and tactor, and an evaluation of tactor designs.

Acknowledgements

This work was supported, in part, by the National Science Foundation under awards DGE-0654414 and IIS-0746914. We thank Dr. David Strayer and Nathan Medeiros-Ward for helping to recruit test subjects, Sarah Bell for proctoring the experiments, and Charles Stewart for helping develop and build the apertures.

References

1. Gleeson, B.T., Horschel, S.K., Provancher, W.R.: Perception of Direction for Applied Tangential Skin Displacement: Effects of Speed. Displacement and Repetition, Trans. on Haptics (2010) (in Press)
2. Gleeson, B.T., Horschel, S.K., Provancher, W.R.: Design of a Fingertip-Mounted Tactile Display with Tangential Skin Displacement Feedback. Trans. on Haptics (2010) (in Press)
3. Tsagarakis, N.G., Horne, T., Caldwell, D.G.: Slip Aestheasis: A Portable 2D Slip/Skin Stretch Display for the Fingertip. In: Proc. Eurohaptics (2005)
4. Kuchenbecker, K.J., Ferguson, D., Kutzer, M., Moses, M., Okamura, A.M.: The Touch Thimble: Providing Fingertip Contact Feedback During Point-Force Haptic Interaction. In: Proc. Haptic Symposium, pp. 239–246 (2008)
5. Provancher, W.R., Cutkosky, M.R., Kuchenbecker, K.J., Niemeyer, G.: Contact Location Display for Haptic Perception of Curvature and Object Motion. The Intl. Journal of Robotics Research 24, 691–702 (2005)
6. Salada, M.A., Colgate, J.E., Lee, M.V., Vishton, P.M.: Fingertip haptics: A novel direction in haptic display. In: Mechatronics Forum Int'l Conf., pp. 1211–1220 (2002)
7. Webster III, R.J., Murphy, T.E., Verner, L.N., Okamura, A.M.: A novel two-dimensional tactile slip display: design, kinematics and perceptual experiments. Trans. on Applied Perception 2, 150–165 (2005)
8. Norrsell, U., Olausson, H.: Human, tactile, directional sensibility and its peripheral origins. Acta physiologica scandinavica 144, 155–161 (1992)
9. Vallbo, Å.B., Johnsson, R.S.: Properties of cutaneous mechanoreceptors in the human hand related to touch sensation. Human Neurobiology 3, 3–14 (1984)
10. Johansson, R.S., Valbo, A.B.: Detection of tactile stimuli. Thresholds of afferent units related to psychophysical thresholds in the human hand. J. of Physiol. 297, 405–422 (1979)
11. van der Horst, B.J., Kappers, A.: Curvature discrimination in various finger conditions. Exper. Brain Research 177, 304–311 (2007)
12. Peters, R.M., Hackeman, E., Goldreich, D.: Diminutive Digits Discern Delicate Details: Fingertip Size and the Sex Difference in Tactile Spatial Acuity. J. of Neuroscience 29, 15756–15761 (2009)

Understanding the Haptic Experience through Bodily Engagement with Sculptural Ceramics

Bonnie Kemske

Affiliated with the Museum of Archaeology and Anthropology, Cambridge University
mail@bonniekemske.com
www.bonniekemske.com

Abstract. This paper presents an on-going research project undertaken by an artist-researcher who uses both investigation into haptic theory and the creation of ceramic objects to increase our understanding of the experience of touch. It asks the question, "How and in what way can an artist contribute to understanding haptics?" The artistic journey began with an interest in the textured surface of ceramics. Physiological, anthropological, and philosophical perspectives were interwoven with studio practice, resulting in the creation of 'cast hugs', ceramic sculptures made through the use of the artist's body. The physical qualities of the ceramic objects positively engaged participants' haptic abilities to distinguish shape, to discriminate texture, temperature, and weight, and to engage their sense of proprioception. It was found that when these senses were fully stimulated, emotions, memories, and associations were strongly evoked.

Keywords: haptic art, tactile art, touch art, tactile ceramics.

1 Introduction

Touch is a full-body experience. Yet, in conceptualizing touch we often concentrate on engaging the hand alone, and hence create objects to touch that do not engage many of the body's impressive and varied haptic abilities. The artwork presented in this paper developed from a by-practice PhD undertaken at the Royal College of Art in London[1]. These new PhDs have developed to go beyond what Christopher Frayling has called "research into art" or "research through art" (traditional forms of research modelled on scientific paradigms) to what he termed "research for art" [1], a new approach that requires innovative and individual methodologies[2]. Within this framework I set out to create a methodology that would concatenate stages of theoretical knowledge and studio practice. I used various approaches, such as empirical assessment, the principles of Grounded Theory [2], and finally, a reflective and emergent writing style that intertwined the understandings gained from philosophical texts with the phenomenological experience in the studio. My aim was to create artworks that would entice viewers into becoming touchers and then to deliberately engage a

---

[1] After ten years as a professional ceramist producing tactile artworks, I undertook the PhD, entitled "Evoking Intimacy: Touch and the Thoughtful Body in Sculptural Ceramics", which was awarded in 2008.

[2] Personal communication, 2003.

A.M.L. Kappers et al. (Eds.): EuroHaptics 2010, Part II, LNCS 6192, pp. 303–308, 2010.
© Springer-Verlag Berlin Heidelberg 2010

greater spectrum of the body's senses of touch. The research resulted in the creation of 'cast hugs', artworks made *by* and *for* the body, that evoked an aesthetic moment that I have called "grounded sensuality" [3].

2 The Artistic Journey: From Seeing to the Embrace

2.1 The Material Qualities of Clay and the Body's Senses of Touch

The journey starts with the fired clay surface. Fired clay has many positive tactile qualities: it can be sculpted into an infinite number of shapes; it can hold a texture from rough to smooth; it can be light or heavy; it can be responsive in terms of temperature; and because it is used functionally for objects that we use daily, it is a material that is comfortably familiar.

Having a solid grasp of the material qualities of fired clay, the next step in the project was to develop an understanding of human physiology and the mechanics of touch. Learning about the body's differing senses of touch and the differing distribution of those senses across the body led to the two-point discrimination threshold test, a neurological test that uses a calliper-like instrument to determine the widest measurements at which individuals perceive two points as one point across the body [4]. Original evaluations by others of tactile clay tiles led me to understand that touch, although an experience common to us all, is also utterly unique to each individual. I realized that although much could be learned from gathering empirical assessments of the artworks, ultimately I would need to evaluate the works personally and subjectively, as there was no universal touch aesthetic to be found. This approach was supported by earlier art-based research [5].

I had my two-point discrimination thresholds measured to find which areas of my body were most sensitive to tactile discrimination. From this, a series of small textured hand-held forms to be run across the body were made, creating differing sensations from the same forms and textures. One particularly effective sculpture was made to be run over the cheek and onto the lips, the form feeling smooth on the cheek and leaping to sudden texture as it reached the lips.

However, the two-point discrimination threshold test does not measure all of haptic experience. It was decided that larger artworks were needed to engage our other touch senses. Anthropologist Nigel Barley has shown that some African women potters make pots that fit their bodies to facilitate carrying [6]. Emulating this I created forms to be held against the body, texturing them from fine to coarse, according to where they were placed against the skin. Drawing upon the knowledge of traditional Japanese Tea Ceremony potters who often under-fire their work so it remains porous and therefore reactive to temperature, I also low-fired the sculptures.

My own and other's verbal responses to these early sculptures reinforced the need for a subjective approach to the project. I became more attentive to the physical and mental experience of creating the objects. Here is an account of my making the forms directly on my own body: *"The clay is cool but warms quickly against my bare skin. It feels snug, contained, comfortable, caressed. There is a strong sense of immediacy and intimacy...Until I lift it away from my body it exists solely as part of me. This piece is an object to me (the subject), but why doesn't it feel like that? Why does it feel like it is part of me?"*

These insights led to French phenomenologist Maurice Merleau-Ponty's "lived experience" [7], which I understand as there being no experience (sensation or thought) that is not experienced through the body, and his concept of "chiasm" [8], which I perceive as "an ever-flowing merging and shifting between touching and being touched, a blurring of the boundary between the body and the object it holds" [9].

2.2 The Physical Attributes of the Artwork and How They Engaged the Body

Back in the studio, having decided it was important to privilege the tactile senses over the visual, I used my body alone to create the works, devising a technique of sitting with my arms and legs wrapped around a large plaster-filled latex balloon until the plaster set, creating 'cast hugs', embodiments of the space of the embrace.

The cast forms that were chosen to be developed into sculptures echoed human shoulders, thighs, and buttocks, creating a sense of the familiar. In exhibition individuals were enticed to explore them to determine their shape. Because of common inhibitions few comments were made about the similarities between the sculptural shapes and the human body, although some visitors did metaphorically translate this into more 'acceptable' terminology. One visitor remarked, *"What's our best experiences? Those of holding our babies – the warmth, the way they fit up against you, their preciousness. This evokes that."* Others used different metaphors and similes: *"Without thinking, I stroke it against my cheek. The smooth and meandering surfaces and their weight are just right and remind me of mammal babies."*

The sculptures were textured to activate our ability to distinguish tactile qualities. Many people commented on this. For example, *"The textured ones are therapeutic because there's a lot to investigate. The smooth ones are more soothing."*

After trials with lighter artworks, the sculptures were made to be heavier, better stimulating the touch receptors that perceive pressure. The weight of the work seemed to evoke a feeling of comfort: *"It's an amazing experience. It feels like it's breathing for you, like you've stopped breathing and it's doing it. It's the weight. The weight feels like it goes forward, not down. It's very therapeutic – I feel relaxed now."*

Proprioception is defined as the ability to feel the body's position in space. In this work, however, the aim was to engage proprioception by orienting one's body to the shapes of the rigid sculptures. Visitor remarks reflect this: *"I like the way the hardness makes me move around and fit my body to it, rather than the other way around. It makes me aware of muscles and my body that I'm not normally aware of."*

Fig. 1. The haptic experience: gallery visitors interacting with 'cast hugs'

Hot and cold neural receptors were activated as the artworks absorbed body heat and began to warm. Surprisingly, this resulted in a sense of reciprocity with the artwork. *"At first it feels cold, but very quickly you can feel it becoming warm. And as you move your hands over it, you can feel where you've been holding it. So you have a sense of how you are changing it as much as it is affecting you. It's responsive."*

2.3 Beyond the Physical

Underlying all the physical attributes I strove to incorporate in the artwork was my intention not to stimulate the nociceptors that respond to pain; I sought to bring a sense of comfort to the haptic experience. Many people remarked that the experience made them feel a sense of well-being. Words were used such as: *"gentle"*, *"sensual"*, *"intimate"*, and *"satisfying"*. One visitor said: *"The weight feels safe and reassuring. It feels significant. Also, the texture is important. Calming."*

Visitor comments suggest that the experience of holding and caressing the sculptures elicited much more than a physical response. For example: *"It makes me feel slightly more important because now I have a purpose; I am looking after something important."* and *"The curves of the objects made me think of my family when I touched them, and gave me tears. A very warm feeling."*

The issue of tactile memories and associations was articulated by visitors. Memories surfaced through contact with the artwork, and associations were made with other touch experiences the individuals had had. *"They remind me of large stones in my village in Iran where women in labour press their bodies against the stone to take away the pain."*

The physical comfort generated and the emotions evoked in caressing the artwork are what led me to term the experience one of "grounded sensuality". People reported a sense of 'rightness' when they settled the artwork against their bodies. *"When you get it in the right place, it works. It rests on you, feels comfortable."*

This last comment echoed my own making experience, where I felt an existential blur between the casts (objects) and me as maker (subject). This was further elucidated through Merleau-Ponty's words that "...there is overlapping or encroachment, so that we must say that things pass into us as well as we into the things." [10] When embracing the artworks, individuals reported they felt the artworks were incorporated into a direct perceptual experience of their bodies. *"It feels like it's become part of me."* This is a kind of expansion of the self. *"Pressing the shape into my body felt as if I was hugging an extension of myself."*

Visitor observation led to understanding that although the experience is personal and subjective, it also can be shared. Strangers came together to talk about their experiences, to make suggestions about interacting with the artworks, and to share the works with each other. This comment expresses one aspect of the experience: *"The hug is about a closeness, sharing an emotional charge. It's important that it's been hugged before – a shared hug. The hug gives you emotional energy."*

3 Understanding the Haptic Experience

In exhibition, although a few individuals did not engage with the artwork, most people did not hesitate to interact with the sculptures, using their bodies to embrace the artforms. My experience of making the 'cast hug' was thereby transferred to the person experiencing the finished artwork. However, individuals did not simply replicate the making, but encountered the artwork in new and creative ways. A sculptural work of art, created by an artist experiencing one set of sensations, results in as many new experiences as there are individuals to interact with it.

Visitor comments suggest that the artworks achieved their objective, that is, that the physical encounter with the sculptures engendered in many individuals a positive haptic experience, resulting in their being made more aware of their body's touch responses through the engagement of an unarticulated touch aesthetic that evoked tactile memories and associations.

The physical properties of the sculptures contributed to this outcome, but just as importantly, the same qualities that stimulated physical responses also elucidated tactile memories and associations that led to emotional responses[3]. This is what hapticity is: the total touch experience that is comprised of both the physical and psychological qualities of touch. Through touch, shadowy memories of intense physical intimacy can be evoked, as seen in comments such as *"Snuggling up next to an object that 'fits' with your body is quite intimate yet strange, as you are not the only person who 'fits' with that object....It's like sharing the same intimate moment that is experienced by many others but at different times in different places – people with different associations, experiences and backgrounds."* This sharing of a common experience draws on our deep human instinct to form relationships and communities.

4 Conclusions

This paper presents an artist-researcher's journey that sought to find a way to engage individuals' haptic senses to promote a sense of well-being. It started with an investigation into the fired clay surface and ended with the creation of 'cast hugs', which gallery visitors willingly handled and caressed. The positive experiences engendered through interaction with the artwork occurred because the sculptures engaged much more than just the touch of the hand. Engaging a broader range of haptic senses through the use of the body allowed for emotional memories and associations to be more fully evoked.

Approaching the subject of touch theoretically, then allowing the theory to direct developments in the studio, in which the tactile senses are privileged over the visual in a very personal haptic experience of making, has led to the creation of sculptural artworks that enhance the haptic experience of art on many levels. Artworks created in this way engage a higher level of haptic involvement, one that goes beyond the physiological and accesses an unarticulated tactile aesthetic that is realized through the metaphoric interpretation of touch memories and associations of other intimate moments of physical contact with objects, whether they be inanimate or human. The creation of art such as this is dependent upon the direct use of the artist's body, and hence, the full engagement of the artist's haptic senses. This approach to haptic research is primarily aesthetic, rather than scientific or technological, yet understanding

---

[3] In this usage, emotion does not imply sentimentality. Rather, it is understood as a core human response that determines how we live our lives and the decisions we make from moment to moment.

the experiences of both the artist and the gallery visitor, in particular, the sense of the subject/object 'blur', could have wider implications within the world of haptic design and technology.

Acknowledgement. Photographs by Adrian Newman.

References

1. Frayling, C.: Research Papers: Research in Art and Design. Royal College of Art 1(1) (April 1993)
2. Glaser, B.G., Strauss, A.L.: Discovery of Grounded Theory: Strategies for Qualitative Research. Aldine de Gruyton, Hawthorne (1999)
3. Kemske, B.: Towards a Touch Aesthetic, Intersections. In: Association of Art Historians Annual Conference, April 2-4, Manchester Metropolitan University (2009)
4. Sinclair, D.: Mechanisms of Cutaneous Sensation. Oxford University Press, Oxford (1981)
5. McNiff, S.: Art-based Research. In: Knowles, G., Cole, A. (eds.) Handbook of the Arts in Qualitative Research: Perspectives, Methodologies, Examples and Issues, p. 30. Sage Inc., Thousand Oaks (2008)
6. Barley, N.: Smashing Pots: Works of Clay from Africa. Smithsonian Institution Press, Washington (1994)
7. Merleau-Ponty, M.: The Primacy of Perception and Other Essays on Phenomenological Psychology. In: The Philosophy of Art, History and Politics, p. 37. Northwestern University Press, Evanston (1964)
8. Merleau-Ponty, M.: The Visible and the Invisible: Followed by Working Notes, p. 266. Northwestern University Press, Evanston (1968)
9. Kemske, B.: Embracing Sculptural Ceramics: A Lived Experience of Touch in Art. Senses & Society 4(3), 342 (2009)
10. Merleau-Ponty, M.: The Visible and the Invisible: Followed by Working Notes, p. 123. Northwestern University Press, Evanston (1968)

Development of Haptic Microgripper for Microassembly Operation

Shahzad Khan, Ton de Boer, Pablo Estevez, Hans H. Langen,
and Rob H. Munnig Schmidt

TU Delft, 3mE Faculty, PME Department
Mekelweg 2, Delft, The Netherlands
s.khan@tudelft.nl, deboer.ton@gmail.com,
P.EstevezCastillo@tudelft.nl, H.H.Langen@tudelft.nl,
R.H.MunnigSchmidt@tudelft.nl

Abstract. In recent times, dimensions of consumer products have decreased, with components sizes ranging down to micrometers/nanometers. In case of microproducts that are produced in low-medium quantities with many variants, the automation of their assembly process may not be economically profitable. On the other hand, the purely manual approach is not sufficient to fulfill the task with high efficiency since a human operator has limitations for the force and precision requirements. In order to overcome these difficulties, tele-haptic micro-assembly systems are a promising approach. One of the bottlenecks on the development of such a system is the micro-gripper, which should be able to perform pick-and-place of micro-objects with diverse sizes and sense the grasping force. In this work, a developmental effort to build a mechanical micro-gripper capable of sensing grasping force and transferring these forces to the human operator using a 1-DOF master device is presented. Experimental results concerning pick-and-place of micro-objects are demonstrated.

Keywords: Haptic microgripper, microassembly, teleoperation.

1 Introduction

With the advancement of recent technologies, there is a strong trend towards the miniaturization of many products, down to the micrometer and sub-micrometer range. One big challenge on the production of these products lies on the assembly of micro-parts coming from different processes or technologies: in the assembly of products consisting of micro parts, the assembly process can add up to 80% of the production costs [1]. The traditional ways of macroassembly processes, by automated positioning robots, are not always applicable, due to the requirements of high precision motion, high tolerances, and the sticking of parts to the end-effectors [2][3].

Micro-assembly is often performed manually by hand (with the support of tools) or by (semi-) automated machinery. Unfortunately, the manual approach often fails in the force and precision requirements. Moreover, the process may lead to non-consistent products and cause excessive strain to the human operator. Automated assembly systems are more reliable in terms of yield, but are not always economically profitable, especially in case of low batch production. Thus, a semi-automatic scheme

A.M.L. Kappers et al. (Eds.): EuroHaptics 2010, Part II, LNCS 6192, pp. 309–314, 2010.
© Springer-Verlag Berlin Heidelberg 2010

is favorable and is achieved by the inclusion of the human operator in the loop to perform microassembly through tele-operated systems [4] [5]. The approach is an interesting alternative to both the pure manual and the automated assembly, but the lack of force feedback increases the risk of damaging the micro components.

In order to overcome these difficulties, a tele-haptic assembly system [6] [7] approach is adopted in which the operator receives different kinds of feed back (e.g. visual, force reaction, etc.). The use of force feedback to the human operator could lead to an improved execution of human based assembly operations, in terms of time, efficiency and reliability. Moreover, it would avoid damage of the fragile parts or the micro gripper and would allow for dexterous manipulation of micro-objects. The presence of the human, opposite to the more rigid approach of automatic micro-assembly, improves the flexibility of the system due to its capability to plan, adapt, and react to unexpected situations during the assembly process.

One of the bottlenecks of this schema lies in the development of a microgripper capable of gripping objects with diverse sizes and to sense the grasping force. Different approaches have been taken to tackle this problem [8]. This paper focuses on the development of a mechanical microgripper capable of estimating the grasping force and transferring this force to the human operator using a 1-DOF master device. The developed 1DOF system is demonstrated by performing pick-and-place of micro-objects. The project was initiated by MicroNed program [9] and lies within the Microfactory cluster in the workpackage IIIB which deals with haptic application in Microsystems [10].

The Section 2 of this paper explains the design of the microgripper and Section 3 describes the experimental setup. In Section 4 the microgripper is demonstrated with the pick-and-place operation of the micro-object using human assistance. Finally, Section 6 concludes the paper and discusses future directions.

2 Design of the Microgripper

The mechanical design of the custom built sensorized micro-gripper is shown in figure 1(a). A base part is holding two aluminum fingers of 5mm x 1mm x 0.5mm, actuated by DC micromotors (Faulhaber BLDC 0206). The gripper arms are directly mounted on the shaft of the motor to reduce backlash and friction in the system. A photo-interrupter device is utilized as position sensor to sense the displacement of the gripper arms and is mounted on the rear-ends of the arms.

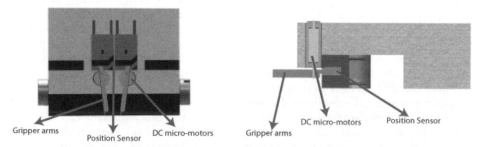

Fig. 1. (a) Mechanical design of the gripper module (b) Side view of the position sensor

Two brushless DC micro-motors have been utilized to drive the two arms of the micro-gripper. Thanks to the linearity between the current flowing through the coils and the delivered torque, a current measurement is used to estimate the grasping force between the arms and the micro-objects. Dynamics effects and non-linearities due to friction and play in the mechanisms may distort this relation. Even if this work does not consider such effects, they must be taken into account in the model if increasing the accuracy is a concern. Two optical sensors measure the absolute position of the respective gripper arms as shown in figure 1(b). The output of the optical sensors depends on the amount of light blocked by the gripper arms, providing a measurement of their displacement.

3 Description of the Experimental Setup

A 1DOF haptic teleoperation system is developed as a proof-of-concept for the micro-gripper. The device is integrated with a previously developed master device for pinching tasks [11], a control structure and a human-machine interface. The overall schematic of the system is shown in figure 2. A simple two-channel bilateral controller in Position-Force scheme (direct force feedback) is utilized. The human operator dictates the position reference to the slave device through the master device by varying the distance between the gripper fingers. This displacement is sensed by the LVDT sensor and feed to the dSpace controller board. The algorithm controls the slave position, while using the optical sensor as a feedback. The slave force measurement is transferred back to the master device, where a force sensor closes a local control loop. In that way, the human operator feels the resistive forces corresponding to the grasping forces at the slave side. One CCD camera is employed to visualize the top view of the slave side for human-machine interface along with the real-time data from the dSPACE controller card.

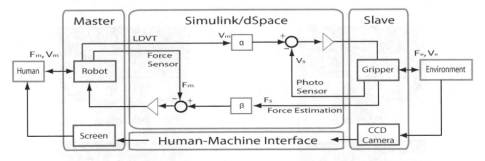

Fig. 2. Overall schematic of the experimental setup

A factor "alpha" is used to scale the position commands from the operator to the slave, while "beta" scales the forces from the slave to the master side. In the ideal condition, the steady state condition of the bilateral controller should be Eqn. (1).

$$X_s = \alpha X_m \tag{1}$$
$$F_m = \beta F_s$$

X_m, X_s denote the master and the slave position respectively and F_m, F_s denote the master and the slave force respectively. A value of $\alpha = 0.031$ is selected to provide very fine motion on the slave side for relatively larger displacements of the master. In order to protect the parts and match the acting and sensing ranges of master and slave, forces are scaled by a factor $\beta = 6000$. The resulting rendered impedance does not mirror that of the remote environment, being in this case much higher in order to protect the micro-parts. This can be adjusted depending on the task requirements.

The micro objects lie in an off-the-shelve *(x,y,z)* stage which performs the required displacement in the millimeters range. This system is currently driven independently and not integrated in the control schema.

4 Experimental Validation of the Micro-gripper Concept

To validate the experimental setup, snapshots of single pick-and-place operation of micro-sphere (SiLibead of type 9405) of diameter 0.5 mm using the haptic interface are shown in figure 3(a) till 3(d), while the corresponding position/grasping force tracking is shown in figure 4.

At t = 0 the experiment starts with the gripper placed in open position. Between t = 3.5s and t = 8.3s the gripper is commanded to fully closed position which is reached at t = 5.3s, and back to the initial state without any interaction with micro-object. The rise in the forces at the slave side is caused by the friction in the actuator. At t = 18s the micro-object is moved in-between the gripper arms using the xyz-stage. The gripper is closed until significant force is felt by the human operator to ensure that the micro-object is grasped firmly which occurs at t = 30s. From t = 30s till 57.5s, the micro-object is grasped firmly in air and the base stage is moved to the desired location. Finally, at t = 59s the micro-object is dropped at the pre-defined location and the grasping force becomes zero.

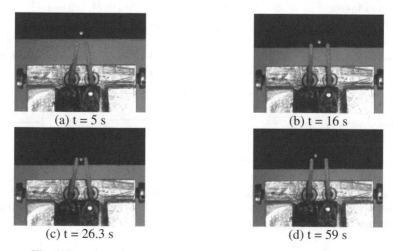

(a) t = 5 s   (b) t = 16 s

(c) t = 26.3 s   (d) t = 59 s

Fig. 3. Snapshot of single pick-and-place operation of a micro-sphere

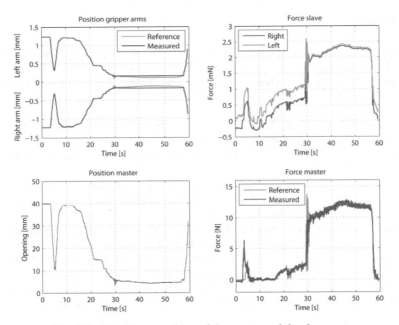

Fig. 4. Position/force tracking of the master and the slave system

5   Conclusion and Future Works

In this work, a developmental effort to realize a microgripper with force feedback mechanism has been demonstrated. Moreover, as a proof-of-concept a 1DOF haptic master device has been interfaced, and experimental results concerning pick-and-place of micro-objects using a haptic interface have been demonstrated.

Methods for measuring the interaction forces in the microenvironment are no readily available, and gripping, releasing and positioning mechanisms are currently been studied. The design of a master device specially tailored to the application has also produced interesting results [10]. It is also necessary to understand the effect of certain mechanical design decisions on the operator experience. Preliminary studies in virtual environments have analyzed the effect of different operation and assistance modes, mechanical architectures and specifications on the user. In order to extend and verify these studies, an of-the-shelve 4DOF assembly station is been set by joining micropositioners, microgrippers and a master device. Once the integrated assembly system is developed, further studies must be conducted to asses the impact of the use of force feedback in tele-operated microassembly tasks.

Acknowledgments. The authors would like to acknowledge the financial support from MicroNed [9], and technical discussions with Prof. Dr. F.C.T. van der Helm.

References

1. Staiger, A., Degen, R.: Micro-assembly technologies and applications. IFIP International Federation for Information Processing 260, 257–263 (2008)
2. Fantoni, G., Porta, M.: A critical review of releasing strategies in microparts handling. In: Fourth International Precision Assembly Seminar IPAS 2008, Chamonix, February 11-13 (2008)
3. Menciassi, A., Eisinberg, A., Izzo, I., Dario, P.: From 'Macro' to 'Micro' Manipulation: Models and Experiments. IEEE/ASME Trans. on Mechatronics 9(2), 311–320 (2004)
4. Kunt, E.D.: Design and Realization of a Microassembly Workstation, MS Thesis, Sabanci University (2006)
5. Mitsuishi, M., Watanabe, T., Nakanishi, H., Hori, T., Watanabe, H., Kramer, B.: A tele-micro-surgery system across the Internet with a fixed viewpoint/ operation-point. In: IROS 1995, Pittsburgh, Pennsylvania, USA (August 1995)
6. Khan, S., Sabanovic, A.: Force Feedback pushing Scheme for Micromanipulation Applications. Journal of Micro-Nano Mechatronics 2009 (2009)
7. Khan, S., Sabanovic, A., Nergiz, A.O.: Scaled Bilateral Teleoperation using Discrete-Time Sliding Mode Controller. IEEE Transaction on Industrial Electronics (2006)
8. Cecil, J., Vasquez, D., Powell, D.: A review of gripping and manipulation techniques for micro-assembly applications. International Journal of Production Research 43(4), 819 (2005)
9. http://www.microned.nl
10. Estevez, P., et al.: A Haptic Tele-operated system for Microassembly. In: IPAS 2010, Fifth International Precision Assembly Seminar, France (2010)
11. Fritz, E.C., Christiansson, G.A.V., van der Linde, R.Q.: Haptic Gripper with Adjustable Inherent Passive Properties. In: Proceedings of EuroHaptic 2004, Munich Germany, June 5-7 (2004)

A Haptic Gearshift Interface for Cars

Eloísa García-Canseco[1], Alain Ayemlong-Fokem[1],
Alex Serrarens[2], and Maarten Steinbuch[1]

[1] Eindhoven University of Technology, Faculty of Mechanical Engineering,
Control Systems Technology Group,
PO Box 513, 5600 MB Eindhoven, The Netherlands
[2] Drivetrain Innovations BV, Croy 46, 5653 LD Eindhoven, The Netherlands
{e.garcia.canseco,m.steinbuch}@tue.nl,
a.ayemlong.fokem@student.tue.nl,
serrarens@dtinnovations.nl

Abstract. This paper presents a two degrees–of–freedom haptic interface that uses force control to reproduce the behavior of a customary lever and gearshift in automotive applications. The haptic simulation of the gear selector lever has been done by the appropriated design of virtual artificial potential functions. These functions contain parameters that have intuitive physical meaning and that can be easily adjusted to change the force sensations fed to the user. To validate our approach, experiments have been carried out.

Keywords: haptic device, gearshift, automobile.

1 Introduction

The automotive industry is experiencing not only a strong enhancement of automation in primary driving tasks, e.g., automated gear shifting, lane-keeping systems, adaptive cruise control, park-assists, automatic hill-hold, brake-by-wire, etc, but also, the introduction of more auxiliaries and interior functions, e.g., USB-connectors, mp3 players, navigation, among others. These trends lower the driver's workload significantly, and draw the driver's attention more and more to the interior functions of the car. Adding more functionality to vehicles increases driver satisfaction or pleasure, however, it can also lead to a significant increase of driver distraction. Haptic cues might offer a promising and relatively unexplored alternative to give warnings and other messages to the driver, and also to aid drivers in the execution of their driving tasks.

The term "haptic" comes from the Greek word *haptesthai*, which refers to the sense of touch. Accordingly, haptic interfaces are devices that provide humans with the means to act on their environment, by generating mechanical signals that stimulate the human touch senses [1].

In the recent years, the automotive industry has been taking a keen interest in haptic [2]. Car makers such as BMW, Audi, Lexus, Nissan and many more have already installed haptic interfaces in their automobiles. Haptic devices in the car can be classified in two categories [3]: a) devices that are constantly in contact with the driver, for instance, the haptic steering wheel [4,5,6,7,8,9], the Nissan haptic gas pedal, and the

A.M.L. Kappers et al. (Eds.): EuroHaptics 2010, Part II, LNCS 6192, pp. 315–320, 2010.

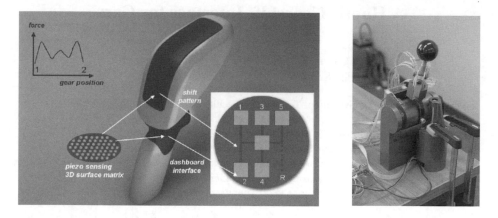

Fig. 1. (left) Haptic gearshift interface concept. (right) 2–dof haptic interface.

haptic car seat. Some of these devices use vibration to give the haptic feedback and they can be used to give warnings to the driver; b) devices that the driver must actively touch. Examples are buttons, knobs, levers and tactile displays, such as the BMW iDrive [10], the Immersion TouchSense [11]. See also [12,13,14,15] for other applications of haptic in automotive environments.

In this paper we investigate a controlled haptic force feedback shift lever that can accurately reproduce the behavior of a customary gearshift during driving, and that might also be used to control interior and comfort functions in the car (Fig. 1). As stated in [12], the primary advantage of haptic levers over customary gear selectors is their ability to reproduce the behavior of manual, automatic or semi–automatic transmissions by simply changing the virtual environment, i.e., the force profiles (haptic patterns in Fig. 2).

2   Description of the System

The main parts of the system are illustrated in Fig. 2 and can be summarized as follows.

2.1   The Haptic Interface

The haptic interface (Fig. 1 (right)) is a two degrees–of–freedom mechatronic device, whose working principle is based on the self–locking property of a worm pair transmission [16]. Without actuation, it is therefore impossible to force the worm to rotate by applying a force to the lever mounted on the worm gear. That is, the operator experiences infinite stiffness of hitting a wall when there is no current fed to the electrical actuator. Vice versa, the actuator is able to move the worm gear and lever around their rotation axis rather easily. The transmission ratio from worm to worm gear can be very large, offering thus a good speed reduction and smaller work load on the actuators. One advantage of this worm pair transmission is the low power consumption, more feedback force requires less power and there is no consumption at all when the lever is kept at its rest position [17].

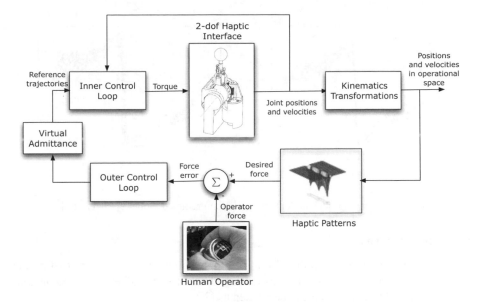

Fig. 2. Control scheme for the haptic simulation of a gear selector lever

The link between the hardware and software is provided by the hardware server and controller board that come along with the dSpace© software. The DS1102 controller board provides the inputs and output ports. This controller board is connected via a 62–pin SUB-D connector cable to the hardware server, which is build as a standard PC card. The dSpace© software contains the *Controldesk* testing environment, the *RTLib1102* real time interface Simulink© library blockset and the Texas Instrument TMS320C ANSI C compiler.

To implement model–based control strategies on the system, the dynamical model of the haptic interface has been obtained in the Euler–Lagrange framework (see for instance [18]) as

$$\mathbf{M}(q)\ddot{q} + \mathbf{C}(q,\dot{q})\dot{q} + g(q) + \tau_f = \tau - \mathbf{J}^T(q)f_e,$$

where $q \in \mathbb{R}^2$ is the vector of joint displacements, $\dot{q} \in \mathbb{R}^2$ is the vector of joint velocities, $\mathbf{M}(q) \in \mathbb{R}^{2\times2}$ is a positive definite inertia matrix, $\mathbf{C}(q,\dot{q})\dot{q} \in \mathbb{R}^2$ is the vector of centripetal and Coriolis torques, $g(q) \in \mathbb{R}^2$ is the vector of gravitational torques, $\tau \in \mathbb{R}^2$ is the vector of actuation torques, $\mathbf{J} \in \mathbb{R}^{3\times2}$ is the Jacobian matrix and $f_e \in \mathbb{R}^3$ is the interaction force vector with the environment. The friction torque $\tau_f \in \mathbb{R}^2$ is given by

$$\tau_f = \left[\tau_c + (\tau_s - \tau_c) \exp\left(-\left| \frac{\dot{q}}{\dot{q}_s} \right|^\delta \right) + b|\dot{q}| \right] \tanh(\lambda\dot{q}), \tag{1}$$

which corresponds to a modified static friction model with Stribeck velocity [19] (Fig. 3), where $\lambda \in \mathbb{R}$ and $\delta \in \mathbb{R}^2$ are adjusting parameters, and the constant vectors $\tau_c, \tau_s, \dot{q}_s, b \in \mathbb{R}^2$ represent the coulomb friction coefficients, the static friction coefficients, the Stribeck velocities, and the velocity coefficients, respectively.

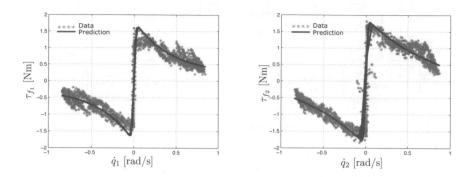

Fig. 3. Friction empirical model versus friction predicted model $\tau_f = [\tau_{f_1}, \tau_{f_2}]^T$

2.2 Force Patterns

We have borrowed some inspiration from [20] to design the haptic patterns that mimic the behavior of a desired gearshift transmission. These force profiles are based on generalized sigmoid functions and can be written as [20]

$$U_d(p) = \sum_{i=1}^{M} \prod_{j=1}^{N} f_{sig_i}(\phi_j(p)), \tag{2}$$

where $p = [x, y, z]^T$ is the position vector of a point in space, $\phi_j(p)$ is a surface function and

$$f_{sig_i}(\phi_j(p)) = \frac{1}{1 + \exp(-\gamma\phi_j(p))}$$

is the generalized sigmoid function. The value of γ depends on the application at hand [20]. In our case, the value of γ is related to the user's preference for force magnitude.

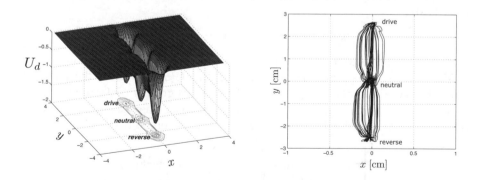

Fig. 4. (left) Virtual potential energy function $U_d(x, y)$ that mimics an automatic gearshift. x and y represent the position of the lever in the horizontal plane xy. The desired force patterns are generated from the negative gradient of U_d as $f_d = -\frac{\partial U_d}{\partial p}$. (right) Experimental results.

The two main advantages of this technique are on one hand, the smoothness of the force field, due to continuous first and higher order derivatives, and on the other hand, the easy adjustment of the magnitude and effective range of the potential field. To generate the desired attractive forces, the negative gradient of equation (2) is computed as

$$f_d(p) = -\frac{\partial U_d}{\partial p}.$$ (3)

Fig. 4 (left) illustrates the artificial potential fields which have been designed to replicate the behavior of an automatic transmission.

2.3 Experimental Results

As depicted in Fig. 2, we have implemented a hierarchical control scheme consisting of two loops: the inner–control loop is a position controller with friction compensation based on inverse dynamics control [18]. This controller computes the input torques as a function of the joint positions and velocities. The outer control loop is a PID force controller with anti–windup [21]. This force controller compute the necessary set points as a function of the measured human force and the force generated by the haptic pattern in order to provide a haptic feeling to the operator. Fig. 4 (right) shows the experimental results for the automatic gearshift. The picture has been drawn during 20 trials in which the user changes the gear many times randomly. We notice that the movements are constrained by the force patterns generated by eq. (3), see also Fig. 4 (left).

3   Conclusions and Future Work

We have presented the preliminary results of a haptic interface that can be used to test different automobile gearshifts. Current work is ongoing to implement the force patterns of semi–automatic and manual gearshift transmissions. In the same spirit of [13], we plan to develop a graphical user interface, were users can easily determine the behavior of the gearshift, and select the desired force profiles.

Acknowledgments. This research is supported by the SenterNovem IOP Man—Machine Interaction Project MMI07105 "Control solutions for human–in–the–loop user interfaces" and by DTI Automotive Mechatronics BV.

References

[1] Hayward, V., Astley, O.R., Cruz-Hernández, M., Grant, D., de-la Torre, G.R.: Haptic interfaces and devices. Sensor Review 24(1), 16–29 (2004)
[2] Bigelow, S.J.: Haptics make it happen. Smart Computing (2004)
[3] Hjelm, J.: Haptics in cars. In: Seminar Haptic Communication and Interaction in Mobile Contexts (2008)
[4] van Erp, J.B.F., van Veen, H.A.H.C.: Vibro-tactile information presentation in automobiles. In: Proc. Eurohaptics 2001, Birmingham, UK, pp. 99–104 (2001)

[5] Enriquez, M., Afonin, O., Yager, B., Maclean, K.: A pneumatic tactile alerting system for the driving environment. In: Proc. of the 2001 Workshop on Perceptive User Interfaces, pp. 1–7 (2001)

[6] Ho, C., Tan, H.Z., Spence, C.: Using spatial vibrotactile cues to direct visual attention in driving scenes. Transportation Research Part F: Traffic Psychology and Behaviour 8(6), 397–412 (2005)

[7] Toffin, D., Reymond, G., Kemeny, A., Droulez, J.: Influence of steering wheel torque feedback in a dynamic driving simulator. In: Driving Simulation Conference North America, Dearborn, MI, USA (2003)

[8] Mohellebi, H., Kheddar, A., Espie, S.: Adaptive haptic feedback steering wheel for driving simulators. IEEE Transactions on Vehicular Technology 58(4), 1654–1666 (2009)

[9] Steele, M., Gillespie, R.B.: Shared control between human and machine: Using a haptic steering wheel to aid in land vehicle guidance. Human Factors and Ergonomics Society Annual Meeting Proceedings 45, 1671–1675 (2001)

[10] Bernstein, A., Bader, B., Bengler, K., Künzner, H.: Visual-haptic interfaces in car design at BMW. In: Human Haptic Perception: Basics and Applications, pp. 445–451 (2008)

[11] Immersion corp., http://www.immersion.com

[12] Bengoechea, E., Sánchez, E., Savall, J.: Optimal cost haptic devices for driving simulators. In: Redondo, M., et al. (eds.) Engineering the User Interface, pp. 29–43. Springer, Heidelberg (2009)

[13] Gil, J., Díaz, I., Iturritxa, E., Prieto, B.: A haptic interface for automobile gearshift design and benchmark. In: Ferre, M. (ed.) EuroHaptics 2008. LNCS, vol. 5024, pp. 906–911. Springer, Heidelberg (2008)

[14] Angerilli, M., Frisoli, A., Salsedo, F., Marcheschi, S., Bergamasco, M.: Haptic simulation of an automotive manual gearshift. In: Proceedings of 10th IEEE International Workshop on Robot and Human Interactive Communication, pp. 170–175 (2001)

[15] Frisoli, A., Avizzano, C., Bergamasco, M.: Simulation of a manual gearshift with a 2-DOF force-feedback joystick. In: IEEE International Conference on Robotics and Automation, Proceedings 2001 ICRA, vol. 2, pp. 1364–1369 (2001)

[16] Serrarens, A.: Gear changing device for automotive applications. Patent AF16H5904FI (2005)

[17] van Diepen, K.: Dynamic haptic control for a 1–dof shift–by–wire system. In: Confidential DCT 2008.71, Eindhoven University of Technology, Eindhoven, The Netherlands (2008)

[18] Spong, M., Vidyasagar, M.: Robot dynamics and control. Wiley, Chichester (1989)

[19] Olsson, H., Astrom, K., de Wit, C.C., Gafvert, M., Lischinsky, P.: Friction models and friction compensation. European Journal of Control 4 (1998)

[20] Ren, J., McIssaac, K.A., Patel, R.V., Peters, T.M.: A potential field model using generalized sigmoid functions. IEEE Transactions on Systems, Man and Cybernetics–Part B: Cybernetics 37(2), 477–484 (2007)

[21] Astrom, K., Haaglund, T.: Advanced PID control. ISA–The Instrumentation, Systems and Automation Society (2005)

Proprioceptive Acuity Varies with Task, Hand Target, and When Memory Is Used

Stephanie A.H. Jones[1], Katja Fiehler[2], and Denise Y.P. Henriques[1]

[1] Centre for Vision Research & School of Kinesiology and Health Science York University,
Toronto, Ontario, Canada
[2] Philipps University Marburg, Marburg, Germany
sahj0812@yorku.ca, fiehler@staff.uni-marburg.de,
deniseh@yorku.ca

Abstract. Participants completed a series of seven tasks to assess proprioceptive acuity of each hand. Proprioceptive localization was fairly accurate and precise. Constant error and precision differences were found as a function of the task, movement of the hand target, the hand being localized, and localization from memory.

Keywords: Proprioception, reach, reproduction, estimation, task factors.

1 Introduction

Although planning a reach to a proprioceptive target (e.g. a hand) incorporates proprioceptive information from the target and the reaching hand, reach tasks are often used as means to explore proprioceptive acuity [e.g. 1, 2, 3]. To circumvent this problem, Jones et al. [4] presented a novel proprioceptive estimation task in which participants indicated the felt location of a hand target (either left or right) relative to visual references or their body's midline. They sought to determine if behavioural differences would arise between a task in which the central nervous system (CNS) used proprioceptive information to plan a goal directed movement to the hand target and a more perceptual task in which no such planning was required. Much like visual information [5], research has suggested differential processing of proprioceptive information for perception and action [6]. Jones et al. [4] found no differences across these two task types. Our purpose was to (1) systematically compare this proprioceptive estimation task to a reach task and (2) to expand on the findings of Jones et al. [4] by comparing this estimation task to a spatial reproduction task (described below) using the same subjects and the same target locations. Our third, novel, aim was to examine if proprioceptive acuity would differ between online and remembered proprioceptive localization in our estimation task. While decays in proprioceptive memory have been shown in reach tasks [7], it was unknown if such decays would also occur when the proprioceptive information was not used to guide a goal directed movement. Our fourth aim was to compare the left and right hand-targets and active and passive placement of the hand-target prior to localization.

A.M.L. Kappers et al. (Eds.): EuroHaptics 2010, Part II, LNCS 6192, pp. 321–326, 2010.

2 Method

2.1 Subjects

Fifteen self- reported right handed participants (9 males; Mean age = 22.2 yrs) volunteered to participate in the present experiment.

2.2 Experimental Setup and Procedure

A schematic of the experimental set up is shown in Figure 1. Participants sat on a height adjustable chair in front of a 90 cm high table (Fig. 1A and C). Participants rested their head on a chin rest located 40 cm above the table top (not shown in figure). Participants grasped the vertical handle of a two-jointed robot manipulandum (Interactive Motion Technologies Inc., Cambridge, MA) with their unseen hand (either right or left); the thumb rested on top of the robot handle (1.4 cm in diameter) and the handle was at approximately waist level (Fig. 1A and C). The robot manipulandum either moved the hand passively, from the start position (body midline, 23.5cm in front of the body; shown in 1D) in a single direction to one of the target positions (12 cm from the start position, in front of the body midline, or 5 cm left or right of body midline; Fig. 1 B and D), or restricted participants' active movement along a straight constrained path until the hand reached the target location (constrained paths shown in 1D). In our proprioceptive estimation tasks, a computer screen projected visual references (1cm in diameter, Fig. 1B) onto a reflective surface above the robot handle (Fig. 1A). A touch screen® (Keytec Inc., Garland, TX) was used to record reach endpoints in our reach tasks (Fig. 1 C and D). Participants could see their reaching arm in the dimly lit room. The target hand/arm was covered using a cloth in all tasks.

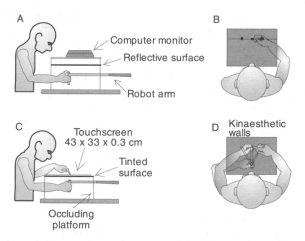

Fig. 1. (A) Side view of the experimental setup used for the proprioceptive estimation tasks. (B) Above view of the visual reference locations for the proprioceptive estimation tasks (same as target locations used in the reaching and reproduction tasks). (C) Side view of the experimental setup used in the reaching and reproduction tasks. (D) Above view of the target locations for the reaching and reproduction tasks.

Participants localized the unseen left or right hand using one of three task types: estimation, reach, or reproduction. In the proprioceptive estimation tasks, the hand target was actively or passively moved from the start position to a location to the left or right of one of three visual references (Fig. 1B). The visual reference appeared once the hand target reached this designated location, and participants indicated if the felt position of the hand was to the left or right of this reference (a 2 alternative forced choice task, 2AFC) [4]. In the remembered proprioceptive estimation task, participants actively placed and returned their hand to the start location before the visual reference appeared; participants indicated if the remembered location of their hand was to the left or right of this reference. In the proprioceptively guided reach tasks, the hand target was actively or passively moved from the start position to one of the three target locations (same as reference marker locations). Participants then reached with the opposite hand to the felt location of the hand target, or in the case of the remembered reach task (always active movement), reached to the remembered location of the hand target (Fig. 1D). In our reproduction task, participants reproduced the spatial location of the hand target using the same hand (always active movement and remembered). Participants actively moved the hand target (guided by the robot) to a target position and then returned it to the start. Constraints on movement (applied by the robot) were then removed; participants moved the hand target back to where they felt it had been using the robot. For the reaching and reproduction tasks, subjects moved to each target with each hand 40 times, for a total of 240 trials for each of the four tasks.

2.3   Assessing Proprioceptive Localization Accuracy and Precision

In our estimation tasks, a 2AFC adaptive staircase algorithm was used to adjust the position of the hand target across trials depending on the subject's pattern of left or right responses [see 4]. For each reference location there were two corresponding staircases, for which the hand target began either 3 cm left or right of the reference marker, which were adjusted independently and randomly interleaved (three pairs of staircases – left and right for each reference - each made up 50 trials, for a total of 150 trials for each estimation task). We fitted a logistic function to the responses for each reference marker (pair of staircases), for each participant, in each condition. Thus, for each reference marker, we computed the bias (the point of 50% probability), which is a measure of accuracy, and the uncertainty (the difference between the positions where the hand was judged left or right of a reference marker 84% of the time) which is a measure of precision [see 8]. In the reaching and reproduction tasks, the horizontal difference between the actual location of the hand target and the reach or reproduction endpoint was computed.

We conducted two 2(hand: left or right hand) x 2(task: estimation or reach) x 2(movement: active or passive) x 3(target: left, center, right) RM ANOVAs to compare both biases and precision across the estimation and reach tasks. We use separate RM ANOVAs to compare accuracy and precision among the remembered tasks (reach, estimation, reproduction). Alpha was set at 0.05 and pairwise comparisons were Bonferroni corrected.

3   Results

Figure 2 displays average biases (solid symbols) as a function of task (bar color), target location (shape of the symbols), for the left hand-target (top) and right hand-target (bottom). If participants perfectly estimated the felt location of the hand target, the symbols would fall on the horizontal black line at zero. The length of each box represents the precision of localization. In the proprioceptive estimation paradigms (green bars), the ends of the box are the locations where participants judged the hand target to be left (bottom of the box) or right (top of the box) of the target location 84% of the time (encompassing the middle 68% of the distribution of estimates). In our reach and reproduction tasks, the ends of the box represent the bias ± 1 standard deviation (also the middle 68% of the distribution) [8].

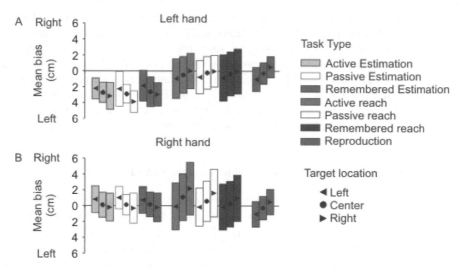

Fig. 2. Average biases (in cm) for the left (A) and right (B) hand targets as a function of task type, movement, and target location

3.1   Task Type

Our first aim was to compare the three measures of proprioceptive acuity. Overall, horizontal errors were deviated more leftward in the estimation tasks than in the reach and reproduction tasks. Reaches were also significantly less precise (blue bars) than estimations (green bars) and reproductions (red bars). As discussed below, these differences between conditions also varied with hand target and target position.

3.2   Localization from Memory

Our second aim was to examine proprioceptive localization from memory. Participants were less precise when reaching to the remembered location of a proprioceptive target (dark blue bars) than when reaching online (light blue solid and open bars). No differences were found between online and remembered estimation conditions (light solid and open, and dark green bars). When comparing among remembered tasks (remembered estimation – dark green solid bars, remembered reach – dark blue solid bars and reproduction – red bars), no accuracy differences were found. But, remembered reaches were significantly less precise than reproductions and remembered estimations, although reaches were found to be less precise than estimations and reproductions overall (as stated above).

3.3 Hand Target

In our active and passive reach, and estimation tasks, horizontal errors for the left hand were biased to the left (green and blue bars top panel) and horizontal errors for the right hand were biased to the right (green and blue bars bottom panel). Overall, reaches to the right hand (left hand reaching) were significantly less precise than reaches to the left hand (right hand reaching).

3.4 Active and Passive Movement of the Hand Target

No differences in horizontal error or precision were found between the active and passive conditions in our reach and estimation tasks.

3.5 Target Position

Horizontal errors were deviated more leftward for the right target location (rightward pointing triangles) and more rightward for the left target location (leftward pointing triangles) in our active and passive reach (light blue and dark blue open bars), and reproduction tasks (red bars). Precision did not differ across the target positions.

4 Discussion

This is the first comprehensive comparison between reach and reproduction tasks, and our estimation task. Overall, while participants were fairly accurate and precise when localizing an unseen hand, we found that proprioceptive acuity differed across tasks and task parameters. Reaches were significantly less precise than estimations and reproductions, regardless of whether active or passive movement was used, or localization occurred from memory. This finding suggests that proprioceptively guided reach tasks (goal directed movement tasks) may elicit noisier estimates of hand target position. For example, processing proprioceptive information about the target and reaching hand, and the need to synthesize that information to plan a goal directed movement, may introduce more variability for proprioceptive guided reaching. As such, unless the primary aim of a study is to examine sensory processing for goal directed movements, measurement methods that are perceptual (such as our estimation task) may be more appropriate for drawing general conclusions about how well we can localize a body part in space. Our results suggest a slight disadvantage (in precision) when localizing a proprioceptive target from memory in a reach task [9, 12]. Greater variability was also found in the remembered reach task as compared to the other remembered tasks, but this could not be separated from the overall greater variability found for reaches. Research has previously reported that reaches made to the left hand are deviated leftward and reaches made to the right hand are deviated rightward [2, 3, 4, 10], but it has been unclear whether such biases would persist if the proprioceptive localization task did not include a goal directed movement. We and Jones et al. [4] have found that these biases are consistent in our estimation task. These biases may not be due to the reaching hand; participants seem to truly perceive their left hand to be more leftward and their right hand to be more rightward. The discrepancy between previously reported accuracy differences between active and passive placement of the hand target [1, 13] and our findings may be because of the method used to place the hand target in our task. Our robot manipulandum limits noise introduced into the somatosensory system from extraneous movements (e.g. as compared to when a hand is passively moved by an experimenter, or self-guided using tactile or instruction cues). Also, active and passive placements of a proprioceptive target do not always differ [4, 14]. Contrary to some reach tasks [3], we did not find any differences in precision across target positions. Although like others [11], we did find differences in accuracy: errors were biased to the right for the left target and left for the right target, regardless of hand target.

References

1. Adamovich, S.V., Berkinblit, M.B., Fookson, O., Poizner, H.: Pointing in 3D space to remembered targets I. Kinesthetic versus visual target presentation. J. Neurophysiol. 79, 2833–2846 (1998)
2. Sarlegna, F.R., Sainburg, R.L.: The effect of target modality on visual and proprioceptive contributions to the control of movement distance. Exp. Brain. Res. 176, 267–280 (2007)
3. van Beers, R.J., Sittig, A.C., Denier van der Gon, J.J.: The precision of proprioceptive position sense. Exp. Brain. Res. 122, 367–377 (1998)
4. Jones, S.A., Cressman, E.K., Henriques, D.Y.: Proprioceptive localization of the left and right hands. Experimental Brain Research (2009), doi:10.1007/s00221-009-2079-8
5. Goodale, M.A., Milner, A.D.: Separate visual pathways for perception and action. Trends in Neuroscience 15, 20–25 (1992)
6. Dijkerman, C.H., de Haan, E.H.F.: Somatosensory processes subserving perception and action. Behav. and Brain Sciences 30, 189–239 (2007)
7. Wann, J.P., Ibrahim, S.F.: Does limb proprioception drift? Exp. Brain Res. 91, 162–166 (1992)
8. Reuschel, J., Drewing, K., Henriques, D.Y.P., Rösler, F., Fiehler, K.: Optimal integration of visual and proprioceptive movement information for the perception of trajectory geometry. Exp. Brain Res. 201, 853–862 (2009)
9. Desmurget, M., Vindras, P., Gréa, H., Viviani, P., Grafton, S.: Proprioception does not quickly drift during visual occlusion. Exp. Brain Res. 134, 363–377 (2000)
10. Haggard, P., Newman, C., Blundell, J., Andrew, H.: The perceived position of the hand in space. Percept and Psychophysics 68, 363–377 (2000)
11. Fuentes, C.T., Bastian, A.J.: Where is your arm? Variations in proprioception across space and tasks. Journal of Neurophysiology 103, 164–171 (2009)
12. Jones, S.A.H., Hideg, C., Henriques, D.Y.P.: Paper presented at the Society for Neuroscience, Washington, DC (2008)
13. Laufer, Y., Hocherman, S., Dickstein, R.: Accuracy of reproducing hand position when using active compared with passive movement. Physiotherapy Research International 6, 65–75 (2001)
14. Monaco, S., Kroliczak, G., Quinlan, D.J., Fattori, P., Galletti, C., Goodale, M.A., Culham, J.C.: Contribution of visual and proprioceptive information to the precision of reaching movements. Exp. Brain Res. 202, 15–32 (2009)

Size-Change Detection Thresholds of a Hand-Held Bar at Rest and during Movement

Gabriel Baud-Bovy[1], Valentina Squeri[2], and Vittorio Sanguineti[2,3]

[1] Vita-Salute San Raffaele University & IIT Network Research
Unit of Molecular Neuroscience, San Raffaele Foundation, Milan, Italy
[2] Italian Institute of Technology, Genova, Italy
[3]University of Genova, Italy
baud-bovy.gabriel@hsr.it, valentina.squeri@iit.it,
vittorio.sanguineti@unige.it

Abstract. We measured the minimum transient change of length of a bimanu-
ally hand-held bar that could be detected. A bimanual haptic interface was used
to haptically render the bar in a static condition and two dynamic conditions involving discrete movements. The detection thresholds were much lower in the
static (< 2 mm) than in the dynamic conditions (> 10 mm). This finding
suggests that our proprioceptive acuity markedly decreases during movement.

Keywords: proprioception, position sense, bimanual hand movement, grasping.

1 Introduction

Kinesthesia is classically divided into a position sense and a movement sense [1].
Studies involving tendon vibrations and ultra-slow movements have shown that it is
possible to dissociate these two senses to some extent [2]. In addition, it is necessary
to further distinguish between a *static position sense*, the perception of joint angle in
absence of movement, and a *dynamic position sense*, the perception of joint angle
during movement [3]. In fact, it has been proposed that different neurophysiological
mechanisms might underlie *slow position percepts* during movement at very
low velocities and *fast position percepts* for moderate-to-fast velocities because the
detection thresholds for passive movements increase markedly at low speeds [2].

Classical paradigms to study proprioception include the reproduction with the same
limb of a location, posture, or distance and the detection of passive movement of the
other limb. Relatively few studies have investigated the precision with which one
knows the position of his limb during voluntary movement. The question is difficult
since there is no obvious way of reporting the perceived position of a limb during
movement. Some have measured the precision with which humans indicate when the
unseen hand passes through a target angle [3]. Others have measured passive movement detection thresholds with actively contracted muscles [4].

In this research, we asked participants to indicate whether the length of a virtual bar
that they held by its extremities with both hands increased or decreased in a static and
two dynamic conditions. To prevent the possibility of using static cues in the dynamic
conditions, the change of bar length was brief so as to occur during the movement.

A.M.L. Kappers et al. (Eds.): EuroHaptics 2010, Part II, LNCS 6192, pp. 327–332, 2010.
© Springer-Verlag Berlin Heidelberg 2010

2 Material and Methods

2.1 Subjects

Six right-handed subjects (1 male, 5 females, age = 27.17 ± 1.18 y), with no known neuromuscular disorders and naïve to the task, participated in the experiment. All participants gave their informed consent prior to testing. The study was approved by the local ethics committee.

2.2 Experimental Setup and Procedure

The experimental setup was a bimanual manipulandum with a large elliptical work-space (80 x 40 cm) made of two 2-degrees-of-freedom parallelogram mechanical structures, each powered by two direct-drive brushless motors [6]. The manipulandum had low intrinsic mechanical impedance at the end-effector (inertia <1 kg; negligible viscosity and friction). It provided a high level of back-drivability and a good isotropy (manipulability index = 0.23 ± 0.02; force/torque ratio = 2.21 ± 0.19 N/Nm) with a large available force level at the handle (continuous force: 50 N; peak force: 200 N) allowing for experiencing a wide range of haptic stimuli. The controller consisted of three nested loops with a 16-kHz sampling rate (current loop) and 1-kHz rate (imped-ance control loop), plus a 100-Hz virtual reality loop. The software environment was based on Python, RT-Lab® and Simulink®.

The participants stood in front of the manipulandum and grasped its handles with the arms flexed (see Fig. 1B). A virtual bar (0.15 m) linked the two handles. The virtual bar was modeled as a linear spring, connecting the two handles of the manipu-landum (stiffness = 2500 N/m and damping = 30 N/m/s). The participants controlled the movements of the bar, which could move freely in the horizontal plane throughout the experiment. Depending on the trial, the length of the virtual bar was linearly in-creased or decreased over the course of 0.25 s and then linearly brought back to its initial length over the course of the following 0.25 s. The transient duration of the stimulus (0.5 s) prevented the use of static cues.

A screen was positioned horizontally above the manipulandum to show the posi-tion of the bar while hiding the hands. The bar was represented by a white rectangle with fixed dimensions (0.15 x 0.04 m) aligned with the actual position of the virtual bar. The screen was also used to indicate the reference position in the static position, and the initial and final positions in the dynamic conditions (see Fig. 1).

At the end of each trial, subjects were asked to indicate whether the length of the bar had lengthened or shortened (forced choice response). The intensity of the stimu-lus (i.e. the size and direction of change of the virtual bar length) was controlled by two interlaced QUESTs that targeted 17% and 83% percent of *positive* responses (i.e., "bar lengthened") respectively. This procedure ensures that the subject is tested with stimuli near the "corners" of the psychometric function, which is crucial to obtain a reliable estimate of its slope [7].

All subjects were tested under three different experimental conditions, the order of which was counterbalanced across subjects. Each experimental condition included 80 trials. In the static condition (ST), the participants had to keep the virtual bar above a visual displayed grey bar (0.15 x 0.04 m) at the center of the screen throughout the trial (see Fig. 1). When the bar was well centered and aligned, the bar color changed

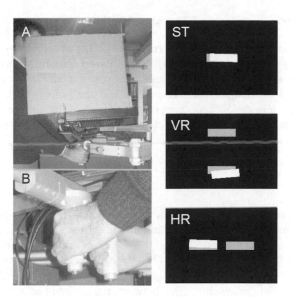

Fig. 1. Left: Side view of the experimental setup. The monitor lies horizontally above the manipulandum (*A*). The participants hold the handles mounted at the extremity of each robotic arm (*B*). **Right:** Visual feedback provided during three experimental conditions. The grey bars denote the desired position of the virtual bar in the static condition (*ST*) or the starting and target positions in the dynamic vertical (*VR*) and horizontal (*HR*) condition. The white rectangle denotes the visual feedback about the current position of the virtual bar. In all conditions, the color of the virtual bar changed to yellow for 0.5 s when the stimulus was delivered. In the dynamic conditions, its color changed to green to indicate when to initiate the movement (see text).

from white to green. Then, 1 s later, it became yellow during the presentation of the stimulus before returning to the white color. At this time, participants had to give their response.

In the dynamic conditions, the stimulus was delivered while the participants moved the bar in the horizontal plane along the sagittal or lateral direction. These two movements directions are referred to as the vertical reaching (VR) and horizontal reaching (HR) conditions respectively. Two grey bars (0.15 x 0.04 m) separated by 0.2 m were displayed on the monitor screen to define the initial and final positions (see Fig. 1). The trial started when the participant had aligned the virtual bar with the starting position. Then, the virtual bar turned to green, which indicated that the participant should move the bar toward the target position. When 25% of the entire path was covered, the bar changed color (to yellow) for 0.5 s, to indicate the moment of the stimulus delivery. The desired movement duration was set to 1.2 s with a tolerance of ±0.3 s. When the actual duration movement satisfied this constraint, target bar became pink; otherwise, a text message indicating whether the movement had been too slow or too fast appeared on the screen. Instantaneous velocity was monitored to insure that participants initiated and finished with a full stop.

2.3 Psychometric Function and Threshold Definitions

A psychometric function (cumulative normal probability distribution) was fitted to the pooled responses of the two QUESTs by likelihood maximization. The detection threshold (ΔL) was defined as the difference between the stimulus value that elicited 75% of positive ("bar lengthened") responses and the point where the bar did not appear to change length (50% of positive responses). The difference between the point where the bar does not appear to change length and the point where the length of the bar did not change physically is the constant error or bias.

3 Results

Participants generally performed the desired movement in the prescribed time. The average movement time and movement amplitude was 1.31±0.11 s and 0.20±0.01 m in the VR condition, and 1.49±0.11 s and 0.23±0.02 m in the HR condition. The peak velocity reached 0.47±0.15 m/s and 0.42±0.01 m/s respectively. At the time of the delivery of the stimulus, instantaneous bar velocity was 0.41±0.13 and 0.33±0.08 m/s, respectively. The average absolute error between the desired and actual lengths of the virtual bar was 0.94 ± 0.28 mm (0.6 ± 0.17 mm in the static condition and 1.11 ± 0.34 mm in the dynamic conditions).

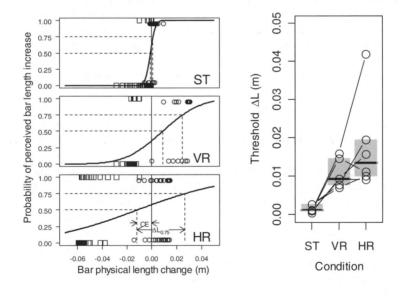

Fig. 2. Left: Psychometric functions of one subject in the static and dynamic conditions. The data points identify the subject's responses (0="bar shortened", 1="bar lengthened") to the stimulus values computed by the QUEST targeting 17% (*squares*) and 83% (*circles*) of "bar lengthened" responses. Thin dotted lines indicate the bar length changes that correspond to the constant error (CE) and detection threshold ($\Delta L_{0.75}$). The solid vertical line indicates the point where the bar did not change length. **Right:** Thresholds of individual participants (dots). The thick horizontal line and gray box correspond to the median threshold and interquartile range.

Figure 2 shows the psychometric functions fitted to the responses of a subject in the three conditions. The slope is much greater in the static than in the dynamic conditions. In other words, this subject was better able to detect and identify the direction of changes of bar length in the static condition than in the dynamic conditions. This observation holds true for all subjects who participated to the experiment. The average (±SD) threshold was 1.6±0.9 mm, 10.7±3.7 mm and 17.9±12.4 mm in the ST, VR and HR conditions respectively. The difference was statistically significant between the ST and VR conditions (paired-sample t-test, $t_5 = 5.37$, $p = 0.003$) but not between the two dynamic conditions ($t_5 = 1.684$, $p = 0.153$). In the latter case, there was a marked threshold increase (>1.5 cm) in the HR relative to the VR condition for two subjects, and a moderate increase (>0.3 cm) for two other subjects.

The average constant error was –0.4±0.5 mm, 1.8±6.4 mm and –2.5±17.6 mm in the ST, VR and HR conditions. At population level, none of these values differed statistically from zero (one-sample t-test, $p > 0.1$). However, in the dynamic conditions, there were considerable differences across participants. For example, the participant in Fig. 2 was equally likely to response that the bar increased or decreased in condition HR when the bar length decreased by 6 mm. In fact, for lateral movements, the constant error (CE) ranged between –20 and 28 mm depending on the participant.

4 Discussion

In this experiment, the stimuli consisted in a brief variation of the distance between the two hands. To compare our results with passive movement detection studies [8], we recomputed the thresholds in degrees by assuming that the change of bar length corresponded to a humeral rotation with a forearm length of 35 cm. In the static condition, the thresholds observed in this experiment ($\tan^{-1}(0.002/0.35) = 0.33°$) were slightly larger than the threshold (0.1°) for the detection of a passive movement at the elbow or shoulder joint at speed above 2 °/s. The difference might be due to the fact that the lengthening/shortening speed of the bar ($0.33°/0.25s = 1.32$ °/s) was slightly slower than the passive movement velocities yielding the lowest detection thresholds (> 2 °/s), but still faster than the limit where these thresholds rise steeply (<1 °/s). In the dynamic conditions, the thresholds were much larger (>1.7°) despite the fact that the shortening/lengthening velocity actually increased in these conditions ($1.7°/0.25$ s $= 7$ °/s).

The main finding of this study was that the identification thresholds for a transient shortening or lengthening of the bar was higher during movement, as compared to a static condition. Our results also gave some indication that the detection thresholds for the direction of change of bar length might be more difficult to assess when the movement direction coincided with the orientation of the bar (HR condition) but additional research is needed to confirm this observation.

The lower thresholds in the static condition might seem to contradict previous observations that proprioceptive acuity decreases in passive conditions [9]. However, our static condition differs significantly from the passive conditions used in posture matching or movement detection tasks where the limb is often completely relaxed. In our study, participants supported the weight of their arm and maintained a firm bimanual grasp. More recent studies have pointed out that the difference observed between passive and active conditions in movement detection tasks disappears if the muscles have been properly conditioned in the passive condition [10]. In fact, it has been recently proposed that proprioceptive acuity could be greater during passive movements than during contraction [4]. This notion is supported by the finding that the perception of an electrically evoked muscle twitch decreases during voluntary movement [11] and by the observation that humans can predict when the unseen hand passes though a visual target equally well during passive and active movements [3].

The large difference between the static and dynamic conditions in our study could be explained by the difficulty for the perceptual system to extract information about the ongoing movement from information about the length of the bar and/or additional noise present in afferent signals during movement [10]. Finally, it is also possible that the need to control the reaching movement reduced the attentional resources available for the detection task. To address this issue, we intend to measure the thresholds during a continuous movement requiring less control.

References

1. Proske, U., Gandevia, S.C.: The kinaesthetic senses. J. Physiol. 587(17), 4139–4146 (2009)
2. Cordo, P.J., Gurfinkel, V.S., Levik, Y.: Position sense during imperceptibly slow movements. Exp. Brain Res. 132, 1–9 (2000)
3. Cordo, P., Carlton, L., Bevan, L., Carlton, M., Kerr, G.K.: Proprioceptive coordination of movement sequences: role of velocity and position information. J. Neurosc. 71(5), 1848–1861 (1994)
4. Proske, U., Wise, A.K., Gregory, J.E.: The role of muscle receptors in the detection of movements. Progress in Neurobiology 20, 85–96 (2000)
5. Casadio, M., Sanguineti, V., Morasso, P.G., Arrichiello, V.: Braccio di Ferro: a new haptic workstation for neuromotor rehabilitation. Technol Health Care 14(3), 123–142 (2006)
6. Watson, A., Pelli, D.: QUEST: a Bayesian adaptive psychometric method. Percept Psychophys 33, 113–120 (1983)
7. King-Smith, P.E., Rose, D.: Principles of an Adaptive Method for Measuring the Slope of the Psychometric Function. Vision Res. 37(12), 1595–1604 (1997)
8. Hall, L.A., McCloskey, D.I.: Detection of movements imposed on finger, elbow and shoulder joints. J. Phsyiol (Lond) 335, 519–533 (1983)
9. Gandevia, S.C., McCloskey, D.I., Burke, D.: Kinaesthetic signals and muscle contractions. TINS 15, 62–65 (1992)
10. Wise, J., Gregory, J.E., Proske, U.: The effects of muscle conditioning on moment detection thresholds at the human forearm. Brain Research 735, 125–130 (1996)
11. Collins, D.F., Caeron, T., Gillard, D.M., Prochazka, A.: Muscular sense is attenuated when human move. J. Physiol (Lond) 508, 635–643 (1998)

Haptic Feedback of Piconewton Interactions with Optical Tweezers

Cécile Pacoret[1,2], Arvid Bergander[1], and Stéphane Régnier[2]

[1] Sensory and Ambiant Interfaces Laboratory, CEA LIST, F-92265 Fontenay-ax-Roses, France
[2] Institut des systèmes intelligents et robotique, Université Pierre et Marie Curie, CNRS UMR 72222, F-75005 Paris, France
pacoret@isir.fr, a.bergander@ieee.org, regnier@isir.fr

Abstract. Haptic feedback for micro- and nanomanipulation is a research area of growing importance with many potential applications in micro- and biotechnology. Past research often involves the coupling of atomic force microscopes to haptic devices, but the results are not satisfactory. We propose to adopt a different approach, which consists of contactless manipulation, in particular by using optical tweezers, coupled with a haptic feedback device. In this article, we describe the potential of such a tool and show with some first experiments of stable interactions between micro-particles.

Keywords: micromanipulation, optical tweezers, haptic feedback, bilateral coupling.

1 Introduction

Grasping and placing precisely micro- and nano-parts are still arduous and costly micromanipulation tasks. Haptic force feedback may help greatly to detect contacts, thus allows a control between objects interactions and increases the efficiency and safety of the tasks. But not all usual micromanipulation tools are well suited for coupling with haptic interfaces.

An atomic force microscope (AFM) beam for instance is used to move an object and to measure the interactions thanks to cantilever deflection. The AFM tip seems to be well suited for pushing microobjects, but its large size is disadvantageous. They obstruct the microscope view during manipulation and the adhesion forces are also important on its surfaces and the samples stick to the tip. Even though particular strategies have been developed applying surface treatments or using two tips [1], the haptic rendering is poor and limited to one axis and simple tasks.

Our goal is to show that a rational choice of micromanipulation techniques and strategies may help greatly the haptic perception (see Fig. 2a.). Optical tweezers are a judicious choice for this purpose, they allow a simple coupling which is transparent and stable. In the following we will briefly explain the basic principle, followed by a presentation of the coupling scheme and finally present an experimental setup with first results.

A.M.L. Kappers et al. (Eds.): EuroHaptics 2010, Part II, LNCS 6192, pp. 333–338, 2010.

2   The Micromanipulator Choice

2.1   Microworld Interactions

In the microworld, the weight of micro sized objects is negligible compared to surface effects. Consequently inertia is insignificant and acceleration is very high. The objects are subject to different interactions : adhesion, electrostatic forces and viscous drag in liquid. Miniaturized tools like micro-grippers or AFM cantilever have a large surface compared to the handled object and thus surface interactions are big which means large adhesion forces.

Other techniques seem to be better suited, which is why "contactless" techniques begin to hold the interest of the research community [2]. Many micro-tools are airborne and employ effects of potential fields. Electromagnetic tweezers [3] and optical tweezers [4] allow a three-dimensional control respectively of a magnetic bead and a dielectric bead in liquid medium only. Contactless manipulation can be used directly without any adhesion effects, but the trap beads are also used to indirectly manipulate random shape objects. A contact occurs in this case between the small trapped micro-tool and the sample, with small adhesion effects.

As the interactions between a trapped micro-tools and the indirectly manipulated sample can be measured, it is interesting to feed back them to the operator. We have selected optical tweezers as manipulator, because, in water, the dynamic is damped and the interactions are scalable and interpretable for the human range. Secondly, the most delicate operations are in the domain of biology where optical tweezers are widespread.

2.2   Laser Manipulation Flexibility

Optical tweezer with force-feedback have been investigated in the past. Arai realizes an experiment with real force-feedback on a trapped particle in a liquid medium free of obstacles [5]. Basdogan proposes a virtual haptic guidance to help the docking of particles [6]. In this paper, we will show the full potential of this flexible tool using a real force feedback when the trapped particles encounter an obstacle thanks to our stability improvements.

Optical tweezer's properties come from the laser source. The light going through a spherical object produces a force. If the bead's refractive index is superior to the environment one, the bead is trapped on a convergent laser focal point. Using a high numerical aperture microscope objective, researchers build since 1986 [7] powerful traps to displace nano- and micro-objects like cells [8], viruses and crystals.

Multiple traps allow more complex applications like holding directly nanowires, microfabricated tools [9], or indirectly random shaped objects [10]. In that case, fast beam deflectors (scanners, acousto-optical-deflector) or diffractive actuators (spatial light modulator, SLM) may be used and coupled to multiple haptic interfaces for a collaboration of the two hands, fingers or more than one operator.

Optical tweezers also have good properties for visual control of the manipulation : they are small and do not disturb the manipulation view. Moreover, they are compatible with other optical microscopy allowing three-dimensional view or DNA visualizations (confocal and fluorescent microscopy [8]).

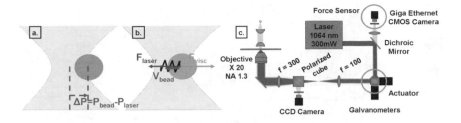

Fig. 1. a. Spring-damping model of the optical trap. **b.** Force balance on an optical tweezers trapped bead. F_{laser} and F_{visc} are respectively the optical force and the viscous drag. V_{bead}, P_{bead}, ΔP and P_{laser} are respectively the speed, the displacement of the bead, its relative position to the laser and the laser position. **c.** Laser and light optical path. The laser beam (pumped Ytterbium fiber, 1064 nm) is deflected by galvanometers (Cambridge technology, Inc), oriented by a telescope to a high NA objective (Olympus, x40, NA. 1.3). A first video camera shows the scene and a second high speed video camera (Dalsa CMOS, 1000fps for 80×80 pixels) is used for position measurements process by a custom C++ program.

2.3 Force Measurement

Optical tweezers are also precise force transducers. The literature [4] describes abundantly the properties of their model : the trap behaves like a three-dimensional spring. To obtain the force applied on the trapped object, a measurement of the relative position of its center to the laser spot is sufficient (see Fig. 1a.):

$$F_{laser} = -K \cdot (P_{bead} - P_{laser}) \tag{1}$$

where K is the trap stiffness, F_{laser} the optical force, P_{bead} et P_{laser} respectively the object and the laser positions. Interferometer, photo-detection or video image processing may be used as position detector and the calibration of the trap stiffness may be obtained with the viscous drag model or the power spectrum method [4]. The calibration errors are not critical for the haptic sensation, as we will see the stiffness can be integrated in the force gain of the direct coupling (see section 3.1). In fact, the laser force measurement gives an image of the other external forces (F_{micro}) as the force balance shows. The dynamics effects are negligible thanks to the object size (see Fig. 1b.):

$$F_{laser} + F_{micro} = M_{bead} \cdot \ddot{P}_{bead} \approx 0 \implies F_{micro} = -F_{laser} \tag{2}$$

Using this equation, the force fed back to the operator by means of an haptic interface is the opposite of the measured laser force. Viscous drag and obstacles such as the surface of a micro channel, larger micro objects or even the Brownian motion due to thermal effects can thus be haptically rendered.

3 Direct Coupling for Good Stability and Transparency

3.1 Non-contact Micromanipulation and Coupling

Our optical tweezers installation (see Fig. 1.c.) includes a laser (1064 nm), an actuator that deflects the light beams (galvanometers), a telescope and an high numerical aperture objective (NA = 1.3). White light is used to image the bead on an high speed video

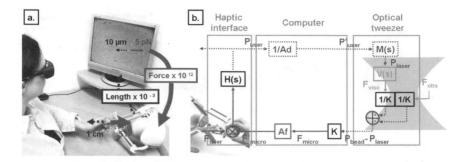

Fig. 2. a. Concept of haptic micromanipulation. **b.** Automatic scheme of the direct coupling between the optical tweezer in Laplace formalism : H(s), M(s) and V(s) are respectively the transfer function of the haptic interface, of the actuated mirrors and of the viscous model. K, Ad, Af are respectively the trap stiffness, the position gain and the force gain.

camera. This sensor is centred on the laser beam thanks to optical path design and allows a direct measurement of the bead's relative position. Using the stiffness model, the force is obtained from this position detection.

This particular design and the chosen high speed components (galvanometers and the triggered fast image processing system) allow the actuation and the position detection of two or three beads. Moreover, the good performances of this tool are an advantage for the stability of closed loop system.

Haptic coupling is a close loop system and benefits of delay optimisation of its components. Even if the optical tweezer was linked to a low cost commercial haptic interface (Falcon by Novint), a direct coupling was used without instabilities. The coupling links consist of simple homothetic gains : in position, Ad and in force, Af (see Fig. 2a.). They are chosen in a way that the handle displacements match optical tweezer workspace and microworld amplified forces are perceptible by human hand ($> 1N$). This coupling method is the most transparent, but may lead to instabilities which can be very important in the case of "contact" micro-manipulator [11].

To prove it, we study the closed loop stability of the coupling (see Fig. 2b.) by applying the Routh-Hurwitz criterion. For the trap stiffness (10^{-7} N/m), object dimensions ($R=2 \cdot 10^{-6}$ m) and viscous drag ranges ($6\pi \cdot \mu_{water} \cdot R$), the system remains stable for large homothetic gains. For $Ad = 10^4$ (centimeter convert to micrometer), the force gain may safely be set to $Af = 10^{12}$, which allows piconewton perception.

3.2   Experimental Proof

In order to improve system response speed [12] and the transparency, we build a dedicated optical tweezer installation. Fig. 3a. shows its response to two constant speed ramps. The viscous drag sensation is highlighted and proportional to speed: the user feels a bigger mechanical resistance as he moved the handle faster. Small oscillations on this curve are the random noise characteristic of the Brownian motion on the trapped bead.

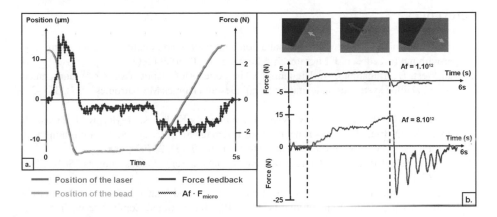

Fig. 3. a. Response of the system to constant speed ramps ($Ad = 10^4$, $Af = 2 \cdot 10^{12}$). The displacement of the laser (blue), of the bead (green) and of the haptic interface (scaled, purple) are presented in comparison with to feedback forces in Newton (blue). **b.** Response of the system to a wall contact. The user force feedback is shown for different force gains : in the first graph $Af = 1 \cdot 10^{12}$ and in the second graph $Af = 8 \cdot 10^{12}$ ($Ad = 10^4$).

In order to prove that the system remains stable in presence of an obstacle, we push a 5 μm bead on the wall of a 100 μm silicon cube. The first graph of Fig. 3b. show the force feedback to the user for a force gain of $1 \cdot 10^{12}$. The sensation of contact is efficient, the user does not push more than necessary to feel the wall. He can pull the bead away with a transparent sensation of the damped dynamic.

The second graph, in contrast, shows what happens if the force gain is higher. Sudden change of ΔP results in a damped oscillation. This situation must be avoided for the manipulation comfort and safety. Optimising our system for better stability allows us to keep it safe from resonant mode of the direct coupling scheme till the precision range of piconewton perception ($2 \cdot 10^{12}$).

4   Conclusion and Perspectives

In this paper, we have presented a system for haptic micromanipulation based on optical tweezers. The high degree of transparency achieved thanks to the stable direct coupling is an important improvement for this contactless micromanipulator. The two coupling parameters are easy to tune and the high force gain allows good haptic perception of piconewton forces even in the exploration of an obstacle.

Optical tweezers are widespread in biology laboratories and the study of single molecules or cells may benefit from the feedback of force information to the operator's hands. They are also affordable [13] for undergraduate pedagogical projects, and the force feedback may help understanding microworld phenomena.

First experiments show already the potential of these flexible tools. A three-dimensional force feedback system is possible with holographic actuator (SLM) and confocal technology. We focus our future work on the multi-trap force feedback and work on user studies in order to highlight the efficiency of this instrument.

References

1. Xie, H., Régnier, S.: Three-dimensional automated micromanipulation using a nanotip gripper with multi-feedback. J. Micromech. Microeng. 19, 075009 (2009)
2. van West, E., Yamamoto, A., Higuchi, T.: The concept of Haptic Tweezer. A non-contact object handling system using levitation techniques and haptics Mechatronics 17(7), 345–356 (2007)
3. Fisher, J.K., Cribb, J., Desai, K.V., Vicci, L., Wilde, B., Keller, K., Taylor, R.M., Haase, J., Bloom, K., O'Brien, E.T., Superfine, R.: Thin-foil magnetic force system for high-numerical-aperture microscopy. Review of Scientific Instruments 77(2), 23702 (2006)
4. Neuman, K.C., Block, S.M.: Optical trapping. Review of Scientific Instruments 75(9), 2787–2809 (2004)
5. Arai, F., Ogawa, M., Fukuda, T.: Indirect manipulation and bilateral control of the microbe by the laser manipulated microtools. In: IEEE/RSJ International Conference on Intelligent Robots and Systems, vol. 1, pp. 665–670 (2000)
6. Basdogan, C., Kiraz, A., Bukusoglu, I., Varol, A., Doğanay, S.: Haptic guidance for improved task performance in steering microparticles with optical tweezers. Opt. Express 15(18), 11616–11621 (2007)
7. Ashkin, A., Dziedzic, J.M., Bjorkholm, J.E., Chu, S.: Observation of a single-beam gradient force optical trap for dielectric particles. Opt. Lett. 11(5), 288 (1986)
8. Konig, K.: Laser tweezers and multphoton microscopes in life sciences. Histochem Cell Biol. 114(2), 79–92 (2000)
9. Arai, F., Endo, T., Yamuchi, R., Fukuda, T.: 3D 6DOF Manipulation of Micro-object Using Laser Trapped Microtool. In: Proceedings of the 2006 IEEE International Conference on Robotics and Automation (2006)
10. Whyte, G., Gibson, G., Leach, J., Padgett, M., Robert, D., Miles, M.: An optical trapped microhand for manipulating micron-sized objects. Opt. Express 14(25), 12497–12502 (2006)
11. Bolopion, A., Cagneau, B., Haliyo, S., Régnier, S.: Analysis of stability and transparency for nanoscale force feedback in bilateral coupling. Journal of Micro - Nano Mechatronics (2009)
12. Pacoret, C., Bowman, R., Gibson, G., Haliyo, S., Carberry, D., Bergander, A., Régnier, S., Padgett, M.: Touching the microworld with force-feedback optical tweezers. Opt. Express 17(12), 10259–10264 (2009)
13. Smith, S.P., Bhalotra, S.R., Brody, A.L., Brown, B.L., Boyda, E.K., Prentiss, M.: Inexpensive optical tweezers for undergraduate laboratories. American Journal of Physics 67(1), 26–35 (1999)

Pressure Is a Viable Controlled Output of Motor Programming for Object Manipulation Tasks

Camille Williams[1], Daniel Shang[2], and Heather Carnahan[3]

[1] Institute of Biomaterials and Biomedical Engineering, University of Toronto, Canada
[2] Department of Kinesiology, University of Waterloo, Canada
[3] Department of Occupational Science and Occupational Therapy, University of Toronto, Canada
camille.williams@utoronto.ca, dshang@uwaterloo.ca,
heather.carnahan@gmail.com

Abstract. While force output is discussed as the predominant controlled output of the motor program for object manipulation, various studies have demonstrated that local pressure distribution at the fingerpad and coefficient of friction at the finger-object interface are also important for grasp control. We investigated the role of local pressure as a possible controlled output during a lift-hold-replace task. Participants lifted one of two masses with either normal or slippery contact surfaces using one of two grip postures that varied contact area. Grip force data was collected by a force/torque transducer while pressure and contact area data were collected using a Tekscan flexible sensor. Grip force and pressure both increased with increased mass or reduced friction while contact area increased with reduced friction and use of the flat grip posture. Additionally, grip force was significantly affected by a friction-grip posture interaction, whereas pressure was significantly affected by a mass-grip posture interaction.

Keywords: Force; Pressure; Finger; Haptic; Grasp control.

1 Introduction

Object manipulation tasks, an essential component of one's interaction with the environment, allow one to transport objects, use tools or explore an object's properties. These tasks consist of a sequence of specific sensory events linked to specific mechanical contact events – subgoals – separated by action phases. For a simple object manipulation task such as grasping an object, lifting it from a stable surface, holding it above the surface for a given period of time and then replacing it, the action phases may be described as reach, load, lift, hold, replace, unload and release [1]. In order to produce the desired movements the brain utilizes instructions contained in motor programs to coordinate a sequential activation of muscles [2]. Motor program instructions are informed and adjusted through anticipatory planning, aided by visual cues and sensorimotor memories of previous interactions with the same or similar objects. This allows the fingers to apply the appropriate grip forces (normal to the object's surface) and load forces (tangential to the object's surface) to ensure a stable grasp, that is, prevent slips or loss of the object while avoiding muscle fatigue and damage to

A.M.L. Kappers et al. (Eds.): EuroHaptics 2010, Part II, LNCS 6192, pp. 339–344, 2010.
© Springer-Verlag Berlin Heidelberg 2010

the object or hand. When the hand interacts with an object, tactile afferents innervating the hand provide information about the physical properties of the object such as shape as well as information about hand-object contact such as friction. Mismatches between the expected feedback from the sensory afferents can trigger corrective changes in the grip-to-load force ratios as well as update the internal representation of the object's properties or hand-object contact for use in future interactions with the same or similar objects [1].

In most discussions of object manipulation and grasp control, force and its derivatives, such as grip force rate, are the only discussed outputs of motor programming. Slip detection and control has also been postulated as a strategy for stable grasping [3]. The authors found that the slip sensor provided a clear signal of slippage while the applied force varied only slightly with respect to the level of incipient slip. Soft tissue strain energy minimization has also been identified as a candidate control scheme [4]. The authors used finite element analysis to refine their hypothesis: given a tangential load, the central nervous system seeks to minimize strain energy in the contact region by varying the normal force. They admit, however, that this hypothesis does not explain the dependence of the safety margin on friction or feed-forward control. Closer examination of other grasp control studies indicates that pressure (force applied per unit area) may also be a viable output of the control scheme that involves the motor program.

One study that explored the relationship between grip control and grip forces demonstrated that grip forces were highly dependent on the coefficient of friction [5]. The main mechanisms of friction that pertain to viscoelastic materials such as skin are adhesion and hysteresis. Adhesion refers to the formation of local bonds at the asperities of the surfaces and hysteresis refers to the delayed response of a material to the forces acting on it. As a result, increasing the contact area between two objects may increase the coefficient of friction [6]. The contact area of the finger may increase because the compliance of fingerpads allows for deformation of tissue, which also distributes force and reduces slip. However, Cadoret and Smith [5] assumed that the compliance of the fingertips and its effect on the control of grip forces were nullified because the grip forces exceeded the range of compliance. This is because the area of contact between a finger and a solid surface plateaus at approximately 1 N – lower than the grasp forces involved in their study (~3 – 8 N). Nonetheless, it should be noted that object manipulation (grasping) begins in the compliant region. Another study investigating the coordination between the grip and load forces during object manipulation used local anaesthesia to examine the adaptation of force coordination to changes in friction. Their results suggested that small localized slips may be explained by unequal pressure distribution across the finger-object contact area as a result of the viscoelastic properties and curvature of the fingerpad skin [7].

Consequently, in the present study we investigated whether pressure might be a controlled output of the motor program during a manual grasp-lift-replace task. We expected to see effects of our independent variables on all measured variables (force, contact area and pressure). While with our design, it is not possible to completely dissociate these three variables, we would like to demonstrate that both pressure and force are variables that must be considered in the programming of object manipulation.

2 Methods

Eight university undergraduate students participated and were required to grasp then lift an object and hold it for 10 seconds. The object was instrumented with an ATI Gamma Force/Torque transducer system (ATI Industrial Automation, Gerner N.C., U.S.A.) that measured the applied grip force. Wrapped over the contact surfaces was a Tekscan (Boston, MA, USA) pressure-sensitive sheet that measured total pressure and finger contact area in real time, sampling at a frequency of 100 Hz. It had 62 sensels per square centimeter and a standard pressure range of 2,413 kPa.

The experimental design included three factors: object mass (350 g, 550 g); friction between the object and fingers (normal, slippery); and grip posture (pinch, flat). For the slippery condition, talcum powder was applied to the fingertips and the apparatus to reduce friction at the finger-object interface as done previously [5], [8]. The grip posture was altered in order to change the contact area between the object and the fingers. The pinch grip used the tips of the fingers while the flat grip used the finger-pads. Prior to the first trial, participants washed their hands with soap and water and dried them thoroughly to reduce oil build-up on the hands. Eight trials were performed for each condition resulting in a total of 64 trials for each participant. Trials were performed in a blocked fashion and counterbalanced across participants. Each block was preceded by a familiarization trial which allowed the participant to develop a haptic reference for the object's properties. All dependent variables were analyzed in separate repeated measures analyses of variance. All effects significant at $p < .05$ were further analyzed using the Newman Keuls methods for posthoc comparison of means.

3 Results and Discussion

Table 1 provides a summary of the statistically significant effects. The analysis of maximum applied grip force revealed significant effects of mass and friction (Fig. 1A). As expected, the heavier mass and slippery conditions resulted in increased grip force. A friction-grip posture interaction shows that grip force was the greatest in the

Table 1. Summary of statistically significant effects

Dependent Variable	Significant Effects	$F(1, 7)$ values	Significance
Force (N)	Mass	22	$p < .01$
	Friction	42	$p < .01$
	Friction x Grip Posture	6.5	$p < .05$
Pressure (kPa)	Mass	35	$p < .01$
	Friction	5.7	$p < .05$
	Grip Posture	114	$p < .01$
	Mass x Grip Posture	11	$p < .05$
Contact Area (mm^2)	Friction	9	$p < .05$
	Grip Posture	52	$p < .01$

slippery-flat grip condition and least for the normal-flat grip condition (Fig. 2A). The similar and higher grip force values for both grip postures in the slippery conditions may be caused by a more cautious approach to the task. In contrast, for the normal friction conditions there is a greater difference between the grip force values for each grip posture. It is possible that the pinch grip posture required a greater grip force because reduced compliance of the fingerpad in this posture limited fingerpad deformation and increase in contact area which usually contributes to grasp stability.

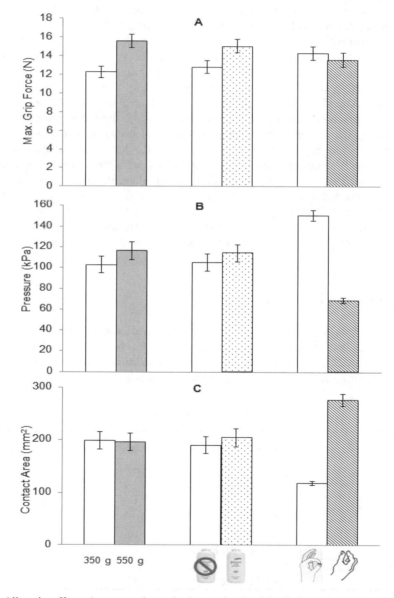

Fig. 1. All main effects (means and standard error bars) of the independent variables (mass, friction and grip posture) on grip force (A), pressure (B) and contact area (C)

Analysis of the contact pressure showed that increasing mass, reducing friction or using a pinch grip all increased the contact pressure (Fig. 1B). Additionally, there was a significant interaction between mass and grip posture: greater contact pressure was applied to stabilize the heavier mass while using the pinch grip (Fig. 2B). Analysis of index finger contact area revealed significant effects of friction and grip posture such that reducing friction or using the flat grip led to an increase in contact area (Fig. 1C). This supports the increase in contact pressure due to the pinch grip posture since the compliance and therefore contact area of the fingerpad is reduced with this posture.

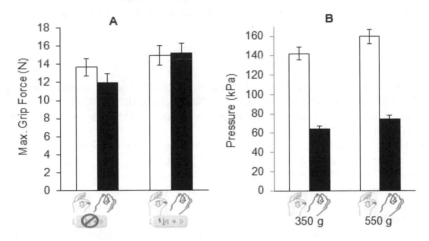

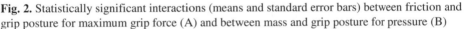

Fig. 2. Statistically significant interactions (means and standard error bars) between friction and grip posture for maximum grip force (A) and between mass and grip posture for pressure (B)

It was demonstrated that there were differential effects for the three measured variables (force, pressure and contact area). These three measures are not independent, yet they were influenced in different ways by the manipulations of mass, friction and grip posture. Thus, it is possible that the motor control system is not only responsible for force production, but pressure at the finger tips as well. Based on these findings we should consider the possibility that pressure can be a controlled variable.

There is some neurophysiologic evidence that supports the notion of multiple control variables (i.e., force and pressure). In the glabrous skin on the palm of hand, the slow-adapting type 1 (SA 1) afferent nerve fibres have been shown to code for texture and small feature discrimination and, upon microstimulation, induces a faint uniform sensation of pressure [9]. SA 1 afferents supply the Merkel complex, which has a small circular receptive field ($2 - 100$ mm^2) with distinct borders, displays high sensitivity to indentation stimuli in a discrete area and responds to local forces [10], [11], [12]. The pressure perception values for a constant one point discrimination task has been reported as 0.1 g/mm^2 (0.1 kPa) [13] – much less than the pressures encountered in this study. In contrast, the force generated by a muscle is detected mainly by Golgi tendon organs located in the tendon of the muscle, in series with the muscle fibre. With this in mind, we suggest that control of force alone does not account for finger deformation or the area of contact between an object and the fingers, and that the control of pressure is a likely candidate.

4 Conclusion

While further studies would be required to fully describe the role of pressure as a controlled output for various object manipulation tasks, the results highlight that we cannot ignore pressure as a potential controlled variable. There are some variations of environmental conditions that result in changes to force but not pressure and vice versa.

Acknowledgements. This project was supported a research grant awarded to H. C. from the Natural Sciences and Engineering Research Council of Canada.

References

1. Johansson, R.S., Flanagan, J.R.: Coding and use of Tactile Signals from the Fingertips in Object Manipulation Tasks. Nature Reviews. Neuroscience 10, 345–359 (2009)
2. Schmidt, R.A.: Motor control and learning: A behavioral emphasis, 3rd edn. Human Kinetics, Champaign (1999)
3. D'Alessio, T., Steindler, R.: Slip Sensors for the Control of the Grasp in Functional Neuromuscular Stimulation. Medical Engineering Physics 17, 466–470 (1995)
4. Pataky, T.C.: Soft Tissue Strain Energy Minimization: A Candidate Control Scheme for Intra-Finger Normal-Tangential Force Coordination. J. Biomech. 38, 1723–1727 (2005)
5. Cadoret, G., Smith, A.: Friction, Not Texture, Dictates Grip Forces used during Object Manipulation. J. Neurophysiol. 75, 1963 (1996)
6. Tomlinson, S.E.: Review of the Frictional Properties of Finger-Object Contact when Gripping. Proceedings of the Institution of Mechanical Engineers Part J. Journal of Engineering Tribology 221, 841 (2007)
7. Johansson, R., Westling, G.: Roles of Glabrous Skin Receptors and Sensorimotor Memory in Automatic Control of Precision Grip when Lifting Rougher Or More Slippery Objects. Exp. Brain Res. 56, 550–564 (1984)
8. Saels, P.: Impact of the Surface Slipperiness of Grasped Objects on their Subsequent Acceleration. Neuropsychologia 37, 751–756 (1999)
9. Haeberle, H., Lumpkin, E.A.: Merkel Cells in Somatosensation. Chemosensory Perception 1, 110–119 (2008)
10. Johansson, R.S.: Tactile Sensibility in Human Hand - Receptive-Field Characteristics of Mechanoreceptive Units in Glabrous Skin Area (1978)
11. Dargahi, J., Najarian, S.: Human Tactile Perception as a Standard for Artificial Tactile Sensing - a Review (2004)
12. Macefield, V.G.: Physiological Characteristics of Low-Threshold Mechanoreceptors in Joints, Muscle and Skin in Human Subjects. Clinical and Experimental Pharmacology & Physiology 32, 135–144 (2005)
13. Dellon, E.S.: Human Pressure Perception Values for Constant and Moving One- and Two-Point Discrimination. Plast. Reconstr. Surg. 90, 112–117 (1992)

Part IV
Performance and Training

A Comparison of the Haptic and Visual Horizontal-Vertical Illusion

Jacqui Howell, Mark Symmons, and Dianne Wuillemin

Monash University, Churchill, Australia, 3842
Jacqui.Howell@arts.monash.edu.au, Mark.Symmons@marc.monash.edu.au,
Dianne.Wuillemin@arts.monash.edu

Abstract. Participants attempted to create squares of four different sizes in two orientations in one of three modality conditions - physically adjusting a tangible template while blindfolded (haptic condition), directing the experimenter to adjust the template (vision condition), or adjusting the template themselves without the blindfold (mixed-mode condition). The side of square was robustly overestimated, resulting in a rectangle elongated in the horizontal direction - evidence for the horizontal-vertical illusion. There was no difference in the illusion's strength as a function of modality conditions or orientation.

Keywords: Horizontal-vertical illusion, vision, haptics.

1 Introduction

In the horizontal-vertical illusion (HVI) a horizontal spar is perceived to be shorter than an equivalent length vertical spar (or the vertical is perceived as longer than the horizontal). In previous studies the stimuli have most commonly been presented as L or inverted-T figures (e.g. [1,2]). As is the case for many illusions, the effect and extent of the HVI has been investigated primarily in the vision domain [1,3]. However, some have found that the illusion also exists haptically. Late blind participants (loss of sight after first year of life) show a similar susceptibility to the illusion as blindfolded sighted participants [4] but early blind participants (loss of sight before or within the first year of life) were more susceptible [5]. Radial arm movements have been found to be overestimated in comparison to tangential movements [6,7,8,9]. Bean's [10] seems to be one of the earlier publications describing a haptic HVI, and there have been a number of other papers since though there remains a number of unanswered questions, including whether the haptic HVI exists for squares in addition to traditional L and T figures. Several studies have found more illusion in L and T figures presented in the horizontal compared to the fronto-parallel plane [11,12,13].

Comparing vision and haptics, in terms of horizontal-vertical illusion strength, has produced varying results. Taylor [14] found that haptics produced greater illusion than vision, however Tedford and Tudor [2] found that vision produced more illusion than haptics. An explanation for this variance could rest in the different methods used for data collection, though what that explanation might be is unclear. Taylor had participants select L and inverted-T figures with equal horizontal and vertical lengths from

A.M.L. Kappers et al. (Eds.): EuroHaptics 2010, Part II, LNCS 6192, pp. 347–352, 2010.

amongst seven alternatives, whereas Tedford and Tudor instructed participants to nominate whether the vertical or horizontal length of inverted-T figures was longer.

The visual HVI has also been observed in solid squares/rectangles whereby rectangles elongated horizontally were often perceived as being square [15] and squares were often perceived as horizontal rectangles [16]. However, the range of sizes used for squares has not been as extensive as for L figures. For example, McManus' [15] squares were 10.5 cm and Sleight and Austin's 2.5 cm on a side. This might at least partially explain the relative weakness of the HVI for squares compared to that found for L figures - less than 2% for the former versus up to 10% for the latter [1]. Several studies have found that larger HVI figures (10 cm) produce more illusion than smaller figures in haptics [17,18]. However in vision the results are not as consistent, with one study finding medium T figures (7.5 cm) produce more illusion than small (5 cm) and large (10 cm) figures [19]. Another potential factor seemingly not systematically assessed as a function of size and modality is the orientation of the stimulus with respect to the explorer's body, a variable that has been shown to influence the amount of horizontal-vertical illusion obtained for both vision [1] and haptics [11,12,13].

Drawing a number of factors together in one experiment, in the current study the HVI is presented both haptically and visually as squares/rectangles, with a systematic evaluation of the effect of stimulus size, and orientation with respect to the observer. It is expected that a vertically oriented stimulus presented visually would demonstrate greater illusion than oriented horizontally, and this pattern will be reversed when the stimuli are presented haptically. Due to the inconsistencies regarding the influence of stimulus size on the visual and haptic HVI, no specific level or direction of performance is predicted. Finally, due to the conflicting findings comparing vision and haptics [14,2] no difference between modalities is expected.

2   Method

The experiment described here is a factorial design. The between-subjects variable was modality, which consisted of three levels - haptics, vision, and a mixed-mode condition involving both modalities. Square size was a within-subjects variable - participants were asked to create squares with sides of size 3, 5, 7 and 9 cm (in counterbalanced order). The orientation of the stimulus was an additional within-subjects variable, with participants forming squares in horizontal or vertical planes directly in front of them, again in counterbalanced order. Each participant created a total of eight squares. All tasks were untimed and participants received no feedback on their performance.

A single set of stimuli was used throughout the conditions and consisted of a pair of 32 by 25 cm cardboard sheets from which a 20 cm square was cut from the corner to form two block-L shapes. The shapes were free to slide across each other in an overlapping manner to form an enclosed square (or rectangle) shape ranging in size up to 20 cm^2 (see Fig 1).

In the haptic condition 10 blindfolded volunteers aged 19 to 48 years ($M = 31, SD = 11$) were asked to "create" squares of 3, 5, 7 or 9 cm using the cardboard cut-outs. The edges that formed the inner target square of the cut-outs were lined with puff paint to form a more tangible surface. When making horizontal squares the participant simply

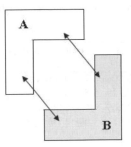

Fig. 1. Cardboard cut-outs that could be overlapped to form a square up to 20 X 20 cm

raised their hands to indicate they were satisfied that they had formed a square of the re
quested dimensions. When operating in the vertical plane the participant used a wall as
a working surface and verbally indicated when they had completing making a square so
that the experimenter could fasten the cut-outs in place before the participant removed
their hands. In either case the experimenter measured the x- and y-dimensions (or base
and side) of the shape while the participant waited to undertake to the next trial.

In the vision condition 10 volunteers aged 21 to 58 years ($M = 32, SD = 14$) created
the same set of squares by instructing the experimenter to move the cut-outs. In the
mixed-mode condition 10 volunteers aged 20 to 51 years ($M = 38, SD = 13$) created
the same set of squares but manipulated the cut-outs themselves with unfettered vision,
thus both haptic and visual information was available to them.

3   Results

Table 1 presents means and standard deviations for the three modality conditions as
percentage error for the vertical and horizontal orientations. Percentage error was calculated whereby scores represent the percentage of overestimation/underestimation
between x- and y-dimensions. A positive percentage error indicates error in the direction of the classic HVI where the y-dimension is perceived as being longer than the
x-dimension.

With percentage error exceeding zero for all three modalities, it would seem that a
HVI effect is evident. Table 2 contains percentage error scores as a function of modality
and requested square size.

Table 1. Means and standard deviations of percentage error of squares created in vertical and
horizontal orientations for three modality conditions

Condition	Vertical		Horizontal		Overall	
	M	SD	M	SD	M	SD
Haptics	10.4%	20.9%	18.7%	27.6%	14.5%	24.6%
Vision	9.3%	12.8%	5.6%	13.1%	7.5%	13.0%
Mixed-mode	7.0%	6.8%	5.3%	5.9%	6.2%	6.4%
Overall	8.9%	14.6%	9.9%	18.9%	9.4%	16.8%

Table 2. Means and standard deviations of percentage error for different square sizes created in three modality conditions

Square size	Haptics		Vision		Mixed-mode		Overall	
	M	SD	M	SD	M	SD	M	SD
3 cm	19.8%	33.0%	8.7%	9.0%	8.2%	17.7%	12.2%	22.5%
5 cm	7.8%	22.2%	5.5%	5.9%	11.1%	13.4%	8.1%	15.3%
7 cm	18.4%	20.0%	6.6%	5.0%	7.9%	10.3%	11.0%	14.1%
9 cm	12.1%	21.1%	3.9%	4.1%	2.6%	8.0%	6.2%	13.7%

A mixed design ANOVA, in which the between factor was modality and within factors were square size and orientation, revealed that there was no significant difference between length estimates made using haptics ($M = 14.5\%, SD = 24.6\%$), vision ($M = 7.5\%, SD = 13.0\%$) and in the mixed-mode ($M = 6.2\%, SD = 6.4\%$) $[F(1,27) = 0.3; p > .05]$. There was also no significant difference between squares made in the vertical and horizontal orientation $[F(2,27) = 1.7, p > .05]$. There was however, a significant difference for the square size factor $[F(2.5, 66.2) = 4.3, p < .05]$[1], though there was no obvious trend (see Table 2). There was a significant interaction between modality and orientation $[F(2,27) = 3.8, p < .05]$ such that squares created in the horizontal orientation resulted in lower percentages of error in all modality conditions except haptics, where the trend was reversed. There was also a significant interaction between modality and square size $[F(4.9, 66.2) = 2.5, p < .05]$[2], however again there was no obvious trend.

The following analysis compares the x- and y-dimension length estimates to what would be expected if length estimates were accurate (i.e. an error score of 0). One-sample t-tests using signed error scores revealed that the x-dimension ($M = 1.2$) and y-dimension ($M = 0.7$) length estimates were significantly different from zero when haptics was used to create squares $[t(79) = 5.4; p < .05$ and $t(79) = 3.7; p < .05$, respectfully] - in the absence of an illusion the x- and y-dimensions should be equivalent. In the vision-alone condition the x- ($M = 1.9$) and y-dimension ($M = 1.0$) length estimates were also significantly different from zero $[t(79) = 6.8; p < .05$ and $t(79) = 3.7; p < .05$, respectfully]. When squares were created in the mixed-mode condition x- ($M = 0.8$) and y-dimension ($M = 0.5$) length estimates were also significantly different from zero $[t(79) = 3.9; p < .05$ and $t(79) = 2.4; p < .05$, respectfully].

The following analysis compares the x-dimension length estimates to y-dimension length estimates. If the HVI plays no part in the creation of squares then it should be expected that the x- and y-dimension length estimate are not significantly different. Paired-sample t-tests using signed error scores revealed that x-dimension length estimates ($M = 1.2$) were significantly larger than y-dimension length estimates when haptics was used to create squares ($M = 0.7$)$[t(79) = 5.3; p < .05]$. When vision was used to create squares x-dimension length estimates ($M = 1.9$) were significantly larger

---

[1] As the assumption of sphericity was not met for the square-size factor (Mauchly's $w = 0.609, p < .05, df = 5$), Greenhouse-Geiser values were used.

[2] As the assumption of sphericity was not met for the square size factor (Mauchly's $w = 0.609, p < .05, df = 5$), Greenhouse-Geiser values were used.

than y-dimension length estimates $(M = 1.0)[t(79) = 5.3; p < .05]$. When squares were created in the mixed-mode condition x-dimension length estimates $(M = 0.8)$ were significantly larger than y-dimension length estimates $(M = 0.5)$ when the participant guided the experimenter in creating squares $[t(79) = 9.2; p < .05]$.

4 Discussion

Substantial inaccuracy in the judgement of length and therefore shape in the perception of squares using vision and haptics has been shown here. As the y-dimensions were frequently made shorter than the x-dimensions (and/or the x-dimensions longer than the y-dimensions) it was demonstrated that the horizontal-vertical illusion (HVI) does influence the creation of squares. This finding is consistent with that of McManus [15], who found that participants visually selected rectangles elongated in the horizontal direction when selecting the "perfect" square from a set. Here the HVI produced similar effects in visual guidance, vision alone and haptics conditions, increasing the robustness of the illusion already demonstrated in HVI figures [1,11].

It was hypothesised that orientation (vertical versus horizontal) would affect the amount of error obtained in squareness judgments. The results did not support the hypotheses, instead revealing there to be no difference resulting from square orientation. This finding is inconsistent with both Avery and Day [1] and von Collani [12] who found orientation influences HVI extent for vision and haptics respectively, though they both used L and T figures. Embedding the L figure as part of a square in the current experiment seems to have negated the orientation effect but it is not clear how or why.

The finding that the HVI influences vision and haptics is consistent with Taylor [14] and Tedford and Tudor [2] who used traditional HVI figures, and with other studies using a variety of spatial illusions in blind and blindfolded participants [10,20]. One explanation for the similarity of such illusions across vision and haptics is that different modalities may rely on the same areas of the brain for spatial processing or use the same principles to interpret the environment.

References

1. Avery, G.C., Day, R.H.: Basis of the Horizontal-Vertical Illusion. J. Exp. Psychol. 81(2), 376–380 (1969)
2. Tedford, W.H., Tudor, L.L.: Tactual and Visual Illusion in the T-Shaped Figure. J. Exp. Psychol. 81(1), 199–201 (1969)
3. Morinaga, S., Noguchi, K., Ohishi, A.: The Horizontal-Vertical Illusion and the Relation of Spatial and Retinal Orientations. Jpn. Psychol. Res. 4(1), 25–29 (1962)
4. Heller, M.A., Brackett, D.D., Wilson, K., Yoneyama, K., Boyer, A.: Visual Experience and the Haptic Horizontal-Vertical Illusion. Brit. J. Visual Impairment. 20(3), 105–109 (2002)
5. Heller, M.A., Joyner, T.D.: Mechanisms in the Haptic Horizontal-Vertical Illusion: Evidence from Sighted and Blind Subjects. Percept. Psychophys. 53(4), 422–428 (1993)
6. Cheng, M.F.: Tactile-Kinesthetic Perception of Length. Am. J. Psychol. 81(1), 74–82 (1968)
7. Davidson, R.S., Cheng, M.F.H.: Apparent Distance in a Horizontal Plane with Tactile-Kinesthetic Stimuli. Q. J. Exp. Psychol. 16(3), 277–281 (1964)

8. Reid, R.L.: An Illusion of Movement Complementary to the Horizontal-Vertical Illusion. Q. J. Exp. Psychol. 6, 107–111 (1954)
9. Wong, T.S.: Dynamic Properties of Radial and Tangential Movements as Determinants of the Haptic Horizontal-Vertical Illusion with an L Figure. J. Exp. Psychol. Human. 3(1), 151–164 (1977)
10. Bean, C.H.: The Blind have "Optical Illusions". J. Exp. Psychol. 22, 283–289 (1938)
11. Day, R.H., Wong, T.S.: Radial and Tangential Movement Directions as Determinants of the Haptic Illusion in the L Figure. J. Exp. Psychol. 87(1), 19–22 (1971)
12. von Collani, G.: An Analysis of Illusion Components with L and T-Figures in Active Touch. Q. J. Exp. Psychol. 31, 241–248 (1979)
13. Deregowski, J., Ellis, H.D.: Effect of Stimulus Orientation upon Haptic Perception of the Horizontal-Vertical Illusion. J. Exp. Psychol. 95(1), 14–19 (1972)
14. Taylor, C.M.: Visual and Haptic Perception of the Horizontal-Vertical Illusion. Percept. Motor Skill. 92, 167–170 (2001)
15. McManus, I.C.: The Horizontal-Vertical Illusion and the Square. Brit. J. Psychol. 69, 369–370 (1978)
16. Sleight, R.B., Austin, T.R.: The Horizontal-Vertical Illusion in Plane Geometric Figures. J. Psychol. 33, 279–287 (1952)
17. Heller, M.A., Calcaterra, J.A., Burson, L.L., Green, S.L.: The Tactile Horizontal-Vertical Illusion Depends on Radial Motion of the Entire Arm. Percept. Psychophys. 59(8), 1297–1311 (1997)
18. Heller, M.A., Joyner, T.D., Dan-Fodio, H.: Laterality Effects in the Haptic Horizontal-Vertical Illusion. B. Psychonomic Soc. 31(5), 440–442 (1993)
19. Harris, K.M., Slotnick, B.M.: The Horizontal Vertical Illusion: Evidence for Strategic Factors in Feedback-Induced Illusion Decrement. Percept. Motor Skill. 82, 79–87 (1996)
20. Fry, C.L.: Tactual Illusions. Percept. Motor Skill. 40, 955–960 (1975)

Setting the Standards for Haptic and Tactile Interactions: ISO's Work

Jan B.F. van Erp[1], Ki-Uk Kyung[2], Sebastian Kassner[3], Jim Carter[4],
Stephen Brewster[5], Gerhard Weber[6], and Ian Andrew[7]

[1] TNO Human Factors, Soesterberg, The Netherlands
jan.vanerp@tno.nl
[2] ETRI POST-PC Research Group, Daejeon, Korea
kyungku@gmail.com
[3] Technische Universität Darmstadt, Germany
s.kassner@emk.tu-darmstadt.de
[4] Computer Science Department, Un. of Saskatchewan, Saskatoon, Canada
carter@cs.usask.ca
[5] Glasgow Interactive Systems Group, Un. of Glasgow, UK
stephen@dcs.gla.ac.uk
[6] TU Dresden, Dept. Comp. Science, Dresden, Germany
Gerhard.Weber@inf.tu-dresden.de
[7] HF Engineer, United Kingdom
andyand@talktalk.net

Abstract. Tactile and haptic interaction is becoming increasingly important and ergonomic standards can ensure that systems are designed with sufficient concerns for ergonomics and interoperability. ISO (through working group TC159/SC4/WG9) is working toward international standards, which are being dual-tracked as both ISO and CEN standards. This paper gives an update on the status of the work in progress and the recently published International Standard on tactile/haptic interactions. Active involvement of experts is sought for work on terms and definitions and measures to characterize devices and operator capabilities.

Keywords: guidelines, haptics, human computer interaction, standards, tactile.

1 Introduction

Ergonomic standards go beyond providing consistency and interoperability. They help enhance usability in a number of ways including: improving effectiveness and avoiding errors, improving performance, and enhancing the comfort and well-being of users. Ergonomic standards provide a basis for analysis, design, evaluation, procurement, and even for arbitrating issues of international trade. Material providing guidance on the design and use of tactile and haptic interactions is sparse [1, 2]. Therefore, an ISO expert group has been working on standards documents for haptic interaction since 2005. ISO TC159/SC4/WG9 reported on its progress at several conferences

A.M.L. Kappers et al. (Eds.): EuroHaptics 2010, Part II, LNCS 6192, pp. 353–358, 2010.

[3, 4, 5] and published its first standard in 2009 [6]. Here we provide an update on our ongoing work and the work items that will start in the near future:

- ISO 9241-900 Introduction to tactile and haptic interactions will be a technical report providing an overview of the 900 series. It will be regularly updated to include references to the various parts of the 900 series and to other standards containing guidance relevant to tactile and haptic interactions. Work on this item has not started yet.
- ISO 9241-910 Framework for tactile / haptic interactions which will include a detailed list of terms and definitions. This is work in progress and more details are given in Section 2.
- ISO 9241-920 Ergonomics of human-system interaction - Guidance on tactile and haptic interactions. This document has been accepted and published as an International Standard, the first standard on haptics (see Section 3).
- ISO 9241-930 Haptic / tactile interactions in multimodal environments will provide guidance specific to immersive and other multimodal environments. This work has not started (see Section 5).
- ISO 9241-940 Evaluation of tactile / haptic interactions will provide guidance on evaluation methods suited for evaluating tactile and haptic interactions. This work is in progress and the current status is elaborated in Section 4.
- ISO 9241-971 Tactile / haptic interfaces to publicly available devices will provide guidance relating to specific accessibility concerns of using tactile / haptic interaction in public environments and systems. Work on this item has not started (see Section 5).

As of 2010, the following countries are actively participating in WG9: Canada, USA, UK, The Netherlands, Sweden, Germany, South Korea, and Japan. Drafts produced by WG9 go through a thorough review process including rounds of commenting and voting on the drafts by National Technical Advisory Groups.

2 Framework for Tactile and Haptic Interaction

This part of the standard series provides a framework for understanding and communicating about various aspects of tactile/haptic interaction. It contains definitions, structures, models, and explanations that are used in other parts in the series and provides general information about how various forms of interaction can be applied to various user tasks.

There have been several efforts to define terminologies for haptics [7, 8]. While there is no difference between haptic and tactile in most dictionary definitions [9], many researchers and developers use *haptic* to include all haptic sensations and limit the use of tactile to mechanical stimulation of the skin. We adopted a similar distinction, also reflected in Figure 1. The science of haptics and the creation of haptic devices depend on knowledge of the human body, especially its capability to sense both touch to the skin and kinaesthetic activity in the limbs and body joints. Figure 1 shows the relationship between the components that make up the field of haptics.

The framework document defines interaction elements and task primitives for haptic interaction. Users can carry out application tasks by employing one or more task primitives enabled by the haptic device and its associated software. Task primitives are provided by system functionality to users as tools for carrying out the tasks for which the device is designed. In any task, the user should be able to *search, gain an overview, navigate, target, select and manipulate.*

The framework document also contains recommendations for ergonomic design guidelines of haptic interaction for individuality, interaction space, accessibility and resolution. In addition, this part of the standard series introduces physiology of haptics, application areas of haptics, device types and selection criteria.

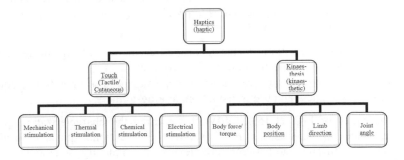

Fig. 1. The components of haptics. "Touch" includes such diverse stimuli as mechanical, thermal, chemical and electrical stimulation to the skin. The "kinaesthetic" sense can be matched by kinaesthetic activity by which a user exerts force or torque on an object external to the active body part.

3 Guidance on Tactile and Haptic Interactions

The document on guidance on tactile and haptic interaction has been accepted by the ISO members as an International Standard and is published by ISO in 2009 [6]. This standard contains guidance in the following areas:

- Applicability considerations for haptic interactions, including: limits to effectiveness, workload considerations (efficiency), user acceptance considerations (satisfaction), meeting user / environmental needs (accessibility), health and safety considerations, and security and privacy.
- Tactile/haptic inputs, outputs, and/or combinations, including: unimodal and multimodal use of haptic interactions, intentional individualization, and unintentional user perceptions.
- Attributes of tactile/haptic encoding of information, including: using properties of objects, using perceptual attributes, and combining attributes.
- Content-specific encoding (what to encode), including: encoding and using textual data, encoding and using graphical data, encoding subjective data, and encoding and using controls.
- Layout of tactile/haptic objects, including: resolution, separation, and consistency.
- Interaction, including: interaction tasks (such as navigation, selection, and manipulation) and interaction techniques (such as moving objects, possessing objects, and gesturing). Guidance for specific haptic interactions related to reading tactile alphabets and notations suitable for blind or deafblind people are handled by Unicode and other national standards.

4 Measures to Characterize Haptic Devices and User Capabilities

Characterizing physical properties of haptic/tactile interaction is fundamental in the specification, design and evaluation of haptic/tactile devices and interactions. Characterization may range from applications such as the development of new devices to the checking of contractual requirements. Due to this importance, we are working on methodologies that can be applied to perform characterization and evaluation tasks. The methodology mainly comprises the definition of sets of measures and corresponding measurement setups. The goal is to provide a set of measures and setups that can be effectively applied. We will cover:

- physical measures specifying technical properties of devices e.g. in the field of mechanics, electronics, computation and control theory,
- human performance measures related to perception, speed of operation, frequency of errors, effectiveness and user satisfaction, amongst others.

Current activities of ISO TC159/SC4/WG9 regarding the characterization of haptic/tactile devices and interactions are focused on the definition of physical measures. At this stage we differentiate between three levels of complexity: "elementary measures", "compound measures" and "derived measures". A few basic examples are given in Table 1.

Table 1. Examples of physical measures

Level of complexity	Measure	Example/ application
Elementary measures	force, time, temperature, distance, ...	perceptual thresholds, maximal/minimal capabilities of users and devices, resolutions, ...
Compound measures	speed	e.g. maximal speed of a device's handle
	frequency	perception of vibration is frequency depended, e.g. [10]
	thermal conductivity, ...	material constant, ...
Derived measures	impedance	e.g. mechanical behaviour of a user
	transparency	transmission performance
	roughness, ...	various measures such as R_a, R_z, R_q, and R_{sk}, ...

Haptic/tactile devices and interactions may be characterized by numerous parameters because the interaction is often bidirectional [11]. This distinguishes haptic devices from visual and auditory displays where information is presented unidirectionally. This bidirectional interaction leads to a coupled system and derived measures such as mechanical impedance Z (ratio of force F to speed v, see formula 1) and transparency T (a measure and stability criterion from a control theory point of view as introduced by Hannaford [12, 13], see formula 2) might be applied to rate the performance of a coupled haptic system as shown in figure 2.

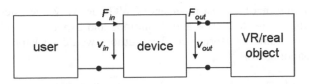

Fig. 2. Two-port representation of a coupled haptic/tactile system transmitting force and speed

$$Z = \frac{F}{v} \; . \qquad T = \frac{F_{out}/v_{out}}{F_{in}/v_{in}} \; . \qquad\qquad (1, 2)$$

Other measures such as "force" or "distance" can indicate perceptional thresholds, sensory resolutions (e.g. two-point discrimination on a Braille display) or other human capabilities such as maximal forces a user can exert on a device. Ergonomic measures may be used for formative or summative evaluation. For example, the multimodal nature of applying and analyzing haptic mock-ups [14] and prototypes requires an adaptation of other ISO 9241 documents related to user centered design.

Overall, up to forty measures are currently being discussed. This number of possible measures indicates the complexity and variety of haptic/tactile perception and interaction. We are also developing two scenarios to demonstrate the application of particular measurements. One scenario on a 3D force feedback display and one on a large tactile display with 7200 pins.

5 Future Objectives

TC159/SC4/WG9 has identified two additional areas for future work: the use of haptic interactions in multimodal environments (potential 9241-930) and public environments (potential 9241-971). While the other standards in the 9241-9xx series focus almost exclusively (with the exception of a few high level guidelines in 9241-920) with haptics, these two new areas both focus on the combination with haptics with other modalities. 9241-930 will provide the more general of the two sets of guidance, focusing on where combinations of modalities are intended to be used simultaneously by a user (such as immersive environments) and will consider multi-modal issues (such as allocation of function to different modalities). 9241-971 will focus on the accessible use of haptics in public environments, where the users might not be able to interact via other available modalities. It will consider systems where users are or are not allowed to connect their own assistive technology. The start of these activities is dependent on finding suitable experts to work on them and on obtaining suitable research and expert opinion that could be used in them.

6 Getting Involved

TC159/SC4/WG9 is continuously working on ensuring that all guidelines are technically correct and feasible. You can get involved as an expert member of TC159/SC4/WG9 actively developing drafts of the planned work items. Independent from actively being involved, the members of WG9 are very interested in your opinions on tactile/haptic-related terms and definitions and experience with measures for haptic devices or human performance. The authors would be happy to get you involved in the ongoing work.

Acknowledgment. This work was supported by the IT R&D program of MKE/KEIT [2009-F-048-01, Contact-free Multipoint Realistic Interaction Technology Development] and The Netherlands Organization for Applied Scientific Research TNO.

References

[1] Van Erp, J.B.F.: Guidelines for the use of vibro-tactile displays in human computer interaction. In: Proceedings of Eurohaptics 2002, pp. 18–22 (2002)

[2] Van Erp, J.B.F.: The multi-dimensional nature of encoding tactile and haptic interactions: From psychophysics to design guidelines. In: Proceedings of the Human Factors and Ergonomics Society 2006, pp. 685–688 (2006)

[3] Carter, J., Van Erp, J.B.F.: Ergonomics of tactile and haptic interactions. In: Proceedings of the Human Factors and Ergonomics Society 2006, pp. 674–675 (2006)

[4] Van Erp, J.B.F., Carter, J., Andrew, I.: ISO's Work on Tactile and Haptic Interaction Guidelines. In: Proceedings of Eurohaptics 2006, pp. 467–470 (2006)

[5] Van Erp, J.B.F., Kern, T.A.: ISO's work on guidance for Haptic and tactile interactions. In: Ferre, M. (ed.) EuroHaptics 2008. LNCS, vol. 5024, pp. 936–940. Springer, Heidelberg (2008)

[6] ISO: Ergonomics of human-system interaction – Part 920: Guidance on tactile and haptic interactions. ISO 9241-920:2009. ISO, Geneva (2009)

[7] Srinivasan, M.A., Basdogan, C.: Haptic in virtual environment: Taxonomy, research status, and challenges. Computer and Graphics 21(4), 393–404 (1997)

[8] Oakely, I., McGee, M.R., Brewster, S.A., Gray, P.D.: Putting the feel in look and feel? In: Proceedings of Conference on Human Factors in Computing Systems, pp. 415–422 (2000)

[9] Merriam-Webster Online Dictionary, http://www.merriam-webster.com/dictionary/

[10] Gescheider, G.: Psychophysics: Method and Theory. Halsted Press, Mahwah (1976)

[11] Hayward, V., Maclean, K.: Do it yourself haptics: part I. IEEE Robotics & Automation Magazine 14, 88–104 (2007)

[12] Hannaford, B.: A design framework for teleoperators with kinaesthetic feedback. IEEE Trans. Robot. Automat. 5, 426–434 (1989)

[13] Adams, R., Hannaford, B.: Control Law Design for Haptic Interfaces to Virtual Reality. IEEE Transactions on Control System Technology 10, 3–13 (2002)

[14] Miao, M., Köhlmann, W., Schiewe, M., Weber, G.: Tactile Paper Prototyping with Blind Subjects. In: Altinsoy, M.E., Jekosch, U., Brewster, S. (eds.) HAID 2009. LNCS, vol. 5763, pp. 81–90. Springer, Heidelberg (2009)

Vibrotactor-Belt on the Thigh – Directions in the Vertical Plane

Yael Salzer, Tal Oron-Gilad, and Adi Ronen

Human Factors Laboratory
Dept. of Industrial Engineering and Management
Ben-Gurion University of the Negev, Israel
{yaelsa,orontal,adiro}@bgu.ac.il

Abstract. This multiple phase research examines the utility of the thigh as a placement for a vibrotactile display in the cockpit. The initial phase of this research is presented hereby. Vibrotactile displays designed to convey horizontal directional waypoints or warnings are commonly situated on the torso of the pilot. Here, an eight-tactors belt prototype fixed around the thigh of a seated operator was used to convey vertical directional waypoints. Localization accuracy was examined. Analysis revealed that vibrotactile cues embracing the thigh are discriminated in a similar manner to the torso, providing initial evidence that vibrotactile signaling on the thigh can provide directional cues in the vertical plane.

Keywords: orienting, vibrotactile display, vertical plane.

1 Introduction

Tactile displays introduce impending solutions to limitations in visual data processing, or malfunction in visual data perception in the cockpit environment [1, 2]. Vibrotactile displays have been thoroughly examined as means to communicate spatial data such as directional waypoint [3], guidance cues for target acquisition [4], threat marking, areas to avoid, to convey distance from a conceptual boundary (e.g., in helicopter or UAV landing) [5,6] or as an alert for collision [7]. Several body parts were used; amongst them were the tongue and fingers [8], arms [9], hands [4], thigh [7, 10] and torso [3, 5]. For example, tactors placed underneath the seated body of the vehicle driver, actuating the dorsum of the thigh, conveyed direction of a possible collision [7] or assisted in navigation [10]. Nevertheless, the most common locus for vibrotactile displays remains the torso [5, 6, and 11] which maintains a good notion of direction in the horizontal plane [12, 13] and does not interfere with clothing and equipment, allowing the user's hands to be free for other tasks [14]. The torso was also utilized to convey vertical spatial orienting, such as the work of van Erp and colleagues [5] who applied vibrotactors on the shoulders and buttocks of the pilot in a hovering helicopter to aid control over altitude and drifts.

In this work we examined the thigh, as a potential locus for directional orienting, within the vertical plane. To the best of our knowledge no previous study addressed

A.M.L. Kappers et al. (Eds.): EuroHaptics 2010, Part II, LNCS 6192, pp. 359–364, 2010.
© Springer-Verlag Berlin Heidelberg 2010

the thigh's vertical directional capabilities in the way utilized here. First we examined the ability to recognize the location [15] of a vibrotactile stimulation embracing the thigh, and then determined which region along the thigh provided more accurate localization. We examined the localization with different burst durations and pulse repetitions which could later be utilized to encode information [16]. The tactor display prototype was developed by a joint venture of Israel Aircraft Industries (IAI), Lahav Division and Ben Gurion University of the Negev (patent pending 11/968,405).

2 Method

2.1 Participants

Sixteen female and 25 male undergraduate students (age 22 to 30, mean 26.7) participated in the experiment for course credit.

2.2 Apparatus

The experimental system consisted of a tactor controller Eval2.0 (by Engineering Acoustics Inc. (EAI)) regulating eight EAI-C2 tactors stitched to an elastic fiber strip, 6 cm apart from each other. The flexibility of the fiber guaranteed unified spacing between the tactors when stretched around the thigh. To mimic pilots' natural clothing, participants wore a standard pilot suit. The tactor belt was worn on the right thigh over the suit. Active noise-cancelling headphones (ATH-ANC7, Audio-Technica) shielded possible noise from the vibrating tactors. The experimental system ran on a 2.8GHz Dell DHM desktop computer with Windows XP operating system. A designated program in E-prime2.0 activated the experimental procedure.

Intouch 5-wire resistive touch screen panel integrated into a 19" Samsung 920 IBM LCD screen was used as the pointing device. Participant responded by pressing on virtual buttons displayed on the screen. Eight virtual buttons (1.5 cm radius) equally spaced in a circular form (8.5 cm radius), each button corresponding to a single tactor according to its relative location on the thigh (see Figure 1). To illustrate, the virtual button at 9 o'clock corresponds to the tactor located on the medial surface of the thigh (Figure 1, tactor 7). Since vibration is best perceived at the frequency of 250Hz [17]

Fig. 1. Left: Midsagittal cross section of thigh (gray ellipse) and relative location of tactors (gray disks). Center: Positioning of the participant and apparatus. Elastic tactile belt mounted on right thigh. Right: Virtual buttons (circles) displayed on the touch screen.

and frequency has no affect on the quality of localization [13]; the frequency of vibration was either a continuous 250Hz (perceived as a continuous "buzzz") or a pulsed 250Hz (with 10Hz or 5Hz beats perceived as "buzz...buzz...buzz", these are 50ms:50ms on-off and 100ms:100ms on-off, respectively). Those three signals are very distinguishable. The touch screen was placed on a table in front of the participant; the sitting position of the participants was adjusted so that each of the buttons was easily reached (see Figure 1).

2.3 Experimental Design

Four within participants variables were defined: signal duration (200ms, 400ms, 600ms or 800ms), signal type (continuous, 5Hz pulsed or 10Hz pulsed), location on the thigh (close to the knee, middle of the thigh, and closer to the groins) and inter trial interval (ITI) (1500ms, 2500ms or 3500ms). In each trial one of the eight tactors was randomly activated; altogether, each tactor was activated 45 times, thus each combination of variables was introduced 10 times within an experimental block (regardless of the tactor location or ITI).

2.4 Procedure

Participants were given time to familiarize with the association between the vibrotactile stimulation and the corresponding virtual buttons on the touch screen. In the experimental block the participant was given a localization task, in which only the response accuracy (ACC) was collected. As a trial began, a tactor was activated. The participant's response was to press the matching virtual button on the touch screen based on her directional judgment. Accuracy value was set to 1 if the correct button was chosen, and zero otherwise. The next stimulation was applied within a random ITI to prevent possible adaptation to the rhythm of stimulations. For each location on the thigh, a practice block of 16 trials was followed by 120 trials of the experimental block. The order of loci was counterbalanced among participants.

3   Results

Generalized linear mixed model (GLMM) fit by the Laplace approximation with all four experimental variables; Thigh location (3) X Signal type (3) X Duration (4) X ITI (3), was conducted. Main effects were found for *thigh location* ($F_{(2, 78)}$=12.487, p=.00002) and *signal duration* ($F_{(3, 117)}$=3.9470, p=.01008). Mean accuracy when tactor belt was located near the knee was highest (M=0.78, SD=0.16), significantly better compared to the middle of the thigh (M=0.71, SD=0.2) (p<0.001) which was significantly better than by the groins (M=0.66, SD=0.23) (p=0.042). Contrast examination of signal duration revealed a significant contrast ($F_{(1,39)}$=11.46, p=0.0016) between signal duration of 200ms (M=0.70 SD=0.21) and the durations of 400ms, 600ms and 800ms (M=0.72 SD=0.21, M=0.73 SD=0.21 M=0.73, SD=0.20, respectively). No significant difference was found between the later three.

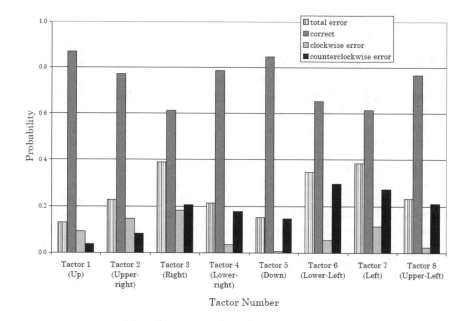

Fig. 2. Accuracy and error probability by tactor position on the thigh. Total error probability rates were separated into clockwise and counterclockwise errors.

Post hoc comparisons evaluate the accuracy of each separate tactor (See Figure 2) regardless of loci on thigh. There was no significant difference between tactors 1 and 5 (frontal and dorsal). There was no significant difference between tactors 2, 4 and 8 and no significant difference between tactors 3, 6, and 7. Tactors 2, 4 and 8 were significantly more accurate than tactors 3, 6 and 7 ($p<0.001$). The frontal and dorsal tactors were significantly more accurate than tactors 2, 4 and 8 ($p<0.001$). The mean accuracy of localization across all tactors was 72%. By allowing a deviation range of one virtual button to the left or right of the correct virtual button, localization accuracy raised to 98.5% (SD=0.01). These finding would be further discussed.

Participants were asked to report on their subjective experience. It was commonly said that the axial tactors (1, 3, 5 and 7) were easy to recognize, the frontal and dorsal (1 and 5) being the easiest. Localization of the diagonal tactors (2, 4, 6 and 8) was perceived with more difficulty.

4   Discussion

The aim of this experiment was to evaluate the localization of the vibrotactile stimulations embracing the thigh. The frontal and dorsal tactors placed on the thigh were perceived most accurately. The tactor located more to the sides of the thigh were perceived as less accurate; medial and lateral thigh was perceived least accurate. Subjective inputs collected from the participants confirmed these findings. Interestingly, these results are in line with previous work which demonstrated that both the accuracy acquired for torso localization and the perceived direction provided by tactile stimulation on the torso are less variant and more accurate the closer the stimulus is to the naval or spine [12, 13, 15]. Tactor location accuracy ranging from 78% down to 66% resembles results reported by Cholewiak and colleagues [18] who achieved 74% success rate when mounting 12 tactors around the waist. Their accuracy improved up to 97%, as the number of tactors in use was decreased.

It should be noted that in the current study, the response of the participant was collected using buttons as discrete means. The buttons were spread 45° degrees apart, corresponding for a range of 22.5° to either side. This response manipulation does not allow an evaluation of a continuous and/or overlapping range for the perceived localization of tactors. Nevertheless, calculating the accuracy within a permitted range of one distinct button to the left or right of the target button resulted with a very high accuracy score of 98.5%. When keeping in mind that the strength of tactile cues is not necessarily in being highly punctual (i.e. pinpoint on the target) but rather by providing higher benefits in enhancing general alertness and orienting attention toward the required direction [19], the results are satisfying for such a paradigm. Hence, this research phase demonstrated that the thigh could potentially be utilized for spatial orientation of the vertical plane, best perceived near the knee.

In conclusion, this work provides the foundation to further examine the usage of the thigh for directional orienting in the vertical plane. Once this potential was established, it is essential to clarify whether vibrotactors' orienting signals are beneficial when accompanying the auditory and visual signals already assimilated in the cockpit and further on, with the dynamic body posture and orientation changes which occur during flight. Orienting in the vertical plane may be exploited to assist pilot's elevation control, navigation or provide means of alerts. Combined with a horizontal plane orienting device the system may act as a complete three dimensional orienting system essential for aviation and space vehicles.

Acknowledgement. This work was supported by the IAI Israeli Aerospace Industry, Uri Paz-Meidan, Technical Monitor (upaz-meidan@iai.co.il). The views expressed in this work are those of the authors and do not necessarily reflect official IAI policy.

References

1. Lintern, G., Waite, T., Talleur, D.A.: Functional Interface Design for the Modern Aircraft Cockpit. The International Journal of Aviation Psychology 9(3), 225–240 (1999)
2. Van Veen, H.A., van Erp, J.B.: Tactile Information Presentation in The Cockpit. In: Proceedings of the First International Workshop on Haptic Human-Computer Interaction, pp. 174–181 (2000)
3. Van Erp, J.B., van Veen, H.A., Jansen, C., Dobbins, T.: Waypoint Navigation with a Vibrotactile Waist Belt. Transactions on Applied Perception 2(2), 106–117 (2005)
4. Oron-Gilad, T., Downs, J.L., Gilson, R.D., Hancock, P.A.: Vibrotactile Guidance Cues for Target Acquisition. IEEE Transactions on Systems, Man, and Cybernetic part C: Applications and Reviews 37(5), 903–1004 (2007)
5. Van Erp, J.B., Veltman, J.A., van Veen, H.A., Oving, A.B.: Tactile Torso Display as Countermeasure to Reduce Night Vision Goggles Induced Drift. In: RTO HFM Symposium on Spatial Disorientation in Military Vehicles: Causes, Consequences and Cures, RTO-MP-086, Spain (2002)

6. Jennings, S., Craig, G., Cheung, B., Rupert, A., Schultz, K.: Flight-Test of a Tactile Situational Awareness System in a Land-based Deck Landing Task. In: Proceedings of the Human Factors and Ergonomics Society 48th Annual Meeting, pp. 142–146 (2004)
7. Fitch, G.M., Kiefer, R.J., Hankey, J.M., Kleiner, B.M.: Toward Developing an Approach for Alerting Drivers to the Direction of a Crash. Human Factors 49(4), 710–720 (2007)
8. Bach-y-Rita, P., Kercel, S.W.: Sensory Substitution and the Human Machine Interface. Trends in Cognitive Sciences 7(12), 541–545 (2003)
9. Cholewiak, R.W., Collins, A.A.: Vibrotactile localization on the arm: Effects of place, space, and age. Perception & Psychophysics 65(7), 1058–1077 (2003)
10. Van Erp, J.B., Van Veen, H.A.: Vibrotactile In-Vehicle Navigation System. Transportation Research Part F 7, 247–256 (2004)
11. Cholewiak, R.W., McGarth, C.: Vibrotactile Targeting in Multimodal Systems: Accuracy and Interaction. In: International Symposium on Haptic Interfaces for Virtual Environment and Teleoperator Systems (HAPTICS 2006), p. 64 (2006)
12. Van Erp, B.F.: Presenting Directions with a Vibrotactile Torso Display. Ergonomics 48(3), 302–313 (2005)
13. Van Erp, B.F.: Absolute Localization of Vibrotactile Stimuli on the Torso. Perception & Psychophysics 70(6), 1016–1023 (2008)
14. Gilson, R.D., Redden, E.S., Elliott, L.R.: Remote Tactile Displays for Future Soldiers, ARL-SR-0152 (2008)
15. Cholewiak, R.W., Brill, J.C., Schwab, A.: Vibrotactile Localization on the Abdomen: Effects of Place and Space. Perception & Psychophysics 66(6), 970–987 (2004)
16. Jones, L.A., Sarter, N.B.: Tactile Displays: Guidance for Their Design and Application. Human Factors: The Journal of the Human Factors and Ergonomics Society 50, 90–111 (2008)
17. Verrillo, R.T.: Vibrotactile Thresholds for Hairy Skin. Journal of Experimental Psychology 72(1), 47–50 (1966)
18. Cholewiak, R.W., Brill, J.C., Chwab, A.: Vibrotactile localization on the abdomen: Effects of place and space. Perception & Psychophysics 66(6), 970–987 (2004)
19. Eriksson, L., van Erp, J., Carlander, O., Levin, B., van Veen, H., Veltman, H.: Vibrotactile and Visual Threat Cueing with High G threat Intercept in Dynamic Flight Simulator. In: Proceedings of the Human Factors and Ergonomics society 50th Annual Meeting 2006 (2006)

Accuracy of Haptic Object Matching in Blind and Sighted Children and Adults

Ans Withagen[1], Astrid M.L. Kappers[2], Mathijs P.J. Vervloed[3],
Harry Knoors[3,4], and Ludo Verhoeven[3]

[1] Royal Visio, National Foundation for the Visually Impaired and Blind, Huizen,
The Netherlands
[2] Helmholtz Institute, Utrecht University, The Netherlands
[3] Behavioural Science Institute, Radboud University Nijmegen, The Netherlands
[4] Royal Kentalis, Sint Michielsgestel, The Netherlands
answithagen@visio.org, a.m.l.kappers@uu.nl,
{m.vervloed,l.verhoeven}@pwo.ru.nl, h.knoors@kentalis.nl

Abstract. In this study a haptic object matching task is used to examine the accuracy of identification of the object dimensions: texture, weight, volume and exact shape in four different participant groups: congenitally blind adults, sighted adults, congenitally blind children, and sighted children. The results show that age is more influential for the accuracy to identify object dimensions by touch than the visual status.

Keywords: Touch, children, tactual exploration, blind, object dimension.

1 Introduction

Object identification is generally based on visual inspection. One searches for familiar visual features to recognize an object. Normally, a visual glance suffices for this purpose. However, for some people objects have to be explored by other senses, for instance because they lack vision. For blind persons the sense of touch is essential for object identification and manual explorations are necessary for concept development. Prominent object dimensions such as volume, weight, shape and texture, can be distinguished by haptic manipulation alone. Vision is not necessary, although past visual experience might be helpful. Touch also conveys different information about tangible objects than vision. Through haptic exploration one achieves more detailed material information. For instance, texture, compliance and heat flow, are more easily accessible by touch than vision. Compared to vision, relatively little is known about haptic object identification and the developmental trajectories of haptic skills [1].

In the present study, matching objects by different object dimensions is studied in children and adults. An additional aspect of touch that is included in this study, is familiarity with the sense of touch. Congenitally blind persons are more experienced in using touch to identify objects than sighted persons, because they often have to rely on touch because of the absence of sight. One could assume that this experience is an advantage. However, the lack of visual experience to assist the haptic manipulations

A.M.L. Kappers et al. (Eds.): EuroHaptics 2010, Part II, LNCS 6192, pp. 365–370, 2010.

can also be a disadvantage. Visual memory and visual imagery are not available for blind people. This study will focus on the influence of haptic and visual experience on the accuracy to identify object dimensions by touch.

Klatzky, Lederman and Metzger [2] were among the first researchers to describe the way people identify familiar objects by touch. Objects were identified by participants both rapidly and accurately. In a sequel to this study Lederman and Klatzky [3] gave a match-to-sample task to blindfolded participants. Hand movements were observed during object exploration. The haptic strategies depended on the object dimension that was tested. They termed these haptic strategies "Exploratory Procedures" (EPs). Each EP was especially suited for gaining information about certain object dimensions: enclosure for estimating size, unsupported holding for weight, lateral motion for texture, static contact for temperature, pressure for hardness, and contour following for exact shape.

Most studies on the accuracy of judgements on tactile dimensions were carried out with adult participants and not children. One of the few exceptions is a study by Klatzky and colleagues [4] who observed preschool children while judging tool functions of objects. In that experiment, children could apply both visual and haptic exploratory procedures. They showed that children executed specialized exploratory procedures to extract relevant tool properties. The children had an appropriate repertoire of EPs and used these to extract relevant information. They used adult-like patterns of exploration to examine the different dimensions. Based on the results and previous work, they pointed out 'the importance of active haptic exploration in acquiring knowledge about objects, whether or not vision is present' (Klatzky & Mankinen, 2005, 248).

Hatwell [5] studied school-aged children's ability to recognise objects both visually and haptically. She compared the results of congenitally blind and (blindfolded) sighted children on a shape recognition task. The visual performance of 7 years old sighted subjects was superior to that of 12 to 14 years old blindfolded sighted and blind subjects who had to solve the task by touch. Vision seemed to be superior to touch, even in the youngest children. That study highlighted the quantitative differences in performance between haptic and visual recognition of shapes.

Lederman and Klatzky's well known 1987 study [3] was never carried out with children, nor with blind persons. The current study fills this gap and describes the accuracy of performance in the same object matching task by children and adults, both congenitally blind and sighted for the dimensions Texture, Volume, Exact Shape and Weight. Next the experimental design will be described and the results presented with regard to accuracy. The discussion focuses on the effects of blindness and the differences between adults and children.

2   Methods

2.1   Participants

Sixty-one participants took part in the experiment, all naïve to the aims of the experiment. The participants were divided into four groups:

1.   16 congenitally blind adults (mean age = 39)
2.   15 sighted adults, matched on age, gender and level of education with the blind adults (mean age = 39)

3. 15 congenitally blind children, attending mainstream schools (mean age = 9)
4. 15 sighted classmates of the blind children, matched on age, gender and level of education (mean age = 9).

2.2 Material

Four object sets with regard to texture, weight, volume and exact shape were reproduced from the original object sets of Lederman and Klatzky [3] with permission of the authors. All the objects were unfamiliar, meaningless and functionless objects and therefore difficult to label. Each object set consisted of 16 three-dimensional stimuli (see figure 1 for an example).

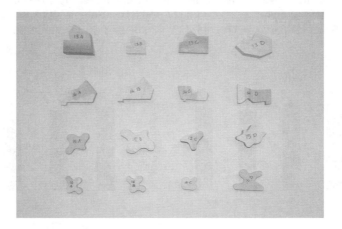

Fig. 1. Object set 'Exact Shape', with at the left side the standard objects. The second item in each row shows the test stimulus that matches the standard best on the required dimension, in this example "exact shape".

Each set comprised of one standard object and three comparison objects, of which one was the best match, but not identical to the standard. By changing irrelevant object dimensions for the task at hand some confusion was purposely introduced into the experiments.

2.3 Procedure

During the experiment, the participant sat opposite the experimenter with a curtain hanging between the participant and the experimenter. As a result, the participant was not able to see the stimuli that were given to him. Participants were asked to put their hands stretched out on the table, with the palms upward. As soon as they received the stimuli in their hands; the participants were allowed to manipulate the objects.

Every condition started with a practice session, in which the participants could practice the procedure of matching one of the objects with the standard. The experimenter first presented a standard object, which they were allowed to explore for one of four object dimensions: texture, weight, volume, or exact shape. Next, the three comparison stimuli were given consecutively and the participants were asked which

368 A. Withagen et al.

of the three best matched with the standard. There was no time limit for responding. Participants had to answer verbally after exploring the three comparison stimuli. No feedback was given. The order in which the participants received the stimuli was randomized but blocked per condition. All trials were repeated three times and the mean of the four trials was taken as the dependent variable.

3 Results

Four oneway ANOVAs were carried out on the mean scores of the four tasks with group as the independent variable. The results are shown in figures 2-5.

For all tasks there was a significant main effect for group (Texture: $F_{(3,57)}=$ 3.370, $p= 0.025$; Weight: $F(3,57)=3.831$, $p=0.014$; Volume: $F(3,57) =3.677$, $p = 0.017$; and Exact shape: $F(3,57) = 11.432$, $p<0.001$). Post Hoc multiple comparisons

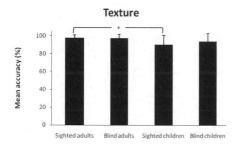 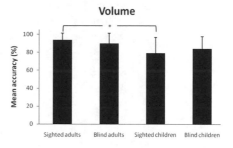

Fig. 2. Mean Percentage Accuracy for Texture. Error bars indicate standard deviations (SD), asterisk indicates significant group difference ($p<0.05$).

Fig. 3. Mean Percentage Accuracy for Volume. Error bars indicate standard deviations (SD), asterisk indicates significant group difference ($p<0.05$).

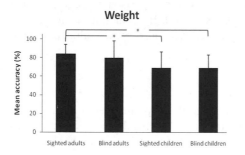 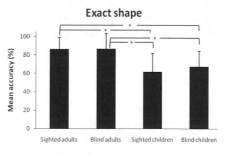

Fig. 4. Mean Percentage Accuracy for Weight. Error bars indicate significant group differences ($p<0.05$).

Fig. 5. Mean Percentage Accuracy for Exact Shape. Error bars indicate standard deviations (SD), asterisks indicate significant group differences ($p<0.05$).

with the Tukey test to correct for chance capitalizations showed significant differences between sighted adults and sighted children for Texture ($p=0.035$) and for Volume ($p=0.016$); for Weight between sighted adults and both sighted children ($p=0.044$) and blind children ($p=0.044$); and for Exact shape between sighted adults and both sighted children ($p<0.001$) and blind children ($p=0.006$), and between blind adults and both sighted children ($p<0.001$) and blind children ($p=0.004$).

Correlation analyses between the scores (transformed into Z-scores) of the four groups on the different object dimensions showed that there was just one significant correlation: for the blind children there was a moderately strong correlation between the object dimensions Volume and Exact Shape of $r = 0.56$ ($p = 0.029$).

4 Discussion

The current study partially replicated the classical experiment of Lederman and Klatzky[3] with congenitally blind adults and children and compared them to the performances of sighted adults and children. Four object dimensions were examined (texture, weight, volume and exact shape) with exact replica's of the original objects of Lederman and Klatzky [3]. The accuracy of the different groups on the four object dimensions was examined in a match-to-sample task. The main interest of the present study was to investigate the influence of age and the absence of sight on accuracy.

On all the four object dimensions the children performed significantly poorer on accuracy than the adults. There were no significant differences found between the same age groups of blind and sighted individuals. Age seems more important than the visual status of the participants. Especially 'Exact Shape' appeared to be a significantly more difficult task for children than adults. For the adults 'Weight' was the most difficult object dimension to match followed by exact shape. Exact shape might be difficult for children because of the number of acts necessary to make decisions about exact shape, the fact that their hands are still small or because of immature spatial perception. In the post hoc multiple comparisons there were more significant differences found between the sighted children and adults (texture, weight, volume and exact shape), than between the blind children and sighted adults (weight and exact shape). Age had far more influence on the accuracy to identify object dimensions by touch than visual or tactual experiences.

However, there are some differences in the performances of the blind and sighted groups noticeable. The sighted children and adults performed significantly different on all the object dimensions. The blind children and blind adults performed only significantly different on the dimension 'Exact Shape', which might be explained not only by the tactual strategies they use, but also by the cognitive complexity of the task. Possibly the differences in performance between the sighted and blind children in relation to adults can be explained by the tactual training the blind children received in early childhood. Individual variation is large in both groups of children but also in the group of blind adults. The large variation also explains the lack of significant difference scores.

Accuracy levels in the current study were comparable with the data from Lederman and Klatzky (1987). Texture was easiest to match and Weight the most difficult. In the current study, percentage accuracy for Weight seemed somewhat higher than in the study of Lederman and Klatzky. However, individual variation was also largest for the dimension Weight, so this difference is probably not significant.

Future analyses should make clear which other aspects affect accuracy, such as for instance, response latencies and the use of different Exploratory Procedures.

Acknowledgements

The authors acknowledge the contribution of dr. Lederman in the design of the stimulus materials for this study and thank all participants, parents and teachers for their time and participation. The research on which this article is based, was supported by a grant from the Novum Foundation; a non-profit organization providing financial support to (research) projects that improve the quality of life of individuals with a visual impairment.

References

1. Klatzky, R.L., Lederman, S.J.: Object recognition by touch. In: Rieser, J.R., Ashmead, D.H., Ebner, F.F., Corn, A. (eds.) Blindness and Brain Plasticity in Navigation and Object Perception, pp. 185–208. LEA, New York (2008)
2. Klatzky, R.L., Lederman, S.J., Metzger, V.A.: Identifying objects by touch: An expert system. Perception & Psychophysics 37, 299–302 (1985)
3. Lederman, S.J., Klatzky, R.L.: Hand movements: a window into haptic object recognition. Cognitive Psychology 19, 342–368 (1987)
4. Klatzky, R.L., Mankinen, J.M.: Visual and haptic exploratory procedures in children's judgements about tool function. Infant Behavior & Development 28, 240–249 (2005)
5. Hatwell, Y.: Form perception and related issues in blind humans. In: Herschell, R.L., Leibowitz, W., Teuber, H. (eds.) Perception, pp. 489–519. Springer, New York (1978)

The Core Skills Trainer: A Set of Haptic Games for Practicing Key Clinical Skills

Sarah Baillie, Neil Forrest, and Tierney Kinnison

The Royal Veterinary College, University of London, Hawkshead Lane, AL9 7TA, UK
{sbaillie,ndforrest,tkinnison}@rvc.ac.uk

Abstract. A new approach to teaching the skills used by health professionals during hands-on (palpation-based) examinations and procedures is reported, where students practice individual 'core' skills by playing haptic computer games. These core palpatory skills were identified through interviews and a survey of clinicians and include determining size, firmness, shape and moving and thinking in 3D. A learning environment using haptic force-feedback technology (The Core Skills Trainer) was created that consisted of a set of eight computer games, one game for each core skill. Concepts from computer gaming were used to help engage students in the learning process including acquiring points, losing lives, different levels of difficulty and high scores tables. Each game has three levels of difficulty to support progressive improvement and the player's ultimate task is to become proficient in all the core skills.

Keywords: Clinical training, core skills, computer games, simulator.

1   Introduction

Hands-on skills are central to the clinical work of many health professionals who use their hands to examine patients (i.e. palpation). Simulators are now widely used to provide trainees with alternatives to practicing these palpatory skills on patients. Many simulators (physical and virtual reality) are procedure specific, i.e. designed for learning a particular clinical task or examination. An example of such a simulator is the veterinary trainer 'The Haptic Cow' [1]. While teaching the core curriculum with the cow, a more generic approach was sometimes adopted because a number of students' career aspirations were not in farm animal medicine, but rather equine or small animal practice. To make the training relevant the instructor would focus on the 'core' haptic skills (e.g. determining relative size or detecting differences in stiffness) that were applicable to other species and techniques, but were being learned in the context of the cow. A logical next step was proposed: the development of 'The Core Skills Trainer', a training tool for learning the palpatory skills that are the fundamental 'building blocks' for many palpation-based procedures and examinations. In human medicine, training for the component skills of minimally invasive surgery (MIS) has been provided [2] but a similar approach for palpation has not been undertaken. The Core Skills Trainer aimed to fill this niche, providing generic palpatory skills training (initially for veterinary education) in an engaging and enjoyable format: a set of haptic computer games, one for each core skill.

A.M.L. Kappers et al. (Eds.): EuroHaptics 2010, Part II, LNCS 6192, pp. 371–376, 2010.

2   Identifying the Core Skills

The first step was to identify the core palpatory skills. A preliminary list was drawn up using information from the literature, including object properties explored through touch as researched by Weber [3], Lederman and Klatsky's exploratory procedures (EPs) [4] and from our own work with veterinarians [5]. A clinical perspective was established initially by interviewing doctors and veterinarians. They were asked to identify the core skills used when performing palpation-based examinations and procedures. The list was then refined and compiled into a survey sent to veterinarians. The recipients were asked to decide whether each skill was core to their clinical work and to provide examples of when the skill was used. At the end of the survey a free text section was provided for respondents to enter additional core skills not represented in the list.

Fifty-five veterinarians responded. Six of the eight provisional core skills were considered of clinical relevance by the majority of respondents (Fig. 1). Comments on the skills indicated that hand movements for certain techniques are restricted primarily to one dimension, e.g. pressing an object to assess stiffness, or could be in three dimensions, e.g. to find and identify structures. The skill of thinking in 3D was related to processing information gathered during complex tasks including palpating 'blind' (e.g. during an internal examination) and building a 3D mental image, say of the overall anatomy. In the free text section a further skill emerged, classified as 'detection of movement', e.g. a pulse.

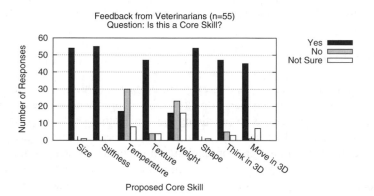

Fig. 1. Veterinarians' responses to a survey designed to identify core skills

3   Software Development

3.1   Requirements Overview

The Core Skills Trainer, a series of haptic computer games, was developed to enable trainee health professionals to practice the core skills identified by clinicians. A games environment was used to capitalize on the students' competitive nature and encourage them to practice and improve. A key requirement was that students should be able to use the trainer independently, so that its use was not limited by the need for a technician or tutor. A fundamental advantage of the core skills approach is that each skill is applicable to many different clinical procedures or tasks. Therefore, each game had to remain abstract from a specific clinical context. This also afforded greater freedom in terms of games design.

3.2 Design and Implementation

Based on the survey of clinicians, five games were developed, each focusing on a different haptic perception task (recognizing an object's stiffness, differentiating between objects based on size, identifying shapes, comparing textures and detecting movement). A further three games were created that incorporated aspects of 3D thinking and movement (two games focused on controlling force/pressure in a single dimension and one on movement around a 3D maze). The games were designed to be appealing, for example in one game, to teach the use of controlled pressure, the player's application of force controls the flight of an airplane. Objects including stars and bombs appear at different altitudes which need to be collected or avoided. In another game (the 'Texture Game') the player follows a path across a grid (Fig. 2; left) by feeling for the 'most textured' squares (texture is represented by dynamic and stick-slip friction). In this paper, the Texture Game will be used to illustrate the process by which all eight core skills games were developed. The challenge was to create fun game concepts, whilst ensuring that the skills taught were relevant to a range of clinical procedures. Veterinarians were regularly involved to help guide clinical relevance.

Fig. 2. The Texture Game (left), one of the eight core skills games developed and a student using The Core Skills Trainer (right)

Concepts from conventional computer games such as scoring points, losing lives and unlocking levels of increasing difficulty are used to engage the player and encourage competition. Each game has three levels of difficulty. The first and second levels present the same task, but the second is more difficult and should require repeated practice to complete. The third or 'expert' level adds an extra challenge (e.g. in the Texture Game the player feels the friction effect on a sphere rather than a flat surface). The games were designed to balance the use of psychophysics (to measure performance) with the gaming principals that the training should be fun and quick. For example, a psychophysical discrimination protocol is used as the basis for a game to teach size perception, however the number of questions is limited and the concepts of points and lives are added.

The Core Skills Trainer was implemented in C++ with H3DAPI [6] and uses a PHANToM Omni (Fig. 2; right). The Omni was chosen as a tradeoff between cost and performance. However, the software was designed to be independent of haptic device type, so that if a more suitable device became available, it could easily be supported. Preliminary user testing was conducted with each game to initially set difficulty levels. The expert level of the Texture Game was modified to use a psychophysical staircase algorithm to estimate a player's perceptual limit. Incorrect (less 'textured') spheres had a constant dynamic friction coefficient of 0.2 (as rendered by the HAPI God Object Renderer [6]), while the friction of the correct (most 'textured') sphere varied in steps of 0.03, decreasing after a correct answer and increasing after an incorrect answer. Three experienced haptic users participated and the resulting average Weber fraction of 34% was used to provisionally set the difficulty of the Texture Game.

A menu system was created to allow the players to access the games and view their overall progress. To enforce the idea that the skills are 'building blocks' for clinical practice and players need to acquire them all, an image of a clinician is gradually revealed as the player completes each game. To encourage the player to practice each skill equally, a game may become temporarily locked if it is played more often than the others. To avoid usability issues combining the use of a haptic device and a mouse, an interface was developed which used virtual haptic buttons, allowing the menus to be navigated using the haptic device.

Automated demonstrations are provided, during which the haptic device actively guides the student's hand through an example game (using PlaybackLib [7]). On-screen text and graphics explain key points during the demonstration.

3.3   User Testing

Development included an iterative process of user testing, involving student volunteers from the Royal Veterinary College (RVC), London. The goals were (a) to improve usability and (b) to refine the levels of difficulty. Each participant played 1-3 different games during a session lasting 30-60 mins and was instructed only to ask for assistance as a last resort. An observer made notes during the session and the participant answered a questionnaire immediately after using the trainer. Scores, lives and success rates were used to help assess the appropriateness of difficulty levels, which were revised during user testing.

3.4   Results

Fifty-nine veterinary students participated in the user testing and completed the questionnaire. When asked if they would like to use the trainer again, 91% answered 'yes', 7% 'not sure' and 2% 'no'. Similarly, 88% would recommend it to others (12% answered 'not sure'). Most found the haptic buttons easy to use giving a median rating of 9/10 for ease of use. Participants enjoyed the experience, giving a median score of 8/10 for fun. In a free text section, one participant remarked: "It is a new way of learning to listen to your sense of touch". Participants gave a median rating of 8/10 (averaged for all games) when asked how appropriate they thought the level of difficulty was (i.e. not too hard or easy). However, during the course of user testing, the difficulty was adjusted in reaction to feedback and scores. Some participants commented that the clinical relevance of the skills was not immediately apparent. Also, at first some participants had difficulty operating the haptic device, particularly moving in 3D.

3.5 Refinements Based on User Testing

An interactive tutorial was developed to help players get used to the haptic device and practice moving in 3D. The tutorial introduced special features of the user interface (virtual haptic buttons and the haptic device guiding the hand during the automated demonstrations) and allowed the player to experience different haptic surface properties. Various aspects of the haptic buttons were refined to improve usability; the raised sides of the buttons were rendered smooth and sloped to prevent the haptic cursor catching and the surfaces of the buttons were assigned a high static friction to prevent the cursor from slipping. A 'Skills Context' button was added in each game to highlight the clinical relevance of the particular core skill. During user testing, qualitative and quantitative feedback (scores, lives and success rates) helped identify games and levels that were too easy or hard. Difficulty parameters (such as the differences between the friction coefficients in the Texture Game) were adjusted based on this feedback.

4 Discussion

A game-based haptic simulator was developed for trainee health professionals to practice core palpatory skills, which were identified by clinicians as being important in clinical practice. User testing conducted with veterinary students suggested that the trainer was easy and enjoyable to use and a number of refinements were implemented including more explanation of clinical context.

The skills used during palpation-based examinations and procedures are difficult to teach and learn because often the techniques are so familiar to the tutor that they become subconscious. Only by repeated practice can students learn to effectively 'listen' to their sense of touch. By ensuring that students can use the trainer without assistance, The Core Skills Trainer can be made available more frequently and so better support this kind of repeated and personal practice.

The core skills approach is appealing as the training is potentially relevant to a large number of different clinical procedures. The abstract games environment means that unlike many procedural simulators, no prior theoretical knowledge (e.g. anatomy) is required, so training can be provided earlier in the curriculum. However, it is not yet known how core skills learned in abstraction would transfer to more complex clinical procedures involving integrating several core skills and other knowledge. Further studies will help to establish how best to combine the core skills approach with training on procedural simulators and real patients. Veterinary and medical students are not currently selected on their manual or palpatory skills, so early exposure to training tools such as The Core Skills Trainer would help students identify skills they need to improve and offer a safe and appealing environment in which to practice. Students and teachers could track skills development using scores provided by The Core Skills Trainer.

The trainer is currently being used with students at the RVC to investigate how it can be incorporated into a curriculum, and preliminary feedback from both veterinarians and students is encouraging. Further studies will attempt to objectively assess the effectiveness of the training provided, beginning by examining learning effects within the games environment. Future work will also include the identification of other disciplines that could benefit from the trainer. The abstract nature of the core skills and their presentation in a games environment mean that adapting The Core Skills Trainer for other skills domains is feasible. Any profession where manual dexterity and haptic perception are important, such as human medicine, dentistry and physiotherapy, could potentially benefit from the trainer with modifications. More generally, a similar combination of game-based learning and haptics could be used to engage students in other areas of learning, not only manual and haptic perception skills training.

References

1. Baillie, S., Mellor, D., Brewster, S., Reid, S.: Integrating a Bovine Rectal Palpation Simulator into an Undergraduate Veterinary Curriculum. J. Vet. Med. Edu. 32(1), 79–85 (2005)
2. Mentice MIST, http://www.mentice.com/ (accessed: January 11, 2010)
3. Weber, E.H.: E.H. Weber on the Tactile Senses. Erlbaum (UK) Taylor & Francis, p. 260 (1834, translation 1978)
4. Lederman, S.J., Klatzky, R.L.: Hand Movements: A Window into Haptic Object Recognition. Cogn. Psych. 19, 342–368 (1987)
5. Forrest, N., Baillie, S., Tan, H.Z.: Haptic Stiffness Identification by Veterinarians and Novices: A Comparison. In: Proc. of WorldHaptics, pp. 646–651 (2009)
6. H3D.org – Open Source Haptics, http://www.h3dapi.org/ (accessed: January 11, 2010)
7. Crossan, A., Williamson, J., Brewster, S.: A General Purpose Control-Based Trajectory Playback for Force-Feedback Systems. In: Proc. of EuroHaptics, pp. 585–588 (2006)

A Measuring Tool for Accurate Haptic Modeling in Industrial Maintenance Training

Paolo Tripicchio, Alessandro Filippeschi, Emanuele Ruffaldi, Franco Tecchia,
Carlo Alberto Avizzano, and Massimo Bergamasco

Scuola Superiore Sant'Anna, Pisa, Italy
p.tripicchio@sssup.it

Abstract. In the context of training for industrial maintenance the capturing and modeling of interaction forces are important elements that allow to characterize the skills of users. This paper describes a device that can be used for acquiring such forces for later use in the context of a training system. The device has been designed for managing the force ranges and the precision required by typical maintenance operations and it can be easily adapted to different type of tools. The paper discusses also the calibration of the device and presents a case study in which actions from different users are being captured.

Keywords: haptic modeling, ergonomics, sensing tool.

1 Introduction

Industrial Maintenance and Assembly is a very complex task. Usually, these tasks involve the knowledge of specific procedures and techniques for each machine. Each technique and procedure requires cognitive memory and knowledge of the way the task should be performed as well as fine motor "knowledge" about the precise movements and forces that should be applied. The dominant skills involved in these tasks are cognitive, and they reflect the operator's ability to obtain a good representation of how to perform each of the steps of a task and the correct order to perform them, which is reflected in their hierarchic organization. But, in many cases , assembly and disassembly operation may involve also motor-control skills which importance is often underestimated. Example of such skills is the capacity to undertake precise movements and controlling the forces applied, especially during the manipulation of delicate parts, in which potential damage can occur when adverse force/movement is applied. For this very reason a multimodal industrial maintenance and assembly platform is in development [1] in the scope of the EU project SKILLS with the intention of providing an efficient and accurate training system for the transfer of skills involved in such specific tasks. In order to faithfully replicate the interaction user-machinery within the virtual world, i.e. in a way perceptually equivalent to the real maintenance job, there was the need of capturing exact forces and torques profiles exerted during the performance of a skilled maintainer. This is less trivial than it may appear as, to the best of our knowledge, there are not on the market universal force measuring tools suiting the range of usages normally involved in assembly and disassembly. To achieve a good data recording of possible interaction forces exchanged during assembly a unique measuring tool

A.M.L. Kappers et al. (Eds.): EuroHaptics 2010, Part II, LNCS 6192, pp. 377–384, 2010.

was then developed and the preliminary evaluation of recorded data is presented here. The developed measuring tool allows to adopt the same tool handle for several maintenance tools uniforming the forces and torques readings and making use of low cost sensors. This allows to build efficient haptic rendering model for the contact during operations like screwing with a screwdriver or tightening with a wrench. Next section will present related work in the topic. After, a discussion of the device realization and calibration is presented. In section 5 a setup that shows the usage of the tool is depicted and retrieved data are analyzed to show capabilities of the device. Last section introduces future works and summarizes the conclusions.

2   Related Work

In [2] is explained that the repeated performance of tasks develops a motor memory. The creation of such motor schemes involves a gain in performance [3] such that the preservation of the exact motor components involved to execute a task is essential for developing skills. To replicate the correct motor actions in a virtual reality training platform a precise haptic modeling of the interaction is essential. Some specific works exists that have analyzed the tool handle shape and how it influences performance for instance in the specific case of a screw driving torque task [4]. It is indeed demonstrated that a discrete number of injuries occurring at the hand can be avoided if the hand tools were ergonomically well-designed [5]. Other ergonomics studies focus on the quantification of the forces applied with or by hand tools [6]. In particular the paper from McGorry describes a device for measuring gripping forces and the moments generated by a hand tool. The present paper starts from these studies and develops a new force measuring tool capable of streaming force and torque values to a remote computer for later analysis.

3   Device

The device (Fig. 1) has been designed to be used in industrial maintenance tasks where different operations and tools are involved. Therefore it is composed of a base that can be plugged with different tools. Since the most common operation is screw driving, as a first step the device has been equipped with a screwdriver and with a wrench (Fig. 1). According to [7] maximum values of torques in screw driving task carried out with a screwdriver do not exceed 6 Nm. The maximum diameter of screws, tightened by means of a wrench in the target application [1], is 8 mm. Thread calculation formulas and empirical relations for screw driving tasks [8] lead to consider 36 Nm be the maximum bending moment applied. These values have been used for the design of the device.

The base is composed of three parts (1-3 shown in the right side of Fig. 1): the handle, the sensing system, and the electronics.

Handle. It has two functions: it provides a shield for the sensors, and it is the interface for the user. For the accuracy of the measurement the user should grasp only this part of the device.

Sensing system. It is composed of strain sensors and of an interface where sensors are attached. This system can read bending moments in the range ±36 Nm and torques

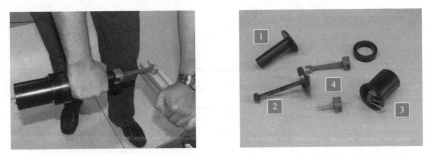

Fig. 1. The assembled device with wrench tool (left) and the components (right)

in the range ±6 Nm. It is not sensible to normal stress if forces are less than 150 N (both in tension and compression). The resolution is 0.2 Nm for the bending moment and 0.2 Nm for the torque. Sensors employed are Vishay uniaxial strain gauges, whose main feature is the low hysteresis. The interface where the sensors are attached is the part 2 shown in Fig. 1: on the shaft two full Wheatstone bridges (A and D) are mounted to measure out deformation due to bending, whereas between the shaft and the circular external ring three ribs house two further bridges (B and C) for the torque sensing. On the opposite side of the ribs is the tool interface, tools are mounted on by means of two screws.

Electronics. It is composed of three parts housed by the large cylindrical cover. The Board with instrumentation amplifiers that is mounted directly on the sensors' interface in order to minimize risks for strain gauges movements. Amplifiers employed are Burr Brown INA2141 whose gain G is set to 100. The Battery, mounted on a plate framed to the cover, that is charged without disassembling the device thanks to the socket on the cover. The Board with microcontroller and transmission module. The microcontroller is the PIC 18F4420 manufactured by Microchip, data are coded with 10 bits resolution. Data are sent to the PC via Bluetooth, transmission frequency is $300 Hz$.

4   Device Design and Calibration

The main specification for the design is the measurement of force and moment applied by the user in screw driving with a wrench and the measurement of torque applied when screw driving with a screwdriver. The sensors' interface has been designed to measure both bending moments and torque, without being sensible to direct stress. The material chosen for this part is the AISI 630(17-4 PH), stainless steel commonly used in strain gauges' applications. The sensors' interface is divided in three zones: the tool interface, the shaft for measuring bending moment, and the cylindrical base, that is used to house the amplifiers, to measure torques and to assemble the handle.

Bending Moment. For the shaft design the user is supposed to grasp only the handle. Shaft transversal section is an l by l square. Pressure on the handle is modeled by means of a force $\mathbf{F}$ and a moment $\mathbf{M}$. According to Fig. 2 $\mathbf{F}$ is supposed to be directed along y and applied at a distance d from the element origin. Components of $\mathbf{F}$ along x and z are

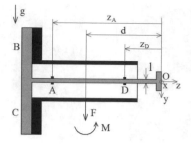

Fig. 2. Free body diagram for bending moment load condition. The uppercase letters A–D refer to the strain gauges, while the tool attachment is the point O.

not considered: F_x does not produce strain where strain due to F_y is maximum, F_z produces a negligible strain that is anyway erased thanks to the strain gauges' placement. Distance d is fixed because the handle dimension does not allow to vary too much the position of the hand. Moment **M** is supposed to be directed along x, strain due to M_y is zero where sensors are placed, strain due to M_z is supposed to be negligible. According to Euler-Bernoulli beam equation the strain, in the $(Oxyz)$ system, at a given point P is:

$$\varepsilon_P = \frac{M_P z_P}{E J} \tag{1}$$

where

$$M_P = M - F(z_P + d) \quad \text{and} \quad J = \frac{l^4}{12} \tag{2}$$

Two values of M_P are needed to obtain F and M. Given M_A and M_D, F and M result

$$F = \frac{M_D - M_A}{z_A - z_D}, \quad M = M_D \frac{d + z_A}{z_A - z_D} - M_A \frac{d + z_D}{z_A - z_D} \tag{3}$$

For the accuracy of these indirect measurement points A and B should be as far as possible. Therefore bridges have been placed at about $2l$ distance from changes of section in order to avoid geometrical nonlinearity effects and, at the same time, to maximize the distance among sensors.

Torque. Since nonlinearity effects cannot be avoided, strain of the ribs has been estimated with FEM. In Fig. 3 (a) the strain due to torque is shown (amplified). There are four zones where strain gauges can be attached. Since these zones are very narrow one redundant Wheatstone bridge has been mounted. Load conditions investigated are pure torque, torque/direct-stress , and bending moment in order to verify respectively that strain is large enough to be accurately measured, direct stress does not affect the measure, and strain due to bending moment is not critical. Figure 3 shows the results of the analysis, torque is 6 Nm, bending moment is 36 Nm and normal force is 150 N. All loads are applied to the tool interface. The three points are verified: strain is about $800 \mu\varepsilon$ under pure torque condition; strain varies less than 3% when compression is applied; strain is less than $1200 \mu\varepsilon$ (sensors' fatigue limit) in all conditions.

Fig. 3. Equivalent strain (Von Mises) for (a)pure torque, (b)torque and direct stress, and (c)bending moment

Inertial Properties. The device has been designed to work in real tasks, hence it is necessary that it is perceived as commonly used tools as much as possible. Among the variables that affect this perception, the size and the inertial properties have been considered in the design of the instrument. The materials of the handle, of the tools and of the cover for the electronics have been chosen in order to place the center of gravity of the instrument as close as possible to the center of the hand, to minimize mass and to minimize the moment of inertia with respect to the axis n shown in Fig. 2. The handle diameter is the same of the screwdrivers involved in the target application, the length allows a human hand to completely grasp the handle. Tools are mounted on the sensors interface by means of two screws. Holes are dimensioned and placed in order to keep contact between the interface and the tool, in this way backlash is always avoided.

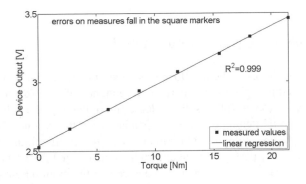

Fig. 4. Calibration curve for bending moment condition

4.1 Calibration

Assumptions and design analyses results were verified by means of a calibration. The device was loaded under three different conditions: bending moment, pure torque, and compression. Figure 5 shows the schemes for the first two conditions. In each case the handle was blocked by means of a clamp. Force were applied by means of calibrated weights, the uncertainty on the load (moment or force where the sensors are placed) is less than 3%. The system was loaded in the range ±6 Nm for pure torque, ±21 Nm

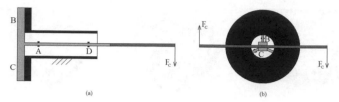

(a)   (b)

Fig. 5. Calibration layout for the conditions (a)Bending moment and (b)Pure Torque. The upper-case letters A–D refer to the strain gauges, while F_C is the applied force.

for bending moment, and $150 Nm$ for compression. Load steps were $0.5 Nm$ for torque, $3 Nm$ for bending moment, and $20 N$ for compression. After each step load was set to zero to verify hysteresis and the trials were repeated three times to assess the reliability of the measure. Both torque and bending moment sensors' response is linear ($R^2 > 0.997$ in all cases), hysteresis was not appreciated. Output O_P available for each sensor is

$$O_P = O_P^0 + \Delta O_P \tag{4}$$

where O_P^0 is the output due to bridge offset, ΔO_P depends on the gauge factor(GF) and on the tool mounted and it must be recorded at the beginning of the measuring session as:

$$\Delta O_P = 1024 GF \, G \varepsilon_P = k_p M_P \tag{5}$$

Numerical values (Nm^{-1}) of k_p for sensors A,B,C,and D are are respectively 11.19, 17.19, 17.38, and 10.50.

5   Acquisition System and Data Analysis

To analyze the capabilities of the developed tool a simple evaluation test has been performed. The test requires the user to perform a sequence of release and tightening of bolts with the wrench tool as follows: first release and tightening of a bolt parallel to the ground and then the tightening of a bolt perpendicular to the ground. The users were asked to perform the task with the right arm and with not specific timing requirements. We selected 7 voluntary users, all male and right handed, aged 23-30. During the task we recorded the interaction forces using the device and the motion by means of a motion capture system. In particular a VICON MX-20+(OMG plc, UK) infrared motion capture system, configured with 7 cameras each having a resolution of 2 megapixels, was employed. The VICON system uses infrared strobes mounted around the cameras to track the position of retro-reflective 6-mm markers running at 200Hz with a resulting position resolution less than 0.5 mm. We used a configuration of 7 markers, of which 3 were placed over the device and 4 over the user: front chest, left and right shoulder and right elbow. Figure 6-left displays the phase diagram relative to forces and torques during the execution of the three subtasks. From this plot the separation of the single movements performed during the task is visible. It is then possible, from the acquired data, to perform a segmentation and to distinguish each step of the complete task. Figure 6-right shows instead the last subtask performed by one of the user as recorded by

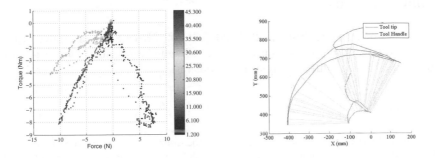

Fig. 6. Single user interaction during the task. Force/Torque plane (left) during the execution of the three subtasks with color as time. Motion of the handle (right) during vertical tightening projected over the plane parallel to the ground.

the motion capture system. To perform this step with a correct movement (as a skilled person will execute it) we expected the users to produce an action of pure flexion, with minimal torque. Figure 7 presents the distribution of torques for every user, showing only half of them performed the task as expected, resulting in a mean of the average torques of $0.1Nm$. However, all of them exerted a peak force of $-10N$ to tighten the bolt. With these results we can easily distinguish between experienced and novice users.

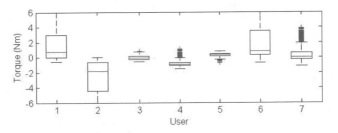

Fig. 7. Plot of torque values generated by the 7 users during the third subtask

6 Main Conclusions and Future Work

The capturing of interaction forces poses several challenges because of portability and ranges of forces, in particular in domains like industrial maintenance. In this paper we have presented a device for capturing and discussed the design decision, integrating a first stage of evaluation. Future work will focus on the modeling of the interaction force in specific tasks, and the integration of the device in the context of an augmented reality training system. The other future challenge is in the haptic rendering of the interaction force using a haptic interface.

Acknowledgments

The authors would like to thank the IST-2006-035005-SKILLS EU Integrated Project, that deals with the multimodal acquisition, modeling and rendering of data signals for the transfer of skills in different application domains.

References

1. Casado, S., Engelke, T., Gavish, N., Gutirrez, T., Rodrguez, J., Snchez, E., Tecchia, F., Webel, S.: A training system for skills transfer involved in industrial maintenance and assembly tasks. In: Gutirrez, T., Snchez, E. (eds.) SKILLS 2009 International Conference on Multimodal Interfaces for Skills Transfer, Bilbao, Spain, pp. 129–134 (2009), Number ISBN:978-84-613-5456-5
2. Schmidt, R.: A schema theory of discrete motor skill learning. Psychological Review 82(4), 225–260 (1975)
3. Christopher Wickens, J.H. (ed.): Engineering Psychology and Human Performance. Pearson, London (1999), Number 9780321047113
4. Kong, Y., Lowe, B., Lee, S., Krieg, E.: Evaluation of handle shapes for screwdriving. Applied Ergonomics 39(2), 191–198 (2008)
5. Lewis, W., Narayan, C.: Design and sizing of ergonomic handles for hand tools. Applied Ergonomics 24(5), 351–356 (1993)
6. McGorry, R.: A system for the measurement of grip forces and applied moments during hand tool use. Applied Ergonomics 32(3), 271–279 (2001)
7. Kong, Y., Lowe, B.: Evaluation of handle diameters and orientations in a maximum torque task. International Journal of Industrial Ergonomics 35(12), 1073–1084 (2005)
8. Juvinall, R.C., Marshek, K.M.: Fundamentals of machine Component Design. Wiley, Chichester (2005)

Control Strategies and Performance of a Magnetically Actuated Tactile Micro-actuator Array

Jérémy Streque[1], Abdelkrim Talbi[1],
Philippe Pernod[1], and Vladimir Preobrazhensky[1,2]

[1] Joint International Laboratory LEMAC:
Institute of Electronics, Microelectronics, and Nanotechnology
(IEMN – UMR CNRS 8520) – PRES Lille Nord de France, EC Lille, Cité Scientifique,
BP 48, 59651 - Villeneuve d'Ascq Cédex, France
jeremy.streque@centraliens-lille.org, abdelkrim.talbi@iemn.univ-lille1.fr,
philippe.pernod@iemn.univ-lille1.fr,
vladimir.preobrajenski@iemn.univ-lille1.fr
[2] Wave Research Center of Prokhorov General Physics Institute, RAS, Russia

Abstract. Tactile display devices must fulfill various technical requirements for tactile stimulation, and present a good compactness for handheld applications; control strategies must also be defined in order to optimize their efficiency. This paper focuses on the control strategies of a 4x4 tactile highly integrated magnetic micro-actuator array offering a resolution of 2 mm. This device is dedicated to provide both static and dynamic tactile sensations, from DC to a 350 Hz.

Preliminary perception tests were led on this device and confirm the effectiveness of the device and its ability to deliver meaningful tactile sensations. Two matters were investigated. The first one concerned spatial localization of tactile stimuli, while the second one was related to the evaluation of the device capacity to create easily detectable temporal stimuli. The considered control strategy also aimed at decreasing power consumption while increasing actuation forces.

Keywords: MEMS, Magnetic Micro-actuators, Tactile display, Control strategy.

1   Introduction

1.1   Context and Background on Tactile Devices

Many applications in the fields of Virtual Reality and Human-Computer Interaction have recently heightened the need for tactile devices aimed at the reproduction of tactile sensations. Beyond teletaction and realistic tactile stimulations, tactile sensations are also promoted as a new communication channel, through a tactile iconography easily linked to emotions or abstract information [1].

Vibro-tactile devices form a category of tactile displays dedicated to the reproduction of tactile sensations like textures. They provide delimited vibrations to the skin, mostly through an array of actuators [2]. Most of them provide vertical vibrations, with variable amplitudes and frequencies of vibration. The devices with the better spatial resolutions

A.M.L. Kappers et al. (Eds.): EuroHaptics 2010, Part II, LNCS 6192, pp. 385–391, 2010.

(reaching 1 mm) and large frequency ranges, up to 400 Hz [3], are often too bulky for any commercial development.

Some studies defined control strategies for their own tactile devices ; they could have different purposes. The STReSS device [4], based on laterally actuated piezoelectric comb arrays, was optimized for embossment detection like bumps or edges [5] and its potential roles in mobile interaction were studied. Some control strategies were also defined for the VITAL device, in order to link tactile stimuli display with emotions [6].

1.2   Tactile Specifications for This Device

The mechanisms of tactile sensation are explained by the sensitivity of various mechanoreceptor networks in the skin, and by neurophysiological interpretation of these stimuli. The global bandwidth of the mechanoreceptors involved in touch extends to a few hundred Hz, for a spatial resolution down to 0.5 mm [7,8].

The presented tactile display device was designed for applications of texture discrimination or tactile iconography, with high dimensional constraints in order to allow its integration in various systems (mouse, gloves, stylus, etc.). The spatial resolution of its actuators is currently set to 2 mm, but can reach 1 mm without any change in design and fabrication. Its actuation bandwidth extends from DC to 350 Hz, for main mechanoreceptors stimulation.

A study on haptic device requirements [9] estimates that the pressure exerted by a tactile device must be higher than 60 mN/cm^2 in order to efficiently stimulate the fingertip mechanoreceptors. According to the resolution set to 2 mm, each micro-actuator must provide forces of about 2.5 mN in order to reach this threshold. The tactile device presented in this study was designed with respect to these requirements, for continuous-wave sinusodal signals. Higher instantaneous forces can be provided when using lower duty cycles, for the same power consumption.

2   Device Presentation

The current tactile device belongs to the family of solutions called Micro-Magneto-Mechanical Systems[10,11,12]. It is based on the simultaneous use of ultrasoft highly deformable membranes and high force and high displacement magnetic micro-actuators arranged in array.

These membranes are made of an elastomer similar to PDMS (Poly-DiMethyl-Siloxane), and that presents better mechanical properties: its elongation at break is over 800%, four times higher than the PDMS one.

This prototype is composed of a 4x4 magnetic micro-actuator array with a 2 mm resolution. It covers an area slightly smaller than 1 cm^2 (typical fingertip surface). Each micro-actuator is actuated by coil–magnet interaction (Fig. 1). Complete details on the device design and its characteristics are provided in [13,14]. Tables 1 and 2 respectively sum up main dimensional and performance data.

The final device was inserted in a 20x20 mm^2 Silicon microfabricated packaging, with 3.3 mm in height (Fig. 2). For the test sessions that were led, the device was kept without any other packaging, like a pointing or handheld device. A 4 mm high aluminum heatsink was added below the device in order to improve heat dissipation.

Table 1. Micro-actuator geometry

Magnet	Diameter	1 mm
	Height	500 μm
Coil	Inner diameter	500 μm
	Outer diameter	1.7 mm
	Length	1.8 mm
Pin	Diameter	500 μm
	Height	250 μm
Coil–Magnet gap		400 μm

Table 2. Micro-actuator performance

Actuation bandwidth	DC–350 Hz
Max. RMS Current	800 mA
Max. instantaneous current	3 A
Deflection/current ratio[1]	60 μm/A
Force/current ratio[1,2]	2.8 mN/A
Crosstalk ratio[3]	>25 dB

[1]Deflection and force amplitudes measured for sinusoidal currents (RMS).
[2]Based on membrane stiffness: 46 N/m.
[3]Deflection ratio between an actuated membrane and its next neighbor.

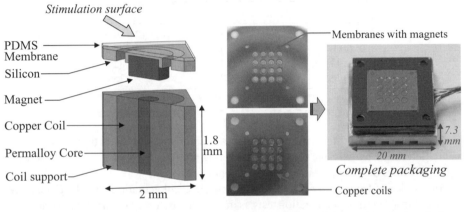

Fig. 1. Sectional view of a micro-actuator

Fig. 2. Integration of the tactile display device into its packaging

The 16 micro-actuators can be indivually driven by a specific power supply unit. The micro-actuators were also equipped with small pins on the center of their membranes, in order to provide more perceptible and localized tactile stimuli.

3 Perception Tests

3.1 Spatial Localization of Tactile Stimuli

Preliminary tests were performed in order to confirm the efficiency of the device, by checking the spatial localization of some stimuli. For each test, four actuators out of 16 were actuated, in one of the four corners of the array. The 7 participants were asked to put the forefinger of their preferred hand on the tactile device, without moving it on

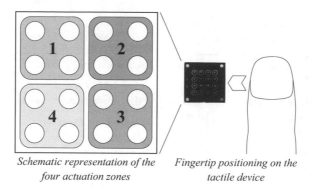

Schematic representation of the   *Fingertip positioning on the*
four actuation zones   *tactile device*

Fig. 3. Perception test: four actuation zones are defined, and only one is triggered for each test; the participants try to determine the active zone

Table 3. Results from the preliminary tests for spatial localization of tactile stimuli

Participants	1	2	3	4	5	6	7	All
5 Hz	12	11	11	11	9	9	12	89%
50 Hz	12	11	12	12	11	11	12	96%
250 Hz	9	10	11	11	9	10	9	82%
Burst	12	8	11	10	7	6	9	75%
All tests	94%	83%	94%	92%	75%	75%	88%	86%

the actuator array. The fingertip was insured to be centered on the active surface. They had to determine which zone was actuated among the four corners of the actuator array. Figure 3 shows the four possible actuation zones for each test.

Four series of tests were achieved, based on different actuation signals. Each series consisted in 12 random localization tests as mentioned before. The first three series used 5 Hz, 50 Hz and 250 Hz signals for the actuators. Their amplitude was fixed to 400 mA RMS, while the device is designed for maximal RMS currents of 800 mA. The fourth series used 250 Hz burst signals, with a repetition period of 200 ms (corresponding to 5 Hz) and a burst length of 20 ms (for a duty cycle of 10%).

Table 3 shows the results of these localization tests, following the actuation signals and according to the participants' perception of the tactile stimulation. The number of good answers (out of 12 tests) is given for each participant and each series of tests. The last line sums up the four series and gives the score for each participant. The last column shows the score for each series of tests, for the group of participants. Globally, 86% of the spatial recognition tests were successful. It validates the use of this tactile device for delivering spatially defined tactile stimuli.

3.2   Rest Times and Pulse Signals

The following tests were focused on the control strategies allowing to display signals at a given frequency, with maximal efficiency. Only one actuator was used for this test session.

First, it was noticed that tactile stimulation induced by a continuous-wave sinusoidal signal often decreases with time. Rest times were periodically introduced between each sinusoidal pattern in order to prevent this phenomenon. Participants were asked how long time they could feel a significant stimulus when wave forms (a) and (b) were respectively used (see Fig. 4). For these tests, the repetition period was chosen to be 1 second, with different rest time ratios. Table 4 shows that rest times significantly improve the temporal effect of tactile stimulation.

Then, square signals were used instead of sinusoidal ones, allowing to change their duty cycle. Different duty cycles were used in order to decrease power consumption, without changing the main frequency of the stimuli.

Table 4. Influence of rest times on the temporal effects of sinusoidal stimuli – mean durations with 400 mA amplitude

Signal Frequency	10 Hz	100 Hz	250 Hz
No rest time	20 s	7 s	9 s
Rest time = 20%	50 s	30 s	28 s
Rest time = 40%	> 1 min	> 1 min	45 s
Rest time = 60%	> 1 min	> 1 min	> 1 min

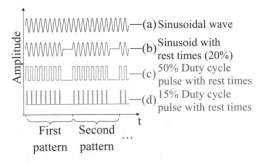

Fig. 4. Scheme presenting control signals with rest times and duty cycles

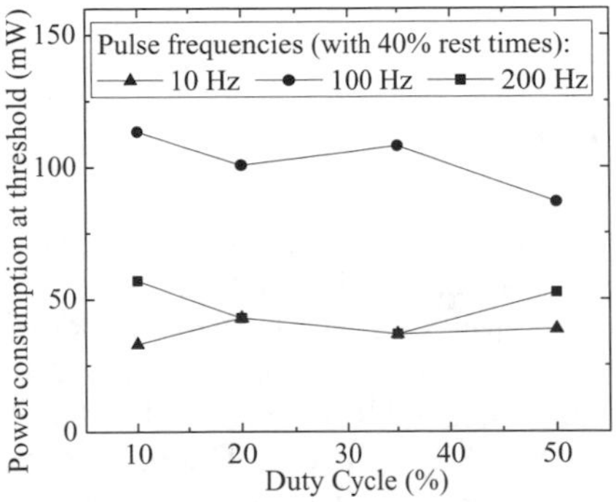

Fig. 5. Minimal power consumption at detection thresholds vs. duty cycle, for different actuation frequencies (rest time = 40%)

Wave forms like (c) and (d) (Fig. 4) were used. Figure 5 shows that the level of power consumption necessary to reach the detection threshold did not depend from duty cycle. 10 Hz pulses were detected for a power consumption as low as 40 mW.

Other tests were made to compare the efficiency of stronger stimuli with different duty cycles, while power consumption was kept constant. Low duty cycles (10 or 20%) were noticed to be more efficient than higher duty cycles (35 or 50%). It shows the interest of low duty cycles in terms of power consumption.

4 Conclusion

The capabilities of a MMMS tactile display device based on MEMS microfabrication techniques and elastomeric materials were presented. Test sessions for spatial localization confirmed the efficiency of this device for the display of spatially defined tactile sensations. This paper also showed the interest of pulse-based signals rather than standard sinusoidal signals, in terms of frequency and power consumption. Detection thresholds do not deteriorate when low duty cycles are used, and tactile perception can be improved without increasing power consumption.

The role of periodic rest times was also noticed as positive for extended use of the device. Rest times at a given ratio (typically 40%) allow to decrease power consumption by the same ratio, while improving the tactile device rendering. Such a device could be particularly efficient for tactile iconography or pattern display, like dynamic generation of Braille characters.

Acknowledgments

This work was supported by STIMTAC Project from IRCICA (Institute of Research on Hardware and Software Components for Information Technology, CNRS), and by Centrale Initiatives Foundation from École Centrale de Lille and École Centrale de Nantes.

References

1. Hafez, M.: Tactile interfaces: technologies, applications and challenges. The Visual Computer 23(4), 267–272 (2007)
2. Benali-Khoudja, M., Hafez, M., Kheddar, A.: VITAL: An electromagnetic integrated tactile display. Displays 28(3), 133–144 (2007)
3. Summers, I.R., Chanter, C.M.: A broadband tactile array on the fingertip. The J. of the Acoustical Soc. of America 112(5), 2118–2126 (2002)
4. Pasquero, J., Hayward, V.: STReSS: A practical tactile display system with one millimeter spatial resolution and 700 hz refresh rate. In: Proc. Eurohaptics Conf., Dublin, Ireland (2003)
5. Luk, J., Pasquero, J., Little, S., MacLean, K., Lévesque, V., Hayward, V.: A Role for Haptics in Mobile Interaction: Initial Design Using a Handheld Tactile Display Prototype. In: Proc. ACM Conf. on Human Factors in Computing Systems, Montreal (2006)
6. Benali-Khoudja, M., Sautour, A., Hafez, M.: Towards a new tactile language to communicate emotions. In: Proc. Virtual Concept Conf., Biarritz, France (2005)
7. Johnson, K.O.: The roles and functions of cutaneous mechanoreceptors. Current Opinion in Neurobiology 11(4), 455–461 (2001)
8. Biggs, S.J., Srinivasan, M.A.: System requirements - haptic interfaces. In: Stanney, K.M. (ed.) Handbook of Virtual Environments: Design, Implementation, and Applications, ch. 5, vol. 2. Lawrence Erlbaum Associates, Mahwah (2002)
9. Hale, K.S., Stanney, K.M.: Deriving haptic design guidelines from human physiological, psychophysical, and neurological foundations. IEEE Comput. Graph. Appl. 24(2), 33–39 (2004)

10. Pernod, P., Preobrazhensky, V., Merlen, A., Ducloux, O., Talbi, A., Gimeno, L., Viard, R., Tiercelin, N.: MEMS magneto-mechanical microvalves (MMMS) for aerodynamic active flow control. Journal of Magnetism and Magnetic Materials (2009), doi:10.1016/j.jmmm.2009.04.086
11. Ducloux, O., Viard, R., Talbi, A., Gimeno, L., Deblock, Y., Pernod, P., Preobrazhensky, V., Merlen, A.: A magnetically actuated, high momentum rate MEMS pulsed microjet for active flow control. J. Microtech. Microeng. 19(11), 115031-1-7 (2009), doi:10.1088/0960-1317/19/11/115031 (available online October 20, 2009; published November 2009)
12. Pernod, P., Preobrazhensky, V., Merlen, A., Ducloux, O., Talbi, A., Gimeno, L., Tiercelin, N.: MEMS for flow control: technological facilities and MMMS alternatives. In: Morrison, J.F., et al. (eds.) IUTAM Symp. on Flow control and MEMS held at the Royal Geographical Society, Dordrecht, Netherlands. IUTAM Bookseries, September 19-22, vol. 7, pp. 15–24. Springer, Heidelberg (2008)
13. Streque, J., Talbi, A., Pernod, P., Preobrazhensky, V.: New Magnetic Micro-Actuator Design Based on MEMS Elastomer and MEMS Technologies for Tactile Display. IEEE Transactions on Haptics (2010)
14. Streque, J., Talbi, A., Viard, R., Pernod, P., Preobrazhensky, V.: Elaboration and Test of High Energy Density Magnetic Micro-Actuators for Tactile Display Applications. In: Proceedings of the Eurosensors XXIII Conference on Procedia Chemistry, Lausanne, Switzerland, vol. 1(1), pp. 694–697 (2009)

Muscular Torque Can Explain Biases in Haptic Length Perception: A Model Study on the Radial-Tangential Illusion

Nienke B. Debats, Idsart Kingma, Peter J. Beek, and Jeroen B.J. Smeets

Research Institute MOVE, Faculty of Human Movement Sciences, VU University, Amsterdam
n.debats@fbw.vu.nl, i_kingma@fbw.vu.nl, p.beek@fbw.vu.nl,
j.smeets@fbw.vu.nl

Abstract. In haptic length perception biases occur that have previously been shown to depend on stimulus orientation and stimulus length. We propose that these biases arise from the muscular torque needed to counteract the gravitational forces acting on the arm. In a model study, we founded this hypothesis by showing that differences in muscular torque can indeed explain the pattern of biases obtained in several experimental studies.

Keywords: haptics, length perception, radial-tangential illusion, torque.

1 Introduction

Our senses provide us with pieces of information concerning our surroundings. These pieces are not necessarily veridical. If one regards perception as a process in which relevant sensory signals are combined into a single perceptual estimate (e.g., [1]), illusory perception boils down to the blending of (a) biased sensory signal(s) into this estimate (thus causing its non-veridicality). Therefore, to understand an illusion, one has to uncover the source(s) of this biased sensory input.

An example of non-veridical perception in the haptic domain is the radial-tangential (r-t) illusion. For clarity, imagine the top view of a standing person's head as the center of a wheel. The spokes of the wheel indicate the radial directions, with the tangential directions orthogonal to them. In 1954, Reid first showed a bias in the perceived extent of arm movements ([2]). Subsequently, it was shown that the direction of arm movement expressed in trunk-centered coordinates (radial vs. tangential) was fundamental to this bias ([3, 4]): arm movements executed in the radial direction were consistently overestimated, whereas tangential movements were underestimated. Thus, when an observer explores an L-shaped haptic stimulus by sequentially tracing the two legs with a finger, the radial segment (standing leg) is perceived to be shorter than a tangential segment (lying leg) of equal length. For an L-figure to feel 'square', a 13-22% longer tangential segment is required ([5]). This overestimation of radial versus tangential lengths is referred to as the r-t illusion.

Over the past five decades, several studies have identified specific factors that alter the degree of over- or underestimation of haptically perceived length (for a review,

A.M.L. Kappers et al. (Eds.): EuroHaptics 2010, Part II, LNCS 6192, pp. 392–397, 2010.
© Springer-Verlag Berlin Heidelberg 2010

see [6]). First, the overestimation of a radially orientated segment increases with its length ([7, 8]). Second, the strength of the radial-tangential illusion depends on the type of exploratory movements. Whole-arm movements induce large perceptual biases, whereas finger-and-hand motions alone induce no bias ([7]). Furthermore, for whole-arm movements the strength of the illusion varies with stimulus length (e.g., [7, 8]) and stimulus orientation ([8, 9]).

It has been hypothesized that the described perceptual biases are caused by differences in movement time between radial and tangential movements ([8, 10]). This hypothesis was recently falsified [5]; it was shown that the radial-tangential illusion was not affected by manipulations of movement time. In this study we advance a gravity-related source of sensory information for the biases. By means of a model simulation we will demonstrate that this single source of information can explain that the magnitude of the perceptual bias depends on the geometry of the task.

Sensing the position of one's limbs in space is called kinesthesis. Arm kinesthesis is greatly affected by manipulations of the position of the arm's center of mass (CM) ([11, 12]). Gravitational forces on the arm can be thought of as a single force vector that acts at the CM. The horizontal distance from the CM to the shoulder joint is the moment arm of the gravitational force, and hence it determines the muscular torque that is required to counteract gravity and keep the arm at a constant vertical height. Given the influence of CM position on perceived arm position, it is conceivable that muscular torques are used by the central nervous system as a cue in limb kinesthesis and potentially also in other haptic tasks that involve limb movement ([13, 14]).

Whenever the arm moves in a radial direction, the position of CM changes such that the moment arm of the gravitational force differs between the start en end positions of a movement. Thus, during a radial movement, increasing (or decreasing) muscular torque is required to maintain the arm at a constant vertical height. In contrast, no changes in moment arm and thus muscular torque accompany tangential arm movements. We hypothesized that a difference in torque magnitude between the start and end position of a movement (ΔTorque) might cause biased length perception. More specifically, a positive ΔTorque would bias toward an overestimation of length, and vice versa. In the current study we founded the ΔTorque hypothesis by comparing its predictions with length perception biases as reported in literature.

2 Methods

We built a simplistic model of the arm to obtain predictions from the ΔTorque hypothesis. This model simulated arm movements over haptic stimuli (line segments) of varying length, position, and orientation. Our analysis consists of a qualitative comparison between patterns of biases predicted from the model, with patterns of biases reported in the literature. We will do so for three different studies ([7-9])

The model. The simulated arm consists of two straight body segments (the upper arm and the lower arm plus hand), and two joints (the shoulder and the elbow, see Fig. 1). The two body segments are of equal length. Furthermore, the segments move in the horizontal plane. In other words, the model simulates 2-dimensional arm movement with elevated elbow at shoulder level. Hence, the required hand position fully determines the shoulder and elbow angles. From the simulated arm positions we determined CM positions. Muscular torque was calculated as $m \cdot g \cdot d$, with m representing the total mass of the arm in kg, g the gravitational acceleration (9.81m/s^2), and d the distance in meters between CM and the shoulder (i.e., the moment arm of gravitational force $m \cdot g$). Note that the radial and tangential directions in this model are in fact defined relative to the shoulder rather than the body midline. Yet, when we refer to radial and tangential directions we will do so in the conventional way, that is, with the directions defined relative to the vertical axis of the body.

Model parameters. Calculated values for muscular torque depend on the length and mass of the two body segments. For the current study we used the measures as obtained from one of the authors. Length of the two body segments was 0.26m, body mass 62kg, and the sagittal distance from body midline to the shoulder was 0.17m. We used standard anthropometrical data ([15]) to calculate the CM of the separate body segments.

3   Results

Overestimation of radially oriented stimuli: the effect of stimulus length. The model was simulated tracing a radially oriented haptic stimulus from its proximal to its distal end. We simulated four different stimulus lengths: 7.5cm, 15.2cm, 22.8cm, and 30.5cm, as in Experiment 1 by Wong ([8]; 90° condition in the Horizontal-Front plane). The proximal end was positioned at a distance of 0.12m from the body vertical axis. The model is shown in Fig. 1 with the smallest (left panel) and the largest stimulus (middle panel). The light and dark grey arm represents the start and end orientation, respectively. White circles represent the CM of the separate body segments; grey diamonds represent the CM of the total arm. The dotted lines represent the moment arm of the gravitational force.

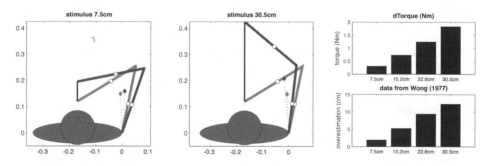

Fig. 1. Model predictions compared with experimental findings for the effect of stimulus length on perceptual biases in haptic length perception. Units on the axis of two left panels are meters.

The forward movement of the hand over the body midline causes the moment arm of the gravitational force to increase. Hence, ΔTorque is positive for these radial movements. The model reveals a pattern of increasing ΔTorque with increasing stimulus length (top right panel), and thus it predicts increasing length overestimation. In line with this prediction, Wong found a pattern of increasingly overestimated stimulus lengths (bottom right panel).

The r-t illusion: the effect of stimulus length. A shape that is generally used to study the r-t illusion is the figure L (e.g., [7]). We simulated the model with an L-figure positioned symmetrically at a distance of 0.3m on the body midline. Absolute values of ΔTorque were calculated because participants in pertinent experiments were often instructed to trace both of the L's legs back and forth. If both movements have an equal ΔTorque, then no difference in biased length perception is expected. Otherwise, the movement with the largest ΔTorque is expected to be overestimated relative to the other.

In Fig. 2, the model is shown tracing a 10.2cm stimulus in the radial (left panel) and tangential (2nd panel) direction. There is a difference in ΔTorque for these two movements (3rd panel), that is, it is largest for the radial movement. Hence it is predicted that the radial leg is overestimated relative to the tangential leg: the r-t illusion. To test the effect of stimulus length on the illusion, we simulated L-figures of 2.5cm, 5.1cm, 7.6cm, and 10.2cm, as in Experiment 3 by Heller and colleagues ([7]; Right Hand, Elbows-Up condition). The model predicts that the magnitude of the illusion will increase with increasing stimulus length (top right panel). This pattern was indeed found experimentally (bottom right panel).

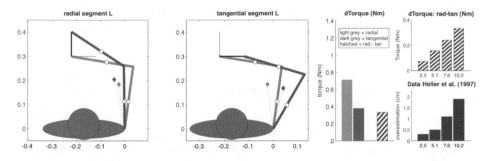

Fig. 2. Model predictions compared with experimental findings for the effect of stimulus length on the r-t illusion. Units on the axis of two left panels are meters.

The r-t illusion: the effect of stimulus orientation. Deregowski and Ellis ([9]) demonstrated that the magnitude of the r-t illusion depends on stimulus orientation. In Experiment 1, they presented an L-figure at 7 orientations: 0°, 15°, 30°, 45°, 60°, 75°, and 90° relative to the body-midline. Thus, for 15°-75°, the direction of the L's legs is a combination of radial and tangential components. A staircase method was used to determine the length at which the standing leg and the lying leg (7.5cm) were perceived equally long. We simulated this experimental setup (see Fig. 3) with a 7.5cm stimulus at a distance of 0.4m on the body-midline. The difference in ΔTorque was calculated for the standing leg minus the lying leg (top right panel). The model predicts a decreasing overestimation of the standing leg's length, and a shift to negative overestimation (i.e., underestimation). More specifically, the model predicts that overestimation changes sinusoidally with the orientation angle. The predicted non-linear pattern of overestimations shows a striking similarity with the experimentally obtained pattern (bottom right panel).

Fig. 3. Model predictions compared with experimental findings for the effect of stimulus orientation on r-t illusion. Units on the axis of two left panels are meters.

4   Discussion

We hypothesized that ΔTorque could explain biases in haptic length perception in general, and the r-t illusion in particular. There was a striking similarity between the ΔTorque patterns derived from our simple arm model and patterns of experimentally obtained perceptual biases. The findings strengthen the hypothesis that the brain uses ΔTorque as a cue in haptic length perception, despite the consequence of biased perception.

Put simply, ΔTorque represents the difference in muscular torque needed to actively counteract gravity at the two endpoints of a movement (i.e., there is no ΔTorque for a supported arm). It is thus a measure of effort. Effort has previously been suggested to relate to biases in haptic length perception ([5, 8, 16]), yet no experimental support was found. Importantly, these authors considered muscular effort in the plane of motion. That is, the torque needed to move the limb against the resistance of its own inertia. This measure mainly depends on the angular acceleration of the movement, whereas ΔTorque depends on the elbow angle (it is the elbow angle that determines the distance between CM and the shoulder). Our current findings revealed that gravity-related muscular effort is a good candidate to account for biases in length perception.

There is a seemingly crucial limitation to our study. The model that we used to calculate ΔTorque was simplified to obtain a unique solution for arm position given stimulus location; we omitted the wrist and considered all movements as if executed in the horizontal plane, which differs from the experiments described. Without any simplification, calculating ΔTorque is a two-dimensional problem in essence. The moment arm of the gravitational force is a vector in the plane spanned by two orthogonal axes that are orthogonal to the gravitational axis (i.e., the horizontal plane). Thus, modeling arm movement with the forearm below shoulder level equals to modeling a shorter upper arm. This will decrease the absolute ΔTorque values but not the patterns that we currently used for comparison with experimental results. Therefore, we believe that the comparisons made in this model study are valid.

This model study has not touched upon all aspects of biased length perception. For example, the r-t illusion was found to be larger for inverted-T-figures than for L-figures (e.g., [9, 17, 18]; but see also [7]). This difference was found to result from the underestimation of bisected stimuli ([18]). We certainly do not exclude that multiple sources of biased information may provide cues for haptic length perception and thus contribute to r-t illusion in haptic length perception as well.

References

1. Drewing, K., Ernst, M.O.: Integration of force and position cues for shape perception through active touch. Brain Res. 1078(1), 92–100 (2006)
2. Reid, R.L.: An Illusion of Movement Complementary to the Horizontal - Vertical Illusion. Q. J. Exp. Psychol. 6, 107–111 (1954)
3. Cheng, M.F.: Tactile-kinesthetic perception of length. Am. J. Psychol. 81(1), 74–82 (1968)
4. Davidon, R.S., Cheng, M.F.H.: Apparent Distance in a Horizontal Plane with Tactile-Kinesthetic Stimuli. Q. J. Exp. Psychol. 16(3), 277–281 (1964)
5. McFarland, J., Soechting, J.F.: Factors influencing the radial-tangential illusion in haptic perception. Exp. Brain Res. 178(2), 216–227 (2007)
6. Gentaz, E., Hatwell, Y.: Geometrical haptic illusions: the role of exploration in the Muller-Lyer, vertical-horizontal, and Delboeuf illusions. Psychon. Bull. Rev. 11(1), 31–40 (2004)
7. Heller, M.A., et al.: The tactual horizontal-vertical illusion depends on radial motion of the entire arm. Percept Psychophys 59(8), 1297–1311 (1997)
8. Wong, T.S.: Dynamic properties of radial and tangential movements as determinants of the haptic horizontal–vertical illusion with an L figure. J. Exp. Psychol. Hum. Percept. Perform. 3(1), 151–164 (1977)
9. Deregowski, J., Ellis, H.D.: Effect of stimulus orientation upon haptic perception of the horizontal-vertical illusion. J. Exp. Psychol. 95(1), 14–19 (1972)
10. Armstrong, L., Marks, L.E.: Haptic perception of linear extent. Percept Psychophys 61(6), 1211–1226 (1999)
11. van de Langenberg, R., Kingma, I., Beek, P.J.: Perception of limb orientation in the vertical plane depends on center of mass rather than inertial eigenvectors. Exp. Brain Res. 180(4), 595–607 (2007)
12. van de Langenberg, R., Kingma, I., Beek, P.J.: The perception of limb orientation depends on the center of mass. J. Exp. Psychol. Hum. Percept. Perform. 34(3), 624–639 (2008)
13. Gentaz, E., Hatwell, Y.: Role of gravitational cues in the haptic perception of orientation. Percept. Psychophys 58(8), 1278–1292 (1996)
14. Wydoodt, P., Gentaz, E., Streri, A.: Role of force cues in the haptic estimations of a virtual length. Exp. Brain Res. 171(4), 481–489 (2006)
15. Winter, D.A.: Biomechanics and motor control of human movement, 2nd edn. John Wiley & Sons, Inc., Chichester (1990)
16. Marchetti, F.M., Lederman, S.J.: The Haptic Radial-Tangential Effect - 2 Tests of Wongs Moments-of-Inertia Hypothesis. Bull. Psychonomic. Soc. 21(1), 43–46 (1983)
17. Day, R.H., Avery, G.C.: Absence of the horizontal-vertical illusion in haptic space. J. Exp. Psychol. 83(1), 172–173 (1970)
18. Millar, S., al-Attar, Z.: Vertical and bisection bias in active touch. Perception 29(4), 481–500 (2000)

The Effect of Coulomb Friction in a Haptic Interface on Positioning Performance

Koen Crommentuijn and Dik J. Hermes

Human-Technology Interaction Group,
Eindhoven University of Technology, The Netherlands
{k.j.crommentuijn,d.j.hermes}@tue.nl

Abstract. The effect of Coulomb friction in a haptic interface was investigated for a simple positioning task. A custom 1-DOF interface was used, for which the Coulomb friction was varied from virtually zero to .70 N. The interface was operated using the wrist and fingers. Results based on the numbers of errors, completion times and subjective ratings show that, for this type of interface and task, Coulomb friction between .15 and .42 N is optimum.

Keywords: Coulomb friction, haptic interface, human performance, positioning task.

1 Introduction

A common design goal for a haptic interface is to minimize friction (e.g. [1]), as friction will attenuate the force output. Sometimes this is realized through clever mechanical designs (e.g. [2]) and sometimes through sending compensating force commands to the actuators (e.g. [3]). Both methods of reducing friction, however, have their limits. They can be too costly, result in concessions for other characteristics, or induce system instability. Considering the haptic interface as an output device, a certain amount of friction in the haptic interface could be acceptable, depending on the haptic information required to perform a certain task. Considering the haptic interface as an input device, some amount of friction could even be advantageous [4]. This study focused on the latter, and was aimed at determining whether there is an optimum level of friction for which humans can use an interface most accurately, quickly and comfortably.

Richard and Cutkosky [4] investigated the effect of real and simulated friction on performance in a positioning task. They concluded that friction could be simulated well and that some amount of friction could aid in a positioning task. However, as only a limited number of friction settings were tested, it remained unclear if an optimum had been found. Berkelman and Ma [5] investigated the effect of simulated friction on the time to complete a 2-dimensional positioning task. From their study it can be concluded that a small amount of additional friction in a haptic interface does not have a large effect on completion time for a positioning task. Since, for example, friction was simulated using an unspecified third-party implementation of a friction model, the question if and at what level an optimum occurs, remains unanswered.

Friction is a complex phenomenon, and a model thereof is often divided into multiple components. Within this study the focus was on Coulomb friction, which is

A.M.L. Kappers et al. (Eds.): EuroHaptics 2010, Part II, LNCS 6192, pp. 398–405, 2010.

generally defined as a constant force opposite to the direction of movement [6]. For a realistic simulation of friction, however, a friction model also needs to define a force for when the haptic interface is not in motion; i.e., a static friction force. A Karnopp model has been implemented as it proved to be a suitable model for simulating friction on a haptic interface [4, 6].

It was expected that a small amount of friction would give the users better control over their movements when handling a mass. The positive effect was expected because friction will cause a predictable constant deceleration when no external force acts upon the mass. A second explanation is that, with friction, more force is necessary to move a mass, filtering unintentional movement. For both explanations of the expected positive effect, the mass of the haptic interface is of importance and could interact with the effect of friction. The effect of the mass of the haptic interface on positioning performance was, therefore, included in this study.

Similar to Richard and Cutkosky [4], a Fitts' Law task was chosen to evaluate positioning performance quantitatively. Additionally, a small questionnaire was used to assess friction and mass subjectively. It was expected that performance would benefit from a small amount of Coulomb friction, but that beyond a certain level performance would decrease again. It was also expected that more friction would be needed when the mass of the system was increased, as friction is expected to aid in the deceleration of a mass.

2 Method

2.1 Apparatus

The haptic interface used in this study was a custom designed 1 degree-of-freedom 'joystick'. The interface has a linear range of 80 mm, and is actuated by two linear motors. A special feature is that friction is virtually absent due to the use of air bearings (see figure 1). The experiment ran on a regular PC with a 17" LCD screen placed at approximately 70 cm from the viewer. The screen had a resolution of 1280×1024 pixels, and one pixel measured 0.2625×0.2625 mm. The movement of the cursor was scaled by a factor four. Friction and inertia were simulated at 1000 Hz on a Target PC (dSPACE DS1103-06). The calibration of the force-output of the system was verified with a resolution of .01 N.

2.2 Simulation of Friction and Mass

In this experiment two virtual masses were connected to the haptic interface. The first mass was connected to the interface using a position-force scheme. A friction force, computed using the Karnopp model, acted on this virtual mass. The computed friction force was also fed back to the user through the haptic interface. The second mass was used to increase the apparent mass of the interface. It was connected to the interface using a position-error scheme. The haptic interface, virtual masses and connecting dynamics can be described by the following set of equations in the Laplace domain.

Haptic Interface $\qquad m_{HI} x_{HI} s^2 = F_{ext} + F_f + \lambda F_{vc,2}, \qquad \lambda \in \{0,1\}$

Virtual Mass 1 $\qquad m_{VM,1} x_{VM,1} s^2 = -F_{vc,1} + F_f$

Virtual Mass 2 $m_{VM,2}x_{VM,2}s^2 = -F_{vc,2}$

with $F_{vc,i} = \frac{bs+k}{\tau s+1}\left(x_{VM,i} - x_{HI}\right),\qquad \tau = \frac{1}{2\pi f},\qquad i \in \{1,2\}$

The Karnopp friction model can be represented as follows in the time-domain:

$$F_f = \begin{cases} -F_c\,\mathrm{sign}(\dot{x}_{VM,1}) & \text{if } |\dot{x}_{VM,1}| > DV \\[2mm] -F_{vc,1} & \text{if } |\dot{x}_{VM,1}| < DV \text{ and } |F_{vc,1}| < F_c \\[2mm] -F_c\,\mathrm{sign}(F_{vc,1}) & \text{otherwise} \end{cases}$$

The Coulomb friction force F_C [N] and gain λ were varied in the experiment. Gain λ was set to either 0 or 1, to disable or enable additional simulated mass, respectively. F_{ext} [N] is the external force that acts upon the interface. The stiffness k and damping b of the virtual couplings were set to 10,000 N/m and 100 Ns/m, respectively. The low-pass filter frequency f was set to 210 Hz. DV, a velocity band for which the velocity is considered zero, was set to .001 m/s.

2.3 Design

This study used a 5x2x3x3 within-subject design. There were four independent variables: Coulomb friction, additional simulated mass, target distance, and target width. Five levels of Coulomb friction were tested: .00, .15, .25, .42 and .70 N. The joystick mass was varied by disabling or enabling an additional simulated mass, resulting in an apparent mass of .53 and 1.03 kg, respectively. Targets were presented with three different widths and at three different distances (see figure 2).

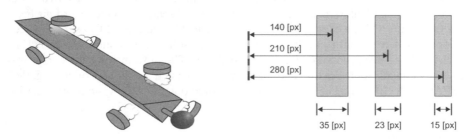

Fig. 1. Joystick with air-bearings   **Fig. 2.** Target width and distance values

The experiment consisted of 48 blocks of 28 positioning tasks (3 distances x 3 widths x 3 repetitions, plus one starting target). One setting for Coulomb friction and additional simulated mass spanned four blocks. Thus, for each experimental condition 12 tasks were performed (4 blocks x 3 repetitions per block). The presentation order of the settings for Coulomb friction and additional simulated mass was randomized across participants. The presentation order of the target distances and target widths were randomized per block. Eight blocks were used to train participants. For each task the completion time and the number of errors were measured. After completing each setting, participants had to rate the joystick on accuracy, speed, pleasantness and lightness, using a 7-point Likert scale.

2.4 Participants

Twenty-three paid participants (17 male, 6 female), with no obvious physical impairment, participated in the study. The average age was 20.4 years, with a range of 18 to 24. Only one participant was left-handed.

2.5 Procedure

Participants used their right hand to control the joystick and move the cursor, and their left hand, by pressing the spacebar on a keyboard, to indicate that the cursor was positioned over a target. An arm support was used to limit the arm movement to the wrist and fingers. A task was completed only after the target was successfully 'hit'. Participants were instructed that avoiding errors was more important than maximizing speed.

3 Results

3.1 Analysis of Errors

On average participants made .075 errors per task. A Repeated Measures ANOVA was performed with mean error rate as dependent variable and Coulomb friction, additional simulated mass, distance to target, and target width as independent variables. Significant main effects are summarized in table 1.

Table 1. Significant main effects for mean error

Variable	df	F	p
Coulomb Friction	1.88, 41.33*	30.89	< .001
Mass	1, 22	5.26	.032
Distance	1.57, 34.44*	9.25	.001
Width	1.36, 29.86*	15.99	< .001

*Greenhouse-Geisser correction applied, because the sphericity assumption was violated.

All four independent variables had significant effects on the number of errors made. Pairwise comparisons revealed that, in the conditions without friction, more errors were made than in conditions with any amount of friction ($p < 0.001$; Bonferroni corrected). Figure 3A shows that more errors were made when additional mass was simulated. Figure 3B shows that the more distant and the smaller the target, the more errors were made. Three interaction effects also proved significant, but, because the effect sizes were relatively small (partial $\eta^2 < .21$), these effects are not discussed here.

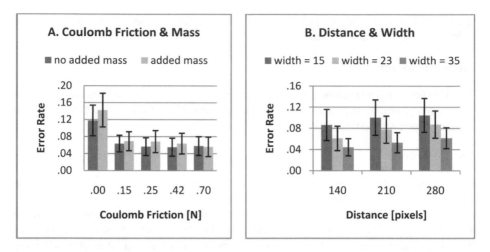

Fig. 3. Effect of independent variables on error rate with 95%-confidence intervals

3.2 Analysis of Completion Time

Tasks in which the participants made errors were excluded from the completion time analysis. The overall median task completion time was exactly 1000 ms. A Repeated Measures ANOVA was performed with median time as the dependent variable and Coulomb friction, additional simulated mass, distance to target, and target width as independent variables. Significant main effects are summarized in table 2.

Table 2. Significant main effects for completion time

Variable	df	F	p
Coulomb Friction	2.74, 30.36*	18.23	< .001
Mass	1, 22	80.47	< .001
Distance	1.60, 35.27*	387.25	< .001
Width	1.33, 29.35*	590.73	< .001

*Greenhouse-Geisser correction applied, because the sphericity assumption was violated.

All four independent variables had significant effects on the median completion time. Pairwise comparisons revealed that in the conditions without friction the completion time was longer than in conditions with any amount of friction ($p < 0.001$; Bonferroni corrected). Figure 4A shows that the median completion time was larger when additional mass was simulated. Figure 4B shows that the more distant and the smaller the target, the more time it took to 'hit' the target. Also five interaction effects proved significant, however, only the interaction effect of Mass x Width, had a notable effect size ($F(1.53, 33.76) = 26.99$; $p < .001$; partial $\eta^2 = .55$). Inspection of the

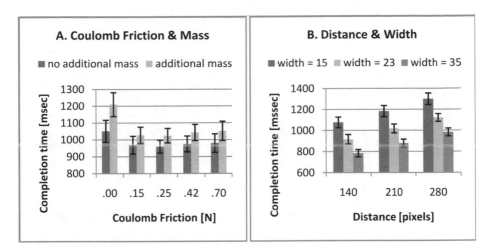

Fig. 4. Effect of independent variables on completion time with 95%-confidence intervals

data showed that this interaction effect was due to the fact that the negative effect of mass on completion time was stronger for the smaller targets.

3.3 Analysis of Subjective Ratings

Four repeated measures ANOVAs were carried out for the four different ratings: accuracy, speed, pleasantness and lightness. Significant results are summarized in table 3 and visualized in figure 5. Coulomb friction had a significant effect on all ratings. Pairwise comparisons revealed that: (1) the speeds for Coulomb friction settings .15, .25 and .42 N were rated higher than for Coulomb friction setting .70 N, (2) the accuracy for Coulomb friction setting .00 N was rated lower than for the other settings, (3) pleasantness was rated higher for Coulomb friction settings .15, .25 and .42 N than for settings .00 and .70 N, and (4) each decrement in Coulomb friction was rated as lighter (all p-values were Bonferroni corrected and smaller than .05). Additional simulated mass resulted in a lower accuracy rating and in a lower pleasantness rating, but had no significant effect on the speed ($F(1,21) = 2.58$, $p = .12$) or lightness ratings ($F(1,21) = 0.03$, $p = .86$).

Table 3. Significant effect for the four ratings

Variable	Measure	df	F	p
Coulomb Friction	Speed	2.3, 48.29*	7.76	0.001
Coulomb Friction	Accuracy	4, 84	23.93	<0.001
Coulomb Friction	Pleasantness	4, 84	24.8	<0.001
Coulomb Friction	Lightness	2.88, 60.53*	47.71	<0.001
Mass	Accuracy	1, 21	25.34	<0.001
Mass	Pleasantness	1, 21	25.01	<0.001

*Greenhouse-Geisser correction applied, because the sphericity assumption was violated.

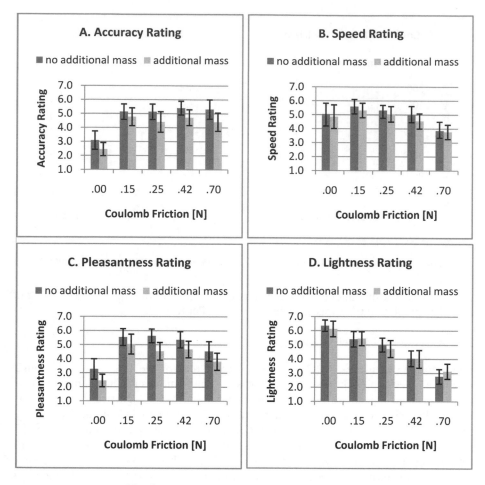

Fig. 5. Subjective ratings with 95%-confidence intervals

4 Discussion

It was expected that performance would benefit from a small amount of Coulomb friction, but that beyond a certain level performance would decrease again. The quantitative performance measures; i.e. the number of errors and completion times, indeed show that, compared to the .00 N setting, performance improved with a small amount of Coulomb friction, but, within the range tested, no level was found beyond which performance decreased. Examining the subjective measures, however, showed that participants rated the highest friction setting lower on speed and on pleasantness. By combining these results, it is concluded that, for this type of interface, Coulomb friction in the range of .15 and .42 N is optimum.

Richard & Cutkosky [4] concluded that performance with their custom haptic interface was better when the Coulomb friction was set to 4.3 instead of 0.8 N. That amount of friction is higher than we found in this study, which is likely due to the fact that their interface was operated using the shoulder and elbow.

When the apparent mass was increased from 0.53 to 1.03 kg, more errors were made and tasks took longer to complete. The negative effect of the additional simulated mass increased when the targets became smaller. The conditions with this simulated additional mass were also rated lower on accuracy and on pleasantness. Strangely, the additional simulated mass did not result in a lower rating on lightness. It was expected that the optimum level of Coulomb friction would increase for a larger mass. No significant indication was found, for any measure, that the additional simulated mass influenced the optimum level of Coulomb friction.

Based on these results, Coulomb friction within the range of .15 to .42 N is advised for input devices operated with the wrist and fingers. Within this range, the positioning speed and accuracy are highest, and the input device is rated most pleasant. For haptic interfaces, for which an accurate presentation of haptic information is important, friction can be reduced to .15 N, but levels of Coulomb friction lower than this should be avoided.

Acknowledgements. This work was supported by a grant from the Dutch Ministry of Economic Affairs (IOP-MMI/SenterNovem). The authors thank Dennis van Raaij and Ron Hendrix for their extensive technical support.

References

1. Lee, J.H., Eom, K.S., Yi, B., Suh, I.: Design of a New 6-DOF Parallel Haptic Device. In: Proc. IEEE ICRA, Seoul, Korea, pp. 886–891 (2001)
2. Hollis, R.L., Salcudean, S.E.: Lorentz Levitation Technology: A New Approach to Fine Motion Robotics, Teleoperation, Haptic Interfaces, and Vibration Isolation. In: Proc. 6th Int'l Symposium on Robotics Research, Hidden Valley, USA (1993)
3. Bernstein, N.L., Lawrence, D.A., Pao, L.Y.: Friction Modeling and Compensation for Haptic Interfaces. In: Proc. 1st Joint EuroHaptics Conf. and Symp. on Haptic Interfaces for Virtual Environments and Teleoperator Systems, Pisa, Italy, pp. 290–295 (2005)
4. Richard, C., Cutkosky, M.R.: The effects of real and computer generated friction on human performance in a targeting task. In: Proc. ASME IMECE 2000 Haptics Symposium, Orlando, USA, pp. 1101–1108 (2000)
5. Berkelman, P., Ma, J.: Effect of Friction Parameters on Completion Times for Sustained Planar Positioning Tasks with a Haptic Interface. In: Proc. 2006 IEEE/RSJ International Conf. on Intelligent Robotics and Systems, Beijing, China, pp. 1116–1121 (2006)
6. Olsson, H., Åström, K.J., de Wit, C.C., Gäfvert, M., Lischinsky, P.: Friction Models and Friction Compensation. European J. Contr. 3, 176–195 (1998)

Is the Touch-Induced Illusory Flash Distinguishable from a Real Flash?

Tom G. Philippi[1,2], Jan B.F. van Erp[2], and Peter Werkhoven[1]

[1] Utrecht University, Department of Information and Computing Sciences, Padualaan 14
3584 CH, Utrecht, The Netherlands
[2] TNO Human Factors, Kampweg 5, 3769 DE, Soesterberg, The Netherlands
{tom.philippi,jan.vanerp,peter.werkhoven}@tno.nl

Abstract. When the presentation of a single flash is paired with that of 2 taps, a second, illusory, flash is sometimes perceived. We presented participants with 1 or 2 flashes paired with 1 or 2 taps and asked them to report the number of flashes. In experiment 1, we used the response categories 1, 2, 3 and analyzed the responses to 2 consecutive illusory flash trials (1 flash, 2 taps). The chance to report 2 flashes was 70% when their preceding answer was 2 and only 10% when it was 1 (p < .001). This effect can occur when participants' percept neither fits the 1 or 2 response category. In experiment 2, we introduced a new response category, viz. 'something different from 1 or 2 flashes' and found that observers used this category in 50.0% of the illusory flash trials, while 2 real flashes were reported as 2 in 87.3% of the trials ($\chi2 = 116.62$; p < .001). We conclude that the percept of an illusory flash differs from that of a real flash.

Keywords: Touch-induced illusory flash, touch, vision, cross-modal, illusion.

1 Introduction

The sound- and touch-induced visual illusions occur when two beeps (B_2) or two taps (T_2) are presented concurrently with a single flash (F_1); in roughly half the trials two flashes are reported [1,2,3]. The second of these two flashes is considered an illusory flash. Among other things, this illusion shows that touch can affect visual perception.

For some time, it has been debated whether the increase in the number of flashes reported for the F_1T_2 and F_1B_2 stimuli is the result of a genuine perceptual effect or whether it is the result of a response bias or other artifact [3,4]. Recently, McCormick and Mamassian [5] found that the sound-induced illusory flash is partially attributable to a change in visual sensitivity and showed that the illusory flash has a measurable contrast, which indicates that the illusory flash indeed has a perceptual basis. Their finding is consistent with earlier EEG studies which show that the activity in the visual cortex associated with perceiving the sound-induced illusory flash differs from the activity of perceiving just a single flash [6,7].

One of these EEG studies [7], however, also reports that the activity in the visual cortex associated with the sound-induced illusory flash differs from the activity associated with perceiving a real second flash. This suggests that the sound-induced

A.M.L. Kappers et al. (Eds.): EuroHaptics 2010, Part II, LNCS 6192, pp. 406–411, 2010.

illusory flash may not look like a real second flash, a notion that is also supported by the recent work of Rosenthal, Shimojo and Shams [8]. They investigated the effect of feedback on the sound-induced illusory flash and reported that although feedback could not eliminate the sound-induced illusory flash, participants who received monetary feedback indicated that there were 'subtle differences' between the illusory percept induced by the F_1B_2 stimulus and the percept of two flashes induced by the F_2B_2 stimulus.

We hypothesize that the perception of a real second flash differs from the perception of the flash induced by touch. That is, we think that the illusory flash percept induced by the F_1T_2 stimulus differs from the percept of two flashes induced by the F_2T_2 stimulus as well as the percept of a single flash induced by the F_1T_1 stimulus. Possibly, the illusory flash percept may look like something different from or something in between the percept of a single flash and the percept of two flashes. For example, the second, illusory flash might be perceived as weaker, shorter, less defined or as (more) merged with the first flash. However, none of the illusory-flash paradigms offered observers the possibility to report possible perceptual differences between a real and an illusory flash since only the response categories 1, 2, 3, … are used.

In experiment 1, we employ the usual response categories (viz. 1, 2, 3, …) and investigate the response to illusory flash trials (i.e. F_1T_2) that are directly preceded by a F_1T_2 trial in which the observer reported an illusory flash or by a F_1T_2 trial in which the observer reported a single flash. Our reasoning for this is as follows: if an observer perceives the illusory flash in an illusory flash trial as different from either the percept of one flash or two flashes but he or see is forced to categorize the stimulus, he or she will probably use the same categorization if the next stimulus is perceived as similar. However, if the presentation of an illusory flash trial is perceived as purely a single flash or two flashes, than the response will not depend on the preceding response.

In experiment 2, we introduce a new paradigm in illusory flash research. Instead of only allowing participants to report 1, 2, 3, … flashes, we allowed them to report a percept which didn't look like either one or two flashes, but like 'something different'. If the percept of the touch-induced visual illusion is not equal to that of the percept of two flashes participants should be able to discriminate these two quite accurately. Since the differences between the touch-induced illusory flash and a real flash may be subtle, only participants familiar with illusory flash experiments were admitted in this first pilot study.

In both experiments we limit our data analyses to the stimuli of interest. These are the F_1T_1, the F_1T_2, and the F_2T_2 stimuli. An analysis of the complete behavioral data of experiment 1 will be presented elsewhere [9].

2 Experiment 1

Twelve participants (mean age 24.3, 6 females) participated in experiment 1. They all had normal or corrected-to-normal vision, reported normal sense of touch and gave their written informed consent prior to participation.

The experiment was conducted in a dimly lit and sound-attenuated room. Participants sat in a chair approximately 52 cm in front of a monitor displaying a fixation cross. Visual stimuli where displayed by a white LED, which was positioned eight degrees below the fixation cross. Tactile stimuli were presented to the right index finger by a Mini-Shaker 4810 (Brüel and Kjær, Nærum, Denmark) located to the right of the monitor. Any sound generated by this device was masked by constant pink noise played through loudspeakers; participants also wore foam plugs.

Visual stimuli were presented with a luminance of 80 cd/m2 and had a duration of 10 ms. Tactile stimuli, also with a duration of 10 ms, consisted of single 100 Hz sine-wave taps with an amplitude of 0.06 mm and an acceleration of 25 m/s². Nine different stimuli were presented consisting of all combinations of 0, 1, or 2 flashes and 0, 1 or 2 taps. Presentations of two flashes or taps were separated by a 60 ms interval. In bimodal presentations the flashes and the taps were presented simultaneously when their number was equal, but when there number was unequal the single flash or tap was paired with the first flash or tap in the other modality. Five hundred ms after stimulus presentation, the fixation cross was replaced by a question mark to indicate to participants that they could give their response during a 2 s period.

Participants were provided written instruction at the start of the experiment asking them to report the number of flashes they perceived via a keypad, and to ignore the number of taps. Prior to the experiment, participants were familiarized with the task by judging the number of flashes in ten visual stimuli. All participants succeeded to judge at least 90 percent correctly in one or two blocks and were consequently presented with another block consisting of 90 stimuli. This block was presented to test their susceptibility to the flash illusions. Once participants completed the above trials, electrodes were applied to record their electroencephalogram (EEG), which was used to answer another research question [9]. All participants observed at least 4 illusions in the 20 illusion trials and were admitted in the main experiment. The main experiment consisted of ten blocks of 135 trials each. In each block, each of the nine stimuli was presented 15 times, resulting in 150 repetitions for each stimulus. Stimuli were presented in random order. In between blocks, participants were allowed to take short breaks. The experiment lasted about four hours.

2.1 Results and Discussion

The left panel of Fig. 1 displays the mean response for the F_1T_1, F_1T_2, and F_2T_2 stimuli. A stimulus (3) repeated measures ANOVA revealed a significant effect on the number of flashes perceived ($F_{(2, 22.03)} = 114.90$, $p < .001$). Post-hoc Tukey HSD analyses revealed that the responses to all stimuli differed from each other (all p <.001). A touch-induced visual illusion was reported in 40.3% of the presentations of the F_1T_2 stimulus, which is in the usual range [1,2,3,6].

To assess our hypothesis we analyzed to what extent reporting a touch-induced illusory flash affected reporting a touch-induced illusory flash in an immediately succeeding F_1T_2 trial. We displayed the results in the right panel of Fig. 1, together with the effects of reporting a single flash in F_1T_1 trials and reporting two flashes in F_2T_2 trials on perceiving a touch-induced illusory flash in a succeeding F_1T_2 trial. A stimulus and response (4) repeated measures ANOVA revealed a significant effect on the number of flashes perceived in the succeeding F_1T_2 trials ($F_{(3, 48.92)} = 6.49$, $p < .001$).

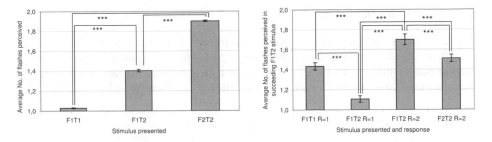

Fig. 1. The left panel displays the average number of flashes reported for the F_1T_1, F_1T_2 and F_2T_2 stimuli. The right panel displays the average number of flashes reported in F_1T_2 trials which succeeded F_1T_1, F_1T_2 and F_2T_2 trials with specific responses (R). Significant differences are indicated by asterisks. *** denote a p-level of .001.

Post-hoc analyses revealed significant differences between the effects of all stimulus and response combinations (all $p < .001$) except between the effects of the F_1T_1 trials where response was one and the F_2T_2 trials where response was two ($p = .30$).

The above analyses show that the chance to report an illusory flash increases by 75% (i.e. from 40.3% to roughly 70%) when the trial was preceded by a F_1T_2 trial where the response was two. Similarly, the chance to report an illusory flash decreased by 75% (i.e. from 40.3% to roughly 10%) when the trial was preceded by a F_1T_2 trial where the response was one. These effects are consistent with our hypothesis: if participants perceived the visual percept accompanying the illusory flash stimulus as neither a single flash nor as two flashes and were forced to respond with a natural number a response bias can be expected. The effects of preceding F_1T_2 trials on the touch-induced visual illusion also contrast with the effects of perceiving a single flash in F_1T_1 trials and perceiving two flashes in F_2T_2 trials on the touch-induced visual illusion, further suggesting that the percept accompanying the F_1T_2 stimulus differs from the percepts accompanying the F_1T_1 and the F_2T_2 stimuli.

3   Experiment 2

Four participants (mean age 27.7, 1 female) participated in experiment 2. All participants had normal or corrected-to-normal vision, reported normal sense of touch and were familiar with the illusory flash experiments.

Experiment 2 was largely similar to experiment 1, except for the following. Only those four stimuli consisting of 1 or 2 flashes and 1 or 2 taps were presented. Furthermore, in bimodal presentations with an unequal number of flashes and taps, the single flash or tap was presented in between the two flashes or taps instead of paired with the first tap or flash. These were presented 20 times each and in random order. Participants were instructed to report the number of flashes, but they were also explained about the illusory flash effect and instructed to press '9' on the keypad whenever they perceived more than one flash, but less than two. Prior to the experiment, participants were presented with about 30 stimuli until they felt they were sufficiently familiar with the stimuli. Participants wore a Bilsom 770 headphone instead of earplugs to mask the sound of the tactile actuator. Experiment 2 lasted about 15 minutes.

3.1 Results and Discussion

Fig. 2 displays the distribution of responses for the F_1T_1, F_1T_2, and F_2T_2 stimuli. A Friedman ANOVA revealed that the stimuli presented significantly affected the response distribution ($\chi^2 = 116.62$; $p < .001$). In fact, multiple comparisons showed that the response distributions for each stimulus differed significantly (all $p < .001$).

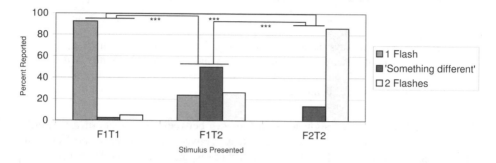

Fig. 2. Figure 2 displays the response distributions for the F_1T_1, F_1T_2, and F_2T_2 stimuli. Each colored bar represents the percentage of reports for each stimulus that fell in that category. Significant differences are indicated by asterisks. *** denote a p-level difference of .001.

The near perfect (~90% correct) perception of the number of flashes in the F_1T_1 and F_2T_2 stimuli is in the usual range of visual numerosity judgment [1,2,3,6,7,10,11].

As a result of the introduction of a new response category, participants no longer report to perceive two flashes in roughly half the illusory flash trials. Instead, they often report that the percept induced by the F_1T_2 stimulus is neither equal to the percept of a single flash nor to the percept of two flashes, which suggests that the illusory flash does not look like a real, second flash. Furthermore, our manipulation appears to have increased the chance to perceive an illusory flash to about 75% (i.e. an illusory flash is perceived whenever the response is 'something different' or 2), indicating that the effect is more robust than previously thought.

Interestingly, the F_1T_2 stimulus still induces the percept of a single flash and the percept of two flashes, each in about 25% of the trials. This has several implications. First, the frequent occurrence of reports of a single flash prevents drawing the conclusion that participants may have reported 'something different' whenever they perceived one flash together with two beeps. Second, the frequent occurrence of reports of two flashes suggests that the differences between the touch-induced illusory flash and two flashes are also 'subtle'. Alternatively, it may indicate that the strength of the illusory flash varies per occurrence. In other words, the illusory flash may not simply be present or absent, but could be 'more or less' present. This could also explain the increase in the chance to perceive an illusory flash reported in this study; weak illusory flashes, which were classed as 'something different' would likely have been classed as a single flash when such a response category would not be available.

4   Conclusion

We provide evidence that the percept of a touch-induced illusory flash is not equal to the percept of a real, second, flash. Perception of an illusory flash is affected by the absence or presence of an illusory flash in preceding illusory flash trials. No effects of the preceding trial were found for all other stimuli. Furthermore, we show that participants can quite accurately discern the illusory flash from a real second flash if they are allowed to use a new response category besides 1, 2, 3, namely "something different from the percept of 1 and 2 flashes". This indicated that observers can perceptually distinguish a touch-induced illusory flash from real flash, which is consistent with earlier reports indicating that the sound-induced illusory flash may perceptually differ from a real flash [7,8].

References

1. Shams, L., Kamitani, Y., Shimojo, S.: What you see is what you hear. Nature 408, 788 (2000)
2. Violentyev, A., Shimojo, S., Shams, L.: Touch-induced visual illusion. Neuroreport 16(10), 1107–1110 (2005)
3. Shams, L., Kamitani, Y., Shimojo, S.: Visual illusion induced by sound. Cogn. Brain. Res. 14, 147–152 (2002)
4. McCormick, D., Mamassian, P.: Response biases in the illusory-flash effect. J. Vision 5(8), 878a (2005)
5. McCormick, P., Mamassian, P.: What does the illusory-flash look like? Vis. Res. 48, 63–69 (2008)
6. Shams, L., Kamitani, Y., Thompson, S., Shimojo, S.: Sound alters visual evoked potentials in humans. NeuroReport 12(17), 2852–3849 (2006)
7. Mishra, J., Martinez, A., Sejnowski, T.J., Hillyard, S.A.: Early cross-modal interactions in auditory and visual cortex underlie a sound-induced visual illusion. J. Neurosci. 27(15), 4120–4131 (2007)
8. Rosenthal, O., Shimojo, S., Shams, L.: Sound-induced flash illusion is resistant to feedback training. Brain Topogr. 21, 185–192 (2009)
9. Philippi, T.G., De Winkel, K.N., Van Erp, J.B.F., Werkhoven, P.: Touch-Induced illusory flash alters activity in the visual cortex (Submitted)
10. Werkhoven, P.J., Van Erp, J.B.F., Philippi, T.G.: Counting visual and tactile events: The effect of attention on multisensory integration. Atten. Percept. Psychophys. 71(8), 1854–1861 (2009)
11. Philippi, T.G., Van Erp, J.B.F., Werkhoven, P.J.: Multisensory temporal numerosity judgment. Brain Res. 1232, 116–125 (2008)

Haptic Recognition of Non-figurative Tactile Pictures in the Blind: Does Life-Time Proportion without Visual Experience Matter?

Samuel Lebaz[1], Delphine Picard[1,2], and Christophe Jouffrais[3]

[1] University of Toulouse II, EA4156 Octogone-ECCD,
Pavillon de la recherche, 31058 Toulouse
[2] Institut Universitaire de France
[3] IRIT, CNRS & University of Toulouse, France
{samuel.lebaz,delphine.picard}@univ-tlse2.fr, jouffrais@irit.fr

Abstract. The present study tests whether age at onset of total blindness and the proportion of life-time without visual experience affect the haptic processing and recognition of tactile pictures in a sample of 20 totally blind adults. We also examine the type of mental strategy (visual, non-visual) used to perform the haptic recognition task. The results indicate that haptic processing of non-figurative tactile pictures may be efficiently achieved with different levels of visual experience and different strategies in totally blind adults. Interestingly, they also reveal interplays between strategy and the proportion of life-time without visual experience.

Keywords: Haptic recognition; Raised-line pictures; Strategy; Visual imagery; Blind.

1 Introduction

Our sense of haptics may be mobilized to retrieve useful spatial information from raised-line pictures. These 'tactile pictures' [1] have a potentially high utility for blind people since they can use them to retrieve information about objects, places, spaces, and shapes [2]. Different types of tactile pictures have been designed and tested experimentally with blind adults, including figurative raised-line drawings (see [3] for a review), tactile maps [4] and diagrams [5], and tactile shapes and patterns [6]. A recurrent but not systematic finding showed that late blind subjects often outperformed early blind adults in tactile picture perception tasks [7]. This finding pertains to the current debate about the role of visual experience and visual imagery in tactile picture perception. This debate disputes two theories on haptic raised-line pictures identification. The theory founded by Lederman and co-workers [8] assumes that raised-line drawing identification is achieved via visual imagery. In contrast, Kennedy [2] argues that picture identification by touch is possible without visual experience and visual imagery, despite being difficult.

In the present study, we asked a sample of 20 totally blind adults to haptically explore non-figurative raised-line pictures, and to decide whether pictures in a pair were

A.M.L. Kappers et al. (Eds.): EuroHaptics 2010, Part II, LNCS 6192, pp. 412–417, 2010.

similar or different (delayed haptic recognition task). Non-figurative pictures were preferred to figurative drawings which may impose additional difficulties to blind subjects who are not familiar with visual drawing conventions [8, 9]. We examined whether the haptic processing of non-figurative tactile pictures varies according to age at onset of blindness (AOB) and the proportion of life-time without visual experience (P). Both parameters may offer a much more precise view of inter-individual differences in tactile picture processing than the usual binary classification into early and late blind groups. We reasoned that if visual imagery and visual experience facilitate the processing of tactile pictures - as predicted by Lederman's theory [8] - haptic recognition performance should be positively correlated with age at onset of total blindness, and negatively correlated with the proportion of life-time without visual experience. Indeed, age at onset of blindness and the proportion of life-time without visual experience may constrain the mental strategy (visual or non-visual) used by blind adults to perform the haptic recognition task. Haptic recognition performance may be lower in blind adults who used non-visual strategies compared to those who relied on a visual imagery strategy.

2   Method

2.1   Participants

The volunteers were 20 totally blind adults (9 women; 11 men; mean chronological age: 37 years, SD: 13). Aetiology of total blindness included retinitis pigmentosa (3), retrolental fibroplasia (4), retinoblastoma (2), infectious disease (4), optic atrophy (1), glaucoma (4), retinal detachment (1), and accident (1). None of the participants suffered from a known neurological dysfunction in association with their visual impairment. The age at onset of total blindness varied from 0 to 25 years. Proportion of life-time without visual experience (P) was calculated for each participant as follows:

$$P = [(CA - AOB) / CA] \tag{1}$$

with CA = chronological age, and AOB = age at onset of blindness. A ratio of 0.10 indicates that the person had spent 10% of his/her life without visual experience. The observed ratio varied from 0.22 to 1.

2.2   Material

The stimuli consisted of 40 non-figurative raised-line pictures (size: 20 cm length) made from a combination of 6 segments (2 horizontal, 2 vertical, and 2 oblique

Fig. 1. Example of *identical (see left)* and *different pairs (see right)* of stimuli used in the haptic recognition task

segments). Each single stimulus was printed on a Swell paper and heated so that the trace got embossed (1 mm height). Two series of 10 pairs of stimuli were used. Each series included 5 identical and 5 different pairs. Fig. 1 shows an example of the identical and different pairs used in the haptic recognition task.

2.3 Procedure

The haptic recognition task involved two series of 10 test trials each, plus two additional training trials. For each trial, participants first explored a tactile picture from top (starting with the circle) to bottom, using the index finger of their dominant hand. Once the picture was fully explored, participants lifted their finger for a 5 sec (retention) delay. Afterwards, they had to explore a second picture using the same procedure as the one described above. The task was then to decide whether the second picture was similar to or different from the first one. The presentation order of the two series of trials was counterbalanced across participants. At the end of the session, the experimenter interviewed the participants in order to determine the mental strategy (visual or non-visual) they had employed to encode and memorize the tactile pictures. A free-answer method was employed following the mirror technique used by Cornoldi et al. [10]. Although the procedure of self-report is not exempt from bias due to its subjective (introspective) components, such a procedure has successfully been used in previous research studies including blind individuals (see [10, 11]).

3 Results

Scores for hits (correct recognitions) and false alarms (i.e. reporting identical when the stimuli were different) were computed for each participant. Haptic recognition performance was measured by the index of discriminability A', which is used in signal detection theory [12]. It was computed according to Grier's formula [12]:

$$A' = \frac{1}{2} + [(y - x)(1 + y - x) / 4y(1 - x)] \tag{2}$$

where y stood for the probability of a hit and x corresponded to the probability of a false alarm. This index ranges from 0 to 1, with 0.5 indicating responses at chance level, and 1 indicating maximum discriminability.

The results (see Fig. 2) showed that blind participants were quite successful at the haptic recognition task (mean discriminability = 0.78, SD = 0.16). Linear correlation analyses indicated that haptic recognition performance was not significantly related to the participants' age at onset of blindness ($r = 0.32$, $p > 0.05$; see Fig. 2A), nor to the proportion of life-time without visual experience ($r = -0.40$, $p > 0.05$; see Fig. 2B). Blind participants mostly used non-visual strategies (65%), and a minority had recourse to a visual imagery strategy (35%) to deal with the haptic recognition task. Non-visual strategies included spatial, kinesthetic, and/or verbal coding of the tactile information. Among the 13 blind subjects using non-visual strategies, 5 used spatial coding, 2 used spatial and kinesthetic coding, 2 used spatial and verbal coding, 2 used verbal coding, and 2 used kinesthetic coding. Strategy (visual versus non-visual) was not significantly related to haptic recognition performance ($r = 0.37$, $p > 0.05$). However, strategy significantly correlated both with the participants' age at onset of blindness ($r = 0.86$, $p < 0.05$), and the proportion of life-time without visual experience

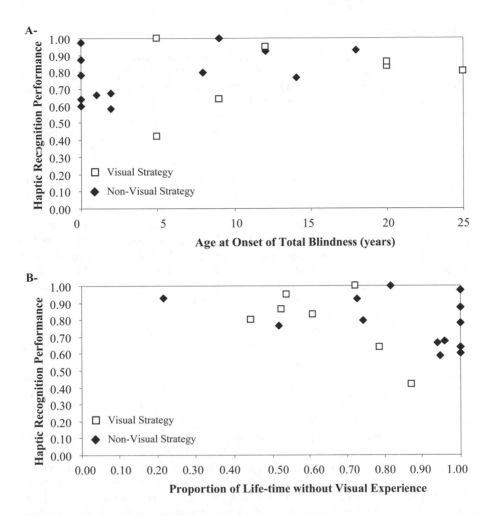

Fig. 2. Haptic recognition performance for the 20 blind subjects according to: **A**- Age at onset of blindness, and **B**- Proportion of life-time without visual experience. Participants who used a *visual strategy* are represented with *white squares*, whereas those who used *non-visual strategies* are represented with *black diamond*.

($r = -0.84$, $p < 0.05$). Closer look at the data (see Fig. 2A and Fig. 2B) revealed that participants who used a visual imagery strategy had a significantly higher mean age at onset of blindness (mean = 17 years, SD = 5) than participants using non-visual strategies (mean = 3 years, SD = 3) (Man-Whitney test [13], $p < 0.05$). Conversely, participants who used a visual imagery strategy have spent a significantly lower proportion of their life-time without visual experience (mean = 0.51, SD = 0.15) than participants who used non-visual strategies (mean = 0.90, SD = 0.10) (Man-Whitney test, $p < 0.05$).

4 Discussion

Contrary to our hypothesis, the present study showed that haptic recognition perform-ance does not depend on age at onset of blindness or on the proportion of life-time without visual experience. This finding is quite surprising because previous studies have shown differences between early and late blind subjects in tactile picture recog-nition tasks [7, 3]. Our study also shows that haptic recognition performance does not depend on the strategy (visual or non-visual) used by blind subjects. This result is in line with [11] who observed that early and late blind as well as sighted individuals reached similar performance although they used different strategies. Visual and non-visual strategy may be equally effective in facilitating recognition of the tactile pictures as well as equally ineffectual. In future studies, the reliability of mental strategies obtained with self-report procedures might be tested using additional tech-niques, such as interference techniques. Interestingly, our data show that the strategy used to encode the tactile pictures highly depends on age at onset of blindness and on the proportion of life-time without visual experience. Previous reports have shown that mental imagery varies according to age at onset of blindness [14, 15]. Our study is the first study to reveal the precise interplay between strategy use and the propor-tion of life-time without visual experience, a parameter (P) that is worth assessing and/or controlling in studies involving totally blind participants.

Illustrating this interplay, the set of black diamonds on the right side of Fig. 2B corresponds to a group of blind subjects that had a very short visual experience (less than 10% of lifetime). These subjects exclusively used non-visual strategies to encode and recognize the tactile pictures and reached a good level of performance. A possible explanation of this result is childhood amnesia, a period of life (0-3 years) during which experience, including visual experience, affects behavior but cannot be brought to conscious memory later. The worse haptic recognition performance (0.42) corre-sponds to a 39 years old woman who became blind at 5 years of age. In spite of hav-ing a very short visual experience (ratio of 0.87, white square on the right side of Fig. 2B), she persisted in using a visual imagery strategy to fulfill the task but get low scores. Conversely, a 23 years old subject who was blind at the age of 18 years old (ratio of 0.22, black diamond on the left side of Fig. 2B) reached a very good per-formance (0.93), though relying on non-visual strategies. Interestingly, this latter subject knew she will inevitably get blind and may have voluntarily developed non-visual strategies to subserve haptic recognition.

Altogether these results showed that subjects who spent 40 to 80% of their lifetime without visual experience are able to encode and recognize simple tactile pictures, regardless of the strategy (visual or non-visual) they use. When the proportion of non-visual experience is important (more than 90%), blind subjects tend to rely on non-visual strategies to encode and recognize the tactile pictures. The presence of only one late blind with a Recent Loss of Sight (RLS) in our study prevents us from concluding about the type of mental strategy these specific subjects use for haptic recognition. Future and complementary work could test a substantial sample of late blind with RLS (i.e. 0% to 20% of non-visual experience) in order to assess whether: 1/ like our unique subject who was suffering a degenerative disease, they actively and quickly develop non-visual strategies to compensate for inevitable loss of vision; or 2/ on the contrary, when they suffered an unexpected loss of vision (i.e. by accident), they preferentially rely on a visual imagery strategy.

References

1. Eriksson, Y.: Tactile Pictures: Pictorial Representations for the Blind. Gothenburg University Press, Gothenburg (1988)
2. Kennedy, J.M.: Drawing and the Blind. Yale University Press, New Haven (1993)
3. Heller, M.A.: Tactile Picture Perception in Blind and Sighted People. Behav. Brain Res. 135, 65–68 (2002)
4. Caddeo, P., Fornara, F., Nenci, A., Piroldi, A.: Wayfinding Tasks in Visually Impaired People: The Role of Tactile Maps. Cogn. Process. 7, 168–169 (2006)
5. Jehoel, S., Ungar, S., McCallum, D., Rowell, J.: An Evaluation of Substrates for Tactile Maps and Diagrams: Scanning Speed and User Preferences. J. Vis. Impair. Blind. 99, 85–95 (2005)
6. Bailes, S.M., Lambert, R.M.: Cognitive Aspects of Haptic Form Recognition by Blind and Sighted Subjects. Br. J. Psychol. 77, 451–458 (1986)
7. Heller, M.A.: Picture and Pattern Perception in the Sighted and Blind: The Advantage of the Late Blind. Perception 18, 379–389 (1989)
8. Lederman, S.J., Klatzky, R.L., Chataway, C., Summers, C.: Visual Mediation and the Haptic Recognition of Two-Dimensional Pictures of Common Objects. Percept. Psychopsys. 47, 54–64 (1990)
9. Thompson, L.J., Chronicle, E.P.: Beyond Visual Conventions: Rethinking the Design of Tactile Diagrams. Br. J. Vis. Impair. 24, 76–82 (2006)
10. Cornoldi, C., Tinti, C., Mammarella, I.C., Re, A.M., Varotto, D.: Memory for an Imagined Pathway and Strategy Effects in Sighted and in Totally Congenitally Blind Individuals Acta. Psychol. 130, 11–16 (2009)
11. Vanlierde, A., Wanet-Defalque, M.C.: Abilities and Strategies of Blind and Sighted Subjects in Visuo-Spatial Imagery. Acta. Psychol. 116, 205–222 (2004)
12. Grier, J.B.: Nonparametric Indexes for Sensitivity and Bias: Computing Formulas. Psychol. Bull. 75, 424–429 (1971)
13. Mann, H.B., Whitney, D.R.: On a test of whether one of two random variables is stochastically larger than the other. Annals of Math. Stat. 18, 50–60 (1947)
14. Postma, A., Zuidhoek, S., Noordzij, M.L., Kappers, A.M.: Differences between Early-blind, Late-blind and Blindfolded-sighted People in Haptic Spatial-Configuration Learning and Resulting Memory Traces. Perception 36, 1253–1265 (2007)
15. Hollins, M.: Styles of Mental Imagery in Blind Adults. Neuropsychologia 23, 561–566 (1985)

Preliminary Evaluation of a Haptic Aiding Concept for Remotely Piloted Vehicles

Samantha M.C. Alaimo[1,2], Lorenzo Pollini[2], Alfredo Magazzù[3],
Jean Pierre Bresciani[1], Paolo Robuffo Giordano[1], Mario Innocenti[2],
and Heinrich H. Bülthoff[1,4]

[1] Max Planck Institute for Biological Cybernetics, Spemannstraße 38
72076 Tübingen, Germany
[2] Dept. Electrical Systems and Automation, University of Pisa,
Via Diotisalvi 2, 56126 Pisa, Italy
[3] Cantieri Magazzù, Via Parrini 17, 90145 Palermo, Italy
[4] Dept. of Brain and Cognitive Engineering, Korea University, Anam-dong, Seongbuk-gu,
Seoul, 136-713 Korea
{samantha.alaimo,jean-pierre.bresciani,
paolo.robuffo-giordano,heinrich.buelthoff}@tuebingen.mpg.de,
{lpollini,mario.innocenti}@dsea.unipi.it,
amagazzu@magazzu.com

Abstract. This paper shows a preliminary experimental evaluation of a novel haptic aiding for Remotely Piloted Vehicles. The aerodynamically-inspired haptic feedback law was named Conventional Aircraft Artificial Feel, and was implemented as a variable stiffness spring. The experimental set-up comprises a fully nonlinear mathematical model of the aircraft, a visual display and a haptic device (a 3 DoF Omega Device). The tests, performed using a set of 18 naïve subjects, show the validity of the proposed approach.

Keywords: Remotely piloted vehicles, experimental evaluation, artificial feel.

1 Introduction

The aim of this research is the investigation of possible haptic aidings for Remotely Piloted Vehicles (RPV). Nonetheless similar techniques could be employed in similar fields like Fly-By-Wire (FBW) piloted commercial aircrafts or helicopters.

The FBW system employed both in large airliners and in military jet aircraft, dispenses all the complexity of the mechanical circuit of the mechanical flight control system and replaces it with an electrical circuit. The FBW makes use of an electronic passive sidestick, in place of the conventional control stick which was connected to the actual aerodynamic surfaces via mechanical linkages. The sidestick is in general implemented as a spring system with constant stiffness that makes the force felt by the pilot stronger as the displacement of the stick increases independently from the particular aerodynamic situation (velocity, load factor). Sometimes the sidestick may provide an artificial vibration of the stick (*stick shaker*) and some acoustical/visual

A.M.L. Kappers et al. (Eds.): EuroHaptics 2010, Part II, LNCS 6192, pp. 418–425, 2010.

warning that makes the pilot to know that the limits of the flight envelope are going to be reached [1].

Completely artificial feel had become essential with fully powered controls [2]. There was considerable speculation about what elements of natural feel should be emulated, coupled with the natural desire to minimise the cost and complexity of the feel devices. The possibilities included control force variation with dynamic pressure (Q feel), speed (V feel) or control deflection only (spring feel), also potentially augmented by devices such as bobweights and downsprings which were already familiar on conventional aircraft. Manual controls also fulfill the role of a tactile display. The human hand can interpret loading forces appearing on the handgrip in terms of demands imposed on the system and its expectable response, enabling the pilot to develop a beneficial phase lead [3].

Artificial feel had become fundamental in addition to the visual cueing in the context of Remotely Piloted Vehicles. Recent work [4] has shown using a rather complex remote piloting and helicopter obstacle avoidance simulation that an appropriate haptic augmentation may provide the pilot a beneficial effect in terms of performance in its task (to fly from waypoint to waypoint as accurately as possible in an obstacle-laden environment). The authors extensively studied the problem of force feedback (injecting an artificial force on the stick which pulls the stick to fly away from the obstacle) and stiffness feedback (changing stick stiffness to oppose less or more strongly to motion when approaching an obstacle) and concluded that a mixed force-stiffness feedback is the best solution. This type of haptic augmentation systems for RPVs was designed in order to help directly the pilot in his/her task by pulling the stick in the correct direction for the achievement of the task or by changing stick stiffness in order to facilitate or oppose to certain pilot's actions [4], [5]. We may group the class of all Haptic Aidings, like the one just described, which produce forces and/or sensations (due to stick stiffness changes for instance) aimed at "forcing" or "facilitating" the pilot to take some actions instead of others under the name Direct Haptic Aiding (DHA).

The sense of touch could be used instead, as originally intended in haptic research, to provide the pilot with an additional source of information that would help him, indirectly, by letting him know what's happening in the remote environment and leaving him the full authority to take control decisions. Thus this research aims at designing novel haptic augmentation schemes which increase the situation awareness, that is to infer a better knowledge of system status and of its external disturbances. This approach requires that the operator is somehow capable of understanding the meaning of a specific haptic feedback and to translate it into a cue which, in turns, will help him/her to perform the task. We may call this class of Haptic Aidings, which is clearly complementary to the previously described one, as Indirect Haptic Aiding (IHA).

An Indirect Haptic Aiding scheme implies that the haptic feedback must trigger the pilot prior knowledge of the force response/dynamics of the vehicle he/she is piloting; as a consequence, the impact of pilot training with a specific force feedback must be accurately understood.

An example of a haptic aiding scheme that follows the IHA concept is shown in the next section.

2 The Conventional Aircraft Artificial Feel

In order to test the IHA concept, we decided to create a benchmark taken form the aerospace field. A typical trouble of remote piloting an RPV is the lack of situation awareness because of the physical separation between the pilot (inside the Control Ground Station, CGS) and the airborne RPV. Currently the remote pilot has got just a visual feedback (visual displays). In case an external disturbance or a fault affects the RPV, that on a conventional aircraft would produce a perceptible effect on the stick, the pilot has to understand this situation by looking at the output of the instruments only. Thus we decided to study if it is possible to improve the pilot situation awareness by adding a haptic cue, which is a force feedback on the control sidestick of the CGS, which is, to a certain extent, similar to the actual force he/she would feel on a conventional mechanically steered aircraft. As a matter of fact, a pilot flying a mechanically steered aircraft feels aerodynamic forces on the stick, which are generated on the actual control surfaces. The simple fact that the pilot feels the load factor (ratio between lift and aircraft weight) helps him to avoid flight conditions which might be dangerous for the aircraft structure. As another simple example, stall may happen during a steep climb maneuver; while approaching the stall condition the stick becomes looser informing the pilot of the risk to lose aircraft control. Furthermore, external disturbances like wind gusts which may be very dangerous if not appropriately and suddenly compensated in a constrained mission environment (e.g., a urban canyon), would produce an immediate effect on the stick.

Useful information like load factor, "distance" from stall and external disturbances cannot be read by the pilot on the GCS cockpit instruments; thus the Conventional Aircraft Artificial Feel (CAAF) haptic aiding scheme was designed in order to provide the pilot with a richer information with respect to the visual display only. The experiments performed try to show and assess analytically that these additional haptic information help the pilot from a performance point of view.

2.1 Forces on the Stick of a Mechanically Driven Aircraft

The force felt by a pilot on the aircraft control column of a mechanical Flight Control System (FCS) during a manoeuvre depends in a very complex manner from all the aerodynamics characteristics of the aircraft, the current state of the aircraft (speed, angle of attack etc.) and of course from stick deflection.

A simplified expression for the force felt by the pilot of a mechanically driven aircraft is [6]:

$$F_S = \eta C_h q S_e c_e G_e = (C_{h0} + C_{h,\alpha}\alpha_h + C_{h,\delta}\delta_e) \cdot q S_e c_e = K_e \cdot \delta_e + F . \qquad (1)$$

Where $K_e = C_{h,\delta} S_e c_e q$ and $F = \left(C_{h,0} + C_{h,\alpha} \cdot \alpha_h\right) \cdot S_e c_e q$.

The coefficients in (1) are: C_h is the elevator hinge moment, q is the dynamic pressure of the aircraft, S_e and c_e are the surfaces and the chord of the elevator and G_e is a gearing factor (with units) to convert moments to force and includes the geometry of the control mechanisms, pulleys, push-rods and cables. C_{h0}, $C_{h\alpha}$ and

$C_{h\delta}$ are respectively the elevator hinge moment coefficient at zero lift, the elevator hinge moment coefficient derivative with respect to tail angle of attack changes and with respect to the elevator deflection changes.

This choice is appropriate for studying the longitudinal dynamics of the aircraft (pitch and altitude motion). Thus, we designed an experiment where the pilot has to perform a simple altitude regulation task.

2.2 Implementation on a Haptic Device

In order to keep the force expression simple and easy to implement in a haptic device the force was assumed to be dependent on the two most important variables for defining the flight envelope: dynamic pressure and load factor.

The dynamic pressure is defined as $q = \frac{1}{2}\rho V^2$ where ρ is the air density and V is the airspeed. The load factor $n = \frac{L}{W}$ is defined as the ratio of the lift L to the weight W of the aircraft.

To implement the above-mentioned stimulus on a haptic device, it is necessary to express the total force F_S to be felt by the pilot as a combination of an external force component F_E and a variable stiffness spring with deflection of the stick δ_S and stiffness K.

$$F_S = K \cdot \delta_S + F_E .\tag{2}$$

In order to avoid oscillations of the haptic device a damping term was added:

$$F_S = K \cdot \delta_S + F_E + K_D \cdot \dot{\delta}_S .\tag{3}$$

Where K_D is the damping constant and $\dot{\delta}_S$ is the velocity of the stick. In order to reproduce the force n the stick felt by the pilot during maneuvers on the longitudinal plane the stiffness K was selected as:

$$K = K_f \cdot \left[K_q \cdot q + K_n \cdot (n-1) \right].\tag{4}$$

Where K_q and K_n are the weights of the dynamic pressure and the differences between the manoeuvre and the one of horizontal flight $(n-1)$ respectively and K_f is a constant gain which determines the "amount" of force feedback.

The gains K_q and K_n was tuned heuristically and the external force was set to zero. Note that the stiffness in (4) contains a dependence on load factor which was not present in (1); the reason for this is to make the pilot aware of the aircraft load factor changes. The final expression of the haptic feedback force becomes then:

$$F_S = K_f \cdot \delta_S \cdot \left[K_q \cdot q + K_n \cdot (n-1) \right] + K_D \cdot \dot{\delta}_S .\tag{5}$$

This expression of the haptic feedback (5) was named Conventional (for mechanically-driven) Aircraft Artificial Feel (CAAF) by its aerodynamically inspired nature. This type of force feedback, in analogy to what found in the artificial feel literature [2], [6] could be addressed as a QN-feel system since the force it generates is proportional to both dynamic pressure (Q) and load factor (N).

3   Methods

In order to test the CAAF (5) concept, a simulated flight experiment was set-up. A fully non linear aircraft simulator was used to provide a realistic aircraft response. An aircraft simulator was implemented using a Matlab/Simulink simulation. The selected aircraft model was a De Havilland Canada DHC-2 Beaver implemented using the Flight Dynamics and Control Toolbox [7]. We prepared a simple control task: the aircraft is flying level in trimmed condition and at constant altitude (*300 m* altitude); a disturbance (a -5° elevator impulse lasting 0.5 seconds) is artificially injected at time t=9.5 seconds (the injection time is the same for all the subjects), and the aircraft initiates a motion according to its Phugoid mode. The Phugoid mode is one of the basic longitudinal flight dynamic modes experienced during the transient phase of an aircraft. It is characterized by complex and conjugate poles that produce a lightly damped oscillation in the aircraft longitudinal variables (velocity, pitch angle, altitude, etc). During these oscillation modes, the dynamic pressure changes because of a change in of the velocity and the load factor changes because of a change in the lift.

The pilot's task is to keep the aircraft leveled, not oscillating, to restore the initial altitude and to keep it as constant as possible. During this task, the pitch and altitude oscillations of the Phugoid mode have to be damped by the pilot using the stick. Figure 1 shows, as an example, the time history of the aircraft altitude in two cases: free aircraft oscillating according to the Phugoid mode and aircraft controlled by the pilot.

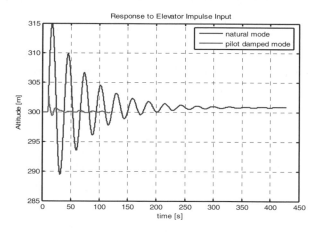

Fig. 1. Aircraft Longitudinal Modes

3.1   The Experimental Test Bed

An experimental test bed was setup in order to test the performance of a set of naïve subjects during the altitude regulation task described above. Figure 2 shows the experimental test bed comprising of a video display and a haptic device.

Fig. 2. The experimental test bed

The visual screen displayed during the experiment was a reproduction of a real one; it was designed to be as similar as possible to conventional aircraft head-down display. The display, in white on a black background, shows the relevant variables in the task (pitch, altitude, speed) and the variable to be regulated (altitude) with a red reference mark for the set points: 300 meters for altitude and trim condition (about 5°) for the pitch.

The selected haptic device is the widely used Omega.3 Device; it was used to simulate the control column of a mechanical driven aircraft (Figure 2). The Omega.3 Device with 3DOF was chosen in order to simulate the forward-backward motion of the control bar since only one degree of freedom was needed. The maximum force of 12 N which the Omega.3 Device can generate was considered appropriate for the experiment.

3.2 The Experiment

The goal of these tests is to proof whether adding the CAAF kinesthetic (force) cue to the visual cue (a simulated cockpit) improves the control. In particular we wanted to assess in an analytical way the differences in pilot performance in the two cases: with and without CAAF; thus the performance of the subjects (dependent variable) was measured through the IAE (Integral Absolute Error) between the current and desired altitude; a smaller IAE would indicate a better pilot performance in damping the Phugoid mode.

18 subjects (aged 23 to 43, mean 30.7) participated to in the experiment. All had normal or corrected-to-normal vision. They were paid, naive as to the purpose of the study, and gave their informed consent. The experiments were approved by the Ethics Committee of the University Clinic of Tübingen, and conformed with the 1964 Declaration of Helsinki.

The experiment consisted of thee different force conditions: No Force on the end-effector (0) (gravity compensation and K=0, F_E=0), Simple Force (1) and Double Force (2) (twice as much force as in the Simple Force condition achieved by doubling the K_f gain). Each condition was run as a separate block, i.e., the experiment consisted of three successive blocks. The order of presentation of the blocks was counterbalanced.

In total, the experiment lasted from 60 to 90 minutes (including instructions and breaks between blocks). Figure 3 shows sample altitude trajectories taken from one of the experiments; the Simple Force case shows clearly a better performance.

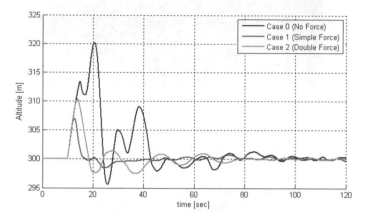

Fig. 3. Comparison of altitude trajectories

4   Results

Mean IAE values were entered in a one-way repeated measures analysis of variance (ANOVA) [No force, Simple force, Double force], which revealed a significant effect of the force factor [$F(2, 34) = 7.932$, $p<0.01$]. Figure 4 shows that the participants were the least variable (performed best) when a simple force was applied, the most variable (performed worst) when no force was applied, whereas providing a double force gave rise to 'intermediate' results.

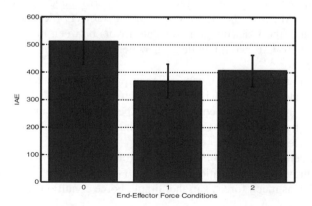

Fig. 4. Performance (mean and standard deviation) for the 3 Force conditions (0: No Force, 1: Simple Force, 2: Double Force)

Post-hoc tests using Bonferroni correction for multiple comparisons ($p<0.05$) indicated that the performance with force (both simple and double) was significantly less variable than without force. In other words, providing CAAF force significantly improved piloting performance as it reduced the variability of the control.

We also assessed the effect of the order of presentation of the blocks with a one-way repeated measures ANOVA [First Block, Second Block, Third Block], which revealed no significant main effect of the order of presentation. In other words, the variability of the performance was comparable irrespective of the order of presentation.

5 Conclusion

The aim of this experiment was to test whether providing Indirect Haptic Aiding could constitute a valuable help for pilots. Participants were provided with haptic cues via a newly developed Conventional Aircraft Artificial Feel. We measured how this type of cueing affected the piloting performance in the Phugoid mode damping task with a simulated aircraft. Our results clearly show that the CAAF facilitates control in this task. Indeed, participants' performance significantly improved when haptic cueing was available. As none of the participants had any experience with piloting, our results suggest that this type of aiding is rather 'natural', as beneficial effects can be observed without any previous learning. In line with these convincing initial results, we are currently investigating the amount of additional information transferred to the operator via the CAAF variable stiffness haptic feedback as compared with other types of haptic aidings (e.g., constant stiffness).

References

1. Tischler, B. (ed.): Advances in Aircraft Flight Control—Mark. Taylor & Francis, London (1996)
2. Gibson, J.C., Hess, R.A.: Stick and Feel System Design. Advisory Group for Aerospace Research & Development. AGARDograph 332. Canada Communication Group, Hull, Canada (1997)
3. Lippay, A.L., Kruk, R., King, M., Murray, M.: Flight Test of a Displacement Sidearm Controller. In: Annual Conference of Manual Control, June 17 (1985)
4. Lam, T.M., Boschloo, H.W., Mulder, M., van Paassen, M.M.: Artificial Force Field for Haptic Feedback in UAV Teleoperation. IEEE Transactions on Systems, Man and Cybernetics, Part A: Systems and Humans 39(6), 1316–1330 (2009)
5. Lam, T.M., Mulder, M., van Paassen, M.M., Mulder, J.A., van Der Helm, F.C.T.: Force-stiffness Feedback in UAV Tele-operation with Time Delay. In: AIAA Guidance, Navigation, and Control Conference, Chicago, Illinois (August 2009)
6. Roskam, J.: Airplane Flight Dynamics and Automatic Flight Cotrols Part I, DARcorporation Design, Analysis, Research, 120 East 9th Street, Suite 2, Lawrence, Kansas 66044, USA (2001)
7. Rauw, M.O.: FDC 1.2 - A Simulink Toolbox for Flight Dynamics and Control Analysis, Zeist, The Netherlands (1997) (2 edn. Haarlem, The Netherlands, 2001)

Haptic Adjustment of Cylinder Radius

Astrid M.L. Kappers

Utrecht University, Helmholtz Institute, Physics of Man,
Padualaan 8, 3584 CH Utrecht, The Netherlands
a.m.l.kappers@uu.nl

Abstract. Haptic curvature discrimination experiments have typically been done with relatively small stimuli (at most hand-sized) placed on a table. In daily life, however, we often handle large curved objects (think of basket balls), which we usually hold with two hands. Here, I focus on the question how well shape information from the two hands is integrated. I investigated subjects' ability to adjust the distance between two large cylindrical shells in such a way that the two shells together would perceptually form a circular cylinder. All subjects were able to perform this task in a consistent way, but adjustments were often far from veridical. As deviations were often larger than discrimination thresholds, I hypothesize that they are either due to systematic biases in curvature perception or to mis-estimations of the distance between the hands. These results contribute to our understanding of haptic shape perception.

Keywords: Shape, curvature, bimanual perception.

1 Introduction

Haptic manipulation objects is an important aspect of dealing with our environment. In this respect it is of interest to investigate how well we are able to perceive shapes. Most quantitative studies focus on curvature discrimination performance with usually finger-sized [1,2] or hand-sized [3,4,5,6] stimuli. The current study uses stimuli that simulate objects that are much larger and would typically be handled with two hands. The main research aim is to investigate how well shape information derived from the two hands can be integrated.

In a study in which hand-sized stimuli were placed next to each other, bimanual curvature discrimination performance was found to be worse than unimanual performance [4]. However, in another study in which the stimuli were placed upright as if touching a large object, bimanual thresholds were in the same range as unimanual thresholds reported in other studies [7]. In the latter study, distance between the stimuli and relative placement of set-up and subject were not of influence on the threshold, but they caused subject-dependent biases (physically the same curvatures presented right and left could be judged as different).

For hand-sized cylindrical objects, humans are very sensitive to small deviations to a circular cross-section [8]. By just grasping cylinders, aspect ratios of 1.03 could be distinguished from 1.00 (circular cross-section). It was hypothesized that subjects are apparently sensitive to small variations in curvatures, as rectangular blocks with similar aspect ratios could not be distinguished. Aspect ratio discrimination experiments are

A.M.L. Kappers et al. (Eds.): EuroHaptics 2010, Part II, LNCS 6192, pp. 426–431, 2010.

not feasible with very large objects, due to handling limitations for both subject and experimenter. Therefore, I chose a matching paradigm in the present study, using an adaptation of the set-up of [7]. The following questions were addressed: How well are subjects able to adjust the distance between two cylindrical shells so that together they form a virtual circular cylinder? Does this depend on the orientation of the virtual cylinder axis? Does this depend on the position of the subject with respect to the set-up?

2   Methods

2.1   Set-Up

The set-up consisted of a rail with two vertical plates on which cylindrical shells could be fixed, such that their curved sides faced outwards (see Fig. 1 for a schematic drawing and details about dimensions). The rail was positioned on a small table. The distance between the cylindrical shells could be adjusted by the subjects by pushing or pulling the shells towards or away from each other. Within the rail the two plates were connected by a steel thread that caused them to always move symmetrically with respect to the center of the rail. The adjusted radius could be read off with an accuracy of 1 mm. In different conditions, the subject was seated at positions C, R, or L, so that the set-up was in the center, to the right or to the left of the subject, respectively (see Fig. 1).

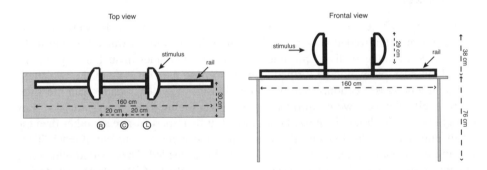

Fig. 1. Schematic drawing of the set-up. In the top view, the virtual cylinder axis is vertical; in the frontal view, the virtual cylinder axis is horizontal.

2.2   Stimuli

The stimuli consisted of a series of pairs of cylindrical shells, manufactured on a computer-controlled milling machine out of a compound of polyurethane foam and artificial resin (Cibatool BM 5460). The shells had a square bottom (29×29 cm) with a thickness of a few cm. Their curvature varied in a systematic way, such that the radii of the virtual circular cylinders that could be formed with a pair ranged from 15 to 85 cm in steps of 5 cm. The shells could be positioned in the set-up in two orthogonal ways, such that the virtual axis of the cylinder would either be horizontal (see Fig. 2 left) or vertical (see Fig. 2 right).

Fig. 2. Subject adjusting the radius. Left: horizontal orientation of the virtual cylinder axis and moderate value of the physical radius. Right: vertical orientation of the virtual cylinder axis and large physical radius. In both examples the subject is seated in the center position.

2.3 Subjects

The subjects were 6 adult students (3 females) at Utrecht University. Their age ranged from 20 to 23 years. Two females (EH and FS) were lefthanded, the others righthanded as assessed by means of a standard questionnaire [9]. All participated on a voluntary basis and they received a financial compensation for their time. They were naive with respect to the task and the research aims.

2.4 Procedure

Before subjects entered the experimental room, the set-up and shells were covered. Subjects were blindfolded and seated on a stool. They were instructed to adjust the distance between the shells by pushing the inner or outer sides in such a way that the virtual cylinder that would be formed by extrapolating the curvature of the two shells had a circular cross-section. They were not allowed to systematically scan the sides of the shells. Subjects were informed that they were allowed to "pass" a trial if they thought the shells should be moved closer to or further apart from each other than the set-up allowed, or if due to their limited arm span, the shells became out of reach. Time was unlimited, but in practice about 40 s per trial was needed. They started with a few practice trials, but they did not receive any feedback. A block of 30 trials consisted of 15 different radii in two orientations (horizontal and vertical) in random order. Per session of about an hour two such blocks could be measured. Three subjects (EH, ET and ME) participated in all conditions C, R and L, the other three only took part in condition C. The former subjects received blocks of different conditions in pseudorandom order. All blocks were presented eight times, resulting in a total number of trials of either 240 or 720 per subject (i.e. 4 or 12 hours, respectively).

3   Results

Although the number of trials for each combination of radius, orientation and condition was always 8, the actual number of settings was often less due to passes of the subject (see Procedure), especially for the higher radii. Therefore, instead of taking the average of the actual settings, the median (taking into account the passes) was taken as the

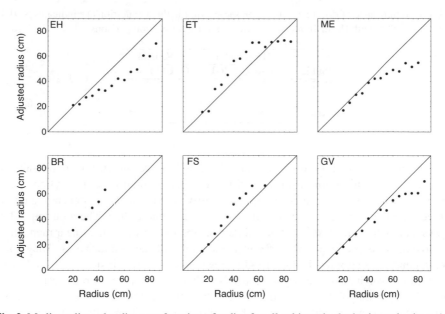

Fig. 3. Median adjusted radius as a function of radius for all subjects in the horizontal orientation in the center condition. The solid line indicates what would be veridical.

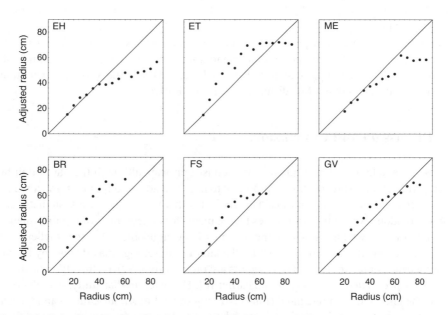

Fig. 4. Median adjusted radius as a function of radius for all subjects in the vertical orientation in the center condition. The solid line indicates what would be veridical. Note the similarity for each subject with the setttings for the horizontal orientation in Fig. 3: subjects that under(over)estimate here, also do so in the horizontal case.

Table 1. Significance of differences between settings in the three conditions (* indicates $p \leq 0.05$ and ** $p \leq 0.005$, with Holm-Bonferroni correction for multiple comparisons)

Subject	Horizontal			Vertical		
	C-R	C-L	R-L	C-R	C-L	R-L
EH	*					
ET	*	*				
ME	**	**		*	**	**

more informative quantity. In Figs. 3 and 4 the results are shown for all six subjects in the center condition, for the horizontal and vertical orientations of the cylinder axis, respectively. It can be seen that settings are mostly not veridical and, depending on the subject, are either under- or overestimations of the actual radius. The adjusted radius shows a monotonic increase with actual radius, albeit not always in a linear manner.

Most subjects preferred the horizontal orientation of the cylinder axis. They commented that especially for the larger radii, they would be sitting inside the virtual vertical cylinder, which made the task introspectively harder. However, paired t-tests (p-level 0.05) show that only for subjects ME and GV the difference between the horizontal and vertical medians was significant ($p \leq 0.005$ in both cases). The results shown in Figs. 3 and 4 are also representative for the results obtained in the R and L conditions. In the R condition, the difference between the horizontal and vertical settings was significant for all three subjects (EH and ET $p \leq 0.005$; ME $p \leq 0.05$), in the L condition only those of ET ($p \leq 0.005$).

In Table 1 the results of paired t-tests between the settings in the C, R and L conditions can be seen. For the horizontal orientation, R and L settings are significantly smaller than the C settings (except C-L for subject EH). For the vertical orientation, only the settings of subject ME differ ($R<C$; $L<C$; $R<L$).

4 Discussion and Conclusions

Subjects are able to perform this task in a consistent way, although they are often far from veridical. In this respect, it is important to note that adjusted radius shows a monotonic increase with physical radius. This indicates that the settings are systematic and not just random, which in turn implies that subjects are indeed integrating information derived from the two hands to form the concept of one large object. For the smaller radii, most settings are almost veridical, but for the larger radii settings may deviate by factors ranging from about 0.6 to 1.5. These factors are rather different from the high sensitivity to small aspect ratio differences found earlier [8]. However, in that study, stimuli could almost be enclosed with one hand (thus involving much higher curvatures) and, probably just as important, a discrimination paradigm may be more sensitive than a matching paradigm. The present deviations cannot be caused by curvature discrimination limitations, as discrimination thresholds are often smaller [7]. Likely explanations are that the deviations are either caused by misestimations of the distance between the two hands, systematic biases in curvature perception and for the higher radii, limited arm span.

The results obtained for the two orientations and the three different positions of the subject with respect to the set-up show subject-dependent differences. These differences are comparable to the biases found in [7], in which these were attributed to possible differences in scanning length of the right and left hands. Future studies would need measurements of hand movements to shed light on the influence of these movements on perception.

Acknowledgments. This work was partially supported by the EU project no. 248587, "THE Hand Embodied". The author thanks Jan Koenderink for discussions about the experimental design.

References

1. Goodwin, A.W., John, K.T., Marceglia, A.H.: Tactile discrimination of curvature by humans using only cutaneous information from the fingerpads. Exp. Brain Res. 86, 663–672 (1991)
2. Gordon, I.A., Morison, V.: The haptic perception of curvature. Percept. Psychophys. 31, 446–450 (1982)
3. Davidson, P.W.: Haptic judgments of curvature by blind and sighted humans. J. Exp. Psychol. 93, 43–55 (1972)
4. Kappers, A.M.L., Koenderink, J.J.: Haptic unimanual and bimanual discrimination of curvature. Perception 25, 739–749 (1996)
5. Louw, S., Kappers, A.M.L., Koenderink, J.J.: Haptic detection thresholds of Gaussian profiles over the whole range of spatial scales. Exp. Brain Res. 132, 369–374 (2000)
6. Pont, S.C., Kappers, A.M.L., Koenderink, J.J.: Similar mechanisms underlie curvature comparison by static and by dynamic touch. Percept. Psychophys. 61, 874–894 (1999)
7. Sanders, A.F.J., Kappers, A.M.L.: Bimanual curvature discrimination of hand-sized surfaces placed at different positions. Percept. Psychophys. 68, 1094–1106 (2006)
8. Van der Horst, B.J., Kappers, A.M.L.: Using curvature information in haptic shape perception of 3D objects. Exp. Brain. Res. 190, 361–367 (2008)
9. Coren, S.: The left-hander syndrome. Vintage Books, New York (1993)

The Effects of 3D Collocated Presentation of Visuo-haptic Information on Performance in a Complex Realistic Visuo-motor Task

Dror David Lev, Roman Rozengurt, Tami Gelfeld, Alex Tarkhnishvili,
and Miriam Reiner

Technion-Israel Institute of Technology
{dlev,tgelfeld,mreiner}@technion.ac.il,
{rrozengurt,early33}@gmail.com

Abstract. Ten operators had to complete a complex visuo-motor task in two extreme presentation conditions, 2D dislocated display and 3D collocated display. Using 3D collocated display operators had better total time performance as well as improved error time performance. In all conditions learning occurred. Error-time improvement following training in the 3D collocated condition carried over to a following 2D dislocated condition but there was no carry over following a block of 2D dislocated display.

Keywords: Haptics; sensory-motor integration; eye-hand coordination.

1 Introduction

Current tele-operation interfaces, like laparoscopic displays, provide a two-dimensional (2D) visual display of the remote operation field, displaced from the haptic manipulators. This is different from direct operation systems where the eyes are focused on the hands and 3D visual and haptic information overlap in space. Still, operators adapt to these differences and are able to complete their tasks in the unnatural environments despite the perceptual and inter-sensory discrepancies. A standing question is how performance adapted to artificial environments fares with performance in more realistic environments in the completion of visuo-motor tasks.

Previous studies ([1][2][3][4][5]) have attempted to evaluate such adaptations using methods similar to early perceptual adaptation experiments [6][7] and simple manipulation tasks (e.g., reaching in straight line). Results show that performance with the more realistic 3D vision is better than performance adapted to 2D vision [3] and that collocated display can introduce significant performance benefits over performance adapted to dislocated displays [4], but not in any case [5].

Researchers that inquire into the processes of hand pointing/reaching, introduce visuo-haptics dislocation in order to disentangle vision and proprioception [8][9][10][11]. In these studies visual and proprioceptive feedback are artificially made unaligned to enable quantification of the independent contribution of vision and proprioception to the control of manual motor actions. The findings of the artificial misalignment studies indicate that "the brain chooses sensory inputs so as to minimize

A.M.L. Kappers et al. (Eds.): EuroHaptics 2010, Part II, LNCS 6192, pp. 432–437, 2010.
© Springer-Verlag Berlin Heidelberg 2010

errors arising from the transformation of sensory signals between coordinate frames" [10] (in the abstract). This suggests coordinate transformation minimization as a unifying principle in brain processing, with the purpose of minimizing related errors [10]. Applying the same logic to 2D (vision) - 3D (haptics) transformations predicts less errors in brain processing if the coordination frames of vision and haptics match (e.g. both 3D). In the same vein, matching the representation in space (co-location) should induce less errors than displacing visuo-haptic information. The problem of coordinate transformation in the current study is aggravated by the high complexity of the visuo-motor task.

All the tasks in the studies discussed above are simple reaching tasks (save the rotation tasks in [8]). This is adequate when the aim is to investigate the underlying processes of manual control, but is insufficient when alternative displays of working environments are being considered [12]. Simple tasks, similar to computer-mouse manipulation, are indeed pervasive but are fundamentally different from complex tasks like unmanned aerial vehicles control or minimal-invasive-surgery. In such complex tasks and environments the effect of different display alternatives is of major concern.

The task of laparoscopic surgery is a good candidate for the study of alternative displays in complex visuo-motor tasks due to the vast amount of ergonomic studies taken in this field, many of which employed virtual reality techniques [13][14][15][16][17]. Furthermore, these studies were explicitly occupied with the effect of visual display dimensionality (2D vs. 3D) and visual display location on the operator (surgeon) performance [14][15][16] or task difficulty [13][17]. In one survey, expert surgeons indicated depth perception as an important technological challenge for laparoscopy system improvement, although opinion is not conclusive regarding 3D display [17]. In a recent literature review it was reported that for the inexperienced surgeon "loss of three-dimensional visual depth cues forms a major obstacle for the effective use of instruments, creating fundamental psychomotor problems of hand-eye coordination" ([14], p. 210). On the other hand, empirical test of the benefit of 3D visualization showed significant decrease in performance, apparently due to technological insufficiency [15]. Zheng and colleagues [16], who conducted an experimental study of co-location presentation manipulation, conclude that collocated display could improve surgeon performance, relative to performance with dislocated presentation. Thus, the results and recommendations vary, depending on the specific study of laparoscopic surgery ergonomics, and its particular methodology.

To pertain to real-world tele-operation tasks in complex environments a novel task has been developed. The new task replicates a laparoscopic surgery with a complex model of a tube that resembles a gut embedded in a picture that mimics the internal of the abdomen (see Fig. 1). The environment includes a 3D haptic device and two types of visual feedback. The 3D visual display is provided co-located with the haptic device (Col-3D) and the 2D visual display was positioned in-front of the operator, resulting in a dislocated visuo-motor presentation (Dis-2D).

If, indeed, Col-3D is beneficial to complex visuo-motor manipulations then it is expected to induce reduced performance time and/or reduced erroneous performance time, compared with Dis-2D. Additionally, it is expected that, after practicing with Col-3D, shifting to Dis-2D will deteriorate performance time and/or erroneous performance time. In the same vein, shifting to Col-3D after practicing with Dis-2D is expected to show improvement in performance time and/or in erroneous performance time.

2 Method

***Participants*:** Eight women and two men aged in the range between 25 years old and 45 years old participated in the experiment. They were lab members or people acquainted with lab members, who were paid for participation.

***Input/Output (I/O) system*:** In all conditions 3D haptics was captured and rendered by a Phantom Omni ("SensAble") force-feedback device. The gut was haptically rendered using the lab's proprietary application-programming-interface (API) which is based on OpenHapticsAE 3.0. Dislocated 2D vision was provided by a 19" liquid-crystal-display (LCD), wall mounted 2m above the floor and 2.4m away from the manual effector. Collocated 3D vision was provided by a 17" cathode-ray-tube (CRT) projecting on a mirror covering the Phantom and the operator's hands. Participants used shutter glasses for looking at the mirror to get a 3D visual image virtually placed where their hands are. The visual display was rendered using the lab's proprietary API, based on OpenGL 2.1. The 2D image of the 3D model target was provided by this API.

***The target*:** The 3D gut is a trivial Torus Knot with parameters q=1.5 and p=1.0 (see Fig. 1). It creates a complex tube with three 3D twists.

2.1 Procedure

The participant sat in front of the system and was given a demonstration task of 3-5 minutes in order to familiarize themselves with the system. The experimental phase started with an explanation of the task and continued with two blocks of 31 trials each. Half of the participants (n=5) worked with a 3D visual display collocated with haptics in the first block and with a 2D dislocated visual display in the second block of trials. The other five participants were presented with the opposite order of blocks.

***The task*:** Participants were presented with a visual display of a complex tube (see Set Up section and Fig. 1) and were told it represents a gut. They were asked to move a small ball, a virtual cutting tool, through the virtual gut and use it to dissect a lump in the other end of the gut. The participant was asked to do it as quickly as possible, but without touching the gut's wall, to avoid the risk of hurting it with the cutting tool.

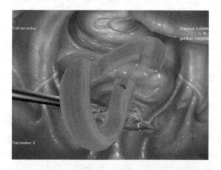

Fig. 1. A (2D) screen-shot showing the virtual gut embedded in a virtual abdomen. Overlaid text provides additional feedback to the participant: amount of trials elapsed, time from the beginning of the trial and the accumulated time of touching the gut's wall.

Measures: Two performance measures were analyzed, the Total-time to complete the task (move the cutting tool from the beginning of the gut to its end, where the lump was) and the Error-time, the aggregate of time periods the cutting tool touched the gut wall during task completion.

3 Results

Fig. 2 presents the learning curves for both measures of performance, in the left panel the Total-time measure, and in the right panel the Error-time measure. The learning curves are the power-functions fitted to the data of all the participants in each condition. In all the conditions curves of improvement are evident.

The statistical evaluation considered the average performance in each condition, using a two-way mixed ANOVA. For both dependent measures (Total-time and Error-time), display condition (within participants) and presentation order (between participants) were used as the independent factors.

Looking at the relations between the learning curves one first notices that the circles (Col-3D) are always below the squares (Dis-2D) which is a manifestation of the predicted advantage in performance of the Col-3D condition over the Dis-2D. Indeed, the average time it took to complete the task under Col-3D (17.5 sec, $SD=8$) was significantly (p=0.001) shorter than the average time that was needed to complete the task under Dis-2D (30.9 sec, $SD=19$). Similarly, the average Error-time was significantly (p=0.0001) shorter in the Col-3D (0.85 sec, $SD=1.1$) than in the Dis-2D (5.35 sec, $SD=5.31$).

Considering the order of blocks, in the learning curves of the Total-time measure the white (first block) and black (second block) lines lie practically one above the other and the statistical analysis reflects that. Performance time in the first block (24.4 sec, $SD=15.4$) did not differ significantly (p=0.70) from the performance time in the second block (24 sec, $SD=17$). Neither was the interaction significant (p=0.91). But in the learning curves of the Error-time measure the white (first block) and black (second block) overlap for the Col-3D display, but it seems that in the second block

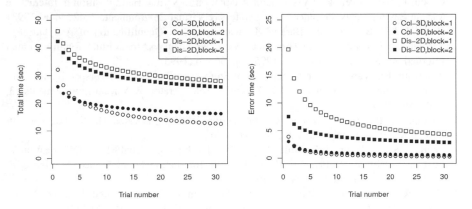

Fig. 2. Learning curves for the Total time measure (left panel) and Error time measure (right panel) over all participants in the different presentation conditions and experiment blocks.

(black) performance is improved. This is supported by the statistical analysis. In the first block average Error-time was larger (3.8 sec, *SD=5.6*) than the average Error-time in the second block (2.4 sec, *SD=2.6*), this difference is found to be significant (p=0.04) and the interaction is also found to be significant (p=0.06).

4 Discussion

As hypothesized, collocated display with 3D vision (Col-3D) facilitated performance more than dislocated feedback with 2D vision (Dis-2D). Furthermore, in all conditions learning occurred, for both measures of performance. For the Total-time measure there was no carryover of learning from one condition to the other. For the Error-time measure, an initial training under the Dis-2D condition had no effect on further performance under the Col-3D condition. On the other hand, an initial training with Col-3D display improved the starting point of training with Dis-2D, but this initial gain dissipates by the end of the training block.

Col-3D stimuli are different from Dis-2D stimuli in two aspects, visual dimensionality and the degree of visuo-motor overlap in space (collocated or dislocated). Reduced visual dimensionality and inter-sensory dislocation introduce complementary discrepancies between visual and haptic coordinate frames. Previous studies of visuo-motor integration concluded that transformation of sensory signals between coordinate frames impedes performance [10]. The current study replicates these findings and suggests that generalization of training can suffer as well.

Acknowledgement

This work is supported by EC fund Immersence 027141.

References

1. Groen, J., Werkhoven, P.J.: Visuomotor Adaptation to Virtual Hand Position in Interactive Virtual Environments. Presence: Teleoperators & Virtual Environments 7, 429–446 (1998)
2. Rolland, J.P., Biocca, F.A., Barlow, T., Kancherla, A.: Quantification of Adaptation to Virtual-Eye Location in See-Thru Head-Mounted Displays. In: Virtual Reality Annual International Symposium (VRAIS 1995), pp. 56–66 (1995)
3. Arsenault, R., Ware, C.: The Importance of Stereo and Eye-Coupled Perspective for Eye-Hand Coordination in Fish Tank VR. Presence: Teleoperators & Virtual Environments 13, 549–559 (2004)
4. Swapp, D., Pawar, V., Loscos, C.: Interaction With Co-Located Haptic Feedback in Virtual Reality. Virtual Reality 10, 24–30 (2006)
5. Teather, R.J., Allison, R.S., Stuerzlinger, W.: Evaluating Visual/Motor Co-Location in Fish-Tank Virtual Reality. In: IEEE Toronto International Conference - Science & Technology For Humanity 2009 (2009)
6. Held, R., Efstathiou, A., Greene, M.: Adaptation to Displaced and Delayed Visual Feedback from the Hand. Journal of Experimental Psychology 72, 887–891 (1966)

7. Kornheiser, A.S.: Adaptation to Laterally Displaced Vision: a Review. Psychological Bulletin 83, 783–816 (1976)
8. Ware, C., Arsenault, R.: Frames of Reference in Virtual Object Rotation. In: Proceedings of the 1st Symposium on Applied Perception in Graphics and Visualization, pp. 135–141. ACM, Los Angeles (2004)
9. Saunders, J.A., Knill, D.C.: Visual Feedback Control of Hand Movements. J. Neurosci. 24, 3223–3234 (2004)
10. Sober, S.J., Sabes, P.N.: Flexible Strategies for Sensory Integration During Motor Planning. Nature Neuroscience 8, 490–497 (2005)
11. Sober, S.J., Sabes, P.N.: Multisensory Integration During Motor Planning. J. Neurosci. 23, 6982–6992 (2003)
12. Ben-Porat, O., Shoham, M., Meyer, J.: Control Design and Task Performance in Endoscopic Teleoperation. Presence: Teleoperators & Virtual Environments 9, 256–267 (2000)
13. Berguer, R., Forkey, D.L., Smith, W.D.: Ergonomic Problems Associated With Laparoscopic Surgery. Surgical Endoscopy 13, 466–468 (1999)
14. Silvennoinen, M., Mecklin, J.P., Saariluoma, P., Antikainen, T.: Expertise and Skill in Minimally Invasive Surgery. Scandinavian Journal of Surgery 98, 209–213 (2009)
15. Wentink, M., Jakimowicz, J.J., Vos, L.M., Meijer, D.W., Wieringa, P.A.: Quantitative Evaluation of Three Advanced Laparoscopic Viewing Technologies: a Stereo Endoscope, an Image Projection Display, and a TFT Display. Surgical Endoscopy 16, 1237–1241 (2002)
16. Zheng, B., Janmohamed, Z., MacKenzie, C.L.: Reaction Times and the Decision-Making Process In Endoscopic Surgery. Surgical Endoscopy 17, 1475–1480 (2003)
17. den Boer, K., de Jong, T., Dankelman, J., Gouma, D.: Problems With Laparoscopic Instruments: Opinions Of Experts. Journal of Laparoendoscopic & Advanced Surgical Techniques 11, 149–155 (2001)

Visuo-haptic Length Judgments in Children and Adults

Knut Drewing and Bianca Jovanovic

Institute for Psychology, Giessen University, Otto-Behaghel-Str. 10F,
35394 Giessen, Germany
{Knut.Drewing,Bianca.Jovanovic}@psychol.uni-giessen.de

Abstract. If participants simultaneously feel an object and see it through an anamorphic lens, adults judge object size to be in-between seen and felt size [1]. Young children's judgments were, however, dominated by vision [2]. We investigated whether this age difference depends on the magnitude of the intersensory discrepancy. 6-year old children and adults judged the length of objects that were presented to vision, haptics or both senses. Lenses reduced or magnified seen length. With large intersensory discrepancies, children's visuo-haptic judgments were dominated by vision (~90% visual weight), whereas adults weighted vision just by ~40%. With smaller discrepancies, the children's visual weight (~50%) approximated that of the adults (~35%)–and a model of multisensory integration predicted discrimination performance in both age groups. We conclude that children focus on a single sense, when information in different senses is in conflict, but can combine seemingly corresponding multisensory information in similar ways as adults do.

Keywords: Visuo-haptic integration, Size perception, Development.

1   Introduction

Perception is based on multiple sources of sensory information—we simultaneously and continuously obtain sensory inputs from our eyes, ears, and the skin. Some of the inputs provide information about the same physical property. We can, for instances, both see and feel the size of an object. Several studies have shown that adults integrate such redundant visuo-haptic information according to a weighting scheme. In contrast, young children seem to be dominated by information from one of the senses [2, 3]. It has been suggested that such dominance reflects a lack of multisensory integration processes per se in the children's developing perceptual system [3]. Alternatively, children might have failed to relate the inputs from the different senses to each other. In the extant developmental studies, stimuli were presented in ways that might have interfered with the assumption that the multisensory information belongs to the same object.

Misceo and colleagues [1, 2] used an anamorphic lens to induce intersensory discrepancy between the seen and the felt size of an object. In this paradigm participants view objects through the lens while manually grasping them through a hand-concealing cloth. Then, they select a match from a set of comparison objects. When adults do this task, the size of the match is in-between the seen and the felt object size (~30 – 70% visual weight = shift from felt towards seen length). 6-year old children,

A.M.L. Kappers et al. (Eds.): EuroHaptics 2010, LNCS 6192, Part II, pp. 438–444, 2010.

however, exhibited nearly complete visual dominance (~80% visual weight). However, in these studies a quite strong lens was used that halved seen object size. Stimuli with such large discrepancies might not be representative for natural multisensory processes, because large discrepancies provide a cue suggesting that information from the different senses does not belong together.

Another recent developmental study [3] induced just very small intersensory discrepancies between vision and touch. Again, about 6-year old children (but not adults) displayed almost unimodal dominance: Haptic dominance in a size discrimination task (~20% visual weight, Age Group 5) and visual dominance in an orientation discrimination task (~90% visual weight, Age Group 6). However, in this study, participants examined a pair of objects attached to the front and rear surfaces of a panel so as to simulate a single object protruding through a hole; the participants felt the one in back while viewing the one in front. With this method it is not apparent to the participant that haptic and visual inputs stem from the same object [4].That is, also the setup in this study provided cues that might have hindered the young children to relate the visual and the haptic inputs to each other.

We tested our objection to the previous studies. We studied visuo-haptic length judgments using the lens technique, because with this technique the common origin of haptic and visual input is immediately apparent. The lenses induced either large (Exp. 1) or small (Exp. 2) visuo-haptic discrepancies. We expect that with small intersensory discrepancies children can use inputs from both senses–as adults do.

2 Experimental Methods

In a two-interval forced choice task 6-year old children and adults compared the length of different standard stimuli (of 20-30 mm length) to a set of comparison stimuli. Standard stimuli were presented either to haptics (precision grip), to vision or to both senses; comparison stimuli were always only felt. In visuo-haptic conditions we used cylindrical reducing and magnifying lenses in order to dissociate seen from felt length (factor 1.5 in Exp. 1; factor 1.25 in Exp. 2, width was not affected). Using the method of constant stimuli, we assessed length judgments by the points of subjectively equal length (PSE). In addition, we measured 84%-discrimination thresholds (just noticeable difference, JND).

Participants. Adult participants were mainly sampled from Giessen University, children from different kindergartens in the regions of Hagen (Exp. 1) and Giessen (Exp. 2). We collected data from 40 adults and 45 children. However, we removed the data from 15 participants, who did not finish the experiment or had outlier values (+/- 3 σ). The final sample of Exp. 1 included 24 children (mean age 6;1 [years; months]; age range 5;0-6;11; 50% female; 66% right-handed) and 21 adults (mean age 33 years; range: 18-51; 52% female; 86% right-handed). The final sample of Exp. 2 included 11 children (mean age 5;6; range 5;1-5;11; 36 % female; 73 % right-handed) and 13 adults (mean age: 25 y.; range: 20-34; 62% female; all right-handed).

Apparatus and Stimuli. The entire apparatus was mobile and the experiments were conducted in a quiet room in the respective kindergartens, the university or elsewhere. Participants sat–vis-à-vis to the experimenter–in front of a table. On top of the table were side-by-side two "presentation boxes". The experimenter placed one stimulus at the bottom of each box. Participants could look at the stimulus through diving goggles and an exchangeable lens; a blind in the box occluded left-eye views. Simultaneously, participants could feel the stimulus through soft cloth at the sides of the box. Stimuli were rectangular plastic plates that were covered with a red-colored smooth film (1 mm high, 20 mm wide, length 14-36 mm). A custom-made computer program pre-scribed the presentation order and collected the participants' responses.

Design and Procedure. The design comprised the between-participant variable Age Group (Children vs. Adults) and the within-participant variables Modality (Haptics, Vision, Haptics + Vision) and Stimulus Set. The standard stimuli used in the different Modality conditions based on two different physical stimuli; a shorter one that was visually presented via a magnifying lens (Set: short-magnified) and a longer standard that was combined with a reducing lens (Set: long-reduced). In Exp. 1 the physical stimuli were 20 mm and 30 mm long. Thus, haptic standards were 20 and 30 mm long. For visual presentation the 20 mm-stimulus was magnified and the 30 mm-stimulus reduced by a factor of ~1.5 (seen length ~30 and ~20 mm). In Exp. 2 physi-cal stimuli were 20 mm and 25 mm long and optically magnified or reduced by a factor of 1.25 (seen length ~25mm and ~20mm). Participants compared the length of each standard stimulus several times to different comparison stimuli (details in Tab. 1). The experiment was divided into three parts. Each part involved three blocks of trials, one block for each Modality condition. The order of Modality blocks was bal-anced across participants. Each block contained each standard/comparison pair once. The order of presentations in each block was randomized, preventing adaptation in visuo-haptic conditions. The experiment was conducted in 2-3 sessions of less than 30 minutes duration each.

Table 1. Size of comparison stimuli for each standard in both experiments

Condition	Standard stimulus	Comparison stimuli	Number of comparison stimuli
Experiment 1			
Haptics or Vision alone	~20 mm	14-26 mm	7, steps of 2 mm
	~30 mm	24-36 mm	7, steps of 2 mm
Haptics & Vision	20 & ~30 mm	16-32 mm	9, steps of 2 mm
	30 & ~20 mm	18-34 mm	9, steps of 2 mm
Experiment 2			
Haptics or Vision alone	~20 mm	16.25-23.75 mm	7, steps of 1.25 mm
	~25 mm	21.25-28.75 mm	7, steps of 1.25 mm
Haptics & Vision	20 & ~25 mm	17.5-27.5 mm	9, steps of 1.25 mm
	25 & ~20 mm	17.5-27.5 mm	9, steps of 1.25 mm

In each trial participants first explored the standard stimulus. In haptic conditions participants felt the standard for about 1-2 sec. They were instructed to grasp with the thumb and the index finger of their dominant hand. In visual conditions participants looked at the standard for about 2 sec. In visuo-haptic conditions participants grasped the standards while looking at it, keeping visual and haptic presentation times approximately equal to the unimodal conditions. Afterwards participants felt the com-parison stimulus in the other presentation box and, then, told the experimenter which of the two stimuli they had perceived as being longer. The experimenter guided the participant through the procedure and entered the participant's response in a computer program. Between trials the experimenter changed the stimuli and lenses in the presentation boxes as indicated by the computer program.

Data analysis. We determined individual psychometric functions for each standard and each Modality condition. That is, we plotted the proportion of trials in which the standard was perceived as being longer than the comparison against the length of the comparison. The PSE is defined as the amplitude of the comparison stimulus at which either stimulus is equally likely to be chosen. The JND is defined as the difference between the PSE and the amplitude of the comparison when it is judged longer than the standard 84% of the time. We fitted cumulative Gaussians to the psychometric functions using the psignifit toolbox for Matlab which implements maximum-likelihood estimation methods [5]. The parameter μ of the Gaussian estimates the PSE, and, σ estimates the JND.

3   Results

We will consider the results from the two experiments in a common section.

PSEs (Fig. 1 &2): As should be the case, PSEs from the haptic conditions were, on average, close to the actual values of the physical stimuli and did in neither experiment differ between age groups (ps>.15; ANOVAs of haptic PSEs with variables Age Group, Stimulus Set). Also, PSEs from the visual conditions by and large matched the values that we had expected from the optical magnification and reduction of the physical stimuli.

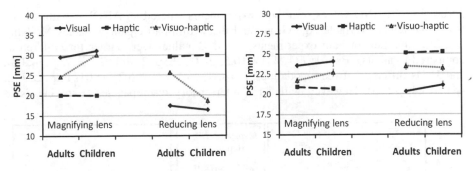

Fig. 1. PSEs in Exp. 1 (*left*) and Exp. 2 (*right*) as a function of Age Group, Modality and Stimulus Set. Error bars (partly covered by data points) indicate standard errors.

The PSEs from the visuo-haptic conditions were in-between the PSEs from corresponding visual and haptic conditions, indicating some combination of the discrepant visual and the haptic information. We analyzed the visuo-haptic PSEs by determining the weight w of the visual relative to the haptic information, as follows (unimodal PSEs were estimated by the group means),

$$w_{Vision} = (PSE_{Visuo\text{-}Haptic} - PSE_{HapticGroup}) / (PSE_{VisionGroup} - PSE_{HapticGroup}) . \qquad (1)$$

In Exp. 1 visual weights (Fig. 2) slightly differed between the Stimulus Sets ($F(1, 43)$) = 9.2, $p<.001$, ANOVA with variables Age Group, Stimulus Sets). More importantly, visual weights were significantly larger for the children as compared to the adults ($F(1, 43) = 73.4$, $p<.001$). In Exp. 2, only the effect of Age Group was significant, $F(1, 22) = 5.7$, $p<.05$. Again, the visual weight was higher for children than for adults. A direct comparison of the two experiments revealed that the age effect on visual weight is significantly more pronounced with large as compared to small intersensory discrepancies (interaction Age Group X Experiment, $F(1, 65) = 6.4$, $p<.02$, ANOVA with variables Age Group, Experiment; individual weights in the analysis are averages over Stimulus Sets). This interaction can be led back to differences between the children groups, $F(1,33)=22.1$, $p<.01$, whereas the adult's weights did not significantly differ between experiments ($p>.2$).

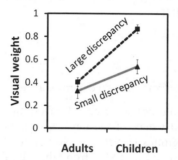

Fig. 2. Visual weights as a function of Age Group and Discrepancy (averaged over Stimulus Sets)

JNDs (Fig. 3): JND values from both experiments entered an ANOVA with the between-participant variable Age Group and the within-participant variables Modality and Stimulus Set. In both experiments, the JND values were larger for children as compared to adults, (Exp. 1: $F(1, 43) = 10.5$, $p<.01$, Exp. 2: $F(1, 22) = 12.5$, $p<.01$), and JNDs differed between modalities, (Exp. 1: $F(2, 86) = 6.2$, $p<.01$, Exp. 2: $F(2, 44) = 3.4$, $p<.05$). However, with large intersensory discrepancies (Exp. 1), visual

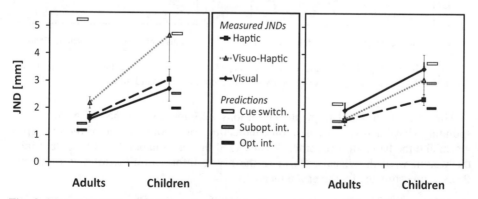

Fig. 3. Measured JNDs and different predictions for multisensory from unisensory JNDs in Exp. 1 (*left*) and 2 (*right*) as a function of Age Group, Modality

and haptic JNDs did not significantly differ, but visuo-haptic JNDs were significantly larger than both unimodal JNDs. In contrast, with small intersensory discrepancies, visual-haptic JNDs did not reliably differ from the unimodal JNDs, only visual JNDs were larger than haptic ones (post-hoc t-test, Bonferroni-adjusted, $\alpha=.05$).

4 Discussion and Conclusion

In the present study, we investigated how adults and 6-year old children combine seen and felt object length. We studied visuo-haptic judgments in two experiments introducing a large or a small discrepancy between seen and felt length. In adults, the contribution of vision to the judgment was moderate (30-40%) and did not reliably depend on the magnitude of the intersensory discrepancy. In contrast, the children's judgments were dominated by seen length (~90% visual weight) for large discrepancies, but approximated the adult's results for small discrepancies (~50%). We, hence, conclude that children–in contrast to adults–concentrate on a single sense, here vision, when information in two senses is in large conflict, but can use inputs from different senses when these seemingly correspond to each other.

But how was the input from the different senses used? Did participants integrate the inputs from the two senses in each trial according to a fixed weighting scheme, as usually reported for adults [6]? Our JND measures are informative on this question, because they assess uni- and multisensory judgment variance. With trial-by-trial integration multisensory variance can range from a minimum below the unisensory variances (=optimal integration; multisensory benefit) up to the variance of the "worst" sense (if that sense's weight is set to one). In contrast, when participants switch between the senses from trial to trial and never integrate (=probabilistic cue switching), multisensory variance can range from a minimum of the variance of the "best" sense (if that sense is always used) up to a variance that exceeds the unisensory variances (as the intersensory discrepancys adds variance to the judgment). We found that with large intersensory discrepancies visuo-haptic judgments were more variable (larger JNDs) than the "worst" unisensory judgments. Thus, a fixed integration scheme cannot explain these data. In contrast, with small intersensory discrepancies multisensory judgments did not reliably differ from unisensory judgments, which is consistent with both a fixed trial-by-trial integration and cue switching.

Hence, we attempted to quantitatively predict the multisensory JNDs from the unisensory JNDs. We used a) a model of optimal integration with optimal weights [6], b) an integration model using the (possibly suboptimal) weights that we had measured and c) a probabilistic cue switching model (probabilities for using each sense were equated with measured weights). Details of the model calculations are described in [6, 7][1]. Figure 3 shows the results. As expected, with large intersensory discrepancies visuo-haptic JNDs were, on average, higher than predicted from both models of integra-

---

[1] We slightly adapted the procedures: Because comparison stimuli were only felt, the present JNDs assess the standard's variance (visual, haptic, or visual-haptic) plus a haptic variance for the comparison. We estimated the standard's variance under the assumptions that variances of comparison and standard are uncorrelated and that the comparison's variance equals that of the haptic standard. Predictions were based on individually averaged values (collapsed over Stimulus Sets). Weight estimates were confined to be between 0 and 1.

tion, independent of the age group (ANOVA with variables Value [Predicted vs. Measured] and Age Group; Value: ps <.01, Value X Age Group: ps >.05). The childrens' average multisensory performance was well predicted by probabilistic switching between the senses, whereas adults performed better than predicted by the switching model (ps<.05 for Value, Value X Age Group, post-hoc t-tests: t<1 for children, p<.01 for adults). The adults' "intermediate" performance might hint at some mixture between switching and integration behavior or at fluctuations in an integration scheme. Overall, we conclude that large discrepancies hindered a proper integration in both adults and children.

In contrast, with small intersensory discrepancies multisensory JNDs were well predicted by the integration model that used the measured weights. This model's predictions did not reliably differ from the measured values, independent of the age group (F's<1 for effect of Value, Value X Age Group). Optimal integration predicted lower JNDs than we observed, whereas switching between the senses predicted higher JNDs (Value: ps<.05, Value X Age Group, ps>.1). Thus, for small intersensory discrepancies the data reject models of cue switching and optimal integration. They rather suggest that both adults and children integrated visual and haptic information according to a fixed, but suboptimal weighting scheme. We conclude that already 6-year old children can integrate multisensory information in similar ways as adults do, if the inputs clearly relate to each other.

References

1. Hershberger, W.A., Misceo, G.F.: Touch dominates haptic estimates of discordant visual-haptic size. Percept. Psychophys. 58, 1124–1132 (1996)
2. Misceo, G.F., Hershberger, W.A., Mancini, R.L.: Haptic estimates of discordant visual-haptic size vary developmentally. Percept. Psychophys. 61, 608–614 (1999)
3. Gori, M., Del Viva, M., Sandini, G., Burr, D.C.: Young children do not integrate visual and haptic form information. Curr. Biol. 18, 694–698 (2008)
4. Miller, E.A.: Interaction of vision and touch in conflict and nonconflict form perception tasks. J. Exp. Psychol. 96, 114–123 (1972)
5. Wichmann, F.A., Hill, N.J.: The psychometric function: I. Fitting, sampling, and goodness of fit. Percept. Psychophys. 63, 1293–1313 (2001)
6. Ernst, M.O., Bülthoff, H.H.: Merging the senses into a robust percept. TiCS 8, 162–169 (2004)
7. Nardini, M., Jones, P., Bedford, R., Braddick, O.: Development of Cue Integration in Human Navigation. Curr. Biol. 18, 689–693 (2008)

Presentation of Positional Information
by Heat Phantom Sensation

Jun Oohara[1], Hiroshi Kato[1], Yuki Hashimoto[1], and Hiroyuki Kajimoto[1,2]

[1] The University of Electro-Communications, Japan
[2] Japan Science and Technology Agency
{oohara,hiro.kato,hashimoto,kajimoto}@kaji-lab.jp

Abstract. In this study, we investigated the "heat phantom sensation" induced by thermal stimulation of two points. Phantom sensations are tactile illusions induced at a point between two or more stimuli, and have been demonstrated to occur in the event of vibration stimulation. However, their induction by thermal stimuli has not been fully investigated. We confirmed the existence of a heat phantom sensation using two heat stimulators, and succeeded in presenting the heat source image at an arbitrary position by changing the temperature ratio.

Keywords: Funneling illusion, Heat sensation, Phantom Sensation, Tactile illusion.

1 Introduction

Progress in the field of communications due to the development of information technologies means that people increasingly need to communicate by means other than direct interpersonal contact. Various types of devices have been developed to achieve remote interpersonal communication, most of which are based on visual and auditory modalities. Recent studies, however, have proposed the use of haptic interfaces to communicate between remote users [1], [2]. Most of these have been based on the use of force or vibratory tactile sensations. However, to transmit emotional information, physical properties related to the autonomic nervous system, such as temperature and humidity, are important.

In this study, we investigated temperature sensation, which can be generated using relatively low cost devices.

1.1 Background

Previous studies on temperature presentation have mainly focused on the display of material properties [3], and most of them involved presentation of the sensation to the hand or finger. Our tactile interpersonal communication, however, is not limited to the hands; we can touch the whole body, and temperature displays should thus be designed

A.M.L. Kappers et al. (Eds.): EuroHaptics 2010, Part II, LNCS 6192, pp. 445–450, 2010.
© Springer-Verlag Berlin Heidelberg 2010

to achieve whole-body stimulation. However, displays to large areas are associated with increased costs and more bulky systems.

During tactile communication, although a sensation may be felt over a wide area (the 'display position'), since we can be touched anywhere on the body, the area of the stimulus (the 'display area') is not necessarily large, since one cannot touch large areas of our body simultaneously with his/her hands. The requirements of the system are thus summarized as follows:

(1) The display position should be widely distributed.
(2) The simultaneous display area does not need to be large; possibly about the size of a palm.
(3) The system needs to involve as little hardware as possible.

The aim of this study was therefore to present temperature information to an arbitrary position, using a small number of devices.

One possible solution is to use phantom sensation. Phantom sensation [4] (sometimes referred to as funneling [5]), whereby a sensation is generated midway between two stimuli, is known to occur for vibratory sensation. Our question is, whether this phenomenon is also observed by thermal stimuli.

On the other hand, spatial ambiguity of the thermal sense called thermal referral was well known [6], [7]. This phenomenon is observed as follows: if the middle finger touches an object at normal temperature while the forefinger and ring finger touch warm objects, then the middle finger also feels warm. A similar phenomenon can be observed using cold objects. This reported thermal referral can be explained by simple spatial summation. However, no studies have reported the ability to present the stimulation at an arbitrary position, which is an important characteristic of phantom sensation.

Let us call the subjective temperature sensation other than real heat sources, "heat source image". Analogous to the phantom sensation induced by vibration, we speculated that the position of the heat source image could be controlled by changing the temperature ratio of the two stimuli. We have referred to this phenomenon as heat phantom sensation (h-PhS). This study aimed to confirm this ability to alter the position of the heat phantom sensation.

2 Experimental Setup

Two Peltier elements were used for thermal stimulation. They stimulated two points on the forearm (Fig. 1). The elements were embedded in an acrylic sheet of the same thickness to produce a flat surface, and thus eliminate any effect of contact with the elements on positional perception. Each Peltier element measured 40 mm × 40 mm, with a 90-mm gap between them (130 mm distance between the centers of the heat sources). Three temperature sensors (film thermistors) were used to measure the skin temperature. These were located on each element and in the intervening gap.

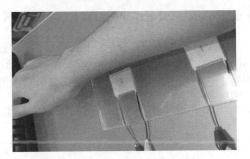

Fig. 1. Two Peltier elements were used to heat the skin. The elements were embedded in an acrylic sheet of the same thickness to produce a flat surface.

3 Perception of Heat Source Image

This experiment was designed to confirm if a heat source image was elicited between the two heat sources, and to investigate the lowest temperature required to produce the funneling illusion.

The participants included five adults (A–E), aged 22–23 years. They have knowledge of funneling by vibration. They were asked if they could feel a heat source image when they put their forearm across the two heat sources. When the temperature of the two heat sources (two temperatures are the same) was increased, all participants reported the sensation of a heat source image. The experiment was repeated five times for each participant. We did not limit response time, and one trial took about 1-3 minutes. Subjects knew the approximate location of the two Peltier elements, but as the elements were hidden by their arms, they could not see the elements during the experiments.

Fig. 2 shows the threshold temperature for the phenomenon. The graph also shows the skin temperature midway between the two points.

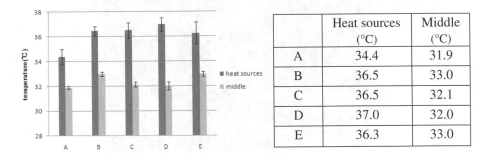

	Heat sources (°C)	Middle (°C)
A	34.4	31.9
B	36.5	33.0
C	36.5	32.1
D	37.0	32.0
E	36.3	33.0

Fig. 2. Threshold temperature for producing a heat source image, and skin temperature midway between the two stimulation points in participants A–E

It was confirmed that the heat source image was elicited in all participants. The average threshold temperature was 36.1°C. The temperature midway between the two heat sources was 32–33°C (approximately normal skin temperature), and the heat source image was thus clearly an illusory sensation.

4 Presentation of Positional Information by h-PhS

This experiment was designed to determine if the position of the illusion could be controlled, as with other PhS. The results of the preliminary experiment showed that an h-PhS was generated at temperatures $\geq 37°C$. Moreover, it is known that heat perception becomes painful at temperatures $>43°C$ [8], [9]. The temperatures of the two heat sources were therefore varied within the range 37–41°C. The temperature combinations are shown in Table 1.

Table 1. Combination of temperatures

Stimulation No.	wrist side (°C)	elbow side (°C)
1	41	37
2	40	38
3	39	39
4	38	40
5	37	41

Stimulations using the different temperature combinations were administered to the participants in random order, and they were asked to identify the position of just the heat source image (Fig. 3). The participants included five adults, aged 22–23 years. The same participants A-D and a new participant F instead of E attended the experiment.

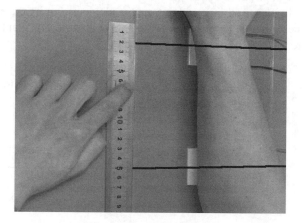

Fig. 3. Participants identified the position of the image

Fig. 4 shows the results of experiment. The two bold lines indicate the central positions of the two Peltier elements. The graph confirmed that the position of the heat source image changed according to the temperature difference between the two heat sources.

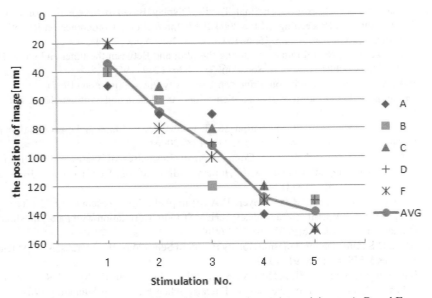

Fig. 4. Perceived position of heat source image in participants A–D and F

5 Conclusions

As described in previous studies, we observed that heat stimulation at $\geq 37°C$ applied to two points on the forearm generated a heat source image that was perceived in an area without thermal stimulation.

Although several studies have reported a positional ambiguity effect of temperature perception called thermal referral, they did not demonstrate the ability of the heat source image to be presented at an arbitrary position. On the other hand, we observed that the position of the illusory image could be controlled by changing the temperature ratio.

These results confirm that h-PhS shows the basic characteristics of PhS, and suggest that temperature funneling is based on a mechanism similar to the funneling of vibratory sensations. Further studies are underway to produce spatially distributed temperature sensations using a small number of devices, based on the h-PhS phenomenon observed in this study.

Acknowledgment. This work was supported by SCOPE (092103992).

References

[1] Brave, S., Dahley, A.: InTouch: A Medium for Haptic Interpersonal Communication. In: Extended Abstracts of CHI 1997, pp. 363–364. ACM Press, New York (1997)
[2] Sekiguchi, D., Inami, M., Kawakami, N., Maeda, T., Yanagida, Y., Tachi, S.: Robot-PHONE: RUI for Interpersonal Communication. In: ACM SIGGRAPH 2000 Conference Abstracts and Applications, vol. 134. ACM Press, New York (2000)

[3] Yamamoto, A.: Control of Thermal Tactile Display Based on Prediction of Contact Temperature. In: Proceedings of the 2004 IEEE International Conference on Robotics & Automation (ICRA 2004), pp. 1536–1541. IEEE, New York (2004)

[4] von Békésy, G.: Neural Funneling Along the Skin and Between the Inner and Outer Hair Cells of the Cochlea. J. Acoust. Soc. Am. 31, 1236–1249 (1959)

[5] Békésy, G.: Sensory Inhibition. Princeton University Press, Princeton (1967)

[6] Green, B.G.: Localization of Thermal Sensation: An Illusion and Synthetic Heat. Percept. Psychophys. 22, 331–337 (1977)

[7] Ho, H.-N., Jones, L.A.: Contribution of Thermal Cues to Material Discrimination and Localization. Percept. Psychophys. 68, 118–128 (2006)

[8] LaMotte, R.H., Campbell, J.N.: Comparison of Responses of Warm and Nociceptive C-fiber Afferents in Monkey with Human Judgments of Thermal Pain. J. Neurophysiol. 41, 509–528 (1978)

[9] Tillman, D.B., Treede, R.D., Meyer, R.A., Campbell, J.N.: Response of C Fibre Nociceptors in the Anaesthetized Monkey to Heat Stimuli: Correlation with Pain Threshold in Humans. J. Physiol. 485(Pt 3), 767–774 (1995)

[10] Alles, D.S.: Information Transmission by Phantom Sensations. IEEE Trans. Man-Machine Systems MMS-11(1), 8–91 (1970)

[11] Barghout, A., Cha, J., El Saddik, A., Kammerl, J., Steinbach, E.: Spatial Resolution of Vibrotactile Perception on the Human Forearm when Exploiting Funneling Illusion. In: International Workshop on Haptic Audio-Visual Environments and Games (HAVE), Lecco, Italy, November 7-8 (2009)

Haptic Playback: Better Trajectory Tracking during Training Does Not Mean More Effective Motor Skill Transfer

Maxim Kolesnikov[1] and Miloš Žefran[2]

[1] Sensory Motor Performance Program,
Rehabilitation Institute of Chicago, Chicago, IL, USA
m-kolesnikov@northwestern.edu
[2] Department of Electrical and Computer Engineering,
University of Illinois at Chicago, Chicago, IL, USA
mzefran@uic.edu

Abstract. In this paper the performance of a haptic playback system with two different control algorithms was experimentally investigated. Accuracy of tracking the reference position and force trajectories of each system during training was examined, and their effectiveness in teaching a hybrid sensorimotor skill with significant position and force components was compared. It was determined that superior tracking performance during training does not necessarily indicate superior effectiveness in motor skill acquisition.

Keywords: Haptics, haptic playback, motor skill acquisition, adaptive training, performance enhancement.

1 Introduction

To learn a sensorimotor skill it is necessary to master two of its complementary components: position and force. In order to acquire the skill successfully one must be able to accurately reproduce both the position and force trajectories. These components can be easily recorded with the aid of tracking devices and force sensors. Once such recording is performed by an expert and stored in a file, it can be used as an aid to recreate the same experience for someone not familiar with the task. We use the term *haptic playback* to refer to such capability.

One way to take advantage of haptic technology for training is to use it during the reinforcement stage of a skill acquisition process. Traditionally, in this stage the involvement of an "expert", an individual who had already mastered the skill, was necessary. Under the expert's guidance the student would have to repeat the procedure numerous times until her ability to perform it would improve to a level when independent execution becomes possible. With haptics technology it is possible to have the role of an expert in the reinforcement stage performed by a haptic simulation system.

In this study we show that there is no direct relationship between the tracking precision of a haptic playback system and its effectiveness as a tool in motor skill transfer.

A.M.L. Kappers et al. (Eds.): EuroHaptics 2010, Part II, LNCS 6192, pp. 451–456, 2010.

2 Haptic Playback

Various approaches to haptic playback exist. Due to causality limitations it is impossible to display with the haptic device both the position and force information for a single dimension, that is why most approaches to date [1,2,3] have been focused on haptically displaying either position or force trajectory while providing the information about the other through a different modality (e.g. visual display). These methods usually focus on certain specific applications. Another approach [4] is to present to the student only the position trajectory and assume that with the small position error the correct force information will be obtained. This approach is problematic for environments with sharp transitions between stiff and non-stiff regions.

In order to evaluate the effectiveness of haptic training for teaching of a sensorimotor skill, we use haptic playback methodology formalized by Corno and Žefran [5]. In this methodology a visual display is used to communicate position data to the user and a haptic interface is used to display forces. Haptic playback is formulated as a control problem where the displayed position target and force signals are computed by a controller so that the user tracks the desired trajectories. Control strategies in this case are formally described as

$$\begin{bmatrix} p_0(t_i) \\ F_{act}(t_i) \end{bmatrix} = \begin{bmatrix} p_d(t_i) \\ -F_d(t_i) \end{bmatrix} - \mathbf{W} \begin{bmatrix} p(t_i) - p_d(t_i) \\ F(t_i) - F_d(t_i) \end{bmatrix}, \tag{1}$$

where p_0 is the displayed position of the visual target, F_{act} is the force displayed by the haptic device, p and F are the actual position of the device and actual force applied by the user, p_d and F_d are the desired position of the device and desired force to be applied by the user, and $\mathbf{W}$ is a matrix of coefficients describing particular control strategies. Haptic training with two different haptic playback controllers was involved in this experiment.

3 Methods

Participants: The pool of participants consisted of 30 volunteers, 19 male and 11 female between the ages of 20 and 56. The median age of participants was 26. Every participant reported a normal or corrected to normal vision, a normal sense of touch and no known history of neurological disorders. One participant was left-handed while others were right-handed. The experiment was approved by the Institutional Review Board of the University of Illinois at Chicago.

Apparatus: Visual information was displayed on a 17" CRT monitor (Dell Inc., Round Rock, TX) placed approximately 60 cm from the user. Haptic guidance was presented via a PHANToM Premium 1.0A haptic device (SensAble Technologies, Woburn, MA) placed on a table beside the monitor. Subjects were asked to hold the stylus of the haptic device like a pen with the fingers of their dominant hand and to place the elbow of their dominant arm on an armrest.

Experimental Task: The task chosen for this experiment was to cut a square piece of thin membrane-like material along the shown trajectory in a virtual environment using

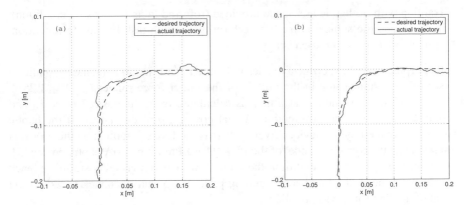

Fig. 1. (a) Typical pre-training trajectory of a subject. (b) Post-training trajectory.

a sharp rod as a cutting tool. Simplified graphical models for the material and the tool were developed in X3D (ISO/IEC 19775) and incorporated into the haptic simulation. The stylus of the haptic device was used to control the movement of the rod in the virtual environment. Only the tip of the rod could make a cut.

To advance the cutting rod's position in the direction of applied force the user had to apply the force with the magnitude in the optimal range $[1, 1.5]$ N. Directional noise angle, uniformly distributed in the range $(-3, 3)$ rad, was introduced for forces with the magnitude outside the optimal range. Hysteresis switch function with the thresholds at 0.5 and 0.8 N prevented the rod from moving when low forces were applied. Viscous environment with damping $k_v = 50$ Ns/m was assumed to compute the velocity of the rod as a function of the effective applied force. A trajectory which has a vertical component, followed by a curved component and a horizontal component was chosen for the experiment (see Figure 1 for sample trajectories).

Experimental Conditions: The following three conditions were employed in a random placement design:

1. Haptic training with the assistance of the *crossed controller* [5] (referred to as *CC* condition in the remainder of this work) when $\mathbf{W} = \begin{bmatrix} 0 & K_P \\ K_F & 0 \end{bmatrix}$, $K_P > 0$, $K_F > 0$. This controller is known to perform well in tracking the correct position and force trajectories of the user in planar tasks when the tool is reduced to a point [5]. When setting the position and force gains stability issues [5] and data from pilot study were taken into consideration; the gains were set to $K_P = 0.03$ m/N and $K_F = 10$ N/m.

2. Haptic training with the assistance of the *modified coupled controller* [6] (referred to as *MCC* condition) when $\mathbf{W} = \begin{bmatrix} 0 & 0 \\ K_F & 0 \end{bmatrix}$, $K_F > 0$ and F_d is calculated from the interaction with the virtual environment, which implies that it is not the recorded force. This simpler and more conservative approach may be better suited for many applications since it eliminates the need to measure forces applied by the user. Force gain was experimentally set to $K_F = 50$ N/m.

3. Training with no haptic assistance provided (referred to as *Unassisted* condition).
   In this mode the subject trained to perform the cutting task by simple repetition.
   Framework (1) was not used here.

For the purpose of this experiment the desired force F_d in Equation (1) in CC condition
was set to a constant value in the middle of the target force range: $F_d(t_i) = 1.25$ N.
Desired position p_d of the rod at time t_i is calculated from the desired force F_d and
damping k_v, assuming uniform motion. Actual position p of the handle of the haptic
device was provided by the device drivers, whereas the force F applied by the user was
estimated from the dynamic model of the PHANToM Premium 1.0A haptic device [5].

In all three experimental conditions the subjects were given visual position feedback
in the form of the desired and actual cutting paths. No visual feedback based on the
amount of applied force was provided.

Experimental Procedure: Each participant was introduced to the device and verbally
instructed on the experimental task. Instructions emphasized the fact that there existed
an optimal range of velocities with which one should advance the cutting tool to minimize the errors in the trajectory. However, no quantitative description of optimal velocities and forces was given to subjects.

Then the subject was asked to perform the task 2 times without any assistance to
obtain the baseline data before training. After that, the training session was initiated in
which the subject participated in 7 training trials under either CC, MCC or *Unassisted*
training conditions depending on the group the subject was randomly placed in (there
were 10 subjects in each group). Testing stage followed the training stage. In the testing
stage participants were again asked to perform the task 2 times without any assistance
(see Figure 1 for typical pre- and post-training trajectories).

During the trials the position of the haptic device, the forces applied by the user and,
for training trials under CC and MCC conditions, the position of the visual target and
the guiding force exerted by the device were recorded for analysis at a rate of 40 Hz.
Due to the smooth nature of the task this rate was sufficient to capture its dynamics.

4   Data Analysis

Each task performance trial is analyzed individually offline and the error measure E is
computed as the area between the desired and actual cutting trajectories.

Effectiveness of learning is assessed through the skill gain parameter. Skill gain G is
computed as a difference between the average error of the pre-training testing trials 1
and 2 and the average error of the post-training testing trials 10 and 11:

$$G = \tfrac{1}{2}(E_1 + E_2) - \tfrac{1}{2}(E_{10} + E_{11}), \tag{2}$$

where E_m denotes the error measure computed for the mth trial. To analyze force tracking performance during training the force error measure E_F is computed as a backward
Euler approximation of the integral of the force error over time. Since the reference
training procedure used under CC and MCC conditions is always the same, there is no
need to normalize the force error with respect to the trial duration.

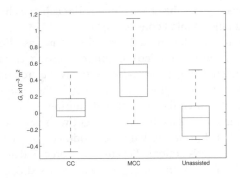

Fig. 2. Mean values, 25th and 75th percentiles, and data range of skill gain G for each condition

5   Results

Skill gain scores G are combined into three groups, corresponding to each of the three training conditions. This allows to analyze the effectiveness of learning under each condition. Mean pre-training errors among the three groups were analyzed using a one-way analysis of variance (ANOVA) test which concluded that they are not significantly different, $F(2,27) = 1.70$, $p > 0.05$.

The null hypothesis is that all skill gain measurements are drawn from the same distribution. A one-way ANOVA reveals a significant difference among the three training methods under investigation, $F(2,27) = 6.09$, $p < 0.01$, thus rejecting the null hypothesis. Mean values, 25th and 75th percentiles and data range of skill gain G in three groups are given in the boxplot in Figure 2. Mean skill gains were found to be equal to $\{0.066, 0.433, -0.020\} \times 10^{-3}$ m^2 for CC, MCC and *Unassisted* training conditions respectively. Tukey's test shows that the minimum pairwise difference between means that must be exceeded to be significant at $\alpha = 0.01$ is 0.439×10^{-3} m, thus MCC training is significantly more effective than the *Unassisted* training, while the advantage of using CC training over the *Unassisted* training is insignificant.

To analyze the subjects' performance during training, position and force error measures are calculated for each training run as described in Section 4. Two-tailed T-tests reveal that the individual mean position error measures in training runs under CC and MCC conditions are not considerably different, $t(18) = 2.00$, $p > 0.05$, however the individual mean force error measures under these conditions differ significantly, $t(18) = -6.58$, $p < 0.01$, with means being equal to 1.72 and 2.72 Ns for CC and MCC training conditions respectively.

6   Discussion and Conclusions

Analysis of experimental data in Section 5 suggests that during training the crossed controller performs better than the modified coupled controller in tracking the force component of the task trajectory, while the performance of the two controllers is not significantly different in tracking the position trajectory. This observation is consistent with prior results indicating that the crossed controller achieves better trajectory tracking during training than the coupled controller [5].

However, as we found out, the crossed controller is not as effective in terms of its training potential as the modified coupled controller. There are two main reasons for this phenomenon. First, good tracking accuracy achieved by the crossed controller comes at the expense of introducing an intentional discrepancy in the position of a visual target. Secondly, even though the force the subject feels during training is the same in case of both controllers if the user tracks the visual target with perfect accuracy, the causes of that force are different. In training with the modified coupled controller the force is directly caused by the user's actions, because the force is determined by the user's motion in a virtual environment. In training with the crossed controller, however, this relationship is not direct, because the force the user feels is computed by the controller and it is not immediately affected by the user's actions.

Our results are consistent with recent observations [7] suggesting that error reduction during training is not sufficient to achieve good performance during independent execution of the task. Motor skill acquisition is a highly complex process, where other factors such as the visual information perceived by the user and the impedance of the environment come into play.

Acknowledgments. This research was partially supported by NSF grants CMS-0600658 and IIS-0905593.

References

1. Yokokohji, Y., Hollis, R.L., Kanade, T.: What you see is what you feel – development of a visual/haptic interface to virtual environment. In: Proc. of IEEE Virtual Reality International Symposium, Los Alamitos, CA, pp. 46–53 (1996)
2. Henmi, J., Yoshikawa, T.: Virtual lesson and its application to virtual calligraphy system. In: Proc. of IEEE International Conference on Robotics and Automation, Leuven, Belgium, pp. 1275–1280 (1998)
3. Kikuuwe, R., Yoshikawa, T.: Haptic display device with fingertip presser for motion/force teaching to human. In: Proc. of IEEE/CNF International Conference on Robotics and Automation, Seoul, Korea, pp. 868–873 (2001)
4. Williams II, R., Srivastava, M., Conatster Jr., R.R., Howell, J.N.: Implementation and evaluation of a haptic playback system. Haptics-e 3(3), 1–5 (2004)
5. Corno, M., Žefran, M.: Haptic playback: Modeling, controller design, and stability analysis. In: Proc. of Robotics: Science and Systems, Philadelphia, PA (2006)
6. Kolesnikov, M., Žefran, M., Steinberg, A.D., Bashook, P.G.: Haptic virtual reality simulator for sensorimotor skill acquisition in dentistry. In: Proc. of IEEE International Conference on Robotics and Automation, Kobe, Japan, pp. 689–694 (2009)
7. Li, Y., Patoglu, V., O'Malley, M.K.: Negative efficacy of fixed gain error reducing shared control for training in virtual environments. ACM Transactions on Applied Perception 6(1) (2009)

Author Index

Printing: Mercedes-Druck, Berlin
Binding: Stein+Lehmann, Berlin